Popular Culture: A User's Guide, International Edition is a lively and engaging introduction to popular culture. It provides the tools and knowledge for an analysis of the contemporary cultural landscape across a range of disciplines, from literary theory and cultural studies to philosophy and sociology.

The text covers a broad range of key topics, such as the underlying socioeconomic structures that affect media and our consciousness, the politics of pop culture, the role of consumers, subcultures and countercultures, and the construction of social reality. It examines the ways in which individuals and societies act as consumers and agents of popular culture. It is also filled with a variety of helpful learning features including case studies, real-life examples, suggested activities, boxed features on specific topics, and a glossary of terms. *Popular Culture* helps readers navigate the complexities of twenty-first century popular culture, arming them with the awareness and ability to critically evaluate everyday life and practices.

IMRE SZEMAN is Canada Research Chair of Cultural Studies and Professor of English and Film Studies at the University of Alberta, Canada. He is also Adjunct Professor of Visual and Critical Studies at the Ontario College of Art and Design University, Canada. He is the founder of the Canadian Association of Cultural Studies and a founding member of the US Cultural Studies Association. He is the author or editor of more than 16 books, including *Cultural Theory: An Anthology* (Wiley Blackwell, 2010) and *After Globalization* (Wiley Blackwell, 2011).

SUSIE O'BRIEN is Associate Professor in the Department of English and Cultural Studies at McMaster University, Canada. Her research and teaching focus on postcolonial and environmental cultural studies. She has published on postcolonial literature, the slow and local food movements, scenario planning, and the temporality of globalization. She is co-editor of *Time, Globalization and Human Experience* (forthcoming 2017).

Popular Culture

A User's Guide, International Edition

Imre Szeman

Susie O'Brien

WILEY Blackwell

This edition first published 2017
© 2017 John Wiley & Sons, Inc.

Edition History
Adapted from *Popular Culture: A User's Guide*, Third Edition, by Susie O'Brien and Imre Szeman, published by Nelson Education Ltd. Copyright © 2014 by Nelson Education Ltd.

The right of Imre Szeman and Susie O'Brien to be identified as the authors of this work has been asserted in accordance with law.

Registered Office
John Wiley & Sons, Inc., 111 River Street, Hoboken, NJ 07030, USA

Editorial Office
9600 Garsington Road, Oxford, OX4 2DQ, UK

For details of our global editorial offices, customer services, and more information about Wiley products visit us at www.wiley.com.

Wiley also publishes its books in a variety of electronic formats and by print-on-demand. Some content that appears in standard print versions of this book may not be available in other formats.

Library of Congress Cataloging-in-Publication Data

Names: Szeman, Imre, 1968– author. | O'Brien, Susie, author.
Title: Popular culture : a user's guide / Imre Szeman, University of Waterloo, Canada, Susie O'Brien,
    McMaster University, Canada.
Description: International edition. | Hoboken, NJ : John Wiley & Sons, Inc., 2017. |
    "Adapted from Popular Culture: A User's Guide, Third Edition [published in 2014 by Nelson Education]." |
    Includes bibliographical references and index.
Identifiers: LCCN 2017011125 (print) | LCCN 2017026179 (ebook) | ISBN 9781119140368 (pdf) |
    ISBN 9781119140375 (epub) | ISBN 9781119140337 (cloth) | ISBN 9781119140344 (pbk.)
Subjects: LCSH: Popular culture.
Classification: LCC HM621 (ebook) | LCC HM621 .S995 2017 (print) | DDC 306–dc23
LC record available at https://lccn.loc.gov/2017011125

Cover Image: Courtesy of Jessica Sabogal
Cover Design: Wiley

Set in 10/12pt Warnock by SPi Global, Pondicherry, India
Printed in Singapore by C.O.S. Printers Pte Ltd

10   9   8   7   6   5   4   3   2   1

Contents

Preface: A User's Guide to *Popular Culture: A User's Guide*

The goal of *Popular Culture: A User's Guide* is to provide readers with an introduction to the critical study of popular culture. Our aim is to give readers the analytical tools to understand the everyday texts and practices that surround them, as well as their own roles as consumers of and participants in popular culture.

Why does anyone need a guidebook to popular culture? Don't we all already know not only what is meant by popular culture, but also how to consume and use it? Guidebooks are supposed to make mysterious lands with unusual customs more familiar, or help us learn how to navigate complex tasks (like building a deck or planting a good-looking garden) with greater ease. Popular culture, on the other hand, is, well, *popular*. When it comes to watching films, listening to pop music, shopping, or sucking down cups of coffee, we believe that we know exactly what we are doing and why we are doing it. Like our native tongue, popular culture is something we know how to "speak" without resorting to lessons, audiotapes, courses, or guidebooks. So what can a user's guide tell us about popular culture that we don't already know?

In many respects, it is precisely the intimacy and familiarity with which we engage in contemporary popular culture that require critical reflection, exploration, and analysis. After all, knowing how to speak a language because we are immersed in it does not mean that we are necessarily able to read or write it, or that we understand its syntax and structure. Reading and writing take an enormous amount of effort to get right. And once we have learned how to read, we are faced with other questions, such as how written language on a page can convey information about real and imagined worlds.

As with language, so, too, with popular culture. Because we are immersed in it, popular culture is both uniquely accessible and frustratingly opaque; it is hard to get a critical purchase on something we inhabit so completely and, most of the time, more or less unconsciously. To help us understand the "syntax" and "grammar" of popular culture— the unacknowledged but crucial structures that give popular culture its shape, meaning, and significance—this book attempts to help readers see this familiar terrain more acutely and with greater insight. Our familiarity with popular culture tends to hide some of its most important features and its relationship to broader social, political, and economic currents. *Popular Culture: A User's Guide* will help readers see parts of the contemporary cultural landscape that they may have been looking at all along without really perceiving them.

This book aims to take readers beyond the "commonsense" approach to popular culture, an approach that is defined by an odd mix of cynical knowingness and complacency. We are working from the premise that readers today possess an unprecedented level of media literacy. We are all aware, for example, that certain forms of media, such as advertising, operate according to particular agendas that may or may not reflect our own interests, and we also believe that we are smart enough to resist. This book seeks to create a level of awareness that goes beyond cynical complacency, not only to make readers aware of the underlying socioeconomic structures that determine the shape of media and, by extension, consciousness, but also to make them recognize the myriad ways in which popular culture manages to maneuver around these structures. We want to give students the tools to understand their role not just as consumers, but also as agents of popular culture.

We also want to showcase the full range of activities and practices that can be considered part of contemporary popular cultural experience. Unlike "high culture," which is generally understood to refer to a discrete body of books or artworks that are unified by their adherence to specific aesthetic and cultural codes, the field of popular culture is diverse and uneven, comprising texts and practices ranging from commercial media to subcultural styles to the activities of everyday life (eating, shopping, drinking coffee, recreational activities, etc.).

Many books about popular culture are actually surveys or overviews of academic or theoretical *approaches* to the study of popular culture. In other words, what such books offer is a roughly historical account of a specific academic discipline (what is now often called cultural studies) and the individuals and theories that have been important to the development of that discipline. While we certainly discuss and make use of many of the most important theories of popular culture, we have chosen to emphasize practical strategies for understanding and interpreting the popular. Working from case studies and examples, this book aims to provide readers with a critical vocabulary and methods of analysis that will allow them to perform independent readings of cultural texts extending far beyond the sampling we offer here.

The specific analyses we provide in each chapter exemplify ways of using and adapting critical and theoretical materials to address the issues and problems at hand. The text is organized mainly around broad themes rather than specific genres or forms of popular culture (television, music, film, etc.), and is bookended by chapters that focus on the prehistory of contemporary popular culture (Chapter 1) and on the complexities that the current historical context introduces for the study of popular culture (Chapters 9 and 10).

A number of other features make this book a distinctive contribution to the study of popular culture. There is, first, an emphasis throughout on the politics of popular culture—that is, on the way in which popular culture is always connected to practices and discourses related to the exercise of and struggle over power and recognition in contemporary society. Second, there is an unapologetically Canadian flavor to this book. One reason for this is practical: both authors grew up, and currently work in, Canada. Though we have both lived and worked elsewhere, and much of our research is focused on places outside of Canada, the premise of this book that popular culture is ordinary and familiar compels us to approach the topic through our own everyday experiences. For that reason, many, though by no means all, of the case studies and examples we draw on are Canadian. Or Canadian*ish*: the fact of the matter is that popular culture in Canada has historically always included radio and television, and films and books from around the world—alongside and in conjunction with homegrown programming and cultural production, but often at the expense of our own cultural producers. This situation of being on the periphery, culturally speaking, is not unique. Many, if not most, people share the experience of being both outside the pop culture mainstream and also deeply engaged with it; this is likely true even for people who live in the English-speaking cultural centers of the United States and the United Kingdom, though it may be harder to articulate without the convenient signpost of a geographical border. While the border that marks our

Canadianness slips in and out of view, we hope this book highlights the fact that, in the study of popular culture, what you see and do not see often depends on where you are looking from.

Finally, to help our readers work through *Popular Culture: A User's Guide*, we have incorporated a number of pedagogical features. Important terms and concepts are listed in a glossary at the end of the book and highlighted in **bold** on their first appearance in the text to allow readers to cross-reference with ease. Each chapter contains one or more suggested activities and questions that are intended to get readers to think further about particular subjects and to apply them to their own experiences. In course use, these Suggested Activities may form the basis of oral or written assignments. Close-Ups in each chapter clarify key concepts, theories, or movements, and may also form the basis for further study and investigation. Each chapter ends with a list of suggestions for further reading or viewing. These titles include other introductory texts that may deal with the same material in a different way or with a different emphasis, as well as original works by scholars and theorists referred to in the chapter.

Like the writers of any guidebook, we hope that readers use our maps and recommendations of places to visit and things to think about as a jumping-off point for the elaboration of their own maps of the landscape of popular culture. The authors would be the first to admit that not only are there plenty of things they have not seen, there are places they do not yet even know exist.

Susie O'Brien
Hamilton, Ontario
Imre Szeman
Waterloo, Ontario
February 2017

Acknowledgments

Susie: To EN/CSCT 1B3 and 1CS3 TAs for coming up with amazingly inventive ways to bring the subject matter of this book to life, and to my students, for their engagement, enthusiasm, and suggestions for how to improve this book, my teaching, and my wardrobe. Special thanks to Jesse Arseneault, Amber Dean, Nick Holm, Mary O'Connor, Simon Orpana, Scott Stoneman, Helene Strauss, and Carolyn Veldstra for insight and inspiration and some great guest lectures, and to Bridget Mountford, for invaluable editorial suggestions as well as reminders about why and how pop culture matters.

Imre: To my colleagues at the University of Waterloo and elsewhere who continue to make it interesting to spend time sorting through the (sometimes alarming) complexities of our contemporary moment: Brent "Brett" Bellamy, Sarah Blacker, Nicholas Brown, Jeff Diamanti, Dan Harvey, Eva-Lynn Jagoe, Sean O'Brien, Michael O'Driscoll, Andrew Pendakis, Stuart Poyntz, Mark Simpson, Will Straw, Justin Sully, Jennifer Wenzel, Sheena Wilson, and Heather Zwicker.

1

Introducing Popular Culture

Approaching Popular Culture

"Let's go get a coffee."

Every day, throughout much of the world, this phrase is uttered thousands of times, by different people—students, teachers, construction workers, lawyers, mothers, retail clerks, unemployed people, old people, young people—and in different social contexts, such as work, breaks from work, dating, interviews, therapy sessions, or hanging out. Going for a coffee is a major part of popular culture, not only in the sense that it is such a common practice, but also in that it means so much more than the literal act of tossing back a hot caffeinated beverage: in fact, "going for coffee" need not involve drinking coffee at all. So what does it mean? And what is it about coffee drinking that makes it part of popular culture while other equally common practices—like, say, yawning or mowing the lawn—are not? Or are they part of popular culture, too?

These are the kinds of questions this book sets out to answer—not by offering a comprehensive account of what fits in the category of popular culture and what does not, but by helping us to think about the question of *why* popular culture is such a critical part of contemporary life. For this reason, it might be misleading to call this book a "user's guide" to popular culture. A standard user's guide to, say, the smartphone that you may have just received for Christmas (which happens all the time in television commercials, less often in real life) tells you everything there is to know about the specific object that you have in your hands, what its functions are, and what it can and cannot do. Popular culture is not like that. For one thing, popular culture is a far more difficult "thing" to pin down than a smartphone or an IKEA desk; it is constantly changing shape, shifting locations, assuming new identities and new tasks and functions. The goal of a user's guide to popular culture is to provide culture's users—that is, all of us—with a way to think about popular culture that is flexible and supple enough to allow us also to think about its changes and redefinitions, and to figure out what is at stake in the definition of popular culture. How can we learn to read and participate in—to *use*—what is popular in a way that strengthens our understanding of ourselves and the world we live in? This book approaches these questions through the analysis of texts (objects that we can interpret, just like a book) and practices (things that we do): seeing movies, listening to songs, watching television shows, playing sports, going shopping—and drinking coffee.

The purpose of this introduction is to lay out a working definition of popular culture, to outline a few key concepts that will reappear in later discussion, and to give you a diagram of the way this book is put together—a "guide to the guide"—that should help make the task of piecing the bits of popular culture together a productive one. We also offer a rough guide to the field of cultural studies (see Close-Up 1.2) for readers who want to

Popular Culture: A User's Guide, International Edition. Imre Szeman and Susie O'Brien.
© 2017 John Wiley & Sons, Inc. Published 2017 by John Wiley & Sons, Inc.

delve further into the question of how popular culture has come to be seen as something significant and tricky enough to require a user's guide. Just be forewarned: by the end of the book, you will still be left with extra parts and you will likely end up with a concept of popular culture that looks different from that of your neighbors. But trust us: this is a good thing…

Defining Popular Culture

Like most things that form a big part of our daily lives, popular culture is familiar and obvious at first glance, but very complicated as soon as you start to think about it in any detail. Before we outline the concept of popular culture that informs this book, we suggest you take a couple of minutes to try to come up with your own working definition. When we've conducted this exercise in introductory university classes, a typical range of ideas tend to come up: popular culture consists of those things—products, texts, practices, and so on—that are enjoyed by lots and lots of people; popular culture is commercial culture (as opposed to, say, "high" culture, which people today still tend to associate with the things they imagine that rich people who own yachts like to do, like listen to opera or go to the symphony); popular culture consists of the traditional practices and beliefs or way of life of a specific group; and, finally, the most wide-ranging definition of all, popular culture is simply the practices of everyday life.

What is interesting about these definitions is not just their range but their differences—differences that are shaped to a large degree by the way we understand the terms "popular" and "culture." It is worth taking the time to think about these different ideas, but not so we can dismiss some of them to identify a correct definition. Like most other important social concepts—concepts such as democracy, progress, justice, civilization, and so on that produce the shape of the societies we live in—it does not really make sense to hope for a correct definition that would likely solve the puzzle of all of these different meanings by establishing the essential one supposedly lurking in their midst. Rather, we want to suggest that popular culture is informed by *all* of these perspectives, not just in the sense that each is partially true, but also in the sense that the tension between them is fundamental to understanding the meaning of popular culture today. So before we erect a definition of popular culture that we can all feel comfortable inhabiting, we need to think about this tension. This may initially seem to be a frustratingly circuitous and unhelpful route to finding out the "facts." However, such meanderings are a critical part of the study of culture, in which the question of meaning is never evident but always up for negotiation and disagreement.

What Is Culture?

When we ask our students to track the word "**culture**" as it is used in the media and other sources, two things tend to emerge: (i) culture (along with variations such as multiculturalism) gets mentioned *a lot*, implying that it is a significant concept in our society, and one that we likely can't do without; and (ii) it appears in many different, often contradictory, contexts, suggesting that exactly *how* it signifies is hard to pin down. When we talk about culture in the sense of building opera houses, the word obviously means something different than when we talk about Western culture or youth culture, national culture or business culture. Culture in the first sense—the one that fits with opera houses, ballet, and Shakespeare, which for convenience we'll call capital-C Culture—focuses on what we usually think of as high-end creative production: artistic pursuits that are enjoyed by an elite minority as opposed to more accessible leisure activities, such as sports. These kinds of cultural productions are those that have over time (they are often associated with the past) assumed an especially privileged place in the collection of ideas and artifacts that comprise a cultural *tradition.*

A second definition encompasses a much broader understanding of culture as a whole way of life of a society or a distinct subsection of society: along with art, it encompasses everyday rituals such as meals, work, religious observances, sports, sex, family, and friendship. Implicitly opposed to "nature," which we associate with biology (the things we share with the living nonhuman world), "culture" in this context refers to the practices that define us, collectively and in distinct groups, as human. This definition of culture, or something close to it, informs the disciplines of the social sciences—particularly anthropology, which until recently tended to focus on the cultures of preindustrial societies. When we go on vacation to experience other cultures, it is this sense of culture that we are making reference to: a glimpse into a different way of life organized according to its own principles and around its own unique practices.

The Mass Media

Interestingly, neither the familiar humanities definition of culture nor the one employed by traditional anthropologists adequately encompasses the experience of living in a postmodern capitalist society—the experience of most of us who teach and study those subjects—which is a way of life increasingly dominated by the mass media. Not only do the mass media tend to fall outside the definitions of culture centered around elite artistic production or the practices of ordinary everyday life; they also are frequently cited as the thing that threatens to destroy culture in both these senses: while one set of critics laments the dumbing-down of Shakespeare to satisfy the tastes of a mass audience in Hollywood productions such as *William Shakespeare's Romeo and Juliet, O* (based on *Othello*), or *10 Things I Hate About You* (based on *The Taming of the Shrew*), another warns of the corruption of "authentic" grassroots cultures by the global entertainment industry, which has made it more difficult to find cultures that are all that different from our own in our travels. While they come from different places, what these criticisms have in common is an element of nostalgia, a feeling that something has been lost, that a once pure realm of culture has become contaminated by commerce. It is the desire to understand this world-contaminated-by-commerce that motivates the relatively new discipline of *cultural studies*, into which this book fits (and whose development as an academic field is discussed in more detail later in this chapter).

Objects of Study

To avoid the limitations of earlier definitions of culture, **cultural studies** defines its object of study in very broad terms. One definition, offered in *Key Concepts in Communication and Cultural Studies*, describes culture as "the social production and reproduction of sense, meaning and consciousness. The sphere of meaning, which unifies the spheres of production (economics) and social relations (politics)" (O'Sullivan *et al.* 68). This is a useful definition insofar as it manages to encompass a wide variety of "meaning-producing" practices and technologies, including both traditional definitions of culture—fine art and everyday practices—and mass media. Of course, while the incorporation of these diverse meanings into one functional frame might give us a quick snapshot of what it is that cultural studies actually *studies*—the kinds of things that it looks at and why it is that it looks at them—it is difficult to ignore that the different conceptions of culture that are named in this definition are historically not only different but also *contradictory*.

Rather than seeking to smooth over these contradictions, cultural studies is interested in actively teasing them out and laying them bare. It is committed to an understanding of culture that does not just expand on earlier definitions to include practices, objects, and people that tended, for different reasons, to get left out (such as television game shows, science fiction novels, or skateboarding), but also thinks about why and how such inclusions and exclusions occur in the first place. This means that cultural studies thinks deeply about the connections between culture and the spheres of politics and economics, and seeks to understand how that realm of activity concerned with "meanings, pleasures, and identities" shapes (and is shaped by) relations of power. Among the key questions that are raised by the contradictions between the different definitions of culture cited above are: How is culture produced (made by a society) and reproduced (passed on by a society into the future)? Who makes culture? For whom is it made? This brings us to the other half of the concept of popular culture (Fiske 1).

What/Who Defines the Popular?

Having wrestled with the complicated problem of what constitutes culture, the meaning of "popular" seems much more straightforward, at least initially. Derived from the Latin word *popularis*, which means "of, or belonging to the people," "popular" is often used in a contemporary context to describe something that is liked by a lot of people. For example, when an authoritative source cites *NCIS* as the most popular show on television, based on ratings in 20 nations ("TV Guide"), we can assume, reasonably, that a lot of us like slick crime dramas shot in glamorous settings. But when we start to look a little further into how the word "popular" is used today, it becomes obvious that it has to do with more than numbers—that the words "popular" and "the people" don't refer to absolutely everyone, but to a particular group to whom a certain quality or value is attached.

A couple of examples will serve to illustrate this. First, a number of major art museums have recently come under fire for abandoning their mandate to promote serious art in favor of "popular" blockbuster shows guaranteed to fill up the galleries (and the museum shop). Recent examples of this phenomenon include the *Art of Star Wars* exhibition that toured galleries in Japan, Singapore, Scotland, and England between 2002 and 2004, and *Diana, A Celebration*, a tribute to the late Princess Diana that drew crowds at museums in Toronto, Fort Lauderdale, and Dayton, Ohio, from 2006 to 2014.

Art and museum critics are not all happy about the trend of blurring high and popular culture. As George Neubert, former director of the San Antonio Museum of Art and the Sheldon Memorial Art Gallery, puts it:

> A lot of museums are now torn between two extreme opposite philosophies....One feels it has to compete with pop culture and mass culture to be relevant and for the big E, education, with lots of well-intentioned outreach and participatory programs. It does for a short moment bring up the numbers, but I wonder how meaningful those are in the long term. (Wolgamott)

A counterargument can be easily mounted in favor of the museums' decision to show more "popular" work: as a public space, the museum should respond to the preference of people in general rather than to the tastes of an overly educated minority to whom museums have typically catered. Since these latter tastes are often seen to be disproportionately supported by state subsidy of the arts, this argument also often concerns the appropriate allocation of tax dollars and the need for the arts sector to be more market driven. While a cultural institution can readily apply to governments for support of a show on Leonardo da Vinci's sketches, it is harder to justify showing off concept drawings of the dark Sith, Darth Maul, even if this is what the public might "really" want to see. In this case, the "popular" is evoked both as a democratic principle *and* as a judgment about who can make sense of "real" art. By including more "popular" shows, the museums invite more people inside them—but not, of course, to see the kinds of art objects they were initially designed to exhibit (see Figure 1.1).

Figure 1.1 Many museums now embrace elements of popular culture. *The Art of Video Games*, an exhibition at the Smithsonian Institute in Washington, DC, included a physical installation as well as an online, interactive component. Source: *The Art of Video Games* exhibition at the Smithsonian American Art Museum, March 16, 2012–September 30, 2012

Another example of the slipperiness of the concept of the popular concerns the use of the related word "people" in the context of political protest. International political meetings, from the G20 to Rio + 20, frequently encounter opposition in the form of "people's summits" organized by activist groups. In this example, the word "people" connotes something like democratic or grassroots or ordinary, in contrast to the powerful minority of state leaders and corporate CEOs. While government leaders denounce the organizers of such meetings as "special interest groups" (versus "democratically elected" leaders), activists counter these claims by highlighting governments' subordination of social justice to corporate agendas and the resulting failure to represent the interests of the people. The term "people" here becomes the symbolic linchpin of a battle to gain the moral high ground over the substantive issues under debate. As with the art museum, the word "people" and its derivative "popular" are used here to convey something roughly opposite to "elite," though the *value* of those terms means something entirely different in each context.

So we can add a couple of new elements to our understanding of the word "popular." First, it tends to carry with it connotations of value that are implicitly contrasted with the value of what it is *not*, though those values are seen differently depending on who is talking and in what context. Second, as is particularly evident in the latter example of people's summits, the question of who or what constitutes the popular is tangled up with questions of power.

With this in mind, let's return to the apparently simple usage of "popular" with which we began this section and think about it in a little more detail. Who are the people who define the "popularity" of *NCIS*? Are they the unenlightened masses who lack the ability to discriminate between schlock and substance? Are they discerning viewers exercising their consumer choice? Or are they engaged in an act of political activism, employing the cultural resources of *NCIS* to construct an agenda for crime prevention or progressive social change? The slightly ludicrous quality of the last possibility raises a quite serious question about how we understand the popular: What kind of agency—that is, possibility for self-motivated activity or action—is involved on the part of "the people" in determining or defining something to be "popular"? This question has particular significance when we start to talk about popular culture.

What Is Popular Culture?

Common uses of the term "popular culture" reflect in interesting ways our understandings of the two separate words we discussed above. The most familiar use of the term "popular culture" identifies it with the entertainment produced through and by commercial media (television, film, the music industry, etc.) that have the economic and technological capacity to reach large, demographically diverse, and geographically dispersed audiences. Popularity is measured, in this case, by patterns of **consumption**: it refers to the things we buy (or watch, or listen to, etc.). A somewhat different use of "popular culture" defines it in terms not of consumption but production: popular culture is what "the people" make, or do, for themselves. This definition fits fairly closely with the anthropological definition of culture as "the practices of everyday life."

Both of these definitions differ quite clearly from the elite capital-C Culture defended by cranky art patrons. Apart from this, however, their connotations are quite different and even oppositional: "do-it-yourself" popular culture is explicitly different from the culture that is produced by large corporate entities whose interest in the everyday practices of their consumers is shaped by their need to figure out how best to sell them things.

Indeed, the kind of culture produced by the commercial media is often seen as threatening the culture of everyday life by diverting people's desire for fulfillment—a desire that can ultimately be satisfied only by productive activity—into habits of passive consumption.

Folk Culture and Mass Culture

To distinguish clearly between these two different forms of cultural production, critics will sometimes use the terms "folk culture" and "mass culture." **Folk culture** refers to those cultural products and practices that have developed over time within a particular community or socially identifiable group and that are communicated from generation to generation and among people who tend to be known to one another. It tends to be seen as the direct expression of the life experiences shared by its creators and their audience (Nachbar and Lause 15; Grossberg, Wartella, and Whitney 37). **Mass culture**, on the other hand, is produced for an unknown, disparate audience. While the transmission of folk culture is generally technologically simple (e.g., face-to-face, oral communication), mass culture depends on electronic (or mechanical) media to convey its message to the largest possible audience in order to secure maximum profit, which is its ultimate goal. These terms can serve to make useful distinctions between kinds of cultural production, highlighting the differences between, say, an Aboriginal dot painting and an MTV rap video. On even a superficial examination, however, the differences start to look a little fuzzy. Aboriginal paintings have been reproduced in forms ranging from mugs to T-shirts to high fashion. These uses are frequently condemned as appropriation or cultural theft—a justifiable charge in the many cases where Aboriginal artists are compensated poorly, or not at all, for the use of their work. But in the increasing instances where Aborigines direct and control the marketing of traditional art, complaints may have more to do with romantic, non-Aboriginal conceptions of primitive authenticity than they do with concerns about cultural ownership or legitimacy. Rap music, for its part, is now a multibillion-dollar industry, but one that emerged relatively recently from the African American street culture of the South Bronx. In each of these cases, it is difficult to identify the precise moment when folk culture metamorphosed into mass culture. The attempt to maintain a strict division is not just tricky in a practical sense, but also, arguably, some-what suspect **ideologically**, an issue explored in more detail in Chapter 5.

The desire to preserve a folk culture safe from the corrupting influence of commerce is often inflected by a nostalgic desire to return to a (mythical) moment of history in which cultural and social identities were secure and cultural boundaries were clear. When this desire is extended to a socially and economically disadvantaged group, as in the two examples above, the situation becomes even more complicated. While it might be argued that the preservation of folk culture is a matter of community survival, the unhappiness of white collectors at the move toward mass-produced art may be motivated by concerns that have little to do with Indigenous peoples' autonomy and more with how the value of their own art pieces will be affected. A less crudely **materialist** motivation for consumer nostalgia in this case might be a well-intentioned, if racist, aesthetic investment in the image of the "noble savage." This imaginary figure conjures up a purer, more natural world outside Western commercial culture while occupying a comfortable place within it.

However seemingly progressive the cause that is being (or has been) promoted in the name of "the people," "folk culture" remains a term whose peculiarly heavy ideological baggage should set off alarm bells every time we hear or read it; the same alarm bells that should go off when we hear politicians invoke the mythical category of "ordinary working folks." Just who are these "ordinary" people? This is not to say that we need to abandon completely the idea of folk culture and all its troublesome derivations. Like mass culture, it retains some value as a descriptive term to designate particular kinds of cultural production, especially when referring to a time before our present capitalist moment—a moment when **authenticity** and commercial value are increasingly impossible to disentangle, when there is a sense in which, as one critic puts it, "*all* culture is mass culture" (Denning 258, emphasis added). We explore this idea a little further in Chapter 5.

Suggested Activity 1.1

Does commercialism destroy the authenticity of a cultural product or practice? Or does the authenticity of an object or practice increase its commercial value and potential? What does it mean if it is possible for us to answer both of these questions affirmatively? How does the divide between authenticity and commercial value work in the case of a practice like ecotourism and an object like the first release of an indie band on its own label?

The Culture of Everyday Life

To signal this ambiguity, and to avoid producing a definition of popular culture that falls too clearly on the side of celebrating the folk or denigrating the masses, we might define popular culture as something like "the communicative practices of everyday life" (where "communicative practices" comprises all those activities concerned with the production of meaning: talking, writing, social rituals such as eating, shopping, dancing, music, visual culture, sports, fashion, etc.) that are shared among many members of a society, including and especially those who are not particularly socially, economically, or politically powerful (see Figure 1.2). This somewhat clumsy definition accomplishes three things: (i) it signals the inclusion of mass media alongside, and even within, the practices

Figure 1.2 "Culture" includes not only artistic and commercial creative practices and texts, but also aspects of everyday life, such as the rituals that surround food. Source: © Corbis/SuperStock

of everyday life, without determining in advance what relationship it has to those practices; (ii) it emphasizes the *meaningful* nature of popular culture—meaningful in the
sense that it is important, as well as in the sense that it is concerned with the production
of sense and social value; and (iii) it highlights the issue of power that always and overtly
dogs the production of culture in general and popular culture in particular.

The Politics of Popular Culture

Why is power such a central issue for understanding popular culture? As we have already
tried to suggest, culture is bound up closely with other aspects of human existence. As "the
sphere of meaning which unifies the spheres of production (economics) and social relations
(politics)" (O'Sullivan *et al.* 68), culture is concerned not just with individual tastes and
desires, but also with the fundamental organization of society—with the distribution of
material and symbolic power. Culture both reflects and influences social organization and
the distribution of power. In the early twenty-first century, in most parts of the world, the
dominant economic system is **capitalism** (for more on capitalism, see Close-Up 1.1). This
means that the key characteristics of capitalism, including both its wealth-generating
capacity and the patterns of inequitable distribution on which that capacity depends, help
determine the shape of culture. This is particularly true for popular culture.

Close-Up 1.1 Capitalism

Capitalism is an economic system based on private ownership of the means of production
and distribution, and geared toward the generation of profit. It is the dominant economic
system in the world today. It is not the only economic system that has ever been in place,
nor is it likely to be the last way in which human beings organize their economies, despite
some claims to the contrary.

Loosely definable as a system of private enterprise whose primary aim is the production of profit, capitalism has been developing since at least the fifteenth century and
underwrites many of the economic and cultural institutions that we take for granted
today, such as private property, individual freedom, and the imperative of economic
growth. Our tendency today to see these features of capitalism as not only positive but
also *natural*—the products of human nature rather than consciously worked-out ideas—
makes it harder to see its less desirable aspects, such as social fragmentation, the unequal
distribution of wealth, and the conversion of everything (including life itself) into something that can be bought or sold.

These brutal elements of capitalism were particularly evident during the heyday of
European **colonialism** from the seventeenth to the nineteenth centuries. During this
period, the exploitation of resources and enslavement of people from the non-European
world helped make possible the massive accumulation of wealth enjoyed by a relatively
small percentage of Europeans. This in turn fueled the Industrial Revolution, in which both
the productive and the destructive elements of capitalism were further intensified.

In capitalist economies, the means of creating, distributing, and exchanging wealth lie
mainly in the hands of individuals and corporations (which in North America have the legal
rights of individuals—see Close-Up 5.2), rather than in public or state hands. The value of
goods and labor is defined not by their social usefulness or significance, but by how much
they can be exchanged for. The main goal of individuals in capitalism is to maximize the
profit or the wages they receive. Proponents believe that, through the dance of supply and
demand, goods and services are optimally and efficiently distributed throughout society.

Detractors point to the growing gap between the wealthy and the poor, whose life activity is often organized to generate even more wealth for those at the top.

Postmodern—also referred to as postindustrial or late—capitalism is distinguished by the fact that by comparison to earlier eras of capitalism, there is now a far greater emphasis on the exchange of information and services (e.g., software and banking) as opposed to hard goods (e.g., steel and cars) in an economy that has become globally integrated.

In fact, one could argue that capitalism does not just inform particular *versions* of popular culture, in the sense of sustaining some dominant narratives (e.g., the story of success through hard work) and disabling others (e.g., the triumph of the group over the individual) or by enabling certain kinds of technological innovation. *Capitalism enables the production of popular culture, period.* We will go on to trace the historical evolution of the relationship between capitalism and popular culture in Chapter 2. For now, it is sufficient to note that the economic and social struggle that is intrinsic to capitalism is fought, to some extent, on the terrain of popular culture.

File Sharing

A simple example will serve to illustrate the kind of struggle we're talking about. Through much of the twentieth century, the evolution of the global, but particularly North American, music industry was a story of skyrocketing profits. This story culminated in the introduction of the CD, which forced consumers to pay considerably more than what they had paid for vinyl LPs (with what many agreed was only a marginal improvement in sound quality), not to mention shelling out for expensive new sound systems. As promised price reductions never materialized, a quiet groundswell of annoyance with the recording industry began to grow. It seemed like a classic case of the customer getting cheated by corporations. Then, in the late-1990s, using the same digital technology that enabled the development of the CD, peer-to-peer file-sharing services such as Napster crept onto the scene, allowing people to swap music files on their computers without paying a cent. The recording industry fought back on two fronts, launching a series of lawsuits in a bid to recoup lost profits and creating programs that would enable users to download individual songs, albums, movies, television episodes, and series for (relatively) low fees. Meanwhile, determined file sharers—"pirates," in industry parlance—continue to find new ways to use the technology and the decentralized structure of the Internet to outmaneuver their relatively cumbersome, slow-moving corporate opponents.

The story of the changing dynamics of music and film distribution is a complicated one, with seemingly clear battle lines between "the people" and "corporations" blurred by such issues as the rights of musicians and filmmakers to get paid for their work, the accessibility of technology, and its implications for the construction of the community. Moreover, it isn't clear what effects the trend toward increasingly individualized, **privatized** music and film might have on our shared public culture (see Chapter 10 for further discussion of intellectual property and digital culture).

Suggested Activity 1.2

What are your feelings about file sharing? Does it constitute theft, as the film and music industries claim and the law increasingly confirms? Or is it a legitimate, even a virtuous form of genuinely popular culture? Do you see this shift in the way consumers access cultural products as empowering to producers, or does it threaten their livelihoods?

Popular culture in this example is not simply an arena in which the disempowered fight back, defining themselves out from under corporate power. Neither does it work simply to maintain those structures by reining in resistance, bringing it back under the umbrella of the dominant ideology of consumer capitalism. Rather, it is subject to a constant struggle over pleasure, profit, and, ultimately, the distribution of social and economic power in the world.

Power Relationships

This dimension of struggle means that it is impossible ever to fix the meaning of popular culture in terms of a collection of objects or practices, or in terms of a single group who can be said to possess them. We need to understand it, as cultural theorist Stuart Hall puts it, not as "a mere descriptive inventory—which may have the negative effect of freezing popular culture into some timeless descriptive mould—but [as] the relations of power which are constantly punctuating and dividing the domain of culture into its preferred and its residual categories" ("Notes" 234). What is true for the objects and practices of popular culture is also true for those who use and/or participate in them. If, as another critic, John Fiske, has claimed, "popular culture is the culture of the subordinated and disempowered" (4), this does not mean that it is possible to identify, by means of a simple checklist, who is "in" and who is "out." Rather than existing in a stable form as the property of a single group, power moves between and among individuals and institutions; this movement is registered with particular intensity in the domain of popular culture. In the absence of the certainty of clear categories, we are left with the less comfortable but more expansive framework of a series of open-ended questions. In evaluating the significance of popular culture, we always need to ask: "Who says what, how, to whom, with what effect and for what purpose?" (Williams, qtd. in Burke 218).

Why Study Popular Culture? A Brief History of Cultural Studies

In one sense, cultural studies boils down to a bunch of theories and methodologies that help us find the answers to these straightforward questions. To understand why they're *good* questions—and less straightforward than they might seem—a bit of perspective is necessary. The very brief history of cultural studies that follows offers such a perspective. In the process, it might also help begin to answer a question you might have asked yourself (with gentle prodding from family or friends, perhaps): What is the point of cultural studies? Why not do something more respectable/useful/career enhancing/*real*?

Every year, a couple of reports appear in the media about some new and outrageous course that has made it onto the curriculum of some university or college. In the 1980s, it was a sprinkling of courses on Madonna and feminism; now such a course is more likely to be on reality television, social media, or the cultural politics of fat. Less remarkable than the appearance of these courses is the fact that they still raise eyebrows. Only a few decades ago, the idea of a course on popular culture in general would have been unthinkable—the equivalent of bringing a case of beer into class and asking students to contemplate the meaning of drinking in their lives while getting happily buzzed. The fact that popular culture is more or less comfortably entrenched in the halls of higher learning while some aspects of it—certain celebrities, particular practices—are still excluded raises questions that are relevant for our discussion in this book: What counts as worthwhile knowledge in our culture? What is the relationship between popular culture and education? How has this relationship changed? Why has it changed?

Close-Up 1.2 Cultural Studies

Looser in its parameters than conventional disciplines such as psychology or history, "cultural studies" is, as one practitioner puts it, "a term of convenience for a fairly dispersed array of theoretical and political positions which, however widely divergent they might be in other respects, share a commitment to examining cultural practices from the point of view of their intrication with, and within, relations of power" (Bennett 33). It embraces a definition of culture that includes—in addition to conventional "texts" such as books—television shows, music, advertising, and ways of life (in the sense of concrete practices such as shopping, eating, drinking, fashion, etc.), as well as more abstract structures such as language, beliefs, "the contradictory forms of 'common sense' which have taken root in and helped to shape popular life," and the institutions that surround them (S. Hall "Gramsci" 26).

This broad definition of culture obviously contains a complex mix of elements—social, linguistic, political, economic; indeed, the study of popular culture might be described in one sense as the study of the interrelationships among what were once seen as discrete fields of existence. As such, cultural studies embraces a number of different disciplines, including literary studies, film studies, political science, anthropology, sociology, and communications studies, and employs a variety of methodologies: close reading, ethnography, content analysis, population surveys, and historical research.

Popular Culture Invades the Classroom

In Chapter 2, "The History of Popular Culture," we talk about the development in the mid to late nineteenth century of a distinction between high, or capital-C, Culture and popular culture. Among the engineers of this divide were "rational recreationists"—religious and charitable groups bent on "improving" the lower classes—and education experts such as Matthew Arnold, who saw in "culture" a way to knit society together and soften the edges of the materialism infecting, in different ways, the middle and lower classes. Strangely, it was from this clearly hostile move against popular culture that the impulse to understand it—an impulse that informs this book—was born.

Sneaking in through the Back Door

Matthew Arnold and his followers saw mass media (understood in the form of such things as popular novels) as leading to social disintegration through the replacement of spiritual with commercial values. They were particularly concerned with what they saw as the crass materialism of the new middle class and the degeneration of working-class morals. Behind this critique lay a powerful resistance to **industrialization** and nostalgia for an organic agrarian society in which people knew one another (and, not incidentally, knew their own place; **class mobility** was not a feature of this society). As people moved away from the supporting structures of church and community into the alienating and anonymous environment of the city, it was argued, they became vulnerable to all sorts of corrupting influences. Implicit in this position is a view of the masses as childlike in their ability to be easily led. The problem, as cultural conservatives saw it, was that they were being led by the wrong forces. The beneficial influences of the classic works of Culture, which discouraged the pursuits of materialism by offering more spiritual forms of sustenance, were being replaced by **commodities** that, in their form (cheap paperback novels, pop songs played on the gramophone) as in their content, seemed to celebrate values of easy pleasure and instant gratification.

These critiques grew throughout the early decades of the twentieth century as new cultural technologies and modes of production facilitated easier distribution of forms of popular culture such as fiction, movies, music, and eventually television. Recognizing that it was impossible to shield impressionable minds from this trash, early twentieth-century educators such as F.R. and Q.D. Leavis suggested that schools should focus on training students' tastes to help them discriminate between true culture and its "multitudinous counter-influences—films, newspapers, advertising—indeed the whole world outside the class-room" (Leavis and Thompson 1). Such discrimination, they argued, was essential to the development of a sensitive moral character.

The course of study they proposed featured such inspiring study questions as "'Modern publicity debases the currency of spiritual and emotional life generally': Discuss and illustrate" (121). The target of these "discussion" questions (which don't leave a whole lot of room for discussion!) is both the products of popular media culture and the ignorant masses who consume them. Education in taste, then, is, as Pierre Bourdieu was later to point out (see Chapter 5), an education in class discrimination. That many of the students themselves came from the class they were now being taught to despise was something not taken up by the Leavises or other educators of the time.

In the Leavises' educational program, popular culture made it onto the curriculum as an example of a social problem—like alcohol, say, or bad hygiene—that could, with the proper techniques of discipline and avoidance, be successfully banished. In a way, though, these efforts were defeated by their own intentions: bringing popular culture into the classroom both acknowledged and promoted its legitimacy as a powerful social force.

The Democratization of Culture

The Leavises' approach to culture was unashamedly elitist. F.R. Leavis's 1930 work, *Mass Civilization and Minority Culture,* painted a picture of a society clearly divided, in which the cultured minority on the inside, the world of "*us,*" fought valiantly to preserve itself from the degenerate populace on the outside, the world of "them." These certainties began to break down after the Second World War, when an increasingly diverse university student body started to challenge the boundary between "us" and "them." Particularly significant was the arrival of a large number of (mostly male) working-class students. Many of these were adults who, because of the war or for economic reasons, had deferred their education. They brought along with them a whole raft of knowledge and experiences that did not conform to elite conceptions of Culture.

Williams, Hoggart, and Thompson

From this group, three figures emerged as particularly influential in the development of the more inclusive vision of "culture" that would come to define cultural studies. Raymond Williams and Richard Hoggart, scholars of English literature, and E.P. Thompson, a historian, all began their university careers as scholarship students from working-class backgrounds. Williams's and Hoggart's later experiences working as adult-education tutors confirmed their sense that the dominant scholarly understanding of culture was far too narrow and exclusive to encompass the rich and complex fabric of their students' lives.

While the work of these three theorists is characterized by important differences of disciplinary perspective, approach, and argument, some of the central general implications of their work can be summarized here. First, all three established the legitimacy of working-class life as a subject of academic study, expanding the boundaries not just of culture but also of history to include experiences traditionally dismissed as insignificant. In the process, they also refined the definition of culture, moving away from a "literary-moral" to a more anthropological understanding of it as "the 'whole process' by means of which meanings and definitions are socially constructed and historically transformed." In this new definition, "literature and art count as only one, specially privileged, kind of social communication" (Williams, qtd. in S. Hall "Cultural Studies and the Centre" 19).

For Hoggart and Williams in particular, literature and art retained their significance as embodiments of important human values. Part of their projects recalled the efforts of F.R. Leavis in their determination to expose students to classic works of literature in order to enhance their literacy and, by extension, their understanding of the broader cultural contexts that shaped their lives. They all shared, to a certain extent, Leavis's elitist disdain for the products of the **culture industry**, enhanced by nostalgia for an earlier, more innocent (and partly imaginary) time when culture had yet to be totally corrupted by commerce. Hoggart and Williams broadened Leavis's focus, however, in their extension of the principles of literary criticism, especially the techniques of close reading, to a wide range of popular texts—songs, magazines, newspapers—and in their emphasis on the connections between these texts and other aspects of everyday life: leisure activities, family relationships, gender roles, and so on. They also differed from Leavis in the crucial respect that, while Leavis wanted to preserve the terrain of minority culture against the threat of "mass" civilization, they sought to enhance democracy by developing the cultural literacy of ordinary people, helping them to understand the substance of their own lives.

One important area of conflict between, and even within, the works of these theorists concerns the relationship between the individual and broader institutional and social structures. While histories "from below" such as Thompson's tried to foreground working-class experience, and also to highlight the **agency** of working-class people in shaping their own lives, his work was also characterized by a recognition of the way in which agency is shaped and constrained by broader economic relations. Williams and Hoggart, though equally interested in the conditions that would allow working people to become the subjects of their own history, rejected what they saw as the economic determinism of traditional **Marxism**, insisting on the substance and autonomy of culture as a shaping force. Debates about the relative power of individuals and the structures that constrain them, the role of ideology in determining hierarchies of cultural value, and the shaping effects of economics on culture (and vice versa) became increasingly urgent in the context of a rapidly expanding culture industry. The establishment of the new Centre for Contemporary Cultural Studies at the University of Birmingham (headed by Richard Hoggart) in 1964 engaged these questions with a specific focus on the study of media and youth subcultures—a diversity of subjects that marked the ambiguity of popular culture as defined simultaneously from above and below.

The Americanization of Popular Culture

The changes that were occurring in Britain in the years following the Second World War were part of broader, global upheavals. One significant change resulted from Britain's shift from a dominant to a subordinate political and economic power in relation to the United States as the new leader of the "free" (i.e., noncommunist) world. Combined with the position of media dominance that the United States had occupied since the early twentieth century, the new configuration of global power meant that, from the 1950s onward, global popular culture increasingly had an American face.

British cultural critics had a mixed reaction to these changes. In the 1950s, art critics working at the Institute of Contemporary Arts (ICA) established a working group to study contemporary trends in architecture, visual culture, and other forms of popular art. They were particularly interested in—and, generally, excited by—the growing influence of American popular culture on British culture. Their approach was different from most of the other critical responses to the culture industry, which were just that: critical.

In the United States itself, serious interest in popular culture was motivated by an unlikely source: the **Cold War**. The contest between communism and capitalism spurred a push in American universities to study, and thereby promote, the **liberal** democratic values that represented the American way of life. American studies programs sprang up that were at first mostly committed to the teaching of American "high" culture—literature and art, along with the triumphant narrative of American history.

Soon these programs began to acknowledge the importance of the media in communicating democratic values through popular culture. The tendency to view the new media culture in a celebratory mode, as the embodiment of America's democratic spirit (as opposed to the culture of censorship and repression that was seen to exist in Russia), competed with concerns about the capacity of the commercial media to lure audiences into habits of unthinking **consumerism**. Concerns about subliminal advertising (see Chapter 5) played a large part in the move to incorporate media studies into university curricula.

While worries about the capacity of the media to weaken society's moral fiber by bombarding it with images promoting sex and shopping preoccupied many American educators, the explicit *American*ness of the media also concerned many critics outside the United States. This vaguely defined quality was seen to shape not just the content of a popular culture that promoted values of liberalism, **individualism**, and consumerism, but also the way in which it was produced and distributed. Improvements in communications technology, in conjunction with American economic and cultural expansionism, granted the products of the American culture industry unprecedented access to the rest of the world. This development spawned fears about **cultural imperialism** (see Chapter 9), as well as the growth of critical media studies in Britain and elsewhere.

The Decolonization of Culture

Challenges to the comfortable dominance of the model of British Culture advanced by Matthew Arnold and the Leavises came not just from a shift in power away from Britain toward the United States, but also from more widely dispersed challenges to the world order associated with decolonization (see Chapter 7). The challenge was not only from the renaissance of other traditions, such as the African and South Asian cultures that had been submerged during the colonial period, but also the necessity—highlighted by anticolonial activists such as Mohandas Gandhi and Frantz Fanon—for European culture to confront the contradictions that lay at the heart of its cherished ideals of freedom and **progress**. Around the same time, women's and labor groups, along with the civil rights movement in the United States, had begun to highlight the fault lines of **race** and gender that defined the supposedly universal norms and values of liberal democracy.

What Is an Education For?

In addition to their broad consequences for society as a whole, these social justice movements, which came to a head in the massive protests launched in the United States, France, and Mexico in 1968, had an enormous impact on higher education. Along with anticolonial and labor rights activists, students were among the strongest participants in the protests. Their chief demand—for a greater role in determining the shape of their education—was in part an expression of anger about the detachment of the world inside the university from what was going on outside it: lectures celebrating the values of freedom, civilization, and human dignity did not fit with the realities of violent conflict such as the Vietnam War, human rights abuses, and environmental destruction. If academic institutions were to serve any useful role in advancing human understanding, they needed to acknowledge the bankruptcy of many of their foundational principles.

The crisis of higher education sparked by the social movements of the 1960s had an intellectual as well as an institutional dimension; indeed, it highlighted the connection between those dimensions by revealing the ways in which privileged forms of knowledge were bound up with structures of power. This is one of the key insights of the cultural moment known as postmodernism, which brought about what one theorist described as a "crisis of legitimation" (Lyotard 26): once the most fundamental beliefs of Western culture are shown to be the product not of timeless truth but of particular social arrangements, they and the structures of authority that uphold them crumble, taking with them the possibility of *any* universal, objective truth.

Culture Wars

The somewhat grandiose term **culture wars** refers to fights that took place in humanities departments of American universities in the 1980s—fights that spilled over into the arenas of media and public policy—between a traditional idea of Culture and the forces of **postcolonialism**, feminism, and postmodernism that sought to undermine it. While the move was sometimes characterized as a campaign simply to replace the Western canon— the preserve of Dead White Males—with a new and eclectic selection of texts, from works by women of color to Hollywood films, what was actually at issue was not so much the works themselves, but the structures of authority that sanctioned some forms of culture while dismissing others.

One important challenge to those structures was a shift in emphasis from Culture to cultures—a rhetorical shift that expressed more substantial changes in focus. First, and most generally, this marked a move away from the humanities/literary critical definition of culture toward a more anthropological one. This entailed both an extension of the term from its traditional focus on works of art to embrace the practices of everyday life, and a recognition of the existence of multiple cultures, existing within and between societies. The idea of culture was thus transformed from something timeless and universal to a historically determined, and thus constantly changing, phenomenon with local and global dimensions. The myth of a unified *English* culture, which frequently lurked behind the "universal" label, began to waver in the face of the recognition of the many *sub* cultures—youth culture, for example, or gay culture—on whose exclusion it was based. At the same time, the invisible lines of race (white) and gender (male) that marked traditional definitions of culture—including the more inclusivist, working-class definitions proposed by Williams and Hoggart—began to emerge through the pointed critiques of women and **minorities**, who had been stuck somewhere on its margins.

The opening out of the idea of culture in response to the claims of its excluded others occurred in conjunction with the arrival in Britain and North America of successive waves of immigrants from the former colonies, including many who ended up working and studying in universities. Some, like the Jamaican-born Stuart Hall, who succeeded Richard Hoggart as director of the Birmingham Centre for Contemporary Cultural Studies, helped to define new directions in cultural studies by, among other things, insisting on its global dimensions and on the necessary connectedness between intellectual work and politics.

Who won the culture wars, then? The persistence of undergraduate programs that still require English majors to take a course in Shakespeare suggests that the ideological magic of "Culture" has not entirely been exorcised. However, the enormous growth in cultural studies programs would seem to suggest that history is on the side of the culture critics. This might look like a victory for feminism and postcolonialism against conservatism—but, as should be clear by now, the relationship between culture and power is never that simple.

Culture and Economics—The Postindustrial Revolution

As in the late eighteenth and nineteenth centuries, the social and political upheavals that marked the late twentieth and early twenty-first centuries were accompanied by economic and technological changes, which have made culture a very different thing than it was 100 or even 30 years ago (for a broad discussion of these changes, see Chapter 10). As with the Industrial Revolution, the weakening of old regulations, in conjunction with the decline in traditional structures of authority, created new freedoms. However, these also eroded structures that had served to nurture and not just to suppress the development of diverse forms of popular culture.

The extension and intensification of market forces granted greater powers to private interests, but weakened the imaginary and actual power of public institutions. The university, one of the key sites for the distribution of what Pierre Bourdieu calls *cultural capital*, is affected particularly strongly by these shifts, in terms of the way its resources are allocated, as well as the role it is seen to play in society. While that role was traditionally conceived as one of nurturing future citizens—a goal facilitated by ensuring students had a solid grounding in the humanities, English (or American) literature in particular—the idea of university is now more likely to conform to the much less romantic vision of a factory for the production of workers in the global knowledge economy. Students, according to this model, are seen not as junior members of an academic community to which they are bound by an **idealized** commitment to learning or becoming "cultured," but as consumers—and, ultimately, products—to be bought up by the corporations that play an increasing role in funding, and thereby shaping, the universities' basic operations.

According to the essentially commercial logic of this model of education, resources cannot be wasted on those departments or faculties that are concerned with abstract values such as citizenship or critical thought. These departments—English, for example, or philosophy—are forced to rationalize their budgets and to modify their course offerings to favor those that can be taught by a few faculty members to a large number of students from a variety of different disciplines. Here, then, is one institutional explanation for why courses in popular culture are quietly popping up alongside (and sometimes in place of) more traditional courses in subjects such as, say, medieval history: they are popular in the same commercial sense that *NCIS* is popular, which is to say they are profitable.

This poses a challenge for cultural studies scholars, whose aim, as we have suggested throughout this book, is not simply to affirm the value of commercial culture, nor—equally simply—to denounce it, but to map its place within a constellation of signifying practices that correspond to underlying relations of power. That constellation is constantly shifting, which means that we need to remain constantly alert to the social and political significance of *all* of our cultural roles, including the role of students and teachers of popular culture. Why—personally, institutionally—are we doing what we are doing? What other subjects *might* we be studying if we were not studying popular culture? What are the educational implications of the growing popularity of popular culture courses?

Why This? Why Now? Why Me? A Couple of Final Arguments for the Importance of Studying Popular Culture

To sum up the last few sections, there are lots of reasons why you are reading a textbook on popular culture instead of (or maybe in addition to) Chaucer's *Canterbury Tales*, or Joseph Conrad's *Heart of Darkness*. First and foremost are the political and social changes that, over the course of the twentieth century, demanded a radical rethinking of the intellectual foundations of "culture" and its connection to other areas of life. These changes have shaped society in general and education in particular. On a more pragmatic level, schools, colleges, and universities have changed their curricula in response to economic pressures, so that what is considered valuable in educational terms is increasingly determined by what is profitable. Those are large, impersonal, and, in the latter case, cynical reasons for why popular culture is suddenly a popular thing to study.

We would also encourage you to think about this in more personal terms. One compelling reason to study popular culture is that it is everywhere. To borrow an expression from T.S. Eliot, if most academic study is about helping to make the strange familiar, studying popular culture is a process of making the familiar strange. This can be a pretty uncomfortable experience, since it involves taking what feels most natural and pleasurable and subjecting it to detached inquiry. Actually *studying* popular culture helps us to move beyond a range of typical reactions to it: (i) unconscious consumption (which is only a theoretical position, since most consumers have achieved some level of critical consciousness); (ii) contemptuous dismissal—"popular culture is trash, so I avoid it" (an equally mythical position, since it is virtually impossible to live entirely outside commercial culture); and (iii) cynical consumption ("I *know* this is garbage, but I like it anyway"—or, stranger, "I like this *because* I know it is garbage"). Most of us probably respond to culture in a way that is something like the third position. A variation on this position is the belief that, while other people are vulnerable to the messages of popular culture, *we* are smart enough to see through its manipulations.

While it might seem to make this position appear even more valid, studying popular culture usually leads to a different conclusion, revealing the culture industry to be both less and more powerful than we initially imagined. Cultural studies unmasks and to a certain extent disables the power of commercial culture by helping us recognize the narratives, genres, myths, and **discourses** that convey its values—values that tap into fundamental beliefs about ourselves, our relationships with others, and society at large.

Yet, as cultural studies also emphasizes, culture is not just about texts, about how the products of the commercial media are put together, and how certain meanings are produced, but also about how we consume those products, what we actually *do* with them. The title of this book, *Popular Culture: A User's Guide*, reflects our belief that not only is it possible for all of us to learn to *use* popular culture more effectively, in the sense of actually shaping it in productive ways, but also that it is vital that we do so. As Stuart Hall puts it, "There is something *at stake* in Cultural Studies, in a way that I think, and hope, is not exactly true of many other very important intellectual and critical practices" (S. Hall "Cultural Studies and Its Theoretical Legacies" 278).

Many cultural studies practitioners go further, stressing a key connection between doing cultural studies and engaging in political activism—as distinct from other kinds of study, which stress mere "technocratic competence" (Freccero 5). The study of popular culture is necessarily political, in the sense of being concerned with the distribution of social and economic power in society. It is important to recognize, however—in spite of the prescriptivist tone of what we've just said about why you *should* want to do cultural studies—that each of us approaches the study of culture in different ways, and that students and teachers of popular culture are often situated quite differently in relation to the subject, based on factors such as age, class, experience, and temperament. For students, what often proves most illuminating (or, for some, simply irritating) about taking a course in cultural studies is its revelation of the connection between popular culture and power. For teachers, one of the insights that proves most strangely elusive—one that they often need to be reminded of by students—is that popular culture is about pleasure. Figuring out what happens at the intersection of those forces of power and pleasure is perhaps the principal value of studying popular culture.

As this is a particularly busy intersection, we find it helpful to access it through a few relatively straightforward paths or angles of approach. On the broadest level, these angles might be identified as *representation*, the process of making meaning from sign systems that encompass anything from words and images to physical structures (cars, buildings, cities) to fashion accessories; *production*, which encompasses the individual and corporate entities involved in the creation and distribution of cultural products, including the technologies through which they are produced and reproduced; and *consumption*, which involves the economic, technological, and physical processes by which different audiences derive meaning from cultural products.

Of course, these categories—the subjects of Chapters 3, 4, and 5, respectively—can't help but bleed into one another. The texts and practices of culture are inseparable from the means of technological production or from what individual audiences do with them—nor can they be separated from what are conventionally regarded as noncultural realms of existence such as economics and politics. Lest popular culture begin to sound like everything (or nothing), let's try to pin it down more firmly by returning to our original example of drinking coffee. An examination of this practice through the lenses of representation, production, and consumption can help us understand how popular culture operates, drawing us in as producers and consumers and working, literally, to reshape the world.

Coffee as Popular Culture

Coffee is a part of culture to the extent that we can ask "What does coffee *mean*?" Coffee is not, in other words, just "a liquid brown drug" (L. H. Cohen 10), but part of a complex set of social rituals. The significance of coffee is hugely determined by context: its meaning shifts depending on whether we are drinking it at home or in a café, from a mug or a Styrofoam cup. Its significance also varies depending on whether we are alone or with friends and in what other activities we are engaged: a social meeting, for example, or a late-night cram session—in which case it might really be coffee's status as a "liquid brown drug" that we are seeking (see Figure 1.3).

Figure 1.3 What is in a cup of coffee? More than a "liquid brown drug," coffee derives its meaning within interconnected networks of representation, consumption and production. Source: © Alexcrab/ iStockphoto

But even then, when the physical properties of coffee are arguably more important than its symbolic properties, it is *still* more than just a drug. After all, if it were just a stimulant we were after, there are obviously other, more powerful options out there. The fact that most of us are probably inclined to reach for coffee rather than, say, amphetamines speaks to more than the question of availability or a fear of being arrested for possession. In fact, these questions (why is caffeine legal while amphetamines are controlled and pot is illegal?) are themselves tied up in the culture of coffee—what it means in a broader social context. To answer them, along with the broader question of how coffee comes to be part of culture, we need to look at coffee in the context of representation, production, and consumption.

The Representation of Coffee

To say that coffee "signifies"—that it refers to something other than its literal, physical substance—is not to say that it has some kind of intrinsic or inherent meaning. Rather, coffee acquires different, specific meanings as it is incorporated within different economic and social practices. It therefore makes sense to ask not just *what* does coffee mean, but also *how* does it acquire meaning, and under what circumstances?

To talk about the meaning of coffee is to talk about how it operates in systems of **representation**, which translate a world of objects into one of sense, significance, and values. So what kind of significance or value is attached to coffee?

Suggested Activity 1.3

Take a few minutes and write down some of the meanings attached to coffee in your life. What kinds of associations does it have and how are they marked by their differences from and similarities to those of other things you ingest (water, milk, beer, etc.)? How do these associations change depending on the context—where, when, with whom, in what circumstances you're drinking coffee? (Or *not* drinking it; strangely, this exercise may be easier if you're *not* a coffee drinker: it's easier to critically analyze a cultural practice if you're detached from it.)

The Mythology of Drugs

We discuss the significance of **mythology** in more detail in Chapter 3. A key aspect to think about for now is the ways in which cultural mythologies tap into the underlying social structures of a culture, including its relations of power. To understand how this works, we can think for a moment about the cultural or *mythological* difference between coffee and some of the other drugs we cited above. Coffee, alcohol, and marijuana are all drugs (i.e., they all have mind- or body-altering properties), but they *signify* differently. The most obvious significance concerns their legality: as legal substances, coffee and alcohol fall fairly comfortably within the realm of things our culture accepts and condones as part of social life. Marijuana, which remains illegal in many jurisdictions, currently does not. As cannabis activists along with many health professionals point out, this different status is not justifiable on the basis of each drug's physical properties: marijuana is not, in other words, inherently more harmful than beer; rather, its status is determined within broader political and social structures (see Figure 1.4).

Of course, part of the mythology associated with different drugs *is* influenced by their physiological properties: the fact that caffeine is a stimulant—conducive, at least in theory, to productivity—while alcohol and marijuana are more conducive to relaxation explains in part why coffee is tolerated in most workplaces while booze and pot (even the names connote sin!) are not. While the different physiological states induced by these different drugs, and even their social effects, might be indisputable, what is less easily explained is why our society places a higher value on productivity and stimulation than on relaxation. Thinking about this question puts us in the realm not of nutrition or health, but of culture and representation.

The Production of Coffee

Clearly, the mythologies surrounding coffee, alcohol, and marijuana—mythologies that influence, as they are influenced by, their legal status—do not exist in a vacuum. Rather, they are generated out of real, material processes: social, political, and economic. This becomes clear when we think about the differences in how coffee operates symbolically (i.e., what it represents) in the cultures of the North, where coffee is consumed in such large volumes, in comparison to the cultures of the South, where it is produced.

In the Global North, along with Australia, New Zealand, and a growing number of other countries, coffee is entangled in the lifestyle of postindustrial society: it is fuel, pleasure, instant gratification, relaxation. In many parts of the Global South, coffee is an

Figure 1.4 When researchers in the United States experimented with giving drugs to spiders, they found that caffeine had a more severe effect than marijuana, resulting in much more sparse, haphazard webs. Source: Noever, R., J. Cronise, and R. A. Relwani. "Using spider-web patterns to determine toxicity." *NASA Tech Briefs* 19.4 (1995): 82. Published in *New Scientist* magazine, April 29, 1995

equally integral part of life, associated not (or not only) with pleasure, but more substantially with labor and the basic conditions of life. Those social rituals surrounding coffee that *do* exist in the South are shaped by an awareness of its economic as well as its cultural significance. For example, among some coffee-growing cultures in Tanzania, coffee has an almost religious significance associated with the *amagdala,* or "life force," of the coffee grower, such that the death of a coffee tree was traditionally taken as an omen of its owner's death (Hyden, qtd. in Weiss 96).

The History of Coffee in Western Culture

In the Global North, by contrast, coffee's role in the global economy is something that most of us, unless we're involved in the stock market or even more directly in coffee sales, are only dimly aware of. Yet its popular cultural significance is profoundly shaped by the history of its production, in conjunction with European colonialism in the seventeenth century as well as with more contemporary processes of **globalization** (see Chapter 9). A brief discussion of this history helps to illuminate some of the ways in which coffee signifies today.

The story of coffee's arrival in the West from the Middle East in the seventeenth century is part of the history of European colonialism. The importation of coffee was part of the much bigger process by which European nations sought to fuel their economies by finding new resources to develop, satisfying and promoting the desires of European consumers and creating new markets for European manufactured goods. Coffee entered European popular culture via the eighteenth-century institution of the coffeehouse, a new meeting place described by one historian as "*the* site for the public life of the eighteenth-century middle class, a place where the bourgeoisie developed new forms of commerce and culture" (Schivelbusch 59). Patronized mostly by commercial agents such as merchants and insurance brokers, coffeehouses were places for both socialization and the transaction of business. Both functions came together in the establishment of a connection between coffeehouses and newspapers. Coffeehouses such as the famous Lloyd's of London (now more familiar as the financial institution it eventually became), established at the end of the seventeenth century, often became centers of journalism, thus linking cornerstones of eighteenth-century public life—industry and print capitalism.

Coffeehouses became sites for the development of capitalist society in more direct ways, as Brad Weiss points out, through the drinking of coffee itself. As both a consumer good and a drink that promoted sobriety, coffee could be enlisted in the encouragement of good middle-class values—values such as "clear-headed rationality, alertness and restraint"—that were not associated with the "rude" pleasures of ale. In short, coffee, "through the short, sudden burst of energy and concentration it supplies is the original therapy for the micro-management of bourgeois personality" (Weiss 101). Coffee was thus enlisted in the reconstruction of the working day associated with the Industrial Revolution (see Chapter 2), as "coffee breaks" became a means of both marking and *making* time that is now routine in labor practices. Coffee fulfills nicely the goal of defining a break from work that is taken in order to make work more effective—a direct conversion of leisure into productivity.

Coffee and Colonialism

If it is no exaggeration to say that coffee contributed to the growth of European and North American economies over the past 200 years, it can also be connected to the *under*development of many Southern nations. While colonialism has now formally ended (in most places, in the middle of the twentieth century), trade regulations preferential to the economies of dominant nations force developing countries to adopt agricultural practices that consign them to continued poverty. Coffee is a good example of a cash crop whose growth is encouraged in places like Central America to satisfy North American consumers. Coffee has replaced the traditional crops that once allowed the region to feed its own people, forcing them instead to import food produced and/or processed elsewhere and, in many cases, causing severe environmental degradation. While growing coffee once offered a relatively decent living to many farmers, its falling price on the world market due to overproduction means that farmers in places like Haiti are struggling to survive.

The effects of fluctuating coffee prices, so critical for producers, are barely felt at the retail end. A 2004 report states:

> For every pound of coffee that sells in the U.S. for between US\$2.69–8.49 (depending on quality) a Guatemalan farmer receives less than 35 cents and the coffee picker less than 14 cents. Put another way, an entire crop of Guatemalan coffee earned one producer US\$8,500 which sold (notionally) for three quarters of a million dollars retail in the U.S. (Simons 85–86)

The principal reason for the growing discrepancy between the wealth of primary producers and retailers is the growing concentration of power in the coffee industry, which is now dominated by just four companies—Nestlé, Kraft (owned by tobacco company Philip Morris, which has been rechristened Altria Group), Sara Lee, and Procter & Gamble—which are able to exercise disproportionate control over the wages received by growers and the prices paid by consumers.

These economic circumstances, which have a big impact on the day-to-day existence of coffee farmers, have until recently been remote from the experience, or at least the consciousness, of the average North American coffee drinker. While we might feel a momentary twinge as we fork over the price of a sandwich or a beer for a Styrofoam cup full of burnt beans and water, our unease is quickly forgotten as we sink into the comfy chairs of our favorite coffee bar, dimly but pleasantly aware of the hum of activity around us as we enjoy moments—or hours—of leisure away from the demands of work, home, or school. That enjoyment might be diminished by a too acute awareness of the economic context in which we are drinking our coffee: part of the magic of the experience of consumption—a magic that is invoked, with variations, whether we are trying on a new dress, drinking a steaming latte, or driving a new car—is its ability to bury the crude facts of the economic transaction we have engaged in beneath the mythology surrounding the item we have just bought. The increasing availability of fair-trade and shade-grown coffees might be seen as a hopeful counter to a trend of unconscious consumption; by inviting us to equate "good" coffee drinking with political activism, these labels could also be seen to be working a different variety of magic.

The Consumption of Coffee

We use the word "magic" deliberately to describe the experience of consumption. Karl Marx (1818–83) employed the term **commodity fetishism** to describe what happens under a capitalist system in which material objects are bought and sold: commodities come to stand in for relationships between people as symbols of meaning and value, while people and social relationships themselves become objectified (they are turned symbolically into objects). In premodern culture, a "fetish" is an object that is believed to have magical powers or that excites erotic feeling. Commodity fetishism, then, is literally the attribution of a magical or sexual power to a commodity, assigning it a value that has no logical connection either to the human labor that produced it or to the usefulness of the object itself, but is derived from the abstract system of exchange that determines that such-and-such an object is worth so many dollars. Commodities don't acquire these "magical" properties by accident, of course; rather, the properties are generated by sophisticated marketing campaigns that tap into prevailing social mythologies. In fact, in a commerce-driven society, the language of marketing increasingly works to *shape* mythologies, thereby defining and creating new values and desires as much as it tries to appeal to already existing ones.

We can get a sense of how this process works by looking very briefly at the mythologies evoked by two different coffee chains that inspire different coffee cultures—the proudly cosmopolitan Starbucks and staunchly Canadian Tim Hortons—and then comparing them with the "third-wave" coffee culture that predominates in Australia and New Zealand. Each works through systems of *representation* that conceal relations of economic *production* in order to enhance the consumer experience. The significant differences between the "magic" of Starbucks and that of Tim Hortons reflect a contemporary consumer culture that differs from earlier forms of mass culture in the way it draws on, and indeed seeks to promote, individualized **identities** (see Chapters 6 and 7) defined largely by lifestyle. The concept of lifestyle, discussed in more detail in Chapter 4, is most easily associated with Starbucks, which indeed deserves some credit for promoting it. The secret of lifestyle marketing lies in the way the product falls into the background of a mythology, one centered on the consumer's attitudes and practices and the identities they imply. While the attitudes or practices may have ethical or **aesthetic** overtones—for example, concern about the environment, a love of art—the overriding premise is one of individualism, expressed through consumer choice.

Starbucks

For a company like Starbucks, the mythological value of individualism is paramount, and it is represented not just through the diversity of blends available, but also through the careful structuring of the whole consumer experience. While it is difficult to generalize across outlets, some of the signal features of Starbucks outlets are dim, natural-looking (as opposed to fluorescent) lighting; movable furniture, often mismatched but clearly designed with an eye not just to comfort or utility but also to style; serve-yourself cream, milk, sugar, and so on; and an aura of creativity, whether signaled by the presence of large murals featuring art or poetry or by individual paintings available for sale. The presence of other sale or display items—designer mugs, dishes, even books or CDs—emphasizes that the Starbucks experience is not about just having a cup of coffee but is an act of self-expression, entry into a privileged and sophisticated world.

Launched in Seattle in 1971, Starbucks is now a truly global corporation—global in terms of its expansion throughout Western Europe and Asia Pacific, but also in terms of the image it projects of the urbane, cosmopolitan consumer. Located mostly in large cities, in areas patronized mainly by middle- and upper-class, educated consumers (e.g., Starbucks outlets are often near, if not affiliated with, university campuses), it aligns itself with the values of style, mobility, and progressive thinking. These values emerge all the more strikingly when we compare Starbucks with Tim Hortons, a chain started in Hamilton, Ontario, in 1964 and named after the late hockey player who founded it.

Tim Hortons

If the "magic" of Starbucks is associated with globalization and progress, Canada's ubiquitous coffee chain, Tim Hortons, is strongly nationalist in flavor even though it was bought by the US chain Wendy's in 1995 and spun off to shareholders in 2006. This mythology is intensified by a long association between Tim Hortons and the Canadian Armed Forces (see Figure 1.5), an association emphasized in marketing campaigns such as the 1999 television ad featuring Canadian soldiers on a ship somewhere in the Persian Gulf, gratefully receiving a massive shipment of Tim Hortons coffee. In contrast to the foreign, slightly scary location of the Middle East (signaled in the ad by jerky camera footage of a chaotic market scene, accompanied by vaguely Arabian-sounding music), Tim Hortons is a piece of home, something that presumably, like the Canadian military, "you can always count on." The soldiers in the ad are almost all men, and the servers who appear briefly to pay tribute to "our boys" overseas are all women, dressed in the familiar brown of the Tim Hortons uniform.

The world represented in the Tim Hortons ad is strikingly different from the ambience of Starbucks, evoking traditional values of the nation defended by a strong military, traditional gender roles, and clear boundaries between the familiar and comfortable and the foreign. This atmosphere is replicated in Tim Hortons restaurants, in which the comfortably padded but immovable benches, functional (and easy to clean) Formica tables, and fluorescent lighting convey an atmosphere of order and uniformity. The institutional flavor of the décor is softened somewhat by the service dynamic, in which the largely female staff deliver your coffee just the way you want it—within fairly limited parameters.

Figure 1.5 The image of Tim Hortons as an emblem of Canada persists in media coverage of the coffee's arrival on a military base in Kandahar, Afghanistan, in July 2006, in response to intense lobbying by the troops. Source: © All rights reserved. AR2007-A050-0016 reproduced with the permission of DND/ CAF 2016

Though the chain has expanded its selection of both food and beverages in recent years, the emphasis here is not on choice, and certainly not on style, so much as on comfort, embodied in the familiar combination of coffee and doughnuts. In fact, the mythology of Tim Hortons is arguably defined in obvious, even self-conscious opposition to the snazzy ambience of Starbucks, and revels in its preservation of old-fashioned, working-class family values against the tide of globalization, speed, and the blurring of traditional identities.

Of course, *both* of these mythologies are constructions—imaginary replications of the world rather than accurate reflections of it. Nevertheless, they *work*, through the dynamics of consumption—a dynamic increasingly central to the formation of popular culture—not just to sell coffee or doughnuts, but also to create compelling pictures of everyday life and of human relationships that are increasingly indistinguishable from "the real thing." What is interesting about our comparison of Tim Hortons and Starbucks is not so much their differences as the similarities that are concealed beneath those differences: both are large **multinational** corporations that capitalize on cheap labor and resource costs in the South to generate significant profits in the North; both derive the bulk of their profits by selling coffee and sugary baked goods—products that might not do a lot for anyone's health, but are staples in a traditional North American diet; and both are major parts of the popular cultural landscape.

Yet for all its symbolic identification with globalization (see Chapter 9 for further discussion), the global reaction to Starbucks in particular has been mixed. In 2008, the company closed 61 of the 84 outlets it had recently opened across Australia, officially citing the global economic slowdown as the reason. But other commentators suggested that Starbucks just didn't mesh with Australia's own coffee culture, which rejected "gimmicky" drinks like caramel lattes in favor of good strong coffee (Raslan, qtd. in Edwards and Sainsbury). Though chains like Bean Bar and Gloria Jeans are successful in Australia, the mythology of coffee there is less tied to a specific company than it is to a style of drink—the flat white—which, originating in Australia and New Zealand, has begun to circulate globally, and to acquire symbolic significance as a marker of a sophisticated appreciation for pure coffee, uncorrupted by branding or the aggressive addition of syrup and whipped cream (Symons).

The flat white is one hallmark of an approach to coffee that has come to be identified as the "third-wave" (Skeie; Cho), a style of production, preparation, and consumption defined very explicitly against a post–Second World War "first-wave" of instant, freeze-dried coffee, and a "second-wave," exemplified by Starbucks and the rise of the espresso machine. In the second-wave, according to this narrative, the focus is consistency, achieved by the mastery of a now standard technique of coffee making enabled by state-of-the-art machines. Defenders of the third-wave, many of them baristas, challenge what they see as the second-wave emphasis on automation, calling instead for a much closer attention to the place of origin and vintage of the bean—much like wine! The belief at the heart of the third-wave is that while in the old days "coffee was 'consumed' rather than 'enjoyed,'" the chief achievement of the third-wave is "letting the coffee speak for itself." In line with contemporary food trends emphasizing raw food and artisanal preparation techniques, this philosophy *appears* to dispense with mythology in favor of an absolutely authentic experience. Rather than seeking a uniform cup of coffee, its proponents suggest, consumers should be educated to appreciate the unique flavor produced by different beans, crafted by a dedicated barista. That respect for difference extends, in the third-wave, to a suspicion of any claims of an authorized method or system, and a strong respect for individual opinion—except maybe a preference for Starbucks or (perish the thought!) instant coffee.

Here is where things get tricky, though. Mythology operates most successfully when its mythological qualities—historically produced values and beliefs—are least visible. It is relatively easy to unpack the mythologies that circulate in ads, especially when, as in the example of Tim Hortons, the values being promoted are highly conventional (e.g., traditional gender roles). It is much harder to challenge the aura of naturalness that surrounds a form of consumption that grounds itself in an opposition to corporate culture and appeals to a standard of taste defined by purity and simplicity. We discuss the politics of taste in further detail in Chapter 6. For now, it is enough to note that all of our practices of production and consumption inevitably negotiate, in some combination of complacency and awareness, acceptance and resistance, the uneven terms of capitalist society. A key ingredient in third-wave coffee culture seems to be the kind of elitist disdain for standardization that characterized earlier waves of mass culture critique. Thinking in more structural terms, participation in the third-wave not only requires money (artisanal roasts cost quite a bit more than coffee purchased from a thermos at the gas station— often even more than Starbucks!), the excellent taste it signifies also demands an aesthetic training that is not universally accessible.

And It All Boils Down To…What *Is* in a Cup of Coffee?

Based on this quick (drive-through?) analysis of coffee, we might come up with a fairly depressing reading of popular culture. Dominated by practices of consumption, much of our experience of popular culture is tangled up in relations of economic exploitation— relations that are concealed by the mythologies and ideologies of capitalism, to which we are helpless, caffeine-addicted victims. Of course, this is a partial picture, and one that is contradicted by the practice of coffee drinking itself.

While there is no escaping the consumerist aspect of coffee drinking, this practice— more, perhaps, than many other aspects of commercial culture—highlights the possibilities for different kinds of consumption. For example, at a time when people are increasingly diverted by home entertainment, cafés can, at least in theory, serve as public spaces for the promotion of community, much as they did in the eighteenth century. It is easy to exaggerate this function: with its comfy chairs, free newspapers, and generally artsy aura, the image of the contemporary coffeehouse is as much a product of slick marketing as genuine community. However, it *is* possible to recall some of the positive aspects of public culture in private space, not by "seeing through" the lifestyle concept of places like Starbucks, but by taking it at its word. In other words, it is possible to sit in a Starbucks reading for hours with an empty cup in front of you, and the culture of the café (a culture Starbucks itself has actively nurtured) is such that no one's likely to ask you to leave. "Going for a coffee" need not mean actually going for a coffee—a concept that places like Starbucks have successfully promoted, sometimes at the cost of their own profits.

Coffee's evolution into a highly charged commodity brings it within the realm of popular discourse, thus creating new channels of meaning and knowledge and new forms of "anticonsumerist" consumerism. The success in recent years of the Fair Trade Federation and other cooperative ventures that seek to preserve the natural environment while ensuring that coffee producers receive a fair price for their products has been motivated by activists in conjunction with consumers themselves. The overwhelming commercial power of corporations such as Starbucks, while contributing to some extent to the growing gaps in wealth that characterize the coffee industry, has also shed a strong and sometimes harsh light on the industry, forcing it to change in productive ways. Coffee's third-wave reflects some of these significant critiques.

Mythology, then, works not just to contain, but also to spark and activate new forms of resistance, not all of which are constrained by the harness of corporate culture. Popular culture isn't just coffee purists sipping their flat whites, poets and students staring at their laptops while their lattes grow cold; it's also the bricks through the window at Starbucks and Niketown, the creators of ads raising consumer awareness about the "real" price of coffee, and the customers who happily imbibe the "lifestyle" of the café, sitting around in animated conversation for hours without actually buying anything. The relationship between these different faces of popular culture is part of what this book will examine.

Our study of popular culture occurs at a historical moment in which there is no human activity that is free from capitalism, commodification, and the profit motive. No space in people's everyday life remains outside these economic processes. This is most apparent in the case of culture and communication, which have become totally commercialized. By the same token, culture and communication have come to dominate the economy, with the result that, as Fredric Jameson observes, "No society has ever been saturated with signs and messages like this one" (Grossberg *et al.* 53).

Many contemporary cultural critics see this shift as a wholly depressing situation, representing the end of collective culture and its replacement with a society of atomized individuals who are consumed by the drive toward self-gratification at the same time as they are entirely colonized by consumerist ideology. These critics despair over what they see as the erosion of people's ability to think critically, to produce and create things for themselves in a context where everything is supplied for them, subject to their ability to pay for it. A less bleak view, and one that we share, is that while commercial culture's grand promise to provide fulfillment and liberate individual and social potential is essentially an empty one, there are, within its intricate networks of power, all kinds of opportunities for creativity and even resistance. Through a series of concrete examples, the remainder of this book develops an idea of popular culture as a process defined by the often contradictory but sometimes collaborative interests of private and public interest, of commerce and creativity, of capitalism and community. Its ultimate goal is to provide tools that will help you to think about your own place in this compelling and sometimes invisible matrix of possibilities.

Suggestions for Further Reading

During, Simon. *The Cultural Studies Reader*. 3rd ed. London: Routledge, 2007.

Edgar, Andrew, and Peter Sedgwick, eds. *Key Concepts in Cultural Theory*. 2nd ed. London: Routledge, 2007.

Fiske, John. *Understanding Popular Culture*. 2nd ed. London: Routledge, 2010.

Gilbert, Jeremy. *Anticapitalism and Culture: Radical Theory and Popular Politics*. Oxford: Berg, 2008.

Grossberg, Lawrence, Cary Nelson, and Paula Treichler. *Cultural Studies*. London: Routledge, 1992.

McRobbie, Angela. *The Uses of Cultural Studies*. London: Sage, 2005.

Miller, Toby. *A Companion to Cultural Studies*. Oxford: Blackwell, 2006.

Mookerjea, Sourayan, Imre Szeman, and Gail Faurschou, eds. *Canadian Cultural Studies: A Reader*. Durham, NC: Duke University Press, 2009.

Storey, John, ed. *Cultural Theory and Popular Culture: A Reader*. Athens: University of Georgia Press, 2006.

Szeman, Imre, and Tim Kaposy. *Cutural Theory: An Anthology*. London: Wiley-Blackwell, 2010.

2

The History of Popular Culture

Taking It from the Streets

On January 7, 2002, in Hamilton, a mid-sized city in Ontario, Canada, a man and his 10-year-old son appeared in court to defend themselves against charges of playing touch football and hockey on the street. Responding to the complaints of a neighbor who had become tired of retrieving balls from her garden, police charged the father with violating a municipal bylaw banning the playing of games on city streets. The case became a cause célèbre across Canada, as hockey fans and defenders of the right to play in public places called in to radio talk shows and wrote letters to the editor expressing their outrage. The neighbor had a different perspective, maintaining, "It is not about hockey, it is about property rights. It's about trampling my family's garden" ("Fighting"). The case was eventually thrown out because the judge determined that the Crown could not prove its case that the man and his son had been playing a game on city property. City councillors promised to look into revising the bylaw.

This case relates to our study of popular culture in a number of ways. First, it's about an aspect of popular culture—informal recreation—that tends to get ignored in favor of an emphasis on the commercial products of mass media. Second, it features sport, whose relationship to "culture" of any kind is often questioned. Finally, this local, even trivial-seeming case has echoes throughout the world: in 2012, police banned an 8-year-old British boy from playing football outside the house because he kicked "too loudly" (Wrenn); Spain's 2013 "Citizens' Security" law, among other bans against public gatherings, proposed fines from €100 to €1,000 for "the practice of games or sports activities in public spaces not designed for them" (Mills); and US communities in Kentucky, Nevada, New Jersey, New York, Ohio, Oregon, and Pennsylvania have banned basketball hoops from streets, citing safety concerns ("Communities"). Critics note the irony of these laws in countries (like Spain) whose professional sports teams have many players who honed their talents playing ball in the street. But even leaving aside the thwarted futures of future pros, it is clear that bans on street sports have particularly harsh consequences in communities where the absence of private driveways or playgrounds means that there is really nowhere else to play. More broadly speaking, this story concerns the critical issue of public space: Who gets to use it and how? How are rights concerning the recreational use of public space balanced against laws protecting private property? These questions and issues lie at the heart of contemporary popular culture. They are, in a sense, what makes it distinct from earlier cultural forms (see Figure 2.1).

We begin this chapter with the story about road hockey as a way of entering an exploration of how popular culture evolved into the form we recognize today. Beginning with a look at traditional (pre-1830) recreation, we trace some of the broad cultural changes that

Popular Culture: A User's Guide, International Edition. Imre Szeman and Susie O'Brien.
© 2017 John Wiley & Sons, Inc. Published 2017 by John Wiley & Sons, Inc.

Figure 2.1 Recalling traditional "grassroots" forms of recreation, a game like street hockey exists in a complicated relationship with contemporary commercial sport. Source: © Rick Eglinton/Toronto Star via Getty Images

led to a rupture between communal enjoyments, such as "street" games, and commercial entertainment. We also look at the development of the institution of "culture" as a refined and exclusive preserve, remote from the "low," physical entertainment of the streets. And finally, in relation to the previous two developments, we look at the struggles that, beginning in the early nineteenth century, determined the shape of popular culture—struggles over work and leisure, over the emerging class structure, and over public space.

Among the questions we will be asking in this chapter are: How is contemporary popular culture different from what came before? What factors—economic, social, and political—contributed to the development of popular culture as we know it today? How is the development of popular culture tied to the broader history of the disappearance of public space? How are relationships of power, particularly class and gender, mediated through culture? Returning at the end of the chapter to the example of street hockey, we suggest that while the answers to these questions may have changed over time, the issues they touch on remain critical to an understanding of popular culture from the nineteenth century to the present day.

Making the Streets Safe for Commerce

In 1835, a small item was added to the English Highway Act, imposing a fine of up to 40 shillings for playing "at Football or any other Game on any Part of the said Highways, to the Annoyance of any Passenger" (qtd. in Malcomson 141). The amendment to the act was part of a bigger movement toward the limitation and management of public space, a movement that had a major impact on the organization and practice of popular culture. As we suggested in Chapter 1, the tension between democratic or popular will and corporate control—the question, in other words, of who owns or produces the space in which we live our lives—continues to be the primary force defining popular culture today. The prohibition of street football reflects a small but significant moment in that conflict.

The reallocation of public space, which was strongly contested at every turn, occurred in conjunction with a whole series of other changes—economic, spatial, and social—that came about during the Industrial Revolution, from about 1830 to 1900. To understand the magnitude of those changes, we'll take a brief look at what life was like before. Much of our discussion in this chapter focuses on the United Kingdom, where the effects of these tumultuous changes were experienced first and most intensely.

Popular Recreation before 1830

Beginning around 1830 in Britain (though it is hard to pin down an exact date), popular recreation underwent some fairly rapid and dramatic changes from the forms that had existed, with few variations, since the Middle Ages. In a primarily farming economy, recreation was closely tied to work in the form of holidays and festivals associated with particular times in the agricultural calendar and everyday social interactions that occurred as part of farm labor. Games, dances, and entertainments were largely public, in the sense that anyone could participate, and they took place on lands customarily shared (at least to some extent) by the community as a whole. Along with work, recreation tied the community together through activities whose form and meaning had been established through long tradition. Perhaps the most notable difference from popular culture today is that traditional recreation was mostly homemade, consisting of sports, games, and dancing that required little in the way of organization and equipment. Life in the towns may have involved more diverse and complex entertainment, but in general, urban forms of leisure were not all that different from rural forms, with social activity strongly tied to work, and both work and leisure still strongly influenced by the traditions and rhythms of the agricultural economy.

There is a tendency to view this early form of popular culture through the rosy haze of nostalgia, to represent it as somehow purer (since it was less commercialized) and more wholesome and community minded than, say, television or video games. It is undeniably true that preindustrial recreation was in many ways more active than contemporary forms of entertainment, in terms of both the creativity and the physical effort demanded of its participants. It also served an important role in maintaining strong community relations, uniting workers of both sexes and all ages.

Harder to romanticize from a contemporary perspective are the brutally violent elements of "blood" sports involving animals, such as bullbaiting and cockfighting, and the high level of social conformity that recreation demanded. While holiday practices such as decorating and dancing around the maypole were condemned by Protestant reformers of the time as incitements to "lasciviousness" and "ribauldrie" (qtd. in Malcomson 9), they ultimately served the conservative cause of courtship. While unsupervised trips to the woods to gather May flowers may have offered lots of opportunities for sexual activity, these did not translate into sexual *freedom*: when these encounters led to pregnancy, as they often did, the outcome was shame for the woman—marriage if she was lucky, but in any case a confirmation of traditional gender roles.

The Bonds of Community

The communal and strongly ritualized form of traditional popular culture reflected a highly stratified society in which leisure, like work, expressed clear distinctions between the ranks of laborers and landowners, with virtually no possibility for social mobility. However, what was in one sense a bigger gulf between socioeconomic categories than exists today was partly bridged by a tradition of patronage, in which the ruling class recognized a duty of care toward those on whose labor they depended. This meant that, among other things, wealthy landowners tolerated and in some cases actively facilitated the recreational activities of their workers (by granting time off, for example, or allowing the use of their land for sports and festivals). This occasional relaxation of social discipline served the landowners as well as the workers, partly because both groups inhabited the same small communities, and also because giving workers an outlet for play made it much less likely that they would challenge the ruling class's authority.

In sum, romantic images of entertainment in preindustrial society are in some senses accurate: fun was mostly free, even when closely bound up with the economic activities of the community; it reflected a strong attachment to the natural world; and recreation fostered connections between people. On the negative side, the conservative and traditional nature of recreational activities allowed only occasional ritual challenges to social authority and tended to emphasize social solidarity over individual pleasure or inclination (e.g., among the entertainments surrounding courtship, there were no alternatives for men or women who were not interested in heterosexual coupling). Finally, traditional recreation, with its strong emphasis on blood sports, reflected the hardship and brutality of farm laborers' lives—brutality enacted most violently on animals.

Capitalism and the Industrial Revolution

The Industrial Revolution brought with it a new culture—new pleasures and identities, but also new kinds of brutality. One of the key preconditions for the development of popular culture in its contemporary form is the economic system of capitalism, which, throughout the eighteenth and nineteenth centuries, was dramatically altered and intensified by a series of events that came to be described as the Industrial Revolution. (For more on the development of capitalism, see Close-Up 1.1.) Of the many social and cultural consequences of the Industrial Revolution, the banning of street football might look pretty trivial. However, this example offers one illustration of the effects of industrialism on the organization of physical space and social relations. We will look at some of these effects in more extensive detail in the section that follows.

Redefining Cultural Spaces

The 1835 ban on football in the streets was one minor event in a succession of restrictions of communal space by state or private interests happening in conjunction with changes associated with the developing capitalist economy. Among the most far-reaching of these changes was the series of Enclosure Acts that converted common grazing land to much smaller, private holdings in order to make the land more economically productive. This practice, which, as its name suggests, involved enclosing formerly open spaces with fences, affected popular culture in very direct ways by placing physical constraints on certain kinds of activity. It also influenced popular culture more generally, changing the relationship between work and play and reconfiguring people's sense of community.

First and most obviously, enclosure placed an obvious restriction on the kinds of recreation that could take place. No longer was it possible, for example, to engage in the vast games of football that used to occur with unlimited players (and few rules) between villages located up to five kilometres apart. Even more modest recreations—for example, the dances and wrestling matches that tended to be organized around particular times of the agricultural year, such as mowing or harvesting—were gradually discontinued as the fields on which they were once performed or played were closed off to the public. Beyond the significance of the loss of these specific activities was the severing of a vital link between agricultural work and recreation. As landowners fenced off property with the aim of increasing its economic productivity, a vital connection between the creative realms of work and play was lost. More generally, the reorganization of space that resulted from enclosure changed the way people related to one another. Not only did it accentuate divisions between the landholding and laboring classes, it also made it harder in general for people to connect with one another, resulting in the fragmentation of traditional forms of community.

Urbanization

In addition to the privatization of mostly rural land represented by enclosure, the process of **urbanization** contributed significantly to the reduction of open spaces available for recreation, since land was expropriated for the building of industrial infrastructure. As fields disappeared with no new playgrounds to replace them, it became harder to find places to hold outdoor sports, festivals, and other forms of public gathering. Urbanization also affected the production of popular culture in more indirect ways. One of the most obvious changes people experienced as they moved from the country to the city was a change in their living spaces. For poor working people in particular, life in the city meant coping with crowded and unsanitary conditions. An 1844 newspaper report describes a typical slum:

> There are whole streets…which are neither flagged, paved, sewered, nor drained; where garbage and filth of every description are left on the surface to ferment and rot; where pools of stagnant water are almost constant; where the dwellings adjoining are thus necessarily caused to be of an inferior and even filthy description; thus where disease is engendered, and the health of the whole town perilled. (qtd. in Engels 49–50)

The huge influx of workers to the city meant that housing had to be built quickly and cheaply. At the same time, wealthy industrialists wanted to be spared the sights and smells of crowded working-class slums; thus factory workers—in their small, identical houses, crammed together on tiny lots—lived in more or less segregated neighborhoods interspersed with upper- and middle-class enclaves.

But the marginalization of the poor was not only physical. In the complex middle-class values of the day (values that still hold sway, if you believe the ads for household cleansers), physical dirt corresponded symbolically to spiritual impurity and immorality. As convictions about the inherent character deficiencies of the poor became institutionalized, backed up by new sciences of hygiene and public health, the poor suffered from simultaneous moves to banish them from sight and to subject their behavior to increasingly vigorous policing. These social constraints, combined with actual space constraints, powerfully reduced people's freedom and mobility.

However, the crowded conditions of working-class slums also fostered new forms of social and political solidarity. Courtyards, which functioned as sort of communal backyards, became gathering places in which people could find some respite from the isolation and loneliness that are the paradoxical by-products of life in a crowded city. For some, "allotments" (rented gardens) provided space to grow flowers or food and to recall, in however modest a way, the pleasure of outdoor life. As cities grew, though, and the demand for space increased, most of these allotments were swallowed up by development.

The one other obvious location for outdoor recreation was the street, which had the advantage of more space and light than the courtyards, but the disadvantage of the presence of the police, who were charged with putting a stop to recreational activities that threatened to disrupt more "legitimate" commercial activities.

The Pub as Community Space

The lack of public space, combined with the excess of official **surveillance** in what little space there was, contributed to the growth of what became the center of urban community—the pub. In addition to camaraderie and beer (which, besides being cheap and satisfying, was generally safer than the drinking water), the pub supplied comforts such as heat, light, and toilets that were frequently superior to what people had at home. Indeed, the density of pubs was greatest in the poorest areas (Best 220). Pubs were often associated with particular professions, as shown in names such as The Weaver's Arms or The Sailor's Dickey. In general, however, they can be seen as part of the trend in urbanization toward the separation of places of work and places of recreation.

Along with the class segregation and crowding that characterized urban life, this fragmentation of a formerly more organic existence undermined familiar forms of identity, community, and popular recreation. At the same time, it fostered new forms of sociality, as well as new forms of social freedom. The positive flipside of the anonymity that went along with life in the big city was increasing privacy—if you kissed a stranger in a pub, your Great Aunt Ethel, neighbors, and minister wouldn't necessarily all be there to see it and tell your parents. Moreover, the layout of the city, in which people's homes tended to be some distance from their places of work, commerce, and leisure, helped to create a new kind of mobility, both literal and symbolic. Of course, the expansion of opportunity was often more abstract than actual, particularly for women and the poor, who were prevented by a lack of economic power and an excess of social discipline from enjoying the liberation from custom and greater freedom of movement enabled by life in the city. In general, however, the process of urbanization contributed to the trend of expanding individual freedom that was to shape social life over the course of the nineteenth and twentieth centuries.

Industrialism

The term "Industrial Revolution," generally used to refer to the period in British history from approximately the mid-eighteenth to the mid-nineteenth century, describes the transition from an agricultural and small-scale commercial society to one based on organized mechanical production. While the term "industry" is often used to refer specifically to factory production as distinct from other kinds of organized work, it is also sometimes used to describe the increasing capitalization, organization, and mechanization of what were formerly thought of as nonindustrial kinds of work: farming, for example, or—more significant for our purposes—culture. (We will discuss the implications of this shift in more detail in Chapter 4.) In contrast to the relative stability of earlier modes of production, industrial enterprises require major investments of capital to generate growth. They also require a large and disciplined workforce, trained in the performance of repetitive, specialized tasks. The Industrial Revolution thus marked a significant change not only in the *mode* of production—the physical process used to generate the necessities of life—but also in the *relations* of production, or division of labor.

In the preindustrial economy, not only was work closely integrated with other aspects of life, workers also had a strong sense of connectedness to their labor and its products. In preindustrial agriculture, for example, workers were involved in every stage of production, from planting to harvest, and, crucially, they had at least some degree of ownership of the process, including small holdings of land. The same is true now of craftspeople, who own and/or have direct control over their workshops, as well as every aspect of the production of their finished crafts. The critical difference for workers in industrial society is that their labor is detached (or, in Karl Marx's terms, alienated from the larger process of production: rather than having any direct economic stake in the products of their labor, they receive only a small hourly wage and their activity is focused on one single fragment of the final product).

New Modes of Production

This style of work was a key part of the new production process known as **Fordism** (after Henry Ford, who pioneered it), a form of assembly-line labor that proved to be extremely efficient at churning out products, from cars to household furnishings. However, the factors that contributed to the high quantity and uniform quality of products had a much more negative effect on the human participants in the process. Fordism worked on the principle of *mechanization*, a process that aimed to turn every facet of the economy, including human society itself, into the equivalent of an efficiently run machine. The consequences of this restructuring of labor reverberated far beyond the factory walls. Fordism is now widely understood to refer not just to a particular mode of production, but also to a form of social organization based on discipline, uniformity, and atomization ("atomization" describes a social structure defined by separate individuals rather than by a vision of the community as a whole).

The mechanization of society was accompanied by what we might term the "mathematicization" of human life. As historian Eric Hobsbawm puts it, "Arithmetic was the fundamental tool of the Industrial Revolution. Its makers saw it as a series of sums of addition and subtraction: the difference in cost between buying in the cheapest market and selling in the dearest, between cost of production and sale price, between investment and return" (*Industry* 61). As with the mechanical innovations of Fordism, the mathematical precision of the new economy extended to social relations as a whole, with relationships between employer and employee, individual and community, increasingly determined less by custom or the incalculable interactions of character and circumstance than by relations of money, or what is often called the cash nexus.

The ideal of an economy in which human labor is enmeshed obediently and productively with machines is not so easily accomplished in reality. To ensure a compliant workforce, employers and legislators collaborated in drafting a series of new regulations and other disciplinary innovations, both inside and outside the workplace, to ensure worker obedience. Perhaps the most effective form of regulation was the extremely low wages workers were paid, which meant that they had to work long hours just to earn enough to feed themselves. Workplace discipline was reinforced by such technological innovations as the punch clock, which secured the cooperation of workers in policing their own attendance at work. In instituting such forms of on-the-job discipline, employers were motivated by the (reasonable) belief that, given a choice, most people would prefer to spend their time at play rather than work. A raft of social measures sought to correct this attitude, including *master and servant laws*, which prescribed jail time for workers who violated the terms of their contracts, and *poor laws*, which "took care of" the unemployed by incarcerating them in workhouses.

Poverty, once seen as a consequence of unfortunate circumstances to be remedied by the assistance of the community, came to be read as a sign of personal failure or moral weakness.

The Production of the Working Class

A more abstract but farther-reaching goal of the new laws was the radical alteration of culture, with the aim of creating a society devoted not to the goal of working hard enough to live, to put food on the table, but to that of feeding itself to work harder, to produce profits. One of the dominant mythologies in contemporary society is the idea that individual effort is always ultimately rewarded with economic and social success. (For a discussion of mythology, see Chapter 3.) This mythology developed in conjunction with the industrial economy. However, it was hard to sustain during the early days of the Industrial Revolution, when the fundamental inequality on which capitalism depends was so starkly evident: by definition, an economic system designed to produce a surplus requires that the majority of laborers are paid less than what their labor is actually worth, and in the early stages of industrialism this amounted to less than the barest living wage for many workers. While preindustrial society had also been characterized by inequality, bonds of custom connected the rich and the poor—sometimes through patronage and sometimes through force, but the two groups were always in close relation with one another. Industrial society effectively broke these bonds, producing a new kind of class consciousness.

According to E.P. Thompson, one of the foremost historians of English working-class history, "class" comes about when a group of people,

> as a result of common experiences (inherited or shared), feel and articulate the identity of their interests as between themselves, and as against [others] whose interests are different from (and usually opposed to) theirs. The class experience is largely determined by the productive relations into which men are born—or enter involuntarily. Class-consciousness is the way in which these experiences are handled in cultural terms: embodied in traditions, value-systems, ideas, and institutional forms. (10)

It is worth pausing on this definition to grasp elements of class that are often overlooked in contemporary uses of the word, which either equate class simply with wealth—"low class" equals "poor"—or link it to a quality of morality or style, as in "That lady may be rich, but she's got no class." Thompson's definition is important in emphasizing that (i) class describes a material relationship to the wealth-generating structures of society; specifically, it distinguishes capital's owners from its laborers; and (ii) one's class position has a determining influence on one's identity and social orientation. To be class conscious is to recognize the role of class in determining those aspects of one's existence—a recognition that goes against the dominant ideology (see Close-Up 2.1).

Working-Class Consciousness

The Industrial Revolution coincided with the expansion of working-class consciousness, which expressed itself in a richly interwoven set of practices (well documented in Thompson's *The Making of the English Working Class*) including sports, games, conversation, eating, and drinking that took place both in private homes and in working men's clubs. While women were included in some of these activities, on the whole working-class

---

Close-Up 2.1 Ideology

"Ideology" is a term that we will make use of throughout this book. It is a concept with many shadings, but with a relatively simple idea at its core. At the most general level, "ideology" refers to the process by which the set of values and beliefs that bind individuals together in a society become "naturalized." The belief and value systems of any given society are the outcome of *history*; that is, of collective human activity that gives shape in large and small ways to the characteristic features of a society. Ideology names those social and political processes that directly and indirectly mask or hide this historical process by making everyday life seem natural, inevitable, and unchangeable. The claim that capitalism is the only rational form of economic organization is often ideological in this way, especially when what this claim suggests is that history was inevitably moving toward a worldwide capitalist system anyway: people did nothing to bring it about and can do nothing to stop it. This is false, and ideology is often at work in attempts to make false statements sound not only like the truth, but also like common sense.

A more restricted meaning of ideology that is related to this one has to do with the difference between how things appear to be and what they are really like. Ideology names the processes through which the real conditions in which people live are obscured by other ideas and beliefs, usually for the sake of maintaining political and social power.

---

leisure activities, like other aspects of English culture, were strongly masculinist in character, an element that was often glossed over by early work in cultural studies that tended to cast working-class culture in overly romantic terms.

Suggested Activity 2.1

Drawing on your personal experience and general knowledge, try to answer the following questions: Is class consciousness a significant force in the world today? Where and how is it manifested? How, if at all, is politics shaped by class concerns? Are hopes for radical social transformation expressed today, and if so how? What role does popular culture play in promoting or subduing these hopes?

Even though it displayed the sexism of its time, one of the distinctive aspects of nineteenth-century working-class culture was its highly developed political consciousness, a sense of the urgency and possibility of radical political and economic transformation. Attempts to effect such a transformation took many forms, from the Luddite rebellions of 1811–13, in which workers smashed the machines that were replacing their labor, to the Chartist movement in the 1830s and 1840s, which was concerned primarily with political reform, to the less formally organized trade union movement. What most of these movements had in common was a strong sense of *collectivism*, or worker solidarity, and a demand for expanded democratic rights. (See Chapter 7 for a discussion of changes in working-class consciousness in the twentieth and twenty-first centuries.)

Workplace Reform

In the latter half of the nineteenth century, slowly and often through an uneasy alliance with employers' own desires for change, these movements achieved some important workplace reforms, including laws restricting working hours and the establishment of

Saturday half-holidays. (In the first half of the century, many factory workers worked a 72-hour week, with only Sundays off. Even this brief respite often meant nothing to working women, for whom Sunday was the only day available to do washing and other domestic tasks.) These, in combination with bank holidays, gradually extended to other professions and came to replace traditional holidays, resulting in a clearer, more generally shared division between work and leisure, if not exactly less time at work.

The one other significant change in the latter half of the nineteenth century that created new possibilities for popular culture was a gradual increase in wages. As with the other changes, this reform came about both because workers agitated for it and because the system demanded it: as capitalism became more efficient at producing goods, more consumers were required; hence the need for higher wages (see Chapter 5).

The social impact of these changes—improvements, really—to working conditions was far-reaching and complex. Besides providing an obvious outlet for enjoyment and relaxation, the formalization of "free" time outside of work also influenced in subtler ways how people understood themselves and related to one another. The new distinction between spheres of work and home played a big part in establishing the almost sacred significance of the nuclear family, a development that had a particular impact on women. While she was still in all likelihood required to contribute to the household economically, the woman of the house assumed a new and arguably more difficult role as symbolic guardian of the family's moral and spiritual health. This expectation, expressed as part of a more general middle-class ideology of moral discipline, functioned in odd concert with the limited expansion of workers' freedoms: with the expansion of leisure time (and buying power) came new ideological pressures toward social conformity.

Perhaps more significantly, the extension to the poor of some limited forms of relief from the systemic deprivation they suffered arguably worked to mute demands for more substantial forms of social justice. Once arrived at, working-class consciousness remained precarious, never achieving the revolutionary expression that Marx projected. One common explanation of the decline in working-class political culture attributes it to the hegemonic success of commercial culture, a development that we discuss further below. It is important not to discount the role of class solidarity, though, both as a catalyst for subsequent forms of political consciousness (discussed in more detail in Chapter 7) and as a critical dynamic in the production of popular culture as an ongoing process of social struggle.

Popular Recreation and Resistance

So, by the end of the nineteenth century, in fulfillment of one of the clichés of capitalism, some of the fruits of the Industrial Revolution had begun to "trickle down" to the working classes. The benefits were hard won, though, and had to be struggled for against the efforts of the ruling class to rein in the pleasures of their social inferiors. While the ruling classes had long been concerned with how the poor enjoyed their off-work time, these concerns took on a new urgency in the Industrial Revolution. The charge against frivolity was led by the middle classes (small factory and shop owners and other capitalists whose wealth derived from their business activities and investments and not from inherited wealth and property, as was the case for the traditional ruling class). This group, whose economic interests and ideology of productivity increasingly came to dominate society, directed their stern disapproval at both the "parasitic ruling class" *and* the "reckless carousing of an irrational working class" (Bailey 76). That this disapproval was qualified by a contradictory desire among many middle-class people to *join* the leisure activities of the "parasitic ruling class" did not make things any better for the working classes, whose own recreation became the target of stringent surveillance and discipline. These efforts at control, which ranged from outright prohibition to more subtle forms of persuasion and direction, were never entirely successful, as they were met at every turn by working-class resistance to interference in their way of life.

Rational Recreation

In a bid to keep the behavior of the "unruly masses" in check, many towns established new or enlarged police forces, charged with strictly enforcing new regulations against blood sports and street games, and arresting people for such vague offenses as vagrancy, trespass, and desecration of the Sabbath. While strong middle-class support existed for the establishment of "a good police" and "set of laws," many of the most dedicated moral reformers also believed that "if possible, the effects of such laws should be produced, almost insensibly, and without the appearance of force: for force will hardly ever answer the end proposed in this land of liberty" (qtd. in Malcomson 97).

The move toward subtler, less overtly coercive means of social control reflected a new cultural complexity that was developing in the shadow of the Industrial Revolution. One paradoxical element of a society that in many instances produced new forms of servitude for working people was a strong emphasis on individual liberty. This critical element of capitalist ideology took on a slightly different—and, from a ruling-class perspective, less desirable—flavor in growing democracy movements. The call for individual freedom had been an important part of the middle class's rise to power, against the pillars of tradition and inheritance that had worked to sustain the dominance of the aristocracy. However, the prospect of extending the privilege to the lower classes and thus risking powerful challenges to a social order built around their own dominance was a source of much middle-class anxiety. Though they were committed in principle to the goal of general social freedom, particularly in the domain of leisure, they were not willing to leave the working classes to determine their own forms of recreation, which might challenge the prevailing moral standards or social hierarchy.

With a primary aim, then, of keeping the lower classes out of the pub—or, worse, the trade union or Chartist halls—significant groups of concerned middle-class citizens got together to promote what they called "rational recreation." Some groups, such as the Society for the Suppression of Vice and the Lord's Day Observance Society, had a strongly Christian bent. Others—many of which were dominated by women—were more loosely organized around the aim of providing forms of public recreation in which people of different classes could mingle, with the poor benefiting from the good influence of their betters. In all cases, there was a strong impulse toward diversion—that is, the sponsorship of sports and activities that would draw interest away from undesirable pastimes: drinking, traditional games, blood sports, and so on. Thus, part of the rational recreationist mandate was the promotion of so-called counter-attractions, including trips and exhibitions scheduled to conflict with the old, discredited forms of pleasure.

The inspiration for this project was not entirely cynical: some middle-class people may have been moved by a genuine desire to alleviate the severe restrictions that had been imposed on workers, and also to heal the fractured class relations brought about by industrialism. It was hoped—naively, maybe, and with a mix of motivations both compassionate and self-serving—that the inequalities that marked the workplace could be temporarily forgotten in forms of recreation designed to be inclusive. The main goal was not inclusivity, however, but "improvement" in the form of intellectual, moral, and spiritual development. In all the activities and organizations promoted by the rational recreationists—concerts, educational institutes, and (increasingly toward the end of the nineteenth century) libraries and museums—there was a strong emphasis on encouraging intellectual as opposed to physical pursuits, the latter being regarded as base and uncivilized.

Matthew Arnold

The efforts of the rational recreationists were accompanied by an elevation of capital-C Culture as a powerful, almost mystical stimulant of moral and spiritual growth. Poet and critic Matthew Arnold (1822–88) was one of the foremost proponents of a program of education that would instill civilized virtues in the masses by exposing them to "the best that has been thought and known in the world" (70). Culture, which up until this time described a general process of cultivation, now encompassed a set of objects, artifacts of supposedly timeless and universal value, exposure to which would encourage the student to transcend his petty and narrow materialist (we might read "class") interests to recognize his place in the universal—or at least the national—order. The title of Arnold's most famous work of cultural criticism, *Culture and Anarchy*, gives a clear sense of the social chaos he foresaw if the guardians of culture failed in their aims.

The power of Arnold's definition of Culture lies partly in its emptiness: its value can't be measured by any precise criteria, but those of discriminating tastes—like Arnold himself, presumably—know it when they see it. It worked as a powerful social ideology, one that influenced literary education until well into the twentieth century, through its contradictory gestures toward universality and hierarchy: Culture was precisely that which united everybody, but its *value* rested in its being understood by only the educated few.

Ambivalence, Appropriation, Resistance

The contradictions that characterized Arnold's definition of Culture informed the project of rational recreation as a whole, a project that was only partly successful. To the extent that rational recreation was meant to bring classes together with the aim of cultivating a community defined by middle-class tastes and morals, it was an almost total failure. In part, the failure stemmed from middle-class ambivalence about what they were attempting to do. The impulse to smooth relations between the classes was always complicated by the desire of the middle class to forget their own working-class origins and confirm their alliance with aristocracy.

This was achieved partly by the promotion of sports and leisure activities from which working classes were excluded. In the case of some sports, such as golf, cost alone was an impediment to participation. For others, such as rowing—once a popular working-class activity—amateur associations drew up rules prohibiting participation from "artisans, mechanics or labourers" on the pretext that the physical nature of their labor would give them an unfair advantage (Bailey 140). Moves toward the democratization of other cultural activities, such as the theater, were countered by the physical segregation of audiences through prohibitive prices at certain events or through restrictive conditions of attendance. Museums, for example, were initially closed on Sundays, which was the only day most working-class people had free. The move to extend opening hours was opposed by some on the grounds that the lower classes were not yet ready for capital-C Culture, and so could not be trusted to appreciate it in the right spirit. When museums finally did open on Sundays, to an enormously enthusiastic public, the *New York Times* warned that canes and umbrellas would have to be checked at the door, "so that no chance should be given for anyone to prod a hole through a valuable painting, or to knock off any portion of a cast" (qtd. in L. W. Levine 183).

Suggested Activity 2.2

Consider the following questions: Are cultural activities still segregated today? If so, how is participation formally (or informally) restricted? To whom do restrictive conditions apply?

Middle-class nervousness about the encroachment of the lower classes on their newly won exclusive cultural terrain ironically confirmed that, in some ways, the rational recreationists were more successful than they could have hoped: working-class people not only subscribed enthusiastically to programs of self-improvement, but also, not surprisingly, showed a strong desire to run the programs themselves. A general appetite for knowledge, along with huge improvements in literacy associated with the move toward compulsory primary education, helped to blur boundaries between workers and their middle-class benefactors in ways most of the benefactors never anticipated. From the mid-1880s onward, many social clubs and mechanics' institutes (popular educational organizations) were independently run by their working-class members. Some had quite politically radical aims; many ended up focusing far more on recreation than education, in clear opposition to the vision of their founders. While the continuing need for financial sponsorship ensured that the wealthy still had some hand in running things, historical research suggests that the lower classes took what they wanted from the activities and societies offered them, making over rational recreation for their own purposes in ways that were often quite different from what their sponsors intended. Accepting middle-class sponsorship, in other words, did not necessarily mean accepting middle-class values (Cunningham 128).

Booze and Blood Sports

While many aspects of the rational recreationist program were **appropriated** by the working classes, people in general strongly resisted attempts to reform and regulate traditional forms of leisure (see Figure 2.2). Drinking was notoriously hard to curb— even on the job—and blood sports and street games survived in spite of official prohibition and the promotion of alternatives. Prizefighting, or bare-knuckle boxing, is an example of one sport that flourished in spite of attempts to curb it, which ranged from fining publicans who promoted it to charging fighters themselves with assault and, occasionally, homicide. (Echoes of the tensions surrounding prizefighting can be detected in contemporary debates about mixed martial arts.) The lengths to which its participants would go to maintain the sport were demonstrated in the famous match between British boxer Tom Sayers and his US counterpart John C. Heenan, in 1860 for what was arguably the world's first international boxing championship, in which the fighters were taken, in disguise, to a secret location outside the reach of mounted police, followed by supporters who left London via a special early-morning train (Bailey 37). While this and other blood sports eventually did decline, there is a lot of evidence to suggest that they persisted throughout the nineteenth century *because of*, rather than in spite of, attempts to outlaw them. (While we like to think we've come a long way since the nineteenth century, the popularity of YouTube videos of amateur locker boxing suggests that perhaps we have not.)

Figure 2.2 Fight between John Jackson and Daniel Mendoza, 1795. Sports such as prizefighting flourished in part because of—rather than in spite of—middle-class moralists' attempts to ban them.
Source: © Heritage Image Partnership/Alamy

As one historian puts it, by the beginning of the twentieth century, "the great majority of London workers were not Christian, provident, chaste or temperate" (Jones 471) and the favored institutions were "not the school, the evening class, the library, the friendly society, the church or the chapel, but the pub, the sporting paper, the race course and the music hall" (Jones 479). The mass demonstrations that greeted attempts to close pubs and shops on Sundays in the 1860s offer evidence of the extent to which popular recreation had come to be regarded as a right to be defended, by force if necessary.

Popular Culture and Politics

This passionate defense of popular entertainment was a source of concern not just to the middle-class reformers, but also to two distinct groups of working-class activists—political radicals and evangelical Christians. Though their aims were very different, what these two groups had in common was a clearly defined vision of a strong and disciplined working-class society whose integrity was undermined by the corrupting influence of mass entertainment.

Pub culture was particularly suspect because of the intoxicating effect of drinking alcohol. The opportunities to get drunk increased substantially with the lifting of the duty on spirits in 1825 and the deregulation of beer sales shortly afterward. Like other moves toward freer trade, this liberalization of alcohol sales had ambiguous consequences for working-class people's autonomy. For the radicals in particular, this and other aspects of popular culture were threatening not just because they were often produced through the patronage of the ruling classes, but also because they consumed energies that might otherwise be directed toward more directly self-improving activities, such as education or the struggle for democracy.

The growth of popular recreation, then, was by no means a uniform or uncontroversial process. Not simply a battleground on which people sought to free themselves from the physical or ideological constraints of industrial society, popular culture was also a critical ground for struggle over exactly how that freedom could or should be pursued. The goal of working-class reformers, whose vision of freedom included the extension of democratic privilege, granting to all people the right to determine the shape of the society they lived in, never quite jibed with the more conservative view of popular culture as a necessary, if temporary, escape from the demands of working life. This conservative view (which finds echoes in the contemporary perception of popular culture as an arena in which to pursue the freedom to "be yourself") did not challenge so much as reflect the entrepreneurial ideology of industrialism. As the most intense suffering associated with the Industrial Revolution passed, and the poor began to glimpse at least the possibility of beginning to share in its benefits, the more conservative view prevailed, assigning popular culture the role of escapist complement rather than radical antagonist to dominant social structures. The increasing commercialization of popular culture played a major role in hastening that trend.

The Production of Commercial Mass Culture—the Birth of the Culture Industry

When we talk about popular culture today, it is generally assumed that we are referring to the products of the mass media—television, film, music, Internet culture, and so on. An important goal of this chapter has been to illuminate some of the currents that swirled around the birth of media culture, shaping it even as they were shaped by it. Thus, even though traditional recreation, working-class culture, and the earnest efforts of the rational recreationists were all largely eclipsed by the power of media culture, the *popularity* of media culture cannot be understood without them. Popularity, you should recall from Chapter 1, is *not*, as the makers of commercial media would have it, simply a measure of how many people buy stuff; rather, it is a shifting and contested arena of power. Commercial culture was an in-your-face challenge to the Arnoldian guardians of "Culture" at the same time as it eroded the tradition and politics of the working class; however, it is in the context of the *persistence* of those alternative cultural strains—elitist attempts to defend their definition of "high" culture and the efforts of ordinary people to shape the meaning of their own experience—that the significance of the commercial media, the most far-reaching cultural development of the last two centuries, must be measured. The concept of **hegemony** (see Close-Up 2.2) has proved most useful to cultural theorists attempting to measure the significance, in political terms, of the explosive growth of commercial culture.

It is tempting to see media culture as truly *popular* in its satisfaction of the desire and will of the people. Nineteenth- and early twentieth-century critics (both working-class activists and middle-class reformers), along with more recent theorists such as Stuart Hall ("Notes"), challenge this assumption, pointing out that the pleasures offered by what came to be known as the *culture industry* (see Chapter 4) are glossy substitutes for the satisfying kind of empowerment that would result from, say, better working conditions, stronger communities, or expanded democratic rights. This does not mean that commercial culture succeeds purely by virtue of trickery, by exploiting people's stupidity; rather, it works hegemonically, through engagement and negotiation with their real desires, which it transforms into shiny novelties—magazines, musical entertainment, films—that can be sold for profit. We will explore the concept of hegemony more fully in subsequent chapters. For now, it is important to keep it in mind as a key element in the successful development of early commercial culture.

Close-Up 2.2 Hegemony

Developed by the Italian Marxist Antonio Gramsci in the 1930s, the concept of hegemony refers to the ability of dominant groups in society to exercise control over weaker groups, not by means of force or domination but by gaining their consent, so that the unequal distribution of power appears to be both legitimate and natural. In other words, hegemony operates not by forcing people, against their better judgment, to submit to more powerful interests, but rather by actively seeking the spontaneous cooperation of subordinate classes in maintaining social relationships that continue their subordination. Hegemony, significantly, is never total, but operates in constant struggle with newly emerging forms of oppositional consciousness. It works not by crushing those forces but by a constant process of negotiation.

So how is popular media culture hegemonic? First, it operates in conjunction (and sometimes in tension) with institutions like the state, the law, education, and the family to legitimate the values of capitalist society—individualism, consumerism, the priority of private versus public interests, and so on. But unlike these other institutions, which sometimes resort to force, commercial culture works almost entirely through the promise, if not the fulfillment, of pleasure. That the pleasures of commercial culture are often opposed by more official institutions—the church, education, and so on—makes them that much more seductive.

A key assumption of this chapter has been that modern popular culture—and, specifically, commercial culture—emerged in the wake of the Industrial Revolution. This is something of an exaggeration: commercial forms of entertainment long predated the nineteenth century: cultural producers such as publishers of pamphlets and ballads, traveling musicians, and other performers did earn a modest living from their work. The major shift in the nineteenth century concerned the forms and scale by which culture was turned into a profitable commodity. Products of the culture industry differed from earlier forms of culture in at least two crucial ways: first, they relied on relatively sophisticated and expensive forms of media technology to reach a mass audience; second, mass media were produced by a **vertically integrated** factory system, supervised by committees or boards of executives and assembled according to complex divisions of labor. This contrasts sharply with traditional cultural forms that tend to be strongly rooted in the working-class community, with performers and their material reflecting the everyday lives of their audiences. Rather than mirroring the actual experiences of any social group, mass media are designed to appeal to as many social classes or class fractions as possible to generate maximum profits for their producers (Naremore and Brantlinger 13).

Several factors combined to make possible the development of a mass entertainment industry. First, a large and concentrated urban population, which by the late nineteenth century enjoyed rising income levels and an increase in leisure time, ensured a captive audience for new forms of popular culture. Second, developments in technology made it possible to produce and deliver entertainment on a vast scale.

Technology

For the media theorist Marshall McLuhan, whose complex insights often get reduced to the single aphorism "the medium is the message," technology—the form, or "medium," of culture—has greater material significance than the content, or "message." This is a fairly radical proposition that few cultural theorists accept in its totality today. However, it offers a useful way into understanding the impact of media technology in shaping our consciousness. Its radicality lies in its suggestion that new media technologies don't just function as the means to create new forms of entertainment or communication; they also literally change us as societies and as individuals, rewiring our perception of and means of engaging with the world.

Suggested Activity 2.3

According to Marshall McLuhan, innovations in media technology—photography, radio, film, television—have all influenced culture and consciousness in profound ways, some, paradoxically, taking us back to preliterate tribal ways of conceiving the world, enabling the creation of the so-called global village. Based on your own and others' uses of contemporary media, how (if at all) do you think that technology enhances or limits different forms of perception and mental or social engagement?

The Engines of Change

The last half of the nineteenth century saw massive changes in the technological landscape of popular culture. By the 1870s, the telephone and phonograph joined a raft of recent inventions including photography, telegraphy, and the railroad, which all worked in different ways toward what one writer termed, with no exaggeration, "the annihilation of time and space" (Solnit 4).

In the United Kingdom, followed by many other countries. the development of a national railway system—not the first thing that usually comes to mind when we think of popular culture—was hugely influential in extending people's physical and imaginative horizons. The most obvious impact of trains was to make travel much easier and more accessible for ordinary people. By the mid-nineteenth century, even working-class families were able to escape the city to spend a few days at the lake or the beach, where they stayed at resorts that offered them all kinds of commercial entertainment. Within the urban environment itself, improvements in public transit made it possible for people to travel between the suburbs and the city at night to attend the theater and, by century's end, the cinema. Besides creating mobile audiences, better transportation fueled the development of popular culture in other, more obvious ways by facilitating the faster, larger, and more extensive distribution of goods and services. The train, in other words, isn't just a mode of transportation; it's also a technology of delivery for products of the industrial economy.

In conjunction with technologies of production, technologies of delivery play a critical role in the development of popular culture. The telegraph, invented in the mid-nineteenth century, revolutionized the delivery of information by enabling the almost instantaneous transmission of information over wires in the form of electric signals. James Carey describes its significance in an interesting way, suggesting that the telegraph

> marked the decisive separation of "transportation" and "communication." These words had always been synonymous, until, that is, it became possible to communicate information immediately from one side of the country to the other. The telegraph revolutionized communication by allowing symbols to move independently of geography and independently of and faster than transport. (213)

It also turned those symbols into viable objects of exchange and, in conjunction with visual technologies such as the camera and film projector, helped create a culture industry founded on mass media. The evolution of that industry, with a particular focus on the development of cinema, is taken up in Chapter 4.

These brief examples show us how industrial technology affected the domain of popular culture by changing the physical processes of production, the kinds of objects that could be produced, and the ways in which they were consumed. It also changed and improved means of distributing cultural goods to a vast audience. In sum, it played a key role in the **commodification** of culture, or its transformation into a collection of products that could be bought and sold.

Regulation, Innovation, Consolidation

Technological development does not take place in a vacuum. The nature of new cultural technologies, the uses to which they are put, who uses them, and who profits by them are questions that are all determined by broader political, economic, and social factors. Critical among these factors are the kinds of regulations—laws, trade agreements, unwritten social rules—that determine the circumstances in which forms of popular culture are produced and consumed. The increasingly liberal trade regulations that characterized British industrial society (developments that were not always matched by a loosening of moral and social restrictions) helped create a climate of entrepreneurial innovation that fueled the development of new forms of popular culture. The period is characterized by genuine rags-to-riches stories of itinerant actors, songwriters, and musicians who emerged from humble beginnings to control small-scale entertainment empires. The same environment that made their enrichment possible, however, also paved the way for the consolidation of ever-larger entertainment conglomerates, effectively shutting the door on the emergence of new independent cultural producers. Though without the global reach of media empires today (whether traditional media companies, such as Rupert Murdoch's News Corp., which owns publishers, newspapers, radio and television stations, and film companies around the world, or new media giants such as Google), mid-nineteenth century British newspaper ownership was concentrated in the hands of a few publishers. Alfred Harmsworth (later Lord Northcliffe), for example, published two papers, *The Daily Mail* and *The Daily Mirror*, whose dubious reputations—critics dubbed the *Mail* "the paper for people who could not think" and the *Mirror* "the paper for people who could not read" (Briggs 9)—did not prevent them from being massively successful, with the *Mirror* becoming for a time the paper with the largest circulation in the world.

The establishment of media empires in the late nineteenth century anticipates the much more significant kinds of **media convergence** that are in evidence today, linking not only forms of media (say, print with television) but also form with content (for example, television networks and sports teams; see Chapter 4). Among the costs of achieving such vast economies of scale, which can (though not always) mean greater efficiency of delivery and higher production values, are a reduction of the diversity of opinion and a dilution of content to satisfy as vast an audience as possible. This latter issue points to one of the most significant consequences of media consolidation in the nineteenth century: the production of a new kind of cultural literacy, based not on an intimately shared knowledge of one's own familiar surroundings, but on a more general social outlook made up of ideas, beliefs, tastes, and opinions shared with a vast group of strangers. The consequences—both positive and negative—of that move toward national and, eventually, global mass culture are taken up in detail in Chapter 9.

Pub Culture and the Music Hall

The expansion of the media industry did not diminish people's appetites for more sensual kinds of entertainment. The pub remained a cornerstone of popular recreation, forming a basis for new entertainment enterprises such as the music hall (see Figure 2.3). While the deregulation of alcohol sales, mentioned above, was a welcome development for pub owners in some ways, it remained difficult to make much money through the sales of food and drink alone in an increasingly competitive environment. Pub owners thus had to resort to other innovations to turn their establishments into profitable commercial enterprises. While many early nineteenth-century pubs were "little more than parlours of private houses," as one historian describes them (Bailey 28), starting around the 1830s changing building regulations led to the establishment of bigger, more commercial pubs—so-called gin palaces. Among the structural elements incorporated into these establishments were bar counters separating customers from liquor and dispensers, thus safeguarding the product and allegedly adding to an atmosphere of professionalism. A more blatantly commercial innovation was the elimination of seats, which encouraged a high volume and rapid turnover of customers. Gas lamps hung outside as well as inside helped draw in customers by extending the territory of the pub into the street (Bailey 29).

The commercial activity of the pub also extended beyond the immediate business of the sale of food and alcohol. As has already been mentioned, pub owners sponsored all kinds of recreational activities, from sports to musical events. Perhaps the most substantial move to transform the institution of the pub into a form of mass culture came with the advent of music hall, in which musical and dramatic performances formed the central component of a comprehensive entertainment package. The experience was enhanced by food and drink, and enjoyed—as pub culture had not been previously—by women as well as men (the wholesome family image was no doubt complicated by the thriving trade in prostitution that its critics maintained was a key sideline of music hall). Like many early forms of mass entertainment, music hall resists easy categorization. While its commercial aspects and the presence of professional performers distinguish it from more traditional forms of do-it-yourself popular culture, it was not yet purely corporate—at least not at first.

Developed out of the more loosely organized "free and easy," in which pub patrons watched—and, more significantly, participated actively in—songs and sketches, music hall represented a bridge between those earlier forms of participatory entertainment and the kinds of mass culture we are more familiar with today, in which audiences tend to be reduced to passive spectators. (A similar cultural transition can be traced in the United States during this period in the development of vaudeville, a slightly **higher-brow** form of musical variety show entertainment, usually served up alcohol free.) In this transformation, producers of commercial entertainment found allies in a middle-class notion of culture that discouraged audience participation in public art as part of a more general campaign against the public airing of "private" feeling—along with a whole range of other activities, such as eating, spitting, nose-blowing, scratching, and farting. While certain

Figure 2.3 The music hall represented a transitional moment in the evolution of "homemade" popular culture into mass culture. Source: © SOTK2011/Alamy

forms of mass culture—in particular, sport—still sanctioned some degree of public participation (as they continue to do today), thus confirming their relegation to a "lower" category of entertainment, the rules of middle-class etiquette proved to be far-reaching in their influence on a general trend to transform audiences from collective participants into passive, individual spectators (L. W. Levine 198–199). Music hall nevertheless retained many of the features of earlier forms of participatory entertainment, with audiences joining in choruses and loudly registering their approval and disapproval of performances.

Significantly, though, music hall has been linked by historians with a moment of decline in working-class democratic movements. Unlike earlier forms of pub culture, in which recreation and politics were often closely bound together with songs and skits blatantly critical of the prevailing class structure, the tone of music hall entertainment tended toward a more conservative acceptance of the dominant ideology of capitalism. Like successive forms of mass entertainment, music hall was not geared toward changing the social order; it offered, rather, a temporary escape from its constraints, a culture not of protest but of "consolation" (Jones 499).

The imbrication of music hall with prevailing economic structures was reflected not just in the transformation of its audiences, but also in the professionalization and organization of its production. In some significant ways, music hall remained rooted in the mostly working-class community that it served, with most of its performers, as well as the songs and skits they performed, coming directly out of that experience. In its ownership, however, music hall came to resemble later forms of corporate entertainment. From the opening of Charles Morton's music hall in 1851, the industry developed quickly, with the first music hall agency established in London in 1858 and others soon following. In 1860, owners of the larger halls formed the London Music Hall Proprietors' Protection Association, which helped establish standards, including common (low) wages for performers. This association, along with the tightening of building regulations, led to the closing of smaller halls and the consolidation of bigger ones. As the larger halls grew more successful, other industries grew up around them, including a thriving music hall press featuring magazines including *Era*, *Magnet*, and *London Entr'acte*. Music hall also forged connections with other forms of entertainment, as proprietors began to invest in multiple ventures, including sport, drama, and (later) the circus, economizing through the construction of ever-larger entertainment complexes that could accommodate a number of activities. In an irony characteristic of the evolution of popular culture, music halls also offered ideal venues for the screening of films—a form of entertainment that eventually came to supplant them. Only a very few entertainers, such as Charlie Chaplin, successfully made the transition from vaudeville to cinema.

Continuities and Changes

We have looked at a number of developments occurring in the domain of popular culture that were strongly influenced by industrialization. The fragmentation—spatial, economic, and social—of an earlier way of life changed the way people related to one another and pursued work and recreation. The struggle of working-class people to define their lives, including labor and recreation, on their own terms met powerful resistance in the form of middle-class reformers and the rise of commercial culture. In general, the growth of mass media involved the intensification of commercialization and concentration of corporate control.

This movement was neither steady nor uniform, however: moves toward consolidating corporate power were routinely challenged by competition and the flourishing of independent operators, as well as by the unionization of performers, technicians, and other employees (these tensions are discussed in more detail in Chapter 4). They were also challenged by those outside the industry—audiences and consumers whose willingness to be passively entertained existed in tension with a powerful impulse to make and do things for themselves. These tensions continue to inform the terrain of popular culture today.

The Organization and Commercialization of Sports

We began our history of popular culture by looking at street football as an apparent casualty of the movement to privatize space and, with it, popular recreation (see Figure 2.4). In many ways, football offers a perfect example of the operation of the forces of corporatization. Proceeding in tandem with moves to ban football from the public streets were efforts to organize it into a successful commercial venture. The sponsorship of "soccer clubs" led to the establishment of organized leagues and the eventual founding of the Football Association in 1863. Considerable effort went into the task of regularizing the rules of the game, though this was not totally successful, as demonstrated by the evolution of two games: rugby and association football, or soccer. (The two games differ widely both in the rules of play and in culture, with the former maintaining a fairly elitist flavour in keeping with its roots in the British public school system, and the latter enjoying a strong working-class following—at least until recently, when commercial success has arguably all but severed the sport from its roots.) Professionalism—that is, the introduction of salaries for players—was legalized in 1855, and clubs began charging admission in 1870, gradually incorporating other commercial enticements such as food, drink, and other entertainment for spectators. As with music hall, a sports media industry soon developed, with Routledge's 1867 *Handbook of Football* helping to foster fan solidarity around a sport that was rapidly becoming institutionalized.

Industrialization also influenced the temporal organization of sports in at least two ways. First, the institution of long and regular working days made it necessary to establish

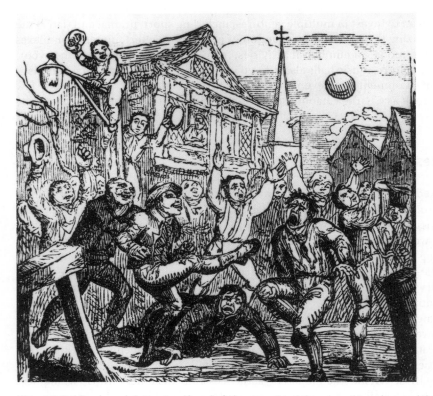

Figure 2.4 A hardy and determined band of players resisted the general trend toward the organization and institutionalization of football. Source: © Rischgitz/Getty Images

rules limiting the duration of play (a significant development in sports such as lacrosse, in which games might once have lasted anywhere from a few minutes to several hours). Second, the marking of time into distinct periods of work and leisure made it possible to establish formal schedules of play, based on the assumption that players and spectators had regularly scheduled time off (Metcalfe 50).

Specialization, Professionalization, North American Sports

Historian Alan Metcalfe also identifies another indirect consequence of the importance of time as part of a general emphasis on quantification: the meaning of sports shifted "from the process, the contest itself, to the product, the record" (51). As a result, the nature of competition changed, with less emphasis on its social aspects and a greater and greater focus on winning. As in other areas of the industrial economy, sport was increasingly shaped by specialization: from a chaotic, collective endeavor in which the different tasks of the game were shared by everyone, players gradually assumed positions in accordance with their specific talents—offense, defense, goalkeeping, and so on (Guttman, qtd. in A. Hall *et al.* 50; see Figure 2.5).

Metcalfe identifies a number of other changes associated with industrialization that eventually contributed to the organization of sports in North America, including the development of transportation and communications technology—the train, the telegraph, and radio and print media—that made it possible not only to arrange contests between far-flung teams, but also to broadcast schedules and results, creating a national audience for sport (52). (From the expansion of national and, eventually, international leagues, we arrive at the contemporary situation in which virtually none of the players on "local" professional teams come from the city—or even the country—in which the team is based. This development, a logical outgrowth of the forces of global capital, changes not only the organization of players, but also the relationship between players and fans, whose relationship to "their" team is an oddly contrived one, connected only arbitrarily

Figure 2.5 The celebrity status and colossal salaries accorded to professional athletes, such as soccer player Lionel Messi, are among the most visible signs of the commercialization of soccer. Source: © Matthias Oesterle/ZUMA Press, Inc./Alamy

to place.) This **deterritorialized** relationship is highlighted by its temporary suspension during international tournaments such as the Olympics or FIFA World Cup, when players are repatriated to their "home" teams, unleashing a whole different order of fan loyalty.

Commercialization alone was not responsible for the wresting of sports such as hockey and football from the people by the elites; in fact, much in the same way as commercial media were challenged by the rational recreationists, professional sports faced strong challenges from amateur associations, connected in particular with private schools and universities (see Figure 2.6). The leagues that were established by the universities especially maintained a strong policy against professionalism, a policy that, recalling the rational recreationists, was motivated as much by an elitist desire to maintain class privilege as it was by a concern for the purity of the sport. Some clubs defined their codes of amateurism according to the exclusion of particular professions and even ethnic groups (see Table 2.1).

In general, nineteenth-century football and hockey amateurists (as distinct from contemporary promoters of amateur sport) were, if anything, more bound up with economic status than professionals, since a strict ban on professionals meant that participation was restricted to those with plenty of time and money. Between them, however, both middle-class amateur associations and corporate owners of professional teams contributed to the creation of a culture of organized sports, based increasingly on spectatorship rather than participation. Indirectly, but most significantly, the propertied interests represented by both the professionals and the "gentleman amateurs" contributed to the decline of public space available for community athletic activity—a development that foreshadows the conflict over street games today.

Figure 2.6 The incorporation of football into schools as part of an ideology of masculine character development was an important step in its institutionalization. Source: © Hulton Archive/Getty Images

Table 2.1 Early definitions of "amateur."

The Amateur Athletic Association of Canada and its successors established the following definitions of an amateur:

1884: An amateur is one who has never competed for a money prize or staked bet with or against any professional for any prize, or assisted in the practice of athletic exercises as a means of obtaining a livelihood.

1896 (add): Or who has entered any competition under a name other than his own.

1902 (add): Private or public gate receipts…who has never, directly or indirectly, received any bonus or a payment in lieu of loss of time while playing as a member of any club, or any money considerations whatever for any services as an athlete except his actual traveling and of selling or pledging his prizes.

1909 (add): Promoted an athletic competition for personal gain.

The above discussion describes a fairly straightforward movement from the loss of public recreation space and the banning of street games to the creation of professional sports and the conversion of players into fans. More recently, the intensification of the commercial imperative in sports has begun to wrest enjoyment of the game away from players and fans alike, as players (in exchange for relatively lucrative salaries, depending on the sport) are subject to being traded (or dropped) at the whim of owners, and attendance at games is (economically) restricted to corporate executives entertaining clients. The biggest winners in professional sport today, arguably, are commercial sponsors, who depend on a still enthusiastic television audience. Yet when we look back to the original English battle over street football, and then forward to the road hockey case in Hamilton, Ontario, the answer to the question of who controls popular culture is more complicated, and more encouraging.

Back to the Streets, Forward to the Present

Street games might, in theory, have been banned in 1835 in Britain, but players were not put off that easily. In Derby in 1845, footballers responded to attempts to stop the annual Shrovetide match by throwing things at the police, including a "brick bat and bludgeon" (one or both of which hit the mayor). Pursued by police, special constables, and dragoons, players ran away to the next village—where, after a vigorous skirmish, they finally surrendered the ball (Malcomson 142). While the footballers eventually lost that contest— with greater police reinforcement in subsequent years ensuring that the tradition was eventually quashed—in other places public protests against the prohibition resulted in the setting aside of public playing fields where the game could continue without interfering with other (commercial) activities.

The modern-day Hamilton street hockey story didn't end quite so violently, and its implications are a little more complicated. Like the English footballers, the player Ryan Kotar and his father enjoyed a partial victory. Their case was dismissed, not because the judge deemed that road hockey was *not* a crime but because of contradictions in witnesses' testimony. The bylaw prohibiting street games still stands, in spite of a motion to Hamilton city council to rescind it. Similar bylaws exist, as we have noted, in many municipalities, though it is questionable how often they are enforced. The tenor of the neighbor's attack on hockey as "totally uncivilized and dangerous" (Clairmont, qtd. by mitch@habs) echoes some of the rational recreationists' charges against street football as leading not only to "moral degradation" among its players, but also to "injury to health, fractured limbs and (not infrequently) loss of life" (qtd. in Cunningham 78). However, the nationwide rallying of community support behind the hockey players, along with their exoneration from charges, would seem to demonstrate a popular determination to keep alive people's rights to enjoy themselves in public spaces. The defense of the hockey players—even by government officials in Hamilton, who promised to try to have the ban struck down—would seem to confirm the survival of grassroots popular entertainment in spite of both attacks from moralists and the expansion of private property rights, including the conversion of sports into a corporate activity.

There are other ways of reading the story, however, that point to both its continuity with and its important differences from the British street football incident. First of all, although this story tended to be represented as a victory for grassroots sports—street hockey as opposed to league hockey or the overly commercialized professional game—the distinctions between the two aren't all that clear-cut. Following the Hamilton incident, the (North American) National Hockey League players rallied in support of street hockey—as much, no doubt, out of a recognition that street hockey nurtures professional hockey fans as out of pure-hearted devotion to the game. In an article calling for the preservation of outdoor hockey rinks, columnist Roy MacGregor touted the value of "being left alone to play the game the way it is played in the imagination," in part because that kind of play nurtures the talent that goes on to win junior world championships and Olympic gold medals. A Canadian Tire television ad played during the 2014 Olympics with the tagline "We all play for Canada" was premised precisely on this idea: that backyard rinks lead to Olympic dreams ("Celebrate").

National Mythology

Victory in such international contests is substantial fodder for the national mythology of Canada, which points to another wrinkle in the story: there is no question that one of the reasons the Hamilton incident received so much press was because the sport in question was hockey—not baseball, not Frisbee, not soccer, but a sport whose restriction, according to one Hamilton city councillor, would be positively "un-Canadian" ("Game On!"). As one supporter put it, "Hockey is Canada's national pastime. When I stumble across kids playing hockey in the street, it brings a smile to my face" (qtd. in Wente). That hockey occupies a significant place in the official mythology of Canada—like football in Spain or baseball in the United States—is indisputable. However, as we discuss in more detail in Chapter 7, national mythologies are not spontaneous expressions of citizenly love. They are, rather, contrived and partial stories whose collective rhetoric conceals the stakes of *power*—both economic and social—involved in their dissemination.

It is in the interests of professional sports and their sponsors that the dream of "the game" be kept alive by powerful images such as the Canadian brewing company Labatt's television commercial in which Toronto commuters spontaneously join in a giant game of street hockey, and the 2002 Tim Hortons calendar that features an image of kids playing a pick-up game on a backyard rink. These heartwarming images are at odds with the sacrifice of public space and resources to the forces of commercialism. Corporate team owners' and sponsors' demands for tax breaks for their teams contribute to this problem by taking funds away from public facilities such as parks and outdoor rinks. Some corporations, including Tim Hortons, *do* make financial contributions to amateur sport, part of a growing trend necessitated in part by the erosion of public support due to commercialization! The underfunding of Canadian amateur hockey, in particular women's hockey, in relation to the vast and increasingly US-dominated entertainment complex of the NHL offers yet another contradiction in the mythology of Canada's "national game." These facts complicate the widely asserted notion that hockey is "a big part of what makes us *us*" (sportswriter Stephen Brunt, qtd. in Wente).

Popular Sports: Who Gets to Play?

As the street hockey story attests, distinctions between grassroots and governmentality, populism and commercialism, are less clear-cut in Canada today than they were in Victorian England. The politics of the popular have also become more complicated: while it's easy to read the 1845 contest over street football in Derby as a contest between "the people" and their political and economic rulers, the question of who constitutes "us"—the people—today is not so simple. We have already mentioned some of the gender implications of the hockey story in relation to the underfunding of women's sport. Sports columnist Laura Robinson goes further to note an unspoken assumption of many of the defenders of street hockey players: when they say "kids," they mean "boys." She goes on to note:

> I can't recall seeing a group of girls commandeering a public street at any time to play any team sport. Boys have always understood that public space is the right space for their physical performance. The theatre of masculinity is public because we have constructed masculinity in a way that demands of men and boys constant physical proof of "who the man is," to use a basketball term. ("Girls" A15)

Nowhere, arguably, is the ideology of masculinity more evident than in hockey, whose increasing violence at the professional and amateur levels has been cause for public concern. Such concern was not, significantly, voiced in relation to the street hockey case, except by the players' neighbor, Nadia Ciuriak—a woman and an immigrant, who was demonized for, among other sins, being "un-Canadian." When she lost her case, columnist Margaret Wente notes, "The neighbourhood boys were directed to wave their hockey sticks triumphantly for the approving cameras." The question of what, or whose, culture triumphed here is ambiguous.

Hockey is also notable for its whiteness. The absence of immigrant and First Nations kids in local leagues—a problem that Hockey Canada is trying to remedy—is attributable partly to the popularity of other sports in recent immigrants' countries of origin, but also to the high cost of participation ("Hockey"). Accessibility remains a key issue for participation in sports, as for popular culture more generally. While the field of sports has expanded to a degree unimaginable to the youths playing football on Britain's fields in the eighteenth century, many barriers—including those we have discussed, defined around categories of class, gender, and race, along with others, such as sexuality and ability—persist to some degree. And the question of space—who gets to play where, how, and with whom—remains critical for understanding popular culture in both the past and the present.

Suggestions for Further Reading

Ashby, Leroy. *With Amusement for All: A History of American Popular Culture since 1830.* Lexington: University of Kentucky Press, 2006.

Betts, Raymond F., and Lyz Bly. *A History of Popular Culture: More of Everything, Faster and Brighter.* New York: Routledge, 2013.

Collins, Tony. *Sports in Capitalist Society: A Short History.* New York: Routledge, 2013.

Cullen, Jim. *Popular Culture in American History.* New York: Blackwell, 2000.

Cunningham, Hugh. *Leisure in the Industrial Revolution.* London: Croom Helm, 1980.

Hobsbawm, Eric. *Industry and Empire: An Economic History of Britain since 1750.* London: Weidenfeld and Nicolson, 1968.

Levine, Lawrence W. *Highbrow/Lowbrow: The Emergence of Cultural Hierarchy in America.* Cambridge, MA: Harvard University Press, 1988.

Malcomson, Robert W. *Popular Recreations in English Society 1700–1850.* Cambridge, UK: Cambridge University Press, 1973.

mitch@habs. "Road Hockey Goes to Court!" *Hockey Talk!* Gameworn.net. 7 Jan. 2002. Accessed 11 May 2012.

Thompson, E.P. *The Making of the English Working Class.* Harmondsworth, UK: Penguin, 1963.

3

Representation and the Construction of Social Reality

Truth2Power

As of October 2012, the website www.urbandictionary.com had 17 definitions for the word "represent." Lodged between "represense" and "Representatard," "represent" is best defined by the contributor Truth2Power. With 249 thumbs up to 133 thumbs down from other contributors and readers, Truth2Power defines "represent" in the following way:

1) Lend physical presence or voice on behalf of a constituency defined by geography or purpose, when such manifestation of presence or voice by the whole of that constituency would be logistically impractical or impossible.
2) Stand in for a person, organization, or principle in a manner prescribed by law or formal custom where knowledge of protocols is specific and germaine [sic] to a particular forum of [sic] jurisdiction. (www.urbandictionary.com)

From a popular culture perspective, we think that Truth2Power has done a pretty good job of defining the term. Truth2Power's definition also offers a window into the way that cultural theorists understand the conceptual background and framework of one of the key terms to understanding popular culture: representation. While some of the actual usages of the word "represent" provided by other contributors to www.urbandictionary.com are a bit, well, questionable, it is more than clear to us that contained within them are the intellectual threads that reach back to the early decades of the twentieth century. For example, we would not encourage you to go home at the end of the semester to tell your relatives that your professors quoted material like this (both from www.urbandictionary.com):

DAD: Your mom wants you to square up this joint, yo.
KID: So you want me to clean my room?
DAD: Dat would be da hizzy.
KID: OK.
DAD: Represent.
Or this:
Represent yo clique, mother fucka.

But we would be pleased if you could see within statements like these, uttered in a vast range of contexts, a discursive, ideological, and political import that has a historical dimension rooted in the way in which language and power are always intertwined in any cultural expression you encounter.

We start this chapter by departing a little from www.urbandictionary.com's focus on the many different ways in which words are used to look at the codes or **sign** systems—the

Popular Culture: A User's Guide, International Edition. Imre Szeman and Susie O'Brien.
© 2017 John Wiley & Sons, Inc. Published 2017 by John Wiley & Sons, Inc.

language—that make representation possible. We look at both the mechanics of sign systems—*how* meaning is generated—and the values or ideologies that determine *what* meanings circulate in particular historical contexts, and with what effects. This process of representation, what may loosely be described as the social production of meaning through sign systems, underpins the fuzzy but firm cultural rules that determine who gets to speak, for whom, and under what circumstances; that is, the words, images, and other signs that we use to define our world both *reflect* and *shape* the relations of togetherness and opposition, love and power, that are possible within it. We begin by looking at the representation of youth, particularly the problem of youth violence.

Constructing a Crisis—the Discourse of Violent Youth

In 2008, *The Australian* carried a story that conveyed the shocking information that "More than half of 12-year-olds have drunk alcohol, and one in 10 has recently carried a weapon or stolen something worth more than $10" (G. Roberts). The shock, if not the outrage, fades a little when we read the story in the context of others appearing in the same period, like a 2008 story on news.com.au, accompanied by a menacing photo of a face partly shrouded in a hoodie, announcing that teenagers "are the most violent Australians" ("Australian"), or the UK *Daily Mail's* assertion that in 2008 "soaring youth crime is linked to rising inner-city gang culture" (Clark). And in the United States in 2007, NBC quoted the US Justice Department as linking "increasing violence among teenagers and other youths" to a "nationwide crime spike" ("Rising"). Such worrying reports, often bolstered by statistics, contribute to a sense of crisis, supporting actions ranging from changes in law making it easier to try youths as adults, to prevention programs such as zero-tolerance policies, and the placement of police officers in schools where they can "nip [bad behavior] in the bud" (Leapman). While there is no evidence that such programs have resulted in a reduction of violent crime (Skiba; Wald and Losen), there is little doubt that the initiative that Henry Giroux calls a "war on youth" has produced many casualties, most of them poor minorities (Giroux "America's"; Kozol). One way to understand this "war" is to look at it through the lens of representation.

Opinion polls are one kind of representation; statistics are another. Not surprisingly, in light of the reports cited above, polls conducted in the late 1990s and early 2000s in the United States, the United Kingdom, Canada, and Australia show a very high level of concern about youth crime (J.V. Roberts). These perceptions do not correlate with statistics. For example, in a UK survey, 75% of respondents believed that youth crime rates had increased over the last two years, when they had actually declined (Hough and Roberts). In the United States, where the "crisis" and associated trend toward harsher sentencing emerged first, 60% of respondents in a 1996 California poll believed that youths were responsible for most of the violent crime recorded by police; the actual proportion of violent crimes committed by juveniles was 13% (Dorfman and Shiraldi). A 2001 review of opinion polls by the Canadian Department of Justice arrived at the following conclusion:

> Canadians' concern with young offenders is not warranted, as statistics indicate that youth Criminal Code offences continue to decrease over the past seven years. Of these offences, more than half are property crimes, and only a few are violent. Despite the low numbers of violent offenders, Canadians are increasingly in favour of mandatory adult trials and serving time in adult prisons for youth convicted of violent crimes such as armed robbery, assault, rape and murder. ("Public")

Statistical data from 2012 shows a continuing decline in youth crime rates in Canada, the United States, and the United Kingdom ("Police"; "Youth Violence"; "Youth Justice").

We present these different accounts of youth violence, which are also different ways of representing the issue, not simply to contrast media hype with the "real" picture presented by statistics, or to challenge the tough-on-crime assertions made by the governments, or to illustrate the inadequacy of data in comprehending the complexity of the truth. Rather, we want to use the "story" of youth violence as a way into talking about representation and the role it plays in the construction of social reality. Questions this chapter seeks to address are: How do language and other sign systems work to signify, or to create, social meaning? How does representation map or produce relations of power? How do different media genres (advertising, news, entertainment) and different types of media (television, print, social media, and the Internet) help shape the production of meaning? How have processes of representation shifted historically? What are the nature and extent of media representation in contemporary global culture? And, finally, how does representation work (or fail) as a means of granting agency to groups and individuals?

Signification—the Production of Social Sense

We have introduced the story of youth violence—a story we return to later in the chapter—in a way that we hope will encourage you to think *counter-intuitively* about representation. That is, rather than reading the stories and statistics as we ordinarily would—as a transparent window on the phenomenon of youth crime—we want to think about the frame, to suggest that the way in which these stories are represented, shaped by specific historical circumstances, has an important role in how the "facts" of our social life are created. Before proceeding to some more examples of how this process works, let's step back and try to get a handle on it from a theoretical perspective.

Broadly speaking, representation involves the social production of meaning through sign systems. Signs are the fundamental units of communication. A sign can be a word, a gesture, a facial expression, an image, a musical note, even an item of clothing—anything that conveys meaning and is recognized as doing so by users of the sign system. Conventional wisdom has it that sign systems, or languages, evolve to communicate preexisting realities. But even a superficial examination of different languages tells us that "reality"—at least, the way reality is organized and understood—differs from culture to culture. Language by itself is not the determining factor here; rather, it is that language, as the central medium of culture, influences the way we perceive the world around us and our place within it.

Structuralist Theories of Representation

The suggestion that language does not simply *reflect* but actually *constructs our understanding of* reality emerges from a shift that occurred in the 1960s in cultural and linguistic theory. The principles underlying that shift are clustered under the general heading of **structuralism**. Structuralist theories are concerned not with *what* words or cultural practices mean, but rather with *how* they mean, according to the structure and rules of the system from which they are generated. One of the first structuralist theorists was Swiss linguist Ferdinand de Saussure, whose semiotic theory has had a significant impact on the study of culture (see Close-Up 3.1).

One of the important aspects of Saussurean linguistics is the distinction it draws between *langue*, or the whole system as it exists on an abstract level, including all possible signs and conventions, and *parole*, the individual utterance or the things we do with language. Subsequent critics point out the artificiality of that separation: languages cannot really be said to exist apart from their specific usage. The distinction between *langue* and *parole* is useful, however, in showing that language, in the form of *parole*, embodies all kinds of possibilities for making meaning, but that those possibilities ultimately exist within a frame—the *langue*—that places a limit on what we can intelligibly say. An obvious example of this limitation is the rules of grammar, which dictate the possibilities for word combination in a sentence.

Close-Up 3.1 Semiotics

Ferdinand de Saussure (1857–1913) was a key figure in launching a move in linguistic theory away from understanding how languages developed historically, or *diachronically*, to looking at them as structures at a single moment in time, or *synchronically*. Saussure was interested in how the individual elements of language—*signs*—worked together, according to rules of selection and combination, to produce meaning. A fundamental principle of Saussure's theory was the premise that the relationship between the two "parts" of a sign—a word (or *signifier*) and the concept it refers to (the *signified*)—is not natural but arbitrary, determined by convention. Meaning is produced not by correspondence between word and world, but by differences within the system. Thus, just as the letters c-a-t are meaningless except in relation to other possible selections and combinations of letters (c-a-r, for example, or r-a-t), the word "cat" derives its meaning—an association with a particular furry animal that says "meow"—by virtue of its *difference* from a series of related words— "dog," "mouse," "lemur," "fish." Meaning here is produced by selecting particular elements from a whole *paradigm* of possibilities and combining them in a particular order, or *syntagm*, according to rules of spelling, grammar, and sense that are specific to each language.

In formulating this theory of language (similar versions of which were being developed simultaneously by the American psychologist C.S. Peirce), Saussure argued for the necessity of a new "science" that would study "the life of signs within a society." This approach, which he termed *semiotics,* has been taken up by theorists of popular culture to read not just spoken language but also television, film, music, fashion, and architecture.

These "rules" pertain not just to basic linguistic functions, but also to broader cultural processes of sense making. Language functions not as an isolated structure within those processes, but as part of a complex social fabric that cultural theorists have sought to illuminate using structuralist principles. Anthropologist Claude Lévi-Strauss (1908–2009), for example, worked to uncover the general cultural structures underlying specific myths in primitive societies. A critical part of his theory derived from Saussure's argument that the process of signification, or meaning making, works according to principles of *difference*, with a particular emphasis on **binary opposition**. In other words, things and concepts acquire meaning through what they are not, through their relation to terms that are more or less opposite and mutually exclusive. The far-reaching cultural consequences of this structuring principle become evident when we look at culturally loaded concepts—the oppositions between culture–nature, say, or man–woman—concepts that crucially define the values not just of "primitive" myths but of our own contemporary culture.

Mythologies

French cultural theorist Roland Barthes (1915–80) uses the word mythology in a much more generalized sense to talk about how sign systems work ideologically to reproduce and legitimate particular social relationships. Barthes elaborates Saussure's theory of how meaning is encoded in signs to take account of the fact that, in addition to their *denotative*, or literal, meanings, signs also assume *connotative*, or mythological, significance. That is, they take on additional associations that are more clearly subjective, charged with a culture's dominant, often unspoken beliefs or values. In his book *Mythologies*, Barthes examines a collection of texts, images, and practices from French mass culture with the aim of exposing the myths that underpin their seemingly natural symbolic significance. Myth, in Barthes's sense, is a form of representation that works to express and, more or less invisibly, to justify the dominant values of a culture at a particular historical moment.

Unlike the relatively simple level of denotation, in which a word or image often corresponds to a single, obvious definition, myth generally brings into play a whole chain of associated concepts (e.g., tree–nature–goodness) by which members of a culture understand certain topics and that help to shape their collective identity. Mythological meanings are generated by the juxtaposition of images and words in particular texts, produced in particular cultural contexts. In one essay, for example, Barthes analyzes a photographic exhibit called *The Great Family of Man*, which toured France in the 1960s. On a denotative level, the exhibit consisted of images of people of different races, wearing clothes that signal different cultural backgrounds, all engaged in simple everyday activities—eating, singing, laughing, and so on. The denotative sign, or literal image, of people laughing in turn becomes the signifier for the **humanist** *myth* of universal human nature—a myth that erases historical conditions of inequality in which actual human beings live. The text uses superficial signs of difference—skin color, dress—that it then brings together into a harmonious, seemingly *natural* whole. This process covers over the actual material and *historical* contradictions that underlie its simple message (Barthes 101). Myth works, Barthes's analysis suggests, to the extent that we read it "straight," accepting unquestioningly its naturalness. The principal goal of his critical reading is to reveal the mechanism behind the myth, "to track down, in the decorative display of *what-goes-without-saying*, the ideological abuse which...is hidden there" (11)—to show how myths are not natural but historical, the product of particular relations of power.

Reading the Headlines

A key focus of Barthes's work is the way in which particular representational technologies—color film, for example—work to create specific ideological effects. Before we move on to talk about visual culture, however, let's try to apply some of the principles of semiotic analysis to some simpler texts: newspaper headlines. The following headline appeared in a Canadian newspaper as part of a story about the introduction of computer software written in Inuit languages (Akin):

FROM IGLOO TO INTERNET: First Nations Gain Entrée to the Electronic Age

These programs, the story suggested, would help facilitate government operations and education in the Canadian Arctic. On a denotative level, the signs in this headline are easily legible, though we might struggle with the metaphor in the last half—what does it mean to "gain entry" to an age? On the connotative, mythological level, the headline is more complex and its seemingly straightforward message more open to question.

Meaning, as we noted above, is produced by the selection and combination of signs. Thus, "igloo" and "Internet," the main signs in the beginning part of the headline, derive their meaning in part from their juxtaposition with one another and in part by the grammar of the phrase in which they appear. What sorts of associations do these terms have in relation to one another?

"Igloo" and "Internet" both come out of distinct cultural and historical contexts that inform their mythological associations. Rather than evoking their specific historical origins, however, these associations tend to be much more vague, subjective perceptions of the cultures they carry: "igloo" is associated with "Inuit"—or perhaps more precisely "Eskimo," since igloos belong to a world that for the most part no longer exists and a time when Southerners' ignorance about the cultures of the North led to the use of the generic term "Eskimo" for all Northern Indigenous peoples. While there is nothing obviously pejorative about "igloo," as there is about "Eskimo" (a pejorative term used by nineteenth-century European settlers, generally thought to be derived from an Algonquin word meaning "eater of raw flesh"), the word does carry connotations that come from the same Southern perspective of the North: it is remote; it is cold; it is barren; it is primitive.

Contrast this with the associations summoned up by the word "Internet": connectedness, speed, modernity, globalization. The sense of the headline, which is reinforced grammatically by the use of the prepositions "from" and "to," is not only one of *opposition* and *contrast* between the two terms, but also of a hierarchical relation in which the movement from one to the other constitutes a progression, a move in the right direction. The positive connotations of the move are also signaled by the phrase "gain entrée," which implies induction into a privileged space, with the suggestion (if we want to really use our imaginations) that the Inuit have finally been brought in out of the cold and into the modern world, after waiting breathlessly on the doorstep of the frozen wasteland of the tundra through much of the twentieth century.

It might be argued that there is actually nothing ideological about the headline at all: that it simply describes what happened—Internet connection arrived in the Arctic—and that it does so using the catchy alliterative words "igloo" and "Internet" to draw readers in. There's no question that headlines work partly through verbal cleverness (rhyming, alliteration, puns, etc.) that has little to do with the sense of what is being conveyed (although we might argue that the compulsion to *be* punchy, to reduce complex stories to simple tags, is itself ideological, reinforcing the primary imperative of the media, which is not so much to inform the public as to sell papers). Word choice has other implications, however, for the ideological frame of the story.

The choice of the word "igloo" as a shorthand for the North, for Inuit society, characterizes that society in a way that, besides carrying certain value-laden assumptions, happens to be false: the igloo, and the hunter–gatherer lifestyle that goes with it, hardly exists any more, a fact that can be celebrated or lamented but that contradicts the picture of the Inuit as a primitive people being catapulted into the twenty-first century. Beyond announcing the introduction into the Arctic of what the sources cited in the story agree will be a useful technology, the headline places the story in a wider frame shaped by mythological assumptions about cultural difference, civilization, and the inevitable and desirable course of globalization and human progress. The issue is not whether these myths are valid or useful; it is that they are *myths*, not naturally given truths—a status that is exposed only by subjecting them to the kind of critical reading that media representations, indeed most conventional uses of language, work against.

Discourse and Power

A semiotic reading like the one we just did focuses on the way in which meaning is generated through the relationships between signs in a text. Of course, the sense of that meaning and its substance—the kind of weight it carries in the world—are determined by the cultural context. This includes a community of readers who share a collection of cultural references, and the broader system of social relations that determines not only what has meaning in a culture, but also who gets to say what, under what circumstances, and with what social effects.

French philosopher and social critic Michel Foucault (1926–84) uses the word "discourse" to describe the way in which speech and writing work in conjunction with specific structures and institutions to shape social reality. Discourse, in Foucault's specialized sense of the word, describes a distinct area of social knowledge and the linguistic practices associated with it. Along with particular subjects and ways of talking about them, discourse also defines broad rules about the context of speech or writing, including who is officially permitted to speak on particular subjects and what kind of authority particular kinds of speech (and speakers) carry. Knowledge, according to this concept of discourse, is constituted through relations of power, which determine what is true, what value is accorded particular kinds of knowledge, and, by extension, what material effects that knowledge will have in the world. Knowledge, in other words, *is* power: it comes into being through the operations of power and it *exercises* power by making things happen (or prevent them from happening, as the case may be).

Science, medicine, and law are all examples of specific discourses that emerge in the context of specific historical conditions and in connection with particular institutions. They are all broadly connected with social power, defining ways not only of talking about but also of managing human subjects, through study, treatment, incarceration, and so on. We will talk more about discourse in Chapter 6 in relation to the construction of identity. For now, the two key points to keep in mind about discourse are (i) its emphasis on the connection between knowledge and power, which legitimates forms of social control over particular groups in society—those deemed unwell, unfit, socially maladjusted, criminal, and so on; and (ii) its incorporation of forms of *representation* with forms of social *practice*, which work in reciprocal relation with one another.

Representing the Youth Crisis

Bearing in mind the concept of discourse along with Barthes's theory of mythology, we are ready to return to the example that began this chapter—the phenomenon of the youth "crisis" and its representation in the media. To understand the dynamics of that representation, we need first to look at the discourses through which the concepts of youth and criminality are defined, and then to look more specifically at how they are reproduced in specific media.

The Construction of Youth

Media representations of the youth problem are shaped by a variety of separate but overlapping discourses through which we have come to understand not just crime but also the phenomenon of youth itself. As debates about shifting age thresholds for things such as sexual consent, drivers' licenses, paid employment, and subjection to the Criminal

Code only begin to suggest, the concept of youth is a slippery one, with no clear biological or cultural grounding in an objective distinction between childhood and adulthood.

Historical research shows that the idea of childhood is a relatively recent one, emerging in the eighteenth century in conjunction with new ideas about education and psychological development. Almost concurrently with the Romantic idea of childhood innocence there arose a concern about juvenile delinquency, a new social problem whose identification was closely tied to the dominant class's determination to educate, reform, and discipline the urban working class (see Chapter 2). Police, health officials, and the newly emerging fields of psychology and sociology collaborated to record, monitor, evaluate, and "treat" wayward youths with the aim of turning them into obedient, productive members of bourgeois society.

The category "youth" emerges more clearly in sociology around the late 1920s, in conjunction with American theories of urban development—and, more specifically, urban breakdown. The commonly identified problems of urban life—alienation, rootlessness, social deprivation—get projected onto youth, a demographic category that is itself thought to be characterized by confusion and social alienation (see Figure 3.1). This urban theory then becomes the model for studies of youth crime and the formation of youth gangs and subcultures (Hebdige *Hiding* 27). While the perspective of most social investigators tended toward sympathy with their subjects, the discipline of sociology collaborated with institutions of education and the police to construct youth as a new target for surveillance, management, and reform.

The dominant perception of youth has changed over the last half-century, largely in response to the targeting of teenagers and, increasingly, children as a huge consumer market. Whether this development has contributed to the empowerment of young people is open to question (see Chapter 5 for a general discussion of consumer culture). In any case, alongside an increasingly youth-centered discourse of marketing, the representation of youth continues to be shaped by sociological and legal discourses that emerged in the

Figure 3.1 A 2002 study that linked piercings with high-risk behavior sparked a raft of headlines like this one, warning "Pierced Girls Are Bad Girls: Study." The caption of the accompanying photo stated "A U.S. researcher says parents, teachers and doctors should view an adolescent's desire to obtain a body piercing as a warning sign, prompting a closer inspection of the teenager's friends and pastimes." Source: © Ollyy/Shutterstock

1950s. The major contemporary discursive development can be seen in the identification of the "new" phenomenon of girl violence, which is a kind of spinoff from the more general category identified below.

Suggested Activity 3.1

"Youth" is not a timeless or objective category, but a concept that emerged within particular discourses, out of particular historical circumstances. Pay attention to where the word "youth" appears, in news or entertainment media, in everyday life, or in academic contexts, and think about the values or assumptions that are attached to it and the discourses that legitimate these ideas. Do the connotations of "youth" differ from those attached to near-synonyms such as "young people," "teenagers," "children," "adolescents," or "kids"? How and why?

The Kids Are Not All Right

The contemporary fascination with youth crime covers up the history of the idea of youth, specifically the timing of its emergence in conjunction with initiatives to tighten social control. It would seem that youth and crime have been linked from the beginning. One of the critical elements of the current stories about violent youths, though, is an emphasis on the *newness* of the phenomenon—not just that youths are more dangerous than they were before, but also that we are seeing the development of new and terrifying forms of violent crime. To understand the construction of the "new" youth problem, it is useful to look at an earlier "new" crisis of violence that occurred in 1970s Britain and has been extensively analyzed by Stuart Hall, Chas Critcher, Tony Jefferson, John Clarke, and Brian Roberts.

In their book *Policing the Crisis: Mugging, the State, and Law and Order*, these writers document the emergence in 1970s Britain of a "new" category of crime—mugging. The word definitively entered British consciousness for the first time following the stabbing death of an elderly man by three men in their early 20s, an event described by a police officer and subsequently in the press as a "mugging gone wrong" (qtd. in S. Hall *et al.* 3). While the term "mugging" had never before been used to describe crime in Britain, it was familiar from its more widespread use in the United States, where it was associated not just with a particular kind of crime—violent robbery—but also with a whole range of broader themes connected to general social breakdown. Following the 1972 incident in Britain, "mugging" quickly came into routine use, appearing in media stories about crimes that actually didn't differ all that much from earlier forms of violent crime, except by virtue of the new and ominous name. Fueling new statistical surveys (which inevitably demonstrated that "mugging" was on the rise), it became part of a broad law-and-order discourse that eventually gave rise to new and tougher criminal penalties and other forms of social control.

The story that Hall *et al.* tell about mugging in their book is an important one—not, they acknowledge, because it tells us why muggings happen or what should be done about them, but because it places the whole issue in a broader context, looking at mugging as a social phenomenon defined not only by the crime itself, but also by society's *reaction* to that crime and the way it is represented. They thus begin their study by looking at the emergence of "mugging" as a label that drags along with it a whole referential context, a whole narrative network overlaid with particular assumptions and values. "Mugging" picked up its symbolic baggage from the history of its usage in the United States, where it "not only dominated the whole public discussion of crime and public disorder—it had become a central *symbol* for the many tensions and problems besetting American social and political life in general" (Hall *et al.* 19). "Mugging" acquired this significance, they go on to say,

> because of its ability to *connote* a whole complex of social themes in which the "crisis of American society" was reflected. These themes included: the involvement of blacks and drug addicts in crime; the expansion of the black ghettoes, coupled with the growth of black social and political militancy; the threatened crisis and collapse of the cities; the crime panic and the appeal to "law and order"... These topics and themes were not as clearly separated as these headings imply. They tended, in public discussion, to come together into a general scenario of conflict and crisis. In an important sense the image of "mugging" came ultimately to contain and express them all. (20)

The term entered the British public vocabulary in this broad, general sense *before* it gained widespread use to describe specific crimes. In other words, "mugging" acquired significance in a *mythological* sense before being applied literally to describe concrete events. And it was in its mythological sense that mugging inspired what sociologists refer to as a "moral panic" (see Close-Up 3.2). The mythology of crime carries along with it a raft of words and images that acquire their significance not alone, but in particular combinations. The killing of Trayvon Martin, an unarmed black teenager, by a neighborhood watch volunteer in Sanford, Florida, highlighted the potency of the hoodie as "sign, screen, expectation and force" (Nguyen). While protesters donned hoodies in solidarity, posting photos of themselves with the tagline "I am Trayvon Martin," talk show host Geraldo Rivera warned parents of black and Latino youths not to allow their children to wear hoodies, lest they meet a similar fate. Many of the well-meaning protesters, who ran the gamut from Harvard law students to members of the basketball team Miami Heat to a pregnant woman, missed what Geraldo made offensively clear: the hoodie symbolizes criminality only by association with minority youths. In other contexts—for example as the unofficial uniform of high-tech workers in Silicon Valley, mostly men, mostly white, led by Mark Zuckerberg, creator of Facebook—it means something else entirely (Hutson).

Close-Up 3.2 Moral Panic

In his book on cultural responses to the 1970s subculture of mods and rockers, *Folk Devils and Moral Panics*, Stan Cohen defines moral panic this way:

> Societies appear to be subject, every now and then, to periods of moral panic. A condition, episode, person or group of persons emerges to become defined as a threat to societal values and interests; its nature is presented in a stylized and stereotypical fashion by the mass media; the moral barricades are manned by editors, bishops, politicians and other right-thinking people; socially accredited experts pronounce their diagnoses and solutions; ways of coping are evolved or (more often) resorted to; the condition then disappears, submerges or deteriorates and becomes more visible. (28)

At its height, moral panic spreads a wide blanket over social experience, interpreting diverse and random behaviors or practices as signs of danger. Regardless of its generally mythological origins, moral panic has real, measurable effects in the form of individual behavior, social behavior, and governmental policy. These reactions to the perceived threat come to play an integral role in (retrospectively) defining its meaning.

New Categories of Crime

In a situation that echoes the mugging crisis of 1970s Britain, the period since the mid-1990s in North America has produced what amounts to a **moral panic** about crime, particularly violent youth crime. A key sign and instigator of that panic is the emergence of apparently "new" categories of crime, each of which carries with it a host of anxieties about general and specific social problems. As with mugging, many of these "new" crimes really amount to the redefinition of old categories: thus, "common assault" became "swarming," "break and enter" became "home invasion," "car theft" became "carjacking," "drive-by shootings" appeared, "serial" rapes and murders became common, and the term "road rage" appeared—all justifying a push for tougher interventions (Page).

Suggested Activity 3.2

Can you think of other words or phrases that have entered (or reentered) public discourse recently to describe "new" social phenomena? In what contexts—in relation to what issues or debates—are they employed? What kinds of symbolic baggage do these words and phrases carry? What ideological assumptions do they rest on? What sorts of social practices do they condemn or legitimate?

These interventions extend beyond harsher penalties for crime to more general policies aimed at youths: dress and conduct codes in schools, extension and intensification of the use of identity cards, curfews (in some places), video cameras in downtown streets, and new regulations designed to prevent youths from hanging out or loitering in public and private spaces such as malls.

Making the News

Before we turn to some specific examples of media representations of youth violence, let's take a general look at the role of the media—specifically, the news—in producing social knowledge. Looking at the news media as a whole helps to illuminate the conditions in which individual stories are produced, as well as showing how particular meanings (particular stories) get favored over others and how they come to assume material significance.

Critical to an analysis of the presentation of events in the news is a recognition that the news is not a transparent window on the world; rather, it is an account assembled from a mass of chaotic data according to particular principles of selection and ordering, framed by internal organizational constraints and broader social codes. It reflects not a single set of interests, but a limited range of interests that tend to support the preservation of existing relations of power—that is, the position of dominant social groups. This tendency should not be understood in terms of a crude conspiracy theory, which sees the news media as always serving the agenda of "the state" or "big business" (though the reliance of the news, like all mainstream media, on advertising and the tendency for news production to be concentrated in the hands of fewer and fewer large corporate owners lead inevitably to a corporate capitalist bias). Even when media empires rest in the hands of outspoken defenders of the political right wing (e.g., Rupert Murdoch), the relationship of news media to forces of social and economic conservatism is generally more subtle, and more mundane, than theories of direct and overt manipulation would suggest. To give but one example, a 2012 study of news coverage of the Keystone XL pipeline (a proposed extension of existing pipelines to ship oil from Alberta's tar sands to American refineries) showed that the media quoted supporters of the project far more than opponents to it (Media Matters).

News-Gathering Structures

News organizations are not monolithic ideological forces; they are complex organizations in which editors and journalists generally exercise a great degree of control over the subject matter and perspective of their stories. Writers do not enjoy absolute freedom (particularly since the terrorist attacks known as 9/11, after which heightened security measures are cited in support of incidents curtailing press freedom, such as the British government's demand, in 2013, that the *Guardian* newspaper surrender or destroy files related to the exposure of illegal British and American government surveillance operations). In general, however, the media's reproduction of dominant ideology stems not from coercion, or even conscious cooperation; rather, it is built into established structures of news gathering. Faced by time and resource pressures, the media rely on a steady supply of stories from reliable, accredited sources; these sources, not surprisingly, usually turn out to be dominant institutions (government, police, the courts) as well as accredited "experts" (academics, think tanks, leaders of interest groups; S. Hall *et al.* 58). As well as being, by virtue of their size and influence, the biggest news*makers* of the day, these sources also set the terms by which stories are *interpreted*, constructing them within frameworks whose dominance conceals their partiality or bias. To satisfy the principle of impartiality, the media will often present two contrasting views, generally reflecting the established positions of dominant political parties, ostensibly representing a conservative and a more liberal view. One problem with the principle of offering "both sides" of a story is that there are often more than two sides, however. Another, less obvious problem with what economist Paul Krugman calls "the cult of balance" is that it gives equal weight to moderate and extremist views, scientific fact, and uninformed or prejudiced opinion ("Centrist"). Whether the "two sides" approach tends to oversimplification or, conversely, the obfuscation of truth, the framework is set by the dominant institution: its perspective determines how the issues are framed, what questions can be asked, and what *doesn't* get included in the discussion.

In reportage of the Gulf crisis that led to the war of 1990–91, for example, the late cultural critic Edward Said notes that discussion in the United States tended to be framed around two options: should the United States attack Iraq immediately following Iraq's invasion of Kuwait or wait to see whether sanctions worked? These two positions crystallized into the official boundaries of discussion when they were erected as the poles of debate between journalists Karen Elliott House and Anthony Lewis on the news and discussion show the *MacNeil/Lehrer NewsHour*. As intelligent and reasoned voices of the respected papers the *Wall Street Journal* and the *New York Times*, respectively, House and Lewis could be trusted between them to give viewers the "whole" picture, a balanced and fair assessment of the possibilities it entailed. Left unexamined in their discussion was the assumption that America *should* intervene somehow, that it "ought *to be in* the Gulf, regulating the behavior of states, armies, and peoples several thousand miles away" (Said *Culture* 293). Consistent with the unquestioned emphasis on the United States, there was virtually no mention of the Arabs "as having something to do with the war, as its victims, for instance, or (equally convincingly) its instigators" (293). The event, rather, was circumscribed, framed in a limited way that was perceived to speak to the interests of its American audience, an audience whose character was not merely reflected but *constituted* through the debate. That is, rather than speaking to a group whose interests were already defined around common goals and values, this news broadcast, in conjunction with ongoing CNN coverage, played a significant role in helping to *define* a consensus around which all American viewers could gather.

Consensus

The process of assuming and building consensus is, according to Stuart Hall *et al.*, a key aspect of news production. "'Consensual' views of society," they explain, "represent society as if there are no major cultural or economic breaks, no major conflicts of interests between classes and groups. Whatever disagreements exist, it is said, there are legitimate and institutionalised means for expressing and reconciling them" (55). The ideological imperatives of consensus building, along with the practical imperatives of news gathering, mean that noncentral, or marginalized, voices rarely get to contribute to the debate. Thus, the educated "expert"/journalist, with privileged access to government sources, becomes the voice of "all of us"—including, presumably, expatriate Iraqi Americans and Canadians whose own "expert" views might be very different. The same rules of consensus building apply to forms of media such as talk radio, in which broadcasters assume a populist, common-sense persona that functions to unite an "us" against "them" (with "them" in this case often caricatured as the "elite" media, "special interest groups," or simply "intellectuals").

Suggested Activity 3.3

Since the mid-1990s, satirical news programs such as *The Daily Show* and *The Colbert Report* have come to dominate the news media landscape, serving as the principal view on current events for many people. One of the chief appeals of these shows is the way they lampoon traditional ways of creating consensus (e.g., by offering a tongue-in-cheek defense of "conservative values"). Even as they reject simplistic or obvious forms of conformity, these shows clearly speak to different models of belonging. How do these models work? Comparing coverage of major news events by satirical and "straight" newscasts, try to identify similarities and differences in the strategies they use to create consensus and the values they reflect and/or try to instill in viewers.

Echoes of the representation of the 1990–91 Gulf War resounded in the 2002 buildup to the war against Iraq. Once more, the terms of the debate were set by dominant interests: "The honest choices now are to give up and give in, or to remove Mr. Hussein before he gets his bomb," as an editorial in *The Economist* put it ("Case" 9). Once again, the news media engaged in the work of consensus building, confirming solidarity with the United States. Of course, the delineation of an inside—"we"—also entails the construction of an outside ("they," i.e., terrorists and their alleged sympathizers) without whom there would be no story. During the 2003 United States–led war on Iraq, the Pentagon-sanctioned practice of "embedding," in which selected reporters were attached to military units, helped to generate sympathetic coverage of American soldiers, and thus to shore up consensus within the news audience about the justness of the war.

Suggested Activity 3.4

While the goal of consensus building characterizes news media in general, the *terms* and *extent* of that consensus differ depending on which media outlet we look at (local versus national television news, for example; public versus commercial; print versus television or the Internet). Take a look at different news media and try to analyze how consensus is assumed or actively enlisted in each case. Around what common beliefs is consensus defined? Who is included, and who is left out? Does the boundary of the community shift depending on the news item?

Media and Youth Crime

Nowhere, perhaps, is the consensus-building function of news more evident than in stories about crime. Crime is a dominant feature in news in part because it so nicely fits the general ideological criteria for what Stuart Hall *et al.* term "news value": it is out of the ordinary; it is dramatic in a tragic way; it is easily personalized; and it can be incorporated into a broader pattern of stories. As with all events deemed newsworthy, the media make crime stories meaningful by identifying them and placing them in a context familiar to the audience—that is, locating them "within a range of known social and cultural identifications" (S. Hall *et al.* 54). The assumption of consensus is obviously an important part of this process: the news is intelligible only to the extent that its audience shares common ideas about how society is defined and how it operates. Consensus assumes the more specific, ideologically charged significance discussed above, depending on the kind of news story being reported. Crime stories are particularly successful consensus builders because, besides being out of the realm of the ordinary, they also fall outside the bounds of community; in fact, they play a key role in defining those boundaries. On the one side is the respectable, law-abiding community—"us"—for whom the victim becomes an innocent and sympathetic embodiment. On the other side is "them"—the accused criminals, who, for reasons both ideological and pragmatic (most people charged with crimes aren't affiliated with journalists' regular "trusted sources"), don't have a voice in their story. Their lack of symbolic representation translates into a more concrete lack of power in the court system, where, as a result of diminishing government funding for legal aid, many people accused of crimes appear in court without a lawyer. Under these circumstances, it has been shown that "they may also be more likely to plead guilty, get convicted and receive stricter sentences" (Tsoukalas and Roberts 87).

Picturing Crime

In its construction of social reality, the news gains its substance through the power of myth. The operation of myth is evident in the photo and caption in Figure 3.2, from a Canadian news story about the Ontario provincial government's proposed Safe Streets Act that came into effect in 2000 (Ibbitson A1). Before we analyze the text itself, we need to make a few observations about the significance of photographic representation. Unlike words, the images in photography do not translate what they signify into an arbitrary code; they are a precise *analogue*, or copy, of the objects they reproduce. This purity of reproduction encourages us to think of photographs as offering a truer, more authentic representation of the world than language is capable of doing; indeed, it is photography's capacity for realism that makes it such a valued part of print media.

Our inclination to trust the evidence of our eyes, for which the photographer functions as a kind of proxy, makes it hard to remember that realism, which describes a mode of representation that is taken to provide a faithful and objective picture of the world, is itself a kind of code or convention. What makes photographic realism so powerful—and so deceptive—as a reproduction of reality is its capacity to capture the constant movement of things and freeze it in a single instant. In that instant, the images captured stand out, weirdly, as more vivid, more intense than our actual experience can ever be. This vividness contributes to photography's seeming ability to convey a world more substantial than that represented by language. The pitfalls of this vividness are twofold: first, it works by tearing objects out of their place in space and time (essentially robbing them of their historical context); second, its apparent naturalness conceals the mediating role of culture in its construction.

Figure 3.2 This photo appeared in the Canadian newspaper the *National Post*, with the headline "Harris Vows to Rid Streets of Pushy Beggars, Squeegees." The caption below the 1999 photo provided further information: "The Tories would amend the Highway Traffic Act to keep 'Martin' from his post at the corner of Spadina Avenue and Queen Street West." Source: © Peter Redman/Toronto Sun, a division of Postmedia Network Inc.

"Culture" here refers to the practices that make the photo make sense. First, it includes the decisions made by the photographer—what to include or exclude, how to frame the subject, what kind of lighting or other technical codes to use, and so on. The increasing ability of photographers to manipulate images digitally (even many compact cameras now boast a "slimming" feature) is only an extension of these cruder aesthetic technologies. Second—and harder to identify—are the multiple cultural resources that viewers bring to bear in interpreting a photograph. With these cautions in mind, we are now ready to look at the photo and caption from the story about creating safe streets.

Those "Pushy Squeegees"

On a denotative level, the photo depicts the view from inside a car, its windshield being washed by a young man in a torn T-shirt. Through the haze of the wiper fluid, a city street is visible. Separately, and even together, the images in the photo could evoke a number of different associations: they are, in semiotic terms, "polysemous." Their meaning is fixed, however, or *anchored*, by the story headline, which reads "Harris Vows to Rid Streets of Pushy Beggars, Squeegees." It is the headline that gives the story its connotative significance and makes it intelligible in a particular cultural context. Conversely, for readers outside major centers who might be unfamiliar with the term "squeegee," the photo clarifies both the activity and the way we are meant to read it, in association with youth, aggression, danger, and so on.

Both the conventional codes of reading and knowledge of the specific context make it clear that the youth cleaning the windscreen is not "Harris" (whom *National Post* readers would recognize as Mike Harris, the then premier of Ontario) but a "pushy squeegee." If the image alone is not enough to convey menace and the threat of violence, the word "pushy" makes it clear that the youth in question is not providing a service but committing an aggressive act (the squeegee being a metaphor for...a switchblade? a club?), while the phrase "rid the streets of" confirms his place in the category of socially useless, even dangerous things. The caption below the photo reads "The Tories would amend the Highway Traffic Act to keep 'Martin' from his post at the corner of Spadina Avenue and Queen Street West." "Martin" is thus not only identified as one of the targets of the legislation, but also is made representative of *all* the beggars and squeegees: men, women, and children living on—and allegedly terrorizing—the streets. The arrangement of the photo works nicely with the grammar of the sentence so that the reader identifies both with the perspective of the camera, which is inside the car, under siege along with the car's driver, *and* with Harris, who embodies the force of law and order with his reassuring vow to make the streets safe again.

We are thus made to feel both vulnerable and reassured: the threat (which is made real in the representation of this story, even if we didn't feel it before) will be taken care of. The meaning of the story and photo are further anchored through their presence in the *National Post*, a paper whose general political slant favors law-and-order policies such as the criminalization of squeegees. The same photo and caption in a different paper—a different frame—might produce a slightly different interpretation.

In its actual context, a story like this one works to elicit public support for political programs like the Safe Streets Act, as well as more generally to reinforce a vision of social order in which "we" are on the inside, protected morally and legally from the onslaughts of those pushy street people. The photo reinforces the division, with the frame of the car window defining a material and ideological fortress between the driver and "Martin," a shadowy figure whose marginality is confirmed by the quotation marks surrounding his name.

Crime on Television

While the newspaper article about the Safe Streets Act uses image and text to turn "Martin" into the poster boy for urban disorder, television and online video employ more complex and expansive codes to weave representations of specific instances of violent youth crime into an elaborate narrative defining a major social issue. While photos promise to deliver a more accurate representation of the world than words, television claims a more privileged place still in its capacity to make connections between images, in a simulation of real-life change and movement. As with photography, however, we need to resist the urge to read television representations naturalistically and instead think about *how* they are simulated.

With television, even more than photography, this means paying attention to the way its status as a commercial medium structures its content. While the function of television clearly changes depending on whether the program being broadcast is a game show, a sitcom, or the news, a common feature of all television programming is the need to produce meaningful information out of an inherently erratic stream of programming; that is, individual television shows need to convey self-contained narratives that mark them off from the general flow of programming and construct meaningful bridges over commercial interruptions. At the same time, the structure of commercial breaks requires that programs be broken down into manageable segments, or "packages," that fit comfortably between the commercials (and it is worth remembering that, from the television industry's point of view, it is the commercials that are the meat and potatoes of the programming: the shows merely provide the hooks to bring in viewers/consumers). The tidy-package imperative, according to which information has to be marshaled into compact (i.e., 10-minute), easily digestible bits, contradicts one of television's key selling points, which is its ability to tell stories—to place images, events, and people into a broader context. These structural imperatives have begun to shift with the increasingly seamless blending of commercials and programming, a manipulation of "reality" that further blurs our perception of crime.

Victoria's Not-So-Nice Secret

This is the mandate of "Victoria's Secret," a documentary that aired in Canada in March 2002 on CTV. The subject is Victoria, BC, a mid-sized Canadian city and provincial capital. Located on Vancouver Island, the city is known for its balmy weather and relaxed pace. Outdoor enthusiasts gravitate to its coastal walking paths and bike-friendly streets, while British institutions like the Empress Hotel's afternoon tea make it a popular destination for cruise-ship passengers. As the show's title suggests, though, with its pun on the provocatively named lingerie retailer, the city harbors some dirty secrets.

The show opens *in medias res*, "in the middle of things," with a shot of a plane landing and a stretcher being unloaded. The sense of crisis conveyed by the opening sequence is heightened by the darkness and even blurriness of the scene, which is filmed in the rain, and by a rapid series of jump cuts from plane to ambulance to stretcher. The images are knitted together by the voiceover, which identifies the scene as the conclusion of a "mercy flight" from Victoria to Toronto, 2000 miles away. The unconscious patient on the stretcher, a teenage boy, is "home for Christmas, but not the way he left." The dramatic events of the story are personalized in the next shot, in which the boy's mother, facing a battery of microphones, explains that her son, who is in a coma, "was very badly beaten up by three guys for no rhyme or reason; he just happened to be in the wrong place at the wrong time." The "wrong place," the voiceover resumes to tell us, is Victoria, BC, "Canada's garden playground."

And the story, as the title suggests, is as much about this place as it is about the terrible plight of the victim. Specifically, it's about Victoria's "dark side" as a city besieged by roving teenage gangs. The threatening quality of these gangs is established by words and images that from the opening shots of the program work to establish clear contrasts between safety and danger, the familiar and the unknown, light and darkness. The world of humane, civilized community and family, summoned up by expressions like "mercy" and "home for Christmas," is contrasted with—and shown to be threatened by—a chaotic underworld, in which anonymous groups of guys—gangs—roam around looking for violence.

The theme of contrasts is set up by initial shots of a tourist's Victoria—a sailboat leaving a marina, golfers playing in the middle of winter, flowers, people drinking tea at the Empress Hotel—accompanied by the voiceover, warning ominously that, while the city is "at first glance, scenic, safe and secure...this is a tale of two cities. It may be hard to believe, but there is a dark side to this city. A violent and dangerous one." Here the image changes dramatically to a scene of the reporter talking to the camera as she walks along what appears to be a dark alley, flanked by walls covered with graffiti. If the mother functions to bring us into the story, presenting a suffering human face with which the viewer is asked to identify, the reporter serves as the controlling perspective of objectivity. In the mode of a correspondent sending dispatches from a war zone, she brings alarming news of a situation that, while barely visible until now, constitutes a pervasive social problem rendered all the more threatening by its manifestation in apparently "random" and "sense-less" acts of violence.

Inciting panic in its viewers, the revelation that there is "a youth gang problem in the midst of Canada's Shangri-la" also offers a kind of comfort, conveyed in the rational, authoritative voice of the reporter, that the problem has been identified, given a label. "These are legitimate gangs," a police officer confirms. "They have a hierarchy; they're wearing colours." The use of the word "legitimate" is interesting, signaling not, clearly, that the gangs are on the side of law and order, but that they fit a template, that they are classifi-able—and hence manageable. No longer random and unintelligible, the problem has assumed a handle we can grasp. And we are persuaded that, though we might not have been conscious of it, this is a problem whose presence we somehow recognized all along: "For too many years, gangs of young people have been allowed to terrorize the streets." This is a cause for outrage that translates into relief that "citizens are now standing up at community meetings demanding action, searching for solutions"—solutions that are forthcoming in the form of police task forces, tougher laws, and pressure on young people to inform authorities about violence, or threats of violence, committed by their peers.

The "Inside versus Outside" Perspective

As well as being a story of contrasts, this is also, like the squeegee article, a story of insides and outsides. "Inside" represents the community, concerned citizens, the media, and television viewers, threatened by an "outside" inhabited by dark and unruly forces, name-less young people who commit acts of violence with "no rhyme or reason." The story also invokes other "insides" and "outsides" in its characterization of Victoria as a place where things like this are not "supposed" to happen. Even the working-class suburb of Esquimault, where two of the assaults occurred, "is a far cry from the mean streets, urban decay and inner-city ghettoes normally associated with street gangs."

At the same time, then, that "Victoria's Secret" might be working to shake its urban or suburban viewers out of their complacency, suggesting that there really aren't "two cities"—we all inhabit the same big, dangerous world—it also serves to shore up bounda-ries, to reassure us that, unlike in the "mean streets" (of Toronto? South Central Los Angeles? Bogotá?), we *do* still live in a community where civilized values prevail. Problems such as poverty and racial tension, summoned up by the word "ghetto," remain "outside," not part of this story or of Canada's garden playground, though they might hover danger-ously nearby, threatening to spill over if we don't monitor the borders vigilantly enough—because the story of youth violence is perhaps above all a cautionary tale about the dangers of complacency, of not attending to signs of social disorder and not treating them seriously enough when we find them.

In looking at "Victoria's Secret" as an example of how representation constructs social reality, we are not trying to suggest that the instances of violence it documents are some-how fabricated or that their effects are negligible. Rather, we want you to think about the process by which the media frames those instances in a particular way, incorporating them within a narrative that draws on and in turn helps to consolidate specific beliefs, emotions, and assumptions. Extending far beyond the specific crimes that the show doc-uments, these beliefs, emotions, and values inform—often unconsciously—our ideas about community, youth, law, and the society we live in. Similarly, a show like "Victoria's Secret" doesn't just inform us about events that are going on in our society; it *re-presents* those events as part of a broad vision of what society should look like. The "facts" of the story are inseparable from—indeed, they are largely manufactured by—values and politics. As an authoritative force in society that holds a near monopoly on social knowledge (in more than one sense, as control over media falls into fewer and fewer hands), the news, particularly in the area of crime, plays an effective role in constructing and delimiting public opinion. To recognize, and critically challenge, the ideologies that underpin dominant constructions of the social order, it is necessary to ask, as Stuart Hall *et al.* do in their book on mugging, a series of questions about the news stories we watch, hear, and read: "'What, other than what has been said about this topic, *could* be said?' 'What questions are omitted?' 'Why do the questions—which always presuppose answers of a particular kind—so often recur in this form? Why do certain other questions never appear?'" (65). In the case of the representation of youth violence, some of the missing questions might be: What kinds of relationships exist between trends in youth crime and trends in adult crime? How does youth crime fit into an overall pattern of youth culture? How does society function (or not) to address the needs of youth in areas such as education, job opportunities, public space, social programs, and so on? How have social views of youth changed? If you think about it, you can probably come up with other questions, other ways of framing the "youth problem."

Truth2Power: The Politics of Representation

As the analysis above suggests, representation has a lot to do with power—with what gets spoken about in what way, and with who gets to speak, on whose behalf. In both the organization of media and the ideological structure of language and other sign systems, representation tends to reproduce existing relations of social power and make them seem natural, hiding the fact that they are the product of complex social histories. The example of media representation of youth violence demonstrates the function of discourse in the maintenance of social order: the simultaneous classification and marginalization of relatively powerless members of society—in this case, youths—works to keep them in their place, through discourse and, more concretely, in the form of laws and social policies.

Enhancing Visibility, Challenging Negative Representation

As the preceding discussion suggests, negative or stereotypical representation has political consequences: it reflects and reinforces the marginality of minority groups. Thus it follows that the political empowerment of subordinate groups in society—youth, women, racial minorities, lesbian/gay/bisexual/trans*/queer (LGBTQ+) people, people who are disabled, poor, or elderly—depends to some degree on changing representations.

This challenge is compounded in many cases by a lack of visibility in the first place. Actor, writer, and director Dylan Marron's Tumblr, *Every Single Word*, drew attention to this problem by posting a collection of videos that splice all the scenes from major films in which actors of color get to speak. The videos are, well, short! A compilation of dialogue scenes from all eight Harry Potter films featuring racialized actors lasted all of 5 minutes and 40 seconds (S. Murphy). In these and other films, as Marron points out, "Casting choices are contributing to a racist system that projects whiteness as 'normal' and erases people of colour" (qtd. in F. Rutherford). Erasure is not the only problem: when racialized and other visible minorities do appear, it is often in roles that conform to stereotypes and/or are subservient to white characters.

Representational Strategies

Over the past several decades some steps have been made toward more inclusive representation. In the case of racialized minorities (and there are clear historical parallels in the representation of women, LGBTQ+ people, and people with disabilities), it is possible to identify a number of different strategies that have attempted—with different degrees of success—to counter dominant codes of white normativity. *Integrationist*, or *assimilationist*, strategies, embodied in films such as *Guess Who's Coming to Dinner* (1967), served metaphorically to invite blacks into mainstream white society on the strength of the reassuring message that "they" are just like "us". *Affirmationist* messages work in a contrary way to emphasize **essentialist** black identities, but in a way that challenges the mainstream. So-called blaxploitation films from the 1970s fulfilled this function. Many popular films and television shows use a combination of these strategies. For example, the enormously popular 1980s television series *The Cosby Show* represented blacks succeeding in white society through their own efforts, but in a way that played down the history and ongoing reality of discrimination, as well as the politics of resistance. In more recent popular culture, stereotypes persist of individual racialized characters such as the "strong black woman"—"the fighter...who don't take shit from no man"—(Harris), perpetuating the bizarre myth that black women (and even black girls—see, for example, *Beasts of the Southern Wild*; hooks) have it made, unlike their white sisters, who are still (also stereotypically) portrayed as attractively vulnerable, girlish, and in need of protection. This myth not only contradicts the realities of black women's higher risk of falling victim of violence and of experiencing health problems including diabetes, heart disease, and depression; it also discourages empathy by failing to represent their "full and complex humanity" (Harris). More sympathetic stereotypes operate in the "black-and-white friendship" film (a few of many examples include *Pulp Fiction*, *Die Hard with a Vengeance*, *Lethal Weapon 1, 2, 3*, and *4, Men in Black 1* and *2, The Shawshank Redemption, The Fast and the Furious, Remember the Titans, The Blind Side*, and *The Help*), which highlights the possibility of overcoming the barriers of race through individual tolerance and understanding (DeMott). These films or shows frequently address racism as an outdated institution that has been (or *is* being, in the case of films set in the past, such as *The Help*) dismantled by a few spunky individuals.

Dominant representations of LGBTQ+ and disabled people follow a different pattern to the one traced above; however, they share an overriding problem of invisibility. A 2012 report compiled by GLAAD analyzing characters on scripted primetime network television shows based on gender, sexual orientation, race, ethnicity, and (dis)ability showed a decrease in the number of LGBTQ+ characters from the previous season. Moreover, only 5 out of 647 regularly appearing characters—less than 1%—had a disability ("Study"). This situation is compounded by the frequent use of nondisabled actors to play characters with disabilities, and the reduction of complexity in favor of stereotypes. Recalling both the "strong black woman" and the faithful black friend in their unidimensionality, "supercrips" (characters who demonstrate exceptional strength and bravery to overcome the limitations of their disability; Shapiro 16) tend to lack the vulnerability and complexity that make characters sympathetic. Instead, they offer sources of inspiration to nondisabled characters, while remaining absolutely, reassuringly different from them.

All of these forms of representation—which can be plotted more or less historically, though remnants of earlier forms persist—arguably aim toward more diverse representation in the popular media. While it is tempting to frame them in terms of an evolutionary narrative toward greater equality, there are problems with each of these counter-narratives. First, the attempt to counter negative stereotypes with more positive ones reverses the hierarchy while leaving the codes of essential identity/differ-ence intact in a way that confirms the complexity and humanity—the unquestioned normativity—of whiteness and able-bodiedness. The "black–white friendship" movie, which avoids stereotypes by constructing highly individualized relationships, is prob-lematic in a different way. By suggesting that the problem of racial discrimination is a matter of individual morality, these films ignore the broader social and material context of race relations: this means that, while overt acts of individual **racism** can be univer-sally condemned, "the more subtle, deeper forms of discursively and institutionally structured racism remain unrecognized" (Shohat and Stam 201). In more explicit social terms:

> The good news at the movies obscures the bad news in the streets and confirms the [US] Supreme Court's recent decisions on busing, affirmative action and redis-tricting....Because black–white friendship is now understood to be the rule, there is no need for integrated schools or...affirmative action. The Congress and state governors can guiltlessly cut welfare, food assistance, fuel assistance...housing money, fellowship money, vaccine money. (DeMott 33)

The obvious criticism to make of these films, then, is that their "realistic" representation of black–white friendship glosses over the real social conditions of black people living in the United States, including disproportionate rates of mortality, poverty, and imprison-ment. Serving as an emblem of already-achieved equality, these films help to legitimate **neoliberal** social policies that contribute to the further marginalization of minority groups.

An increasing number of films, such as France's *The Intouchables* (2011), the Spike Lee film *Red Hook Summer* (2012), and the more recent films *Dope* (2015) and *Dear White People* (2015), counter the postracist tone of much of popular culture by highlighting the economic and social relations of *in*equality that are concealed by the myth of tolerant individualism. Rather than focusing on exemplary characters who rise above their social circumstances (characters who always manage to be a bit richer/smarter/better looking than everyone around them), these films offer a more complex view, one that acknowl-edges the role of culture and economics in shaping individual lives.

By now it should be impossible for you to read the words "real" and "realism" without warning bells going off. However praiseworthy the efforts to create an accurate rather than a simply positive picture of a group or situation, such efforts remain troubled by the shaky "reality" of representation itself, according to which myth and ideology are not simply everywhere present but inescapable. Under these conditions, one could argue that the only way to seriously undermine the politics of representation is to highlight the hid-den conventions and codes on which they are based—much as we did in our semiotic readings of newspaper and television news reports. Feminist critic Laura Mulvey notes, "It is said that analyzing pleasure, or beauty, destroys it" (323). This, she suggests, is the intention of critical scholarship such as her own psychoanalytic reading of Hollywood cinema. It is also the intention of avant-garde cinema—those films, such as *This Is Not a Film, Another Earth*, or Errol Morris's *Tabloid*, for example, that deconstruct, as they represent, dominant codes of representation. Satire is another powerful way to highlight through humorous exaggeration the construction of stereotypes. The 2010 film *Four Lions* is a good example of this genre. Focusing on four British-born jihadists plotting to blow up the London Marathon, the film skewers both fundamentalist religion and Islamophobia. Counter to stereotype, the (hilariously incompetent) would-be terrorists blend in perfectly in their working-class British communities, and are therefore over-looked by the police, who instead seize the ringleader's brother, an innocent Muslim cleric who is totally unaware of the scheme. One danger of such satirical critiques is that the distinction between laughing at and laughing with offensive humor is sometimes murky. The repetition of powerful myths, even if it is done with the aim of critique, always carries the risk of merely reinforcing them. But satire, when it works to critical effect, is another illustration of Mulvey's argument about destroying or demystifying the images that seduce us, reminding us that negative representations cannot be undone without attending to their underlying politics, including the contexts from which they are produced.

Beyond Representation: Who's the Boss?

This points to another issue in media representation: namely, its production. In 2015, racialized minorities would appear to have made significant strides in television and film, with critically acclaimed shows such as *Scandal, Treme, Empire,* and *How to Get Away with Murder* featuring actors of color in lead roles and claiming a growing share of Emmy nominations—though still not many in the lead actor/actress category (Johnson); Viola Davis's 2015 award for lead actress in a drama series made her the first black woman to win in that category. For many media critics, however, the way minority groups are represented is secondary to who controls the production, distribution, and exhibition of those representations. Reports on Hollywood employment practices released by American labor union the Screen Actors Guild in 2007–08 (the last dates for which statistics are available) reveal that minority actors took up only 27% of television and theatrical roles; where they participate at all, it is as performers rather than as producers (Screen Actors Guild). Recently, in films like *Hunger Games* and *Aloha,* we have seen white actors cast in lead roles where the source texts featured characters of a different ethnicity. It is noteworthy that, where ethnicity is not specified in the source text, filmic adaptations tend to default to white. Of the relative absence of racialized characters in the Harry Potter movies, Thomas comments: "J.K. Rowling made a masterpiece....It deals with things like destiny and honor and friendship and empowering yourself through education—those are incredible themes, but those are universal themes. That has nothing to do with whiteness. So why then, are we making it seem as if those universal themes are actually just for white people?" (qtd. in S. Murphy).

The consequences of these historical patterns of representation (using "representation" in a more directly political sense) are not just cultural, in the sense of determining whose stories get told and in what way, but also economic, since it is in production that—celebrity salaries notwithstanding—the real profit in the entertainment industry lies. So while HBO's *The Newsroom* may depict progress in hiring practices, in reality 86.9% of television news directors are white, according to the Radio-Television News Directors Association, and four networks—NBC, ABC, Fox, and CBS—dominate the entire structure of production (Papper). In the words of actor/director Mario Van Peebles, "We have to be in there not just as actors, but as writers and directors—and as development executives and programmers, that's the next goal. Playing basketball's not enough any more, we've got to own our teams. Without economic power, you have no power" (qtd. in Schneller).

Social media has significantly diversified the field of representation, both in terms of who gets represented and who controls representation. Collective projects like the Facebook group "This Is What Disability Looks Like," which posts participants' images that challenge "tragic" and "inspirational" stereotypes of disability, and #BlackOutDay, which flooded social media sites with selfies, gifs, and videos of black people on March 6, 2015, give visibility and voice to groups who are underrepresented or badly represented in mainstream media. Some of these, such as #iftheygunnedmedown, which followed the 2014 police shooting of unarmed black teenager Michael Brown in Ferguson, Missouri, take direct aim at the role of visual culture in supporting institutionalized racism. By juxtaposing ordinary photos of themselves with the question "If they gunned me down, which picture would they use?" participants highlighted the racist codes that determine the "menacing" photos that mainstream media routinely circulate following instances of police violence against black men, women, and children, implying that they somehow deserved it. These representations are arguably making real headway against the overwhelming whiteness of dominant media; it is too soon to tell whether or to what extent they will translate into more material modes of empowerment.

As the preceding discussion suggests, representation has a complex relation to politics. In discussing this relation, we need to go beyond the dynamics of representation itself to understand the contexts in which representation occurs. The next section examines some of the ways in which we might go beyond the simple analysis of texts to understand representation as part of a larger process of creating popular culture.

Contexts of Representation

We have talked a great deal so far about the power of representation, particularly media representation, to construct social reality—literally, to create the world we live in, shaping our beliefs and behavior, fears and desires. It has become commonplace to recognize the role these representations play in our lives, for good or, from the perspective of many commentators, for ill. In the words of one media critic:

> The American industrial-entertainment complex has pretty much replaced the church as the maker and enforcer of values on this continent....We hit 18 having spent more time in front of the TV than at school. We can summon the face of Bruce Willis, the stubble and the crooked smile, more readily and vividly than our own father's. Our heads resound with the voices of strangers. (Grierson 24)

Grierson makes these observations in an article that begins by recalling the death of Reena Virk, a Victoria, BC, teenager beaten unconscious, then drowned by a group of other teens after a party one night. Speaking at a memorial service, Budgie Basi-Reed, a family friend, drew a direct connection between what happened to Reena and the kinds of images that children and teens get bombarded with in television and video games. "Violence," she notes, "has become an acceptable form of entertainment" (qtd. in Grierson 24). In the article that follows, Grierson advances what has become a familiar argument, that brutal media imagery is largely responsible for the creation of an increasingly violent society. Adherents of this thesis cite events like the 2014 shooting of six people in California by Elliott O. Rodger (who then committed suicide); a manifesto written by Rodger prior to the shooting highlighted his love of the video game *Halo*. Adam Lanza, the 20-year-old who killed 26 people at Sandy Hook Elementary School, was also said to be an avid gamer (Terkel).

In the introductory section to this chapter, we began by talking about the role of media in promoting the *idea* that not just violence but youth violence is a growing social problem. We talked about the role of representation—and, in particular, mass media representation—in creating a climate of social fear in which dominant myths about community, morality, race, gender, and age harden into "facts" about youth violence. A critical premise of our argument is that representation plays a determining role in shaping the world we live in. We need now to take a step back from that argument and to recognize the perils in taking it too far. Just as we need to wriggle our way out of the belief that we all like to cling to that we as individuals possess an independent mind that somehow exists prior to language and other cultural forms, we also need to reject the equally common assumption that words and images are all-powerful, that their effects are clear and easily measurable. Interestingly, most of us are able to hold on to both these beliefs at once by maintaining a dodgy distinction between our *own* ability to see through the snares of advertising and other forms of representation and the infinite impressionability of *others*, particularly children, to what they see, hear, and read. We have already tried to show, both in this chapter and the previous one, some of the weaknesses in the assumption that it is possible simply to see around or through ideology. Now we need to tackle the converse theory of mass media manipulation.

The Myth of Mass Media Manipulation

This theory is familiar to all of us in the form of arguments such as Grierson's about the social effects of certain kinds of representation—particularly sex and violence. Gary Bauer, former head of the US Family Research Council and onetime Republican presidential candidate, puts the argument more crudely: "If you expose children to uplifting and noble material, you're more likely to have noble citizens. If children are wallowing in sexual images and violence, that is bound to have an impact on those who are most vulnerable" (qtd. in Lacayo). While this observation seems, on first appearance, to make a certain kind of sense—the images and ideas we are exposed to *do* shape who we are—there are also some obvious problems with it.

Locating Meaning

First, the concept of "uplifting and noble material" assumes, first, that we all agree on what is uplifting and noble and, second, that nobility and upliftingness are somehow inherent, present in some representations and absent from others. The difficulty of making that assessment is shown in the clearly arbitrary criteria by which would-be censors evaluate controversial images, particularly those that feature violence. For example, when Republican presidential candidate Bob Dole issued his famous 1995 rant against Hollywood's "destructive messages of casual violence and even more casual sex," included among his list of good "family" fare was the Arnold Schwarzenegger film *True Lies*. Along with its spectacular violence, the movie gained notoriety for a scene in which CIA agent Harry Tasker (Schwarzenegger), having encouraged his wife (Jamie Lee Curtis) to become a spy posing as a prostitute, poses as a client himself, then has her perform a lengthy striptease before revealing his real identity. "Uplifting and noble" this isn't! However, leaving aside perhaps the most likely reason for Dole's endorsement—at the time a major supporter of the party, Schwarzenegger was the (Republican) Governor of California from 2003 to 2011—we can surmise that the sex and violence pass the test here because the former occurs in defense of family values (Tasker puts his wife through the humiliating ordeal of the striptease as a kind of punishment or test in response to his suspicion that she is cheating on him) and the latter is committed against obvious "bad guys"—their badness signaled, as many commentators noted, by their Middle Eastern appearance.

More recent examples of violence in visual culture that presumably would pass the Dole test are television shows such as *Homeland* or video games such as *Call of Duty*, which depict extreme violence whose use is justified as necessary to the task of keeping good (American) people safe in increasingly dangerous times. Even the more controversial UFC (Ultimate Fighting Championship) expresses a mythological equation of elegantly executed brutality with moral virtue. While a chorus of voices continues to loudly decry the problem of "antisocial violence," the years since 9/11 have seen an increased tolerance in politics and entertainment (realms that are often confusingly blurred) of what is represented as "pro-social violence," including government-sanctioned torture.

The point here is not to suggest that *True Lies* and *Homeland* belong in the *bad* representations bin, not the good one. Rather, these examples reveal that the value and meaning of cultural texts are not qualities that reside objectively within them; they are instead determined in part by the audiences that watch and respond to them. Thus the representation of *True Lies* has a different meaning for Bob Dole than it does for some feminist viewers—including Jamie Lee Curtis herself, who in a 2002 interview included it among roles that she now regretted taking on (Wallace). Similarly, viewers might cringe at the depictions of violence in a show for any number of reasons, including opposition to the cause in whose name it is enacted or an objection to violence in general, but continue to watch out of enjoyment of other elements: the comedy, for example, or the brilliant dialogue or suspenseful plot. The meaning of texts is complicated not just by the complex interplay of signs within them, but by the complex—and often unpredictable—responses of readers and viewers.

Representation and Social Consequences

A second problem with media theories such as Bauer's is his assumption, echoing beliefs of early twentieth-century critics such as F.R. Leavis (see Chapter 1), of a direct relationship between the consumption of particular images and particular social effects. Leaving aside for a moment the undefined (and undefinable) question of what constitutes noble citizenship, the assumption that viewing "good" images will lead to "good" behavior rests on a simplistic understanding of how pedagogy, or the process of teaching and learning, operates. The meanings we take from cultural texts come from a combination of convention—ways of interpreting particular signs that are shared widely among members of a society—and individual subjectivity and experience. What we *do* with these interpretations is also influenced by those diverse factors.

Some studies do draw conclusive links between the consumption of violent media images and aggressive behavior. One of the most compelling of these studies is the work done on violent video games by David Grossman, a US army lieutenant and former psychologist. In his book *On Killing: The Psychological Cost of Learning to Kill in War and Society*, he draws some disturbing parallels between the effects on young people of media, particularly television and video games, and the techniques the military uses to train its soldiers to kill. In particular, Grossman points to two kinds of conditioning that work to desensitize subjects to killing. First, in a process of what is called "classical" conditioning, the military trains its soldiers to find killing acceptable, and even pleasurable, by associating it with rewards. The same process is at work as "children watch vivid pictures of human suffering and death, and they learn to associate it with their favorite soft drink and candy bar, or their girlfriend's perfume or their boyfriend's touch" (Grossman 26).

The second form of conditioning, what psychologists term "operant" conditioning, works by teaching subjects to perform acts habitually, without thinking. Military technology such as flight simulators and moving-target practice help to teach this kind of behavior by offering a rapid series of stimuli that require an immediate—violent—response. The same process is at work in point-and-shoot video games, Grossman notes, in which targets pop up randomly and success depends on the ability to shoot quickly and accurately—without, needless to say, imagining the consequences for the simulated victims. As evidence of the translatability of those skills to real life, Grossman presents the chilling example of a 14-year-old boy in Paducah, Kentucky, who shot up a school prayer group, firing eight shots from a .22-calibre pistol and hitting eight victims, five of them in the head. (The average US law enforcement officer, shooting at a distance of seven yards, has a less than one in five rate of actual hits.) When questioned, the killer, who had never fired a real gun before, admitted to being an avid player of video games. While this is an extreme example of the effects of simulated violence, Grossman argues for a host of more subtle and pervasive effects on children who, if they don't grow up to become killers themselves, become more or less desensitized to the effects of violence, thus creating an atmosphere of bystander tolerance for events like the beating to death of Reena Virk.

Grossman's thesis is a compelling one that seems to suggest that specific kinds of representational *content*—that is, violence—conveyed in a specific *form*—electronic media, and interactive video games in particular—produce undesirable social effects. However, in its reliance on relatively simple "behaviorist" psychological theories, his argument seriously underrates the complexity of the processes by which human beings read and respond to the world around them. Moreover, by placing the burden of proof on the representations themselves, on what they are saying and/or asking users to do, arguments such as Grossman's neglect the broader question of how and under what circumstances people consume this media—on what they *do* with it.

Representation and Imagination

This is not to say that imagination and reality are utterly distinct from one another: they are not, which is why the realm of the imagination is such a potent place. As well as providing a storehouse of images that interpret and mediate the world for us, the imagination—and culture in general—also offers resources that help us to cope with painful aspects of reality in ways that can be both harmful and productive for individuals and society, but are rarely simply one or the other. Representations of violence, which have been around since the beginning of human civilization—though admittedly not in so graphic a form as today—offer a site for particularly complex workings out of fear, aggression, anger, and desire. While it is frequently pointed out that youths who commit violent crimes tend to be avid consumers of violent media, what is not so frequently pointed out—and what is more difficult to measure—is the role such media might play in helping many others to work through feelings of frustration or anger, thus avoiding their explosion into actual acts of violence. As media critic Henry Jenkins puts it:

> The key issue isn't what the media are doing to our children but rather what our children are doing with the media. Eric Harris and Dylan Klebold [perpetrators of a mass shooting at Columbine High School in Colorado in 1999] weren't victims of video games. They had a complex relationship to many forms of popular culture. All of us move nomadically across the media landscape, cobbling together a personal mythology of symbols and stories, and investing those appropriated materials with various personal and subcultural meanings. Harris and Klebold happened to be drawn toward dark and brutal images, which they invested with their personal demons, their antisocial impulses, their maladjustment, their desires to hurt those who had hurt them. (23)

Jenkins goes on to describe a web site constructed by a 16-year-old girl who invited submissions from across the United States of poems and stories based on characters from popular culture. The submissions drew on many of the same media products that had been cited in the Columbine case, particularly the film *The Basketball Diaries*, reading them not as incitements to violence, but as complicated explorations of themes such as love, friendship, and community (23).

Even when popular culture becomes the site of darker imaginings, the connection between fantasy and violence is far from clear-cut. In the atmosphere of fear following the Columbine shooting, however, social authorities were quick to establish a link, establishing "zero tolerance" policies against "violent" forms of cultural expression, ranging from making verbal threats to wearing trench coats. In one notorious case, a Grade 11 student in Cornwall, Ontario, was jailed for more than a month in 2000 after reading aloud in class a story he had written called "Twisted" in which a bullied student plots to blow up his school. The student claimed that the piece was a work of fiction, inspired in part by the work of Stephen King. Many writers, including King himself, leapt to the student's defense, organizing a special forum/fundraiser to draw attention to his plight. Protesting what was clearly a violation of the boy's freedom of speech, many of his defenders were careful to distance themselves from the claim that art has no bearing on reality: a victim of bullying himself (seven of his classmates were subsequently arrested for assault), the student was clearly expressing, in the form of creative fiction, many of his own frustrations and fantasies. To draw a straight line from that expression backward to Stephen King and forward to some future act of violence is, however, to grossly oversimplify the effects of representation on individuals and society.

What Do We *Do* with Texts? The Role of the Audience in Constructing Meaning

As examples such as this suggest, we should think of representation not simply in terms of a collection of texts or images that promote irresistible messages, leading to specific kinds of desirable or undesirable behavior. This is the assumption underlying Gary Bauer's vision, cited above, of children "*wallowing* in sexual images and violence" (emphasis added). This phrase paints a picture of glassy-eyed teens quaffing Coke and munching Doritos in front of endless MTV videos. Besides assuming that this (hypothetical) audience's viewing practices are completely uncritical or reflective, the term "wallowing" also suggests that the *pleasure* they derive from the texts they are consuming is decadent and lazy, and should be viewed with suspicion.

The problem with that idea is demonstrated not just in the web site Jenkins describes, which showcases the creative uses to which some popular culture fans put the texts they consume—and we can all probably think of countless other examples of such creativity, in particular fan groups that construct elaborate new, and often subversive, narratives based on the characters of their favorite shows or films—but also in the documented responses of ordinary viewers, who may characterize themselves as neither hardcore fans nor creative artists. Studies on the use of cultural products, from the original 1980s television series *Dallas* to romance novels to video games, suggest that audiences *read*— rather than passively consume—cultural texts in complex ways, finding in them—often within a single text—sources of fantasy, consolation, irony, and humor.

Encoding and Decoding

Stuart Hall describes this process of reading, or meaning making, in terms of two key operations, *encoding* and *decoding*, which are divided into multiple stages (see Figure 3.3).

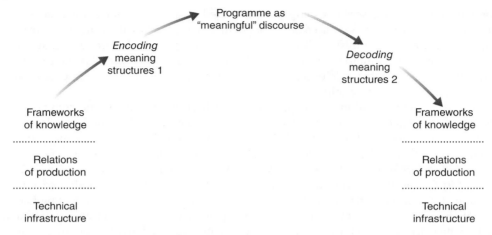

Figure 3.3 Encoding/decoding. Source: Stuart Hall, "Encoding, Decoding," *Culture, Media, Language*, London: Unwin Hyman, 1990, Pg. 94. Reproduced with permission of Taylor & Francis

Focusing on television representations in particular, this model recognizes that meaning does not exist in the heads of creators, or the show itself, in a clear form that then gets distorted, either by technological constraints (a lousy satellite signal, say) or by viewer misinterpretation. Rather, meaning is created and altered at every step along the way, from the way in which producers construct a visual text, using signs and narrative forms supplied by the surrounding culture and their own position within that culture, to the way in which those encoded meanings are transmitted, via particular technologies, and then received and decoded by viewers, once again based on the technologies of the medium as well as on their own individual and cultural storehouse of meanings.

A critical point to note in Hall's theory is that, while it acknowledges a level of agency on the part of viewers, it does not suggest that audiences are free to take whatever meaning they wish from texts. Because the stages at which meaning is produced work interdependently, the way in which messages are encoded places limitations on the way in which they are decoded. Hall identifies a continuum of possible reading positions, ranging from the *dominant–hegemonic*, in which the audience's interpretation of the text is consistent with the ideological codes in which it is produced (in other words, the audience subscribes to the **preferred reading**); to a *negotiated* position, in which the audience accepts the legitimacy of the preferred reading on a general level, but modifies it in light of personal interests or circumstances; and finally to an *oppositional*, or *counter-hegemonic*, reading position, in which the audience understands but rejects the text's code and reads it in light of an alternative code.

Reading a Television Scene

An informal experiment, conducted in one of our introductory popular culture classes, highlighted the operation of these different kinds of readings. In the class, we watched a scene from the popular 1990s television show *NYPD Blue* in which two of the detectives were interviewing a suspect in a murder/drug case (if you're not familiar with *NYPD Blue*, think *Law & Order* or *CSI*, in which scenes like this one occur pretty frequently). Employing the familiar "good cop–bad cop" television formula in which one detective acts sympathetically toward the suspect, appearing to offer refuge from his more aggressive colleague (and thereby hopefully eliciting a confession), the two detectives were alternately coaxing the suspect and yelling at him. Eventually, Andy Sipowicz, playing the "bad cop," loses his temper and starts beating the suspect, a young Latino man, who falls to the floor, shielding his face with his hands. Our understanding of the scene is aided by our knowledge of Sipowicz as a talented cop, plagued with problems with alcohol and a generally bad temper. When asked to read the scene, focusing in particular on the issues of conflict and morality (Is there a "right" and "wrong" being depicted here? Whom do we as audience members identify with and why?), students came up with a variety of different answers.

A dominant–hegemonic reading—one that many students subscribed to—agreed that the morality of the scene was murky, but that it should be read in the context of "standard" police procedure; that is, Sipowicz may have gotten a bit carried away, but a certain amount of force is justified in extracting a confession from a criminal. The assumption that the audience identifies with the police and not with the criminal is primary in a dominant–hegemonic reading of the show. Other students read the scene according to what they identified as a more negotiated position. While not questioning the fundamental rightness of the police's position, they were uncomfortable with the violence depicted (both within the context of the story in terms of Sipowicz's apparent loss of control, and at the level of the show in terms of the representation of violence in general).

A few other students took up a counter-hegemonic, or resistant, reading position, which understood but rejected the premise of the unquestioned legitimacy of the police. These students focused on the status of the suspect as a member of a racialized minority, and therefore as someone in particular danger of being subject to arbitrary arrest and detention. The presumption of innocence—a presumption on which, they pointed out, the criminal justice system was meant to rest in any case—becomes more highly charged in a context in which race is sometimes read as a sign of likely guilt. This reading is oppositional because it refuses the underlying principle of the show, that the police are self-evidently the "good guys," there to protect the citizens (read: "us") against the "bad guys." Rejecting the more or less black-and-white moral code of the show and replacing it with one based on various shades of gray (or, in the case of a few viewers, reversing the code altogether and rooting for the underdogs—the "bad" guys) represents not a misreading but an aberrant, or atypical, form of decoding, one that may signal an explicit mode of oppositional politics.

While this example highlights the practical operation of these different kinds of readings, Hall's model cannot be applied wholesale to every cultural text. Some texts are more susceptible, or "open," to negotiated or oppositional readings than others, depending on such factors as the extent to which they conform to or depart from formula and the range of audience to which they're targeted. We also need to be careful not to try to read Hall's model of encoding/decoding as offering a clear map of distinctive kinds of readings or readers. In practice, the distinction between different kinds of reading, particularly "negotiated" and "oppositional," is often murky, and readers or viewers rarely react in a uniform way to what they consume. In other words, it is possible to object to the representation of women in James Bond movies from a feminist perspective while appreciating the plots as perfect examples of the action formula.

Generally, our reactions to popular culture—even those of us who study it for a living!—are less self-conscious than that, or they are a mix of self-conscious critique and pleasure, even the wallowing kind condemned by Bauer. In addition to being shaped by our experiences and beliefs, our responses to cultural texts are powerfully influenced by the situation in which we watch them. Depending on the mood we're in, our motive for watching (distraction/stimulation/intellectual engagement), the people we're watching with, and even the other kinds of texts we've consumed recently, our response to a given text will be different in different circumstances.

Suggested Activity 3.5

Try to identify the patterns in your own responses to different forms of popular culture. How, and to what extent, is pleasure moderated by critical consciousness and vice versa? How do your responses to popular cultural texts change depending on the nature of the text, the circumstances in which you are watching/reading/listening to it, or the people you are with?

Representation in Contemporary Culture

The fact that the process of making meaning is complex, individualized, and even arbitrary (based, for example, on something as trivial as whether you happen to be watching *Girls* with your dad or your friends) does not mean that it does not have effects. As Stuart Hall's model suggests, material practice is a critical part of the "circuit of meaning," one that determines, as it is in turn determined by, representation. As a broad indication of the connection between reading and social practice, Hall suggests that an increased instance of counter-hegemonic, or oppositional, readings can be taken as both symptomatic and predictive of radical shifts in the political and social landscape. The wide availability of digital video technology has also contributed to a diversity of images. Beginning with the 1987 circulation of a video showing the beating of Rodney King by LA police, we have seen a rise in amateur video documentation of police violence against black people. Coupled with rising evidence showing that the police in the United States treat blacks more harshly than whites (Shears; Rankine), these photos have prompted general questioning of the relationship between ideology and the administration of justice—the kind of questioning, Hall suggests, that can lead not only to a shift in popular culture, but also to significant political change. That the police officers in the Rodney King case—like those in the 2014 case of Eric Garner's choking death at the hands of NYPD officers—were acquitted in spite of the video documentation of their actions suggests that things are not so simple, however. The interpretive biases of viewers (e.g., white jurors), shaped by historical context, play a determining role in representations' meanings and effects.

Political and Ideological Context

Contrary to the commonly held belief of an overall trend toward loosening traditional patterns of social authority, we have seen, especially following the events of September 11, 2001, some strong moves in the opposite direction, toward more unambiguous representations of good and evil, innocence and guilt (think, for example, of how the CIA, until recently represented as beset by corruption, has been rehabilitated, along with the military, in television shows such as *Homeland*, *24*, and *NCIS*). These shifts mirror a more general ideological move toward increased support for practices such as racial profiling—practices that had, until recently, fallen into general disfavor because of their theoretical grounding in crude stereotyping and their practical effect of infringing the civil liberties of minority groups. Changes in political circumstances determine changes in dominant ideology, which in turn consolidate the new political order.

But the relationship between representation and reality that this example highlights goes beyond a comment on the causes and/or effects of particular kinds of representation. The new tolerance of the once discredited practice of racial profiling, a practice that represents an uncritical embrace of the most simplistic form of representation, suggests that the material effects of representation are not consistent over time—that is, the power of representation to influence reality changes, depending on broader circumstances.

To take a concrete, and perhaps overly simplistic, example, representation in the crude form of political propaganda is most powerful in times of economic, political, and social anxiety. It is no accident that Horkheimer and Adorno (see Chapter 4) formulated their culture industry thesis in the context of the buildup of fascism in 1930s and 1940s Germany. A large part of their horror at the potential for mass media to lull people into an acceptance of brutal social regimes stemmed from the fact that audiences of Nazi propaganda *were* being lulled into such a state—to the point of accepting the slaughter of millions of innocent people. What makes Horkheimer and Adorno's thesis particularly provocative is their argument that this media power extended to the United States, where the ideologies of industrialization and progress helped to create a mass media machine and an audience particularly receptive to its products.

Some theorists suggest that contemporary media, which some see simply as the fruition of Horkheimer and Adorno's worst predictions, is characterized by the triumph of representation. That is, we should be focusing concern not on the content of this or that representation, but on the dominance of representation itself as a social, political, and economic force. French theorist Jean Baudrillard puts it this way: "Abstraction today is no longer that of the map, the double, the mirror or the concept. Simulation is...the generation by models of a real without origin or reality: a hyperreal" (166). The phenomenon of hyperreality, of total mediatization, that characterizes contemporary culture goes beyond the paranoid fantasy of the James Bond movie *Tomorrow Never Dies*, in which one media conglomerate tries to seize control of the whole global communications industry. It resembles something more like the vision in *The Matrix*, in which people's experience of reality—even their sense of themselves—turns out to be merely a computer simulation.

Like many good movies, the vision of *The Matrix* is both more and less extreme than the real-life situation to which it alludes. While it would be hard to identify a real-world counterpart of the sinister conspiracy that created the matrix and enslaved people within it, the film offered the possibility of escape, which in the real world proves more difficult. One of the characteristics of the "instantaneity of communication" that characterizes postmodern popular culture is "the incursion of imagery and communication into those spaces that once were private—where the psyche previously had the chance at least to explore the 'other'; to explore, for example, alienation" (McRobbie *Postmodernism* 16). The disappearance of the mental space from which to experience a tension between the world as it is and the world as one would like it to be explains what many people who recall the 1960s lament as a lack of political idealism in contemporary generations.

Virtual Culture

The disappearance of this space also has more immediately dangerous effects. For theorists such as Thomas de Zengotita, the media are absolutely central to events such as the Columbine killings—not because the killers were fans of violent movies or video games, but because they and the surrounding culture were so steeped in the culture of virtuality that the difference between the video "rehearsal" of their murder that they prepared for a class and the actual event was in some significant way immaterial. The air of unreality was not confined to the action of the shooting itself, but extended to the coverage of the event, in which, de Zengotita observes, events had a generic quality, indistinguishable from coverage of hundreds of other depictions of "violence in the heartland," right down to the stock characterization of "correspondents...in moved-to-the-breaking-point-but-professional mode," anchors in "grave-demeanor-reserved-for-inexplicable-evil mode," and so on (56). As for the mourners themselves, de Zengotita asks, "Can anyone doubt that, no matter how authentic their feelings, [they] respond at some level to implicit expectations when the cameras roll? Especially since they have seen this show on TV before; now, suddenly, they are in it" (56).

The idea that representation, and the representational power of the media in particular, is all-pervasive—that we are all somehow watching it or "in it"—raises important questions about our ability ever to critically assess the material conditions of our existence, let alone do anything to alter them. How, and to what extent, is it possible to challenge, or at least creatively intervene in, our symbol- and image-saturated culture? The strategies of **deconstruction** advocated by Laura Mulvey, and taken up in different ways by avant-garde artists, filmmakers, and culture jammers, work to critique not just individual texts or ideologies, but also the codes that underwrite them, thereby robbing visual culture of some of its magic. Many critics have pointed out, however, that the ironic awareness with which we all tend to read images now has outlived its usefulness as a strategy of critique: there is no outside in postmodern culture.

The Trouble with "Truthiness"

We have spoken at length in this chapter about the power of representation—of language and discourse—to define what we accept as truth. At the same time, it is important not to fall prey to the view that there is nothing outside of discourse—nothing, that is, that eludes the scope of power and ideology. Truth, by this reckoning, has disappeared, surrendering authority not to critique but to "truthiness," a buzzword popularized by the comedian Stephen Colbert to describe US President George W. Bush's habit of appealing not to evidence or logic, but to instinct or gut feeling. Taken to its cynical extreme, the dismissal of the traditional concept of truth enables an exercise of power that is totally resistant to the kind of cultural critique we take up in this chapter—a kind of power that does not deny but actually revels in its use of ideology. Under Bush's presidency, the White House came to exemplify this postmodern style of domination. As one of President Bush's aides put it to *New York Times* reporter Ron Suskind:

> [People like you are] in what we call the reality-based community...[i.e.,] people who believe that solutions emerge from your judicious study of discernible reality....That's not the way the world really works anymore....We're an empire now, and when we act, we create our own reality. And while you're studying that reality—judiciously, as you will—we'll act again, creating other new realities, which you can study too, and that's how things will sort out. We're history's actors...and you, all of you, will be left to just study what we do. (51)

These words are chilling; they're also somewhat absurd in their claim to have closed the circuit of discourse and reality. That circuit can never be closed, not just because the world exceeds our ability to represent it, but also because the field of representation is fluid and always subject to contestation and struggle.

Keeping these limits in mind, we argue for the necessity of paying critical attention to the words and images that mediate our social lives. As our analysis of a diverse array of media texts in this chapter demonstrates, these elements of representation—the "signs" of our times—might not point to the truth, but they do tell us, figuratively, where to go (and perhaps more importantly who can go where). Symbolic representation is, in other words, a crucial aspect of *political* representation, a subject that, as www.urbandictionary.com reminds us, informs practically every aspect of our social lives. In analyzing representation, the important issue is not finally whether popular culture offers us truth, but whether it allows us to imagine and enact a more democratic, a more truly *representative* society.

Suggestions for Further Reading

Barthes, Roland. *Mythologies*. Trans. Annette Lavers. London: Granada, 1973.

Berger, John. *About Looking*. New York: Pantheon, 1980.

Hall, Stuart. *Representation: Cultural Representation and Signifying Practices*. London: Sage and Open University Press, 1997.

Mirzoeff, Nicholas, ed. *The Visual Culture Reader*. London: Routledge, 1999.

Radway, Janice. *Reading the Romance: Women, Patriarchy and Popular Literature*. Chapel Hill: University of North Carolina Press, 1984.

Ryan, Michael. *An Introduction to Criticism*. Oxford: Wiley-Blackwell, 2012.

Said, Edward. *Culture and Imperialism*. London: Chatto and Windus, 1993.

Shohat, Ella, and Robert Stam. *Unthinking Eurocentrism: Multiculturalism and the Media*. London: Routledge, 1994.

Sturken, Marita, and Lisa Cartwright. *Practices of Looking: An Introduction to Visual Culture*. Oxford: Oxford University Press, 2001.

4

The Production of Popular Culture

The Business of Culture

Popular culture is big business. Each and every year, trillions of dollars are spent on the production of popular culture and trillions more on purchasing popular cultural objects (music CDs, DVDs, fashion, video games), services (cable and satellite television, Internet providers, personal trainers), and experiences (cinema going, musicals, tourism, restaurants, etc.). With the exception of a few recessionary dips, each year also brings an increase in the size of the contribution of popular culture to the overall economy. In 2011, video game sales in the United States totalled $16.6 billion (a more than $7 billion increase over 2004), while $9.42 billion was spent on movie tickets during the same period. These figures are just the tip of the iceberg when it comes to the overall impact of popular culture on the economy.

While it is difficult to determine with precision the amount that the production and consumption of popular culture contributes to standard measurements of economic performance, such as **gross domestic product (GDP)**, what is certain is that the production of culture has an unprecedented significance for today's economies. For instance, the global stock market boom of the 1990s was fueled to a very large degree by a popular cultural phenomenon: the promise of new services, experiences, and consumer objects (primarily consumer electronics) associated with and generated by the rise of the Internet—new services that investors believed could result in new profits. Many of the companies whose stock valuation rose highest during the 1990s (and correspondingly fell hardest by the end of the decade) were involved in producing the equipment that allows the Internet to function: routing and switching hardware, fiber optics and other kinds of telecommunications infrastructures, and computer hardware itself. But many more were rushing to produce what can only be described as new kinds of cultural experience: new ways of dealing with personal finance, interacting with the government (as immortalized in the documentary *StartUp.com*), communicating with others (blogs, chat rooms), and shopping (for books, groceries, plane tickets, and even, in the case of eBay.com, the ephemera that one usually finds at garage sales). These kinds of cultural experiences would not be possible without the technological infrastructure provided by companies such as Oracle, IBM, and others; at the same time, there would be no need for this infrastructure without public interest in the experiences and services that it enables. Depending on how one chooses to look at it, one could say that the *entire* economy is now dependent in surprising ways on popular culture. As we will discuss in more detail in Chapter 5, the performance of the overall economy has become dependent to an unprecedented degree on consumer spending, especially spending on supposedly

Popular Culture: A User's Guide, International Edition. Imre Szeman and Susie O'Brien.
© 2017 John Wiley & Sons, Inc. Published 2017 by John Wiley & Sons, Inc.

"nonessential" items—the kinds of discretionary purchases that often include forms of popular cultural entertainment and other cultural experiences. But this is equally true of economic *production* itself. As a number of recent writers have pointed out, "Processes of production and systems of organization can be seen…[as] assemblages of meaningful practices that construct certain ways for people to conceive of and conduct themselves at work" (du Gay 4).

It would be a mistake to see production as outside of or exempt from the historical development of popular culture over the past 150 years. The "culture of production"—that is, the guiding production philosophy of the factory or office—has become increasingly important to CEOs and management consultants intent on increasing productivity and profits through the creation of an effective work culture. The ideas that are championed in attempts to reframe work culture—for instance, the airy loft spaces and game rooms associated with the workspaces of the "new" Internet economy—often find their origins in popular culture; even if the links cannot be located directly in popular culture, supposedly "scientific" ideas of business management circulate in and through mass culture, and books on office management have themselves become a part of popular culture consumption, with new fad management ideas emerging as frequently as shifts in fashion (the latest: workstations attached to treadmills and standing desks). The prevalence of these ideas is reflected in the popularity of television shows such as *The Office*, *30 Rock*, and *Mad Men*. They are compelling to the extent that many, many people are conversant with management-speak and the hypocrisies of business and office dynamics.

There is no simple way to separate the production of popular culture from the processes through which it is consumed. The aim of this chapter and the one that follows is not to suggest that production and consumption have to be treated separately, nor that the values and meanings generated in one don't spill over into the other in a perpetual process of osmosis across a very thin and permeable boundary. Rather, we are separating production and consumption only to stress the ways in which each contributes in its own way to the creation of individual and social meaning in popular culture.

Surprisingly, in the history of the academic study of culture, *neither* production nor consumption has been taken seriously enough. For the most part, cultural critics (e.g., literary and art critics) have focused their interpretive and critical energies on the completed objects of culture—novels, poems, artworks, films, songs, and so on—while paying scant attention to the processes that brought these cultural forms into existence (printing presses, the invention of the film camera, recording devices, the factory production of DVDs, etc.) as well as to the multiple uses that consumers make of culture. This has changed dramatically over the past 40 years. Far more attention is now paid to the historical, social, and political contexts in which culture emerges and is read, watched, and heard. Even so, production has been considered for the most part both too generally and too abstractly: the production of culture has been seen as a small segment of economic production in general, and the culture that is produced has been treated as secondary to more primary economic and material forms and forces. To put it perhaps too simplistically, the production of steel and cars has been treated as the "real" economy, whereas the production of films and television shows has been seen as a marginal economic practice.

This chapter looks at the role of production in shaping culture in less abstract terms. While we will consider the big question of how culture is shaped by economics, we will also explore the specific economics of cultural production today in order to think through the ways in which it shapes the experience and meaning of popular culture.

"Money Changes Everything": The Pitfalls of Thinking about Production

We are *all* familiar with discussing popular culture in reference to production. The entertainment section of our daily newspaper contains movie reviews, interviews with television personalities and rock stars, reports on the legal troubles of the rich and famous (e.g., Oscar Pistorius's murder trial; the arrests of Paris Hilton, Nicole Ritchie, and Lindsay Lohan for impaired driving, among other things), and, perhaps, reviews of local theatrical performances and art exhibitions. Just as important, however, are stories that directly describe the economics of popular culture. Each Monday's newspaper reports the previous weekend's box-office grosses in full detail—for example, for the weekend of July 25–27, 2014, the top-grossing movies were *Lucy* ($43.6 million), *Hercules* ($29.8 million), and *Dawn of the Planet of the Apes* ($16.8 million)—and long newspaper and magazine articles on (among other things) the impact of illegal music and movie downloading on each of these industries are regular fare. Indeed, it is often the case that we know *more* about the economics of pop culture than the "content" of pop culture itself: we might know which movies were big hits, and even know some elements of their plots, without ever having set eyes on them.

For example, the releases of successive editions of *Grand Theft Auto* were widely reported, both as financial stories about their unprecedented successes and as (rather typical) stories about the degree to which contemporary culture has continued to degenerate, reaching new lows of violence and amorality. Regardless of how popular the game will become, far fewer people will ever play it than will have heard it reported as a pop culture phenomenon. A similar point can be made about top 10 lists of movie ticket and album sales: while even dedicated movie fans will not be able to take in all the films that circulate in and out of a top 10 list from week to week, one of the functions of the list is to inform audiences about the (financial) importance of cultural objects that they might not see immediately, but are perhaps worthy of their attention at some point, given the attention that other members of the public have bestowed on them.

Economic versus Artistic Success

Reports on contracts, financing deals, and profits and losses in the film, book, and music industry highlight the intimate connection that exists between popular culture and money. The "success" of stars, movies, pop albums, and so on—and not merely their financial success—is very often measured by the number of units sold. Directors who make movies that generate huge profits are more likely to be given the opportunity to direct future movies: one huge financial success early in a career can lead to literally dozens of chances to make future stinkers, all in the hope that the director might recapture the "magic" that led people to empty their wallets in the first place.

Just as commonly, however, financial success is taken by many consumers of popular culture as the inverse of "quality": in other words, the more *financially* successful a product might be, the less *artistically* successful it must be. The band REM's later CDs sold many more copies than their earlier ones; for early fans, the band's move from obscure club band in Athens, Georgia, to heavy rotation on MuchMusic and MTV is seen as a clear sign of a decline in the quality of its music. Examples of this formula abound and have been applied to every aspect of popular cultural experience: the beaches of Negril, Jamaica, were more interesting before resorts arrived; the Notting Hill district of London was hip until the bankers moved in; the Haight-Ashbury district in San Francisco was a

"*I like his earlier work better, particularly the ones I said I didn't like at the time.*"

Figure 4.1 "I like his earlier work better, particularly the ones I said I didn't like at the time."
Source: © Bruce Eric Kaplan/The New Yorker Collection/The Cartoon Bank

site of authentic popular culture, but is now simply a tourist trap of the first order; Beat-era writer William S. Burroughs was cool until he became a shill for Nike. This formula, which places economic success and artistic or aesthetic value in an inverse relationship, offers one common way of theorizing the impact of production on popular culture (see Figure 4.1). Unfortunately, its real utility for serious cultural analysis is limited for a whole number of reasons, not least of which is that it closes off any real attention to the role played by production by deciding on the relationship between production and popular culture in advance.

What is wrong with assuming, for example, that because a film is made in Hollywood it must necessarily be "bad" or uninteresting? After all, isn't this generally true (as anyone who saw *Zookeeper*, *The Tourist*, or *Jack and Jill* must surely admit)? There are a number of different claims or assumptions being made in a statement such as this one that need to be carefully separated out.

First, one of the central assumptions lying behind this connection between money and popular culture is that if the great unwashed masses like something, then it's impossible for it to be good. Put bluntly, such claims continue a tradition of class elitism and snobbery (discussed in Chapter 2) that presumes the intrinsic value of its own opinions while dismissing the crowds lined up for *Ted* (2012) as little more than crude, uncultured people without any form of aesthetic or artistic discrimination. To take popular culture seriously means also to take seriously the whole range of reactions, interests, and values placed on the products of popular culture.

Second, such claims simply aren't true. "Hollywood" cinema—already a far too general term that applies to a vast range of products and production techniques—*has* produced films that are admired worldwide. Films that have been both critical *and* popular successes have been produced throughout the history of American cinema, including those that emerge in many ways from the belly of the beast. "Classical" Hollywood films, which were much admired, for instance, by French film critics after the Second World War, were produced on a kind of filmic factory line whose goal was to produce as many films as possible as cheaply as possible to obtain the maximum profit. The profitability of these films (from the classical Westerns of director John Ford to *film noir*), or of, say, the *Godfather* trilogy or *Jaws*, seems to belie any easy equation between value or sophistication and money.

Third, even what is sometimes considered to be "high" art, from painting to the nineteenth-century novel, was produced in conditions in which money played an important role. Though we continue to have a romantic idea of the artist in which he or she is motivated by considerations other than money (which is why bio-pics of artists, such as *Frida* or *Pollock*, always focus on the suffering and poverty that artists endure), this is largely just that: a romantic fable that tells us more about our own discomfort with the links between money and art than with the real conditions of cultural production during our own or past centuries.

Walter Benjamin

We could go on dissecting the problems of the art–money equation. The main point that we want to articulate, however, is the problem that reliance on this equation introduces into an examination of the role of production in popular culture. As the German philosopher Walter Benjamin (1892–1940) understood clearly, our discussion of cultural products continues to make use of what for him in 1936 were already "a number of outmoded concepts, such as creativity and genius, eternal value and mystery" (218).

These concepts don't seem appropriate for describing a situation in which culture is produced in a new and very different sense than how we might imagine a nineteenth-century painter "producing" a painting (by standing in front of a canvas) or a classical composer "producing" a symphony (angrily stabbing at a piano as his long, curly white locks flip up and over his shoulders). As much as we might confer the status of "genius" on a film director and clap a screenwriter on the back for her great "creativity," a film is produced in a far different way and under far different circumstances than a painting or a musical composition (even in the examples we give above, we are indulging in a romantic vision of artistic creativity perpetuated by the movies). The filmic equivalent of the painter's scrawl in the bottom corner of a painting are the credits that run for minutes on end at the conclusion of a film, detailing all the personnel required to create the finished product—set designers, sound engineers, lighting experts, assistant directors, continuity editors, technicians, accountants, and so on. The myth of the intrinsic value of "independent" films, which generally have lower budgets and are made with fewer personnel, seems to derive from the fact that in these cases it is easier to assert the filmmakers' unique voice or "genius": there are fewer intermediaries to deflect from the director's true vision. In understanding the role of production processes in the creation of contemporary popular culture, it seems essential to move away from these "outmoded concepts" that are addressed to the critical evaluation of popular culture—not because contemporary popular culture is valueless, but because a focus on value tends to obscure the complex ways in which cultural products are produced, which in turn leads us to misunderstand how production contributes to their form, shape, and broader social significance.

To summarize, we need to avoid the common connection that is made between production and value. Concentrating on how something is produced helps us to better understand the object or experience under examination. The fact that popular culture is produced for profit, and, in general, by large groups of people instead of single creative individuals, should tell us right away that understanding popular culture means under-standing the process through which it is made. It doesn't tell us anything on its own, however, about how "good" or "bad" these things are. This is in some ways the wrong question to ask. The right questions would lead us to consider factors such as the stand-ard length of pop songs, the temporal structure of television programming (in which a half-hour television program means 22 minutes of "real" content), and the reasons why there is a disconnect between the collective labor required to produce a film, television program, or video game and the credit bestowed on those involved, which generally goes only to stars and directors. As just one example of this, the individuals who have taken credit for the *Grand Theft Auto* games we discussed above don't even know how to pro-gram! In what sense, then, is this game an expression of *their* creativity and genius?

The Culture Industry Thesis

When we think of "culture" as the kind of thing one might experience while visiting a museum of fine art or going to the opera (while wearing a dapper white suit and sporting a pencil-thin moustache and a monocle, of course), it seems hard to make a connection to "industry"—to the factory, work, and labor. Indeed, as we have touched on before, one of the most powerful definitions of culture that has been passed down to us posi-tions culture as the refined, genteel *opposite* of the crude, utilitarian world of industry. One of Matthew Arnold's worries when he was writing *Culture and Anarchy* (1869) was that the Victorian faith in technological progress and the wealth created by industry was displacing culture from the center of British society. The pursuit of human perfection through encounters with "the best that has been thought and known" was for Arnold of paramount importance; industry was a secondary, less important feature of social life. In his time, this "natural" arrangement had become (in his view) dangerously inverted: "The idea of perfection as an *inward* condition of the mind and spirit is at variance with the mechanical and material civilization in esteem with us" (23). Arnold's famous description of the "pursuit of perfection" as the "pursuit of sweetness and light" (31) is made in deliberate opposition to both the real and symbolic heaviness and dirtiness of nineteenth-century industry. The pristine white space of art galleries, with their untouchable objects and church-like quiet, is just one of the areas where we can see the continuation of this vision of culture—even in those cases where new galleries have occupied abandoned nineteenth-century factories to take advantage of their exposed brick and massive open spaces, such as the Buda Art Centre in Kortright, Belgium, the Tate Modern in London, or the Massachusetts Museum of Contemporary Art in North Adams.

   While it is easier to see popular culture as something that is necessarily produced in a way that the fine arts are not (which is part of the fascination audiences have with the television show *American Idol*), the link between *culture* and *industry* remains mainly a figure of speech. The common use of the terms "film industry" and "record industry" points to the large productive and administrative apparatus that helps to get the band Apocalyptica's funereal heavy metal to the record stores and Steven Spielberg's latest films to the cineplex. Typically, however, these terms do not evoke images of factory workers piecing together jewel cases and etching code into CDs along an assembly line (which isn't how it is done in any case), but only, perhaps, a gentler, kinder form of production—one that takes place in office buildings and studios and is anchored in the productivity and creativity of the "talent." While we all understand that popular

---

Close-Up 4.1 The Frankfurt School

The **Frankfurt School** is the name given to a group of innovative social theorists whose ideas remain important decades after the School was formally dissolved. Though there is no "Frankfurt School" approach to popular culture per se (the individual members agreed on no fixed set of ideas or concepts, and often disagreed with one another), the School's name is used to describe approaches that emphasize the production of popular culture and insist on its ideological constraints. Though not affiliated with the School, many contemporary critics of popular culture—especially critics who look at the influence of television on society, including Thomas Frank, Todd Gitlin, and Mark Crispin Miller—draw heavily on its general arguments.

Established in 1923 at the University of Frankfurt as an independent research center, the goal of members of the Institute for Social Research was the elaboration of a "critical theory" of society. Critical theory has since become the name for a diverse set of practices in social and cultural theory, philosophy, and literary studies. For the Frankfurt School, critical theory was meant to preserve critical reflection on the possibilities and problems of contemporary society as a way of continuing the political work of achieving human freedom.

Members of the Frankfurt School included Horkheimer, Adorno, philosopher Herbert Marcuse, psychologist Erich Fromm, and sociologist Leo Lowenthal. Some of the key texts they produced include Adorno's *Negative Dialectics* and Marcuse's *One-Dimensional Man*.

---

culture is mixed up with business, it nevertheless is only by stressing the connection between culture and industry that we can truly get a sense of the impact of production on popular culture.

The Frankfurt School

The social theorists Max Horkheimer (1895–1973) and Theodor Adorno (1903–69) were the first people to use the term "culture industry" to describe the conditions in which contemporary popular culture was produced (see Close-Up 4.1). In *Dialectic of Enlightenment*, published in 1947, Horkheimer and Adorno pushed "culture" and "industry" together in an effort to create a new consciousness about the changed conditions of cultural production in contemporary societies. It was, at the time, a revolutionary new way of thinking about culture. Over the past 65 years, the *culture industry thesis* that Horkheimer and Adorno advocated has generated an enormous range of debates and discussions. It remains central to explorations of the production of culture, whether as an articulation of an idea that is still important to understanding popular culture today, or as an extreme view about the limits of popular culture with which contrary theories and viewpoints have had to contend.

What Is the Culture Industry?

What is the culture industry? And, perhaps more importantly, what kind of culture does the culture industry create?

The British communications scholar Nicholas Garnham has described the cultural industries as "institutions in our society which employ the characteristic modes of production and organization of industrial corporations to produce and disseminate symbols in the form of cultural goods and services, generally, though not exclusively, as commodities" (25). To put it in a somewhat circular fashion, the cultural industries are the industries of culture—those institutions (generally, corporations) whose product is culture. At one level, it is easy to locate such industries in contemporary society: the institutions that create films, television programs, popular music, video games, and iPhone apps, for example, can all be seen as cultural industries.

But why stop there? While films, television programs, and CDs may be concrete cultural products, there are numerous other institutions that "produce and disseminate symbols in the form of cultural goods and services." For example, the merchandising of sports equipment and clothing is "cultural" in this sense, as are the products of the fashion industry more generally (at all levels, from H&M to Hollister to Harry Rosen) and all the activities and products associated with tourism. But we can even go further and make the claim that the marketing and advertising of *all* consumer products has transformed consumer production in general into cultural industries. "Basic" foodstuffs such as eggs, milk, beef, chicken, and cheese are carefully marketed to consumers as part of a healthy lifestyle. The great cliché of automobile advertising is the link made between vehicles and nature: when you buy an Audi Quattro or Subaru Outback, you're buying not an environmentally damaging mode of transportation but the adventure of the outdoors, and an outdoors that you wouldn't be able to access *except* with these vehicles. Ads for banks and mutual funds commonly feature images of cottages, beaches, or family settings: dealing with these institutions, the images suggest, will secure you the freedom that your life otherwise so clearly lacks. The products of these industries may not be directly "cultural" in the same way as the film industry's are. What these examples should suggest, however, is that today the border between cultural and other industries has become difficult to draw, due in part to the expansion of the field of cultural experience (such that even buying cheese has become culture in some strange way), as well as to the creation of new forms of production, such as marketing and advertising (see Figure 4.2).

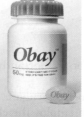

My son used to have his own hopes and aspirations. Now he has mine.

Thanks, Obay™!

From the makers of WhyBecauseISaidSo!™

Figure 4.2 The 2008 "tease and reveal" ad campaign by Ontario Colleges drew attention to common attitudes toward community colleges as a second choice to university programs. The ad was covered a few weeks later with a sticker saying "Luckily, Obay Isn't Real…Explore all the options at ontariocolleges.ca." What makes this ad especially effective is that it plays on common assumptions about the function of advertising, especially as it relates to teens and young adults. The subtext is that parents would need a drug such as Obay just to get teens to listen to them instead of to ads like this one! Source: Ontario Colleges EN_TSA_Aspirations_TSR. Reproduced with permission of Colleges Ontario

Garnham's definition applies to cultural *industries*; Horkheimer and Adorno spoke of a singular "culture industry," a single system that explains the function of culture in contemporary society, both those forms and kinds of culture produced by cultural industries and those that are not. There is little dispute over the fact that culture today is produced (at least in part) through an industrial process. What *is* in dispute is Horkheimer and Adorno's assertion of a single, dominant system of cultural production, and the social, political, and cultural significance that they attribute to this system. Before we can ascertain how successful this thesis is in describing the production of popular culture, we need first to explore Horkheimer and Adorno's theories in greater detail.

Culture, Experience, and the Culture Industry

To fully grasp Horkheimer and Adorno's worries about the culture industry, it is necessary to have some sense of the larger issues explored in the *Dialectic of Enlightenment*. It is a notoriously dense and difficult book, so a brief overview cannot help but miss many of its nuances, especially as a good deal of the energy and effect of the book comes out of the authors' highly stylized and rhetorical mode of writing.

In the introduction, Horkheimer and Adorno describe their task as "nothing less than the discovery of why mankind, instead of entering into a truly human condition, is sinking into a new kind of barbarism" (xi). The legacy of Enlightenment thought with which to a large degree we still live sees history as a process of continual improvement and development—in a word, history is characterized by progress. The narratives of history that we encounter in classrooms, newspapers, government documents, and television documentaries suggest that things are constantly getting "better": once women couldn't vote, but now they can; once humanity could move around the earth only slowly, but now there are jet planes; once there was only semaphore, but now there's the Internet. The political part of this narrative makes the claim that humanity in general is slowly increasing its degree of freedom.

Horkheimer and Adorno object strongly to this "myth" of progress and to the belief in human reason that lies at its core. Far from leading to greater freedom, they see people's lives today as more restricted than ever. Humanity's faith in progress has created an inescapable system of **instrumental rationality** that limits to a considerable degree what we understand and experience, and a domination of nature that threatens the continued existence of the world (see Close-Up 4.2). The historical events that the narrative of progress would see as exceptions to the rule (in particular, the rise of fascism in Europe), Horkheimer and Adorno see as a direct outcome of this narrative. To paraphrase Walter Benjamin, for them every document of civilization is also a document of barbarism.

The culture industry plays an important part in perpetuating the domination of human beings and nature under the guise of increasing their freedom. The subtitle of the chapter on the culture industry in the *Dialectic of Enlightenment* says it all: "Enlightenment as Mass Deception." The culture industry produces culture that is designed to deceive and mislead those engaged in it. What the culture industry creates—what we now describe as mass or popular culture—has for Horkheimer and Adorno only one real function: to reproduce incessantly the values of capitalist culture. In the late nineteenth century, Karl Marx had analyzed the exploitation of workers by capitalists in the factory system. The existence of the culture industry is one of the main reasons why, over the course of more than a century, little had been done about the exploitation of labor. The culture industry deceives by making it difficult, if not impossible, to see the social limits of a life that appears to be filled with an endless degree of consumer choice, and in which one can at

---

Close-Up 4.2 Instrumental Rationality

Instrumental rationality is a complex concept that has a simple idea at its core. In essence, the use of rationality, or reason, in an instrumental fashion suggests the use of the most efficient means to achieve the desired end. Analysis of instrumental rationality is usually associated with the German sociologist Max Weber (1864–1920), whose work had an impact on the Frankfurt School (see Close-Up 4.1) and on the shape of the *Dialectic of Enlightenment* in particular. For Weber, the rise of capitalism introduces instrumental rationality into all spheres of life—not just in economics, but also in politics, culture, and other parts of society. It might seem as if it is a good idea to achieve efficiency in all areas of life. However, there are drawbacks to instrumental rationality, especially when it becomes applied generally. The concept of efficiency is not a neutral one; that is, it implies a certain set of values about the goals of human activity and human life that may in fact contradict other values that people hold dear. The Frankfurt School was critical of instrumental rationality because it eliminated the critical use of reason. Perhaps most dangerously, instrumental rationality can turn into an autonomous force. Even though human beings invented this use of rationality (indeed, they invented the concept of rationality itself), it has come to be treated as an irresistible, unchallengeable fact of nature.

Many conflicts today concern the problems of instrumental rationality. For instance, the "efficient" pursuit of profits and technological development has resulted in considerable damage to the environment. The difficulty that environmentalists have faced in changing the policies of governments and businesses has to do in part with how deeply instrumental rationality is embedded in the structure of these organizations. Similarly, the global push to privatize public services, including transportation, utilities, and, most controversially, healthcare, has been justified in terms of greater efficiency. Those opposed to the privatization of public services oppose instrumental rationality with a different set of values, which emphasize the need to provide collective goods to everyone in society at a reasonable cost.

---

least engage in amusements of various kinds after the work day is done. For Horkheimer and Adorno, these choices and pleasures are false ones, and the function of amusement is little more than "the prolongation of work" (137).

Three Points about the Production of Popular Culture

In their discussion of the culture industry in *Dialectic of Enlightenment*, as well as in related work by Adorno on popular music, three main points emerge about the production of popular culture in the twentieth century.

First, what characterizes popular culture for Horkheimer and Adorno is the **standardization** of cultural production *and* audience reaction to contemporary culture. In the age of the culture industry, culture comes packaged in a small number of predictable forms and genres and is produced by an increasingly limited number of giant corporations for consumption by a global audience. The small number of genres into which music is categorized for download on iTunes (country, rock, alternative, jazz, etc.) and the similarly limited number of film genres and plots (horror, teen films, thrillers, action films, romantic comedies, etc.) are broad examples of what Horkheimer and Adorno seem to have in mind; the fact that today, just as in the 1940s, a small number of major **transnational** companies make the majority of films *and* music available for global consumption suggests that standardization remains a problem for contemporary cultural production.

Standardization of cultural production is necessitated by the mass commodification of culture: there are only so many films that can be made (the number of films produced each year by Hollywood is still surprisingly low) and so many albums that can be recorded, and the available "prime time" space on major television networks is constrained by the temporal limits imposed by the work day. We are all familiar with the effects of standardization. Indeed, one of the great complaints of cultural consumers is that there is so little that is "truly" new being produced for us to listen to, watch, and experience. Even with access to 200 television channels, it is not an uncommon experience to flip through them over and over and still find "nothing" to watch.

This might seem paradoxical or contradictory, since one of the key features of contemporary popular culture is the importance of the "new." Spin an album for a few weeks and its novelty has been used up: we grow bored of it and long for something new to spend our money on. The creation of newness is linked to the perpetuation of profit: as long as the cultural industries have something "new" to offer us, the money will continue to flow in. But the creation of "newness" also presents a problem: how can any cultural producer or industry create genuinely "new" objects for culture consumers? Standardization offers a paradoxical solution to this problem by allowing producers to continue to pass off apparently new objects in old shells: the endless stream of pop love songs, which contain not only the same sentiments but often the same chord progressions and melodies; Britney Spears, Rihanna, and (even) Adele; all *11* films dealing with the hockey-masked horror assassin Jason (if one includes *Freddy vs. Jason*); and iPods in different colors.

Standardization is closely connected with what Adorno describes as **pseudo-individualization**. In his essay "On Popular Music," Adorno suggests that in the case of the popular music of his day, "The composition hears for the listener" (215). This is not meant to be taken literally, of course. The claim being made is that popular music (and popular culture more generally) is so standardized that not only is the audience's response predictable, it is also in a sense "built in" to the cultural product itself. To get a sense of what Adorno has in mind, we need only think of the times when we can feel ourselves being very directly manipulated by cultural objects. The "tearjerker," a movie that leans heavily on sentimentality to hook its viewers, can bring tears to our eyes no matter how trite or predictable its plot might be; a good deal of Top 40 music at any one time seems to rely on recycling licks, hooks, and themes that we like despite ourselves (in the world of the standard pop song, humanity is engaged in the trials and tribulations of dating to the exclusion of virtually every other experience). If pop culture is so effective today at capturing our emotions and desires, it is in part because those emotions and desires have themselves been coded, created, produced, and reproduced by our experiences with popular culture to begin with.

Pseudo-individualization implies the production of a false identity: the experience of a sense of individuality and selfhood that doesn't match up to the experiential depths that these terms usually suggest. To be an "individual," as both philosophers *and* advertisers tell us, is to be separated from the crowd and in control of one's decisions and actions. Everyone is supposedly an individual in this sense—though if that's the case, then it raises the question of who exactly forms the mass or the crowd that an individual distinguishes him- or herself against. A belief in this strong sense of individuality runs deep in contemporary culture, even if almost everyone also believes that popular culture has taken away people's individuality, causing them to pursue one fad and fashion after another, year after year. For Adorno, it is precisely this belief in one's own "real" individuality that constitutes pseudo-individualization. He writes that the "standardization of song hits keeps the customer in line by doing their listening for them, as it were. Pseudo-individualization, for its part, keeps them in line by making them forget that what they listen to is already listened to for them, or 'pre-digested'" (217). Pseudo-individualization is what enables standardization to function. Instead of seeing contemporary popular culture as a landscape in which the directions we can travel are circumscribed and limited, we see (for ourselves, at least, if not for all others) a world of nearly infinite choice that emerges out of our individuality. Pseudo-individualization is the ideological screen that makes a standardized culture seem like a culture of genuine artistic expressions that we interact with in our own supposedly unique way. Standardization and pseudo-individualization pose a problem for Horkheimer and Adorno because of their political implications: they suggest we are free, when the reality is very different.

This leads into the second point they make about the production of popular culture, one that we have already anticipated. In their view, popular culture is produced only to reinforce and maintain the power of the status quo. Not only are the products of the cultural industries uniform and without real artistic merit, but also their aim is not to engage members of the public, but to distract them from reality by drawing attention away from the contradictions and problems of contemporary society. In the case of popular music, Adorno writes that "listeners are distracted from the demands of reality by entertainment which does not demand attention either" (219). The ubiquity of standardized, mass-produced culture, the pseudo-individualization it both produces and invites, and the distraction it creates make it difficult for human beings to confront fully the enormous social and political challenges that face them. To put it bluntly, it is hard to stay focused on the problems of the environment and on the increasing corporate influence of government decision making when there is so much television to watch.

As the political process itself becomes more and more beholden to the structures and systems of popular culture (the sound bite, political advertising, the carefully staged press conference, opinion polling, reality TV–style debates, etc.), it is not surprising to find that people are tuning politics out and exercising their choice in the one arena that appears to allow it: the consumption of popular culture. For Horkheimer and Adorno, the rise of popular culture seems to signal the death of the project of human emancipation. "The idea of 'fully exploiting' available technical resources and the facilities for aesthetic mass consumption is part of the economic system which refuses to exploit resources to abolish hunger" (139); this is, for them, one of the great obscenities of the production of popular culture. There is something genuinely obscene about an economic system that devotes billions of dollars to beer commercials and wrestling spectacles but that seems unwilling to intervene in the increasing polarization of wealth throughout the world, and the lack of resources to treat AIDS in those African nations that have been ravaged by the disease.

Finally, a third, related point concerns the possibilities and prospects of oppositional art and culture. The vision of popular culture that emerges in Horkheimer and Adorno's work is one in which artistic and cultural resistance has all but evaporated. But how can this be? On the contrary: contemporary culture seems to be characterized by all manner of opposition to the standardization of popular culture. The limits and problems of standardized culture form a prominent theme in contemporary art, from Andy Warhol's soup cans to Roy Lichtenstein's pop art drawings, from the photos of Roy Arden to the sculptures of Jeff Koons. The same can be said of contemporary fiction and drama as well. Even within popular culture, it is possible to find criticisms of contemporary culture on television (in *The Simpsons*, *Family Guy*, or *South Park*, for example) and in popular music (from Radiohead to Kanye West—"Couldn't afford a car so she named her daughter Alexis [a Lexus]"). Contemporary culture is also home to numerous subcultural groups that oppose "the way things are." These include pop culture subcultures (e.g., the rave scene and skateboarders—see Chapter 8 for a more detailed discussion of subcultures), but also span the range of activist and extremist groups. There seems to be an awful lot of dissent and opposition going on in a world that is supposedly dominated and controlled through the medium of popular culture. Indeed, for all its popularity, it seems that even the biggest fans of pop culture are frequently disappointed that the things they watch or listen to aren't always as good or interesting as they would like.

Be that as it may, it is worth noting that all of this oppositional activity seems to have left the basic structures of capitalism and popular culture production in place—no matter how much their opponents might wish to do away with them. Horkheimer and Adorno are well aware of the fact that dissidence and dissatisfaction still exist within the system of amusement and distraction that they outline. Indeed, this is to be expected by virtue of the very fact that this system limits human possibilities and expression. The amusements of popular culture might put salve on the wound of human exploitation under capitalism, but they can't heal it: the pain is still there, even if we don't always feel it.

Though the dissatisfactions that are expressed at all the different sites suggested above are real enough, Horkheimer and Adorno believe that there is a way in which such resistance is already factored into the larger system. "Whenever Orson Welles offends against the tricks of the trade," they write, "he is forgiven because his departures from the norm are regarded as calculated mutations which serve more strongly to confirm the validity of the system" (129). Dissidence isn't a problem; indeed, it helps to offset the need to introduce "newness" into the system of standardization. Rebellion keeps the system going. "Real" art, which requires the kind of serious attention that popular culture generally doesn't, might be able to knock us out of our stupor. That this hasn't happened and seems unlikely to happen suggests that such art no longer exists: "high art," the kind that appears in museums and galleries, has also succumbed to the effects of the culture industry, becoming little more than wall decorations for rich people. In the words of Horkheimer and Adorno, "Something is provided for all so that none may escape" (123).

Summarizing Horkheimer and Adorno

If we were to summarize Horkheimer and Adorno's position on popular culture, it would be that its meaning and function is determined primarily at the level of production. By understanding the ways in which popular culture is produced, in this view, we also seem to be able to understand virtually *everything* there is to know about how popular culture works—not just its production but how it is consumed, what it means socially, and so on. From this perspective, analyzing or understanding the meaning of specific cultural objects is pointless. While you might learn that *The Simpsons* is a different kind of cartoon than the old Disney cartoons that Horkheimer and Adorno discuss in *Dialectic of Enlightenment* (134–38), you would have to conclude that the general social function of both is, in the end, the same: the amusements that they generate impede reflection on the realities of our social and political situation. Put bluntly, what popular culture does is distract us from seeing the way things really are.

On one level, this is a powerful point: it lends credence to the central role that popular culture plays in contemporary life. Far from being "mere" amusement, popular culture is at the heart of the production and management of social order. At the same time, Horkheimer and Adorno's view of popular culture is decidedly one-sided (it's all bad). Quality aside, the most superficial comparison of *The Simpsons* and, say, *Bambi* would suggest that this mode of interpretation leaves out a big part of the story of popular culture. While the culture industry thesis offers a systemic analysis of popular culture in contemporary society and draws attention to production as an important site of investigation, there are ways in which it closes off continued critical reflection and exploration—the opposite of what its formulators intended.

Some Problems with the Culture Industry Thesis

As influential as the culture industry thesis has been (and it has exerted a considerable influence, both implicitly and explicitly), Horkheimer and Adorno's analysis of popular culture has been attacked from a number of different positions. Indeed, much of what constitutes the field of cultural studies can be seen as a reaction to the *limits* of this thesis. The insistence within cultural studies on the need to consider the consumption of popular culture emerges in part as a reaction to a view that imagines that what audiences and individuals do with popular culture can be determined in advance at the level of production. Taking popular culture seriously means taking seriously the ability of diverse individuals and communities to interact with popular culture in their own creative ways—within, of course, specific social, cultural, and political limits.

Criticisms of the culture industry thesis can be grouped into three main categories. It is worth reviewing these criticisms (if briefly) to get a sense of how we might move beyond the limits of the culture industry thesis in our explorations of the production of popular culture.

First, and most commonly, Horkheimer and Adorno's culture industry thesis has been criticized as elitist. As Keith Negus puts it:

> Adorno and Horkheimer's view of cultural production has, with some justification, often been portrayed as the pessimistic lament of cultural elitists who were dismayed at what they perceived to be the homogeneity and vulgarity of "mass" taste, and who were concerned that the potential for artistic creativity in music, literature and painting had been co-opted and corrupted by the production methods and administrative regimes of industrial capitalism. (70)

The ubiquity of these criticisms alone suggests that there is something to this point. But criticisms of the elitism of the culture industry thesis actually confuse or conflate a number of points. As we suggested above, it is true that the culture industry thesis does not account for the creativity (or at least the potential creativity) of consumers of popular culture. Yet this does not mean that, on the contrary, Horkheimer and Adorno leave room open for connoisseurs of "difficult" novels or abstract art. Rather, they are equally critical of the political limits of "serious" or "elite" art as well. In "The Culture Industry Reconsidered," Adorno makes a case for the "seriousness" of *both* high and low art. The problem with the culture industry for him is that it attacks high *and* low culture, forcing them together in a way that strips both of their potential to resist total social control. What Adorno identifies as an element of certain forms of avant-garde literature and art he thus sees as residing in the "rebellious resistance" of low culture as well. In other words, it is simply *not* the case that Adorno sees only "high" art as having political potential. The problem with contemporary culture is not that it is "low," but that its political and social effectiveness has declined. If the culture industry thesis is elitist, it is because it prioritizes production to the total exclusion of consumption, and not because it suggests that *Masterpiece Theatre* taken with brandy is superior to football enjoyed with beer.

A second criticism is that the culture industry thesis is historically limited. Like everything else, it is a product of its times and the circumstances in which it was produced. In his introduction to an excerpt from Horkheimer and Adorno's book, Simon During points out:

> It is worth emphasizing that when this essay was written the culture industry was less variegated than it was to become, during the 1960s in particular. Hollywood, for instance, was still "vertically integrated" [in the mid-1940s] so that the five major studios owned the production, distribution, and exhibition arms of the film business between them; television was still in its infancy; the LP and the single were unknown; the cultural market had not been broken into various demographic sectors—of which, in the 1950s, the youth segment was to become the most energetic. (29–30)

Some of the features characterizing the culture industry in the 1940s have returned: there are once again highly integrated forms of cultural production, vertical in some cases, **horizontal** in others (see the discussion of media convergence in Chapter 9). Nevertheless, the fundamental point that During makes is one worth considering. The culture industry thesis was one of the first attempts to analyze the new form of mass-produced culture that emerged by the mid-twentieth century in the United States, Canada, and Europe.

As Bernie Gendron points out, while Horkheimer and Adorno have been criticized for denigrating popular music in the 1940s, the songs produced in the song mills of Tin Pan Alley *did* make use of an extremely limited melodic and lyrical palette. In the intervening years, the production of popular music has changed significantly and in complex ways in reaction to cultural and social shifts, and in accordance with the development of new technologies (in ways that we will discuss later in this chapter). No general theory of the culture industry such as the one set out by Horkheimer and Adorno could sustain the wild shifts that have taken place in popular cultural production. Even if we use the cultural industry model as a rough framework for an analysis of the production of popular culture, we need to be attentive to changes in the conditions in and under which pop culture is and was produced.

Finally, critics have suggested that Horkheimer and Adorno's vision of contemporary social life is far too "totalizing." What this means is that their sense of the extent of the culture industry's influence is too widespread: like the Borg in *Star Trek: The Next Generation*, they seem to insist that all "resistance is futile." Indeed, as we saw above, Horkheimer and Adorno suggest that even resistance to the system of the culture industry is part of the system, too. The truth, however, is that popular culture is a messy and unwieldy object that cannot easily be explained by reference to a single explanatory model.

The Relevance of the Culture Industry Thesis
In many respects, the culture industry thesis extends Marx's assertion that the dominant culture at any given time is the culture of the dominant class; popular culture, then, reflects and supports the power and dominance of that class. But, as Raymond Williams has argued:

> The body of intellectual and imaginative work which each generation receives as its traditional culture is always, and necessarily, something more than the product of a single class. It is not only that a considerable part of it will have survived from much earlier periods than the immediately pre-existing form of society. It is also

that, even within a society in which a particular class is dominant, it is evidently possible both for members of other classes to contribute to the common stock, and for such contributions to be unaffected by or in opposition to the ideas and values of the dominant class. ("Advertising" 320)

While the culture industry thesis may account for a significant degree of the production of standardized culture in contemporary society, it would be a mistake to forget the considerable remnants of "older" forms of culture (opera, classical music, art, "folk" cultures and practices, etc.) and to minimize the anarchic energies of subcultures and **countercultures**: dominant culture is never so dominant as to form the single face of culture at any given historical moment, despite how easy it can be to envision total control by big business.

None of this is to minimize the contribution of Horkheimer and Adorno to the study of popular culture—their general points and the issues they raise remain central to our imagining of contemporary culture. What we can conclude from our lengthy analysis of the problems and possibilities that the culture industry thesis introduces is that, while it is important to consider the role of standardized production, no general theory of production describes the full experience of contemporary pop culture. One of the things that we need to realize is that contemporary cultural production is complex and often contradictory. As the film scholar Gill Branston puts it, "Capitalist products have both an exchange value for their owners and shareholders, and a use value for their audiences, and sometime the two can be fairly far apart" (19). Popular culture is produced in part to make money, but this does not completely determine what it means for its users—nor, for that matter, does it completely determine *why* popular culture is made. We can get a sense of the multiple, complex reasons on both sides of the equation by looking in the next section at historical shifts in production in a single important segment of the culture industry: Hollywood films. The final section of this chapter, "Cultural Production Today," will deal with some recent developments in the production of popular culture (a discussion expanded further in Chapter 9).

Shifting Modes of Cultural Production

This section will highlight the changes in the production and distribution of one cultural form—Hollywood film—over the course of its relatively brief history. It should be obvious enough that forms and modes of production change over time. For one thing, there are technological reasons for these shifts and changes: as new technologies are introduced, the systems of production and distribution of existing forms undergo significant changes.

In the history of recorded music, numerous formats have succeeded one another, including record albums (of various speeds and formats), eight-tracks, and cassette tapes. The heated formal and informal discussions about the superiority of albums versus digital music (the "warm" sounds produced by albums contrasted to the tinnyness of CDs, etc.) seemed to have been resolved, by the 2010s, in favor of records, suggesting that the march of new technological formats is not as straightforward or relentless as it might appear. What is clear, though, is that new technologies shape the creation, circulation, and use of cultural products in significant ways. In the case of film, the introduction of sound and color had implications for the way in which films were produced, and the possibilities of widespread digital distribution (as evidenced by video-on-demand technologies and the online swapping of films through high-speed digital access) promise to change the ways in which films are both shot and screened.

Changes in production result not only from technological developments, but also from social and economic ones. Film became a popular cultural phenomenon in part because it arose at just the right time. By the end of the nineteenth century, leisure time had become a reality for more and more people. Prior to the invention of film, a system of public entertainments in which audience members exchanged money for cultural experiences had also become well developed. Such public entertainments included traveling orchestras, music hall, vaudeville and burlesque shows, magic shows, and amusement parks (see Chapter 2). Film arrived in a social situation in which there were both venues in which films could be screened (e.g., vaudeville theaters) and an audience accustomed to seeing spectacles "performed" for their pleasure.

The Evolution of Hollywood

The history of Hollywood filmmaking can be roughly divided into five main eras: (i) early cinema (1895–1920), which is the period between the invention of film and its organization into an industrial system of routinized production; (ii) the studio system (1920–60), the era of "classical" Hollywood film production; (iii) the so-called Hollywood Renaissance period (1965–75), which describes the period of innovative and edgy film production that occurred between the end of the studio system and its reorganization; (iv) the blockbuster era initiated by Steven Spielberg's *Jaws* (1975), which has continued (for the most part) up to the present; and (v) the present digital era, which continues to change form with each passing year. Each of these eras is characterized by a different relationship among the three main elements of the film industry: *production*, *distribution*, and *exhibition*.

The history that we offer here has to be understood as merely a sketch of a very complex story of a single national cinema. At different times during this history, the national cinemas of other countries have been powerfully active as well, rivaling, and even surpassing, the US movie industry. For example, the Indian film industry, nicknamed "Bollywood" after its base in Mumbai (formerly Bombay), today produces as many feature-length films as all the major Hollywood studios combined, and in the early 2000s, Nigeria's film industry, or "Nollywood," became the world's second largest film industry, putting Hollywood in third place. However, our aim is not to offer an overview of film history in general, but to provide an example of shifting conditions and circuits of cultural production through a single, relatively well-known example.

Early Cinema

The first public film screening took place in Paris on December 28, 1895. It was organized by Auguste and Louis Lumière, who adapted Thomas Edison's Kinetoscope viewing machine, which could be viewed only by single patrons in peep-show fashion in specially designed parlors. Over the next few years, the Lumière brothers screened their films around the world, in various parts of Europe and also in South Africa, Russia, India, Brazil, Mexico, Australia, and Japan. The content of early cinema has been described as "a scatter of inventions" (Williams "British" 14), which ranged from the recording of everyday events and activities (the Lumières' *actualités*, the most famous of which shows a train coming into a station from background to foreground), to early forms of short narrative films, such as Georges Méliès's *A Trip to the Moon* (memorably revisited in Martin Scorsese's 2011 film *Hugo*). The visual vocabulary of filmmaking developed as quickly as the technology of filmmaking itself. By 1916, the director D.W. Griffith had released two full-length features—*The Birth of a Nation* (1915) and *Intolerance* (1916)—that contained many of the visual elements that would come to comprise the classical Hollywood style.

In terms of cultural production, the period of early cinema was a troubled one. As with the development of any new medium, numerous players entered into various parts of the production process, only to be driven out by the ferocious competition over the potential spoils. For the first few years of film exhibition, the greatest degree of control in the cinema business lay with the exhibitors. Since early films were very short, exhibitors chose films offered by numerous producers and assembled longer, custom-made film programs out of the bits and pieces they had purchased. The period from 1905 to 1907 witnessed a boom in the United States in the construction of small theaters (nickelodeons) in urban centers, where a wide cross-section of the public would congregate to watch films. To sustain interest and keep people coming, exhibitors would change films often—sometimes on a daily basis—which produced a boom in film production as well.

As films became longer, control began to shift to film producers. To generate profits from longer (and thus more expensive to make) films, producers began to evolve forms of studio production that allowed for more precise control over the contexts of production (e.g., lighting and, later, sound) and costs. Studio production worked like a factory for films: all of the fixed elements needed to create a film (cameras, lighting, etc.) were located in one place, at which the actors, directors, and staff involved in the film would assemble. Studio production also enabled advance planning of the production process. By 1904, films were no longer sold to exhibitors but rented to them, which allowed producers to retain control over their films and to further extend their profits by reducing the physical amount of film stock they had to produce. By the time of Griffith's films, the era of "factory filmmaking," in which there were clearly defined roles for directors, cinematographers, script supervisors, and so on, was in full swing. Scripts became elaborate blueprints for the production of films, and advances in editing allowed for films to be shot in the cheapest and most efficient manner, and then assembled in the correct order for exhibition.

Some of the major studios still in existence today (e.g., Warner Brothers, Universal, Paramount, and Fox) began as chains of nickelodeons. These exhibitors quickly saw the advantages of producing their own films to ensure a steady supply for their theaters and to bypass the system of competitive bidding for films that drove profits up for producers (who would sell their films to the highest bidder) at the expense of exhibitors. Thus was born the studio system: a system in which a small number of companies became vertically integrated, controlling the production and distribution of films that they would then exhibit in their own theaters.

In 1908, the 10 most powerful US production companies tried to establish a **monopoly** on the industry by setting up the Motion Picture Patents Company, which demanded licensing fees from all film producers, distributors, and exhibitors. A group of rivals who called themselves the Independents fought against the company's dominance. Their strategies included using illegal equipment and imported film stock, and moving as far away as possible from the film industry's home in New York to the then village of Hollywood, California. When the Motion Picture Patents Company was finally forced to shut down in 1915 in response to the finding that it constituted an unfair monopoly, the Independents were in a position to do what so many industry outsiders and renegades have done since and assume a position of dominance (think Bill Gates in the computer industry). Thus, led by Adolph Zukor, the Independents (which eventually became Famous Players Lasky Corp.) quickly came to dominate the industry, integrating production, distribution, and exhibition, raising capital through the stock market, and establishing the Hollywood star system in the process. By 1921, Famous Players Lasky controlled more than 300 cinemas and was itself being accused of monopolistic practices (Briggs 51–52). While the film industry was to change dramatically over the course of the twentieth century, this early struggle between independents and conglomerates, entrepreneurs and monopolistic organizations established a dominant pattern that was to characterize not just cinema, but also the entertainment industry as a whole.

There is one other issue that we need to raise with respect to film production in its early years. In early, pre-sound cinema, film technology *and* films themselves were often imported from Europe to North America. In the first years of film, France, England, and Germany were sites of film production that rivaled the United States. By 1920, however, the United States had established itself as the global center of film production. There are a number of reasons for the sudden dominance of US filmmaking. Most significant was the impact of the First World War (1914–18) on film production in Europe. While film production on the European continent was shut down, US companies rushed to fill the continued global demand for film products. For example, by 1916, 60% of the films shown in Argentina and 95% of the films exhibited in Australia originated in the United States. The establishment of the US film industry in California helped to solidify the Americans' position through the availability of cheap land and nonunionized labor in a perfect climate for year-round production. Finally, the gains that the US film industry made during the war allowed it to spend far more money on production values than its European counterparts, even after the war. This continues to be the case today: the most expensive European-financed film to date was Jean-Jacques Annaud's *Enemy at the Gates* (2001), which was made for $70 million. This is well below the Motion Picture Association of America's figures for the *average* cost of a US feature film, which in 2005 was $90.2 million. (While the current figure is no doubt larger, the secretive world of contemporary Hollywood filmmaking means that production costs are now seldom shared with the public.)

The Studio System

The 1920s was a period of enormous growth in the US film industry. Between 1922 and 1930, investment in the film industry rose from $78 million to $850 million, and average film attendance doubled between 1922 and 1928, from 40 million to 80 million people per week. The studio system marks the fullest expression of the factory film system. The five major studios and the "little three" (see Table 4.1) kept all the staff required to make a film, from actors and directors to cinematographers and stagehands, under exclusive contract to a specific studio. Films were assembled based on the available in-house elements: scripts were assigned to the available directors, cast with those actors who were under contract but not working on other films being made by the studio, and so on. Humphrey Bogart was cast in the lead role of the film *The Maltese Falcon* only because bigger stars were busy doing other projects; such stories of fame by accident in studio-era Hollywood are legion.

The studio era is also characterized by an unprecedented degree of economic and corporate integration in the film industry. Studios owned all aspects of the industry, from production to distribution to exhibition. For example, by the 1930s, Paramount owned 1210 theaters in North America, which would, of course, exhibit Paramount films exclusively. The studio era is also the period in which the major companies, in a bid to outdo one another, built opulent theaters to capture the attention of audiences. As a result of their control over the industry, independent film production in the United States dried

Table 4.1 The studio system (1920s to 1960s).

The Five "Majors"	• Paramount
	• MGM (Metro-Goldwyn-Mayer)
	• Fox
	• Warner Bros.
	• RKO (Radio-Keith-Orpheum)
The Little Three	• Universal
	• Columbia
	• United Artists
Independents	• Samuel Goldwyn
	• David O. Selznick
	• Herbert Biberman
"B" Movie Producers	• Roger Corman, Ed Wood, Russ Meyer

up, with the exception of films put together by a few major producers. Independents found it challenging to get their films financed, mainly because of the difficulty in finding locations to screen their films once completed. Foreign films more or less faded from the US cultural landscape. The themes of movies also narrowed considerably in comparison to cinema's early years, with fictional drama becoming *the* genre of Hollywood filmmaking.

In 1946, Hollywood recorded its highest box-office and attendance figures of all time at a figure of 98 million tickets sold per week. From this point on, however, the studio system entered a precipitous decline that was to endure for the better part of three decades. The film industry encountered two major challenges. First, in 1948, the US Supreme Court ruled that the eight largest studios were guilty of violating antitrust laws enacted at the turn of the twentieth century to prevent the creation of monopolies or oligopolies in American business. The studios were forced to sell off major parts of their assets, in particular their theater chains, which opened the way for independent, nonstudio productions. Second, the mid-1940s to the mid-1960s saw a shift in American movie-going habits. In part this was a result of the movement of the middle classes after the Second World War from the cities to the suburbs, which left many large theaters devoid of the audiences needed to sustain them. In combination with the growth in television ownership (90% of US homes owned a television by the end of the 1950s), the film industry was badly damaged: profits declined by a shocking 74% between 1947 and 1957. The film industry responded to these changes in ways that would begin to bear fruit only from the mid-1970s onward. Films began to be made and marketed for specific segments of the audience: children's films, movies aimed at teens, more serious dramas for adults, and so on. Foreign and "art" films, imported for distribution from abroad, were once again shown, though seldom outside of major urban centers.

Hollywood Renaissance
Before these responses to the decline of cinema going could take hold, the decade between 1967 and 1976 saw a remarkable flowering of US cinema. Eschewing the limits and standard narratives that characterized classical Hollywood cinema, a number of young directors redefined the parameters of film form and content. Often dealing with edgy narratives on contemporary themes, the films of directors such as Robert Altman, Arthur Penn,

Martin Scorsese, and Francis Ford Coppola (all graduates of recently established film school programs) captured the imaginations of a society that was undergoing significant changes as a result of the 1960s counterculture and the social movements associated with this period.

This era of filmmaking is now often lamented as a lost or squandered opportunity for the creation of serious American cinema. The lingering belief in the inherent connection between independent production and quality filmmaking (a connection that has been revived in the recent use of the term "independent" as a term of approbation) originates with the films of this era. While filmmakers were able to exercise a degree of control over their films that harkened back to the days of early cinema, films such as *Bonnie and Clyde*, *The Godfather I* and *II*, *Nashville*, and *Taxi Driver* were nevertheless still produced and distributed under the auspices of major production companies. Whatever their aesthetic successes, these films and their directors continued to be subject to the influence of the remnants of the studio system. Indeed, there is a way in which this era functions as a kind of laboratory in which different models for the reorganization of the film industry could be tested out. The kind of independent production that took place during this period, which brought together all the personnel necessary to create a movie on a film-by-film basis, did create the conditions for more idiosyncratic filmmaking than the old studio-based production system. At the same time, it also created a model for the mode of production that would take place in the blockbuster era that followed.

The Blockbuster Era

Since 1975, there have been numerous shifts and developments in Hollywood filmmaking—so much so that to claim that anyone could describe all the shifts and changes in one general category misses some important nuances. Nevertheless, the dominant idea and ideal of Hollywood film since the breakout success of *Jaws* and *Star Wars* is captured in the idea of the "blockbuster": films that shatter the barriers between market segments and draw crowds who line up around the block. Blockbuster films are crafted as events or spectacles—they are highly anticipated and carefully controlled. To maximize profits, distributors plan the release dates of different films to coincide with periods of high attendance (the Christmas season, early summer, etc.) *or* low attendance (which is when serious or "mature" films are released), and to minimize competition with other blockbuster movies (*Spider-Man* and *Attack of the Clones* were released on separate weekends to avoid an impact on each other's profits, as were *Harry Potter and the Philosopher's Stone* and *The Fellowship of the Ring*). Though no longer organized into oligopolies, as they were during the studio system, during the blockbuster era the majors have once again come to dominate: from 1970 to 1987, films produced by the big studios generated 84% of box office revenues in Canada and the United States. In the first six months of 2005 alone, the major studios—Paramount, Warner Brothers, 20th Century Fox, Disney, Universal, and Sony—took in $3.2 billion at the box office; in 2011, films produced by Paramount, Warner Brothers, Sony/Columbia, Buena Vista, and Universal made up 72% of the market share of film revenue worldwide.

The production process has changed considerably from earlier eras. The big companies, such as Paramount, Warner Brothers, and 20th Century Fox, are now primarily finance and distribution companies. Like much of the rest of the global economy, the production of films has been reorganized into a more flexible system. Production has become the responsibility of individual producers, financed by the old studios, who rent production space, equipment, and personnel on a short-term, film-by-film basis. There are very few stars and directors under "exclusive" contracts to production companies; everything is done on the spur of the moment during available windows of opportunity for directors, stars, and production crew.

The exhibition of films has also changed in ways that have had impacts on the film industry in general. New exhibition spaces have been designed with multiple screens on which a range of movies appealing to different market segments can be screened. Distributors wield enormous power over exhibitors. Especially for popular films, distributors can dictate the number of screens on which an exhibition company must run its films and the minimum length of time for which the films have to be screened. Independent exhibitors have once again faced difficulties in competing for films against large exhibition companies, such as Cineplex Odeon and Famous Players in Canada—one of the reasons that many national cinema productions get comparatively little screen time at home. For example, in 2010, the Ministry of Canadian Heritage reported that the box-office share of English Canadian films was only 1.4% of the total.

Actual film screenings currently make up only one small part of the overall revenue generated through the production and distribution of films. Companies can now recoup costs in numerous ways: through the licensing of secondary screening opportunities (after the opening period but before video distribution); through distribution in the form of DVDs, cable and broadcast television rights, and online streaming services such as Netflix; through various forms of merchandising, especially in the case of children's films; and, finally, even through such mechanisms as the sale of advertising space within movies themselves in the form of product placements (Reese's Pieces in *E.T.*, FedEx and Wilson in *Castaway*, Omega watches and Ford in *Casino Royale*, and POM juice in director Morgan Spurlock's documentary on branding in films, *The Greatest Movie Ever Sold*).

Production and Meaning

This brief history of Hollywood filmmaking highlights the huge number of changes in the industry over the past century. A more detailed history would introduce further divisions and differences in the production process. One of the first things that this history should tell us is that although we might be able to watch *The Birth of a Nation* and *The Fellowship of the Ring* at home on the same evening, they are *not* the same kind of cultural object. We refer to both as "movies" or "films," but we should not forget that they were created under very different conditions. If we obscure this fact (which we all too often do), we risk forgetting the ways in which different systems of production create different forms of popular culture. For instance, the difference in dominant film themes and styles in each era is not simply an accident of history, nor can it be accounted for as shifts that occur on their own (that is, without being influenced by the productive process). At the same time, we need to be cautious about drawing direct lines of influence between style and production. Our aim in this chapter is not to argue for the reduction of theme to the logic of production practice, but to insist that we consider production when we explore the social meanings and significance of popular cultural objects.

A summary of our discussion in this section is provided in Table 4.2.

Cultural Production Today

Just as production techniques and systems have changed over time in Hollywood film, so do they continue to evolve in significant ways in other parts of popular culture. This final section of the chapter looks at recent developments in cultural production that have an

Table 4.2 Production modes and film styles.

Period	Production System	Theme/Style	Representative Films
Early cinema (1895–1920s)	• Independent • International • Power divided between production and distribution	• *Actualités* • Varied styles • Experimental	• *A Trip to the Moon* (1902); *The Birth of a Nation* (1915)
Studio system (1920s–60s)	• Oligopolistic • Vertical integration • American narrative (social conflict/love stories)	• Fictional drama • Classical Hollywood	• *City Lights* (1931); • *Stagecoach* (1939); • *Strangers on a Train* (1951); *From Here to Eternity* (1953)
"Hollywood Renaissance" (1965–75)	• Independent/corporate • "Return" of foreign film • Production	• Experimental and critical • *Cinema verité* • Documentary	• *Bonnie and Clyde* (1967); • *McCabe and Mrs. Miller* (1971); *Mean Streets* (1973); *The Conversation* (1974)
Blockbuster era (1975–present)	• American • High budget • Synergy • Distribution/cross-production • Video/television	• Classical narrative • Special effects • Spectacle	• *Jaws* (1975); *Terminator 2* (1991); *Jurassic Park* (1993); *Lord of the Rings* (trilogy: 2001–2003)
Digital era (2000–?)	• International • High and low budget • Internet distribution	• Mixed genre • New documentaries • Remastered classical foreign films • Digital animation • Digital effects + 3D film	• *Monsters Inc.* (2001); *Bubble (2005); An Inconvenient Truth* (2006); • *Singin' in the Rain* (1952; digitally remastered); • *Avatar* (2009)

Suggested Activity 4.1

In what ways might this production history differ in the case of popular music or other major areas of popular culture (books, tourism, eating out, etc.)? Unlike film, popular music combines a form of craft labor—that is, the labor of a small number of individuals practicing a craft that is in some sense preindustrial—with mass, standardized production. In addressing the question, make sure to keep this point in mind.

---

impact on the ways in which we examine popular culture today. As you will see right away, these developments constitute an extension of aspects of the culture industry thesis and offer important challenges to it. For example, the expansion of the Internet as a means of cultural communication and the growth of the digital production of sound and images offer cultural producers the chance to circumvent the typical channels of cultural production and distribution—a development that we discuss in more detail in Chapter 10. But before we celebrate the birth of a new cyberutopia, we need to be conscious of the fact that these alternative productive practices exist in a world of popular culture production that continues to be dominated by a relatively small number of major corporations. While bands with limited resources can now make their music available to people around the world through the Internet, it remains true that even a considerably weakened music industry has far greater distribution and marketing powers (and so, also, the ability to generate massive profits) than any independent band that relies on getting the word out through YouTube. David Bowie, Prince, Public Enemy, and other major musical acts have attempted to distribute their music solely online with considerably less success than distribution through record stores; the tide may well have turned, however, with Radiohead's success (starting with its album *In Rainbows*) in selling its music directly to fans from its own web site.

Lifestyle Marketing and Market Segmentation

A full-page newspaper ad for Cadillac mimics the timelines that one often finds in art history books. The line begins in the dark recesses of history with an image of the Lascaux cave paintings, which are among the earliest examples of human artistic expression. Next in line is the paradigmatic expression of Ancient Greek sculpture, the Venus de Milo, followed by Leonardo da Vinci's *Mona Lisa* and, closer to the present, a painting by Picasso. Bringing us up to date, at the end of the timeline are photos of three vehicles—the new Cadillac XLR, the CTS, and the Escalade EXT (a truck). The caption to this ad reads: "It seems to be humanity's destiny to find new ways to express beauty. Presenting the latest installment."

It is tempting to dismiss the artistic pretensions of this advertisement: surely a Cadillac is not a work of art in the same sense as the paintings by da Vinci and Picasso. But this would be to miss the real insight the ad offers into the character of contemporary popular cultural production. To an ever-increasing degree, as Celia Lury has argued in *Consumer Culture*, the production of all consumer goods has been subjected to a process of stylization. Consumer objects have become increasingly aestheticized: like art objects, it is as often as not how something "looks" that guarantees that it will sell, *not* what the object actually does or is used for. This stylization of contemporary production, Lury suggests, was achieved via a long process "through the introduction of the principles of fashion to an ever-wider range of products, often following the model developed for the product category of clothing" (61).

Product Packaging

The most common site where this stylization or aestheticization is encountered on a day-to-day basis remains product packaging, whether we think of this in terms of the enticing photographs on cereal boxes or (arguably) the first great form of aesthetic packaging, album cover art. But the link between the stylization of production and fashion goes deeper than this. Mimicking the fashion seasons, new models of automobiles and consumer electronics, such as stereo equipment, computers, and cell phones, are "released" annually or biannually. Bending the supposedly immutable laws of time, the resplendent curves and shiny surfaces of *next* year's car models are available in the summer of the preceding year. Most brands of cell phones and MP3 players are designed with removable faceplates that can be changed and adapted by consumers to coordinate with their clothing or to express their artistic sensibilities. The fashion sense at work in these product lines is exemplified by the success of Motorola's RAZR ("one of the slimmest phones on the market") and the rainbow hues of Apple's iPods or LG's Chocolate MP3 camera phones. The availability at any one time of numerous models of Nike running shoes or sleek modernist household appliances designed by architect Michael Graves for Target stores all point to ways in which style and design have become essential elements of the production process, if not *the* essential element in the design of products for end users. And no one knows this better than the shops connected to art museums, which have used the general stylization of popular culture to boost their profits through the sale of all manner of knick-knacks whose main appeal is not found in their utility, but in their artistic style.

Lifestyle

The increasing prominence and importance of style in popular culture production goes hand in hand with a redefinition of consumption as an aesthetic or artistic exercise. This shift is captured perfectly by the term "lifestyle." The idea that each of us has a lifestyle—a way of living, consuming, and being that uniquely defines us—has come to prominence only over the past several decades. Though "lifestyle" can be used to refer broadly to the way one lives—in the city or the country, having a laid-back personality as opposed to a "work hard, play hard" mentality—the element of style emerges mainly out of what and how one consumes, and especially how one consumes popular culture (see Chapter 5 for an extended discussion of this point). The idea of life being akin to a work of art has a longer heritage, with origins in the mid-nineteenth-century idea of the urban *flâneur* and the figure of the dandy explored by, among others, the writer Oscar Wilde in *The Picture of Dorian Gray*. What has changed is that the expansion of consumption in the twentieth and twenty-first centuries has generalized the belief in lifestyle.

This has had some significant social consequences. For instance, the critic John Seabrook has suggested that as a result of lifestyle consumption, the divisions between high and low culture, between "**highbrow**" and "**lowbrow**," have broken down into what he refers to as "nobrow." In perfect synchrony with lifestyle consumption, Seabrook argues that in nobrow, "Commercial culture is a source of status and currency rather than the thing that the elite define themselves against" (*Nobrow* 106). The question is no longer whether one participates in popular culture; rather, it is *how* one participates in it—and, through the consumer choices that one makes or refuses to make, the kind of lifestyle that one carves out of popular culture.

At one level, we can see the relentless production and consumption of style as a perfect embodiment of the idea of pseudo-individualization that Horkheimer and Adorno describe. The idea that increasingly stylized forms of production have transformed standardized popular culture into a situation in which everyone can assume the role of the "modernist notion of artist as hero, as the advocate of radical values, challenging the consensus of public life and disturbing the complacency of domestic life" (Lury 75) seems to confirm the Frankfurt School's worries about popular culture. But things aren't quite so simple. The stylization of cultural production has extended and enhanced its power and the role that popular culture plays in everyday life and in the economy. But it has also introduced surprising challenges and problems for the producers of contemporary popular culture. As Simon During suggested in his criticisms of Horkheimer and Adorno, contemporary popular culture has becoming increasingly variegated, diverse, and unruly.

In the 1950s, cultural production was, in general, geared toward the mass market as a whole. Since then, there have been greater and greater degrees of **market segmentation**, with the result that cultural producers have to gear their products to increasingly small and specialized segments of the overall group of consumers. This trend has perhaps been most evident in television programming. In the United States, the three major networks have tried to combat declining overall audiences by adopting the techniques of their competitors: cable networks defined around specific lifestyle interests (Outdoor Life Network, Food Network, etc.) or programming to specific demographic groups (e.g., the WB network targets audiences under 35). The segmentation of the consumer market has affected producers of clothing, food, and consumer electronics as well.

As just one example, in an effort to boost its stagnant sales, Coca-Cola Corp. has unveiled an ambitious strategy to design specific beverages for up to 500 clearly defined segments of the market (e.g., children under 3 whose parents will allow them to drink only milk products, teens interested in skateboarding, adults who work long hours but eat healthy foods, etc.), which will be further adapted to account for national and regional differences (Stevenson). On the Web, YouTube is planning a similar saturation of the market by launching hundreds of specialized online channels, each of which will focus on specific hobbies, lifestyles, and interests, such as horseback riding (Seabrook "Streaming").

Of course, the segmentation of the market presents producers with possibilities in addition to problems. There is the potential to tap into new markets and so to expand profits. However, the problems are significant and go beyond, for instance, the energy and coordination required to produce thirty models of athletic shoes instead of one or two. The idea of life as style may in some sense be a false one. But inasmuch as people take it seriously, there is some evidence that they have grown more suspicious of certain forms of advertising and marketing and are resistant to being categorized even in micro-market segments. The more producers need to concentrate on style and the more (and more different) styles they have to produce, the more likely it has become that they will miss the mark when it comes to targeting their intended audiences. In an interview, the heads of three of the major US networks admitted that they had no idea that television programs such as *Survivor* and *The Sopranos* would be hits (Hirschberg 67). Their grasp on what the public "wants" is tenuous at best, and their ability as producers to dictate to audiences seems equally limited, which is attested to by the number of canceled "sure-fire hits" that litter the television landscape each season. One of the reactions to this situation has been an increase in more invasive forms of marketing and advertising that try to grasp the moods and preferences of consumers and audiences in advance of their full cultural expression (for more on this, see our discussion of "cool hunters" in Chapter 5).

Suggested Activity 4.2

How does the reintroduction of "retro" fashions and styles contribute to lifestyle consumption? In *The Conquest of Cool*, cultural critic Thomas Frank suggests, "Retro's vision of the past as a floating style catalog from which we can choose quaint wardrobes but from which we are otherwise disconnected is, in many respects, hip consumerism's proudest achievement: it simultaneously reinforces contemporary capitalism's curious ahistorical vision and its feverish cycling of obsolescence" (227). How does this reinforce, challenge, or expand our discussion in this section?

Copyleft: Challenging Copyright

It is vain for painters or poets to endeavour to invent without materials on which the mind may work, and from which invention must originate. Nothing can come of nothing. (Joshua Reynolds)

Though it has remained a central idea of Western culture since Romanticism, artists and writers do not create authentically only when they do so autonomously—that is, when they are off on their own, away from people and the influence of the society they live in. Such ideas of artistic autonomy might help to reinforce our belief in creative "genius"; what they fail to do is capture the complex ways in which cultural productions are always an expression of the broader social and cultural contexts out of which they originate.

This is a long way of saying that there is no such thing as absolute innovation in cultural production. Rather, as Joshua Reynolds suggested in 1797, cultural production depends on creative borrowing and adaptation; whether this is consciously done or not, it is out of such adaptation that "new" culture is produced, and through such borrowing that cultures remain vibrant and alive.

Sampling

One of the clearest examples of such creative and productive "borrowing" today is in rap and hip-hop music, which often samples previously recorded songs in interesting and provocative ways. For instance, Jay-Z's anthemic "Hard Knock Life" employs the chorus of "It's the Hard-Knock Life" from the musical *Annie*; Kanye West's "Power" draws on King Crimson's "21st Century Schizoid Man"; Maestro's "Stick to Yo' Vision" uses The Guess Who's "These Eyes" in a memorable fashion; and, in the case of "mashups"—the complementary interweaving of two generically different tracks to create something new—there is a sense in which the entire product is sampled, as in DJ Danger Mouse's infamous *The Grey Album*, a fusion of The Beatles' *White Album* and Jay-Z's *The Black Album*. There are similar examples of reusing or borrowing in film remakes (e.g., Gus Van Sant's attempt to produce a scene-by-scene remake of Alfred Hitchcock's *Psycho*), in literary adaptations, and in the visual arts (Douglas Gordon's *24 Hour Psycho* stretches the Hitchcock original to a full day by projecting it slowly frame by frame).

Legal Issues

Since the early 2000s, the use of borrowed materials has begun to run into legal roadblocks. As Sven Lütticken writes, even though "some sort of appropriation of pre-existing material is integral to many forms of contemporary cultural practice these are increasingly under pressure from armies of lawyers" (89). One of the major issues in contemporary cultural production concerns the use and abuse of **copyright** legislation to limit and control free expression. Disputes over copyright today form just one of the many disputes over **intellectual property**, a category that includes not just copyright but also trademarks and patents. For producers of popular culture, there is a great deal to be gained by asserting and maintaining their copyright privileges. As cultural production has become increasingly susceptible to copying and illegal redistribution (something that might have been difficult with a painting is easy with music in the digital era), corporations and cultural producers alike have ever more stridently asserted their copyright in order to control all the profits generated by their products. In many cases, however, it seems that the original intent of copyright has been subverted, and that the eagerness with which copyright claims have been pursued have reduced culture to mere profit making and have made free, unfettered cultural borrowing all but impossible. Only in 2006, for instance, were film professors in the United States given the right to put together clips of films for classroom instructional use.

The Evolution of Copyright

The history of copyright differs from country to country. In the English-speaking world, it first developed alongside book printing as a form of state control or censorship. The Crown granted publishers the right to produce a specific book over a certain period of time, less to guarantee publishers a profit than to get access to and approve its contents. The first violations of copyright were attempts to circumvent state censorship, as in the "forbidden best-sellers" of pre-Revolutionary France that the historian Robert Darnton has explored. Copyright in its contemporary sense "was stimulated by the wish to enable authors to make a decent living and hence be able to create new works" (Lütticken 94). By 1831, copyright legislation in the United States covered books, maps, engravings and etchings, and musical compositions. The goal of limiting the reproduction of these works to the original producer was to boost the indigenous cultural production of the young republic and create a self-sustaining cultural sphere.

While copyright legislation may have been developed to protect cultural producers, in the context of contemporary cultural production copyright seems to have become a tool of those corporations most directly involved in the culture industry. There are two kinds of copyright infringements that need to be separated in our discussion: the first involves direct infringement of existing copyright standards, while the second concerns increasingly suspect challenges to cultural appropriation, parody, and the artistic use of popular culture. The continuing debate over file-sharing services such as Megaupload and the illegal pirating of videos, DVDs, music CDs, and computer software occurring worldwide are examples of the first kind of dispute (see Chapter 1).

There is little question that sharing music files without copyright permission (for example) constitutes copyright violation. What these forms of copyright violation have highlighted, however, is the degree to which copyright works in favor of corporations rather than cultural producers and audiences. In terms of the latter, the practice of music file sharing, popularized by Napster in 1999, constituted a public rejection of a kind of standardized production described by Horkheimer and Adorno: tired of being sold over-priced CDs with a few songs they desired and a bunch of "filler" material, audiences could now access only the songs that they wanted. Napster also presented consumers with a chance to sample music outside of the limited frame of popular music imposed by the marketing and distribution practices of major record labels in an effort to maximize profits. File sharing also brought to light the dirty half-secret of the contemporary music industry, which is that the artists who create the music see very little profit. While the band Metallica sued Napster in a heavily publicized case, other artists saw file sharing as an opportunity to provide their music directly to their audiences, thereby circumventing the music industry altogether.

The second form of dispute over copyright has become more prominent as of late. These are disputes over cultural appropriation of various kinds, and have come to the fore as the idea of what constitutes copyright is stretched further and further. Copyright has now been applied to thematic *similarities*, to original music compositions that supposedly *sound like* something else (as in the case of John Fogerty, former lead singer of Creedence Clearwater Revival, being sued by his former record company for songs on his solo album that sounded too much like that band), and even to bits of lyrics. It now seems as if copyright covers the general *idea* of a product as much as the product itself. Mattel, which jealously guards its major product, Barbie, has been one of the companies to press its claim over its product the furthest. On different occasions, Mattel has sued rival producers of female toy figures on the basis that it "owns" the general proportions of Barbie's surreal measurements (bust–waist–hip); blocked distribution of director Todd Haynes's film *Superstar: The Karen Carpenter Story*, which uses Barbie action figures to tell the life of the pop star, who succumbed to anorexia; ended artist Mark Napier's *Distorted Barbie* project through a threatened suit; and even (though unsuccessfully) took on the band Aqua over its song "Barbie Girl."

Mattel is hardly the only corporation to engage in such practices. The Disney corporation has also sued artists for making use of its iconic images in artworks, and has even effectively blocked publication of a critical biography of Walt Disney himself, on the basis that it would hurt corporate profits by damaging the image of wholesome fun that the company has built up around its **brand**. It seems today that almost every successful pop culture object has been subjected to litigation. The author of the Harry Potter series, J.K. Rowling, has been sued (unsuccessfully) for supposedly stealing the term "Muggle," and she and her publisher have in turn pursued attempts to cash in on the Potter name, as in the case of the parodic Russian novels by Dimitri Yemetz, author of *Tanya Grotter and the Magic Double Bass.*

Who Is Popular Culture For?

The suits over the artistic reuse of popular cultural images and the use of materials for the purposes of parody or criticism raise a more general question about cultural production today: Just who and what is popular culture for? Audiences and artists seem to believe that popular culture, even if produced by large corporations, forms part of the commonly held stock of images, sounds, experiences, and ideas that make up contemporary experience, standing alongside great works of literature and masterpieces of artistic expression. Corporations seem to believe otherwise. For them, cultural production represents profits to be made—or lost, if copyright is not enforced. The bending of copyright in the direction of corporate interests threatens the cultural commons that Reynolds describes in the quotation that begins this section. A great deal of the art made since the beginning of the twentieth century, for example, has made creative use of popular culture, from Marcel Duchamp's "readymades" (the transformation of everyday objects into art) to the surrealists through to rap and contemporary art. These possibilities now seem threatened, as does our more general access to the images of art history, which have been slowly but surely assembled into image data banks by corporations such as Microsoft, which now holds access to the copyright of many artworks. The extension and expansion of copyright benefit few at the expense of many; it constitutes one of the major sites of control over popular culture in the world today.

Computer Software Copyright

One of the most successful responses to the extension of corporate control through copyright has been in the field of computer software, where the stakes over intellectual property have perhaps been the highest. The "product" created by computer software companies is in many respects immaterial: the product as such is not the downloaded file through which one accesses the program, which does not exist physically in the same way that even a film does. Software is also uniquely susceptible to being copied easily and exactly. As such, the software industry has ferociously defended the intellectual property that it has created in order to safeguard its investment both in the products and in the profits they generate. Protecting intellectual property in software has meant that companies have closed off access to the source code of their programs. No one can access this code except other companies that have paid a licensing fee to create programs that work in conjunction, for example, with the various incarnations of the Microsoft Windows operating system.

In response to this closed system, programmers such as Richard Stallman and Linus Torvalds have created forms of free, open-source software such as GNU and Linux. Open-source software can be used by anyone free of charge. Because the software source code is "open"—that is, accessible by everyone—not only can new programs be created to work with Linux by programmers anywhere in the world, but the bugs (or errors) that plague most complex software programs can also be pointed out and repaired in the basic code itself. With free software, the often high cost of programs is mitigated entirely. "Copylefting" is Stallman's innovative way of using copyright against itself. Free software that is made available under a general public license legally requires all software derived from it—"even those that carry only a tiny fragment of the original code" (Stallabrass 144)—to be copylefted; that is, made public and accessible to all.

As cultural production becomes increasingly important to the economy at large, struggles over the ownership of popular culture are likely to become more important. On January 18, 2012, several prominent web sites—including Wikipedia and Reddit—decided to turn themselves off for 24 hours. This blackout was in protest at two proposed pieces of legislation in the United States: the Stop Online Piracy Act (SOPA) and the Protect IP Act (PIPA). Wikipedia and many other web sites and services feel that these acts, which, if passed, would alter the infrastructure of the Internet in favor of copyright holders, impede freedom of thought and expression, as well as the free exchange of ideas. This online protest and the publicity it generated caused SOPA and PIPA to be shelved, at least temporarily.

Digital Production

For much of the twentieth century, the forms of production of popular culture effectively ruled out mass participation in many kinds of mainstream popular cultural production. Producing a film, television program, or record album "independently"— that is, outside of major production systems—was difficult, if not impossible; as we have seen above, the creation of a standard 35 mm film narrative requires the use of enormously expensive equipment, the use of equally expensive fixed capital (in the form of sound studios, sets, etc.), and, finally, a considerable investment in production personnel for the creation of even a modest film. This was true of television programming and music production as well, and was a general rule for most forms of popular cultural production. And production was just one part of the problem; even if one could make an independent film, the ability to distribute and market it to a wide audience was severely circumscribed by the degree of access one had to the "official" or standard systems of popular cultural production.

One of the major recent developments in popular culture has been the introduction of new forms of production and distribution that have challenged and circumvented older modes of popular cultural production. The digital revolution in image and sound production, recording, and distribution promises to change the shape of popular culture in ways that we are still only beginning to experience and understand. There have been a variety of formats that have allowed cultural producers to take control of the production and distribution of their own products, from Super 8 movie cameras to four-track recorders that allowed "garage bands" to produce their own audiotapes. Forms of digital production not only permit more effective distribution of these products—whether via sound and image files shared over the Internet or through the pressing of CDs and DVDs that retain sound and image quality—but also increasingly place "small" or independent producers on a par with major producers, at least in terms of the quality of sounds and images produced. (See Chapter 10 for a more detailed discussion of the implications of these new developments.)

There is effectively no important difference between popular music produced within and that produced outside of the music industry, at least not in terms of sound quality, which is why the challenge of digital production has been felt most acutely to date in music. The music industry continues to struggle with the impact of digital distribution; total revenues dropped from $38.6 billion to $27.5 billion between 1999 and 2008; by 2014 they were down to $15 billion—less than half what they had been 15 years earlier. In terms of film production, however, a gap remains, due in part to the extreme visual density of 35 mm film in comparison to the highest-quality digital video (though this, too, may change), and in part to the cinematic spectacle of special effects (including the reintroduction of 3D) in mainstream Hollywood cinema.

The Impact of New Technologies on Popular Culture

Even so, digital production has had a decisive impact on the production of popular culture, both inside and outside the dominant forms of production. On television, "reality" shows make use of lightweight digital cameras to record perspectives that more traditional production techniques would be unable to capture (e.g., the "helmet cam" used in shooting point-of-view segments in reality and game shows). Since the popularity of *The Blair Witch Project* (1999), major studios have released a number of films shot entirely on digital video, such as James Cameron's *Avatar* (2009), and numerous others that have incorporated digital video into standard 35 mm filmmaking, such as Danny Boyle's *Slumdog Millionaire* (2008). For some filmmakers, digital video has presented an opportunity to rethink the medium of film in a wholesale way by rejecting the limits imposed by standard production practices. Eschewing artificial lighting, sound stages, sets, and so on, filmmakers who have adopted the Dogme 95 manifesto—which calls for a return to single-camera filmmaking with an absolute minimal use of nonnatural lighting and sound (it actually calls for none at all, but this has been difficult to achieve in practice)—have produced a series of films celebrated for their innovation and freshness. In this way, the increasing accessibility of sophisticated production technologies creates vibrant niches for the revitalization (using those same sophisticated technologies!) of earlier, low-tech production methods and styles.

These uses of digital video are hardly revolutionary—that is, we have not yet seen the creation of new genres or completely original narrative modes as an outcome of the new format. But there are spaces and places in which digital video has already played an important new role. The low cost and high quality of digital video have produced an explosion in the production of documentary film, in two different senses of this term. First, digital video has revived formerly flagging feature-length documentary productions, as has (for that matter) the ability of independent companies to distribute documentaries in DVD and online digital formats in place of film stock. Feature-length documentaries that have been enabled by digital video include *Who Killed the Electric Car?* (2006), *An Inconvenient Truth* (2006), and *Gasland* (2010).

Second, digital video has been used by groups and individuals around the world to document social and political realities that mainstream media miss or deliberately avoid reporting. Video has played an important role in documenting the abuse of state power during anti-globalization demonstrations. Mainstream media outlets, including the Canadian Broadcasting Corp., covered the demonstrations against the Free Trade Agreement of the Americas (FTAA) in Quebec City in 2001 largely from the perspective of the government officials who were meeting behind the chainlink fence separating most of Old Quebec from the rest of the city. From this perspective, the use of pepper spray, water cannons, and plastic bullets against the demonstrators was justified by the perceived threat that demonstrators posed to these officials. The tens of thousands of hours of footage shot by the demonstrators with digital video cameras offered a very different view of the demonstrations. Not only did these images highlight the numerous unprovoked attacks on peaceful demonstrators by police, but by allowing the demonstrators to articulate their own views on the FTAA, they challenged the repeated assertions by the mainstream media that the protestors knew almost nothing about what they were demonstrating against. Digital video, whether shot using cameras or cell phones, has played a similar role in political demonstrations throughout the world, including the events in 2011 now collectively identified as the Arab Spring. (See Chapter 10 for further discussion of the role of media in popular resistance movements.)

Through its ability to bypass the systems that defined the production of popular culture for much of the twentieth century, digital production promises to shake up the production of popular culture. Though it is unlikely to redemocratize popular culture to the extent that its most optimistic supporters suggest, it offers at least the potential for new forms of and relationships to popular culture.

Suggestions for Further Reading and Viewing

Branston, Gill, and Roy Stafford. *The Media Student's Book*. 5th ed. New York: Routledge, 2010.

Dorland, Michael, ed. *The Canadian Culture Industries: Problems, Perspectives, and Policies*. Toronto: Lorimer, 1996.

Ellis, Jack C. *A History of Film*. 4th ed. Needham Heights, MA: Allyn and Bacon, 1995.

Hesmondhalgh, David. *The Cultural Industries*. London: Sage, 2002.

Nealon, Jeffrey T., and Caren Irr, eds. *Rethinking the Frankfurt School: Alternative Legacies of Cultural Critique*. Albany: State University of New York Press, 2002.

Negus, Keith. *Producing Pop: Culture and Conflict in the Popular Music Industry*. London: Edward Arnold, 1993.

PressPausePlay: A Film About Hope, Fear and Digital Culture. Dir. David Dworsky and Victor Köhler. Prod. House of Radon, 2012. http://www.presspauseplay.com.

Rosenbaum, Jonathan. *Movie Wars: How Hollywood and the Media Limit What Movies We Can See*. Chicago: A Capella Books, 2000.

Sterne, Jonathan. *MP3: The Meaning of a Format*. Durham, NC: Duke University Press, 2012.

Striphas, Ted. *The Late Age of Print: Everyday Book Culture from Consumerism to Control*. New York: Columbia University Press, 2009.

5

The Consuming Life

Back to "Normal"

In the immediate aftermath of the events of September 11, 2001, a large number of discourses started to circulate in both political circles and among members of the general public. Most of these were concerned directly with the events and their political and economic consequences. To better understand "9/11," discussions began on the concept of terrorism, the responsibility of the West to the rest of the world (especially the degree to which it had evaded this responsibility), the "clash of civilizations" (Islam versus the West), the role of the United States as the world's policeman (and the problems with this role), the problems with and benefits of military action, the implications of the new security measures adopted in a number of countries, and so on.

Perhaps more surprisingly, what also emerged was a debate on the underlying values of Western societies and the appropriateness of these values. In the days and weeks following 9/11, political and business leaders encouraged citizens to continue to shop, travel, and spend money.

For instance, New York mayor Rudolph Giuliani encouraged New Yorkers to "stay calm and go about their business, to 'buy a pizza,...and see a show" (qtd. in S. Jenkins 45). If Americans stop shopping, Giuliani and other political leaders implied, it would mean the terrorists had won. Many leaders expressed the conviction that to go out and shop was important as a means not only of sustaining the economy, but also of defending "our" fundamental cultural values.

Even if statements such as Domenici's captured something real about the economic and social practices important to the contemporary Western way of life, for many people there was something disturbing about this frank admission of the central role played in our lives by consumption and consumerism. In the immediate wake of 9/11, many Americans stopped spending in an apparent attempt (or so the media told us) to recapture more "wholesome" values, whether this was expressed through a reaffirmation of familial relationships or connection to friends, or through a deliberate attempt to "slow down" and appreciate more deeply the days and weeks that we usually race through. Predictably, this decline in consumption caused a slowdown in the US economy. A few years later, however, things were definitely "back to normal": the streets and malls were full of shoppers snapping up, among other things, memorabilia related to 9/11 (T-shirts, postcards, designer clothing, etc.), which appeared quickly in the stores of New York in the days and weeks after the tragedy.

Popular Culture: A User's Guide, International Edition. Imre Szeman and Susie O'Brien.
© 2017 John Wiley & Sons, Inc. Published 2017 by John Wiley & Sons, Inc.

Consumption Patterns

The tragic events of 9/11 offer an example of the importance of consumption to contemporary culture, as well as the profound ambivalence that attends all forms of consumption. We consume endlessly and in multiple ways and forms, and not just when we slide money across a store counter and walk away with a bag of goodies. Consumer spending patterns are carefully monitored by both businesses and governments, since they have a direct impact on the overall state of the economy (see Close-Up 5.1). A tremor in the consumer confidence index, a measurement that tries to anticipate future consumer desires, can produce very real effects, including layoffs, business bankruptcies, and cutbacks to government programs in anticipation of declines in tax revenues.

Close-Up 5.1 The Consumer Confidence Index

In the United States, consumer confidence is measured monthly through a survey of 5000 representative households. The overall score is measured against a baseline of 100 established in 1985 (in September 2002, the index was 93.3). The index is based on responses to five survey questions: (i) an appraisal of the current business environment and (ii) expectations about the business environment six months from the survey date; (iii) an appraisal of current employment conditions and (iv) employment conditions six months down the road; and, finally, (v) expectations about family income six months from the survey date.

This is a survey of subjective feelings about the economic environment. For economists and business leaders, it is important because it is just such subjective reactions to economic circumstances that guide consumer behavior, much more than objective data. This is why there is often a disconnect between economic reports that pronounce the fundamental or underlying strengths of the economy (productivity levels, capital investment, etc.) and consumer behavior that suggests otherwise (decline in stock investments, downturn in consumer spending, etc.).

Critiques of Consumerism

Consumption is a normal, everyday social practice around the globe. In our increasingly complicated world, no one can produce everything they need (if they ever could), so the exchange of goods and services by individuals and institutions is a necessity. At the same time, consumption and consumerism are often treated as social ills. Consumerism has been associated by many critics with the rapid decline in the quality and character of social life, the result being a crass, utilitarian culture dominated by the ultimately empty pursuit of money and goods. Some of the social complexity of consumerism is captured by the fact that this uneasiness with it has become an occasion for further consumption, whether in the form of practices of consumption that express a desire for more "authentic" forms of consumption (organic food, fair trade coffees, holistic medicines, massages, "getaway" weekends, adventure travel, etc.) or through the purchase of cultural goods that criticize consumerism implicitly or explicitly (e.g., films such as *Fight Club*, *American Beauty*, *Super Size Me*, and *The Queen of Versailles*; the music of bands such as Radiohead and Rage Against the Machine; books such as Michael Moore's *Stupid White Men*, Naomi Klein's *No Logo*, Eric Schlosser's *Fast Food Nation*, and so on).

It is common enough to discount these criticisms by pointing out the simple contradiction produced by the sale of goods that criticize consumption (tracts against consumerism that activate further consumerism). Some critics argue that what we might think of as anti-consumerist forms of consumption (buying vintage clothing, for example, or listening only to music by obscure local bands) are not so much critiques of consumerism as they are rebellions against conformity—or what we perceive as the conformity of "the masses" or society in general (see Figure 5.1). The "rebel consumer," as Joseph Heath and Andrew Potter term the person whose buying habits fit this model (108), is really just seeking a pure, extreme form of social distinction (we discuss this aspect of consumerism in more detail below). Heath and Potter do not denounce consumption as a social evil; however, they do dismiss it as an essentially empty practice, one that (unlike politics, for example) is incapable of producing real social meaning or change.

Like the more straightforward anti-consumerist positions they critique, Heath and Potter's argument fails to capture adequately the full complexity of contemporary consumption. Nor do such criticisms manage to locate the ambivalence over consumption within definite geographical and social circumstances. According to the United Nations, in 2012 eight billion people spent less than $2 per day, a figure that should act as a constant reminder of the limits of the discussions of consumption and popular culture both in this chapter and in cultural studies more generally. Around the world, the main problem that people experience with consumption is not that it has come to make their lives empty; that is, not that there is too much consumption, but that there is too little— both of the necessities of life and of a wide range of other goods.

Whether we love it or loathe it, consumption has become a key aspect of social life. If we are to make sense of its social significance and its key role in contemporary popular culture, we need to begin by understanding consumption as more than exchange.

Figure 5.1 The concept of activist shopping enjoys popular support; its capacity to effect democratic change remains limited, though, by the economic framework of consumerism. Source: Original to author

Economic measurements of consumption tend to focus narrowly on the instant of exchange, the moment that money and goods change hands. However, the cultural and social dynamics of consumption extend well beyond the moment of exchange. A study of consumption has to consider what takes place before and after exchange. Why do people engage in the forms of consumption that they do? What do people do with the objects and services that they consume? What symbolic meanings are contained in consumption? How is consumption connected to our deepest emotions, desires, and fantasies? And what are the consequences of the ways we consume? These are the questions that we explore in this chapter.

Suggested Activity 5.1

When do you shop? Do you ever find yourself deciding to "go shopping" to reward yourself, to alleviate stress, to buy gifts for others, and so on? What does it mean when consumption becomes an end in itself—that is, when the point of shopping is not necessarily to purchase any specific item or service, but mostly to engage in the act of consumption?

A Brief History of Consumer Culture

In our introduction to this section, we have used a number of terms more or less interchangeably: consumption, consumerism, and consumer culture or society. In practice, the meanings of these terms overlap considerably; however, exploring contemporary consumption necessitates that we draw some distinctions between them. As we saw in Chapter 4, in social theory, consumption has long been opposed to production. Until relatively recently, scholars have paid far more attention to the processes of production than consumption: consumption has been understood as little more than the completion of the process of production, with production treated as the site at which the most significant social processes take place. As Marx expressed famously in his preface to *A Contribution to the Critique of Political Economy* (1859), it was the "relations of production"—that is, "the economic structure of society" (45)—that for him formed the real foundation of society. How human beings organized themselves productively determined to a large degree the social experiences and cultural possibilities of their society.

Even among sociologists and other social scientists unsympathetic to Marx's view of society, the idea that the form in which human beings organize production (i.e., how they organize their economy) is the most important determining characteristic of society was central to social theory throughout most of the twentieth century. The outcome of this has been that the study of consumption has only slowly emerged from the shadow of production in the analysis of popular culture.

Commodities and Desire

Consumption—all of the practices commonly associated with what happens at the end of production—came to the fore of social studies only when it became clear that a new kind of society was emerging in the twentieth century: a consumer society, a historically unique form of society in which consumption plays not only an important but even a central role. As a general concept describing a particular form of human interaction and kind of social relationship, practices of consumption predate the twentieth century. It is possible, of course, to apply the concept of consumption to exchanges dating back millennia—all the way back to at least the early development of money, and even possibly before that if the most common meanings of consumption are evoked. Nevertheless, it does appear that a significant social shift took place around the end of the nineteenth century as a result of a new focus on the consumption of commodities.

Commodities are objects and services produced for consumption or exchange by someone other than their producers. Almost everything produced for consumption today is a commodity: we work at a specific job producing specific goods and services, whether this involves selling insurance or producing automobiles in a factory, or, in the case of professors, "producing" educated students in a university. Through the exchange of our labor for a salary or wages, we are then able to purchase all the other goods and services we require (food, clothing, utilities, entertainment, etc.)—including, it should be added, those things that we work at producing (insurance salespeople aren't given free insurance, nor are auto workers invited to take home the automobiles they produce).

Human beings have long exchanged goods that they produce for other goods: it has always been difficult to produce everything that one needs (and, certainly, everything that one wants). What has changed, then, is less the fact of exchange than the range of commodities that have become available, the ability of more and more people to engage in wider and wider forms of consumption, and the creation of new wants and desires through advertising and display. The conjunction of these and other factors has produced consumerism, the name for the dominant values and practices arising from, and providing fuel for, life in a consumer society.

The Creation of Consumer Society: Advertising, Credit, Debt

How and when did this new kind of society come into being? While the rise of consumer society is generally associated with the Industrial Revolution, it actually was not until relatively late in the game—the late nineteenth and early twentieth century—that people started to consume in earnest. The obvious reason behind the intensification and extensification of consumption was that the expansion of industry resulted in a massively increased amount of goods produced. Factories became bigger and more efficient, and so could produce more items more cheaply than before, which made widespread consumption possible. But, as the most elementary economic theory should tell us, the relationship between supply and demand does not work this simply or easily.

As Richard Robbins notes in *Global Problems and the Culture of Capitalism*, the rise of consumerism can best be understood not as the natural and inevitable consequence of a burgeoning economy, but rather as a largely *manufactured* response to a specific (and continuing) crisis in the capitalist system of production. To put it simply, industry had by the end of the nineteenth century reached a level of efficiency that threatened to topple the whole economy through overproduction. The production of goods for which there is not an adequate number of buyers is clearly unsustainable and is one of the causes of economic recessions and depressions. To stimulate demand and so avoid a total crisis, it was necessary not just to increase but also to fundamentally change patterns of consumption in order to make buying things a more central part of everyday life. Consumerism is the answer to the inevitability of capitalist overproduction. This change in the way we consume was as much *cultural* as it was economic. That is, it wasn't enough simply to increase wages so that people could buy more with the money they earned. Rather, according to the logic advanced by Henry Ford, one of the most important products of the factory line was the consumers who were produced out of the wages that he paid his workers. In addition to automobiles, Ford created not only the kind of people who could afford to purchase them, but also the kind of people who increasingly understood their lives in reference to possibilities of consumption.

Shifting Values in Western Society

For consumerism to function correctly, what was needed was a revolution in the underlying values of Western society—a shift from thrift and the virtues of parsimony to the come-what-may, carpe diem philosophy of the consumer. This shift is often described—particularly by critics of consumerism—as representing a decided decline in spirituality, accompanied if not actually caused by a rise in materialism. In fact, the relationship between spirituality or religion and materialism is not that simple: they cannot be considered as simply and clearly opposites, the "good" of the spiritual standing above the "bad" of materialism.

At the beginning of the twentieth century, the sociologist Max Weber argued that the materialist "spirit of capitalism" could be located (apparently paradoxically) in Protestant asceticism. While asceticism involves the rejection of worldly temptations, over time the ceaseless labor carried out to increase the glory of God became disassociated from its religious roots, leading to a situation in which "material goods gained an increasing and finally an inexorable power over the lives of men as at no previous period in history" (181). The growth of materialism represented not so much an abandonment of religion as a shift in its orientation, away from guilt and self-denial toward values of self-enhancement and emancipation. This shift was enabled in part by the Enlightenment belief in progress, as well as by the actual alterations in people's material circumstances associated with the Industrial Revolution (see Chapter 2). While traditional religious doctrines, combined with the sheer difficulty of life, tended to rule out the prospect of happiness on earth in favor of an emphasis on the glories of heaven, the ideology of industrialism made secular comfort seem not only possible but also morally good. As James Twitchell puts it, at this point "the culture of consumption replaced the culture of contrition" (230). The "spiritual" redemption of materialism was accompanied by a shift away from the ideas of humility and the subordination of the self to a higher power to an emphasis on the possibility of changing and enhancing one's life through individual will. And if self-enhancement required a new stove or a new pair of shoes—well, so much the better, both for the individual and for the economic well-being of society as a whole.

Still, the conversion of a society organized around thrift and self-sacrifice to one committed to shopping did not come about easily. The birth of consumer society required more concerted and more creative action on the part of manufacturers and government. Richard Robbins identifies a number of key developments that together fueled what was seen as this necessary change. The first of these were developments in retail sales, in particular the invention of the department store. Beginning in Paris with the Le Bon Marché (1852; see Figure 5.2), followed in 1902 by the flagship Marshall Field's store in Chicago, the department store offered a whole new shopping experience: in fact, it was the department store that, more than any other development, turned shopping into an *experience* rather than simply a routine, generally boring duty. Featuring such novel attractions as coatrooms and restrooms, the department store was committed to the enhancement of consumer pleasure and comfort, inviting its mostly female patrons to leisurely browse the aisles while enjoying musical performers or drinking tea. Complementing the structural appeals of the department store was a new emphasis on service, in which sales assistants would welcome customers (the precursor to Walmart greeters), offer advice, and administer general pampering. The emphasis on friendliness,

Figure 5.2 Growing from a small shop founded in 1838, Le Bon Marché in Paris is often considered the oldest department store in the world. This 1928 ad is for a sale on handbags, dresses, and umbrellas. Source: Mary Evans Picture Library 10090746/MEP

however contrived, played an important role in turning an essentially economic transaction into a personal one—an important function in an age in which the relationship between primary producers and consumers was growing ever more distant.

Advertising and Marketing

Perhaps the most significant factors in boosting consumerism were innovations in advertising and marketing. Until the mid-eighteenth century ads were mainly informational, announcing new products and providing more or less straightforward accounts of their qualities, sometimes complete with testimonials from satisfied customers or accredited experts—doctors or pharmacists, for example (this kind of advertising finds echoes today in those ads in which a serious, white-coated commentator, whose credentials appear in print at the bottom of the screen or page, points to simple graphs or other scientific-looking data to show how this particular brand of antacid or painkiller or diaper outperforms the competitors). With the flourishing of competition among manufacturers, the emphasis in advertising changed from informing customers about new products to encouraging them to discriminate between a host of virtually identical brands of the same product. Part of this was achieved by innovations in packaging, beginning with the production of prepackaged goods with labels—Ivory Soap and Quaker Oats were among the earliest such brands, promoted as early as the 1870s (see Figure 5.3).

Over the course of the twentieth century, both packaging and advertising quickly became more sophisticated, as marketers realized that the way goods were displayed and promoted was at least as important in getting people to buy them as their actual substance. Starting around the time of the First World War, marketers began to marshal the forces of psychology to help them develop more subtle and unconscious forms

Figure 5.3 Quaker Oats is an early example of a brand name that has become synonymous with its product. Source: © Granger Historical Picture Archive/Alamy

of persuasion. The most well-known instance of early marketing psychology was the use of so-called **subliminal advertising**, in which, for example, the ice cubes in a glass of Coke were engineered to look like the body of a naked woman, or the word "sex" flashed up on the screen in the middle of an ad for dental floss, disappearing too quickly to be registered on anything other than an unconscious level. While advertisers have dabbled in subliminal messages, the attention paid to this kind of trickery tends to overstate its significance, ignoring the much simpler and arguably more effective use of straightforward images with complex emotional resonances—in other words, Barthes's mythology (discussed in Chapter 2). The need to use mythology in advertising is obvious: the actual objects being sold are not valuable enough in and of themselves to persuade us that we actually *need* them; they therefore need to be associated with something deeper and more intangible to evoke our desire—what Raymond Williams, in "Advertising: The Magic System," terms, simply, "magic."

Since the conclusion of the Second World War, advertising has come to occupy a position of unparalleled dominance, reflecting both the intensification of consumerism and the growth of the information economy—a development we explore in more detail in the last section of this chapter. Advertising is, as Williams puts it, "the official art of modern capitalist society: it is what 'we' put up in 'our' streets and use to fill up to half of 'our' newspapers and magazines: and it commands the services of perhaps the largest organized body of writers and artists, with their attendant managers and advisers, in the whole society" ("Advertising" 336). As such, advertising is both a barometer and a key producer of dominant social values, chief among which is, of course, the value of consumerism itself. Underpinning the myths invoked by the specific signs in any given ad that are meant to compel an attachment to this brand over that brand is another übermyth: that our deepest needs and desires—for love, autonomy, security, freedom, self-development, friendship—can be met by buying something. The pervasiveness of this myth, which we oddly cling to even as we recognize it *as* myth, accounts for the second major development in advertising in the past few decades: the "magic" of advertising has been kicked up to a new level so that it is simultaneously more transparent and more powerful than it was before.

Branding

If advertising was once about cloaking a product in a sparkly glow, disguising its mundane qualities in shimmery illusion, now it achieves its most dramatic effects by eliminating the product altogether—even to the point of announcing the product's redundancy (as in ethical ads by companies like Patagonia that actually plead with us to "buy less"). This is the hallmark of the contemporary art of branding, in which companies vie to sell us not individual products, but lifestyles that are defined by broad patterns of selective consumption. The disappearance of the actual commodity in advertising weirdly confirms the triumph of consumerism, such that "goods"—including entertainment, vacation packages, and services—are thoroughly and inextricably "knitted into the fabric of social life and cultural significance" (Jhally 80).

But the expansion and intensification of consumer society have not been stimulated by the efforts of retailers alone. As Richard Robbins notes, government policy, encouraged by corporate lobbyists, has worked in conjunction with other broad institutional changes to create a cultural climate hospitable to consumption. The introduction of MBA programs and design institutes in the early 1900s, particularly in the United States, marked both the recognition and encouragement of the possibilities for the professionalization of marketing. This in turn led to the formalization of what had once been an informal, vaguely disreputable sector of the contemporary economy into a specialized profession that young people could yearn to one day join: those major advertising firms such as J. Walter Thompson, Young & Rubicam, and Ogilvy & Mather that established Madison Avenue (the stomping grounds of *Mad Men*) as a fixture in the collective unconscious.

Credit and Debt

Around the same time, changing government policies in the United States placed increasing focus on commerce, including the eventual creation of government ministries devoted to researching and promoting its expansion. One major campaign in North America was the drive to get people to buy houses. A 1920s government-issued pamphlet touted the "family values" of owning a detached home, backed by psychological research highlighting the importance of separate bedrooms for each child (Robbins 16). Of course, the boost in home ownership could not be achieved without another major initiative— the expansion of credit. By putting limits on interest payments, making it easier to take out a mortgage or get a car loan, governments and banks have played a crucial role in fueling consumer spending. This had the added benefit, Robbins notes, of bolstering the discipline of the workforce, which was kept in line by the fear of being unable to make credit payments. The ongoing expansion of credit and the desire for home ownership came together with devastating results in 2008's global financial crash (this is discussed in more detail in Chapter 10).

The major cultural effect of policies making credit both easier to get and also more acceptable socially is that being in debt—a situation that was once an occasion for embarrassment—has become a way of life, such that according to one estimate the average household debt-to-income ratio in Australia was 150% of disposable income in 2010. Of course, the even darker side of this picture is that an alarming number of individuals and families live just a hair's breadth away from bankruptcy. The ideology of consumerism, by creating not just an unquestioned right but a moral imperative out of the ownership of stuff, works to conceal, without overturning, huge discrepancies in wealth between the rich and the poor. And in the global economy, this formula applies not just to individuals but to nations as well.

Consumerism is a value system that has rapidly (though unevenly) spread around the entire world. It is most developed in North America, Europe, Japan, and Australia (those areas commonly referred to as "the West"), but it is difficult not to see that aspects of consumerism are present globally. As discussed previously in this chapter, consumerism refers to a complex set of values and practices. What is central to consumerism is the belief that the organization of life around the purchase of commodities is in fact, for all its other problems, the optimal way to address the needs and wants of individuals, and even the best way to allocate social goods. This "belief" is often more implicit than explicit. Explicitly, people frequently express worries about consumption and its social, political, and environmental effects. But through the *practices* that individuals engage in— constrained as these are by the structures and institutions of consumer society—faith in the optimal efficiency of the market is restated day after day around the world. And it is not just the efficiency of market forces that is valorized in consumer society, but the underlying goals of such an economic system, too. The consumer lives in what Ernest Gellner has described as a "society of perpetual growth" (24); the consumer's central goal is to accumulate money so that he or she may purchase and consume ever-increasing quantities of goods and services.

Consumer Culture and Mass Culture

The history of consumer society closely mirrors the history of popular culture offered in Chapter 2. The two histories are intertwined: to a large degree, contemporary popular culture *is* consumer culture. The description of contemporary popular culture as a form of mass culture is one way of capturing the historical novelty of contemporary forms of consumption and their links to the popular. At the beginning of his book *Selling Culture*, cultural critic Richard Ohmann offers a definition of mass culture that can help us to identify the distinctive features of mass and consumer culture and to see the ways in which our ideas and practices of consumption differ from those prior to the end of the nineteenth century. Ohmann describes mass culture as a system characterized by

> voluntary experiences, produced by a relatively small number of specialists, for millions across the nation to share, in similar or identical form, either simultane-ously or nearly so; with dependable frequency; mass culture shapes habitual audiences, around common needs or interests; and it is made for profit. (14)

What does this definition tell us about popular culture and consumerism? There are forms of consumption that are socially or physically necessary: food, clothing, shelter, and so on. In his discussion of mass culture, Ohmann wants to omit these to concentrate on forms of voluntary consumption, specifically on what we have come to refer to as "entertainment."

As we will see below, the meanings that circulate around consumption cannot be limited in quite this way. We all require shelter; this requirement, though involuntary in comparison to our choices of entertainment, is explicitly connected to contemporary forms and practices of consumption through the kinds of shelter we strive for: a big house in the suburbs, a sleek condo in a downtown high-rise, a farmhouse in the country, and so on. One of the interesting things about consumer culture, at least in those countries with relatively high standards of living, is that there is no longer anything "basic" about the necessities of life: we require clothing to keep us warm or shelter us from the sun, but, as we all know, the kinds of clothing that we choose to consume have significant social meanings and implications.

Even though Ohmann's definition is geared toward a characterization of mass cultural entertainment, it still helps us grasp just what is unique about consumer culture. In general, we purchase the objects or services that we consume from the specialists who produce them: for the most part, we don't make our own clothing (we certainly don't make the cloth), grow our own food, or manufacture electronics in our basement. Consumption is dependent on a vast specialization of labor and industry, and on the development of an enormous set of institutions that are geared toward the production and distribution of consumable objects and services: it is no coincidence that the history of the modern corporation parallels the rise of consumer culture (see Close-Up 5.2). There continues to exist a wide range of handmade goods, homemade foods, and so on, but these exceptions merely prove the rule of specialized production.

Further, the things we consume, from T-shirts to soft drinks to televisions, are consumed by millions of others around the world in virtually the same form, with only slight variations from country to country. McDonald's, for instance, has famously modi-fied parts of its standard fast-food menu to account for local tastes or prohibitions against certain food items. On the whole, though, one of the appeals of McDonald's is in fact the almost global standardization of its menu: consumers can expect a Big Mac to taste the

---

Close-Up 5.2 Corporations

Though it might seem as if corporations have been with us forever, they are relatively recent inventions; it is more recently still that they assumed the legal status they hold in most Western countries today.

Corporations first emerged in the seventeenth century through the establishment of chartered corporations, which were given specific missions outlined by an act of government. Such chartered corporations were granted the exclusive right to engage in colonial ventures over a specifically defined geographical space. The economic logic of these corporate bodies was to allow for huge pools of capital to be accumulated to achieve ventures that would have been impossible for small groups to carry out independently. The United States was initially settled by a corporation, the Massachusetts Bay Company, as was a large part of Canada under the auspices of the Hudson's Bay Company.

Early corporations were chartered to fulfill some form of public mission. In the United States after independence, corporations were involved in building bridges, constructing roads, and other activities that now fall to governments. Once corporations began to be involved in raising capital for the creation of private wealth, it became necessary to define their status more formally in legal terms. In a landmark case in 1886, corporations in the United States were defined as "persons" as a result of the application of the 14th amendment to the US Constitution, which was originally designed to protect recently emancipated slaves, to a case involving a dispute over differences in tax rates for individuals and corporations. The 14th amendment states that "no state shall deprive any person of life, liberty or property": once defined as "persons," corporations gained the same rights and protections as individuals. Though corporations have slightly different statuses in different countries, the trend globally has been toward the US model of corporate rights. This nineteenth-century quirk in legal jurisprudence bolstered the strength of corporations immeasurably: corporations have repeatedly appealed to their rights as individuals to strike down laws that attempt to limit or regulate their activities.

---

same in Auckland as it does in Santa Cruz, Munich, or Osaka. Contemporary consumption is premised on such uniformity. It makes little sense to prefer to buy Nikes in one store over another on the assumption that the shoes one can purchase in one location are "better made" than in the other (though they may of course be priced differently).

Simultaneity, dependable frequency, and the creation of habitual audiences are important for understanding the ways in which most forms of popular entertainment are offered up to us for consumption. Television schedules are standardized across nations (*The Walking Dead* or *The Big Bang Theory* don't appear on different nights in Toronto than in Edmonton), NFL games and *Hockey Night in Canada* take place at predictable—and scheduled—times, and Netflix releases new seasons of popular TV series with predictable regularity, allowing viewers to plan binge-watching sessions ahead of time. Both streaming services and film production companies make use of teaser trailers to whet the appetites of audiences far in advance of actual release dates (e.g., the first trailer for *Star Wars: Episode VII—The Force Awakens* was released in November 2014, more than two years ahead of the December 2016 film release date!). What links everything together is profit. Today, consumption almost always involves the exchange of money and almost always occurs in a situation in which it contributes to the creation of profit.

Identifying these general features of consumer society does not mean that it is impossible to find contrary examples or situations. It is not to suggest, as theorists of consumer culture sometimes have, that there are no forms of exchange, social relation-ships, or cultural experiences that are not part of consumerism. Education, religious participation, and forms of "self-produced" entertainment (playing your guitar for your friends) are just some examples of experiences that fall somewhat outside the guiding values of consumer society, even if they are informed by those values (as when education becomes merely a way to secure a high-paying job so that one can buy a big-screen LCD TV). Rather, what we want to draw attention to is that our particular forms of consumption are a recent historical "invention." Only recently did we turn to others to the extent to which we do today to feed, clothe, and entertain us, and find meaning and social significance in the act of doing so.

It is this fundamental shift in the character of consumption that in turn produces a need to explore the new and complex social and cultural meanings generated by consumer society. We will do this by turning now to look at three important ways in which consumption produces the cultural meanings that are an important part of contempo-rary culture: consumption as a means of producing and reinforcing social and cultural distinctions and differences; the connections between consumption and individual iden-tity and agency; and the political meaning of contemporary forms of consumption, which includes the impact of consumption on the social spaces that we now inhabit. Many of the issues raised in this chapter overlap with the explorations of identity (Chapter 6) and representation (Chapter 3).

Consumption as Distinction

As we have already noted, the practice of consumption is not exhausted in the moment of exchange, nor is what is exchanged "used up" or destroyed through consumption, even if this is one of the typical meanings associated with consuming. To consume food means that the food gets "used up" and broken down. But in its social and cultural meanings, exchange is only one part of a larger system of meaning produced in and through con-sumption. *What* we choose to consume and *how* we consume are already pregnant with social significance. The ability or lack of ability to consume certain objects and services, or even to consume at all (in the case of extreme poverty or social and geographical isola-tion), has profound consequences that most of us implicitly understand. For example, we might choose to purchase an automobile that is more expensive than we can really afford because of what we imagine that it enables us to do (climb effortlessly over boulders to the top of a butte where we can survey the endless desert stretching in front of us, as suggested by ads) and what that particular make and model symbolize. Automobiles offer mobility and convenience; they can symbolize youthfulness or hipness, comfort or a con-cern with safety, high economic status or thrift. In the end, however, all automobiles perform the same function—moving people around. The existence of a vast number of brands and models, colors and option packages, and so on suggests that other forces of meaning are at work in an individual's choice of vehicle—forces that may seem more important than (in this example) fiscal responsibility or concern about the environment (in which case the best option might be not to purchase a car at all). *What* we choose to consume in this case highlights certain values (mobility, convenience) at the expense of others (a habitable planet); *how* we do so—what kind of vehicle, what color, what features we add or subtract—immediately brings to light other values or symbolic associations (e.g., the importance of youthfulness in our culture) that are involved in all forms of consumption.

Consumption and Agency

There is one important category in this scenario that needs to be addressed in further detail before we proceed. It is perhaps the central concept at issue in contemporary analyses of consumer culture, and indeed it is essential to consumerism itself. This is the category of agency, the ability of individuals to act as self-conscious, willful social "agents" or actors, and to exert their will through involvement in social practices, relationships, and decision making. (This concept is discussed in more detail in Chapter 6.) Certainly, debates over the ultimate social significance of consumer culture often revolve around questions about the degree to which individuals are able to express their free will or agency in their day-to-day decision making, as opposed to their actions and decisions being relatively determined—decided on in advance as a result of the structures and institutions within which they live.

Analyses of consumerism and consumer practices will differ depending on the degree of real choice that we imagine individuals have in contemporary society. For instance, for the most part, those of us who live in democracies are free to vote for whom we want; on the other hand, that freedom is limited by the degree to which political parties tend to express small variations on the same political themes. We can see this same "non-choice" in our automobile example. You are able to choose the color and make of your car. What is more difficult to "choose" in most North American and Australian cities and towns is to go without an automobile. This is less likely to be the case in Europe, and congestion in major cities everywhere is leading many to forgo cars. However, mass transit systems remain underfunded, and low-density development has made it difficult to go (for instance) from a suburban home to work at a light industrial park, and from there back home, or to shop for food at a supermarket located on a retail strip.

Moving beyond these examples, what feels to each of us like free choice is also heavily determined by our social and cultural backgrounds. Our choices define and are defined by the social categories within which we *want* to situate ourselves and in which we are already situated. There are certain ways in which we have to act and dress in order to "belong" or participate in certain social or career circles. We might in some sense "choose" to belong to these groups; nevertheless, it is important to put aside the idea that there is some kind of *absolute*, unconstrained agency or free choice in consumer society (or any society, for that matter). There is a reason that demographical studies of consumer choice capture patterns of consumption linked to income levels, geographical region, and so on. All of the consumers in an area may be freely choosing to buy one brand of clothing over another, one brand of beer over another. And yet, when grouped together, these individual "free" choices point to similarities in consumer choices that cannot be written off as mere coincidence. There is also a reason why television programs are developed to "deliver" certain target audiences to advertisers interested in selling their products to (say) 19- to 25-year-olds. No one is twisting the arms of young adults to tune in to these shows, but hopefully they do anyway, so satisfying the hopes of both television executives and advertisers.

Understanding the meanings of contemporary consumption involves a comprehension of both the structures and institutions of consumption that define and shape our choices *and* the way in which these choices in turn shape and define these structures and institutions. It is common to understand social structures and institutions as necessarily imposing constraints or limits on behavior. Attending high school, for example, places limits on what you do and where you can go during the day on weekdays. But if schooling limits some behaviors and choices, it also enables a whole range of others (through education, exposure to peers, and extracurricular activities, etc.) and does so in ways that cannot be easily controlled or predicted. The structures of consumption both enable individual consumption and provide restrictions on it in a continuously shifting way: our choices are structured, but this does not mean that they are determined in advance. While realizing that agency and structure always go together, we will look first at some of the structures that consumption produces and reproduces, and then in the next section consider the individual and collective meanings we make through our use of the things we consume.

Taste and Distinction

It is obvious to most of us that the things we own have a meaning above and beyond the simple possession of them. Few if any of us have a sense of the monetary value of all the things around us taken together. But what we do know is that many of the objects we surround ourselves with mean something to us: they may remind us of the person who gave them to us, or they in some way express our individuality—who we are and what we like. The furniture we own, the objects we place on our walls, the music we collect and listen to, the books we display on our shelves, the way our apartments or houses look—all of these objects externalize our own sense of ourselves, whether explicitly or implicitly. What they also do, however, is connect us with others through the subtle forms of **distinction** they produce. For example, if we like the music of Neutral Milk Hotel and Animal Collective, seeing their albums in other people's homes will indicate a connection between them and us; conversely, seeing a rack containing only Céline Dion and Michael Bublé CDs will suggest something very different.

Sociocultural Differentiation

One of the most important ways in which contemporary consumption functions is that it produces systems of sociocultural differentiation. To put this more plainly, what we "choose" to consume *includes* us in some groups and *excludes* us from others. Once again, to a certain degree, what we can consume (or not consume) has always functioned as a form of social distinction. At an earlier point in European history, only the nobility could afford to consume large quantities of meat flavored with exotic spices from abroad; peasants, craftspeople, and city dwellers had to make do with bread and beer.

In comparison to contemporary forms and modes of social distinction through consumption, even up to the end of the nineteenth century a relatively minimal degree of social differentiation was signaled by the consumption of different kinds of commodities. Shops in the late nineteenth century had a limited number of consumer items, few of which were readily identifiable by brand name: coffee, sugar, and other food items came out of barrels rather than in the clearly distinguished packages of a specific brand. To a considerable degree, distinction through consumption is a relatively recent phenomenon, first described by the sociologist Thorstein Veblen in 1899, and more fully theorized and systematized by the French sociologist Pierre Bourdieu in the 1970s and 1980s.

Thorstein Veblen

Veblen's famous analysis of **conspicuous consumption** explored the uses to which "excess" consumption was already being put by the end of the nineteenth century. "Wasted," or excess, consumption was the result of a widespread increase in incomes and consequent expansion of consumption that occurred at the end of that century. For Veblen, "wasted" consumption was not illegitimate, useless, or purposeless. What he was trying to capture by using this term were forms of consumption beyond those that "serve human life or human well-being on the whole" (203). Consumption at the beginning of the twentieth century was becoming "conspicuous"—obvious, noticeable, and visible in order to signal or symbolize class differences and distinctions. As Veblen points out, there are a number of possible categories that could be used to symbolize social differences: moral and intellectual qualities, physical or aesthetic differences, and so on. In the United States and Canada, all of these categories were being subsumed by displays of money. But one need not be rich to be able to render one's forms of consumption visible to other classes. Veblen insisted that there existed conspicuous forms of consumption all the way down to the very poorest groups. A difference between the very rich and the poor and middle class rested in the creation of the category of "taste." Veblen writes:

> The growth of punctilious [precise or demanding] discrimination as to qualitative excellence in eating, drinking, etc., presently affects not only the manner of life, but also the training and intellectual activity of the gentleman of leisure. He is no longer the successful, aggressive male. In order to avoid stultification he must also cultivate his tastes, for it now becomes incumbent on him to discriminate with some nicety between the noble and ignoble in consumable goods. (190)

Pierre Bourdieu

In many ways, Bourdieu's research and writing take up the same themes as Veblen's. Bourdieu, too, is interested in the social uses of consumption as a form of class or group distinction or discrimination. For Bourdieu, whenever we consume—be it images, types of food, music, or art—we are engaging in complex forms of social differentiation, discrimination, and display, whether we realize it or not. We may be aware of being involved in this social "game of distinction," as we most definitely are when we dress up for a job interview, for instance. But for Bourdieu, we participate in this game of social distinction even when we make decisions that seem to express personal or individual choices. The sum meaning of consumption for Bourdieu *is* this game of distinction. "Taste," the faculty that Veblen believed the rich had to cultivate to be able to make accurate distinctions between better and worse forms of consumables, is now something that we all exercise.

Yet even in expressions of our likes and dislikes through consumption, Bourdieu believes that there is a form of social meaning at work. He writes: "Taste is the basis of all that one has—people and things—and all that one is for others, whereby one classifies oneself and is classified by others" (45). Taste appears to be individual; however, not only is it social, but it is also a site at which social power is produced and maintained.

Suggested Activity 5.2

Reflect on your own consumption and the purchases made by your peer group. What forms of distinction can you see yourself engaged in? How is social distinction represented in popular culture? Think, for example, of the importance of forms of display in music videos and in contemporary Pygmalion narratives, such as in films like *Pretty Woman*, *Maid in Manhattan*, *Lars and the Real Girl*, and *Real Women Have Curves*, or the television show *Ugly Betty*. What do such narratives tell us is required, in addition to money, to move from the lower to the upper classes?

Consumption and Power

In his exhaustively researched book *Distinction*, Bourdieu and his research associates perform a number of experiments in which they ask respondents from different economic levels of society (expressed through their job titles) to rank and identify films, pieces of classical music, and photographs, based on their likes or dislikes. Astonishingly, there was a remarkably strong correspondence between the choices individuals made and the socioeconomic groups to which they belonged. There was, for example, a link between supposedly "difficult" music and art and members of higher income groups, while blue-collar workers "liked" more melodic forms of classical music, narrative films versus more experimental films, and so on. This difference in taste between socioeconomic groups has most often been thought to be based on either education or innate ability. Bourdieu saw things differently. He argued that differences in consumption express *only* the way in which consumption has been used to create and reinforce preexisting class divisions. There is no "taste" that is more correct or accurate than any other. Rather, by virtue of their socioeconomic status, groups in power have been able to transform *their* tastes into the legitimate ones by which others are measured. In this way, consumption has placed barriers to class mobility, because in addition to one's economic status, one also has to have correct ideas about what to consume and how to consume it.

There are two things that Veblen's and Bourdieu's theories tell us about contemporary consumption. First, the idea that we consume "freely"—that is, that our choices are somehow entirely our own and are disconnected from larger social structures—is an illusion. Of course, subjectively, it certainly *feels* as if our choices are free. Nevertheless, "Objectively and subjectively aesthetic stances adopted in matters like cosmetics, clothing or home decoration are opportunities to experience or assert one's position in social space, as a rank to be upheld or a distance to be kept" (Bourdieu 57). Second, these theories tell us that one of the primary social meanings of consumption is social distinction and differentiation. Juliet Schor writes:

> Bourdieu argues that class status is gained, lost, and reproduced in part through everyday acts of consumer behaviour. Being dressed incorrectly or displaying "vulgar" manners can cost a person a management or professional job. Conversely, one can gain entry into social circles, or build lucrative business contracts, by revealing appropriate tastes, manners, and culture. Thus, consumption practices become important in maintaining the basic structures of power and inequality which characterize our world. (457)

Bourdieu has claimed that "there is no way out of the game of culture." For this reason, he has sometimes been criticized for theorizing consumption in a way that stresses structure(s) at the expense of agency. Is it always the case that our choices necessitate the adoption of a position in social space? How, then, do societies change and develop? While Bourdieu does have his own theory of the relationship between structure and agency, at their most extreme his views can start to seem like those of Horkheimer and Adorno that we discussed in Chapter 4. "Choice," that is, starts to look completely determined by our own location on an intricate social grid.

We need not take Bourdieu or Veblen as being totally correct about consumption to find a great deal that is useful in their descriptions of the symbolic meaning of consumption. Indeed, one of the things that Bourdieu asserts in *Distinction* is important to our discussion in the next section of this chapter. For Bourdieu, there is no more or less legitimate form of consumption: whatever difference there might be between watching Italian opera on PBS or *Dancing with the Stars* lies not in the intrinsic value of one television program over the other, but in the way in which these choices are mobilized socially. The next section will explore why it is important to see the meaning of consumption as being produced through the uses to which agents put the things they consume.

Consumption, Desire, and Pleasure

It is extremely easy to dismiss consumption as wasteful, pointless, without purpose, and so on. As we suggested at the outset of this chapter, consumption is both a normal part of contemporary societies and yet also a social practice accompanied by feelings of ambivalence, guilt, and uncertainty. When social critics write about the ills and traumas associated with consumer society, the image they project is of a present peopled by indistinguishable drones mystified by the electronic buzz of advertising, grimly doing their duty by dragging themselves through malls and filling up shopping bags with slick-looking black leather shoes, wafer-thin cell phones, and flavored popcorn bought by the bucket—none of which they need. In a nutshell, many critics portray consumer society as a form of Technicolor totalitarianism—the gray dreariness of life in the Soviet Union, lit up only by neon lights and the smiling faces of Gap employees.

Not only do these views miss much of what takes place in consumption, they also presume what consumption means without ever investigating or considering that its meanings may be multiple and vary from place to place. Is contemporary life really so grim and empty? Not at all! Or, at the very least, since life is experienced very differently depending on "an individual's participation in consumption or their practical freedom to exercise choice" (Lury 6), the landscape of consumer culture cannot in any simple way be equated with a gulag of the soul. Through consumer culture, individuals enact their desires and develop new ones; consumption is also a source of enormous amounts of pleasure—especially the consumption of entertainment, whether this involves reading Jonathan Franzen's *The Corrections* or watching any one of Adam Sandler's sublime and sophisticated (!) comedies.

Of course, it is possible to point out (as we will in the next section) that there are rather serious consequences of this kind of pleasure and this system of desire. And it is also possible to assert that the desires and pleasures of consumer culture are not ones that are particularly worth having, or are at best degraded remainders of more lofty and serious feelings and dispositions—the ones that a small subset of humanity experienced at some point in the past while the vast majority of people were engaged in endless labor in terrible conditions.

A more effective rejoinder that does not rely on positions that are difficult to substantiate, or arguments that reenact the legitimation of tastes that Bourdieu criticizes, insists on consumerism as a system that is inscribed in our most intimate pleasures and desires. At the beginning of *Selling Culture*, Richard Ohmann paints the following picture of the consumer in mass culture:

> The advertiser can sell Bill Black an image of himself as a carefree male...because he has already learned from a million other commercials to fill vacancies in his life through commodities, because advertisers have long since inscribed that nexus on his mind, because *they* have to expand sales to cope with the productive capacity that manufacturers have achieved partly by making Bill's job mechanical, which in turn makes him long for autonomy and market-free social relations, which desire

has over decades been fixed to an image of the home as a place of care and refuge, which image drew him into a marriage with impossible hopes, and the burden of these hopes on his wife, along with her own ad-inflated aspirations to be super-woman, has made her resentful and no fun to be with. And so on and on. (12–13)

In this system, there is no space for "real" or "authentic" desires. And this is probably right: all of us are now born into a culture that is consumerist through and through in such a way that renders appeals to "authentic" desires or pleasures as suspect as our desire for pure, unconstrained agency. Still, what such accounts are never able to explain is why consumer culture "fails" so frequently, and why advertisers constantly have to reevaluate their audiences and reconsider the ways in which they might reach them.

To put this slightly differently, "If consumption was simply a reflex of production, what need would there be for design, advertising or marketing expertise?" (du Gay *et al.* 85). One of the errors in thinking about consumer culture is to assume that it is total in the way that Ohmann suggests—that there is no excess, slippage, or contradiction that breaks up the smooth operation of consumerism, or at least produces other forms and moments of social interaction and meaning. To question the absolute power of consumerist ideology does not require a return to "real" or "authentic" desires; rather, what it means is that we need to consider the ways in which individuals create social and individual meaning through consumption—however problematically, however incompletely.

Making Meaning in Use

In the words of the authors of *Doing Cultural Studies*, du Gay *et al.*, consumption needs to be understood to some degree, and in conjunction with our discussion of structure above, as a process of "appropriation and resistance," "an ongoing cycle of *commodification*—where producers make new products or different versions of old products as a result of consumers' activities—and *appropriation*—where consumers make those products meaningful, sometimes making them achieve a new 'register' of meaning that affects production in some way" (103). Consumers don't passively accept the meanings that supposedly come prepackaged with the things they consume—or at least they don't *always* do so. Rather, consumers help to *make* culture in a variety of complex and contradictory ways. First, consumers engage in a process of distinction and discrimination through the things that they choose to consume or not to consume. The landscape of consumer society is littered with products and services that didn't hit their mark: it is estimated that more than 80% of consumer items introduced each year fail. Second, consumers produce meaning at the intersection of the wide range of experiences, practices, and relationships that they are or have been engaged in. The unpredictable connection of these elements creates new possibilities and meanings that can fall outside of the structures of consumption (see Figure 5.4).

It is possible to overstate the agency that individuals engage in through their practices of consumption. Cultural studies has at times gone too far in creating a "vision of consumption practices as inherently democratic and implicitly subversive" (du Gay *et al.* 104). Nevertheless, the fundamental point of insisting on even the possibility of consumer activity (as opposed to passivity) can be substantiated by looking at actual practices of consumption as they occur in specific social situations. (The discussion of McDonald's in Chapter 10 is one example.) To decide that we know the meaning of every situation of consumption from the outset doesn't help us to understand either the ways in which consumption has changed over time or the politics of consumption—that is, the larger social issues that we need to consider whenever we investigate consumption.

Figure 5.4 In the movie *American Beauty*, the now iconic image of plastic bags dancing in the wind became a symbol of beauty for the character Ricky, highlighting the unpredictable intersections of commodity culture and creativity. Source: © AF archive/Alamy

The Politics of Consumption

The most common critical responses to consumer culture have been *normative*: consumer culture has been assessed on the basis of its supposed innate value. Put most simply, is it good or bad for us? Thumbs up or thumbs down? All-Bran (=healthy) or Frosted Flakes (=unhealthy)? For the many boosters who celebrate consumers and consumption as engines for economic growth and the spread of democracy, others decry consumerism and consumption more generally as innate social evils. On the one hand, there are those who say that television (for instance) educates and amuses people, democratically opens up the range of possibilities available to them, puts them in touch with the whole society or even the whole global village, makes them informed citizens, helps them improve their material lives, and so keeps the economy going; and on the other, those who say television creates illusions, destroys literacy and the English language, isolates people from one another, puts them in debt by making them want things they don't really need, and turns them into political zombies (Ohmann 11–12).

The former position tends to be held implicitly, except at times when—as in the post–9/11 crisis—consumers need to be reminded again of the duty and joy of shopping. The latter position is part of a long tradition of normative critiques of mass culture dating back to Matthew Arnold's worries in *Culture and Anarchy* (1869) about the eclipse of an interest in spiritual values through the "vulgar" pursuit of material wealth during the rapid industrialization of Britain in the nineteenth century (see Chapter 2).

Writing in the 1920s, Samuel Strauss spoke directly about the problems of what he referred to as "consumptionism," "a philosophy of life that committed human beings to the production of more and more things—'more this year than last year, more next year than this'—and that emphasized the 'standard of living' above all other values" (qtd. in Robbins 3). The decline of all other values in favor of consumer values was criticized in the 1950s by former advertising executive Vance Packard, who drew attention to the psychological tricks of advertising that led to overconsumption. Every new publishing season brings a raft of critiques of consumer culture more or less along these same lines (such as Robert D. Putnam's *Bowling Alone: The Collapse and Revival of American Community* or, in a different vein, Judith Levine's *Not Buying It: My Year Without Shopping*). Consumerism seems to be a perpetual problem, and a problem that a century of both scholarly and public criticism seems to have done little to resolve.

The Consequences of Consumption

Another way of approaching consumer culture frames the implications of consumerism in a somewhat different way. This is to ask: What are the consequences of consumer society? What is the price of the pleasures we can and do derive from making meanings through our practices of consumption? A response to this question can take various forms, ranging from the philosophical to the empirical.

Philosophically, the capitalist system that gives rise to and perpetuates consumerism has long been seen as a fundamentally alienating system: it is a system in which the pleasures of consumption are purchased for most at the cost of engaging in forms of labor that are antithetical to our real interests and that have become more and more specialized and narrow. In other words, we get to define ourselves through the things we buy only by subjecting ourselves to jobs that in all too many cases hardly represent how we would like to be spending our time.

Empirically, a number of critics have drawn attention to the impact of Western consumerism—a style of consumerism, it should be added, that is quickly becoming global—on other peoples and on the environment. Richard Robbins has explored in detail the global consequences of consumerism through his examination of the development of the sugar and beef industries (194–220). The Western appetite for sugar led to the expansion of the plantation economy in the eighteenth and nineteenth centuries and, correspondingly, to the untold suffering of millions who were displaced from their homelands to serve as slaves on these plantations. The modern beef industry, to take another example, has had an environmentally devastating impact around the world, leading to environmental degradation through the deforestation that often accompanies large-scale ranching, the pollution of groundwater and the atmosphere by waste products, and the spread of disease to both human beings and wild animal populations.

What is perhaps more telling is that we can see the same stories of human and environmental damage if we consider virtually *any* aspect of contemporary consumption, from the use of automobiles (depletion of both nonrenewable resources and the ozone layer, increased human health risks due to smog and high levels of ultraviolet radiation, not to mention the widespread impacts of a warming planet) to the purchase of hip, funky clothing (almost all of which is produced in degrading sweatshop factories in developing countries, a form of labor that approximates slavery even if workers "freely" choose to work in them). At the same time, ever-expanding consumption of consumer items of all kinds has proven to be a key component of the health of national economies and international markets. The growth of new consumer classes in countries such as China, India, and Brazil has been taken as a positive sign of the development of these nations.

In the final analysis, the fact that we are quickly approaching some very real limits in Earth's physical resources makes it increasingly difficult to valorize some of the ways in which consumerism enables agency. To give but one example, we are close to reaching Hubbert's peak (if we haven't already surpassed it), the point at which humanity has used

Figure 5.5 The scale of contemporary production has expanded along with the global increase in the demand for consumer objects and experiences. Source: © 06photo/Shutterstock

up half of the entire planet's petroleum resources. Petroleum not only fuels our cars, heats our homes, and permits our factories to work, but is also used to make plastics, artificial fibers, paints, and so on. What will happen to consumption when we are sliding from Hubbert's peak toward zero remains to be seen.

While this chapter has argued that it is important to take consumerism seriously in order to understand contemporary popular culture, it is just as important to understand the global impact of our "society of perpetual growth." When perpetual growth takes place in a world of limited natural and human resources, serious and inevitable problems will arise. Finding answers to these problems generated by consumption is one of the major challenges of the twenty-first century. The greatest challenge is to try to understand how to mobilize the pleasures and possibilities of consumption, and the way in which consumption can be a place of individual and collective agency, in a manner that also addresses the increasingly terrible consequences of consumption on an accelerated, expanded, and global scale (see Figure 5.5).

A Different Kind of Consumer Culture

In "Towards a New Politics of Consumption," sociologist Juliet Schor proposes a model for thinking past the either–or way in which consumption has typically been addressed. Her proposal is to reorient rather than do away with consumption (which is, as we will see in the final section of this chapter, one of the common critical reactions to consumerism: the belief that the only solution is to do away with it altogether) by addressing one of its key, if undertheorized, aspects.

Contemporary modes of consumption put untold stresses and strains on individuals. Schor believes that there is already an enormous amount of discontent with consumerism;

what is lacking is a way to conceptualize it. Social well-being in a consumer society has always been linked to income levels. The assumption is that the more money you have, the more you can spend and the more satisfied with life you will be. (This is why politicians always employ the rhetoric of tax cuts and new jobs to try to win votes.) What is lacking is a market for "alternatives to status or positional goods" (457): there is a market for things, but not for public goods or more time. In turn, since it is difficult to express one's desires for these kinds of goods in a society where achievement is measured almost solely by monetary wealth, consumer society "underproduces" goods that people find important: a clean environment (since environmental costs are not included in the price of goods), leisure (it is harder to choose more free time over higher incomes in virtually every employment sector), and all manner of public goods (since mass transit is so inadequate, we are forced to use private cars, which in turn leads to a further decline in mass transit since it is used less and less).

A new politics of consumption would try to create a language and a political framework in which it is possible to create an economy of "less work and less stuff" (459). Schor believes that there is a strong demand for such an economy, even if it is difficult to see this because we can participate only in the forms of consumption currently "on offer" (459). She makes seven suggestions, all of which are important to our discussion here.

The first involves the revival of a discussion of the minimal social needs for every individual in society to be fully able to participate in it. Second is a focus on "quality of life" rather than "quantity of stuff," which in turn is related to the third, the need for more ecologically sustainable forms of consumption. Addressing minimal social needs has to be accompanied by more democratic consumption practices; that is (fourth), a way of "de-cooling" high-end products and changing the rules of the game of distinction. Fifth and sixth, a "vast consumer policy agenda" has to put pressure on the development of government policy, including the creation of policy to control the "cultural environment" (ad-free zones, diversity in retailing, etc.).

Seventh is a point that is absolutely crucial to any politics of consumption. Schor points out what Marx insisted on almost a century and a half ago: "Everything we consume has been produced. So a new politics of consumption must take into account the labor, environmental, and other conditions under which products are made, and argue for high standards" (461). *This* constitutes the real agenda for rethinking our consuming lives— lives whose frantic pace, absurdities, and wasted efforts, all in the name of accumulating more stuff faster and faster, are in turn threatening to consume us. The forms that our criticisms take, however, rely all too frequently on the use and abuse of a set of concepts that seem unable to push us out of the dangerous orbit that we have assumed around the planet Consumption; we will look at these concepts below. If we continue our present trajectory, the future explorers who find our remains will come across only a tape with a single sentence recorded on it: "We had compulsions that made us confuse shopping with creativity" (Coupland 11).

Authenticity and Co-optation: *The Merchants of Cool*

Rachel Dretzin and Barak Goodman's *Frontline* documentary *The Merchants of Cool* explores the hypercommodified world of contemporary youth culture. Narrated by PBS correspondent Douglas Rushkoff, who appears in the documentary as a lonely adult figure wandering through the landscape of youth pop culture, the documentary explores a whole range of contemporary marketing and advertising practices that extend their way deep into the lives of one of consumer culture's most cherished subjects—youth. Though the film is now more than a decade old, the dynamics of youth, cool, and consumption explored in it have changed surprisingly little.

The current generation of teenagers is the wealthiest in history. The documentary claims that in the United States in 2000, teenagers spent $100 billion themselves and influenced the spending of another $50 billion. (US teen spending in 2011 was estimated as $208.7 billion.) Since teens generally don't have to pay for the necessities of life, the vast majority of spending went toward forms of what Veblen described as "conspicuous consumption"—CDs, movie passes, soft drinks and fast food, fashion, and video games. For companies involved in producing the objects teenagers consume, there is fierce competition to secure these discretionary dollars. Dretzin and Goodman explore the forms that this competition has taken, as well as the impact it has had on youth culture and contemporary popular culture more generally, to come to some conclusions about the degree to which the values of industry have infiltrated the last remaining cracks and gaps in consumer society.

Defining "Cool"

According to Dretzin and Goodman, teens today respond "most reliably" to "this maddeningly elusive thing called cool." Increasingly, "cool" has been understood as standing in opposition to mainstream consumer products: something that everyone likes cannot possibly be cool. This has created a paradoxical situation for companies that produce consumer products, especially for those that target teens. To ensure sales of their products, they need to appeal to what teens find cool; as soon as they begin to flood the market with their products, a product that started out cool quickly becomes yet another mass-produced object intended primarily to separate teens from their money.

The Merchants of Cool showcases the ways in which companies have tried to search out what youth think is cool in order to capitalize on it; it also shows the transformation of something cool (and thus supposedly *transgressive*, or opposed to the dominant values of consumer culture) into a form of mainstream consumer culture. In the first instance, companies focus on a variety of marketing techniques that employ forms of ethnography. "Cool hunters" are marketers who search out what young people think is cool before it becomes part of the culture at large (or even of youth culture at large). Such cool hunters visit high schools and try to track down "early adopters"—teens who are willing to take a chance in wearing radical clothing, listening to music that might be unpopular with their peers, and decorating their bodies and styling their hair in original ways. They then compile this information into reports that are purchased by large companies, which in turn use the information to try to anticipate the kinds of products and styles teens will purchase.

The filmmakers paint a picture of a present in which marketers, by entering into the lives of teens more and more intrusively, have shortened the time between the expression of an authentic agency with respect to popular culture (teens making their own forms of cool, or reworking parts of existing consumer forms) and when this expression becomes commodified, turned into an experience or object to be bought and sold to as many people as possible. Rushkoff, the narrator, suggests that what is being witnessed in youth culture today is the intensification and extensification of a longer historical narrative of consumer culture. The fundamental "engine" of consumerism (what drives it onward and upward) that the film identifies involves the co-optation by businesses of genuine, authentic forms of cultural expression.

The worry of the filmmakers is that co-optation of authentic forms of popular expression now occurs so rapidly that youth culture no longer has any room to breathe or to develop and grow. And what this in turn implies is that consumer culture is now in danger of becoming total, with social, political, and cultural structures coming to overwhelm the few remaining sites of agency.

We are all familiar with the narrative offered in this documentary. When our favorite indie band signs to a major label or achieves unexpectedly widespread sales or wins a Grammy, or when a reputable film star begins appearing in mass culture schlock (many fans have wondered why Robert De Niro would ever agree to star in *Meet the Parents*, much less *Meet the Fockers*), we can't help but feel as though they have somehow "sold out," trading their artistic authenticity for the comfort of cold, hard cash. This narrative seems to work particularly well in discussions of popular music.

Music Scene Fashion Narratives
Punk in England and grunge in Seattle emerged out of local situations and music subcultures in response to specific social and political contexts. In both cases, punk and grunge styles—which comment on consumer culture's fascination with fashion (punks ripped and defaced their clothing, reassembling items with staples and safety pins; grunge musicians adopted working-class clothing, specifically the iconic lumberjack shirt)—quickly crossed over to the mainstream, or at the very least were transposed to other cultural and subcultural settings. British soccer star David Beckham saw fit to wear a version of the mohawk in the qualifying rounds leading up to the 2002 World Cup; in North America, youth living outside the Pacific Northwest quickly started wearing lumberjack shirts and listening to Nirvana and other examples of the Seattle sound. The narrativization of these kinds of cultural movements implies an early, noncommodified, nonconsumer moment of authenticity, followed by an inexorable process of commercial and cultural **assimilation** of apparently threatening or oppositional discourses into mainstream culture.

Yet while this may be a familiar narrative about the dynamics of contemporary consumption, it is one that passes over a number of issues that we have tried to emphasize here. First, there is a way in which (as with so many other examples of cultural criticism directed toward consumption) this narrative translates into political stasis: since genuine expressions are fated to be assimilated into mainstream discourses, it is pointless even to *try* to make your own forms of popular culture. And, since being popular means being co-opted, it is more or less structurally impossible to spread (say) an anti-consumerist message as widely as possible, as many bands have wanted to do, since once everyone is into something, it must be "bad."

More significantly, this narrative assumes the solidity of two categories that should be seen as both more porous and more incomplete than the "co-optation thesis" implies. The claim that the products of youth culture are *ever* authentic in the first place—or at least authentic in the way that *The Merchants of Cool* implies, outside of consumer culture and in opposition to it—positions youth culture in an impossible place. Punk didn't come suddenly out of nowhere: it was itself already part of a pop culture discourse and has to be seen as "inside" rather than "outside" of consumer culture. (How else would you ever have the idea that you could cause a social and/or cultural revolution by playing your guitar?) Finally, the co-optation thesis displays little faith in the uses to which people put consumer objects. Co-opted culture is imagined as a culture bereft of agency, a position that we explored and challenged above in the section on desire and pleasure.

Counterculture Narratives
One of the most important challenges to the view that consumer culture involves the co-optation of real, genuine, or authentic forms of culture is found in Thomas Frank's

analysis of the supposed co-optation of the politics of the 1960s into consumer culture, a transformation that turned the 1960s' hippies into the 1980s' yuppies. In *The Conquest of Cool*, he focuses on the supposed absorption of the energies of the 1960s counterculture into the language of advertising. He writes, "At the heart of every interpretation of the counterculture is a very particular—and very questionable—understanding of corporate ideology and of business practice...business was the monolithic bad guy who had caused America to become a place of puritanical conformity and empty consumerism" (7).

However, an examination of 1950s and 1960s business culture gives us a very different vision of things: in many cases, business saw the counterculture not as an enemy, but as a symbolic ally in their own efforts to modify and update business practices. The bureaucratized, overly rationalized business environment of the 1950s was producing fewer and fewer gains. The solution was to adopt a model of flexibility and creativity that mirrored the values inherent in the counterculture. Indeed, Frank even suggests that advertisers adopted a critical position on mainstream culture before the radicals of the 1960s. Like the hippies themselves, advertisers and businesses were responding to the fact that "the mass culture critique was, if not populist, enormously popular...by the middle of the 1950s, talk of conformity, of consumerism, and of the banality of mass-produced culture were routine elements of middle-class American life" (11).

What Frank's analysis shows us is that the standard co-optation model, which places the values of the dominant culture and the counterculture (or youth culture) in strict opposition, offers a far too simplistic understanding of both. The popularity of this model, its presence as a cultural commonplace to which we all turn all the time to explain changes in popular culture, has correspondingly skewed our own understanding of it, reinforcing both the overwhelming power and solidity of the structures of consumer culture (the forces of co-optation), and the uncritical presence of those authentic experiences or expressions that are then co-opted.

Suggestions for Further Reading and Viewing

Barber, Benjamin R. *Consumed: How Markets Corrupt Children, Infantilize Adults, and Swallow Citizens Whole*. New York: W.W. Norton, 2008.

Bocock, Robert. *Consumption*. New York: Routledge, 1994.

Clark, David B., Marcus Doel, and Kate M.K. Housiaux, eds. *The Consumption Reader*. New York: Routledge, 2003.

Cook, Daniel Thomas. *The Commodification of Childhood: The Children's Clothing Industry and the Rise of the Child Consumer*. Durham, NC: Duke University Press, 2004.

The Corporation. Dir. Mark Achbar and Jennifer Abbott. Prod. Mark Achbar and Bart Simpson. Vancouver: Big Picture Media Corporation, 2003.

Czech Dream. Dir. Vit Klusák and Filip Remunda. Prague: Hypermarket Film, 2004.

De Graaf, John, David Wann, and Thomas H. Naylor. *Affluenza: The All-Consuming Epidemic*. San Francisco: Berrett-Koehler, 2001.

Gottdiener, Mark. *New Forms of Consumption*. Lanham, MD: Rowman and Littlefield, 2000.

Hastings, Gerard. *The Marketing Matrix: How the Corporation Gets Its Power—And How We Can Reclaim It*. New York: Routledge, 2012.

Hengeveld, Rob. *Wasted World: How Our Consumption Challenges the Planet*. Chicago: University of Chicago Press, 2012.

McCracken, Grant. *Culture and Consumption*. Bloomington: Indiana University Press, 1988.

Princen, Thomas, Michael Maniates, and Ken Conca, eds. *Confronting Consumption.* Cambridge, MA: MIT Press, 2002.

Scanlan, Jennifer. *The Gender and Consumer Culture Reader.* New York: New York University Press, 2000.

Schor, Juliet B. *Born to Buy: The Commercialized Child and the New Consumer Culture.* New York: Scribner, 2005.

Schor, Juliet B. *Do Americans Buy Too Much?* Boston: Beacon Press, 2000.

Schor, Juliet B. *The Overspent American: The Unexpected Decline of Leisure.* New York: Basic Books, 1998.

Schor, Juliet B., and Douglas Holt. *The Consumer Society Reader.* New York: New Press, 2000.

6

Identity and the Body

Identity—a Necessary Fiction?

In the 2005 film *Transamerica*, Bree, a 40-something transgender woman, goes on a road trip from New York to Los Angeles with Toby, a teenage hustler. Along with a number of standard elements of the Hollywood road movie (dodgy transportation, encounters with wacky but sympathetic strangers and stereotypical Midwestern conservatives, frequent fights and misunderstandings), the plot offers a more unusual premise: Toby is Bree's son, fathered by her during a brief encounter before she openly identified as a woman. Bree knows this, but Toby doesn't, believing instead that the prissy middle-aged woman who sprung him from jail is a Christian do-gooder hoping to convert him on the cross-country journey to find his father. Bree has undertaken the trip at the insistence of her therapist, who won't sign the papers giving authorization for her sex-reassignment surgery until she confronts this recently discovered and very awkward part of her past. Much of the critical commentary on this film focused on the theme of transgender issues, which at that point had received little attention in mainstream cinema, and on the impressive performance of cisgender actress Felicity Huffman, best known for her role in the television series *Desperate Housewives*, playing an amab (assigned male at birth) trans woman. In recent years criticism surrounding the appropriateness of casting cis men and women as trans characters in film has received more mainstream attention, as it oftentimes denies trans actors the right to adequately represent their own gender narratives. These elements aside, the film is interesting as a paradigmatic exploration of the traditional Western theme of identity.

The transness of Bree's character accentuates conventional questions about the relationship between identity, behavior, and biology, as well as the political charge these questions have always carried. The film also approaches questions about the role of genetics in defining identity from another traditional angle: the relationship between parents and children. Toby clearly feels, rightly or wrongly (mostly wrongly, as it turns out), that solving the mystery of his birth father will help him resolve confusions about his current life path. The role of the past in defining identity is clearly key to Bree's quest as well, if we accept her therapist's "expert" advice that she cannot move on until she has somehow dealt with her past and the identity she performed. Finally, the film is interesting for the way in which it both addresses and fails to address a question that has emerged in different forms from the eighteenth century until the present: To what extent are identities made up and/or constructed (and perhaps even make-believe) and to what extent are they natural? Are our identities anchored by factors such as sex, gender, and sexual orientation, or are they free floating, subject to change? In the following two chapters, we take up these along with some even more basic questions: What is identity? Why is it so important in contemporary society? What is at stake in the representation and production of identities, individual and collective?

That something *is* at stake is clear to see from the many kinds of popular culture that derive at least part of their meaning from the significance of identity. From magazine ads that appeal to our sense of ourselves as unique individuals to subcultural styles that allow us to create resistant identities (see Chapter 8), popular culture testifies to the centrality of identity in producing meaning and pleasure in our everyday lives. In this chapter, we explore ideas about identity that tend to take up a position somewhere between the poles of essentialism and **social constructivism**. Essentialist theories posit identity as a fundamental, unchanging core of meaning that precedes and transcends culture and politics. Identity derives its sense and legitimacy, according to these theories, through its grounding in nature and/or history, where "history" is seen as an unbroken line of development whose truth is unquestionable. Social constructivist theories, on the other hand, emphasize the cultural and political circumstances in which identities are produced. Social constructivism takes issue with the essentialist premise of identity as something inherent within an individual or group, foregrounding instead the complex *process* through which narratives of identity express broader social relations, including and especially relations of power. Those relations remain invisible to the extent that identities are naturalized or essentialized—that is, represented as outside or prior to particular historical circumstances.

Over the course of the twentieth century, developments in the field of psychology, political theory, and philosophy highlighted some of the logical and practical problems with essentialism, while offering variations on constructivist models of identity. Recent advances in genetics have swung the pendulum back to theories based on biology, or "nature," that seek to explain how we are who we are. Without discounting these theories, much of the discussion in this chapter explores the role of social and political forces in constructing narratives of identity. Genetics might establish broad parameters for what we can do, think, or feel, but it is culture that gives us the ingredients to establish the storylines of who we think we are. To see identity as a form of narrative or story— something made up, rather than given—does not lead us to suggest that it is insubstantial or dispensable. Rather, this chapter demonstrates the symbolic and material weight of identity, both as an ideological force that inserts us into particular roles that we may or may not have chosen in a social script that we do not ultimately control, and as a platform for self-expression that may allow us limited forms of rewriting. The fluid and contradictory nature of human experience further means that we cannot be defined by any simple mechanism of identity—or even multiple identities (e.g., sister, friend, student, musician, bartender); there will always be parts of us, conscious and unconscious, that exceed the narratives that at various times work to explain, shape, or confine us.

A critical issue in debates about the significance and limits of identity is the role of our bodies in determining who we are. The assumption that has prevailed in Western thought since the time of René Descartes (1596–1650)—that mind and, by extension, self and identity were fundamentally distinct from the crude materiality of the body— has been increasingly confounded, in science and in popular thought, by a recognition of the inseparability of mind and body. A sometimes confused vacillation between the two perspectives—mind versus body and mind and body (or, to use a term we define later, *embodied subjectivity*)—characterizes contemporary practices such as health and fitness regimens and forms of body modification, such as tattooing, piercing, and plastic surgery, that view work on the body as a means of self-enhancement. The perception of the body as almost infinitely malleable to our individual specifications, a perception that is in line with broader beliefs about the role of choice in consumer society, is complicated by the recognition that the capacity to fashion our selves and our bodies is not equally available to everyone. The persistence of categories of gender, sexual orientation, and race as markers of identity and social power highlights the complex relationship between culture and physicality, whereby material differences are invested with cultural meanings that in turn have material effects, in the form of unequal pressures and opportunities encountered by members of different groups in their quests for self-definition.

The relationship between identity and agency, or the capacity that each of us has to shape our own life, is a critical problem that informs many of the concerns we explore in this chapter and the following one. Thus, while many of our discussions focus on the way identities function as stories or create meaning, of central importance is the way these meanings operate to produce particular kinds of power and pleasure.

Suggested Activity 6.1

As you read this chapter and the following one, think about the identities that define you—or that you choose to be defined by—and how these identities fit into the bigger symbolic and material networks that articulate the society you live in. When and how do these identities conflict with one another?

The History of Identity—Some Different Theories

The seeming obviousness of the concept of individual identity belies the fact that, until relatively recently (up until the eighteenth century), nobody gave much thought to it. The idea of the individual as a unique self, with deep psychological needs and preferences, held no currency in a social context in which the meaning of an individual life was subordinate to the issue of the survival of society as a whole. Who you were was prescribed not by your own internal qualities or will, but by the role you occupied in the institutions of family, church, class hierarchy, and so on. So why has individual identity come to have such importance in contemporary society? One dominant explanation is that society simply evolved to a point at which people were liberated from tradition-bound structures, and the unique identities of individuals—which had been there all along—suddenly leapt out of their straitjackets of class and religious conformity to claim their fundamental value and significance. It is certainly true that, from the late eighteenth century on, increasing attention was paid to the issue of identity and to debates over the role of nature or nurture in defining it. All these debates were concerned with the meaning not just of individuals but also of society, since the issue of the role of birth or environment in shaping personality had critical implications for social policy relating to medicine, education, and the treatment of criminality.

Identity and the Unconscious

One of the first major bodies of work to concentrate on—and, ultimately, to unsettle—the grounds of identity was the field of **psychoanalysis**, pioneered by Sigmund Freud (1856–1939) in the early part of the twentieth century. Through his work on adult psychiatric problems—essentially, identity disorders—Freud developed a theory, later elaborated on by others, of the stages of identity development that are a critical precondition for the individual's integration into society. Significant to Freud's theory is the emphasis on the way in which identities are not pre-given, or natural, but rather *produced* in order to manage chaotic fears and desires whose expression is socially forbidden. Babies, psycho-analytic theory suggests, have no coherent identities to speak of. Their inner world is defined by an unorganized collection of primal drives and instincts, with no conscious sense of themselves as separate from the world around them. A baby's eventual realiza-tion that the world—most significantly, their mother—is not merely an extension of themselves but a separate being is both a traumatic break and the beginning of the process of socialization, marked by the management and containment of powerful, contradictory impulses toward "the other."

Freudian Theory of Psychosocial Development

Two key moments in the process of psychosocial development are (i) the recognition of sexual difference, which hinges on the presence or absence of a penis (symbolically expressed in Freud's theory as "the phallus")—this recognition imposes social meaning on our early desires, directing us, via fear of paternal authority, away from the forbidden love object of our mother's body; and (ii) the acquisition of language. As a symbolic sys-tem that manages and mediates our relationship to the world, language is an important part of the social machinery that works to channel our desire into socially acceptable forms of adult sexual orientation and gender identity.

In Freud's formulation, these early moments in development, framed by the so-called Oedipal triangle of mother–father–child, lay the groundwork for two distinct ways of orienting the self in relation to others: the first, which comes later to be associated with sexual feeling, involves the desire to possess, or to *have,* the other; the second—what Freud called identification—involves a recognition of a similarity between oneself and the other that inspires the desire to *be* the other. These two drives, which Freud suggests are biologically rooted, are organized, in the process of the resolution of the Oedipal conflict, to reflect "proper" gender identification and sexual orientation: the young boy learns to identify with males and to desire females, while girls, lacking phallic agency, learn to *be* desirable to males and to identify with women. According to Freud, these patterns of desire and identification are reinforced culturally, by the dominant institu-tions of education and family as well as by popular culture (see our discussion of Laura Mulvey's theory of Hollywood cinema in Chapter 3).

However, sexual drives are by nature chaotic—"polymorphous," in Freud's words. So-called civilization demands that we repress socially unacceptable fears and desires into the unconscious. Here they are inaccessible to our waking selves except through occasional chinks in our rational consciousness, where they appear in disguised form as dreams, fantasies, and verbal accidents (or "Freudian slips"). Because they cannot be articulated, these unconscious currents continue to create troubling ripples in our emotional lives, making the stability of both gender identification and heterosexual orientation precarious. The complex mix of love, fear, and aggression that characterizes our relations with others—particularly those closest to us—testifies to the impossibility of ever fully resolving the tensions enacted through the Oedipal conflict. The determina-tion with which we cling to our identities—particularly gender and sexual orientation—is partly a reflection of an unconscious fear of the consequences of acknowledging the ambivalence that underlies them.

Identity and Ideology

The key lesson in Freud for understanding identity is not that it has no grounding in reality; rather, it is that the stable and coherent selves we articulate to the world and to ourselves are constructions, a bit like dams built to control and manage the torrent of chaotic drives and impulses that cannot be assimilated into society. Later psychoanalytic theorists, particularly **feminist** theorists, emphasize the importance of culture in defining psychosexual development, stressing that both the Oedipal complex and its resolution assume the shape they do in Freud's theory not because they represent natural or obvious stages in individual development, but because they are already overdetermined by the values of a patriarchal, capitalist culture that lays stress on the nuclear family, the possession of phallic authority, and the development of the individual.

Marxist Theories of Identity

The suggestion that not just the shape but also the very concept of individual identity is determined in particular cultural, historical circumstances informs the theories of Karl Marx, who, like Freud, understood the construction of identity as a response to underlying forces of which the individual is largely unconscious. For Marx, as for Freud, identity can be understood in one sense as a kind of mythical armor that people assume as a way of coping with the gap between their needs and desires and the social economy. While for Freud repression was the mechanism that shaped identity while concealing its own origins from it, for Marx the primary force in producing identity and consciousness as a kind of empty protective shell was ideology (see Close-Up 2.1). Ideology, you will recall from earlier chapters, is a form of knowledge or belief that is shaped by, while serving to conceal, powerful interests through its representation as natural, or common sense. In the system of industrial capitalism that was gaining force during the time Marx was writing, ideology played a hugely significant role in securing the acceptance of an exploited working class by promoting a belief in the naturalness of the capitalist order and in the freedom of the individual within it.

In Marx's theory, ideology is the (disguised) expression of underlying economic relations. Later theorists, particularly the French theorist Louis Althusser, revised Marx's theory to emphasize the centrality of the social structures—what Althusser termed **ideological state apparatuses (ISAs)**—through which ideology is reproduced. Rather than being absolutely determined by the economy, the realm of culture and ideology, as it is disseminated through institutions such as schools, universities, and the media, comes to have a semi-autonomous or independent role in shaping individuals and society. The new importance accorded to culture means that its effects are more pervasive than Marx suggested: while earlier concepts of ideology saw it as a kind of "false consciousness" that could be enlightened by seeing through it to the *real* economic conditions it concealed, Althusser's revised concept, which was strongly influenced by psychoanalysis, emphasized the impossibility of ever totally liberating identity from ideology.

In particular, Althusser focused on the process he termed **interpellation**, by which individuals are compelled, through a mix of individual psychological and social imperatives, to identify with the social roles offered to them. This happens in a variety of contexts: for example, in the university setting, the architecture of the classroom, modes of academic discourse, and signs and ads around campus all combine to construct a set of relationships between different people. For the institution to function, it requires individuals to take up their assigned places in those already established relationships, not through a system of elaborate rules but through each individual's recognition of and *identification with* their role.

Suggested Activity 6.2

Think about how the educational institutions you have attended work to interpellate you into particular roles as a student and member of society. Elements you might consider include specific material structures of authority, such as the arrangement of the classroom, in which the professor sits or stands at the front while students sit together in a body, as well as the broader institutional structures that shape your expectations of what kind of social position your education, in conjunction with other social forces such as family and class, prepares you to assume.

Drawing on psychoanalysis, particularly the work of the French theorist Jacques Lacan, Althusser locates the roots of this process of identification in the early stages of socialization, in particular the acquisition of language. Particularly critical in this process is the moment Lacan identifies as the *mirror stage*, which corresponds to the child's recognition of itself as a separate being. The mirror stage describes the moment in which the child sees itself reflected in the mirror (which can also be read as a metaphor for the eyes of its mother and the world outside itself) and identifies with that image. What is particularly significant about that moment of recognition, Lacan suggests, is that it is actually a *misrecognition*: the stable, unified figure that the child sees in the mirror—more stable and unified, in fact, than the child itself, whose body and sensations are still relatively uncoordinated—is a reflection, a pleasing image of integrated selfhood that the child can never fully inhabit. The moment of identification, then, is actually a moment of splitting, in which the promise of wholeness is haunted by the impossibility of fulfillment: identity is always characterized by lack. This lack creates the potential for challenging the terms of identity, something we take up later in this chapter.

All Selves Are Not Created Equal

Of course, because the possibilities for identification are defined and limited through their production within unequal social systems, they hold out much more promising opportunities for some people than for others: in other words, identity may be an illusion, but it is an illusion that *works* for some people in a way that it doesn't for others. This inequality is highlighted explicitly in Marx's theory, which shows that the stakes of ideology are different depending on what position one occupies in the class structure, and more implicitly in psychoanalysis, where sexual difference determines the extent and the ease with which identity and authority are available to different groups.

According to both Freud and Marx, then, the process of socialization into a patriarchal, capitalist society not only establishes identity as a crucial focus of self-organization; it also prescribes and delimits what kinds of identities it is possible to adopt. Identity formation is thus both enabling and disabling—*how* enabling or disabling depends largely on the place one is assigned in social hierarchies defined by gender and class.

Feminist Theories

Feminist theory has taken up the insights of Freud and Marx while also showing the limits of psychoanalysis and Marxism in understanding the mechanisms and the politics of gender identity. The concepts of the unconscious and ideology help to explain how gender identity is socially constructed and why it is so firmly entrenched. They explain, in other words, both why it is important to challenge "natural" patterns of identification and desire and why it is so difficult. Forged in an intricate amalgam of biology and culture, women's self-perception as the "other" of male desire cannot be undone by a simple political assertion of equality. Neither is it possible to counter ideological constructions of femininity with some "real" essence of femaleness, since the very notion of gender is shot through with ideology, experienced by each of us at the most basic level of self-perception.

Paradoxically, it is through the inherently fractured nature of women's self-perception that it becomes possible to mount a challenge to conventional ideologies of gender. Assigned a role in culture that is defined not as autonomous or self-sufficient but as always in relation to—"other" than—the normative category of man, women have not historically inhabited the myth of identity as comfortably as men generally do. They are, in the words of feminist Luce Irigaray, "the sex which is not one," a phrase that sums up the construction of women as negative, *less than* whole, desiring subjects, and as irreducible: not "one," but always split between the myth of stable identity and the reality of its fragmentation and flux. While this condition of always incomplete self-affirmation can be seen as disempowering, it also arguably offers a lever through which to tear apart the whole fiction of identity on which **patriarchy** is based. That is, rather than aspiring to the ultimately empty idea of coherent selfhood—an idea that is always haunted by the shadow of the inferior, incoherent other—female identity actually exposes the emptiness of the edifice that has served to shut women out.

Race—The Empty Signifier

The function of race as a marker of identity did not enter Freud's theory, at least not in an obvious way. While masculinity was the explicit standard by which to analyze normal human development, whiteness operated *im*plicitly in the same way: an assumed norm whose claims to universalism betrayed the **Eurocentrism** of early practitioners of psychoanalysis. Frantz Fanon, a Martiniquan psychiatrist who practiced in Algeria during the dying days of the French colonial regime, challenged psychoanalytic theory to take account of the role of race, and the associated practice of racism, in defining identity. His 1952 book, *Black Skin, White Masks*, showed how, in the cultural context of colonialism and its aftermath, racial minorities are driven to define their identities in split and fractured forms. Where fully human identity is characterized by the "unmarked" race of whiteness, being black presents an untenable choice: become fully human by identifying with what you are not and never can be, or be your "self"—in effect a non-self, defined only by difference and negation. At best, this dilemma leads to a strongly conflicted sense of self and community; at worst, it can lead to forms of psychiatric illness. Although Fanon was not overly sympathetic to feminism, his interventions shared with feminist critiques the insistence that identity—along with what becomes defined as mental disorder—must be understood in the context of relations of power. Fanon's insights inform the work of contemporary cultural theorists such as Stuart Hall, who analyze the discursive construction of race (a subject we discuss in detail in Chapter 7).

Identity and Power/Knowledge

A critical premise informing psychoanalytic and Marxist thought, and foregrounded by feminism, is that identity is defined by and through power.

Michel Foucault

French philosopher and social critic Michel Foucault devoted particular attention to this relationship, showing how power both constrains and produces social meaning, especially that privileged site of meaning that is individual identity. One of the crucial ways in which Foucault's theory departs from that of Marx is in his understanding of how power operates in society. While traditional Marxist theory conceives of power as belonging to or wielded by a ruling class (similar to the assumption in early feminist theory that power rests primarily in the hands of men), Foucault saw its function in a much more nuanced way.

Moving beyond the obvious critiques that Marxists and feminists could direct at one another—that class is complicated by gender and vice versa, so power could never be said to rest in the hands of a single identifiable group—Foucault suggested that power is not *possessed* at all; rather, it circulates continuously throughout society, concentrating in different places at different historical moments and constituting particular meanings and identities as it does so. Foucault's theory does not contest Marx's point that power is unequally distributed; rather, it questions the stability of that distribution, emphasizing its fluidity and the ambiguity of its effects. One of Foucault's most significant insights is his observation that power shapes society productively rather than repressively. This does not mean that all the effects of power are good; it means, rather, that power takes the form not only of regulations restricting people's freedom to be, speak, or act a certain way, but also of discourses—whole systems of thought, speech, and knowledge *production* that structure institutional and social practices (see Chapter 3).

Foucault was particularly interested in the late eighteenth and early nineteenth centuries (not coincidentally the same period on which Marx's work focused), a period in which cultivation of the *self* took on a new urgency. As we have mentioned above, before the eighteenth century the idea of individuals possessing complex and meaningful interior lives did not hold much interest. The concept began to gain currency not because people were finally free to "be themselves," but because, in an industrial-capitalist society characterized by the fragmentation of old social hierarchy and the burgeoning of a middle class whose entrepreneurial energies translated into new forms of wealth and freedom for individuals, new forms of social discipline were required to maintain order. As Freud, Marx, and others had already clearly shown, discipline need not take the form of physical force or punishment, or even law; it works most effectively through the largely unconscious internalization of ideas, values, and modes of discrimination that are represented as natural, or "common sense." Thus "discipline," in Foucault's sense, combines what are usually seen as two separate meanings of the word, the first associated with methods of training or techniques designed to enforce obedience, and the second with branches of knowledge (e.g., science, modern languages, philosophy) characterized by particular rules or methods.

By highlighting the connection between forms of knowledge and the exercise of power (significantly, "discipline," can be either a noun or a verb), Foucault emphasizes the material consequences of knowledge as it becomes classified into different discourses—medicine, for example, or the law—that are enacted, or put into effect, through institutions such as hospitals, schools, and prisons. These institutions play a critical role in the reproduction of social hierarchies and in the shaping of individuals through technologies of treatment, training, or punishment. Foucault's work on prisons led to particular insights into the way technologies of discipline that were developed in the eighteenth century led to new forms of self-regulation and management.

An important architectural innovation in eighteenth-century prisons was the *panopticon,* a structure comprising a tower erected in the center of a courtyard with cells arranged all around it (see Figure 6.1). All of the cells were visible from the tower and—more importantly—the tower was visible from all of the cells. The special disciplinary power of the panopticon lay not so much in the power it gave guards to keep an eye on the prisoners, but rather in the effect it had on the prisoners themselves, who had a sense of being constantly under surveillance whether there was anyone in the tower or not. The prisoners' internalization of the disciplinary gaze of the tower represents a concrete model of a more general process, intensified throughout the nineteenth century, in which individuals came to subject themselves to a kind of social scrutiny. They developed, in other

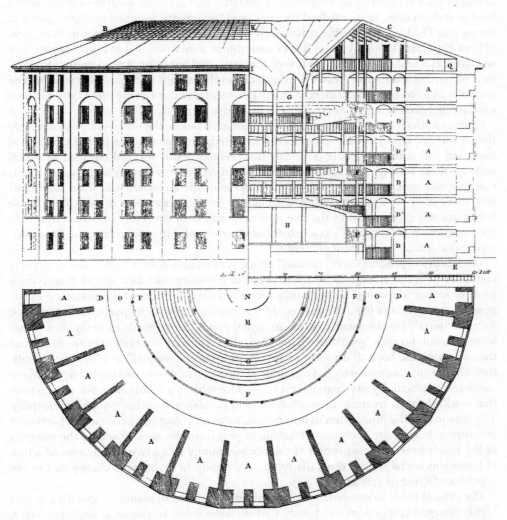

Figure 6.1 Jeremy Bentham's panopticon worked to maintain the effect of constant surveillance whether the central watchtower was occupied or not. Source: Jeremy Bentham, https://en.wikipedia. org/wiki/Panopticon#/media/File:Panopticon.jpg. CC0-1.0 public domain https://creativecommons. org/publicdomain/zero/1.0/

words, what Foucault termed "technologies of the self," modes of conscious self-construction devised in response to naturalized systems of social power. Central to this process of self-construction was an awareness of the physical body, whose control and management is always the ultimate end of power.

The History of Sexuality

The need for a disciplined labor force in an industrial economy, combined with the unstable conditions of life in industrial society—crowded slums, the decline of traditional institutional checks on individual behavior, along with new opportunities for leisure—led to a heightened focus on the body as a critical site of social regulation and discipline. Sexuality thus became a preoccupation in the latter half of the nineteenth century, with a host of moral codes, laws, medical theories, and treatments designed to investigate and manage it. The idea that the Victorians were obsessed with sex is, of course, nothing new. Where Foucault's theory departs from conventional assumptions is in his insistence that sexuality, as a unified collection of drives, fantasies, and behavior, is not a natural foundation of human identity repressed in the nineteenth century and now liberated; rather, sexuality as a coherent idea emerged in the nineteenth century *at the same time and as a product of* its construction as an object of discourse.

Of course, that does not mean that sex did not exist before the nineteenth century, only that it was not constituted as an object of knowledge in the way in which it came to be then and still is today. People obviously had feelings about sex and engaged in sexual activity; these feelings and acts were subject to discussion and representation in literature, popular media, and pornography and, occasionally, to legislation. What differentiated this earlier view was the indistinguishability from other aspects of daily life of those behaviors and characteristics that we now associate with sex. Only in connection with the production of "sexuality" as a subject of discourse did it come to assume its significance as a critical component of identity.

The historical production of "normal" sexuality as an idea does not precede but actually coincides with the emergence of the concept of *homo*sexuality as a way of classifying a form of sexual "deviance." As with other forms of classification whose historical emergence Foucault traces (e.g., the concept of madness, along with its particularly gendered form, hysteria), homosexuality is not an actual condition or mode of being, but rather what Foucault terms a "regulatory fiction," produced as part of a system of social control that works on the basis of drawing a distinction between "normal" and "deviant" identities. This key distinction, which is reproduced through the discourses mentioned above—medicine (particularly psychiatry) and law—underwrites a whole network of practices that work, through treatment, punishment, and exclusion, to enforce social conformity. The reasons for the production of homosexuality as an object of discourse at a particular juncture in history are complex, stemming in part from the need to secure the integrity of the newly emerging institution of the nuclear family as a place for the reproduction of bourgeois social values; thus, the regulatory fiction of sexuality is closely tied to the regulatory fiction of gender.

The critical point to emphasize here is the entanglement of identity—specifically, that highly charged component of identity that we have come to define as sexuality—with power. Power should be understood here not as a mechanism of repression or oppression, as the theories of Freud or Marx would seem to imply, but rather as a force whose impulse to control and regulate is facilitated by its productive capacity, its ability to bring into being new objects, new knowledges.

It is this productive, generative aspect of power that makes it so ambiguous and volatile. The concept of homosexuality, Foucault suggests, did not just underwrite the production of new systems of social control, "it also made possible the formation of a 'reverse' discourse: homosexuality began to speak on its own behalf, to demand that its legitimacy or 'naturality' be acknowledged, often in the same vocabulary, using the same categories by which it was medically disqualified" (101–102). In other words, while the "invention" of homosexuality serves institutional interests, embodying a new object of knowledge and by extension a new tool of social regulation, it also opens new possibilities for modes of identity formation and associated pleasures.

Summary of the Key Theories of Identity

Foucault's insights into the operation of power—that it is all-encompassing, circulating throughout the social body rather than remaining in the possession of particular groups, and that it works not by restriction but by the production of new meanings, new identities, new objects of knowledge—build on the insights of Freud and Marx to tell us some key things about identity: (i) it arises not from within individuals or groups, but from the complex social structures—and, in particular, the relations of power—in which those individuals and groups are situated; (ii) it is historically specific, such that some aspects of identity—individualism, for example, or sexualities—emerge as particularly significant in the context of particular social or economic arrangements; and (iii) it is both imaginary and real: imaginary in the sense that its apparently essential qualities are ideologically or discursively constructed, and real in the sense that those constructions have material consequences in the form of laws and policies, beliefs and actions.

Ideologies of individualism are concretized in laws relating to private property, freedom of expression, and human rights, while discourses of sexuality are implicated in regulations and practices that seek to police or treat so-called deviant forms of sexual behavior (regulations and practices that sometimes conflict with the laws designed to uphold the rights of the individual). The embodiment of the concept of identity in legal, educational, and medical institutions firmly entrenches it as a fundamental principle in Western society. It is not merely those institutional imperatives that make identity so compelling to us as individuals; rather, it is also the way in which our own needs and desires are interpellated, or addressed, by those institutions that leads us to internalize a sense of identity as something we simply cannot do without.

Hegemonic Masculinity, Postfeminism, and the Third-Wave

The whole concept of identity is anchored to a mythic masculine norm. However, the perceived solidity and stability of this ideal do not straightforwardly extend to real experiences of men—even white men. Particularly in the last decades of the twentieth century, economic changes associated with globalization issued a new challenge to conventional ideas of masculinity in North America. The movement of industry offshore (and with it many working-class jobs) has contributed to what is often called the "feminization" of labor—a phrase that refers not just to the influx of women into the global workplace, but also to a shift in the kinds of work available, from manufacturing to service jobs in developed countries, and from agriculture to manufacturing and service in developing countries (Kanji and Menon-Sen). In developed countries in particular, the move from traditionally male industrial labor to softer, so-called women's jobs has been accompanied by a loss of wages and job security (service-sector jobs are far less likely to be unionized), thus threatening the sense of autonomy that undergirds myths of masculinity. While her study has been faulted for unconsciously reinscribing myths of natural white middle-class male authority (see Walzer), Susan Faludi's *Stiffed* offers a lucid account of the new sense of precariousness experienced by American men in the late twentieth century as a result of lost productive capability. In addition to the real erosion of workers' rights accompanying the decline of the manufacturing industry, Faludi documents the identity crisis men suffer as they move away from the sphere of production toward what has traditionally been regarded as the girlie terrain of consumption (put simplistically, shopping).

Faludi's thesis finds many echoes in popular culture since the late 1990s, perhaps most famously in the film *Fight Club.* The iconic scene of the narrator sitting on the toilet, poring over an IKEA catalogue with guilty excitement, expresses what is supposedly every man's secret fear: becoming "a slave to the IKEA nesting instinct." What seems at first to be an elegantly simple solution to this problem—a club in which members heal their wounded masculinity by bare-knuckle fighting—doesn't ultimately offer immunity from the curse of being owned by things, as the club becomes a franchise and then a kind of brand; like the idea of traditional masculinity itself. Culture critic Latham Hunter, however, makes a strong case for seeing in *Fight Club*, and a host of similarly themed 1990s films (*Very Bad Things, Office Space, Falling Down, The Big Kahuna, American Beauty*), a reassertion of the conventional power structures that the fight club so crudely symbolizes. She suggests that, as they mourn the suffocation of the masculine soul within the smooth, bland space of the office cubicle, these films endorse, perhaps even more insistently than 1980s *Rambo*-style action films did, a hegemonic model of masculinity characterized by "amorality and aggression" (Hunter 72).

This model is "hegemonic," critic Richard Connell explains, in the sense that it confers positive value on one exclusive idea of maleness, and because its reinforcement of certain characteristics ("force" and "competence" in particular) "stabilizes a structure of dominance and oppression in the gender order as a whole" (Connell 94; see Figure 6.2). Like other hegemonic ideals (we discuss hegemony in detail in Chapter 2), the persistence of myths of masculinity is not assured, but must always be shored up against resistant myths and realities. Popular men's magazines, for example, convey a mix of macho back-slapping "You go, boy!" confidence and anxiety about the emasculating effects of everyday life. One issue of *Men's Health* contains an article entitled "Yes, You Were Born to Run" that compares recreational runners with African hunters in the Kalahari (Conniff). In the same issue, a quasi-medical report explaining the physiological hazards of sedentary life (i.e., sitting around too much) tries to restore some virility to the desk jockey with an account of the cool things readers likely do while sitting: "watching *24*, tracking your NCAA pool results, or doing pretty much anything on, say, a Bowflex" (Scott).

Other forms of popular culture lay bare the crazy incongruity of traditional ideas about "real" men and the circumstances of contemporary men's lives. The television series *The Office*, for example, satirizes conventional ideas of masculine power through characters such as Dwight Schrute, whose fantasies of empowerment contrast sharply with the smallness and drudgery of his life as assistant regional manager in a paper company.

The implausibility of Dwight's performance of super-potency offers a very crude example of the process whereby the strength of conventional gender identities is undone by their anxious and exaggerated reinforcement. The more extreme the enactment, the less solid the original idea appears. Of course, one risk of parody is that the standard that one is playing with or trying to ironically undercut is actually reinforced through its repetition. The over-the-top bro culture in films like *Superbad, Knocked Up, The Wedding*

Figure 6.2 Gender codes are highly visible in electoral politics. During the 2008 US Democratic primary, candidate Barack Obama was mocked for bowling "like a girl," while his rival, Hillary Clinton, downed whiskey shots in a bar and visited the Indianapolis Motor Speedway. As Hillary Clinton's defeat to Donald Trump in 2016 further confirmed, looking like "one of the boys" is a requisite for political success in North America. Source: © Alex Wong/Getty Images

Crashers, and the *Hangover* and *Anchorman* franchises is an example of the ambiguity of satire. In each film, a supporting cast of immature, sexist guys highlights by contrast the slightly more progressive main character. The optimistic explanation for the huge appeal of these movies is that we enjoy rooting for the nice guy and we're laughing *at* rather than *with* his boorish friends. Ironic humor is never that simple, though, and the idea of masculinity represented in these films is complicated by the persona of actors such as Will Ferrell, Seth Rogen, and Jonah Hill, none of whom possesses traditional Hollywood leading-men looks. When damaging gender **stereotypes** are enacted by cartoonish versions of gender extremes (this works most clearly in actual cartoons; think Gaston in Disney's *Beauty and the Beast*), it is easy to dismiss them; however, the fat and/or boyish bodies of many of the actors in the current crop of comedies can make their offensive behavior seem goofy and endearing. As critic Scott Stoneman puts it, "How do you make masculinity seem innocuous? Make it fat. Nonetheless, as innocuous as the characters Jonah

Hill and Seth Rogen play seem, the things they say are straightforwardly misogynist" (personal communication). The realism of these films (unlike *The Office*, which is clearly satirical) increases the likelihood of our sympathetic identification with the characters and unquestioning acceptance of the conventions they embody.

Postfeminism

Hegemonic masculinity, in its tough or fat, funny versions, thrives in more or less comfortable coexistence with **postfeminism**. Whether embraced by name or, more often, implicitly supported by a conscious sense of simply being *not* a feminist, the term "postfeminism" implicitly endorses a rejection of the model of feminism, often described as "second-wave," that burgeoned during the 1970s and 1980s. In opposing the second-wave objective of dismantling the structures of patriarchy (such as the sexual objectification of women and their exclusion from or suppression within powerful institutions), *post*feminism expresses some combination of two assumptions: (i) feminism has achieved everything it set out to do (that is, patriarchy no longer exists); and (ii) feminism is an angry, strident political movement that is divisive (anti-men) and anti-pleasure (suspicious of heterosexual sex).

Rosalind Gill defines postfemininism as "a distinctive *sensibility*" whose elements include a return to traditional ideas about natural sexual difference, a celebration of femininity as a bodily ideal, a focus on "individualism, choice and empowerment," and "the dominance of a makeover paradigm" ("Postfeminist" 149). Postfeminism is visible everywhere in popular culture, from magazines like *Glamour* and *Seventeen* to books and shows such as *Pretty Little Liars* and *Gossip Girl*, which foreground fashion and (hetero)sexual attractiveness as key to successful female identity. What makes this emphasis post- or anti-feminist is not so much the concentration on pleasure, particularly sexual pleasure—this is also a focus of contemporary, "third-wave" feminists (who criticize second-wavers for ignoring or dismissing it). Rather, the dominant articulation of "girl power" counters feminism in its biological essentialism (the idea that the genitals one is born with determine one's desires, interests, capacities, sexual orientation, etc.) and emphasis on choice (the idea that individuals have freedom to make their own decisions about dress and social and sexual behavior). What joins these assumptions, covering over their essential contradictions, is a rejection of feminism's assertion that who we are is shaped by the culture we live in and the structures of power that guide us—sometimes enticingly, sometimes by more coercive means—to make particular choices and assume particular identities.

Gill notes a number of elements of postfeminist media culture that undermine the central principle of choice. First, the range of desiring subjects and desirable objects is extremely narrow: "Only women who desire sex with men—except when lesbian women 'perform' for men—but, equally crucially, only young, slim and beautiful women" are celebrated for their sexual autonomy (Gill "From"). Second, Gill notes the many anxieties that form invisible accompaniments to celebrations of female empowerment that are focused on sexuality, including fears of unattractiveness (testified to by YouTube videos with the plaintive plea to strangers to answer the critical question "Am I pretty?") and the loss of attractiveness (e.g., through aging), which is tied to a loss of control over one's appearance, because the equation of sexiness with self-actualization rests on a belief in not just the possibility but the necessity of self-maintenance through the right combination of diet, exercise, fashion, and beauty regimes. Gill challenges the postfeminist assumption of empowerment (women used to dress up for men; now they do it only for themselves) by pointing out, first, that this is an oversimplification of history as well as the present (women were never totally under the sway of men, just as they aren't now completely free of patriarchy), but second, and in a way that resonates with Foucault's theory of power, that women have not overthrown but rather internalized the disciplinary regime that dictates particular compulsory ways of looking and acting. In other words, "What this shift entails is a move *from an external male judging gaze to a self-policing narcissistic gaze*" (Gill "From," emphasis in original).

Questions about the meaning, possibilities, and limitations of women's sexual choice came to the fore in debates about SlutWalk, a series of events that began in Toronto in 2011 in response to a police officer's association of rape with a woman's provocative dress, and has since spread to cities around the world. While fully endorsing the SlutWalk's defiance of the "blame the victim" attitude conveyed in the officer's comment, many feminists expressed skepticism about the potential for empowerment in the word "slut," suggesting that the event "simply repackages sexist imagery in 'empowering' wrapping paper" (M. Murphy). Megan Murphy goes on to note drily, "We already have a word that describes women who support sex, equality, and the end of patriarchal oppression." That word, of course, is not "slut" but "feminist." And some critics have suggested that, contrary to feminist aims, "The view of achieved gender equality promoted by [events like SlutWalk] is idealistic at best, and harmful and silencing at its worst" (Smith).

Being and Doing

Since the 1970s, most children have learned about the conventionally accepted difference between sex and gender by the time they reach middle school: sex refers to biological characteristics (male/female), while gender refers to cultural constructions (masculinity/femininity). The contradictions of postfeminism aside, most of us also learn at an early age that gender stereotypes are inaccurate and limiting: lots of girls are good at math; not all boys like sports. Sex might be given, in other words, but gender is fluid. Of course, this challenge to convention can go only so far: it is generally assumed that, in spite of the existence of a few exceptions, the categories of sex are restricted to two, male and female.

The solidity of this classification system starts to break down as soon as we acknowledge the bodies for which it doesn't work (see Figure 6.3). Those who have both male and female sex characteristics (intersex) or whose gender identity doesn't correspond to the sex characteristics they were born with (including but not limited to: trans*gender, bigender, agender, nonbinary, demigender, two-spirited or *hijra*) obviously expose the limits of the definitions of "man" and "woman," as do, in a less clear-cut way, processes of hormonal and physiological change over the course of an individual's lifetime. The designation of testosterone and estrogen as male and female, respectively, does not account for the fact that both hormones are released by men *and* women, and their presence—along with other secondary sex characteristics, such as the size and function of reproductive organs, facial hair, voice, and physique—alters with age and in response to environmental factors such as nutrition and stress (Shilling).

Giving conceptual shape to these complexities, gender theory, which came to prominence with the work of feminist theorist Judith Butler in the 1980s, emphasizes the mythological characteristics of sex *and* gender, as well as the grounding of the strict classificatory system in a heterosexist power structure. The cluster of institutions that define patriarchy—family, property rights, and laws of inheritance—all express the myth of a "natural," hierarchical division of labor (productive and reproductive) founded on the differential roles and identities of men and women.

Figure 6.3 When the Toronto District School Board mandated curriculum elements challenging homophobia and heterosexism, the conservative Institute for Canadian Values launched a campaign at stopcorruptingchildren.com. When it ran an ad in the *National Post*, portraying a wide-eyed child with the words "Please! Don't confuse me. I'm a girl. Don't teach me to question if I'm a boy, transsexual, transgendered, intersexed, or two-spirited," trans activist Chase Joynt, in collaboration with media artist Alexis Mitchell, parodied it with a poster captioned "Please! Don't insult me. I'm Chase. Teach me to question everything!" Source: Photo courtesy of Chase Joynt and Alexis Mitchell

We can get a sense of the way our culture bundles all these things together when we think about the way the word "sex" works in our language to signify both an activity and an identity. The ambiguity of meaning is arguably not accidental, but rather highlights assumptions about "normal" links between identity and desire (basically, who should do what with whom) and, in a more general sense, the way culture tends to reduce an expansive concept of what bodies can *do* to a much more reductive definition of what they *are*, based simply on the presence of particular physical characteristics. It is the *mythological* attachment of identity to those organs that Butler refers to when she argues that "'sex' is as culturally constructed as gender; indeed, perhaps it was always already gender, with the consequence that the distinction between sex and gender turns out to be no distinction at all" (*Gender Trouble* 7).

The implication of Butler's argument—that sex is not biology but culture—is not that bodies and their differences are immaterial, that sex = gender and both are purely imaginary; rather, what Butler points out is that "the body" as a physical thing is inseparable from ideas about it, from values and norms that have congealed around the concepts of sex and gender. She explains: "I do not deny certain kinds of biological differences. But I always ask under what conditions, under what discursive and institutional conditions, do certain biological differences…become the salient characteristics of sex," noting further that, "When people ask the question 'Aren't *these* [i.e., the capacity for pregnancy] biological differences?' they're not really asking a question about the materiality of the body. They're actually asking whether or not the social institution of reproduction is the most salient one for thinking about gender" ("Extracts"). Of course, these connections and categorizations are not just abstract ideas that scholars in feminist, gender, and **queer theory** *think* about; they get embodied in the way we see ourselves and live our lives. Butler and others employ the concept of **performativity** to describe how social scripts about sex and gender get enacted. The word "performativity" is closely connected to "performance," and the idea of artifice that we associate with the theater is an important element of it. A key difference between performance and performativity, however, is that "performance" conveys the idea of an actor playing a role. With performativity, however, there is no "real" identity prior to its scripted enactment. Performativity is "that aspect of discourse that has the capacity to produce what it names" (Butler "Extracts"); the identities that are thereby enacted are not grounded in a stable or absolute truth, but rather are made to seem "natural" (which is to say, to accord with our cultural expectations) through repeated performance. It is through the dynamic of repetition that identities are confirmed, but also—crucially—destabilized, in the sense that no performance can perfectly and once and for all confirm the truth of the ideal—the myth it is attempting to interpret.

For some people, some of the time, gender identity may be something we inhabit comfortably so that we are hardly aware of it; the idea that we are engaged in interpretation or performance seems bizarre. But when our lived experience resonates awkwardly with cultural norms (this happens to most people at some points in their lives; if one is gay, transgender, or nonwhite, this experience may be more continuous), the performative nature of identity is more visible and, Butler suggests, potentially open to "resignification" or subversion.

As critics of Butler have suggested, however, it is easy to exaggerate the subversive power of performativity. In a cultural context in which the manipulation of conventional gender *style*—in the form of clothes, accessories, hair, and so on—has become an element of high fashion, the political implications of gender role playing can't be assumed in advance. This is particularly true given that the capacity to play around with sex and gender depends a lot on one's social position, including one's race, culture, and class.

The stakes of "passing"—conforming convincingly to accepted ideals of beauty, behavior, and belief—are not the same for everyone.

The 2000 film *Boys Don't Cry* shows the limits of theories of the liberating potential of performativity. The film adapts the real-life story of Brandon Teena, a transgender man. While Brandon's attempts to present as a cis man, portrayed in the film by cis actress Hilary Swank, were by all accounts convincing—he managed to pass as male with a number of girlfriends—the discovery of his biological gender resulted in his rape and murder. Violent instances of abuse such as this are frequent in the LGBTQ+ community and, as well as high suicide rates associated with bullying of gay and trans youth, highlight that, while gender identity may be performative, the social stage on which we perform these identities still forcefully restricts opportunities for improvisation.

Further constraining the flexibility of self-expression is the normative culture of whiteness that pervades not only conventional ideas of sex and gender, but also prevailing sex and gender theory. The concept of **intersectionality**, a term coined by law professor Kimberlé Crenshaw in 1989, offers a vital way to recognize the way in which different—and often unacknowledged—social categories and systems of oppression and power interact to shape identity and agency.

LGBTQ+

Having acknowledged the narrow and constraining power of social scripts around sex and gender, an obvious question might be: Why do we continue to follow them? Particularly for those who want to overcome historical structures of oppression, instead of organizing around such cumbersome labels as LGBTQ+ (lesbian/gay/bisexual/trans*/queer) or LGBPTTQQIIAA+ (lesbian/gay/bisexual/pansexual/transgender/transsexual/queer/questioning/intersex/intergender/asexual/ally), wouldn't it be better to dispense with labels altogether? Foucault's discussion of discourses of sexuality—and discourse more generally—highlights an important reason for the stickiness of labels: they operate not only to restrict, but also to produce meaning and pleasure. In practical terms, the performance of recognizable categories of gender identity *works* socially to organize knowledge, pleasure, desire, acceptance, and inclusion/exclusion. In more political terms, identity labels name sites of struggle around which activists can organize, reclaiming historical terms of condemnation into rallying calls for pride.

Alliances between activists working to end discrimination on the grounds of gender and sexual orientation are not straightforward or obvious, but must be constantly worked out and negotiated. Divisions persist (between, for example, trans-exclusionary feminists who insist on the clarity of the fault line between male and female as a marker of specific distributions of power and trans activists who argue that adhering to the line—even as a strategic fiction—perpetuates forms of exclusion) and agendas do not necessarily coincide.

"Queer" is a word that some activists and scholars embrace to define not just LGBTQ+ orientations, but also a willful rejection of the hegemony of sex/gender normativity. Originally used as a term of denigration (and still seen by many as derogatory), "queer" now signifies for many LGBTQ+ people a liberatory project whose strength lies in its exploitation of the gaps in conventional categories of identity and expression. Though still associated primarily with "same-sexual-object choice," the deliberate, personal, and political reclaiming of the term "queer" can also signal "the open mesh of possibilities, gaps, overlaps, dissonances and resonances, lapses and excesses of meaning when the constituent elements of anyone's gender, of anyone's sexuality aren't made (or can't be made) to signify monolithically" (Sedgwick 8). Queer theory, notes gender theorist Eve Kosofsky Sedgwick, encompasses possibilities "that can't be subsumed under gender and sexuality at all" (9), including race, ethnicity, and postcoloniality.

It Gets Better? Possibly...

Anguished debates over terms and principles might seem at odds with the dominant trend in Western culture, where, barring a few dissenting conservative voices, gender and sexual freedoms appear to be slowly but steadily expanding. Same-sex marriage is legal in a dozen countries and several US states; the "coming out" stories of celebrities are regarded not as scandalous but progressive, if they're regarded at all (Peters); and popular mainstream television series (*Will and Grace, Modern Family, Glee,* and *Orange Is The New Black*) feature gay LGBTQ+ characters. It's not all good yet—especially relating to transgender rights, since television still lacks much trans representation—but it is getting better; this is the dominant media message. However, it is a message that invites critical scrutiny.

In her cleverly titled article "Raise Your Glass If U R A Firework Who Was Born This Way," Lauren Elmore casts a skeptical eye on the burgeoning of "gay anthems" by singers such as Ke$ha, Katy Perry, Pink, and Lady Gaga in the wake of Dan Savage's *It Gets Better* project—an archive of YouTube videos that has attracted millions of viewers and is intended to assure gay youth that the bullying, loneliness, and anxiety they might be experiencing won't last forever, that life will get better. Drawing on the work of queer theorist Jasbir Puar, Elmore critiques the project's aura of liberal privilege and ignorance regarding intersectionality (enhanced by the participation of prominent straight white role models such as Hillary Clinton), which offers a vision of "upward mobility that echoes the now discredited 'pull yourself up by the bootstraps' immigrant motto" (Puar, qtd. in Elmore). Elmore suggests:

> The recent spate of gay anthems, while danceable and memorable, likewise reinforce a one-size-fits-all narrative of overcoming adversity—a fact that seems even more problematic when that reinforcement comes from privileged, heteronormative feminine figures. Secure in their glamorous celebrity, these women can sympathize with queer fans, but it's unclear whether they can empathize with them—their you-go-queers! lyrics and deliberately inclusive video imagery encourage values of self-respect that may come easily only to them and to those who share their privileges.

Touting the values of Oprah-esque individual empowerment, and the promise of assimilation into straight society via a conventional model of economic and social success, these anthems risk reinforcing, rather than challenging, forces of exclusion:

> We might gleefully repeat 'we are all born superstars,' or 'it gets better,' but we don't always think of the ideologies of self, society, and cultural currency that underlie those statements. Listeners, queer as well as straight, may unconsciously take cues from these popular messages and eventually understand them as the dominant vocabulary for understanding queerness—which, in turn, reifies a message of conformity and discourages dissent among the community for whom these messages are ostensibly meant. (Elmore)

This may seem counter-intuitive: aren't these singers actually telling listeners that it's okay *not* to conform, that in fact empowerment lies in being true to oneself and celebrating one's difference from the mainstream? The problem is that the model of difference that is being affirmed accords neatly with conventional neoliberal ideology, a system of values that is increasingly tightly bound to consumerism and capitalism more generally. As noted in Chapter 5, the upshots of living in this system include both growing material inequalities and an increasing, anxiety-inducing pressure to construct a persona that is distinctive (in Bourdieu's sense) yet likably ordinary (or, as Pink might say, being "wrong in all the right ways").

Queer theorist Lisa Duggan calls this straightening out or mainstreaming of sexual minorities "homonormativity." Reacting against not only conservative homophobia but also those forms of gay activism that call for broad social change, this form of politics "does not contest dominant heteronormative assumptions and institutions but upholds and sustains them" (179), taking the concept of equality out of the public, political arena and redefining it in terms of the narrow aim of gaining "access to the institutions of domestic privacy, the 'free' market and patriotism" (179). The legalization of gay marriage and the right to join the military are among the principal goals of a movement that claims to represent "a phantom mainstream public of 'conventional' gays who represent the responsible center" (179).

Lady Gaga and Dan Savage would almost certainly reject the label "conventional," and both have a more expansive view of gay rights than that outlined above. There remains a danger, however, that the chorus of general agreement that meets their messages—that bullying is wrong and that it is okay to be gay, that it gets better—will drown out the voices of those whose experiences don't conform to the model of gay upward mobility being celebrated, and will simplify the problem of social pressure, which is not always clearly personified in the figure of a homophobic thug throwing a gay kid in the dumpster. As one blogger notes:

> Basically [the It Gets Better project] suggests support for queer youth has to stay "on message" and "upbeat." Dissent and diversity does not seem to be encouraged. This is borne out by the vast numbers of videos being uploaded by white, university-educated gay men, in comparison to those from women, transgender people, and working class people, and people from diverse ethnic backgrounds. (QuietRiotGirl)

The issue is not simply the need to expand the "it gets better" narrative to include spokespeople for these groups, but rather the inseparability of the narrative itself from a myth of self-empowerment and overcoming adversity through optimism that does not acknowledge the structures of racial, economic, and cultural privilege that restrict access to this kind of mobility. "The message," as another blogger puts it, is, quite simply "wrong. Sometimes it gets better—but a lot of times it doesn't get any better. Emphasizing that things will improve on graduation is misleading both to young folks struggling and also to people with privilege who are looking on (or looking away)" (Femmephane). Moreover, "Telling people that they have to wait for their life to get amazing—to tough it out so that they can be around when life gets amazing—is a violent reassignment of guilt…[which] quietly but forcefully suggests that if you don't survive, if you don't make it, it's your own fault. It blames the queer for not being strong enough to get to the rosy privileged fantasy" (Femmephane).

Elmore notes that, for all their problems, gay anthems "mark a time and place in LGBTQ history that is pivotal for many lives. Listeners and musicians alike, LGBTQ+ and straight, can celebrate and change with these songs. But the key is combining them with real advocacy to make sure the messages don't fade out with the mix." Puar adds, "It is imperative that this conversation is connected to broader questions of intersectional social justice in terms of race, class and gender. Otherwise, projects like Savage's risk producing such narrow versions of what it means to be gay, and what it means to be bullied, that for those who cannot identify with it, but are nevertheless still targeted for 'being different,' It Gets Better might actually contribute to Making Things Worse."

Identity and Affect

One of the critiques of the It Gets Better project noted above was the pressure "to stay 'on message' and 'upbeat'" (QuietRiotGirl). Though staying positive can be seen in one sense as just smart strategy whatever project one is engaged in, it is worth pausing for a moment to consider how the imperative to be "upbeat" pervades popular culture more generally. In fact, while it may be the case that as the pressure to conform to rigid gender norms and heterosexual orientation has lessened somewhat, the obligation to assume a particular attitude or emotional state, characterized by confidence, cheerfulness, and a flexible, optimistic orientation toward the future, has intensified. The Oprah-authorized imperative "Live your best life" finds support in a raft of prescriptions for how to do just that: appreciate the little things (*The Book of Awesome*); think positively and good things will come to you (*The Secret*); express yourself by belting out a song (*Glee*); press the Like button on Facebook whenever you can…you get the message.

While it might seem perverse to criticize positivity—a value that finds confirmation in a burgeoning academic field of "happiness studies"—some scholars have noted a less rosy side to the optimism boom. The more happiness becomes a cultural—even a moral—imperative, as Sara Ahmed notes, the more it shores up a consensus of a happy "normal" majority, set against a cohort of angry or sad dissenters, who may include not only those who are depressed or grieving, but also those who are excluded from the mainstream by virtue of gender, race, religion, ability, and so on, as well as those who do not desire socially sanctioned "happy objects" (a partner of the opposite sex, marriage, the commodities of conventional success, etc.). The charge of unhealthy negativity can also be brought against anyone critical of the arrangement of power in capitalist modernity. In the context of the happiness imperative, it becomes easy to recast all kinds of political activism in terms of antisocial stereotypes: the "feminist killjoy" (Ahmed 50), the "angry black woman" (67), the "violent activist" (169).

Opposition or critique of any kind is particularly prohibitive in a neoliberal work environment, in which the ideology of entrepreneurial self-advancement combines with an emphasis on networking to stress positive sociality. In such a climate, as Angela McRobbie notes, likability is critical, and it is "not cool" to be negative or "'difficult'" ("Clubs" 523). Against the tides of "cruel optimism," which is how Lauren Berlant describes the condition in which "something you desire is actually an obstacle to your flourishing" (such as a longing for the "good life" amid conditions of growing precariousness; 1), no one is suggesting that it is better to be sad. Rather, recent scholars of **affect**—which refers to mood, emotion, feeling; that is, those states of engagement that exist beneath, around, or to the side of consciousness—encourage an acceptance of ambivalence and what Ahmed calls "queer pessimism," which is not just negativity but "pessimism *about* a certain kind of optimism, as a refusal to be optimistic about 'the right things' in the right kind of way" (162). Escaping the happiness trap, she suggests, unleashes the possibility of other emotions, including "strange and perverse mixtures of hope and despair, optimism and pessimism within forms of politics that take as a starting point a critique of the world as it is, and a belief that the world can be different" (163).

Different Bodies, Different Selves?

As the discussion above suggests, identity is an expression of a turbulent mix of culture and materiality that congeals in the form of the body. This section delves further into the subject of the cultural production of the body, with a particular focus on the relationship between embodiment and agency, which describes our power to act independently in the world, to determine our own meanings, our own actions, our own pleasures.

Embodied Selves

Descartes's famous formula "I think therefore I am" informs the modern notion of identity as defined by the preeminence of mind (consciousness) over matter (the body). Descartes's elevation of the rational mind as the faculty that gives meaning to human life, granting it supremacy over other, nonrational forms of life, informs a dualist philosophy characterized by a series of closely overlapping oppositions—spirit versus matter, mind versus body, reason versus passion, nature versus culture—that map out relations of being and, more significantly, relations of power. Besides laying the groundwork for laws about the protection of private property, this framework has underwritten such dubious social practices as slavery and the subjugation of women on the grounds of a division of living beings into knowing subjects—"man"—and knowable (and possessable) objects.

Postmodernist thought has posed significant challenges to the dualisms that inform the modern concept of identity—and indeed much of modern Western philosophy. In particular, postmodernism has blurred the scientific and/or philosophical certainty of distinctions between subjects and objects, consciousness and matter, that allow us to know the world while remaining abstracted from and superior to it. The destabilization of philosophical dualisms associated with postmodernist thought is reflected by the more general breakdown of structure and hierarchy associated with contemporary social life. As old hierarchies dissolve—and with them any clear sense of identity based on birth, breeding, or old notions of class—the body becomes an increasingly important site for the negotiation of social meaning. In some ways, the new attention focused on the body reflects a move away from seeing bodies as simply containers for identity and toward recognition of the ways in which the self is embodied—at once natural and cultural, physical and psychological.

The Human Body: Natural or Cultural?

Once we start to explore the entanglement of nature and culture in relation to the body, it becomes harder and harder to determine where one ends and the other begins. The body may be a material phenomenon, but the way we experience it is determined by culture. Concepts of health and disease are one case in point. Anthropologist Emily Martin has investigated the role of myth and metaphor in the way science understands the human body—for example, by looking at it as a kind of machine or by employing metaphors of war to describe the operation of the immune system in maintaining health. Thus, we "fight" disease; our white blood cells "seek out and destroy" pathogens. The metaphorical construction of the body has especially interesting social implications in relation to the representation of reproductive processes. Think, for example, of what it might mean for conventional gender mythology if we were to replace the familiar, almost cartoonish image of eager sperm competing to *penetrate* the docile, receptive egg—an image comically rendered in Woody Allen's 1972 movie *Everything You Always Wanted to Know about Sex (But Were Afraid to Ask)*—with what some scientists suggest is a more accurate image of a tiny wiggling sperm being *enveloped* by the much larger egg (Martin). (See Figure 6.4.)

One of the major changes in contemporary society lies in the character of the global economy. Rather than being based on the production of new things, economic transactions increasingly involve nonmaterial commodities: stocks, information, the arts, and services (healthcare, fast food, tourism). The economy, then, is increasingly fueled by culture, and culture, by extension, has become increasingly defined by economics. It is this development that Fredric Jameson refers to in his definition of postmodernism as "the cultural logic of late capitalism."

The economic circumstances that Jameson highlights, along with recent historical developments such as decolonization, civil rights, and feminism, have all contributed to the intellectual and cultural changes now described under the heading of postmodernism. The concept is often used to describe a broad shift in approaches to truth and knowledge, away from the rationality and truth seeking that emerged out of the Enlightenment. Since the late 1950s, the existence of such truths or laws has been challenged. Postmodernism views the search for truth as a project whose real aim is achieving social power and control, and is suspicious of any "grand narratives" or theories that seek to provide the single explanation for how human beings act (such as Freudian psychoanalysis) or how societies function (Marxism, for example).

For the French critic Jean Baudrillard, postmodernism is characterized by the culture of the "simulacrum" (1), a copy without an original, or a sign without a referent, defining a world in which representation is quite simply reality. Many people find this disturbing, signaling the "emptying out" of history, the disappearance of nature, and the impossibility of defining a platform of belief from which to launch individual projects or political movement. For others, the erosion of traditional concepts of identity translates into

Figure 6.4 Traditional images of conception owe less to scientific accuracy than to metaphorical representations of gender stereotypes.
Source: © timquo/Shutterstock

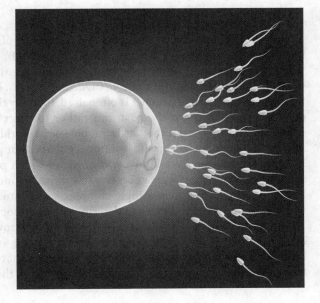

exciting possibilities for the construction of new, multiply defined selves. In general, the way we respond to the breakdown of the old structures of meaning depends on whether our particular identities, defined by the traditional markers of class, gender, race, sexuality, and so on, are empowered or excluded by those structures.

Commenting on the nostalgia for depth and wholeness displayed by many cultural critics, McRobbie says, "The obvious question to ask is which social subjects have had the privilege of being whole, or 'healthy,' and thus fully inscribed in history and in culture?... To lament the decline of full wholesome subjectivity is literally to cast aspersions on unwholesome, un(in)formed, partial and hybridic identities" (*Postmodernism* 4). McRobbie focuses on women, youth, and racial minorities, but the term "hybridic" could also encompass LGBTQ+, migrant, and disabled identities.

Learned "Body Techniques"

Culture not only influences how we understand bodies, it also becomes inscribed on bodies themselves. As sociologist and anthropologist Marcel Mauss (1872–1950) noted, the way in which we conduct such basic activities as sleeping, eating, sitting, walking, having sex, and giving birth should be understood not as natural, but as a series of "body techniques" that are *learned* in particular social contexts and are hence culturally and historically specific. One of the most striking examples that Mauss provides is French women's characteristic style (or technique) of walking, which changed in the 1930s with the arrival of American cinema: the movies carried with them a whole repertoire of fashion comprising ways not just of dressing but also of comportment, of holding and carrying the body.

While French women's imitation of styles of movement associated with Hollywood film might be prompted by an association of the United States with images of energy and freedom, most body techniques serve a much more utilitarian function in relation to the demands of a smoothly running society. In most societies, this means that considerable effort is expended in what Mauss calls "education in composure...a mechanism inhibiting disorderly movements" (474). Thus we learn not only how to move, but also how and when to inhibit movement, techniques that differ significantly by age and gender.

The Self-Controlled Body

The idea that culture exerts a shaping and restraining effect on the body is carried further in the work of sociologist Norbert Elias (1897–1990), who documented the process by which centuries of Western civilization produced the modern, individualized, self-controlled body. In Volume 1 of *The Civilizing Process*, Elias uses the concept of "civilization" not in the sense in which it is often used, to imply the progressive movement beyond the "backward" ways of the past, but rather to describe a series of specific historical changes in Europe, from the hardscrabble social world of the Middle Ages to the court society of the Renaissance, whose influence shapes our present-day culture. In particular, Elias focuses on the shift from a way of life in which physical strength, aggression, and indulgence of appetites were necessary to survival to one in which "polite society" defined by the court dictated increasingly complex social rituals, the successful observance of which played a significant role in determining one's social status.

One of the critical aspects of this shift is a move toward interdependence, such that existence had to be negotiated with an increasing awareness of the effects of one's behavior on others. Thus the civilized body is one that is subject to an expanding set of taboos and social codes, demarcating it sharply from the physical environment and from other bodies. Practices that were once widely tolerated, such as defecating in public or sharing beds with strangers, were subjected to increasingly strict social sanction as a new model of appropriate bodily conduct emerged. This new model was characterized by a broad repertoire of gestures—manners—that signified an observance of social relations, including an overall tendency toward self-restraint and a clear sense of separation between private and public.

Physical Capital and Social Status

Over time, learned behaviors can produce physical effects. Often conforming to conventions that are linked to particular identity categories—gender, for example—these effects can work to embody the stereotype on which the behavior was initially based. For example, in an essay entitled "Throwing Like a Girl," Iris Marion Young identifies a tendency in Western industrial societies for girls to move in ways that are more limited and constrained than the ways in which boys move. In effect, responding to a learned physical orientation that Young calls "inhibited intentionality" (145), girls and women are not inclined to use their bodies' full potential range of strength and motion. Thus, what is often regarded as women's "natural" lack of physical strength and coordination is at least partly attributable to the way in which their bodies are socialized to move (or not) in particular ways. These learned behaviors, ingrained into habit, contribute to the transformation of women's bodies into the stereotypically "weak vessels" they were already imagined to be.

Sociologist Pierre Bourdieu sheds light on the way physical comportment expresses social difference by expanding Mauss's concept of **habitus**. A term connoting both living space and habit, habitus describes the way in which particular social environments are internalized by individuals in the form of dispositions toward particular bodily orientations and behaviors. The concept of habitus thus allows us to talk about the way in which social differences are reproduced at the level of the individual body. Class, Bourdieu suggests, plays a determining role in the development of bodies by influencing such factors as social location and taste (learned habits of discrimination influencing choice of lifestyle, discussed in Chapter 5), as well as more physical aspects of habitus. These differences in turn contribute to the production of different kinds and degrees of social value attached to different kinds of bodies. Value corresponds more or less closely to class, with working-class bodies possessing less value than dominant-class bodies—value here is determined principally by the ability to translate what Bourdieu terms *physical capital* into other forms of capital: economic (money), cultural (education), and social (networks of belonging).

Of course, the different kinds of capital do not map perfectly onto one another. Professional sports, for example, have traditionally offered a venue for men from non-privileged circumstances to convert physical capital into economic capital in a fairly direct way. However, as recent research into the effects of cumulative concussion has confirmed, the heavy toll that professional sports—like most forms of physical labor—exact on the body, combined with their relatively restricted access as a career path, diminishes their significance as an exception to the rule that "white-collar" bodies tend to enjoy more privileged access to forms of economic, social, and cultural capital than do "blue-collar" bodies.

Sport is just one venue in which the dream of class mobility is projected. A whole raft of reality television shows, from the *You've Got Talent* and *Idol* franchises to *Extreme Makeover*, *Toddlers and Tiaras*, and *What Not to Wear*, play on the myth that it is possible, by virtue of talent, spirit, and the right clothes, to be catapulted out of a life of obscurity and struggle to instant popularity, wealth, and fame. However, while these shows seem to celebrate the democratic idea that beauty and stardom lurk inside all of us, the victory of the participants—and the pleasure of the audience—rests on the shadow of failure: the bad fashion choices of the "before" segment of the narrative and the losing acts of other contestants, interpreted (and frequently mocked) by the shows' judges. So while it may be the case that the codes that constrain particular bodies to act in certain ways have loosened, the lines between winning/success and losing/failure remain strong, and the stakes may be getting higher. Possibilities for modifying and even transcending the body have thus become a highly charged cultural and political issue.

Altered States

While people at all times and in all places have sought to change their bodies in different ways, advances in science, combined with the unique pressures of a consumer culture highly biased toward the visual, have contributed to a growing trend for body cultivation and modification. "Body modification" describes practices that include "piercing, tattooing, branding, cutting, binding and inserting implants," as well as less invasive practices such as exercise and diet, that seek to alter "the appearance and form of the body" (Featherstone 1). Whether these practices are motivated by aesthetics, pressure to assimilate, or the need to overcome body dysphoria, whether they uphold or challenge prevailing social norms, and whether they aim toward the accentuation, transformation, or transcendence of the body—and few can be so simply classified—they demand examination in relation to the more fundamental questions of how they contribute to the production of individual and social meaning, identity, and power (see Figure 6.5).

Figure 6.5 Once associated with subcultures, tattoos today have significance as a form of creative self-expression that works in tension with their legibility within conventional codes of gender, sex, class, and so on. Source: © ziggysofi/Shutterstock

Enhancing/Producing the Healthy Body

At the beginning of the twenty-first century, Western cultures have increasingly come to see health as a matter of individual control and responsibility. This trend is reflected in such developments as increasingly stringent legislation on food labeling. Laws requiring uniform labeling on all packaged food (and on restaurant menus in some US states), listing information such as fat content and potential health benefits, make the assumption that health and fitness are largely dependent on wise consumer choices. A variety of factors have contributed to this development. The wide availability of information, due in large part to the Internet, has given individuals much more knowledge and confidence about health-related matters than they had a generation ago, leading to a much more proactive stance in managing their own health. At the same time, both fueling and responding to this trend, a massive consumer industry has sprung up around personal healthcare, promoting everything from so-called nutraceuticals (drug-enhanced foods) to fitness clubs.

Less visibly, but perhaps most significantly, the move toward personal responsibility for healthcare occurs in the context of a regulatory framework that Foucault describes as **biopolitical**. The disciplinary modes of power described earlier in this chapter worked to produce compliant bodies through institutions such as the prison, the factory, and the medical clinic. The biopolitical society that emerged in the late nineteenth century employs new forms of information and knowledge, including statistics and biological science, to enhance, or "optimize," life and health at the level of the population as a whole. Biopolitics does not replace earlier disciplinary modes of control, but works in complex conjunction with them to define "a biological body which is understood less in terms of fate and more in terms of the management and pre-emption of risks, even as something that can be potentially improved" (Braun 9). In contemporary neoliberal society, the state assumes a diminishing role in managing the health of the population, instead enlisting citizens in the task of sustaining national health by taking responsibility for their own health and fitness.

Beyond public health campaigns aiming to inspire, encourage, worry, and/or shame people into exercising, lowering their sugar and salt consumption, and vaccinating their children, a more general social climate is focused on self-improvement as a life project. According to Robert Crawford, the prevailing mythology, which he terms "healthism," situates the problem of health and disease at the level of the individual and "elevates health to a super value, a metaphor for all that is good in life" (365). As it functions to medicalize nearly all aspects of life—from eating, sex, and recreation to childbirth and dying—healthism subscribes to the idea that the facilitation of choice (guided by education and liberated by deregulation) will produce optimal outcomes. Its neoliberal emphasis on individuals and economics does not take account of broader structures and institutions that distribute opportunities for agency and decision making unequally. "Healthism," in Crawford's words, "reinforces the privatization of the struggle for generalized well-being" (365). It also brings into play diverse dynamics in which discourses of consumer choice and pleasure are infused with moralistic messages about responsibility, and normative conceptions of bodies and their capacities (see Close-Up 6.1).

The ambiguity of these messages is reflected in practices surrounding diet and fitness, where the general goal of "health" is overlaid with the complex and often contradictory values of physical and sexual attractiveness (generally associated with pleasure) and moral well-being (frequently defined by discipline and self-denial). In these mixed motivations can be detected the ambivalence about the relationship between self and body

Close-Up 6.1 Disability

Questions about "natural" and "normal" bodies assume particular significance with respect to **disability**. Over the past few decades, the concept of ability has come to replace the language of "normal" versus "abnormal." This generally positive move—a shift from categorizing people according to what they *are* (implying degrees of humanness) to what they can or cannot *do*—has not eliminated practices of discrimination. Disability theorists and activists highlight the way in which conventional ways of looking at disability employ discourses of science and medicine to mask aesthetic and societal factors (e.g., neoliberal ideologies of individual success, institutional constraints, and cultural anxieties about vulnerability and mortality) that privilege the economically productive body. Understood in this way, disability is "not so much a property of bodies as a product of cultural rules about what bodies should be and do" (Thomson 6). Without discounting the value of medical interventions, disability activists and theorists work to challenge conventional ideas of disability as lack or inferiority, ideas that reinforce material barriers to disabled people's participation in society. Disability studies echo the concerns of cultural theories of race, gender, and sexuality that challenge the practice of excluding minorities. With respect to disability in particular, the increasing capacity for geneticists to identify (and treat or eliminate) so-called abnormalities in utero highlight what is at stake in definitions of "normal" identity and ability.

discussed above. While the pursuit of exercise as a form of self-improvement might imply a recognition of an integral connection between body and identity, many practices associated with exercise, including dieting (and its more extreme pathological form, eating disorders), are inspired by the idea of the body as an alien thing, separate and requiring discipline from the self.

What Is Natural/Normal?

Many health practices are founded on ideas about a natural physical state, which regimens of diet or exercise seek to enhance. These ideas are troubled by the burgeoning popularity of cosmetic surgery, which clearly aims less to preserve a "natural" state of health than to produce a "cultural" convention of beauty. Crossing the line from medicine to aesthetics, cosmetic surgery sheds unexpected light on the reliance of both discourses on concepts of *normalization*. Celebrated by many people as a technology of self-expression that allows them to convey an outer image that is more in tune with their inner selves, cosmetic surgery is condemned by others as a biotechnological reinforcement of oppressive gender norms (Balsamo).

The operation of such norms is most clearly evident in such forms of cosmetic surgery as liposuction and breast enlargement. While these procedures may be seen—and, more importantly, may actually *work*—to enhance the self-confidence of those who seek them, they do so at the expense of conscripting them more fully into the prescribed roles of a patriarchal social order.

Some forms of body enhancement work more ambiguously. For example, female bodybuilding seems in one sense to challenge conventional gender codes by rejecting a feminine ideal of ultra-thinness. Maximizing instead of minimizing the body—replacing weakness with strength—bodybuilding represents a form of physical feminine empowerment. On the other hand, the maxed-out body is achieved at a cost of punishing discipline and "self"-denial that, at its extreme, actually compromises the goals of health and fitness.

Of course, bodybuilding is about more than health and fitness: like most fitness practices, it is also about display. For women, whose relationships to their bodies have always been mediated by social codes that define them as objects to be looked at (see Mulvey in Chapter 3), display is at best an ambiguous form of empowerment (Grosz 224). At the same time as it accentuates strength, the culture of bodybuilding still draws attention to the female body as the repository of female worth. As this example demonstrates, body modification practices may challenge social norms, but they cannot avoid negotiating them. Most practices, like bodybuilding, take place in complicated conversations with our historically ambivalent conceptions about mind and body—conceptions that are inevitably tied to ideas about gender and power.

The Politics of Body Modification

Body modification practices also raise other issues of power and agency. As with highly gendered forms of body modification, the practice of surgically altering racialized features to conform to more Eurocentric standards of beauty can be understood in terms of its promotion of empowerment and/or subjugation. The practice of blepharoplasty, in which a fold is inserted to give the eyes a more rounded, open appearance, gained notoriety in Canada after the death of one patient from a botched illicit operation. The incident sparked an unusual degree of media commentary on the powerful and damaging effect of myths of white normativity. A more nuanced perspective on the subject is expressed in Korean Canadian Ann Shin's documentary "Western Eyes," which mixes a critical analysis of racialized aesthetic conventions in pop culture with interviews with women who have undergone the procedure. The women emerge from the film neither as victims of the dominant culture nor as models of self-empowerment, but as individuals struggling to define their identities through conflicting codes of physical beauty and normality.

These codes are not "natural"; neither are they solely cosmetic. The complexity of the issues surrounding medical and/or surgical body modification is evident in relation to sex-reassignment surgeries. Gender may be largely culturally determined, as discussed earlier in this chapter; however, its significance is sufficiently deep and pervasive that gender dysphoria is considered by the medical community to constitute threats to physical health. Many trans people feel that medically transitioning is important to their larger transition process, though not all trans people are interested in or have access to these often expensive surgeries. The decision to undergo a sex-reassignment surgery blurs the distinction between culture and nature in the determination of what constitutes a "normal" identity. It also demonstrates the fraught political implications of body modification: fueled dominantly by narrow cisnormative codes of sex and gender identity, sex-reassignment surgeries are also an issue of acceptance and survival for many trans people.

Transcending the Body?

The possibilities of body modification are taken to their extreme, at the same time as they are critically challenged, in the work of performance artist Orlan, who has subjected herself to nine plastic surgery procedures—including the implantation of horns in her forehead—in order to explore (and explode) classical notions of beauty. Orlan's is a self-conscious parody of more conventional versions of plastic surgery (which themselves assume an extreme form in the more than 20 operations undergone by American talk show celebrity Cindy Jackson in an eerily successful bid to look like Barbie). Declaring "I don't want to be the Barbie Doll" (qtd. in Goodall 160), Orlan seeks instead to expose the arbitrariness, the unnaturalness, of the standards of beauty that have come to define

Western femininity. She does this not in defense of the so-called real body but to expose its nonexistence. The body, Orlan observes, "is obsolete. It is no longer adequate for the current situation. We mutate at the rate of cockroaches, but we are cockroaches whose memories are in computers, who pilot planes and drive cars that we have conceived, although our bodies are not conceived for these speeds" (qtd. in Goodall 151).

Orlan's comment reflects the **posthumanist** position that the concepts of man, self, and body that underwrite traditional ideas of human identity have become untenable as society confronts the inextricable entanglement of nature and technology, human and machine. This is not to say that the body *used* to exist in a more or less natural state that has been disrupted or corrupted by technology, but that the increasing difficulty of drawing distinctions between the human and/or natural and the technological highlights the inadequacy of the once intelligible myth of an autonomous human identity (see Figure 6.6).

Sport is one area where arguments over the almost sacred integrity of the human body are highly charged. Efforts to police the boundary demarcating natural from unnatural bodies result in situations like the 2007 attempt on the part of the International Association of Athletics Federation (IAAF), the world track and field governing body, to exclude South African sprinter and double amputee Oscar Pistorius from the Olympics on the grounds that his prosthetic legs would give him an unfair advantage. According to his coach, Pistorius (who had broken speed records for disabled sprinters, but whose times did not end up meeting the qualifying standards for the 2008 Olympics) faced a number of challenges running with prostheses. If he performed better than other runners, it was only because he worked harder; in Pistorius's own words, "I train harder than other guys, eat better, sleep better and wake up thinking about athletics. I think that's why I'm a bit of an exception" (qtd. in Longman). An IAAF spokesperson defended the organization's argument for excluding Pistorius: "With all due respect, we cannot accept something that provides advantage. It affects the purity of sport. Next will be another device where people will fly with something on their back" (qtd. in Longman). The line between acceptable and unacceptable body modification is constantly shifting; excluded in 2008,

Figure 6.6 Products like Google Glass, billed as a "ubiquitous computer," blur the line between human and technology. Source: © Filip Singer/epa european pressphoto agency b.v./Alamy

in 2012 Pistorius was allowed to compete in both the Summer Olympics and Paralympics. Robert Gailey, an associate professor of physical therapy at the University of Miami Medical School who has studied amputee runners, poses a question for the IAAF: "Are they looking at not having an unfair advantage? Or are they discriminating because of the purity of the Olympics, because they don't want to see a disabled man line up against an able-bodied man for fear that if the person who doesn't have the perfect body wins, what does that say about the image of man?" (qtd. in Longman). (Pistorius's athletics career came to an end when he was charged and convicted with culpable homicide in the death of his girlfriend, Reeva Steenkamp.) Performance-enhancing drugs are mostly banned (yet widely used, as exemplified by the 2012 report of the US Anti-Doping Agency that led to cyclist Lance Armstrong being stripped of his seven Tour de France victories), and so far no restrictions have been placed on golfers or baseball players who undergo laser eye surgery to improve their vision (see Saletan). Given the impossibility of ever establishing an objectively correct standard, the question of who can participate in what athletic activities and under what circumstances has to be approached from a different angle.

Cyborgs

The figure of the cyborg, an amalgam of human and animal and/or living organism and machine, is not simply the imaginary creation of the producers of cyberpunk novels and movies, but an everyday reality embodied in our use of computers and machines. In a significant way, we have not only come to inhabit technology, technology has also come to inhabit us, as theorists such as Paul Virilio have pointed out; he cites as one example the medical use of micro-machines to view, diagnose, treat, and enhance the body. Such innovations have the potential to be socially useful, but also scarily invasive. University of Toronto professor and inventor Steve Mann highlights both the possibilities and the dangers of cyborg technology with wearable cameras and computers that turn the tables on such routine uses of surveillance as store security systems.

For many people, the prospect of an ever-closer relationship between humans and machines invokes utopian ideas of a virtual reality in which individuals and communities are able to transcend the limits of nature and their bodies to enjoy ever greater freedoms. For others, the prospect of a progressive erosion of the integrity of principles such as "humanity" and "nature" is deeply disturbing, heralding a nightmarish world like the one represented in *Blade Runner*, in which the complexity and beauty of our existence are transformed into a bunch of animate machines.

As former athletes such as Oscar Pistorius, artists such as Orlan, and cultural theorists such as Donna Haraway and Steve Mann have shown, however, neither of these visions is ultimately viable. The techno-utopian dream, an extension of the Enlightenment project of harnessing the physical world to human need, relies, like the techno-pessimist vision, on the old idea of a separation between body and mind, nature and culture that is simply not sustainable. Both the technological and the natural ideal are myths forged out of culture, and their ideological frames limit the possibilities for human liberation.

Contrary to the promises of technophiles and purveyors of cosmetic miracles, "Identity has not turned into a free option for all subjects in all situations and all contexts" (Klesse 20). Prevailing structures of gender, class, racial, and sexual inequality mean that everyone does not enjoy the opportunities for self-fulfillment. The limitations on our freedom to define ourselves as we will is also compromised by the fact—of which we are periodically reminded, by environmental catastrophes (some of them human caused) and by the inevitability of death—that we are not just *in* but also *of* nature. This recognition has ramifications for our understanding of not just humans, but also the other-than-human beings we relegate to the category of "animals." For many scholars in the growing field of **critical animal studies** (see Wolfe, for example), recognizing the imaginary nature of the boundary between humans and animals demands not the extension of rights to animals, but rather a radical questioning of the humanists' concepts of identity, consciousness, and subjectivity on which the concept of rights is based. The critical issue, which we have tried to stress throughout this chapter, concerns not whether our identities are born or made, or whether they are defined through or against our bodies, but what they mean in terms of our ability to enhance our own and others' power to act in a world not entirely of our own making.

Suggestions for Further Reading

Ahmed, Sara. *The Promise of Happiness*. Durham, NC: Duke University Press, 2010.

Berlant, Lauren. *Cruel Optimism*. Durham, NC: Duke University Press, 2011.

Bordo, Susan. *Unbearable Weight: Feminism, Western Culture and the Body*. Berkeley: University of California Press, 1993.

Butler, Judith. *Bodies That Matter: On the Discursive Limits of Sex*. London: Routledge, 1999.

Connell, R.W. *Masculinities*. Berkeley: University of California Press, 1995.

Crenshaw, Kimberle. "Mapping the Margins: Intersectionality, Identity Politics, and Violence Against Women of Color." *Stanford Law Review* 43(6), 1991: 1241–1299.

Davis, Lennard J., ed. *Disability Studies Reader*. London: Routledge, 2006.

du Gay, Paul, Jessica Evans, and Peter Redman, eds. *Identity: A Reader*. London: Sage, 2000.

Featherstone, Mike. *Body Modification*. London: Sage, 2000.

Giddens, Anthony. *Modernity and Self-Identity*. Cambridge, UK: Polity, 1991.

Lemke, Thomas. *Biopolitics: An Advanced Introduction*. Trans. Eric Frederick Trump. New York: New York University Press, 2010.

Shilling, Chris. *The Body and Social Theory*. London: Sage, 1993.

Woodward, Kathryn, ed. *Identity and Difference*. London: Sage, 2000.

7

Identity, Community, Collectivity

Who Do You Want Me to Be?

In the pilot episode of the early 2000s television series *The O.C.*, a memorable meeting occurs between Ryan, the kid from the wrong side of the tracks, and Marissa, the troubled, rich Newport Beach girl who will become his girlfriend. Marissa, who is standing at the end of her driveway waiting for her boyfriend, is stunned to see Ryan step out of the shadows and asks, "Who are you?" His suave reply—"Whoever you want me to be"—establishes his enigmatic coolness, and sets the tone for the quests for identity and connection that Ryan and the other characters embark on throughout the series. It is a scene with mythical resonance in its depiction of the arrival of a mysterious stranger into a close-knit, if deeply dysfunctional, community, whose structure is shaken but never destroyed. It is also an interesting scene with which to begin our discussion of identity and community.

Part of the interest in *The O.C.* (aside from a lot of risky sexual and other behaviors) revolves around Ryan's struggle to fit in. The pilot episode sets up his lower-class status by some clear signifiers. The shots of Chino, the town he comes from, are drab and dingy, an impression heightened by the few actions that occur there: Ryan and his brother in an alley at night, smashing the window of a car his brother has talked him into stealing; Ryan's departure from home—a beat-up bungalow with a pickup on the front lawn—after being punched and thrown out by his mother's alcoholic boyfriend; and finally, Ryan making a desperate call from a graffiti-covered phone booth outside a liquor store to Sandy Cohen, the lawyer who has offered to help him. The bleak, featureless drive between Chino and the clean and tree-filled suburb of Newport Beach symbolizes the vast distance between the two worlds—a distance that the show suggests is both hard and, in some ways, weirdly easy to cross. Although he faces some discrimination from Sandy's wife, Kristin, and also from Luke, Marissa's boyfriend (who clearly has other reasons to be hostile), Ryan takes to the easy life, well, pretty easily, enacting the American popular myth of upward mobility. At the same time, he retains his street cred, never losing the aura of romance that comes from his working-class origins.

Ryan's story raises many interesting questions that we attempt to work through in this chapter: How do individuals fit (or not fit) into communities? What are the terms of inclusion and exclusion, and how have these changed over time? How do particular identities conflict with and/or reinforce other identities, both individual and collective? How do they work to reinforce and/or undermine structures of power? In this chapter, as in the last, our underlying concern in studying identity is to explore the way in which identities function in society to help or hinder different people in their efforts to act autonomously or as self-conscious agents.

Generally speaking, a community may be defined as "a social, religious, occupational or other group sharing common characteristics or interests and perceived or perceiving itself as distinct in some respect from the larger society within which it exists" (Dictionary. com). The criteria by which communities are defined—and the significance attached to the defining criteria—vary widely depending on which community is described and who is describing it. It is probably fair to say, though, that we rarely use the word community in a neutral way: there is usually some explicit or implicit *value*, either positive or negative, attached to it. But as the last chapter showed, we also attach a lot of value to the idea of the individual. It is therefore not surprising to find in our investigation of popular culture that communities and individuals operate in complicated tension with one another—a tension that can result in different forms of being and belonging together. We conclude this chapter by thinking about the construction of collectivities, groups of individuals that come together at particular times, for specific, often political purposes. If the word "community" suggests a seamless whole (with the emphasis on "unity"), collectivities are looser and more self-conscious, and while communities are strongly shaped by a sense of tradition, collectivities may be more oriented to the future.

Back to the *The O.C.* In one sense, as the name of the series implies (O.C. is an acronym for Orange County, California), this is a show about community—a particularly exclusive community, as it happens, whose security is maintained by a literal gate. Part of the show's appeal undoubtedly stems from its representation of popular fantasies of how the super-rich live—fantasies that include envy/admiration of their luxury goods, endless leisure, and impossibly hot bodies, as well as schadenfreude (a useful German word that means enjoying someone else's bad fortune) at the scrapes they get into, which tend to be bigger and badder than the screw-ups of ordinary people. It probably doesn't matter much to the audience that it isn't a particularly realistic representation of the community it's supposed to depict: contrary to popular belief, not all rich people are stunningly good looking! More seriously, in the real O.C., in 2005, Asians made up 16.1% of the population and Latinos 32.7% (Kelly), while the characters in the television series are overwhelmingly white. Surely if the show focused primarily on community, some effort would be made to get the demographics right. But then, you could argue that the show isn't really all that interested in community in *that* sense—the sense of the **identity politics** of race; it is just about individuals, getting into and out of relationships and, especially in the case of the teen characters, asserting their independence and figuring out who they are. There is a sense in which the journey Ryan embarks on in the first episode, from the moment he is kicked out of his family's house to where he's standing on the Cohens' expansive driveway telling Marissa that he can be "whoever she wants him to be," is simply a more literal version of the kind of journey of self-discovery that everyone undergoes in one form or another. And although the characters encounter some pretty spectacular roadblocks, from addiction to infidelity to bankruptcy, the general sense of the show conforms to the myth Ryan embodies of the individual as a free agent who enjoys pretty much complete social mobility. Following the time-tested formula of television and movie drama in which "the glamorous impersonates the ordinary" (Mulvey 326), Seth Cohen, Marissa Cooper, and their friends are represented as pretty typical teens. Their neighborhood might be gated, but, so the myth goes, given a little luck and the right attitude, anyone could be a part of it.

Of course, *The O.C.* is just a television show. But as we note in Chapter 3 and elsewhere in this book, television shows and movies reflect—and also *affect*—our values, fears, and fantasies, as well as our sense of identity and community. While *The O.C.* portrays an image of a community made up of radically autonomous individuals united by their lavish lifestyle (and, of course, the money to enjoy that lifestyle), a different picture of the relationship between individuals and communities emerges in the Canadian television series *Little Mosque on the Prairie*. Set in the fictional prairie town of Mercy, Saskatchewan, *Little Mosque* focuses on the relations between a small and close-knit group of Muslims in the town and their non-Muslim neighbors. "Community" in this show is therefore not defined by zip or postal code as it is *The O.C.*, but by religious affiliation. Interestingly, aside from a vaguely defined Anglicanism associated with the church in which the local mosque rents space, the religion of the non-Muslim characters is neither here nor there. The main community boundary in the show is the division between Muslims and non-Muslims. There are, however, lots of sub-boundaries *within* the Muslim group—including one literal separator in an episode that features a debate over whether a partition should be erected in the mosque to divide female from male worshippers. The focus on conflict and complexity between Muslim characters reflects the producers' desire to show non-Muslim audiences that "[the Muslim] community has the same foibles and quirks that any community does" (Dube).

The relationship between individuals and community is very different from that depicted in *The O.C.*, as can be seen in the pilot episode that also centers on the arrival of a stranger. Unlike Ryan, who enters the Cohens' neighborhood under somewhat dubious circumstances, Amaar Rashid (Zaid Shaikh) arrives in Mercy for entirely legitimate reasons: he has accepted the position of imam at the local mosque. In keeping with the romantic outsider motif, Rashid is impossibly good-looking. But where Ryan is able to retain his mysterious allure with his enigmatic reply to the question "Who are you?" Amaar has no such luck. After being interrogated at the airport when a woman overhears him using the words "suicide," "Allah," and "bomb" in a totally innocent phone conversation with his mother, he arrives by taxi in Mercy to be accosted immediately by a reporter, who asks him (in a tone not nearly as friendly as Marissa's in *The O.C.*) "Who are you?" By the time Amaar has patiently provided his name, the purpose for his visit, and assurances that he is not a terrorist to the clearly still suspicious reporter, a crowd has gathered, creating further confusion that Amaar must once again patiently dispel. Where Ryan in *The O.C.* is granted the power and anonymity of being just a guy—"whoever you want me to be"—Amaar is forced to identify himself in order defend his legitimacy against prevailing stereotypes of nonwhite Muslims—a community to which he is inextricably linked, whether he likes it or not. *Little Mosque on the Prairie* challenges those stereotypes, including an assumed association between Muslim faith and a dark, or "Middle Eastern–looking" complexion, with a cast that includes a black Muslim from Africa and a white Muslim convert by marriage. It also depicts the joys and tensions of belonging to a religious community whose laws are subject to debate and controversy from within as well as from without. Conflicts are drawn within and across the Muslim and non-Muslim communities along lines of gender and sexuality. In short, the program treads a precarious line between depicting the "foibles and quirks" that define individuals, and recognizing the ties that bind communities from inside and outside, by choice and by imposition.

The O.C. and *Little Mosque on the Prairie* are clearly very different shows, in content and genre: *The O.C.* is classified as drama/romance, while *Little Mosque* is a comedy with serious undercurrents, inspired by the experiences of the show's creator, Zarqa Nawaz, living as a Muslim in a remote city in Western Canada. Both shows contain elements of realism. However, the point of comparing them is not to determine which is more true to life. In an interview, Nawaz commented that "it rests on my shoulders to get the balance right between entertainment and representing the community in a reasonable way....You have to push the boundaries so you can grow and evolve as a community" (qtd. in

MacFarquhar 1). One conclusion we may draw from this comment is that cultural producers from minority groups (where "minority" is defined not by numbers but by cultural power) feel and/or are held accountable in ways that members of dominant groups are not to the communities they come from for the way they represent those communities: they are more likely to be asked not just "Who are you?" but "Where are you from?" and "What are you doing?" Shows like *Little Mosque on the Prairie* (see Figure 7.1) challenge the myth of liberal individualism in favor of a focus on how community boundaries, variously constructed, enable and constrain our actions, identities, and relationships.

Unlike *The O.C.*, *Little Mosque* makes visible the structural, institutional obstacles to achieving the principle of individual equality. Ultimately, though, the show endorses the notion that, as one Muslim viewer put it, "we're all the same at the end of the day" (Kamal Nawash, qtd. in Dube). What does that mean, exactly? Some cultural commentators argue that the humanism that underlies such statements tends to work to normativize, or establish as a default, the experience and perspective of the dominant group. This perspective tends to flatten out the beliefs, traditional practices, and historical experiences of minority groups in favor of a superficial affirmation of different styles of dress and cuisine as colorful accessories that liven up our otherwise uniform, "normal" way of social interaction (think "Diversity Day" on the television show *The Office*).

Identity politics, or the strategic assertion of a racial or cultural unity, is one response to the marginalization and/or invisibility of minorities that this seemingly universal perspective produces. Unlike the exclusivist identity claims of majority groups, which operate often invisibly to secure existing power imbalances, identity politics challenge the status quo in its explicit bid for recognition and the extension of majority rights to minority groups. The term "identity politics" is often used in a negative way to describe what some critics see as loud demands for special treatment by minority groups. Others, including some members of those groups, contend that *all* rights, claims, and struggles

Figure 7.1 Shows like *Little Mosque on the Prairie* highlight obstacles to achieving equality in hopes of eliminating them. Source: https://www.youtube.com/watch?v=hlFOyOmktFw, screenshot at 13.42

over power emerge from particular locations and particular constellations of identity; identity politics just makes visible the lines of exclusion and belonging. Identity politics can work strategically as assertions of legitimacy and value by groups who have traditionally suffered oppression or marginalization by the dominant culture. A strict emphasis on group belonging can also work negatively, to define meaning by a more or less explicit process of exclusion, as we discuss below.

"The People Who Are Ours"

In a 2002 survey commissioned by the Northern Ireland Community Relations Council, a sociologist interviewed Catholic and Protestant children between the ages of three and six to find out their views on the political situation there (see Close-Up 7.1).

When asked "What do you know about Catholics?" one Protestant child responded, "They're bad. Catholics are different from ordinary human beings because they are badder." In response to the question "What do you know about Protestants?" Catholic children provided similar responses: "They want to kill all the Catholics. They're like Catholics. They do the same things only they're stronger."

These children's perspectives on Irish cultural identity are interesting for what they reveal about the politics of identity in general. First, they highlight the extent to which group membership, like all forms of identification, is defined by the terms of *sameness* and *difference*: Catholics are defined by virtue of their difference from Protestants, by their essential "otherness."

Close-Up 7.1 Bad and Badder

The following is excerpted from a report commissioned by the Northern Ireland Community Relations Council entitled "Too Young to Notice?" (Connolly *et al*. 45). Paul Connolly, a sociologist at the University of Ulster, interviewed 352 Catholic and Protestant children from Northern Ireland about their attitudes to the political situation there. All of the children were between 3 and 6 years of age.

What Do You Know about Catholics?
They rob.
   They're bad. They batter Almond Drive people. Almond Drive—that's where I live.
   Catholics are different from ordinary human beings because they are badder. The police come after them. They make petrol bombs, get petrol at garages, throw them and they blow up.

What Do You Know about Protestants?
They want to kill all the Catholics.
   They're like Catholics. They do the same things only they're stronger. Protestants would take people hostage. The police give them their weapons and make a deal to get the hostages.
   Catholics don't like Protestants, and that's why they don't like them. They're bad.

Why Do You Like or Not Like This Flag?
[After showing the Protestant children an Irish tricolour flag.]
   Northern Ireland flag. You put it up in July. It annoys people when it's waving. A Drumcree flag is the good one and that is the bad one.
   It's the Fenian flag. It's only bad people that have that colour of flag and that's all I know about that flag.

Why Do You Like or Not Like This Flag?
[After showing the Catholic children a Union Jack, the UK flag.]
  I don't like that flag—a sad one—'cause it's bad.
  It has red and blue and white. They burn them, down at a club. Put Union Jack on grass and burned it. All bigguns throw stones at British Police. Just don't like that one.

What Do You Know about the People in This Photograph? Why Do You Like or Not Like Them?
[After showing Catholic children a picture of a Protestant march.]
  Sometimes they march when they're attacking other places and sometimes when somebody's dead.
  They're holding up stuff. They're Orangemen. Because they're going to kill us. They wanted to kill us anyway.
  They came to our road and my daddy said they're Orange bastards!
  Because they're bad. They're police.
  'Cause they be fighting.
  Because they're not friendly.
  They're Orangemen. People tried to kill the Orangemen because they don't like them.
  They're dangerous men. They're evil. They steal money.
  They're not my favourite because they've got all the colours that I hate.
  They're Protestants. They want to march so that they can get the Catholic area.
  I like the people who are ours. I don't like those ones because they're Orangemen. They're bad people. Mummy told me they were bad.

What is particularly significant in the first example in Close-Up 7.1 is the implied norm against which "Catholic" is defined: "Protestant" identity is not mentioned, but is assumed, in its absence, to be synonymous with "human beings." A key characteristic of group identity, particularly though not exclusively in the case of dominant groups, is **ex-nomination**, or failure to acknowledge the distinguishing sign or particularity of that identity. Not mentioning a distinguishing characteristic—like whiteness, say, or, in the case of Northern Ireland, Protestantism—implies that it is just ordinary, the norm. Difference, within this framework, is never neutral; rather, it is conceived as deviation from a standard.

While this form of discrimination can sometimes seem relatively value free (for example, the phrase "nonwhite" to describe blacks or Asians looks innocuous enough, until we start to think about why we rarely hear whites described as "nonblack"), it works implicitly—and sometimes explicitly—on the basis of hierarchy. Hence, the others are "badder" than we are. Critical to the operation of the hierarchy is the operation of stereotype, in which a group or individual is reduced to a few fixed, unchanging characteristics (again, in implicit opposition to the more complex and fluid "normal" identities that we ascribe to ourselves and those identified by a child in the survey as "the people who are ours").

Like Us, Only Worse

What is striking in the stereotypes that are used by the children in the interview in Close-Up 7.1—and what is true of stereotypes generally—is that, regardless of what group is being described, they tend to sound a lot alike. Though some allowance must be made in this example for the age of the interviewees—a 4-year-old has a limited vocabulary to describe deviance—the terms in which they describe "otherness" resonate remarkably with those used by adults. "Badness," or treachery, an absence of morality, and a tendency toward the illegitimate use of violence (as opposed to the *legitimate* use of violence by one's own group) are standard terms of condemnation that establish the place of the other outside the bounds of civil society, while asserting, again by implicit comparison, the moral integrity of "us."

The children's comments also illustrate another interesting thing about stereotypes: one Catholic child's remark about Protestants—"*They're like Catholics. They do the same things* only they're stronger" ("Bad and Badder" 21, emphasis added)—points to the emergence of stereotypes through the tension between difference and *sameness*. Recall the discussion in Chapter 6 of Freud's theory about the contradictory drives that inform relations between "self" and "other": the traumatic separation that marked our entry into the social world means that the stability of our identities always hinges on a tension between the desire for connection with the other and the fear of being consumed by the other. The ambivalent self-construction that underlies the production of stereotypes leads to a representation of the dominant group as simultaneously vulnerable and power-ful in relation to an "other" who is both threatening and weak. Thus, Protestants "do the same things [as Catholics] only they're stronger" because "the police give them their weapons." The moral superiority of the Catholics lies in their victimization at the hands of established power structures. On the other hand, claims to virtue frequently rest on *appeals* to traditional authorities—the law, God, or, in the case of children, parents: "Mummy told me they were bad" (21). The ambiguous positioning of authority as a site of identification (the thing that confirms our status) or source of victimization (the thing that shuts us out) again reveals the precarious foundations of the construction of the self.

Cultural Symbols, Material Contexts

Of course, frequently—as is the case in Northern Ireland—a tendency to ally oneself with or against established powers (and to construct those powers accordingly as legitimate or illegitimate) has a historical basis. As a consequence of centuries of British occupation, an occupation that, in spite of a formal cessation of hostilities between (mostly Protestant) Unionists and (mostly Catholic) Nationalists in 1998, is still rejected by some Nationalists, most of the police force in Northern Ireland is English—that is, largely Protestant.

The ambiguous role of the police in the stories of the children in the interview demon-strates the complex interplay between symbolism and society in the formation of the structures of power. The Protestant child infers the badness of the Catholics from the fact that "the police come after them" ("Bad and Badder" 21). As in most attempts to draw a link between race, culture or **ethnicity**, and criminality, this equation is confused in its attribution of cause and effect: the inference of guilt on the basis of pursuit or arrest is based on an assumption of the objectivity of the police. This objectivity is called into question by the Catholic children's reference to an alliance between the police and the Protestants. Regardless of its accuracy, the reference serves as a reminder of the ideologi-cal context in which power always operates. The role of ideology in determining identity is particularly clear to see in the case of children: we are not surprised when the shaping influence of "Mummy told me" appears behind the veil of personal conviction.

Nevertheless, it is important to resist the temptation to see children as the innocent victims of ideologies that are variously deployed and/or seen through by the rest of us who know better. As we argue in Chapter 3, no one, not even the supposedly impartial administrators of justice (nor, for that matter, the cultural critic!), escapes the discursive networks through which "truth"—including the "truth" of stereotypes—emerges as a function of power. The terms by which group identities are defined are always shot through with ideology, their mythological character highlighted in the arbitrariness of the symbols that convey their substance—for example, the Irish tricolour flag and the Union Jack, which Protestant and Catholic children characterized, not surprisingly, as "bad" and "the colours I hate." As empty of real significance as these symbols may be, however, we cannot dismiss their power, just as we cannot underestimate the material force of ideology as it is expressed in the beliefs and actions of individuals, police, and armies.

Collective Identity and Crisis

Within the context of what have come to be labeled "the Troubles" in Northern Ireland, it is easy to see how group identity comes to take on massive significance. As Kobena Mercer notes, "identity becomes an issue when it is in crisis, when something assumed to be fixed, coherent and stable is displaced by the experience of doubt and uncertainty" (43). It would be a mistake, however, to assume that identities don't matter outside situations of obvious "trouble." The tendency for dominant groups to ex-nominate the signs or myths that designate their specialness means that it is possible for members of those groups to have, or at least to believe that they have, very little invested in belonging to a particular group. They are able to bracket questions of identity because the balance of social power allows *their* identity to pass as universal, unmarked. It is only when the balance of power shifts that it becomes necessary to haul out the symbols, to remind themselves and others what it is that makes them unique.

Particularism versus Universalism

Such a collective identity crisis arguably occurred in the wake of the September 11, 2001, terrorist attacks on the United States, when it suddenly became necessary to reassert the specific meaning of "America," all the while continuing to insist on the universality of that identity. The tension between particularism ("we are like this, we stand for these beliefs, ideas, practices") and universalism ("we are all human beings, except for those who don't do or believe as we do") underlies all definitions of group identity, with the fiction of universality being comfortably indulged in when times are good, and the defense of singularity being invoked when one's position of strength is threatened.

At these moments, as in the crisis following 9/11, people are generally more willing to surrender *individual* civil liberties, such as freedom of speech—liberties that under other circumstances are seen as natural—in order to gain the greater security perceived to be associated with the defense of the group. These defenses take multiple forms, including the tightening of physical or territorial borders, the intensification of policing activity, and the dissemination of myths or ideologies that work to bind the group together and to enforce the exclusion of outsiders.

Looking at identities in crisis serves to remind us of conditions that are more or less critical to the maintenance of *all* identities. Designated through particular practices of representation in which differences are more or less highlighted, identities are always rooted, in the last instance, in relations of power and force. A recent story in the Toronto newspaper *The Globe and Mail* about the arrest of a suspected terrorist carried the headline "Muslim Militant or Family Man: Terrorist Has Many Faces." At times of crisis, practices of racist stereotyping become more widespread, with boundaries between "us" and "them" expressed in the form of binary opposition.

Suggested Activity 7.1
Try to find recent media examples of the representation of *difference* defined by group identity. In what contexts do these representations occur? In what situations are the identities of specific groups promoted (and/or ex-nominated) or stereotyped?

Modern Identities: Nation, Empire, and Race

One of the principal ways of defining identity in the modern world has been through the idea of the **nation.** Historically connected to European practices of colonialism between the sixteenth and nineteenth centuries, nations and **nationalism** remain significant today, both as symbolic guarantees of identity and security and as obstacles to more global connections. Associated with such positive ideals as patriotism, loyalty, and collective strength, nations and nationalism also work—traditionally and today—on principles of exclusion based on race, gender, and sexuality. Beginning with a specific example of how the nation functions in popular culture today, this section goes on to locate those contemporary resonances in a broader historical context.

I Am Canadian

In the Canadian beer company Molson's ad (see Figure 7.2) that came to be known as "The Rant," a young man in a plaid shirt—"Joe"—stands with a microphone in front of a huge crowd and offers a simple, powerful declaration of what it means to be Canadian (see Close-Up 7.2).

Figure 7.2 In 2015, a stenciled image of a hijab-wearing woman accompanied by the text "I am Canadian" began appearing on the walls of buildings in Hamilton, Ontario. This image offers a pointed challenge to the Conservative government's proposal to ban Muslim woman from wearing the niqab (a head scarf that covers their faces) at citizenship ceremonies. Source: Unknown artist, Hamilton, Ontario. Photo: Author

Introducing himself with a stereotypically Canadian, self-effacing "Hey," Joe begins his speech with a few negations of common American stereotypes of Canadians and concludes, positively and triumphantly, by proclaiming "My name is Joe and I AM CANADIAN! Thank you." The ad's instant popularity, measured by increased sales and a flurry of media and popular discussion, was widely attributed to its having expressed, simply and appealingly, the essence of Canadian national identity. Leaving aside the question of whether the ad was an accurate or positive representation of Canadianness (some people, including Ontario's Minister of Consumer and Commercial Affairs Bob Runciman, worried that it constituted "America-bashing"; see "I Am...an Asshole?"), "The Rant" is useful to look at as a particularly powerful example of how nationalist discourse operates, both in the Canadian context and more generally.

On a general level, one of the first things the ad tells us is that having a national identity is not just a matter of being a citizen of a particular state. It is also a strongly felt personal investment in being part of a special community—one defined by particular loves (hockey, beer, nature) and beliefs: in peace, for example, or in social justice. Belonging to a particular nation is not just a passive kind of subjection to an external, predetermined state structure, then, but a form of belief and action that is itself *constitutive*—a defining part of that nation.

Close-Up 7.2 Joe's Rant

"Hey.

I'm not a lumberjack or a fur trader.

I don't live in an igloo or eat blubber or own a dog sled.

And I don't know Jimmy, Sally, or Suzy from Canada, although I'm certain they're really, really nice.

I have a prime minister, not a president.

I speak English and French, not American.

And I pronounce it "about," not "a boot."

I can proudly sew my country's flag on my backpack.

I believe in peacekeeping, not policing.

Diversity, not assimilation.

And that the beaver is a truly proud and noble animal.

A tuque is a hat, a chesterfield is a couch,

and it IS pronounced zed, not zee, zed.

Canada is the second largest landmass, the first nation of hockey, and the best part of North America.

My name is Joe, and I AM CANADIAN!

Thank you." ("I Am Canadian")

Identity as Difference

But at the same time as Canadianness, by Joe's reckoning, seems to be a specific, deliberate thing, there is another sense in which being Canadian—or American, or British, or any nationality—doesn't mean anything in particular in and of itself. It signifies only insofar as it defines a particular *relationship*, one that is defined by connection with other Canadians and—equally importantly—by a *difference* from non-Canadians. The Canadian identity promoted by "The Rant" is one informed by self-conscious awareness of Canada's place in a world of other nations—nations toward which Canada assumes a particular political stance (peacekeeping v. policing), and whose otherness is critical to the definition of the Canadian self.

Of course, the principal "other" in Joe's rant is the United States—or, more specifically, a mythical "America"—whose dominance, and implied aggressive indifference to Canada, is what turns this speech into a rant rather than a simple declaration of patriotism. Like all nationalist statements—indeed, more explicitly than most—Joe's rant is a deliberate act of boundary drawing, establishing what, and more importantly who, belongs inside, and what belongs outside.

The urgency of defending what is often, as here seems to be the case, a fairly vulnerable boundary between "us" and "them" means that the arbitrary, or accidental, aspect of being a part of a particular national community needs to be played down in favor of an image of the nation as an organic whole. One of the chief ways in which this effect of incorporating all national citizens into a single coherent body is achieved in this ad, as in many nationalist statements, is by using the figure of a single individual to stand in for the nation as a whole.

Joe's status as a prototypical Canadian is highlighted by the series of images played on a screen behind him—the Parliament buildings, the flag, a set of individual faces of different races, and a waving crowd (Joe's audience?). By virtue of his placement on the stage, and his possession of a microphone, Joe is the spokesperson or representative of the community represented by these symbols. The choice of "Joe"—a good- but ordinary-looking guy in his late 20s who loves hockey and beer—as that individual is, of course, not accidental, since the target market for Molson Canadian beer is young men between the ages of 19 and 29. Though his name is no longer mentioned, Joe's spirit clearly inspires the television ads that ran during the 2008 Stanley Cup playoffs explaining the "unwritten code in Canada." If you follow the code, the ads explain, "chances are you've left your coat on some pile and knew it wouldn't get stolen; you've never made a move on your buddy's girlfriend;" and "you've grown a beard in the off-season." And (of course) Molson Canadian is your beer ("The Code").

The question of what Joe represents (an alpha male with a sense of irony?) becomes much more interesting when framed in terms of his supposedly exemplary Canadianness, bolstered by the stereotypically masculine symbols of beer and hockey. Associated with a broader collection of mythological images of the nation as a rugged Northern climate, settled by bold pioneers who survived through teamwork and toughness, these symbols create an unmistakably gendered image of the representative Canadian. The picture of Canada and Canadians is also fleshed out in ways that are both more obvious and more subtle: Joe's proud declaration that he speaks "English *and* French," in contrast to implicitly monolingual Americans, draws on the idea of a bilingual and bicultural Canada—an idea that is supported, but also complicated, by his invocation of the idea of *multi*cultural diversity. Though the ad speaks powerfully to the values of inclusivity and difference as central components of Canadian identity, the voices in whom that symbolic "diversity" actually exists do not speak—except in disembodied and homogenized form, *spoken for* by Joe, as the generic (white, male, anglophone) Canadian. How might "The Rant" have signified differently (more or less effectively?) if Joe's words were spoken by a teenage girl, an old woman, a black man, an Asian woman, a person in a wheelchair?

Suggested Activity 7.2

Though some elements of national myth persist over time, others change in response to events, processes, and conflicts within and outside the nation. Assuming it had not been done before, how would an ad along the lines of "The Rant" work today? What changes would be necessary in order to draw a positive audience response? How would the Rant have to be changed if it were created for American, British, or other national contexts? Looking at parodies of this ad on websites such as YouTube offers an interesting window into the ongoing struggle over national meaning (see, for example, "I Am Not Canadian").

Authentic versus Commercialized Culture

When Canadian Heritage Minister Sheila Copps aired "The Rant" at an International Press Institute conference in Boston to demonstrate what culture means to Canadians, some commentators criticized her for confusing "authentic" culture with its corrupt *commercial* form. Copps herself made a distinction between deep and superficial, authentic and commercial, in her assertion that "for Canadians, culture is not just another good. It's not just entertainment. It's the expression of the soul and identity of who we are" (qtd. in Robert MacGregor 282). Leaving aside for a moment the issue of whether and/or how "culture" differs from "entertainment" (an issue touched on in Chapters 1, 2, and 4 of this book), Copps's presentation, and the response to it, raises questions about the relationships between national identity, culture, politics, and economics.

The principal critiques directed at Copps's use of the Molson ad—that it invoked a contrived or made-up identity in place of a genuine one, that it exploited the theme of Canadian identity in order to achieve partisan political goals, and that it ignored authentic national culture in favor of a commercial substitute—all miss a critical fact about nationalism, which is that it is, by definition, informed by a combination of spontaneous feeling and conscious construction. Even more crucially, it is inextricably tied to political and economic concerns, which it helps to influence even as it is in turn shaped by them. These complex relationships are easy to see when we look at nations and nationalism in a historical context (see Close-Up 7.3).

Nations and Nationalism

The dynamics of nations and nationalism are important to understand in the context of discussions of identity. Not only is the nation one of the most globally significant forms of collective identity, but the very concept of modern identity, in its individual and collective forms, is in significant ways tied to the historical emergence of the nation in eighteenth-century Europe.

Much as contemporary economic, technological, and political changes are throwing old identities into confusion, changes in eighteenth-century Europe associated with the Industrial Revolution, developments in technology and communication, and political conflict had a powerful impact on traditional identities.

Simply put, the changes associated with modernity reconfigured strongly hierarchical or "vertical" medieval empires, framed by the ordering principles of dynasty and religion, into a more chaotic collection of "horizontal" states, characterized by their secular, more fluid political and economic organization. As a form of mythological solidarity that transforms a population into a "people," the nation was an important correlate of the modern state brought into being by state force at the same time as it fleshed out the meaning of the state, giving it a sense of purpose and natural rightness. As sociologist Zygmunt

---

Close-Up 7.3 Nations and Nationalism

As a form of what Benedict Anderson terms an "imagined community," the nation is both example and instigator of the process by which identities that are constructed or imagined come to assume the force of *nature*. One useful way to approach the significance of the nation as a source of modern identity is to think about the relationship between nations and nationalism.

Our usual, common-sense way of understanding the relationship is to see the nation—a people defined by collective belonging to an extensive community, usually defined in relation to a specific territory—as primary, with nationalism as a frequent though not inevitable by-product. Recent theories of the development of nations (Anderson; Gellner) suggest that the relationship might best be understood as working the other way around: that is, nations are how the ideological impulse of nationalism is legitimated and given concrete shape.

Bauman puts it, "the state supplied the resources of nation building, while the postulated unity of the nation and shared national destiny offered legitimacy to the ambition of the state authority to command obedience" (683).

Imagined Community, Invented Tradition

Thus, nations can be defined in relation to the machinery of particular states and to the territories they command. This is not a necessary relationship, however, as can be seen in contemporary examples of stateless nations such as Palestinians or Kurds. In fact, the nation, as a concept, derives its historical significance not so much through its grounding in a specific material polity or place, but rather through its unprecedented power to command connections between people spread out over vast distances. Unlike traditional civic groupings defined by village or even city-state, the nation demanded an imagined relationship between a vast body of people, most of whom had never met.

In the eighteenth century, as today, popular culture functioned as an important vehicle of nationalism. The nation became possible in part, Benedict Anderson suggests, because new forms of media such as the daily newspaper helped to create a large group of readers, linked by their capacity to imagine themselves as part of a whole network of unknown others. These readers form the basis of a community, informed by a collection of stories that, through their assemblage in the form of a single text, contribute to the creation of a coherent narrative of the world—a *national* point of view. Language and literacy play critical roles here, too: the rise of print capitalism that spurred the growth of newspapers corresponded with a decline of the privileged status of Latin as the sacred *written* language to which all vernacular or spoken languages were secondary. The production of written texts in the everyday languages spoken by people throughout Europe hastened the breakup of religious empires, while granting real and symbolic significance to the communities defined by distinct vernaculars. Of course, the "community" facilitated by print was strongly linked to literacy, and its contours were therefore shaped by the social as well as the economic interests of educated elites. Nationalism, understood in this way, is inevitably a top-down phenomenon.

Like other modern structures of identification, the nation can be understood as both empowering and restrictive (see Chapter 6). Fueled by the spirit of revolutionary movements against absolutist regimes, expressed most dramatically in the French Revolution of 1789–99, nationalism was based partly on the idea of the rights of "the people" to govern themselves. This ideal became a defining principle in the French and American Constitutions. Its democratic appeal masks the function of the nation as the legitimating ideology of the *state*, whose territorial boundaries are regulated internally and externally by instruments of force—police and military agencies, legal and educational institutions, and political organizations. The two meanings of the nation—as an expression of the ideal of equal citizenship, and as an alibi for state power—function simultaneously, the never fully realized promise of popular democracy working to justify the disciplinary force of the state while concealing the gaps in social and economic power that separate the mass of "the people" from the ruling elites. The compelling symbolism of "we" operates only to the extent that it is supported by forgetting that some of "us" own greater stakes in our collective project than others.

The nation's capacity to work as a collective project depends in large part on its ability to interpellate its members as citizens, enlisting their active and voluntary submission to the greater community. To this end, the idea of the nation must be embodied in a powerful narrative that grounds the present in the past. The principal mechanism for this grounding is what some historians have described as "invented tradition": "a set of practices, normally governed by overtly or tacitly accepted rules of a ritual or symbolic nature, which seek to inculcate certain values and norms of behaviour by repetition, which automatically implies continuity with the past" (Hobsbawm *Industry* 2).

A contemporary example is the controversy that has arisen in many North American communities over the public use of the phrase "Merry Christmas." Every year, a flurry of angry letters to the editor and radio call-ins has greeted the use of secular alternatives such as "Season's Greetings" or "Happy Holidays" on billboards and in other public venues. The gist of these complaints is that these bland greetings are threatening to destroy the tradition of Christmas, a key part of communities with a Christian heritage. History suggests, however, that not only is celebrating Christmas a relatively recent practice, secularism also lays equal claim to being a tradition in many countries around the world, especially those with a liberal political heritage. As historian Alan MacEachern noted in a letter to the Toronto newspaper *The Globe and Mail*, the "Happy Holidays" that adorned the front page in December 2007 was not an example of "political correctness run amok," but rather a variation of a tradition begun in 1925. The letter went on to quote the words of a 1965 editorial explaining why *The Globe* continued to wish readers "Season's Greetings" instead of "Merry Christmas":

> We reach out to each other, for each other is what we depend upon. And so many of our cards now tactfully say, Season's Greetings, for it would not be polite to say Merry Christmas to a Jewish friend or an agnostic friend or an unbelieving-in-anything friend. And they are wanted at the party. It is lonely in this scientific, pragmatic, abundant world.

These sentiments, expressed more than 40 years ago, challenge the idea of Christmas as an essential Canadian tradition that has recently come under attack from non-Christian immigrants, cheerleaders of **multiculturalism**, or cranky secularists: while many people have celebrated Christmas since the arrival of the first European settlers in the country that eventually became known as Canada, the holiday is not simply a unifying national tradition, but rather part of a history of conflict and negotiation about what it means to live together as Canadians. The same can be said for the United States, United Kingdom, and, indeed, for most other countries in the world today.

The stakes of such contests over what counts as national heritage concern more than identity, of course: they also work to legitimate claims to occupy the land. This function is particularly significant in colonial nations such as Canada and the United States, in which histories of the violent displacement of Indigenous people have been neatly covered over by stories of natural inheritance (through the tragic, but inevitable, death of the North American Indian) or of romantic conjoinment. Both stories are merged in Walt Disney's *Pocahontas*, in which the brutality of colonialism (translated, in the film, into an unfortunate instance of cultural misunderstanding) is ultimately overshadowed by a love story that signals the possibility of a new race of "Americans" defined by the harmonious blending of (masculine) Europe and (feminine) North American Indian (see *Mickey Mouse Monopoly*).

Nation and Empire

We have tried so far to show how, while identity in a general sense is predicated on difference—the community of a precariously constructed "us" dependent on an excluded "them"—this is particularly true for nations as a consequence of the historical circumstances in which they emerged. Both nationalism and nation-*states* are products of the Industrial Revolution, as discussed above. The Industrial Revolution was itself dependent on the resources of distant regions of the world, which supplied it with raw materials as well as capital in the form of gold and silver. These regions were not themselves industrialized, and were not to enjoy the benefits of industrialization for a long time, even though they came to assume a crucial role as markets for the products of industry. The economic development of European nation-states, in other words, was fuelled by the *under*development of other parts of the world—Asian, African, and American colonies, exploited for their resources and their labor while they were prevented, through trade regulations backed up by military force, from becoming full partners in the generation of wealth (see Blaut).

The construction of European national *identities* was similarly dependent on the non-European world. The process of secularization and scientific enlightenment that contributed to the breakup of the old religious dynasties was strongly connected to the voyages of exploration undertaken by Spain, Portugal, England, France, and the Netherlands during the fifteenth and sixteenth centuries. As much as these travels were undertaken in search of wealth, they were also driven by a quest for knowledge, and ultimately served to shape an understanding of the physical world and its human inhabitants as more vast and complicated than had previously been imagined. As Europeans came into contact with other, previously unknown peoples, two things happened: on the one hand, other places and cultures were translated and distorted—made to fit, positively or, more often, negatively, into categories of the already known, thus consolidating the universality of European ideas and values. On the other hand, contact with otherness led to a recognition of a multitude of radically different worlds. National identities were shaped by both of these responses to difference: the recognition of **cultural relativism**, whereby, in contrast to the religious view of a single universal truth, differences in belief and practice were seen to be inevitable and perhaps even desirable; and the consolidation of singular **sovereign** identities characterized by an imperative to safeguard and even to extend their sovereignty, by force if necessary.

The West and the Rest

Colonialism was not just an economic and political undertaking in which European nations competed for dominance through the exploitation and settlement of overseas colonies. It was also, importantly, a cultural project, in which these nations sought to extend throughout the world their concept of civilization, defined by the Enlightenment values of scientific rationalism and liberal humanism: the imperative to *conquer* the non-European world was tempered (but, importantly, not contradicted) by the will to *save* it.

Refining and complicating the explicit universality of the colonial vision, according to which all of humanity was marching in the same direction along a single, historically determined road to progress, was its grounding in principles of identity and difference. The humanistic thrust of colonialism, which sought to impart the idea of the natural sovereignty and brotherhood of man, was more seriously undermined by the fundamental principle of *in*equality that structured the whole colonial and civilizing project (see Figure 7.3). Like the

The first step towards lightening

The White Man's Burden
is through teaching the virtues of cleanliness.

Pears' Soap

is a potent factor in brightening the dark corners of the earth as civilization advances, while amongst the cultured of all nations it holds the highest place—it is the ideal toilet soap.

Figure 7.3 Nineteenth-century British ideologies of race and nation are reflected in advertising of the time. While messages like this one would never appear today, advertisements continue to be a potent site for the reproduction of mythologies of collective identity. Source: © North Wind Picture Archives/Alamy

mission of the "rational recreationists" (see Chapter 2), which sought to improve the working classes of England by enlisting them in middle-class programs of education and recreation, the colonial project reflected two connected but irreconcilable assumptions: that of a fundamental equality between humans that could be advanced through education; and that of a fundamental and hierarchical difference between groups that justified the material and ideological domination of the inferior group by the superior one.

Orientalism—Then and Now

That process of anxious drawing and redrawing of boundaries impels the operation of colonial discourse, which produces forms of knowledge and ways of talking about "the other" as a way of securing the identity of the imperial "self." Edward Said uses the term **orientalism** to describe a dominant form of colonial discourse in which a mythologized East, or "Orient," becomes a site for the projection of Western fantasies of otherness as well as a mechanism for Western domination of actual non-Western cultures.

Based on Foucault's formulation of a nexus between knowledge and power (see Chapter 6), orientalism consists of a repertoire of images and ideas that *produce* "the Orient" as an object of Western knowledge and control. Disseminated through a variety of institutionalized forms (travel writing, civil service briefs, government policy documents, journalism, and even "innocent" forms of culture such as art and literature), orientalism played a critical role in European—particularly British—domination of non-Western cultures. It draws on a bank of stereotypical (and frequently inconsistent) qualities— inscrutability, deviousness and treachery, religious fundamentalism and immorality, violence, and excessive delicacy and effeminacy—in order to construct "the oriental" as a fixed, unchanging other, lacking subjectivity or internal variation and condensed in binary opposition to Western consciousness and culture. At the same time as orientalism serves to mark the absolute otherness of Eastern people, thus shoring up the integrity of Western identity, it is also a way of making the foreign familiar, of turning other cultures into objects of Western knowledge.

Contemporary Orientalism

It is easy to dismiss both nationalism and orientalism as products of unsophisticated cultures or bygone eras remote from our contemporary world. However, both persist in Western popular culture in forms that, like other myths of collective belonging, show up more obviously in times of crisis. The term "orientalism" may not signify precisely what it used to; however, the discursive practices it refers to continue in different forms. For example, long after it became unacceptable to typecast black or Native characters as the bad guys, and particularly in the wake of the September 11 attacks on the World Trade Center, films and television shows ranging from Disney's *Aladdin* to the television series *24* continue to draw on stereotypes of the Middle East and/or Arabs as evil and barbarous.

Accompanying the rapid circulation of racist stereotypes and ensuing violence following 9/11, a new academic and popular-knowledge industry for the production of knowledge about Islamic cultures grew up seemingly overnight. Like the eighteenth-century European scholars of the East (actually called "orientalists"), a host of Western experts began appearing on talk shows, producing new books and articles, and reviving old ones that purported to explain the "essential" qualities of Islamic culture (see, for example, Huntington; B. Lewis).

Like their eighteenth-century forebears, these new forms of "knowledge" homogenized a number of vastly different, complex cultures into a single, static classifiable entity, defined by implicit contrast with a more variegated, fluid West. Read in the context of a generalized Western anxiety about the non-West in general, and Islam in particular, the bulk of these studies reinforced a stereotype of Muslim culture as fundamentally different from, and threatening to, Western culture, while also serving to legitimate Western initiatives to *contain* and *manage* the threat. While they might seem remote from acts of racist violence, these discursive forms of "cultural profiling" assume material significance in the form of new customs and immigration, policing, and legal regulations in the United States and Canada that make it easier to detain and deport, arrest, and imprison people on the basis of race or national origin.

Race and Identity

Lurking in the background of much of the preceding discussion is the significance of race, which, for the last 200 years, has been a particularly highly charged means of defining collective identity.

When it first appeared in English around the beginning of the sixteenth century, the word "race" had a fairly neutral meaning, referring simply to different kinds of people or things. By the late eighteenth century, the term was used increasingly to designate fixed, biological, and hierarchical differences between groups of people. It became, in other words, caught up in the currency of power. The science of population that Foucault saw as foundational to biopolitics (see Chapter 6) was essentially racist in character, classifying populations according to biological notions of "fitness" and cultural development based on physical characteristics. The hierarchies constructed in this way helped to legitimate colonial practices of genocide, slavery, as well as eugenics, which aimed to effect "the hereditary improvement of the human race by controlled selective breeding" (thefreedictionary.com). Racism also provided justification for subtler forms of violence, such as residential school systems in Canada and Australia, which forcibly removed Aboriginal children from their families in order to cultivate in them the qualities of human civilization that their own cultures were thought to lack.

Race, then, along with the whole chain of cultural assumptions it drags behind it, is not only inextricably linked to racism (see Figure 7.4); it is directly predicated on it. In other words, "'racism' is not so much a product of the concept of race as the very reason for its existence. Without the underlying desire for hierarchical categorization implicit in racism, 'race' would not exist" (Ashcroft *et al*. 198). One of the critical premises this statement illustrates is that "race" is not a natural, pre-given category, but one that assumes significance in particular historical circumstances to suit particular purposes.

Postcolonial Identities

Regardless of its dubious scientific status, it is inarguable that race, like other markers of identity, *matters* in a cultural, political, and economic sense, affecting not just the way different people are represented based on the group they allegedly "belong" to by virtue of skin color, but also economic opportunities, social freedoms, and even mortality. Confidently forged in colonialism, racism persists in quieter ways in *post*colonial societies, while meeting powerful resistance from those who recognize its lingering effects (see Close-up 7.4).

Close-Up 7.4 Postcolonialism

Beginning with India/Pakistan in 1947, most of Britain's former colonies became independent in the three decades following the Second World War. In a technical way, then, the period from approximately 1950 through to the end of the twentieth century can be referred to as **postcolonial**. Postcolonial*ism* refers to a body of theory that studies literatures and cultures produced in the aftermath of colonialism. So (confusingly), in direct opposition to two other "posts" we have talked about or will discuss in this and the previous chapter—postfeminism and postracism, each of whose belief in the "pastness" of oppression represents a kind of historical amnesia—postcolonialism describes a critical perspective concerned with the persistence of—and resistance to—the legacies of 500 years of colonialism. Postcolonialism is particularly interested in the ways in which people from colonized societies (some of whom still reside in their places of origin, others who have become part of diasporas around the world, with large concentrations in metropolitan centers: New York, London, Toronto) have variously adapted to, appropriated, and transformed the European cultures thrust on them by colonialism.

Figure 7.4 The line between national pride and racism is often blurry. Following a number of incidents of aggression on and off the field in previous tournaments, during Euro 2012 the Union of European Football Associations joined with players in a highly publicized anti-racism campaign. Source: © Tony Marshall/EMPICS Sport

Decolonizing Cultures

In one of the more infamous events of the last age of empire, representatives of the dominant European powers met—in the spirit of cooperation—over a period of a couple of months in 1884–85 to divvy up the territory of Africa among themselves. As a result of what became known as the Berlin Conference, more than 30 newly created states, "superimposed over the one thousand indigenous cultures and regions of Africa" (Rosenberg), were parceled out among France, Germany, England, Italy, Spain, and Portugal. There were no African representatives at the conference. Some 75 years later, much of Africa successfully won liberation from Europe, via independence movements mounted in the name of the "nations" that had so recently and arbitrarily been imposed *by* Europe.

These newly enfranchised citizens faced a significant challenge in affirming identities that would not, somehow, simply echo the hierarchical categories of race and nation that defined colonial discourse. The Négritude movement of the 1950s, for example, challenged both the supremacy of European culture and the arbitrariness of the national boundaries imposed by colonialism, by emphasizing a pan-Africanist identity, inspired by a rich collective history and culture. Instrumental in asserting and demonstrating the legitimacy of Indigenous African and diasporic Caribbean forms of cultural expression, Négritude was also limited by the essentialist mythology of race in which identity is defined (and *con*fined) by a narrowly prescribed set of physical characteristics.

A key task for postcolonial writers and artists was to reaffirm the substance and value of worlds that the colonizers had deemed empty of culture. As Nigerian writer Chinua Achebe put it in a 1975 essay, "The Novelist as Teacher": "I would be quite satisfied if my novels (especially the ones set in the past) did no more than teach my readers that their past—with all its imperfections—was not one long night of savagery from which the first Europeans acting on God's behalf delivered them" (45). At the same time, Achebe, along with other anticolonial writers such as Frantz Fanon, stressed that postcolonial national culture could not appeal to mythological vision of the precolonial past, but must instead reflect the living reality of African people. Out of the violent turmoil of colonialism, critical insights emerged into the "truth" of imagined community. Stuart Hall put it this way:

> Cultural identities come from somewhere, have histories. But, like everything which is historical, they undergo constant transformation. Far from being eternally fixed in some essentialised past, they are subject to the continuous "play" of history, culture and power. Far from being grounded in mere "recovery" of the past, which is waiting to be found, and which when found, will secure our sense of ourselves into eternity, identities are names we give to the different ways we are positioned by, and position ourselves within, the narratives of the past. ("Cultural Identity" 225)

Cultural identities *do* come from somewhere; the roots of culture in place are particularly critical for Indigenous societies. Yet for Hall (Jamaican born, British trained, and one of the founders of cultural studies) and others, postcolonial cultures, and the identities that arise from them, are significantly shaped through movement.

Diaspora and Cultural Hybridity

The term **diaspora** refers to the dispersal or scattering of a people, by choice or by force (and often those motives are blurred), from their homeland to diverse geographical regions. Colonialism itself was a diasporic process, as it involved the movement of millions of Europeans across the globe. For some, such as the convicts transported to Australian penal colonies, the trip was far from voluntary. In the case of many of the colonial settlers, comprising largely poor, marginalized members of their respective societies, relocation to the colonies in search of opportunities was a choice only in the most technical sense.

Arguably the most traumatic process of migration, and one that has become central to contemporary theorizations of diaspora (see Gilroy's *The Black Atlantic*), was the forced exile of thousands of Africans as slaves, who constituted the primary labor force in the American colonies. The new cultural forms that evolved out of that massive uprooting had a profound effect on postcolonial society, particularly in the Caribbean where indigenous populations had been virtually wiped out. The process of global migration initiated by colonialism has accelerated in the years following decolonization, as people from the former colonies have migrated to metropolitan centers, including the settler–invader societies of the United States, Australia, and Canada. These movements have fragmented traditional place-bound communities at the same time as they have created new ones, shaped by complex dynamics of memory, movement, and encounters with new places and cultures

The Musical Diaspora

The dynamics of diaspora have also produced new and powerful forms of popular expression, nowhere more evident, perhaps, than in the realm of music. The dominance of musical forms rooted in ex-African slave culture—jazz, blues, rock and roll—leads one critic to take note of the remarkable situation in which "an utterly exploited and dominated group managed to colonize not European music, which is henceforth relegated to the outermost margins of 'high' culture, but Music itself" (Brown 24). Whether or not the evidence supports such a global claim, one need only look at the contemporary examples of rap and hip-hop as forms that developed not out of only black, but specifically diasporic, culture. "Rap," as Paul Gilroy notes,

> is a hybrid form rooted in the syncretic social relations of the South Bronx where Jamaican sound-system culture, transplanted during the 1970s, put down new roots and in conjunction with specific technological innovations, set in train a process that was to transform black America's sense of itself and a large proportion of the popular music industry as well. (*Small* 125)

Of course, rap and hip-hop have long transcended the borders of the United States, shaping music throughout the world. Groups such as Team Rezofficial and War Party in Canada and Indigenous Intrudaz in Australia use rap and hip-hop as a way to define Indigenous identity, drawing on the social history of those styles to stress similarities between lives lived in the margins of the majority culture. The dynamics of diasporic culture, especially when they are embodied in forms such as music, which is boundary crossing by its very nature, move beyond identities defined by race to illuminate and create wider, more **hybrid** communities.

A late twentieth-century buzzword that retains some of its zing, *hybridity* is often used to describe a condition of multicultural plurality, a happy blend of cultures thrown together in a gigantic global jam session. As theorized by contemporary critics such as Homi Bhabha, however, hybridity describes not just a movement between identities, but also an agitation *within* the notion of identity itself whereby, through cultural exchange, we are forced to recognize the "other" within ourselves. That is, contemporary movements of cultural exchange do not just break down singular identities into multiple and conflicted forms; rather, they reveal that identities were multiple and conflicted all along. Thus, the forces of diaspora, and the forms of cultural hybridity they enhance, powerfully influence the formation of contemporary group identity. As well as reconfiguring the identities of those who have experienced migration in a direct way, the politics of diaspora has shaped the production of community more generally, creating greater fluidity—and sometimes conflict—between collectivities defined by race, class, and cultural tradition.

We need to be cautious, however, not to read the story of identity and community as a tidy linear narrative that moves from enclaves of race and nation to a more open and cosmopolitan global culture shaped by diaspora and hybridity. Identity and/or community formations in the contemporary world are characterized by strong foundations in traditional models of belonging that are constantly being broken, modified, and in some cases reinforced in response to the pressures of globalization (see Chapter 9).

Postnational Identities: Melted, Frozen, Reconstituted

Consumerism, Identity, and Resistance

As we have noted above, the breaking up of traditional identity categories has been accompanied by the resurgence of new forms of nation and identity politics. Many of these movements are informed by strong histories of marginalization that cannot be addressed by a new rhetoric of inclusivity and the erasure of distinct identities. As with all such collective identity projects, they are also beset by problems of exclusion and the suppression of internal differences, such as those explored in *Little Mosque on the Prairie*.

An additional problem with the assertion of more or less homogeneous group identities rests in the danger of commodifying difference—that is, of turning it into an exotic spectacle that not only lacks political agency, but also further disenfranchises minority groups by objectifying them for consumption by the majority. This danger is accentuated in our intensely visual culture, which tends to operate through the *aestheticization* of difference, in which meaning is reduced to pure visual effect. This form of signification is more or less harmful depending on the power of the group whose identity is being portrayed, and the context in which that portrayal occurs—how it is represented, and how and by whom it has been produced.

Through the commodification of culture, "objects and images are torn free of their original referents and their meanings become a spectacle open to almost infinite translation. Difference ceases to threaten, or to signify power relations. Otherness is sought after for its exchange value, its exoticism and the pleasures thrills and adventures it can offer" (J. Rutherford 11).

The Marketing of Difference

Difference has become a major marketing tool, functioning not just to increase profits by appealing to increasingly narrow market segments, but also to reproduce a particular ideological vision that harnesses the happy image of unity through diversity to an individualist ethic of consumerism. Represented most famously in 1980s Benetton ads, which promoted an idealized racial diversity through the presentation of stereotypically white, black, and Asian models dressed in different-colored sweaters, the strategy of difference also defines more recent ad campaigns by companies such as Gap and Nike. These ads convey a message of corporate social responsibility, while carefully abstracting the images they present from any complicating historical contexts. Thus, "difference is stripped of all social and political antagonisms and becomes a commercial symbol for what is youthfully chic, hip, and fashionable" (H. Giroux *Disturbing* 15).

Figure 7.5 With their in-your-face violation of cultural taboos surrounding race and sexuality, Benetton ads have been read as both socially progressive and crassly exploitative of the minority groups represented in them. Source: © 1991 Benetton Group SpA. http://www.benettongroup/media-press/image-gallery/

These representations of difference interact in complicated ways with actual group identity. On the one hand, advertising depends on extensive research in which consumers are polled in an attempt to identify genuine group identities, which then become the basis for the images portrayed in ads. As our discussion of consumption in Chapter 5 emphasizes, however, marketers ultimately do not find so much *create* their ideal consumers, appropriating forms of identity, meaning, and pleasure that are based on memory and lived experience, and shaping them within superficial categories of "lifestyle"—in which being part of a particular tribe (or switching from one tribe to another) is as simple as changing one's shirt or listening to a different band (see Figure 7.5).

This is not to suggest that there is a simple distinction between "real," lived identities and those produced through commercial media; indeed, as Benedict Anderson shows, modern identities are inseparable from the structures of the media and the capitalist economy. Just as forms of early print media such as the newspaper played an instrumental role in the creation of national identities, more recent forms of electronic media have helped to shape postmodern identities. The burgeoning of a global (if primarily English-speaking) Internet culture has helped to facilitate forms of community that are not contained by national borders. At the same time, nations persist, their forms adapting to the changing functions of states in the late capitalist economy.

The Postmodern Nation

Outside the rhetoric of far right political parties and drunken soccer fans, essentialist appeals of the "blood-and-soil" variety do not generally turn up in the language of the modern democratic nation. Does this mean that the "imagined community" at the heart of contemporary nation-states has become more inclusive of difference and more open to outsiders? Not necessarily. The imperative for modern states to foster freedom and be open to global commercial flows (see Chapter 9) persists alongside a preoccupation—heightened since 9/11—with security. A glance at the Government of Canada's web site in June 2012 confirmed these aims: the major stories of the day, represented by three slides that loop across the top of the page, are "Government of Canada Introduces the Faster Removal of Foreign Criminals Act," "PM welcomes all-member support for entry into Trans-Pacific Partnership," and "Harper Government Welcomes Sichuan Airlines' Inaugural Passenger Flight to Vancouver International Airport." What Wendy Larner calls the "spatial imaginary" of the nation has come to be defined by a focus on "mobility, fluidity and networks" (46), which the state seeks not to restrict, but to regulate and enhance the vitality of the population and the systems (economic, political, transportation, communications) that support it. This biopolitical aim (see Chapter 6 for additional discussion of biopolitics) works alongside, and in support of, the imperative of economic competitiveness. With capitalism as the overarching narrative, the concepts of "freedom" and "security" assume a very specific meaning, which favors the goals and activities of business over (for example) environmental protection: thus, the celebration of freer trade with China (including extensive Chinese investments in the Alberta Oil Sands) proceeds at the same time as the government moves to prohibit Canadian environmental organizations from receiving support from foreign "radicals" ("Environmental").

The concept of strengthening the nation through the governance of flows also plays out in obvious ways with respect to immigration. Eugenics—and the idea of race that sustained it—reached its apex in Nazi Germany, and then lost steam; for obvious reasons. But while the idea of hierarchy based on physical characteristics of race may have fallen out of favor, at least superficially, the principles that inform it—such as the belief in a linear path of human civilization, along which some groups have progressed farther than others—persist, even in official government discourse. A striking example is the Canadian Ministry of Citizenship and Immigration, whose official guide for potential immigrants makes a point of explaining that "Canada's openness and generosity do not extend to barbaric cultural practices that tolerate spousal abuse, 'honour killings', female genital mutilation, forced marriage, or other gender-based violence. Those guilty of these crimes are severely punished under Canada's laws" ("Discover").

While no one would suggest that Canada *should* welcome those practices, the appeal to gender equality here provides cover for a crude characterization of "barbaric" foreign cultures. A cynical reading might note that Canada's claims to enlightened handling of violent crimes against women look a bit less sturdy in the face of the 2012 UN inquiry into the disappearance of more than 600 Aboriginal women over the previous two decades, and the indifferent response of Canadian police and government (Talaga). Critics of the *Discover Canada* guide, which was written in 2009 and revised slightly in 2011, note that it differs quite a bit from previous versions in its strong emphasis on military history, British colonial roots, and "what the guide identifies as Canadian traditions, values and culture" (Jafri 2; see also Dhamoon and Abu Laban). The absence of direct reference to race is consistent with a more or less official mythology of "postracism." Like postfeminism (discussed in the previous chapter), postracism, which is reinforced by documents like the Harper Government's 2008 apology to students of Indian residential schools, expresses the belief that racism was a tragic remnant of an unenlightened past, which has now been superseded. The upshot of this myth is that glaring inequalities, such as those expressed in high incarceration rates among racial minorities (in Saskatchewan,

Aboriginal men and women account for 15% of the population as a whole, but 79% of the prison population; S.S. Giroux) and differential sentencing (those found guilty of murder in US states where capital punishment is legal are more likely to receive the death penalty when the victim is white; Dieter 20), cannot be seen as having any connection to historical or institutional forms of discrimination that we have supposedly overcome. Rather, they must be understood in terms of individual, family, or cultural inadequacy (poor self-control, weak parenting, unenlightened/"barbaric" values, etc.).

Even when the ghosts of racism are not evident, the biopolitical discourse that shapes our contemporary culture works in the spirit of "optimizing" the health and productivity of the national population by creating normative scales based on sociocultural fitness, or perceived risk (of school failure, crime, obesity, poor health, etc.). Reliance on such scales as a form of measurement extends across academic disciplines of psychology, criminology, and public health into the media and popular consciousness; such apparently "scientific" categories become quickly translated into categories of exclusion. Because they abandon crude black-and-white stereotypes in favor of slippery, more neutral-sounding modes of discrimination, they can be mobilized in support even of seemingly progressive causes. Thus, an article seeking to challenge negative stereotypes of immigrants as "a drain on society, lazy, and [living] off social assistance" offered what was intended to be a reassuring statistic: "the percentage of low income, recent immigrant adults who had work-limiting disabilities was 11 per cent, significantly lower than the 26 per cent of other low-income Canadians who could not work because of their disabilities" (Wong). It is impossible to read this in the positive light in which it is clearly intended without acknowledging the hierarchies and exclusions on which it is based: in addition to assuming an equation between social assistance and laziness, it suggests that disability is antithetical to citizenship. In trying to validate a certain class of immigrants (wealthy, productive), the article implicitly devalues those—including their struggling Canadian counterparts—who are poor, or unable to work because of a disability.

The discussion above highlights some aspects—we would argue negative aspects—of some contemporary ways of imagining national community. Efforts by Canada, along with governments of other wealthy nations, to restrict further the possibility for immigrants, particularly refugees, to find sanctuary have mobilized groups such as No One Is Illegal—a network of anti-racist activists and church groups based in cities across the world who work on behalf of refugees and those with insecure citizenship status. Members of this group work to counter discriminatory and exploitative work policies (such as low remuneration and denial of basic rights to migrant workers) as well as the global economic inequities (poverty, war, etc.) that exacerbate those conditions and force people to immigrate.

Virtual Belonging

"Can we build a new kind of politics? Can we construct a more civil society with our powerful technologies? Are we extending the evolution of freedom among human beings?" (Katz 68). These stirring questions (in sharp contrast to the ironic tone of Joe's rant) provide the lead-in to an article in the December 1997 issue of *Wired* magazine describing the emergence of a new kind of community—the digital nation. Based on a Merrill Lynch–*Wired* survey of the attitudes and beliefs of users of communications technology—cell phone, beeper, laptop, and home computer—the article set about to describe (and celebrate) the possibilities of digital citizen- or *netizen*ship, a new form of belonging unconstrained by place, gender, race, sexual orientation, or national origin.

Figure 7.6 Social networking sites offer some of the same forms of support and connection provided by traditional communities along with new possibilities of flexibility. Whether they strengthen or threaten those more material connections is a different question. Source: Original to author

If we accept the premise of this article, the explosion of membership in online social networking sites since its publication represents a huge leap for community and even democracy. (We discuss some of the political implications of the Internet in Chapter 10.) With respect to the capacity for digital culture to enhance and extend community, the verdict is mixed (see Figure 7.6). Fifteen years after writing a book that optimistically outlined the liberating possibilities of online social engagement, in 2010 psychologist Sherry Turkle produced the much darker *Alone Together*, lamenting the enlistment of Internet users' social identities by corporate venues like Facebook, and the related impoverishment of communication: in place of meaningful, and sometimes messy, face-to-face encounters we opt for the cleaner, faster mode of tweeting and texting. In contrast to Turkle's argument that computers foster self-absorption and narcissism, other researchers emphasize the possibilities, along with the risks, of the Internet as a space in which youths in particular are cultivating vital skills for navigating the tricky process of identity construction along increasingly porous lines of publicity/privacy (Boyd; see also Valenzuela *et al.*).

Forms of communication clearly play a vital role in defining how we can be in the world and with each other. But whether we see our social bonds deepening and extending or becoming more shallow and brittle, it is important not to overestimate the role of technology without considering the broader social, political, and economic contexts in which particular technologies flourish. The complex processes that can be gathered under the heading of "globalization" (discussed in Chapter 9) form the backdrop to both shifting currents of identity and community and the technologies that support them.

Suggested Activity 7.3

How and to what extent is your sense of identity and community shaped by digital technologies? In your experience, does digital communication enhance and/or restrict possibilities for connection, belonging, and social responsibility?

Deterritorialization/Reterritorialization

The weakening of traditional borders obstructing the flow of information, goods, money, and, to a lesser extent, people has created new forms of community and made it possible to imagine the fulfillment of Marshall McLuhan's idea of a truly "global village." At the same time, the economic and social inequalities that define current global relations—inequalities that are, by most estimates, growing—seriously undercut the utopian ideas presented in articles such as Katz's. These realities, in combination with concerns about loss of cultural heritage, a form of historical belonging that is often grounded in the ecology of particular places, give rise to new forms of nationalism and other models of local community that rival the placeless world of the netizen. While some of these new identities clearly serve to advance the autonomy of their members, others (gated communities, anti-immigrant and fundamentalist groups) in paradoxical cooperation with the *dis*identifying forces of global capitalism that they in principle oppose, serve to further entrench inequality and conflict.

Gates are not the only means of enforcing community homogeneity. Variations of the guide for immigrants produced by the Canadian government represent efforts by municipalities to stave off the unsettling tides of globalization by attempting to enforce strict (often blatantly racist) identity codes. The small agricultural town of Hérouxville, Quebec, prepared a document for newcomers advising them that in Quebec a woman can "among other things, drive a car, vote freely, sign checks, decide for herself" and "dress as she sees fit respecting of course the democratic decency." Conversely, its council would "consider that killing women in public beatings, or burning them alive are not part of our standard of life" ("Hérouxville Town Charter"). Adopted in response to debates over provincial policy regarding the "reasonable accommodation" of religious minorities, the code was widely criticized for its obvious targeting of Muslims. Hérouxville's status as an almost exclusively white, Catholic, francophone community with only one immigrant family—one blogger sarcastically observed: "Well that's a shock. You'd think people would be lining up to move to such a welcoming place" ("Quebec Town")—only strengthened the charges of xenophobia.

While we can be shocked at the naked hostility of the motion (which, it should be noted, attracted some sympathy as well as condemnation), it is important to think about some of the surrounding circumstances. In defense of the document, councillor André Drouin claimed that most of the criticism came from "people of the ruling classes, the elected and the non-elected, and from people considered to be part of the intellectual elite" (Drouin, qtd. in "Bouchard"). Using **populist** rhetoric (see Chapter 1), he defends what he deems to be an expression of democratic will accountable to "'Québecois' particularities" against the powerful, unelected judiciary of English Canada. Not mentioned, but implied, are the urban elites within Quebec, in Montreal in particular, whose accommodation of minorities rarely seems to extend to poor white farmers. As Quebec journalist Alain Dubuc observes:

> We are reminded that the fragmentation of a society can take on several different forms, and that the risk of withdrawal or retreat, which can damage the connection between host society and newcomers, may also divide the host society itself. What

separates the urban and rural worlds can sometimes be more important than what separates communities sharing the same urban space.

The elite—politicians, judges, intellectuals and the media—have elaborated a vision of the relationship between the majority and the various minorities, without bothering to check if the people were following along, and pretending not to see the cracks forming in the self-righteous facade.

We must not forget this other more contentious dialogue, even though it gets a lot less attention, if we want to be able to respond to the kinds of fear and escalation that gives birth to crises such as Hérouxville. (Dubuc A17)

The image of community expressed in Hérouxville is worlds away from that of the television series *The O.C.* with which we began this chapter. Hérouxville is a real place, and "the O.C"—at least as it is depicted in the television show—is not; but it is worthwhile to compare for a moment the two visions, for what they say about the fears and fantasies that shape our imagined communities. At one end of the fantasy extreme is a world of unfettered mobility, in which concerns about individual freedom supersede concerns about cultural identity, democracy, or equality. At the other end is a world of stability and security, in which social interaction is governed by tradition. Though one appears to be more liberal than the other (the standard of "decency" governing women's dress is a bit, well, stretchier in Newport Beach than it is in Hérouxville), both represent themselves as socially progressive. In both fantasy communities, the rules of engagement are unwritten but firmly understood. In different ways, the two fantasies conceal fears of the racial tensions, forms of (post)colonial oppression, and growing economic inequalities that beset real communities, including Hérouxville, Quebec, and Orange County, California.

Community or Collectivity?

Throughout this chapter we have talked about the vitality of community as a site of belonging, and also about its pitfalls, as an imagined enclosure whose strength is seen to lie in its exclusion of and competition with others, whether "others" are defined in national, racial, or religious terms, or simply as outcasts from the category of community altogether. In tension with the segregationist implications of community, there exist alternative ways of thinking about belonging and living with others, some with deep historical roots and others more recent. To reflect the less solid, more self-conscious and mobile character of these groups, it makes sense to give them the different designation of "collectivities."

As we noted in Chapter 2, the working-class consciousness that flourished along with industrialization gave rise to a labor movement whose various factions sought to hasten the end, or at least to soften the effects, of the brutal effects of capitalist exploitation. At least two factors have eroded this consciousness. First, the burgeoning of other social movements, including the Civil Rights movement, feminism, and the gay rights movement from the mid-twentieth century on, came to complicate straightforward narratives of capitalist oppression, as well as unquestioned assumptions about the uniformity of working-class identities and interests. Second, the globalization of production and consumption that has accelerated since the 1970s (see Chapter 9 for a more detailed discussion of globalization) has eroded the conditions that made it possible to collectivize (e.g., job security, the relative fixity of companies' location and organization), at the same time as the neoliberal ideology of individual freedom has made it difficult to imagine not just forms of working-class unity, but any type of solidarity with others.

Thus, while the modes of identity politics noted above continue to create constellations of affiliation and attachment, the "politics" sometimes seems to have faded into the background; meanwhile, "identity" increasingly focuses on taste and lifestyle: the clothes we wear and the music we listen to, what we buy (or don't buy), our hobbies, and our "likes" all offer paths to connect with others—smoothed by social networking sites such as Facebook, Twitter, and Pinterest, which allow us to transcend the narrower, and sometimes less congenial, confines of our immediate social surroundings. Whether digital culture has helped to create a new democratic sphere of global "netizens" is questionable (see Chapter 10 for further discussion of digital culture). It has, however, facilitated the communication of ideas about global collectivity—some of which long predate the invention of the Internet.

Global Belonging

Cosmopolitanism—a mode of thought that emphasizes shared principles of (and obligations to) global humanity that supersede national differences without doing away with them—was first articulated in modern times by Immanuel Kant in 1795. Though it has earned criticism for its Eurocentric assumptions, which risk papering over differences and inequalities in postcolonial society, it retains its imaginative power through creative rewritings in contemporary times—particularly around the concept of hospitality toward marginalized populations (refugees, the homeless, etc.; see, for example, Cheng and Robbins; Derrida).

Ecology, a way of envisioning the world that emphasizes interconnections between human and nonhuman animals, and recognizes the dependence of both on planetary systems, offers another powerful framework for imagining the place of individuals in the wider world. Though it is informed by biological science and the environmentalist movement since the 1970s, it also echoes, sometimes unconsciously (and sometimes crassly and naively), traditional Indigenous conceptions of the relationships that tie people to each other and to other living things and the places that sustain them. Ecology has come to offer a particularly compelling model of global connectedness in the face of problems such as climate change, and environmental risks more generally, which theorists such as Ulrich Beck suggest have an ironically democratizing effect in that "by their nature they endanger *all* forms of life" (22). Here, too, the appeal of ecology's apparently universal inclusivity must be tempered by a recognition of the unevenness of circumstance: environmental benefits, costs, and risks are not allocated equally (think, for example, of the uneven distribution of access to clean drinking water, or the location of polluting industries or waste facilities). Even the assignment of priority around environmental concerns (climate, biodiversity, air quality, or basic sanitation—which is the most urgent issue?) is likely to vary depending on which part of the world, and in what circumstances one lives.

Imagined Collectivities

Thinking about inequality takes us from identity back into the terrain of politics once again, which emerges as an important site of organization at a time when the idea of the social is both eroding and more important than ever. Both the difficulty and the necessity of finding identity through collectivity appear in the joining together, beginning with the 1999 demonstration against a meeting of the World Trade Organization in Seattle, of different groups united by their opposition to economic globalization. Significantly, the people who came together on this and other occasions, some of whom participated in the founding of the World Social Forum in Port Alegre in 2001, included farmers, environmentalists, students, socialists, and anarchist groups that previously had little to do with one another and that differed radically in demographics, geographical base, and even politics. They came together, however, in new and powerful coalitions, united through their critical resistance to neoliberalism. The Occupy Movement represents another such coalition, in which the recognition of shared precariousness unites workers, students, and the unemployed—that 99% of the population that seems not to have benefited from the directions in which the world has been heading for the past three decades or more.

These alliances point to a significant shift in the dynamics of collective identity from the relatively fixed markers of class, nation, and race to more fluid and multiple forms of definition. The celebration of expanding social freedoms can sometimes lead us to over-look growing insecurities that accompany the fluidity of neoliberalism; these insecurities can lead both to the tightening of borders (gated communities, ethnically homogeneous enclaves) and to the formation of new collectivities focused on ideas of social and environmental justice. These collectivities both reflect and influence the generation of identities in the realm of popular culture—identities that may not be explicitly political, but that have concrete political *effects* in the way in which people imagine their places in the world and capacities to effect change.

Suggestions for Further Reading

Anderson, Benedict. *Imagined Communities*. London: Verso, 1983.

Bhabha, Homi. *Nation and Narration*. London: Routledge, 1990.

Brown, Garrett Wallace, and David Held. *The Cosmopolitanism Reader*. London: Polity, 2011.

Code, Lorraine. *Ecological Thinking: The Politics of Epistemic Location*. Oxford: Oxford University Press, 2006.

Hall, Stuart, and Paul du Gay, eds. *Questions of Cultural Identity*. London: Sage, 1996.

Mackey, Eva. *The House of Difference: Cultural Politics and National Identity in Canada*. Toronto: University of Toronto Press, 2002.

Said, Edward. *Culture and Imperialism*. London: Chatto and Windus, 1993.

Said, Edward. *Orientalism*. New York: Vintage, 1979.

Smith, Jackie. *Social Movements for Global Democracy*. Baltimore, MD: Johns Hopkins University Press, 2007.

8

Subcultures and Countercultures

*Not a moment passes without each one of us experiencing, on every level of reality,
the contradiction between oppression and freedom; without each one of us being
caught up and weirdly twisted by two antagonistic perspectives simultaneously.*
(Raoul Vaneigem, *The Revolution of Everyday Life*, 4)

The Mainstream and Other Streams

To a large degree, the way in which we have been addressing popular culture in this book
has been to focus on the dominant or most prevalent forms of culture in the Western
world today. By "dominant" we mean what is usually described as mass culture—forms of
culture that are accessible, widely available, and intended for consumption by as many
people as possible. There is no real mystery about the forms of popular culture that one
might consider to be dominant: Hollywood and Bollywood blockbusters, pop music on
the Billboard Top 40, broadcast television, video games, Google, and so on.

There are two ways in which such things might be seen as dominant. First, if we measure the prevalence of this or that form of culture by the sheer number of people that
listen to it, watch it, or otherwise participate in it (whether this is measured by attendance, sales, or revenue figures), James Cameron's *Avatar* (2009) or Christopher Nolan's
The Dark Knight Rises (2012) would be dominant in ways in which films such as Gary
Burns's *Waydowntown* (2000) or Guy Maddin's *My Winnipeg* (2007) could only hope to
be. Second, dominance can refer to the core set of beliefs, ideas, and identities that are
circulated through forms of popular culture. In this respect, *Waydowntown* might be
seen as an expression of dominant culture, too. Though made on a small budget and
shot in the Western Canadian city of Calgary, the critique of dead-end business culture
articulated in *Waydowntown* shares a great deal with other much more popular films,
such as *American Beauty* or *Office Space* (see Figure 8.1). Even though *Waydowntown* is
an indie film, financed outside of the major studio system, formally and structurally it
resembles the most common forms of movie making (*My Winnipeg*'s mockumentary
style is slightly more adventurous). In this second, wider understanding of dominance, a
small or limited audience is not in and of itself a guarantee that a film or any other form
of popular culture advocates or expresses views and ideas contrary to mainstream,
dominant culture.

While we have tended to focus on the meaning and impact of dominant forms of popular culture, some of the ideas that we have been discussing in the preceding chapters
cannot help but cast doubt on the existence of this very fact—that is, that there is anything

Popular Culture: A User's Guide, International Edition. Imre Szeman and Susie O'Brien.
© 2017 John Wiley & Sons, Inc. Published 2017 by John Wiley & Sons, Inc.

Figure 8.1 Canadian filmmaker Guy Maddin's *My Winnipeg* is a formally inventive and adventurous mockumentary about his hometown, Winnipeg. Source: © AF archive/Alamy

like a single, dominant culture. In Chapter 4, we challenged Horkheimer and Adorno's culture industry thesis, which imagines people as little more than consumers who are completely duped by the nature of the capitalist world in which they live; in our discussion of consumption in Chapter 5, we drew attention to the multiple ways in which people make meaning through their varied practices of consumption; and in our discussion of groups and identities in the previous two chapters, it is clear that identity formation, too, is more complicated than might be suggested by the idea of dominant forms of popular culture.

In the context of these discussions, "mainstream" culture looks a lot less mainstream than we generally tend to imagine when we employ this term. Or to put this another way: one of the things that becomes clear when studying popular culture is that our idea of the mainstream is sometimes less a reality than it is a cultural construction that regulates our activities through the establishment of very powerful cultural norms—norms that everyone adheres to in some ways, but that everyone also contravenes or goes against in numerous others. No one is purely mainstream, not even the characters in the television series *Friends* (who, for instance, revel in free pornography, engage in sexual relationships outside of marriage, and engage in other forms of behavior that belie their otherwise straight, clean-cut image). As popular culture itself has pointed out over and over again, there is an infinity of strange and unusual things happening behind the "normal," everyday façade of white picket fences and suburban garage doors (as you can see in any episode of *Big Love*, *Breaking Bad*, or *Weeds*).

Yet to say that the idea of the mainstream is a creation is not to say that there is no such thing. There *do* seem to be general, widespread patterns of social behavior present within societies that guide both individual and group activity. As we have seen throughout this book, one of the main reasons why scholars have become interested in the study of popular culture is because of the powerful role it plays in generating and regulating social behavior. Scholars are also interested in how popular culture has been used to work *against* dominant ways of behaving and acting, in both the minor ways in which (as we suggested above) everyone goes against the grain of the mainstream in some way, but also in more extreme or direct ways. In this chapter, we will be focusing on groups that challenge the values, ideas, and structures of mainstream culture consciously and directly through their actions and practices: subcultures and countercultures. In their actions and practices, subcultures and countercultures oppose dominant structures that they see as limiting, repressive, and/or problematic. Subcultures and countercultures are engaged in the struggle to create new and different forms of social reality. In many cases, but especially since the Second World War, this struggle has often been directed against popular or mass culture itself; paradoxically, this attack on popular culture has frequently come through the creation of new forms of popular culture, which themselves tend to be absorbed into mainstream culture in a perpetual back-and-forth that has shaped contemporary experience profoundly.

Minority–Majority Relationships

In the next section, we will establish some preliminary distinctions between these two kinds of groups. But first, we need to note that the very idea of subcultures and countercultures immediately reinvokes the idea of a dominant culture that we challenged above. Each of the prefixes "sub" and "counter" implies a number of things, as we will see below. One of the main things that they signify, however, is the relationship of a smaller "culture," however understood, to the larger, defining culture of a given society at a given moment. In other words, whatever else they might signal, the concepts of subcultures and countercultures oppose a minority group to the majority: it makes no sense to speak of a subculture or a counterculture that is "dominant."

Furthermore, this minority–majority relationship is generally an antagonistic one. While it has become common to use the term "subculture" to refer to all kinds of practices and activities that might be considered strange or unusual, we will try to use these concepts somewhat more precisely. For example, people who play Scrabble seriously enough to attend tournaments and vie for national (and even global) championships might be interesting or unusual. But these Scrabble players do not constitute a genuine subculture. Why not? First, players of Scrabble—no matter how attentively or religiously—are, in the end, playing a popular game by its prescribed rules. This stands in contrast to, for instance, writers of "slash fiction," who express their own desires and fantasies by writing original (and often erotically charged) stories that borrow characters from popular televisions shows such as *Star Trek*. Similarly, Scrabble players don't bend a popular cultural form into a different shape—like, for example, the numerous fans who produced and distributed online "improved" versions of George Lucas's *Star Wars Episode I: The Phantom Menace*, or have mocked films, videos, and television programs on YouTube. Through their actions, writers of slash fiction, the creators of the "phantom edits," and YouTube "mockumentarians" all express dissatisfaction with the limits and constraints of popular culture; the same cannot be said of serious Scrabble players, who can easily indulge their passion for the game while being otherwise upstanding, productive citizens.

Of course, the same could be said for our other two examples: a phantom editor by night could well be a university professor by day, and YouTube videomakers can be students, lawyers, doctors, or whatever. What we want to draw attention to here is that a practice should not be considered subcultural unless its aim is to draw attention to the limits of majority practices and to offer new practices or cultural forms as an alternative; having an interesting hobby does not a subculture make. Subcultures and countercultures are both antagonistic; one of the ways of distinguishing between subcultures and countercultures is by looking at the precise nature of their antagonism toward mainstream culture and at the kinds of new forms that they propose as an alternative to mainstream or dominant culture.

After making some general distinctions between subcultures and countercultures, the remainder of this chapter will examine the relationship between popular culture and these groups in three ways. First, it will consider the ways in which sub- and countercultures have been *represented* in popular culture, specifically popular film. There are a few reasons why we have chosen to begin with representations of these antagonist cultures. One of the main ways in which sub- and countercultures are brought into contact with the "dominant," mainstream culture is through popular cultural representations of these practices. Our sense of the possibilities and limits of these groups—a sense that tends to be very different from what the groups themselves believe their aims and goals to be—is often staged within popular cultural forms. While analyzing representations of sub- and countercultures does not give us an accurate account of the practices of these groups, it does help us to understand one of the ways in which these practices become meaningful within popular culture. Starting out with representations also reminds us of the proximity of subcultures to mainstream culture. All too commonly, sub- and countercultures are imagined as being absolutely separate from and unaffected by popular culture. The opposite is in fact the case: often, popular culture has an impact on how subcultural groups stylize or represent themselves. To offer just one small snapshot: the roots of the "gangsta" tough-guy pose that emerges in hip-hop culture can be found in part in the gangster tough-guy pose of *The Godfather* films. In the mid-1990s, rapper Snoop Dogg styled himself "Tha Doggfather," striking a very *Godfather*-esque pose on an album cover. The writers of *The Sopranos* have whimsically depicted its contemporary New Jersey hoods watching and making use of Coppola's filmic trilogy as a source for their own gangster poses; "authentic" roots sometimes have representations at their base.

Following this look at representations of sub- and countercultures, the second emphasis of this chapter is on the politics of subcultures in particular. As we will see below, countercultures are usually imagined as explicitly political; it is harder (at first) to see how a subcultural practice like skateboarding might also be political, if in a different way than an organized march down the streets of a capital city might be. We end the chapter with a consideration of some practices of contemporary activist and countercultural groups, especially their engagement with and use of Internet and new communications technologies (this will be discussed in Chapter 10, too).

Investigating the practices of subcultures and countercultures offers rich insights into the ways in which culture, especially popular culture, operates in the world today. From culture jamming (see Close-Up 8.1 later in this chapter) to the practices of religious countercultures (a category in which one might be able to include everything from Mormonism to the Raelians), from the peace movements of the 1960s to the contemporary techno music–infused Love Parades that fill the streets of European cities each summer, there are numerous groups for whom "culture is deeply political" and "can be used as means of resistance" (Duncombe). In the words of Stephen Duncombe, "In order to strive for change, you first have to imagine it, and culture is the repository of the imagination" (35).

Subcultures and Countercultures: What Is the Difference?

In what way do subcultures differ from countercultures? Are they fundamentally different, or do these two terms point to the same groups, activities, and practices, though in slightly different ways?

To some degree, the distinction between subcultures and countercultures is artificial. Subcultures and countercultures flow fluidly into one another: their boundaries are permeable. As the cultural critic George McKay puts it, "subcultures feed the counterculture—the range of subcultural movements from hippy through punk through rave and others contributes to the increasingly resistant lifestyle or perspective of counterculture" (6). Even so, it is both possible and necessary to draw a distinction between subcultures and countercultures, especially if we want to understand both the relationship that each has to popular culture *and* their impact and influence on mainstream culture. While their aims and activities are often congruent, these terms do point to different kinds of practices and activities, and should not be seen as simply interchangeable terms designating the exact same thing.

One way of gauging this difference is by considering the use of the terms in scholarly studies. A quick library search will show that the term "subculture" is used to describe things as diverse as science fiction fans, communities in Appalachia, gay and lesbian communities, the lifestyle of singles, the practices of minority religious groups, cults, squatters, Japanese Americans, bodybuilders, and food cooperatives. A search under the term "counterculture" pulls up a much more limited range of topics: communes, the 1960s, and what have been described as "new social movements"—groups that are engaged in politics outside the boundaries of traditional political parties (e.g., women's rights, the civil rights movement, environmental groups, the anti-globalization movement, etc.).

Even this first, cursory attempt to separate sub- and countercultures highlights a key difference between the two terms: while subcultures may be political in their aims and activities, countercultures are *explicitly* so. The goal of countercultures is to replace the social and political values and beliefs of the majority with their own values, which they see as unjust, discriminatory, limiting, and regressive. For example, the heterogeneous groups and activities that are commonly referred to by the term "the sixties," from the hippie movement to drug culture, from the struggle for civil rights to the movement against the Vietnam War, were motivated by a common dissatisfaction with dominant social and political institutions and a desire to fundamentally alter these values. The energies that fuel countercultures come from the possibility (and hope) of radically altering the way things are. (Of course, the degree of seriousness with which this possibility is pursued varies greatly.) On the other hand, the power of subcultures comes from the tensions created by the relationship between subcultural practices and the practices of majority culture. Subcultures draw strength from the fact that their practices *are not* those of the rest of the society of which they are a part. As Sarah Thornton has put it, "the defining attribute of 'subcultures'...lies with the way the accent is put on the distinction between a particular cultural/social group and the larger culture/society" (5).

Subcultures

The concept of "subcultures" is a relatively recent one, developed first in the 1940s by a group of sociologists associated with the University of Chicago. These sociologists wanted to better understand the complex dynamics of contemporary Western societies. All large societies are made up of numerous smaller groups of people. While we might belong abstractly to a nationally defined society (English, Americans, Slovenians, etc.), we do so through our participation with concrete groups of people with whom we have something in common. Such groups might include political organizations, churches, ethnic communities, sports teams, and work communities. Subcultures are also groups of people who share something in common. What makes subcultures different than other groups or communities in society is that they are (most commonly) groups that deviate or differ from existing social norms.

Subcultures are typically conceived of as "disenfranchised, disaffected and unofficial" (Thornton 2). They exist "underground," outside of the mainstream of society in minor, if not hidden, tributaries and out-of-the-way spaces that they try to secure as their own. Furthermore, subcultures are often identified with youth groups, and youth culture in particular. In contemporary societies, young people have creatively expressed their dissatisfaction with the social norms that they encounter as they enter adulthood by adopting unconventional practices, lifestyles, and attitudes. Space is also an essential component of subcultures: space within which to meet, to act, to form a community, to forge common bonds. Such spaces can range from underground clubs in semi-abandoned parts of large urban centers (CBGB in the Bowery section of New York, Yorkville coffee houses in the 1960s in Toronto) to open-air festivals (the numerous large concerts held in the United Kingdom in the 1970s, outdoor rave events in Europe and Canada in the 1990s); from the use of public spaces by skateboarders (for example, the poured concrete ramps and stairs of government buildings and art galleries) to the "space" that the Internet has made available for the creation of a wide range of virtual subcultures (for example, *Game of Thrones* fan forums, communities that want to do away with copyright, and online gaming portals like Steam).

Countercultures

The concept of a counterculture is equally recent, though, as with the concept of subcultures, the term has since its invention been used to refer to groups and activities prior to the second half of the twentieth century. "Counterculture" is a term still most commonly used in reference to the politics of the 1960s, especially with respect to the art, culture, and politics generated around the protests against the US war in Vietnam.

Countercultures pose an explicit challenge to the existing order of things. Put bluntly: their goal is to change the world. While this is an explicitly political goal, countercultures cannot be reduced to their political activity alone. There is an important cultural aspect to the activities of countercultures, which distinguishes them from (for example) the actions of nongovernmental political organizations (NGOs) or even most contemporary activist groups. Countercultures have their own privileged set of cultural objects (especially forms of countercultural or "alternative" music) through which they express, articulate, and consolidate their political views (think of the link between some forms of popular music in the 1960s and the activism of the period).

To perhaps an even greater degree than subcultures, countercultures express their politics culturally through a demand for a fundamental revision of lifestyle practices. After all, what makes a culture a *counter*culture is its contravention and contradiction of not just mainstream politics, but also the culture that produces these politics, which can be located in the daily, lived practices of the mainstream. If we use as an example 1960s youth culture (in the United States as well as in much of the rest of the world), this reform of lifestyle was expressed in the adoption of communal living (group living in response to the alienation and individualism of capitalist culture, expressed spatially by massively expanded suburbs), vegetarianism (animal rights and healthy lifestyles), drug use (in opposition to mainstream demands that everyone spend their lives engaged in productive labor), and open sexuality (a challenge to the restrictions of "normal" sexuality and the marriage bond). This list could easily be expanded.

Both subcultures and countercultures take culture seriously. They understand not only that culture can be a way of articulating political views and perspectives, but also that in contemporary society culture plays a crucial role in political expression. In general, both have a tendency to view "dominant" popular culture through the lens of Horkheimer and Adorno's cultural industry thesis (see Chapter 4). One of the things that subcultures and countercultures react to is what they see as the dearth of genuine cultural expression and experience in the age of mass culture. In response, they produce their own forms of culture—their own clothing styles, music, and cultural and political practices—and articulate new ways of living and behaving.

Differences of Scale

The emergence of the concepts of subcultures and countercultures following the Second World War can be linked to the decline of genuine public spaces for political debate and a sense that mainstream political groups were no longer accountable to the public. With so many similarities, what distinguishes sub- from countercultures more than anything else is perhaps the *scale* of their reaction to the gradual impoverishment of contemporary political and social life, which seemed to go hand in hand with the fiscal improvement of life in Western countries; even while most people were better off financially, they felt more and more unhappy socially. Countercultures presume to act on a bigger social canvas than subcultures and are limited neither spatially to specific "scenes" or locales, nor by the dominance of youth within them. For example, contemporary anti- or alter-globalization movements include individuals and groups from around the world, and people of all ages with varying ideas about what needs to be changed and how to change it. What might be seen as loosely connecting these different actors is their insistence that "Another World Is Possible" (the animating phrase of the World Social Forums). The Occupy movement in 2011 took a similarly global form, with people collecting together in hundreds of cities across the world (see Figure 8.2). The slogan of Occupy—"We are the 99%"—drew attention to social injustices and economic inequalities experienced by the vast majority of the planet's population, for whom two decades of neoliberalism have meant the massive enrichment of 1% to the detriment of everyone else.

It is important to emphasize that this difference of scale should not by itself be seen as valorizing the politics of countercultures over subcultures. That is, one conclusion that could be reached quickly is that, because countercultures work out their political commitments more explicitly and engage them more directly, they accomplish more than subcultures. Indeed, while countercultures have not been immune to criticism from any number of vantage points, it has been subcultures that are more commonly viewed (by the mainstream media, for example) as little more than self-indulgent practices engaged in by spoiled youth who will "grow out of it" soon enough, or eccentric adults who are spending their free time engaged in practices that are different from what it is imagined most people are doing (and should be doing). This view of subcultures tends to reduce them to something like fashion trends, which young people engage in energetically only to forget about when another trend arises. One of the main things that scholars who have studied subcultures over the past two decades have shown is that this view is mistaken.

Figure 8.2 Members of Occupy Edmonton were prevented by police from entering campus on the National Day of Student Action (February 1, 2012) to protest higher education funding cuts, high tuition fees, and record levels of student debt. After a public outcry, protesters were permitted on campus the following day. Source: Amber Bracken/Edmonton Sun, a division of Postmedia Network Inc.

If subcultures are not always explicit in their politics, their very existence stands as an implicit rejection of the practices and ways of life of majority culture. As we will see below, subcultures have complex politics, too, even if these are expressed in different ways than in countercultures.

We want to stress two points before continuing. First, the goal here is not to lay out strict definitions for the purpose of setting up a taxonomic or classificatory system into which we would then place various resistant, minority groups. The aim of these distinctions is to offer a broad initial framework within which to consider the specifics of sub- and countercultural practices and actions; simply dividing groups into one or another category is only the first step in trying to understand what is going on. Second, as we have already suggested, there is considerable slippage in these categories. As McKay points out, the counterculture draws on subcultures for elements of its own cultural practices. This slippage will be evident in our discussion in this chapter, and, indeed, is endemic to the study of these groups and their practices.

Artistic Manifestos

As an example of this slippage, it is has become common to treat artists' movements and avant-garde manifestos as expressions of countercultural sentiments. In terms of the rough distinctions that we have drawn here, however, artistic avant-gardes seem more like subcultures. Though artist manifestos gesture to wholesale revolutions in sensibility—as in Tristan Tzara's "Dada Manifesto" of 1918: "I am against action; for continuous contradiction, for affirmation too, I am neither for nor against" (249)—they do so within a relatively restricted social sphere (relatively elite forms of artistic production) and do not always demand a complete lifestyle revolution. (That is, being both for and against contradiction does not mean that one has to give up smoking, or one's sports utility vehicle (SUV), and so on; one can be bourgeois and a dadaist at the same time.)

However, the gesture made to a total social revolution is not insignificant. In a way common to countercultures, a shift in the form and style of artistic production is imagined as having large-scale political effects. The French Canadian (or Québécois) manifesto "Refus Global" (1948) was imagined by the painter who is usually seen as its primary author, Paul Émile Borduas, as *maybe* having had an impact on painting in Canada. However, by making this aesthetic intervention through a "total refusal" of the political, social, and religious verities of its era, the manifesto played an essential role in bringing about the social changes in Quebec now described as the "Quiet Revolution." A similar categorical ambiguity can be seen in the case of punk. While punk is almost always treated as a paradigmatic example of a contemporary subculture, the depths of its critique of contemporary culture, which draws on a wide array of political and countercultural currents and theories, suggests that there is more at work than might be indicated by the term subculture.

One final note: as we have stressed elsewhere, it is unproductive simply to dismiss the activities of subcultures and countercultures on the basis of what we know or think we know about (for example) the incorporation of punk or 1960s culture into our present-day mainstream. As we said in Chapter 4, the phrase "Resistance is futile" doesn't turn out to be true—even for the Borg in *Star Trek*, who tried and failed repeatedly to assimilate Captain Picard and his crew into their mechanized world (a perfect allegory for how many of us see the world of contemporary popular culture: as an unfeeling mechanism intent on absorbing everything organic into its metallic confines). Why, then, should it constitute an adequate way of considering the nature of our responses to popular culture? It doesn't—which is not to say that the practices of subcultures and countercultures are not often contradictory or that they do not have problems. They do, but so does everything else: we should not demand purity of aims or authenticity of intent from subcultures and countercultures—in the contemporary world, it is best to imagine that everything is already contaminated, and go from there.

Suggested Activity 8.1

Given the discussion above, is it possible to identify a counterculture (or countercultures) today? Are the various political groups that oppose capitalist culture today linked by common goals and/or ideas about appropriate counter-lifestyles? How does the idea of a counterculture (or countercultures) fit with the relatively new idea of "alternative" culture (or cultures)? Make a list of subcultures and countercultures—and, for that matter, alternative cultures—and try to think about how and why we refer to these groups with these different terms. Are these categories still a productive way to think about contemporary cultural experience?

Popular Representations of Subcultures and Countercultures

How do we come to understand or know about groups that lie outside the mainstream? Unless we happen to be an active part of a particular subculture or counterculture, our knowledge of it comes to us at second hand, through studies, reports, newspaper articles, and, of course, popular culture. Representation plays a crucial role in how we conceive of these sub- and countercultures. For example, for most of us, our sense of what the 1960s counterculture was like and what its lasting significance has been is based on an accumulated sludge of television and film representations, *Behind the Music* documentaries, and experience with the bits and pieces of 1960s "classic" rock that we play along to on *Guitar Hero*, as opposed to detailed reading of studies of the period. It is just as difficult to think about punk except through the lens of films such as *Repo Man* and *Sid and Nancy*; the music of more recent "punk" bands, such as Green Day and blink-182; and perhaps through reading the obituaries of punk luminaries such as Dee Dee Ramone and Joe Strummer (lead singer of The Clash). These popular representations influence our sense of what subcultures and countercultures are about, what they managed to accomplish, and to what degree they "succeeded" or "failed" (which is a common, if strange, way to think about these cultural forms and practices). We need to be conscious of the significance of representation not because it is possible to get the accurate, authentic "truth" about sub- or countercultures, but because we should be aware of the way in which such representations shade our perceptions and interpretations.

The issue of representation raises another important point, one that we alluded to earlier and will discuss in more detail below. In a complex way, popular representations of subcultures and countercultures play an important part not only in how they function, but also in how we understand popular culture. Our sense of subcultures is that they are hidden from view or that their activities take place entirely unnoticed, in the dark. The truth is somewhat different, as Chuck Klosterman makes clear in his discussion of the very different reactions to the almost simultaneous deaths of two American rock musicians: Robin Crosby, lead guitarist for the early 1980s heavy metal band Ratt, and Dee Dee Ramone, bassist for the seminal New York punk band The Ramones. Crosby's death on June 6, 2002 was almost entirely ignored by the press; on the other hand, Ramone's death a day earlier received a huge amount of coverage—the exact opposite of one might expect based on the album sales of each artist. Despite being—or perhaps *because* they were—members of a fringe subculture, The Ramones were seen as representing a development or shift in US culture that had since come to pass. As for Ratt? Though millions and millions of people bought their albums, the band is now "forgotten" in a way that The Ramones (whom at the time very few listened to) are not.

In popular culture, subcultures tend to be viewed in two dichotomous ways: either as threatening and dangerous, or as the conscience of the mainstream—that is, as the "real" cultural expression of a culture that is otherwise dominated by "bad" commercial culture. There is another division built into this first one. When subcultures are represented as dangerous, they are often also paradoxically characterized as lacking substance: as mere style that constantly changes. Part of what is supposedly dangerous about subcultures, then, is that they attract people to engage in activities that have far less substance and meaning than mainstream culture. This is the exact opposite of what the public (or at least the media) reaction to Dee Dee Ramone's death suggests: that it is the practices of subculture that leave the permanent record for an otherwise insubstantial mainstream culture, which is defined by shifts in styles or fashion in music, film, and so on that are driven not by art but by the market. We will consider these conflicted ways of representing subcultures and countercultures by looking briefly at three films: *Forrest Gump* (1994), *Fight Club* (1999), and *Ghost World* (2001).

Forrest Gump: Subcultural Deviance

The goal of the film *Forrest Gump* is to offer an overview of the American experience following the Second World War. It accomplishes this by a fairly typical cinematic and novelist procedure, using the life of one individual, the eponymous Forrest Gump (Tom Hanks), both to highlight important events and milestones in US history during this period and to explore related shifts in culture and sensibility. Forrest, a fatherless, intellectually challenged Southerner, manages over the course of the film to successfully navigate his way through the real and metaphorical landmines of the past 40 years. His life passes through all of the major events of post–Second World War history, and Forrest comes into direct contact with some of the period's important historical figures. Elvis, a boarder in Forrest's home, adopts his performance style by imitating the inhibited gait that Forrest possesses as an adolescent. Forrest wins a national football championship with Alabama on a team coached by the legendary Bear Bryant; plays a crucial role in the struggle to racially integrate schools in the US South; becomes an inadvertent hero as a soldier in Vietnam; becomes a champion Ping-Pong player; guests on Dick Cavett's television show (where he appears alongside John Lennon); single-handedly invents the running craze; and makes a bundle on Apple stock (he should have waited until the appearance of the iPhone to sell!)—just to name a few of the symbolically charged things he accomplishes.

Forrest represents the adventure that America undergoes during this era and he navigates it bluntly, pragmatically, and successfully. For the most part, then, even as the film examines many of the difficult moments in post–Second World War American social and cultural life, it celebrates US drive and initiative and suggests that more good things are coming in the future. Forrest's life ends in that most typical place in American cinema: back at home, folded into the comforts and security of family life.

No account of the US experience after the Second World War would be complete, however, without some attention to the roles played by subcultures and countercultures in creating this history. In *Forrest Gump*, the activity of subcultures is typified through the life history of the other major character in the film: the love of Forrest's life, Jenny. Through the opposition of Jenny and Forrest, it becomes clear that Forrest represents not *all* of American experience, but merely the experience of mainstream culture; Jenny represents an alternative path through recent US history—the dark side of Forrest's generally blissful (or at least, blissed-out) experience. The film is unambiguous in its portrayal of American counterculture. If Jenny is unable to follow Forrest's path through the major institutions of US life—college, the military, small business, sports, and so on—it is because she has been sexually abused by her father. Her immersion in the counterculture is treated less as a conscious choice than as the consequences of a psychic trauma that she never gets to adequately address. Countercultures and subcultures, the film seems to tell us, are for damaged souls. Jenny drifts through the American underworld: she appears in *Playboy*; while Forrest is in the mud of Vietnam, she gets involved with hippies and peaceniks (who drive a VW van painted with rainbow colors); she becomes involved with the SDS (Students' Democratic Society) in Berkeley, which is led by her physically abusive boyfriend; she becomes suicidal after doing lines of coke as part of the early 1980s "me" generation; and, when she finally shows up again in Forrest's life to introduce him to their son, she tells him: "I have some kind of virus and the doctors don't know what it is and there isn't anything they can do about it." If Jenny's trauma leads her into US counterculture, it is her involvement with it—with *all* of it (missing nothing)—that leads to her death.

It is not difficult to see that the film suggests that subcultures and countercultures are dangerous, destructive, and misguided, especially for those involved in them. In the world narrated by Forrest Gump, happiness and fulfillment are achieved only by following the path of the straight and narrow (which in Forrest's case has the added advantage of putting him into contact with important people, like Presidents Kennedy and Nixon). Forrest's own happiness is impeded only by the fact of Jenny's death, which is the direct consequence of her alternative lifestyle. Forrest's son, who represents the future of American society, is in some respects the product of both the mainstream and the counterculture, of Forrest and Jenny. But what the film actually seems to argue is that America has a future *despite* the presence of the subculture. It is up to Forrest, after all, to raise Forrest Jr. It is not accidental that Forrest Jr. is raised in the same place as his father; for all the things that have happened, the real America perseveres, unchanged by the challenges that the counterculture and history seemed to have posed to it. Near the end of the film, Jenny suggests: "I was messed up for a long time." *Forrest Gump* exemplifies very clearly one of the dominant ways in which subcultures are represented—simply as the actions of misguided, messed-up people.

And yet, there are elements of the film that make us question its representation of American counterculture. Most obviously, it is the character of Forrest himself who causes us to wonder about the narrative we are being sold. Jenny is far more intelligent and self-conscious than Forrest; if Forrest represents the mainstream, then the mainstream is shown to be unthinking—emotional and intuitive rather than reasoned and reflective. Forrest suggests that "for some reason I fit in the army like a round peg." His successes come out of his ability to slide into preexisting systems and institutions; he challenges nothing and accepts everything. In *Forrest Gump*, the options in post–Second World War American society come down to two equally problematic positions: *either* one joins the counterculture and challenges norms and limits, but at the price of one's own happiness, health, and life; *or* one unthinkingly accepts "what is," even if this means participating in an imperialist war or raping the environment (as recorded by Forrest's enormous haul of shrimp in the Gulf of Mexico). This is a false choice, of course: we need not acquiesce to the *either/or* that the film constructs for us. Nor need we accept its stereotypes of the counterculture, even if we should note that it is precisely such representations of sub- and countercultures that inform the way in which many of us view their activities, as well as the people who participate in them.

Fight Club: Fight the Power?

A very different, if equally troubling, view of subcultures is presented in David Fincher's cult hit *Fight Club* (see Figure 8.3). What made the film attractive to critics and audiences when it was first released was that it appeared to offer a unique, critical perspective on the values of capitalist society—in particular, the way in which consumption has come to constitute the main goal and purpose of contemporary society. While criticisms of contemporary reality are actually a quite common theme of American cinema, what made *Fight Club* appear to be different from films such as *The Cable Guy* (1996), *The Truman Show* (1998), and *The Matrix* (1999)—or even a more recent film such as *Wall-E* (2008)— was that it translated critique into action through the creation of an anti-capitalist subcultural movement whose ultimate goal is the violent destruction of the system of global consumer credit. (In the wake of the explosion of consumer credit and the crisis caused by the sub-prime mortgage meltdown in 2008, this would be a more popular movement than ever.)

Based on the 1996 first novel by Chuck Palahniuk, *Fight Club* narrates the story of Jack (Edward Norton), an insomniac, bored corporate drone who finds meaning in his life through his newly formed relationship with Tyler Durden (Brad Pitt), a thrill-seeking everyman. In a number of memorable set pieces, both Jack and Tyler rail against the limits of consumer society. In order to make some connection with people in an unfeeling, individuated society, Jack begins to attend group meetings for people struggling with

Figure 8.3 Brad Pitt gets tough on consumer culture in *Fight Club*. Source: © AF archive/Alamy

various diseases and ailments—none of which he has. Jack's job, which is to calculate the cost-effectiveness of consumer recalls (that is, if the cumulative cost of the lawsuits brought against the company as a result of the malfunction of a product would be less than a recall, they cynically decide against it), is depicted in all its existential horror as a brain-deadening series of unfulfilling routines.

It is only when Jack meets Tyler that he begins to "feel" again. A spontaneous fight in the parking lot of a bar leads to the creation of an underground bare-knuckle club where men can beat their sufferings out of each other and learn to feel something (even if it is pain) in a world that has crushed their sensibilities under the weight of consumerism. This "fight club" forms the genesis for an anti-consumerist army that is assembled by Jack and Tyler; it engages in a campaign that adopts the stratagems of culture jamming (see Close-Up 8.1), but also moves to more violent and direct assaults on computer stores and coffee shops, and, finally, on the corporate headquarters of credit-card companies, which are destroyed in the final frames of the film.

The film and book contain many rich (though problematic) strands that could be followed up and teased out, but perhaps the defining element of the narrative (on which we briefly touch in Chapter 6) is the connection that it makes between consumerism and the decline of masculinity in contemporary society. The fight clubs are an exclusively male domain: it is not just that men need to be awakened out of their consumerist lassitude, but also that by beating each other up they are reasserting a supposedly essential masculine identity that contemporary culture has stripped from them. For Tyler, the real trauma in contemporary life is that men can no longer be "real" men: virile, physical, and firmly in charge of both the family and the culture at large. Contemporary experience has emasculated men and rendered them impotent. What has brought about this situation is nothing other than consumerism itself, which the film repeatedly identifies as a specifically feminine realm, in line with the long-established ideologies of consumerism that we discussed in Chapter 5.

In many respects, the critique of consumerism in *Fight Club* becomes an alibi for an attack on the feminine, especially on the rise of women (and minorities) to positions of power and influence in Western society. The film claims that in a world in which women have at least the potential to be equal to men, men cannot be real men. Instead of working with their bodies in factories, men have to drag themselves to "soft" office jobs and dream of the furniture in IKEA catalogues instead of the supine female bodies one finds in pornography. Changing the world for the better seems to mean putting women back in their place—hardly an instance of progressive politics or a successful criticism of consumerism, which should presumably create a situation in which men *and* women could engage in consumption differently.

Close-Up 8.1 Culture Jamming

Culture jamming is the practice of turning manifestations of consumer culture—in particular, advertising images—against themselves for political ends. By parodying targeted ad images, culture jamming recontextualizes them and offers a different set of associations through which they can be read.

Culture jamming has a double aim: to draw attention both to the problems of specific activities and practices (driving environmentally damaging SUVs, exporting the practice of smoking to the developing world, watching television, subscribing to the damaging beauty ideals promoted by the fashion industry) *and* to the limits and dangers of the larger consumerist and capitalist system that legitimates and promotes these activities and practices. One of the best-known forms of culture jamming is the annual "Buy Nothing Day," held worldwide on the day after American Thanksgiving, which is one of the largest shopping days each and every year. Culture jammers take to the streets not only to dissuade people from shopping, but also to remind them of the troubling link that has been developed between the celebration of family and belonging (everyone gathering together for Thanksgiving) and the orgy of consumerism that follows.

The Canadian magazine *Adbusters* has played an integral role in promoting and celebrating various forms of culture jamming. Indeed, the origins of the Occupy movement have been traced back to a call to action posted in the magazine's blog in July 2011. Examples of its campaigns and ads, as well as those of jammers from around the world, can be found at www.adbusters.org.

Unlike *Forrest Gump*, which demonizes sub- or countercultural resistance even as it highlights its lack of importance to the main script of historical development, *Fight Club* takes the activities and possibilities of subcultures seriously. Only a group outside the mainstream could shake up a world lost in consumerist dogmatic slumbers: Jack and Tyler cannot change things on their own, nor is it likely that mainstream society will change of its own accord. Nevertheless, this representation of a subculture reinforces mainstream ideologies concerning gender roles in a way that makes us question their aims and goals. Of course, in one respect this is indeed an "accurate" portrayal of the very real limits of an engagement with gender stereotypes in many subcultures. For example, women skateboarders have had to struggle with the dominance of this practice by men, while women in punk faced similar limits and problems: even as the punks fought against the capitalist world, women punks had to fight for recognition and respect within the subculture itself. However, representational accuracy is hardly the aim of *Fight Club*: if an engagement with the politics of gender in subcultures emerges as a moral of the film, it is only by reading against the grain of its otherwise deeply patriarchal logic.

Ghost World: Being Ghostly

Terry Zwigoff's *Ghost World* (2001) offers one of the most compelling and original representations of subcultural practices and activities in recent film. The film's title is quite literal; it explores the ghostly world of alternative lives and practices that exist parallel to and overlap with what we generally imagine as mainstream culture. In doing so, the film also offers an incisive look at the assumptions and presumptions that constitute the mainstream, probing the very real limits that it places on individuals and groups in expressing their differences.

Ghost World tracks the entry of two high-school friends, Enid (Thora Birch) and Rebecca (Scarlett Johansson), into adulthood in the summer following their graduation from high school. The film begins with Enid and Rebecca's graduation ceremony and the reception that follows. Both are by-the-numbers affairs, with the valedictorian mouthing platitudes (she describes high school as "the training wheels for the bicycle of life") and the reception being typically amenable to the cool kids and torture for the geeks and nerds. From the way in which Enid and Rebecca snarl and quip their way through their graduation day, it is clear that they are outsiders. For them, the utter kitschiness and predictability of the graduation exercises are a source of amusement.

Unlike typical depictions of those who do not conform to accepted models, both Enid and Rebecca are remarkably self-confident. Being at right angles to the mainstream and its expectations does not isolate them; rather, it gives them a feeling of power as they navigate their way through the clichés and stereotypes of contemporary culture. They are critical of faux enthusiasms and false emotions, without being cynical or dismissive; indeed, the falsehoods with which contemporary society surrounds itself are for them a continual source of interest and amusement. While dining in Wowsville, an "authentic fifties diner," Rebecca turns on the tabletop jukebox and out pours rap music. "Who could forget this greatest hit from the fifties!" she remarks, to the delight of both women.

Can the friends sustain this joyous, devil-may-care attitude as they make the transition from adolescence to an adult world in which there is a price to be paid for nonconformity? This is the key question around which the plot of the film revolves. Following high school, the women endeavor to find their own apartment, which immediately introduces them to a world that demands compromise and shifts in their priorities. To get an apartment Enid and Rebecca need money, which means that they need to find jobs. Rebecca gets a job in a coffee shop, and as soon as she does her sarcasm seems to become tempered by the pragmatic demands of making money and getting through the week. However, Enid's entry to the adult world is delayed by the need to make up an art class that she, a talented artist in her own right, nevertheless failed in her last term. More significantly, over the course of the summer she gets to see deep into the "ghost world" of the film's title by coming into contact with Seymour (Steve Buscemi), whom she describes at one point as "such a clueless dork, he's almost cool."

Seymour is a lonely, middle-aged man whom life seems to have beaten down. He is equally dismissive of a world made up of, at best, people whom Enid refers to as "extroverted obnoxious pseudo-bohemian losers." Seymour seems to have enthusiasm for only one thing: collecting rare 78 rpm records, especially of early blues music. His skill and enthusiasm for collecting music that others do not care about defines him against the mainstream, who express open admiration for the rock band Blues Hammer while ignoring the aging blues legend who opens the show that Enid and Seymour go to see.

At the same time, Seymour's interests also confine him to the ghostly, half-real world in which he exists. When Enid first sees Seymour's room, she stands in complete awe: "This is like my dream room," she says, "I would kill to have stuff like this." Seymour is dismissive: he says that he hates his collection, and suggests that collecting is unhealthy, a problem that one would be better off without.

Enid and Seymour develop a strong relationship, based as much on their common attitude toward what is supposedly the "real" world as it is on any physical attraction or emotional involvement. Up to the final sections of the film, *Ghost World* presents us with a remarkable view of the ghost world that subcultures occupy. Zwigoff successfully showed us, in his earlier filmic depiction of the life of the comic book legend R. Crumb, the world and views of outsiders in a sympathetic, though not celebratory, light. Occupying the real world's ghost world does not come without consequences: Enid and Rebecca's relationship erodes, Enid squanders a chance at a college scholarship by producing a controversial work of art, and Seymour's loneliness and isolation seem to be exacerbated rather than improved when he starts dating Dana, a real estate agent, who buys him his first pair of designer jeans.

In the end, the film appears to imply that no matter how much power Enid's unique attitude yields over the faux–real world she inhabits, it is not enough. Abandoned by all of the people who could have constituted the community of individuals that together produce a sub- or counterculture, Enid leaves town alone on the bus that supposedly never comes. Even in this film, as surely as in *Forrest Gump*, the "real" world appears to have an ultimately irresistible power over all those who try to exist at right angles to it. There is never a firm community of dissenters established, and even where one might expect to find such a community—at Zone-O-Phobia, the comic book store Enid frequents—she and the manager are in constant conflict. "If you really want to fuck up the system," he says, "go to business school. Join a big corporation and fuck up stuff from the inside."

The goal of this section has been to emphasize the various ways in which sub- and countercultures have been represented in dominant forms of popular culture. What we can see from these three very different examples is that while subcultures are celebrated as playing an essential role in history and in social transformation, they are also almost always represented as a problem for society. Sub- and countercultures tend to be represented in relation to dominant culture either as the fringes occupied by those who just can't make it within the mainstream (which is then correspondingly valorized as the domain of "real" values, morals, and beliefs), or as the space in which genuine social discontent is voiced but in the wrong way (violently in *Fight Club*, individualistically in *Ghost World*).

Whatever position different films or television programs take on sub- and countercultures, we can see from these examples that what they in fact highlight are the views of mainstream groups on subcultures—whether dismissive or sympathetic—as opposed to the views and needs expressed in and through sub- and countercultural practices. In other words, these representations tend to present subcultures predominantly as an issue or problem for the mainstream; insofar as these groups also always make use of the discourses and representations of mainstream culture, this has an impact on the nature and shape of sub- and countercultural practices as well. There are two things that we should take away from our analysis of these films: first, our understanding of subcultures is affected by representations of them; second, popular cultural representation plays an important (if seemingly contradictory) role in how participants in sub- and countercultures imagine their own role and engage in their own practices, as we will see in more detail below.

The Politics of Subcultures

There is no society, only individuals.
Former British Prime Minister Margaret Thatcher, qtd. in Keay

Earlier in this chapter, we suggested that even if subcultures are not explicitly political, their activities and practices always contain an *implicit* political stance—a position or attitude toward gaps and absences in the mainstream culture that individuals seek to redress through their involvement in subcultures. At a very general level, the fragmentation of contemporary societies into an enormous range of active subcultures after the Second World War points to a lack of genuine opportunities for communal or group relations *within* the mainstream. Perhaps a better way of putting this is that, since mainstream North American values tend to celebrate individuality above all else, communal forms of relation outside of the typical markers of group identity (such as race, ethnicity, or religion) could not exist except on the outsides or margins of mainstream culture. There are, of course, always groups and subgroups that make up each and every society; but subcultures are something new whose very existence points to problems and contradictions in the way reality is constituted by the powers that be.

For instance, it is no surprise that the contradictory demands and stresses that contemporary society has placed on young people in particular would produce a flourishing range of youth subcultures. These subcultures aim to escape the controlling attentions of an adult society that simultaneously infantilizes young people (wants them to remain children) and encourages them to take on adult behaviors and responsibilities earlier and earlier in life. Participating in a subculture is a way of establishing one's own form of social life, with its own rules that may be very different from or even directly opposed to mainstream adult rules and values. While it may be true, as Sarah Thornton has argued, that "the vast majority of British youth subcultures, past and present, do not espouse overt political projects" (177), it nevertheless seems clear that even if their politics are implicit, such politics constitute an essential and important reason for the creation of subcultures to begin with. George McKay has described it in this way: "One of the things hippy and punk had in common was an oppositional impulse, an idealism or rhetoric of idealism. For both, politics and culture were, or could be, or should be, the same thing" (5). If we are to properly understand subcultures, separating forms of cultural expression from politics proper would be a mistake.

Hiding in the Light

What are the forms that this politics takes? There are many, of course: it is both difficult and dangerous to generalize across the wide range of activities and practices that have been characterized as subcultural. However, there does seem to be one mode of politics that many subcultures have adopted—though, again, they have adopted it in many different ways. In his influential book *Subculture: The Meaning of Style*, Dick Hebdige deftly explores the dual, apparently contradictory relationship that subcultures adopt toward mainstream culture.

The effect of subcultures—both with respect to those "within" them and the majority of members of society "without"—is produced through the adoption of both invisibility *and* visibility. Subcultures hide in the shadows, where one can do whatever one likes away from prying eyes, specifically the eyes of the authorities. But insofar as it also seems essential for subcultures to be able both to mark their difference from mainstream culture *and* to engage critically with the limits of that culture, it is also important for the mainstream to be able to sit up and take notice—to be shocked, in other words, whether by the harsh social reality depicted in rap songs or by the graffiti left on the walls of its garages. Hebdige explains:

> the subcultural *milieu* has been constructed underneath the authorised discourses, in the face of multiple disciplines of the family, the school and the workplace. Subculture forms up in the space between surveillance and the evasion of surveillance, it translates the fact of being under scrutiny into the pleasure of being watched. It is hiding in the light. (*Subculture* 35)

The Arrival of Punk

We have already seen one of the strange consequences of the way in which subcultures "hide in the light." The death in 2002 of Dee Dee Ramone was widely interpreted as the passing of a significant cultural era. And yet, relatively few people ever heard him play, either live or on record, and it would be difficult to make a case that The Ramones had a major impact on the popular music that followed them. How could a supposedly minor cultural practice, hidden out of sight in dank clubs in the Bowery and in the rougher streets of London, end up as a pop culture era or touchstone? The answer: by hiding in the light of mainstream attention. For Hebdige, "subcultures are both a play for attention and a refusal, once attention has been granted, to be read according to the Book" (*Subculture* 35). There is no better example of this than the one he himself draws on: punk music and style, which flourished ever so briefly in the mid-1970s and has since given birth to numerous other "punk" styles.

As might be suggested by the title of Penelope Spheeris's documentary on the Los Angeles punk scene, *The Decline of Western Civilization*, punk represented an all-out assault on the values of mainstream "civilization." One would expect the public to recoil from punk and to respond to its challenge with diatribes against it. This is indeed what happened. In the United Kingdom, punk was treated as a pariah subculture, a dangerous movement that was colonizing the minds of some British youths and that thus had to be brought to a rapid end. But how, then, could one explain the incredible popularity and success of the group that became the whipping boy of anti-punk sentiment, the Sex Pistols? At the height of anti-punk fervor (such as it was), the Sex Pistols' "God Save the Queen" reached number two in the British pop charts, and their album *Never Mind the Bollocks* hit the top of the charts. The anti-establishment Sex Pistols and their ilk were tabloid celebrities throughout the late 1970s; by the 1980s, punk had become such a fixture of the London landscape that popular tourist postcards featured pictures of green-haired punks with ripped clothing to send back to the folks in Saskatchewan ("Greetings from London!").

As we will see in the next section, this is commonly viewed as evidence of punk's *lack* of politics. Yet Hebdige's formula lets us see things differently: it is precisely by being available and open for display to the mainstream that the minority culture of punk was able to draw attention to the very real sources of its discontent with both the values of mainstream culture and its relationship to it. "Hiding in the light" allows subcultures to create, maintain, and nurture their own communities of belonging (by "hiding" in clubs, squats, and even the streets), while also engaging with the culture at large (exposing themselves to the "light" of public opinion by displaying their unique styles on the streets, and their music on the airwaves).

Not all subcultures engage in the same forms of display or do so to the same degree. Many subcultures prefer to remain more hidden than punk. However, secret societies, of the kind featured in Stanley Kubrick's *Eyes Wide Shut* and much beloved by scenarists for James Bond films, do not a subculture make.

Avant-Garde Punk

You don't sing about love to people on the dole.

Johnny Rotten, qtd. in Szatmary 220

Punk has been the subject of numerous scholarly studies, popular books (Greil Marcus's *Lipstick Traces*), films (*Sid and Nancy*), and documentaries (*The Great Rock'n'Roll Swindle, The Filth and the Fury*). As perhaps the first instance of a popular cultural form that seemed to be explicitly political (to a higher and more intense degree than the music of the 1960s), punk continues to fascinate and inspire musicians, audiences, and scholars. Yet for all its influence, the era of punk was remarkably short. Less than a year passed between the British debut of The Ramones on July 4, 1976 (the event widely heralded for kick-starting punk in the United Kingdom) and the emergence of high-end copies of punk fashion, such as the gold safety pins sold at Saks on Fifth Avenue and the stylized rips and safety pins in the gowns designed by Zandra Rhodes for Bloomingdale's, which were already on the market by June 1977 (Szatmary 236).

As we have seen above, the way in which punk (and other subcultures) "hides in the light" makes it political in many more ways than by its subcultural "form" alone. But there are other ways in which punk is political above and beyond this form—the "down with civilization" lyrics of punk music, and the anti-establishment disposition and demeanor of punks themselves. In a way that is too seldom appreciated, subcultures of all stripes draw heavily on a stew of political and cultural ideas and ideals, especially those that have been constructed by other oppositional or subcultural groups of cultures in the past.

The Marxist Influence

One of most important of these has been the tradition of socialist and communist thought. However partially or incompletely, Marx's insistence on seeing the history of society as a "history of class struggles" has remained a core element of the way in which many subcultures understand their social status (Marx and Engels 34): as minority cultures in permanent conflict with the wealthy and their duped middle-class supporters. Subcultures need not take up explicit class-based politics in order to see themselves as belonging to those groups that are systematically disadvantaged by capitalism, nor to make use of the kinds of cultural analysis and forms of cultural practice that such political identification opens up. And socialism is just the beginning. As the example of punk shows us, there is a great deal more going on in subcultures than angry youths spontaneously rebelling against their seniors.

The familiar story told about punk is a cautionary tale that traces the rapid rise of a genuine subculture and its equally rapid co-optation by consumer culture (see Chapter 4 for a discussion of co-optation in popular culture). The threat that punk posed seemed real enough to bring the wrath of the state down on the paradigmatic punk band the Sex Pistols, even before the release of their anti-monarchist anthem "God Save the Queen" in

June 1976. Denounced by Members of Parliament, attacked by the Anglican Church, banned from playing live almost anywhere in England and from having their songs played on British radio, the Sex Pistols nearly brought about the conditions that they sang about in "Anarchy in the U.K." Yet by 1980, Linda Ronstadt, Billy Joel, and even Cher were posing in punk regalia on the covers of their albums.

The quick rise and fall of punk are real enough. Yet what this version of the events misses is the complex political roots of punk culture. The anarchy and chaos of punk music—its fearsome, angry, and terrifically loud sound and its utter rejection of "civilized" values—have tended to reinforce a sense of its spontaneous origins and generally unfocused politics. Punk is now often treated, as it was by a number of its detractors during the punk era itself, as little more than another blip in a long tradition of youthful rebellion expressed through pop music (falling temporally between the threatening sexuality of Elvis and the angst of Nirvana and Eminem).

However, if we were to pull apart any of these forms of rebellion, we would find an enormously rich reservoir of ideas and concepts. Like Dadaism and Surrealism before it, punk understood itself quite self-consciously as a cultural form (in both its music and its style) whose aim was *épater les bourgeois*—to pierce through the sterile drone of bloated 1970s art rock (epitomized by the band Yes) and the flabby corporate culture that was increasingly coming to stand for culture as such. The New York precursors of UK punk music, artists such as the Velvet Underground, Patti Smith, and Tom Verlaine, drew inspiration for their lyrics from the Beat Generation (epitomized by writers such as Jack Kerouac and Allan Ginsberg); from the avant-garde centered around Andy Warhol; and, in the case of Verlaine (aka Tom Miller), from French Symbolist poetry. Though the Sex Pistols famously rejected Patti Smith's literary, avant-garde leanings, the transition of punk from New York to London interjected new political dimensions into punk even as it stripped away others.

It would be possible to continue in this vein for some time. For instance, we have yet to mention the political roots of punk art, which was featured on album covers and posters advertising band performances. Again, the slapdash quality of this art might suggest unfocused, youthful spontaneity. But in reality, punk art drew heavily on the slogans and art of the May 1968 student revolution in Paris, as well as from the tradition of agitational-propaganda (agitprop) aesthetics created by the artists of the Soviet Revolution. Punk was also an importantly hybrid musical form, which drew inspiration (as well as licks) from Jamaican reggae and ska music that "lambasted the racism and capitalism that Britain had imposed on Jamaica" (Szatmary 232). In April and June 1978, The Clash and other bands played to audiences of 80 000 and 50 000 young punks respectively, who came out to show their solidarity with their black brethren against the organization of the racist National Front in Britain. It is clear that there was a whole lot going on in punk— even if most punk musicians relied on only three chords to express themselves.

Situationism: Guy Debord and Henri Lefebvre

In addition to all of its other cultural and political influences, punk is importantly connected to the tradition of Situationism, both in spirit and (as Greil Marcus shows in his history of punk, *Lipstick Traces*) in substance. Malcolm McLaren, the infamous manager and midwife of the Sex Pistols, wanted to use the band to explore the "politics of boredom," a phrase indebted to the Situationist slogan "Boredom is always counterrevolutionary." Situationism explored the new kinds of politics required in a society crushed not by a lack of things (i.e., too little food to feed everyone), but by an abundance of material goods. Situationism played an important role in the May 1968 student revolution in

France, which began in reaction to the US war on Vietnam, but turned into a more general assault on the banality of a post–Second World War capitalist culture that promised so much (less work and more leisure) and delivered so little (boring work and boring leisure).

The May 1968 revolution in France and elsewhere was intimately connected to the spaces of the city (see Figure 8.4). An important element of many subcultural and countercultural political movements—including punk, as well as the strategies of Occupy and the events of the Arab Spring—is the critical eye that they cast on the organization of the spaces of everyday life and its impact on daily experience and social possibilities (for further discussions of space and the popular, see Chapter 9). The sight of punks in London's West End unnerved the well-dressed businesspeople and shoppers who expected certain forms of dress and behavior in public spaces—spaces in which, supposedly, one was free to dress and do as one liked. And protests of all kinds take place in the streets for the same basic reasons: to disrupt established patterns of movement through the city and use of its space, and (like punks) in order to display their discontent in the light of the public view (whether directly or via the media who are drawn to such displays).

It was the perception that spaces of daily life were becoming increasingly bureaucratic and controlled that led French philosopher Henri Lefebvre (1901–91) and French writer and filmmaker Guy Debord (1931–94)—the man at the heart of Situationism—to investigate the structures of the contemporary city and to propose strategies for bringing about a "revolution in everyday life." Both thinkers witnessed at first hand the enormous shift in the rhythms and energies of everyday life that occurred in France in the decades following the Second World War. Paris and other French cities went through a rapid process of rebuilding, expansion, and modernization. Large preplanned housing developments were added to cities around the country—the suburbs with which most of us are

Figure 8.4 "The police post themselves at the School of Fine Arts/The fine arts students poster the street!" This anonymous poster from the May 1968 protests in Paris cleverly connects art, revolution and access to education—and to the streets.
Source: © akg-images

now familiar—and the texture of daily urban life was modified through the introduction of a homogenizing mass consumer culture that came to many people as a shock. In France as elsewhere, the shorthand term for these modernizing developments was "Americanization." Bureaucratic, banal, emptied of life, predictable, routine: both thinkers witnessed the way "the commodity, the market, money, with their implacable logic, seize everyday life" (Lefebvre "Towards" 79), and both wanted to think about ways in which to take life back.

The great theme of Lefebvre's philosophy was the complex and messy events, objects, and happenings of everyday life. He saw everyday life as the space that any philosopher should try to understand: it was there that social structures were experienced and broad understandings about the world and the possibilities of human life were generated. For Lefebvre, the long process of modernization had produced forms of everyday life characterized fundamentally by increasing alienation, lack of creativity, and an artificial separation of human activity into specialized spaces and activities: spaces to live, work, shop, have fun, and so forth. In the nineteenth century, Karl Marx had famously described alienation as the result of workers' separation from the product of their labor. For Lefebvre, this experience of alienation had become part of the very stuff of life, making all experience inauthentic and full of unease. Witnessing the construction of spaces such as a new suburb in the French city of Mourenx—a place made up of "nothing but traffic lights"—Lefebvre asks: "Are we entering the city of joy or the world of unredeemable boredom?" (Lefebvre *Introduction* 119). It is this boredom of the mainstream that gave energy to many subcultural and countercultural movements.

Debord shared a similar view of the world that was being put together out of the ruins of war. He is best known for *Society of the Spectacle* (1967), which has become an important text for scholars and activists alike who are interested in thinking about the deep impact of mass-media images on society. Though the "spectacle" is most often thought to refer to the collection of images that bombard us daily—advertising, television, movies, and the like—for Debord it names "not a collection of images but a social relationship between people that is mediated by images" (12). The spectacle was a form of society in which our experiences and understanding of all social relations were shaped through mass-mediated images. For Debord, spectacular society represented the deepest possible penetration of capitalism and consumerism into everyday life. Like Lefebvre, he saw contemporary life as deeply alienated and alienating. As he writes, "the spectacle is the bad dream of a modern society in chains, expressing nothing more than its wish for its sleep. The spectacle is the guardian of that sleep" (18).

For both Lefebvre and Debord, the alienating, empty feeling that comes from living in the suburbs or from the experience of the consumer city has its roots in larger, structural transformations that have ensured that capitalist society and its pursuit of money are life's primary objective. For Debord, these transformations include changes to the space of the city. As part of the activist art collective called the Situationist International (SI), Debord developed strategies for reclaiming the experience of the city. *Dérive* (or "drift") was a political and social practice that proposed to explore the city in ways very different than those imagined or permitted by the dominant physical and social organization of urban space. To drift through the city instead of following fixed patterns (moving directly from work to home, staying only in the "good" or familiar parts of the city, remaining in public spaces and avoiding the private) produces a very different view of the city within which one lives. The defamiliarization that drifting generates also creates circumstances in which one can critically reflect on the ways in which space is organized—ways that are invisible in the routine of daily life.

In Lefebvre's later work, he also probed all the ways in which urban space had become "a space envisioned and conceived by assorted professionals and technocrats: planners, engineers, developers, architects, urbanists, geographers, and others of a scientific bent" (Merrifield 89). Little space was left that allowed for the creation of genuine differences of experience or meaning; all activity was tied into modern rhythms of work and play, with after-work leisure being little more than a preparation for more work. Throughout his life, Lefebvre was fascinated by moments in which the spaces and rhythms of "normal" everyday life were interrupted, even momentarily, from the bawdy excess of festivals to the occupation of the streets of Paris by students in May 1968. As with the SI's practices of "drifting" through the city in a manner that evaded and challenged its typical spatial organization, Lefebvre believe that these breaks in the everyday allowed for a glimpse into the social construction of everyday life. In so doing, the hope was that it also opened the way for a more radical reconstruction of everyday life and its spaces, and that the energy of festivals could replace the dreariness of contemporary experience on an ongoing and daily basis. Despite the apparently unassailable logic of urban space and the physical and imaginative weight of its accumulated infrastructure—streets, bridges, highways, sewers, spaces zoned for one kind of activity instead of another—life and space could still be different, if alternative forms of being and belonging were posed to the easy, if deadening, character of life in the mainstream.

At earlier points in this book, we have touched on some of the ways in which space and our experience of it are shaped by the social and cultural systems in which we live (we explore this topic further in Chapter 9). In Chapter 6, for example, we discussed the ways in which the space of the panopticon—a prison designed so that prisoners feel that they might always be under surveillance—produced forms of self-conscious regulation and change in behavior. Our discussion in Chapter 5 of the *flâneur*, the strolling urban figure who moves through the city to take in the experiences and pleasures of displays of consumer items and the bodies of other shoppers, is also an example of the ways in which space creates new forms of experience and culture. One of the clearest signs of the degree to which space is organized in ways that shape our lived experience of space *and* the shape and character of popular culture today is the divide between public space and private space. And so it is not surprising that struggles over space are at the heart of a number of subcultural practices, including the activity we focus on next: skateboarding.

The Invention of Skateboarding

So, punk is political. But what about other kinds of subcultural practices? Haven't we stacked the deck in our favor? What about a practice whose politics is somewhat more obscure, if it exists at all? What about, say, skateboarding?

Even though skateboarding has now become a staple of popular culture, it wasn't always a recognized sport with its own stars (like Tony Hawk), brand names, specialist magazines, computer games, ESPN tournaments, and the like. Skateboarding first emerged as a post-surfing pastime in the late 1950s and briefly surged to popularity in 1963, when the national championships were aired on television. It then died out—seemingly just another fad kids' hobby, like the hula hoop. The conditions that saw its revival in the early to mid-1970s highlight the politics that continue to be played out through this seemingly innocuous pastime.

Dogtown and Z-Boys

Stacy Peralta's documentary *Dogtown and Z-Boys* (2002) provides not only an exceptional account of the second birth of skateboarding, but also a compelling narrative of the politics that emerges out of the sport. The film explores the birth of the famous Zephyr Skateboard Team, which would later produce many of the most successful of the first-wave of professional skateboarders. The team hailed from Dogtown, a decrepit, rundown area of West Los Angeles that was quite literally built on the ruins of the American dream: the area had once sported one of the most famous of the many amusement-park piers that lined the California coast. After the park closed in 1967, the area fell into economic decline, leaving the abandoned amusement park and the area around it to "pyromaniacs, junkies and surfers." The team members grew up in this area, mostly in broken families that were never far from bottoming out. Yet, rather than calling Dogtown an urban wasteland, they describe it as a "dirty, filthy paradise."

What made Dogtown a paradise was the degree of control that the youths could exert over their space, both as surfers and then later as skaters. Dogtown was covered with graffitied signs warning outsiders to stay away: "Locals only!" "Go home!" As the Zephyr team began to develop and build skateboards to "surf" their mostly abandoned streets, they also began to stretch their claim over public space to other parts of the city. Because much of California is built on hills or in valleys, many schoolyards in the area had a land-scaping quirk: in order to level out school playgrounds, landscapers had to build in walls of banked asphalt. Though these were fenced off from the public, they became the first rudimentary skate parks, which the Dogtown kids would, on weekends, bike miles and miles to get to in order to practice their new craft. During the mid-1970s, another off-limits space opened up to skateboarding. The prolonged drought in California during this time meant that the numerous swimming pools in the LA area were left empty. Dogtowners began to enter private property covertly in order to skate the abandoned swimming pools, and in so doing risked arrest and imprisonment.

The documentary is careful to highlight the fact that the kids who pioneered contemporary skateboarding were motivated by nothing more than having fun. There was "no promise in it," and they had "no goals, no aspirations." None of them knew what skateboarding would become or what it was accomplishing. Nor did they have a sense that by skating the streets, pools, and hidden and sealed-off spaces of the city, they were doing something more than having a good time. Of course, the consequences of one's actions can easily exceed what one believes one is doing. In a series of influential articles published in *Skateboarder* magazine in 1975, Craig Stecyk made explicit what the Zephyr team had been doing as a matter of course: making new use of the dead spaces created by contemporary culture:

> Skaters by their very nature are urban guerrillas: they make everyday use of the useless artifacts of the technological burden, and employ the handiwork of the government/corporate structure in a thousand ways that the original architects could never dream of. Two hundred years of American technology has unwittingly created a massive cement playground of unlimited potential, but it was the minds of 11-year-olds that could see that potential. (*Dogtown and Z-Boys*)

The disputes that continue to arise throughout North America over the uses that skateboarders try to make of public and private space for a bit of simple recreation suggests that there is something larger at stake in these practices. It might seem a stretch to equate kids interested in doing grinds and flipping their boards with anti-globalization demonstrators who take over the spaces of the city, but in a way both are making the same fundamental demand: "Whose streets? Our streets!" Skateboarding has a politics, too.

From Zines to Blogs

Subcultures and countercultures need spaces in which to meet, share ideas, and live out their differences. The need for space—whether occupied legally or illegally, as through squatter movements that remain active throughout Europe—places some limits on the activities of these groups and also exposes them to the intervention of authorities nervous about the ramifications of the activities of this or that group. For example, both as a result of state and local ordinances and simple demographic realities, it can be difficult to use your BMX bike or skateboard in many big urban centers. This is why you'll encounter groups of teens popping wheelies and jumping off concrete skyscraper and freeway embankments if you take a walk in the middle of the night through the core of Shanghai or St. Petersburg, Russia: 3 a.m. is the only time you can take your BMX to meet a statue of Lenin or Mao.

The spaces required by countercultures and subcultures can be physical—or virtual. Those involved in cultural practices outside the mainstream have always needed a way to communicate their desires, ideas, and opinions, and a mechanism by which to connect up with others in their region and nation (and indeed, around the world) who share their activities, beliefs, and commitments. One of most important such "spaces" for alternative cultural expression have been zines. Self-published, nonprofit, small-circulation magazines (the word from which they draw their name), zines were crucial to the life of countercultures and subcultures from the 1970s to the end of the twentieth century. Zines have an enormous diversity of form and content. Any and all subcultural practices have had zines: fanzines—zines for fans of particular bands, TV shows, artists, and so on—were an initially important form; zines expressing alternative political views and challenges to mainstream definitions of gender and sexuality (as in riot grrrl and queer zines) were another major theme; and texts in opposition to decisions made by government and industry were also prominent. Not all zines were connected to alternative communities or subcultures: they also offered individuals a means by which to engage in self-expression. Though they most commonly combined text and images, whether original work or material reproduced and repurposed from other sources, the form taken by zines is as varied as their content, ranging from sophisticated examples of avant-garde art and design to virtually unreadable, badly reproduced mash-ups of images pulled together from magazines and newspapers.

Scholars who have studied zines have identified several precursors to this genre, from Cold War *samizdat* publications—underground oppositional political texts in the Soviet bloc shared through copying—to the self-publication of pamphlets and manifestos by dissidents and radicals intent on spreading their ideas. What distinguishes contemporary zines from those texts to which they bear at least a family resemblance are the mechanisms through which they were produced and distributed. The ubiquity, ease of use, and affordability of photocopying technology made it possible for zinesters to create mags in which they could say exactly what they wanted, by-passing the editorial gatekeepers at newspapers and in publishing houses; and the existence of independent bookstores and art/cultural centers in most cities, as well as (relatively) low mailing costs, provided a means by which zines could be widely distributed (though many zines were only ever available in the city in which they were produced). Beginning in the early 1980s, maga/zines devoted to reviewing and promoting other zines (such as *Factsheet Five* and Canada's *Broken Pencil*) enabled zinesters to learn about work that they might otherwise never have come into contact with. Early computer bulletin board systems (BBS), listservs, and online forums served a similar purpose, creating a network of zines and zinesters that constituted a vibrant—and increasingly influential—alternative to mainstream cultural publications. Some zines developed such a large readership that they made the jump from zines to "real" magazines, including the UK music and culture publication *Dazed and Confused* and *Giant Robot*, a magazine focusing on Asian and Asian American pop culture.

Though zines continue to be produced and distributed, and though a number of well-established zine events are still held around the world (such as Canzine, held annually in both Vancouver and Toronto), their social and cultural prominence in alternative culture has waned over the past decade. If the advent of cheap photocopying and early home computers and printers (on which some were produced) helped to make zines possible, the Internet, portable computing, and new communications technologies have fundamentally reshaped the 'space' of alternative cultural expression. Zines are starting to disappear from the shelves of independent bookstores—which have themselves become a threatened species due to the Internet—and in the process have become something else entirely. While there are webzines—that is, online sites where one can find the fan content or alternative political energies once expressed in zines, and which in some cases even mimic the form of physical zines in their new virtual homes—for the most part the advent of the Internet has heralded new forms of countercultural and subcultural expression.

These days, almost any group or individual can set up a web site on which they can promote their likes and dislikes, support a cause, or share a story. One might be tempted to believe that the transformation of zines into e-zines has seen them blend and blur indiscernibly into the giant stew of text, images, sound, and video that makes up the Internet. But there is something closer in spirit to zines that forms a distinct subgenre of e-content, and that continues to have a specific connection to the expressions and practices of alternative culture: blogs. As with everything else on the Internet, the subject matter of blogs extends to anything and everything. At their core, blogs are journals made up of a series of discrete posts that invite response from readers. Some blogs are limited to personal reflections akin to diaries; more typically, blogs offer commentary on a specific subject the blogger knows about or is interested in, and in so doing offer their readers a combination of the op-ed page of a newspaper together with useful links and connections to relevant web sites and to other blogs.

Blogs are an astonishing cultural and social phenomenon. The social media information service NM Incite reported that by the end of 2011 it had tracked 181 million blogs, up from 36 million in 2006 (as of 2016, the number of blog posts per day had exceeded 3 million). The numbers of readers of these blogs is at least (according to studies in the United States) fourfold that number, and both figures continue to grow faster than Web use in general. Though variants of what we now call blogs have existed as long as the Internet itself (whether in the form of web pages listing previously surfed links along with commentary or online diaries), the origins of today's blogosphere can be dated back to the August 1999 launch of Blogger, a popular and easy-to-use free blog publishing site (purchased by Google in 2003) available in some 50 languages. Since then the genre of the blog has very rapidly become an accepted (and expected) part of the language and landscape of the Web. In the way in which it is employed on a huge number of official and institutional web sites, the blog has become a kind of shorthand for quick, opinionated commentary. The online version of the *New York Times*, for instance, now includes an enormous range of blogs—a minimum of three blogs (and often many more) to accompany each and every one of the paper's many sections (see http://www.nytimes.com/interactive/blogs/directory.html). But even though blogs have become popularized and commercialized in ways that would have been impossible with zines, they still offer individuals an opportunity to express their views about all manner of subjects—a contribution to and complication of public discourse that is difficult to gainsay, even if its full social and political effects are still difficult to determine.

Having said this, it is important to pay attention to some of the (inevitable) limits of the blog genre. On the one hand, blogs might be seen as a kind of expansion and enhancement of the capacities and reach of countercultures and subcultures; on the other, the sheer number of blogs means that any individual blog is difficult to come across, and the sheer profusion of expression tends to reinforce the myth of the Internet as the ultimate embodiment of the democracy that is assumed to characterize Western societies in general. This is a claim that individual zines and blogs might well want to question and challenge. In her assessment of blogs, critic Julie Rak points out that "even as the corporate use of blogs and the corporatization of the materiality of blog writing have grown, and blogging itself changes, most blog rhetoric still adheres in some form to a version of liberalism which was part of early internet culture. In this form of liberalism, freedom of expression is important, particularly when it occurs outside of institutional attempts to control the flow of information" (172). For Rak, it is not only the case that such liberalism becomes the dominant form of ideas distributed across the Web, but also that blogs work "to attract specific types of community based on similarity rather than differences... identity with the blog genre is based on a balance between the need for privacy (if one doesn't want to be found) and the need for community based on identification with others through sameness" (177). When one considers the nature of zines in light of these comments about blogs, the inevitably liberal character of *both* forms emerges. In each case, the spaces in which zines and some blogs operate exist outside of dominant mass culture; in each case, their intent is to create new communities based on sameness of belief rather than explicitly on confronting mainstream society in a manner that might expand their range of impact and effect; and finally, at the heart of each form is a belief in the capacity and importance of individual expression—an affirmation of liberal individualism, which is to say, the guiding ideology of capitalist society—even if such expression is imagined as attacking the limits of society.

Unlike zines, blogs invite a response on the part of readers: the ability to consider what a writer has opined is a feature of the vast majority of blogs. On the other hand, there are things that zines can do that blogs cannot. The real-world communities and connections that zines produce are often less ephemeral than the virtual worlds within which blogs exist—one in which there is always another blog to which one can jump. And the narrative capacity of some zines to engage in complex critiques of existing social and political forces can be of a different order than that produced by a string of blog posts. There are certainly blogs that are expressions of countercultural and subcultural practices, activities, and beliefs; whether the ease of access to these blogs is generative of alternative culture politics or, given the mass scale of blogs, ultimately defuses its energies and ambitions remains to be seen.

Suggested Activity 8.2

Simon Orpana's "The Art of Gentrification: A Zine About Art, Urban Space and Politics," the zine included with this edition of *Popular Culture: A User's Guide*, tries to puzzle out a key conundrum of contemporary urban life. How can cities grow and develop in a way that benefits everyone in the community? A relatively new resident of Hamilton, Ontario's James Street North community, Simon watches as artists start to move in to take advantage of cheap rents in the dense, urban community of Victorian-era buildings. As they make the area "safe"—that is, more accessible to middle- and upper-middle-class people than it was before—the artists are followed by property developers, whose activity will inevitably drive rents up, forcing both artists and even older members of the community out. It is a classic narrative of gentrification, which is not to say that it is an unproblematic or acceptable one.

By delving into the history of economic theory and the characteristics of life and labor under contemporary neoliberal capitalism, Orpana's zine seeks to come to grips with the tensions and problems that accompany gentrification. Combining text with images, and political and economic theory with laughs, his intent is to inform and persuade as well as to work it all out for himself.

What do you make of Orpana's zine? What did it tell you about gentrification that you didn't know before? How do the ideas expressed in it benefit from taking the form they do (think, for instance, about how and where it was distributed, and to whom, in addition to form, style, and content)? What are the limits of a zine about art, urban space, and gentrification?

We have barely begun to scratch the surface of the possible use that subcultures and countercultures are making—and might yet make—of the new technologies (like cell phones and the Internet) that have entered our world. The role played by new technologies in generating—and inhibiting—political possibilities in something that we will discuss further in Chapter 10.

Suggestions for Further Reading

Austin, Joe, and Michael Nevin Willard. *Generations of Youth: Youth Cultures and History in Twentieth-Century America*. New York: New York University Press, 1996.

Cockburn, Alexander, and Jeffrey St. Clair. *Five Days That Shook the World*. New York: Verso, 2001.

Debord, Guy. *Society of the Spectacle*. New York: Verso, 1996.

Duncombe, Stephen. *Notes from Underground: Zines and the Politics of Alternative Culture*. 2nd ed. Portland, OR: Microcosm, 2008.

Fernandez, Luis A. *Policing Dissent: Social Control and the Anti-Globalization Movement*. New Brunswick, NJ: Rutgers University Press, 2008.

Gelder, Ken. *Subcultures: Cultural Histories and Social Practice*. New York: Routledge, 2007.

Hall, Stuart, and Tony Jefferson, eds. *Resistance through Rituals: Youth Subcultures in Post-War Britain*. New York: Routledge, 1993.

Hebdige, Dick. *Subculture: The Meaning of Style*. London: Methuen, 1979.

Lasn, Kalle. *Culture Jam: How to Reverse America's Suicidal Consumer Binge—and Why We Must*. New York: Quill, 1999.

Marcus, Greil. *Lipstick Traces: A Secret History of the 20th Century*. Cambridge, MA: Harvard University Press, 1989.

Muggleton, David. *Inside Subculture: The Postmodern Meaning of Style*. New York: Berg, 2000.

Redhead, Steve, Derek Wynne, and Justin O'Connor, eds. *The Clubcultures Reader: Readings in Popular Cultural Studies*. Oxford: Blackwell, 1997.

Ross, Andrew, and Tricia Rose, eds. *Microphone Fiends: Youth Music and Youth Culture*. New York: Routledge, 1994.

Roszak, Theodore. *The Making of a Counter Culture: Reflections on the Technocratic Society and Its Youthful Opposition*. London: Faber and Faber, 1970.

Skott-Myhre, Hans. *Youth and Subculture as Creative Force: Creating New Spaces for Radical Youth Work*. Toronto: University of Toronto Press, 2009.

Wark, McKenzie. *The Beach beneath the Street: The Everyday Life and Glorious Times of the Situationist International*. New York: Verso, 2011.

9

Space, Place, and Globalization

The cities will be part of the country; I shall live 30 miles from my office in one direction, under a pine tree; my secretary will live 30 miles away from it too, in the other direction, under another pine tree. We shall both have our own car.

We shall use up tires, wear out road surfaces and gears, consume oil and gasoline. All of which will necessitate a great deal of work…enough for all.
        Le Corbusier, *The Radiant City* 1967; originally published 1935

(Dis)Locations of Popular Culture

To drive west along Wilson Street in the small Canadian town of Ancaster, Ontario, is to experience a journey along the timeline of consumer life in the country. Wilson Street, like many main streets in small and mid-size towns in Canada, is lined with independent shoe and clothing stores, car mechanics, insurance brokers' offices, and a range of Protestant churches. In Ancaster, many of these businesses are housed in nineteenth-century buildings made of blocky stone cut in precise cubes and rectangles. Interspersed among the businesses there are franchises of Starbucks and Pizza Hut as well as some of Canada's most popular fast-food restaurants like Tim Hortons. To somebody new to this area, the presence of the franchise restaurants can seem to be a blight on the quaintness of the town and/or a reassurance that, if you are not feeling up to taking the risk of eating at a local joint, you can always grab a slice and a double-double. For those who are more concerned that the franchises are displacing and replacing smaller, locally based businesses, the presence of McDonald's and other franchises is a reminder that it is virtually impossible to compete with companies whose brands are so well known, whose products' names have become recognized substitutes for everyday consumer goods, and whose corporate mission is to dominate the essential and discretionary spending of consumers. They want your dough, morning, noon, and night.

Further along Wilson Street, where the businesses thin out and where there is still residual evidence of the farms that used to be plentiful in this region, you cross an overpass from which there is very little to engage your eye except for a few stands of trees and an empty field. On the other side of the overpass, on your left, you suddenly come upon the early twenty-first-century version of Ancaster's Main Street. It is a big-box shopping development, virtually identical to ones you'll find in or around Toronto, New York, London, Budapest, or Moscow. The anchor tenant, sitting at the back of the development with a commanding view of the other big-box stores, is a Wal-Mart Supercentre, looking as if its vast length is holding its arms open to embrace the cars, minivans, and SUVs that

Popular Culture: A User's Guide, International Edition. Imre Szeman and Susie O'Brien.
© 2017 John Wiley & Sons, Inc. Published 2017 by John Wiley & Sons, Inc.

move like horse-and-buggy carts up and down the painted lanes of the parking lot. Whether we work there, shop there, or just drive by, this is the landscape in which many of us spend large chunks of our lives.

It is clear to all that the spaces and places we inhabit have undergone changes over time. Older cities and towns offer a visual archaeology of the kinds of spaces that we used to inhabit and the spaces that most of us tend to live in now. To many people, the shift from the old Main Street of mom-and-pop stores and houses bundled close to shops *and* to work—until relatively recently factories and other places of business were mixed in with housing and shopping—to the new main streets that run past shopping malls or along which box stores are conveniently assembled is simply due to progress. More people, more cars, and more technology mean that cities are spread out, highways are lengthened, parking lots are expanded, and stores are ballooned in size to house (for example) the huge number of competing LCD and plasma TVs fighting it out for market dominance. It's natural! It's progress!

Except that it doesn't feel that way to many people. After years of fleeing city cores imagined as crowded, noisy, polluted, and dangerous, many people are opting to forgo long commutes to work in order to live back in the city. In Canada, condominium towers are sprouting up not only in Toronto and Vancouver, but also in small cities of 100 000 people. Vacation trips abroad are rarely to visit the suburbs of cities, but to either one of two poles: "unspoiled" nature in the form of beaches or mountains (we discuss these spaces in more detail below), or the heart of cities whose chief attraction seems to be that they are dense, walkable, and full of the hurly-burly of human activity—cities such as Los Angeles, London, Paris, Istanbul, and Mexico City. Increasingly, people are starting to recognize that since the Second World War, we

> have been building a national landscape that is largely devoid of places worth caring about. Soulless subdivisions, residential "communities" utterly lacking in communal life; strip shopping centres, "big box" chain stores, and artificially festive malls set within barren seas of parking; antiseptic office parks, ghost towns after 6 p.m.; and mile upon mile of clogged collector roads, the only fabric tying our disassociated lives back together—this is growth, and you can find little reason to support it. (Duany *et al.* x)

If this is progress, it certainly doesn't always feel like it. But what can we do about it? Are we supposed to return to a world of country lanes and small shops? Even if we wanted to, most of us couldn't afford it any longer: living in an old stone house in Ancaster or an apartment in Paris is pricey. Even though it might be all around us, space costs, and costs differently depending on how many people want it. That is just the first of the many complicated aspects of space, a thing that we usually take for granted as simply given, as opposed to seeing it as created and recreated by human beings in different ways throughout our history.

Organizing Space and Place

What exactly is space? To begin with, space is a physical reality: the boundless container of everything known and unknown that is referred to as the universe—the "final frontier" invoked by Captain James T. Kirk in the original *Star Trek* series. We tend to think of the thin sheet of breathable atmosphere that we inhabit on Earth as also being primarily made up of space—certainly more limited and bounded than the universe, but the field in which to put stuff (cities, roads, dams, our gardens, our bedroom furniture) and in which we move around. One of the important differences between space and place seems to be that place is "made" space. Space is devoid of content, impersonal, and abstract, whereas place is filled with stuff, made into something, and clearly identifiable (not just a city, but Red Deer, Alberta; not just a room, but my brother's room). As we will see below, there is more slippage between the ideas of space and place than this might suggest, but these are some beginning points at which to look at what space and place mean in and for popular culture.

Suggested Activity 9.1

What are some of the ways in which our organization or imagination of space is expressed in language? Can you think of examples of changes in how we describe space? For example, one way in which geopolitical differences were once expressed was by reference to the "West" (Western Europe, Canada and the United States, and Japan) and either the "East" (the former Soviet bloc) or "the Rest" (the developing world or the "Third World"). Since the end of the Soviet Union, it has become more common to describe the world as divided into "North" (Western Europe, Canada and the United States, and Japan) and "South" (the developing world). What realities do such terms capture and/or obscure (e.g., how can the United States and Japan both be "West"?) Why do we seem to rely on such spatial divisions not only in everyday language but in organizing important political and economic divisions—so much so that they can come to be real?

The ways in which we think about space matter a great deal to how we inhabit and use places and spaces, and how we interact with people across the world—or across our cities. Inevitably, every city has some part of it that is considered to be the "bad side" of town, a side imagined by many as dangerous and thus to be avoided at all costs. It comes as a surprise, then, that in many cases these "bad sides" have crime statistics no worse than other parts of the city; space here works to conceal or to reinforce existing stereotypes about race, ethnicity, and class. The process of **gentrification** is seen by many as an always positive development that transforms the bad side of town into a desirable place to live, such as Queen Street West in Toronto, Crown Heights in New York, or Notting Hill in London. While "upgrading" these older spaces does make them appealing for shopping and hanging out, it also results in a change in the composition of the communities that once existed there. As often as not, the increase in property costs that comes with gentrification results in a change in the ethnic and class composition of these neighborhoods: even if they own their own houses, poor families can find themselves challenged by the rise in taxes that comes with the increase in property values. Activists in many cities around the world have played an important role in raising questions about the spaces and places that would remain for those disadvantaged communities "moved out" as a result of gentrification.

As we can see by this example, the symbolic and imaginative dimensions of space are closely linked to the ways in which space is *physically* organized, and vice versa. In some respects, one could see human activity on Earth as little more than a relentless process by which space has been arranged and rearranged for human use. In 2002, it was estimated that humans had built up more than 32 million kilometers of roadways—more than one-third of the average distance from the Earth to the Sun (*CIA Factbook*). The majority of the world's rivers have been dammed, diverted, and/or rerouted; levees and dikes have been built to hold out water from human habitations or agricultural plains; canals have been cut to connect bodies of water for purposes of navigation (the most famous of these being the 77 km Panama Canal connecting the Pacific and Atlantic Oceans, and the 193 km Suez Canal linking the Mediterranean and the Red Seas); tunnels have been carved into mountains and under waterways (such as the 50 km Channel Tunnel linking the United Kingdom and France); and much of the world's original environment has been refashioned for human use through logging, mining, clear-cutting of forests to expand agricultural lands, and so on. As these physical changes have occurred, the ways in which we experience space and imagine space have changed as well. A trip that a century ago would have taken days by train or horse can now be driven by car in a matter of hours, and jet travel makes the entire world accessible within a day's journey. Rapid communication between distant locations via the telephone and the Internet has further changed how space is organized and experienced. When globalization (discussed later this chapter) is described as "the compression of the world and the intensification of the consciousness of the world as a whole" (Robertson 8), this is a compression that has emerged out of both the physical and imaginative reorganization of space. Even if the physical world is the same size as it has always been, the space on the Earth is certainly smaller than ever.

Private versus Public Space

In Chapter 2 we suggested that one way to understand the development of popular culture is by way of the shifting arrangement of public and private space. The passing of Enclosure Acts in mid-nineteenth-century Britain effectively broke up what was once common land, used for grazing animals and public recreation, into parcels of private property to be used for the generation of profit by individual landholders. Enclosure is both an important example and a useful metaphor for the changes that have occurred in the distribution and use of space over the last two centuries (see Figure 9.1). The commercialization of sports is one example of the impact of this process on popular culture: the loss of public land means not just fewer places to play, but also a big change in the way we play. Recreation today generally means forking out some cash for an experience that is considerably less active than the village football tournaments of nineteenth-century England.

This is not to suggest that we have moved wholesale from a society of fit and rosy-cheeked athletes to a bunch of paunchy couch potatoes wrestling over the television remote (an activity—or lack of activity—that healthcare professionals actually might deem more dangerous than football). Nor has the process of commercializing public space proceeded in a linear fashion from the eighteenth century to today. The hazards of urbanization that we discuss in Chapter 2, including threats to public health posed by crowding and poor sanitation, gave rise eventually to the development of an urban planning industry to manage the structural challenges of making cities work as engines of productivity and as livable communities—goals that are sometimes hard to reconcile and whose outcome may not be what we had hoped for. Among the innovations that cities produced were parks and public swimming pools, places of leisure whose creation—like the projects of the nineteenth-century rational recreationists—sprung from a mix of middle-class motives. In addition to providing outlets for public enjoyment, it was also

Figure 9.1 The Manchester band The Get Out Clause shot a video using only surveillance cameras—an inventive way of putting devices that control and monitor to different uses. Source: © The Get Out Clause

hoped that these sites would divert the working classes from the lure of the pub toward more wholesome physical activity.

Playing in the Park

The construction of parks in North American and European cities was a logical response to dwindling public spaces—a situation that, in 1820s New York, had led to the popularization of cemeteries as retreats from the chaos of the city. Central Park, a 7.8 km^2 green space (eventually expanded to 11.6 km^2) established in 1853 in the heart of Manhattan, became the template for a certain kind of urban oasis, imitated in many cities, though rarely on the same scale. For Frederick Law Olmstead, the landscape architect who designed Central Park (as well as Yosemite, the Niagara Reservation at Niagara Falls, NY, and a whole series of parks in Boston and Buffalo), parks performed a critical social role; spending time in nature "had lasting beneficial physical, mental, and moral effects, particularly if it occurred 'in connection with relief from ordinary cares, change of air and change of habits'" (Olmsted, qtd. in Spirn 93). In contrast to British parks, which Olmsted criticized as mostly the preserve of the privileged, he hailed the creation of Central Park, "the first real park made in this century," as a "democratic development of the highest significance" ("Central Park"). Parks were to be for the enjoyment of everyone, which meant not just provision for mixed activities (in spite of occasional collisions, horseback riders, pedestrians, cyclists, and pleasure vehicles circulated along the trails of Central Park) but, more importantly, the mixing of classes. Olmsted was adamant that parks should be free for all visitors, a view sustained by the condescending belief that looking at beautiful scenery would be good for working-class people's morals (Spirn 92).

The democratic, or genuinely *popular*, character of parks, including Central Park, cannot be assumed or taken for granted, but is rather part of an ongoing struggle. As with many so-called wilderness areas (a topic we cover later in this chapter), the "natural" space of Central Park was achieved through the eviction of the people who lived there, mostly poor African Americans and Irish immigrants. As contemporary cities grapple with the problem of homelessness, it seems inevitable that parks will increasingly become hotspots for conflict over the meaning of living space (in 2005 one expression of that conflict resulted in the beating to death of a homeless man in a Toronto park by three drunk reserve soldiers from a nearby armory; Mathieu). Parks also experience the waxing and waning of the social welfare state, as their upkeep depends on the availability of public funds. In the 1970s, a lack of money and municipal will sent Central Park into a significant decline, to the point where it developed a global reputation as a dangerous place where innocent strollers were liable to get mugged. The situation slowly improved through the efforts of citizens' groups, who raised money, organized volunteer working groups, and lobbied government to repair the decaying infrastructure and rehabilitate natural spaces in the park. The park looks a lot better these days; however, struggle over its meaning as a public space continues.

In 2004, on the eve of a Republican National Convention, the anti-war coalition United for Peace and Justice (UFPJ) applied for a permit to hold a rally in the park. The city refused the application, a decision that was upheld by the Federal Court. Almost no one bought the lame explanation offered by the city, that it would "spoil the grass"; however, the "real" story as represented in screaming newspaper headlines such as "Anarchy Threat to City: Cops fear Hard-Core Lunatics Plotting Convention Chaos" was equally ludicrous (qtd. in Dobbs). The rally, which drew more than half a million people, was eventually held away from the park, in keeping with the request of the organizers' that participants respect the law. However, in the press release it issued before the rally, the UFPJ reasserted Central Park's place as "New York City's town commons, a traditional public forum that belongs to all the people of this city," and declared: "The fight to restore Central Park to public use is far from over and it is just beginning" (United for Peace and Justice). While the size of Central Park, combined with its location in New York City, gives it an emblematic status, the conflicts that define its history find echoes in cities across North America, as walkers, skateboarders, political protesters, dog owners, nature lovers, and wading pool aficionados assert their rights to enjoy urban green space.

Rich Kids Swim, Poor Kids Sink

In comparison with the struggle over parks as places of genuinely popular culture, the politics of swimming pools might seem trivial; however, throughout the century or so of their recent use, public pools have also seen their share of controversy. Public pools or baths—in the early years there wasn't much difference—were built in mid-nineteenth-century Britain (a few decades later in the United States and Canada) as part of a campaign to promote hygiene. Pools were seen as a way to foster both physical fitness and cleanliness: many people could not afford baths in their own homes, and developing medical theories about germs prompted new concerns about sanitation. Civic and medical officials alike were inclined to single out the poor as "a 'smelly' group," and the term "'the great unwashed' was often used for the working classes who were purportedly ignorant on matters of personal hygiene and hence health" (Sigworth and Worboys, qtd. in Sheard 65). There was another compelling reason to build indoor, or at least fenced, pools, which was to shield decent folks from the sight of boys splashing around "nekkid" in city rivers (not to mention protecting the swimmers themselves from hazards of floating objects like rats, condoms, and occasionally decomposing bodies; Cavett).

If ideas about hygiene, not always well informed, were a significant factor behind the creation of public pools, they also influenced the contested issue of who got to use them and under what circumstances. Struggles over public pools mirrored broader social tensions with particular intensity, as they tended to evoke deeply held mythological assumptions about connections between health, cleanliness, sexuality, and morality.

Swimming pools produce a peculiar type of intimacy; as Jeff Wiltse puts it, "people who might otherwise come in no closer contact than passing in the street, now waited in line together, undressed next to one another and shared the same water" (3). Wiltse's book, *Contested Waters: A Social History of Swimming Pools in America*, describes how pools in the Northern United States became flashpoints for turbulent race relations throughout the nineteenth and twentieth centuries. Between the world wars, pools gradually evolved from spare, functional facilities segregated by gender, to lavish recreation centers where men and women would swim and lounge around in deck chairs, sometimes on fake beaches surrounded by palm trees. The erotic possibilities inspired by this environment fueled white anxieties about the mixing of races—specifically, the proximity of black men to white women. Thus began the racial segregation of pools, which persisted until the 1950s and 1960s (consistent with the bogus "separate-but-equal" rationale of other segregation policies, the white pools got the palm trees and deck chairs, while black swimmers had to make do with more spartan facilities). Within the civil rights movement, blacks mounted a successful challenge to the whites-only rule through a combination of activism and litigation. Whatever equality resulted from that challenge was short-lived, as (mostly white) members of the upper middle class retreated from "dirty" and "dangerous" cities to the suburbs, where they built their own private pools. Throughout the 1960s and 1970s, a large number of public pools were allowed to sink into disrepair; some were closed for good, and some reopened as private facilities.

The state of public swimming pools has historically been, and continues to be, a microcosm of the wider North American society. As the neoliberal economic tide of globalization saps the public sector of money and energy, all public facilities—pools, parks, libraries, community centers—are vulnerable. In 2008, the Toronto District School Board, which controls most of the city's pools, announced plans to close many of them over the next two years to deal with a budget shortfall (a drama repeated during Mayor Rob Ford's tenure in 2011 and 2012). According to board officials it came down to a choice between pools and funding for ESL (English as a second language) and Special Education programs. A third option would see private companies such as Canadian Tire enter into partnerships to help keep the pools open. As with other areas of popular recreation, the cost of struggles to preserve public space are borne disproportionately by the poor and by minorities (according to the US Centers for Disease Control, African Americans drown at significantly higher rates than other races, a statistic arguably attributable in part to unequal access to swimming pools; "Water Related Injuries"). The headline of an article in *The Globe and Mail* written by Canadian author Margaret Atwood puts it baldly: "Rich Kids Swim, Poor Kids Sink."

Close Up 9.1 Malls as Public Space?

When they first began to be built in large numbers in the 1950s, enclosed shopping malls were described by many developers as the new commons: a shared public space in which citizens could mingle and meet, encountering one another free from the heat of summer or the frigid temperatures of winter, while also shopping for yoga clothing and squeezing in a plate of Chinese noodles at the food court. And just as in any public space, they could also take photographs of the picturesque store fronts they encountered, zip around on their skateboards, speak their minds about the Iraq War, and assemble for street protests. So why was Stephen Down being led out of the Crossgate Mall in Guilderwood, New York, in handcuffs for wearing a T-shirt saying "Give Peace a Chance"—a T-shirt that he bought from a store in the mall (Kohn 1)?

Well, in part because you can't do *any* of the things we just listed. Malls may be a place where people congregate in large numbers—perhaps even the main space in most cities in which people do get together in large numbers on a regular basis, other than sporting events. But you can't skateboard in a mall (it seems these days you can't skateboard anywhere) or march down the main strip of stores with a placard in your hand; and in many malls security guards will ask you to put away your video camera. But wearing a T-shirt? Down was told by security that he was behaving inappropriately in the space of the mall by wearing a "peace" T-shirt on the eve of the war with Iraq in 2003. In the United States, freedom of political expression is of course guaranteed, but only on *public* and not private property. And malls are spaces that are privately owned, as are many "public squares" adjacent to office towers, airports, apartment complexes, and even the spaces in front of many "public" buildings.

"Public" can be a tricky word, especially when it is connected to "space." Lawrence Lessing has defined the commons as goods or resources "in joint use or possession to be held or enjoyed equally by a number of persons" (19). By this measure, as Margaret Kohn points out in *Brave New Neighborhoods*, her investigation of the increasing privatization of public space, there is less and less space that acts as a "commons" today. "In everyday speech," she writes, "a public space usually refers to a place that is owned by the government, accessible to everyone without restriction, and/or fosters communication and interaction" (11). But right away, it is possible to see all kinds of gaps and problems in this idea of public. Not all government buildings are accessible to everyone, and even national parks are available for use only by those who can pay a fee to enter (in 2016 a daily pass to Banff National Park set a family back CAN$19.60—before fees for camping, fishing permits, etc.). Private spaces such as malls or coffee houses can also foster communication—as long as you keep ordering lattes and bring your "I love America" T-shirt when you do.

Factories and Offices: The Spaces/Places of Work

One of the last areas of life many of us likely think of when we think about popular culture is work: unless we're lucky enough to work in the entertainment industry (a mixed blessing, to be sure), popular culture—in either its commercial or democratic sense—is what we do when we're *not* working. The discussion in Chapter 2 of this book about street football games, pubs, and music halls would seem to support this view of popular culture as distinct from work culture. It is true that in the nineteenth century a change *did* occur as work shifted from fields to factories. Just as a space opened up between work and home (and public and private), leisure and recreation—those practices most commonly understood to be part of popular culture—were increasingly relegated to their own distinct places and times. Taking note of this shift, we include work under the broad category of popular culture for two reasons. First, in a general sense, it's impossible to draw a clear boundary between work and play. Workplaces have their own cultures that express to some degree broader societal trends and in some ways are distinct from them, as we discuss in Chapter 4. Second, the space—and time—of postindustrial work in North America has morphed into other aspects of life in interesting ways. As with so many other aspects of popular culture, movies offer insightful ways to understand what this shifting work space looks like.

The 1936 Charlie Chaplin film *Modern Times* offers a comical/nightmarish depiction of the Depression-era workplace. The main character, played by Chaplin, is listed in the credits simply as "a factory worker," his namelessness reflecting the depersonalized, mechanistic quality of his job. The film opens with a shot of a clock that fills the whole screen, its hands creeping to 6 a.m., or the beginning of the work day. Accompanied by menacing music, the scene changes to show a mass of pigs being hustled somewhere (wherever it is, it can't be nice), which then morphs into a roiling logjam of workers coming out of a subway. The workplace itself is a windowless cavern with exposed pipes, filled with vast machinery that dwarfs the humans who operate it. At the sound of a whistle, a brawny, shirtless foreman flips a lever that sets the whole factory in motion, with the workers clearly expected to fit their bodies to the rhythms of the machines. In stark contrast to the conditions on the factory floor, in an office insulated by a door with a glazed window, sits the company president, who keeps tabs on his workers through a series of closed-circuit television sets. The power structure, organized according to strict hierarchy and maintained through surveillance, seems unimpeachable.

The conflict, or the comedy, in the film starts when the character played by Chaplin, whose job it is to tighten bolts on metal parts as they roll by on an assembly line, can't keep pace with the machinery, which has speeded up following an order from the president. Infinitesimally brief pauses to scratch an itch and brush away a fly disrupt the rhythm of the whole line, an interruption in productivity that the president responds to by ordering that the process be speeded up even more. When the worker tries to grab a quick smoke, the president's face appears on a large screen in the bathroom, ordering him to get back to work. Nor does he get any respite at lunch, as Chaplin's character becomes the involuntary guinea pig for a new device to speed up eating. Harnessed into a machine, his head is held in a kind of vice while a succession of levers spoon soup into his mouth and wipe his face with a napkin, a process that gets faster and faster until he ends up eating a bolt.

In spite of its comedy, the film delivers a powerful critique of the crushing effect of modern work and, by extension, "modern life" (the period that is sometimes said to mark the shift from working-in-order-to-live to living-in-order-to-work), which is symbolized by the physical structure of the factory. The clearest demonstration of the totally inhospitable character of the modern workplace is the scene of Chaplin's character being sucked into the machinery of the assembly line. For a few moments we see him drawn passively (and apparently quite comfortably) through a gigantic gear mechanism: he has become part of it, and it of him. His enmeshment in the machinery of work is shown by his inability to stop compulsively repeating the bolt-tightening motions of his job until well after he leaves the building. At least he *is* able to leave the building, and (following a brief period in a mental hospital) to become caught up (somewhat confusedly) in the events of the day. After accidentally participating in a political protest, being arrested a few times, and finding, then losing, a series of jobs, he walks off into the sunset with his girl into what will clearly be uncertain, but somewhat free, times.

Fast forward to the 1999 film *Office Space*, whose satirical look at contemporary office life offers a productive counterpoint to *Modern Times*. Like the earlier movie, this one opens with the journey to work. As the scurrying pedestrians of *Modern Times* are replaced by cars, the speed of the commute has paradoxically slowed to a crawl. Stuck in traffic, three drivers vent their frustration while a fourth man becomes increasingly agitated waiting for a bus, mumbling "It's late again. If I'm there late again I will be dismissed." A fifth man drives effortlessly into a reserved spot in a parking lot, his customized license plate MY PRSHE accentuating his status (and his obnoxiousness). The journeys are emblematic of the power structure at Initech, the software company where all the men have arrived at work. The low-rise building's bland exterior and mass of cubicles present a much more benign atmosphere than the large and terrible machines of *Modern Time*'s factory. The disciplinary structures also seem less onerous: with no gigantic clock or punch cards to remind him that he is always already late, Peter, the main character, consults his wrist watch while sitting in the semi-privacy of his cubicle. The everyday annoyances of his job—Milton's (the guy at the bus stop) incessant mumbling and radio listening, and an erratic photocopier—pale in comparison to the toll that assembly-line labor takes on its workers. It quickly becomes clear, however, that the apparently relaxed atmosphere and lack of obvious hierarchy mask a power structure that is in some ways more rigid than that of the factory. The audience comes to dread, as Peter does, the appearance of his boss, Bill, casually leaning over his cubicle, camouflaging his orders (to perform seemingly useless tasks, work late, etc.) within falsely friendly colloquialisms: "Hello, Peter, what's happening? Um, I'm gonna need you to go ahead and come in tomorrow [Saturday]. So if you could be here around nine, that'd be gre-e-a-a-t."

In *Modern Times*, the instruments of the factory worker's oppression—piercing whistles, large machines, thuggish foreman, the boss's face and voice on the large screen—are obvious, if hard to resist. In *Office Space* they are much harder to see, concealed as they are behind a veneer of casual equality and the illusion of choice—"*if* you could be here around nine"—as if he could choose not to be. (In fact, Peter does decide to stop working and gets promoted anyway, underlining the emptiness of the contemporary business world symbolized by Initech). Peter's final, triumphant gesture of resistance, in which he, Michael, and Samir smash the photocopier and blow up the building, seems a bit excessive as a response to the gently suffocating ambience of Initech; their rage seems all out of proportion with the innocuousness of the machines that enslave them. The scenes of destruction are also strangely cathartic, however, in part because they're so insistently physical in contrast to the immaterial economy the workers labor within.

One of the odd impressions to emerge from *Office Space* is of the overwhelmingly oppressive nature of the work environment. Even the intimidating and arguably dangerous machinery in *Modern Times* seems less menacing than the warren of portable cubicles that leave Peter and his colleagues simultaneously isolated and exposed. A dominant feature of American business architecture from the 1950s to the 1970s, cubicles were meant to embody the corporate systems they contained. Moves toward more flexible and movable walls might be seen to reflect a progressive shift toward a more open, democratic work environment. Interestingly, in Europe, where an extensively unionized workforce had a consistently stronger influence on labor conditions, "open-plan" offices never did catch on; workers rejected them for the same reason they have become the butt of satire in North America, that they "represent a form of individual housing that neither provided privacy nor fostered interaction" (Christopher Budd, qtd. in Ross 111).

The absence of insulation from creepy managerial intimacy—"Hello, Peter, what's happening?"—is at the benign end of a spectrum of privacy-invading practices at work that include monitoring of computer use, video surveillance, security measures such as retina scanning and fingerprinting, and mandatory drug tests. Less obviously intrusive, but pervasive in its social effects, is the corporate practice of eroding the distinction between workers' status as employees and their private lives. In sharp distinction from the anonymity of the factory, where the worker functions as a cog in the machinery, contemporary corporate culture goes to great lengths to validate and nurture workers as individuals. Going beyond the long-standing practice of recognizing productivity through prominently displayed photos of "Employee of the Month" (allowing some workers at least to rise temporarily above the fray), many companies now boast their commitment to nurturing their employees as "whole people." This can take the form of flex-time, allowing some workers (mostly managers) to organize their work day around other commitments, as well as more proactive efforts to cultivate workers' physical and emotional health. Onsite daycare programs, dry cleaners, restaurants, and gyms help to streamline workers' lives (and ensure that they spend most of them at work), while the sponsorship of newsletters, sports teams, clubs, and faith groups built around employees' own interests harnesses those aspects of individuals' lives that once found expression outside of work.

Some companies go the extra mile to fulfill workers' needs (see Figure 9.2). In 2008, for the second straight year, the search-engine company Google ranked first on a list of Best Companies to Work For compiled by *Fortune Magazine*; as of 2016, Google/Alphabet (the latter being the name of Google's new parent company) had been chosen as the best place to work for the seventh time over the previous decade. In addition to flexible working arrangements and the encouragement of employee input, Google earns praise for having "special and unique benefits that include opportunities, to learn, grow, travel, and have wildly zany fun during the work-day" (see Figure 9.3). As reported by the Great Place to Work® Institute,

Figure 9.2 In 2008, public protests greeted the City of Toronto's announcement of plans to close public pools to save money. Source: © Colin McConnell/Toronto Star via Getty Images

Figure 9.3 More rejuvenating than a coffee break: as part of a move to unleash all the productive capacities—body and soul—of their labor force, a few companies, such as this YouTube office in London, England, have designed spaces for their employees to chill out in. Source: www.google.co.uk/press/images.html

the décor of Google offices encourages much fun. Lava lamps, bicycles, large rubber exercise balls, couches, dogs, press clippings from around the world, projection screens displaying search queries or daily Google events fill the halls and offices. According to an article in the *Seattle Times* entitled "Big Google Ideas Generated Here" (06/24/06): "If the Googleplex exploded, the employees would have a hard time digging themselves out of a shower of pirate flags, action figures, t-shirts with funny sayings, leis, ironic signs, a fringed leather vest, thousands of game pieces, and giant Lego people." ("Why Is Google So Great?")

Of course, perks like meditation rooms and gyms represent the top sliver of workplace benefits. The vast majority of workers labor in far less comfortable conditions. The service sector, where 75% of the Canadian population currently works (according to the Canadian government's Standing Committee on Industry, Science and Technology), may be less dangerous than the factory in *Modern Times*, but lack of benefits and job security contribute to the precariousness of *post*modern workers' lives. At the same time, workers caught in the net of the ever-ballooning, never-stable service industry are expected to invest significant parts of themselves in their work. *Office Space* offers the frivolous example of Peter's waitress girlfriend Joanna (Jennifer Aniston), who is told off by her boss for not wearing the requisite 15 pieces of "flair" (suspenders, buttons, and other forms of "self-expression" that serve as crude indicators of an employee's "fun" quotient). Telemarketing companies that require South Asian callers to adopt "neutral"-sounding American accents are a serious, real-life instance of the way the contemporary workplace (in this case cramped offices in Bangalore, where employees facilitate the magical process of time–space compression) turns the labor force into pseudo-individuals while largely denying their humanity. And, of course, the stresses and physical dangers of factory life have not gone away. The sweet design and functionality of Apple—part of the texture of the world in which work and play are combined for many of us in late capitalist society— suddenly look less sweet when we think about the conditions in which iPads and iPhones are manufactured. A series of news stories in 2011 and 2012 about fatal fires and worker suicides in Chinese factories where Apple products are made brought home to Apple customers (many of whom have bought into the brand image of Apple as not just cooler, but also more progressive than PC users) the heavy costs of the lightness and flexibility that characterize our social space (we discuss this further in Chapter 10).

In *Modern Times*, the comedy in the film and our sympathy for Chaplin's character are driven by his incomplete subjection to the process of mechanization: even when, after escaping the factory, the worker continues compulsively to perform (on people's noses and women's dress buttons) the motions of his assembly-line action of bolt tightening, he does so in the form of a crazy but graceful ballet, expressing his alienation and thereby leaving intact something of his humanity. The subjection of the contemporary worker is arguably more complete. As Arlie Russell Hochschild notes in *The Time Bind: When Work Becomes Home and Home Becomes Work*, the "balance" that many workplaces claim to endorse today tends not to mean what we might think—a balance between home and work—but rather the shifting of the things that used to be associated with home, such as secure relationships, nurturing, interdependence, and recreation, into the workplace, with the result that workers willingly devote more and more time to work and less and less time to home and family responsibilities, which feel increasingly like work (18–21).

It seems that we have today a world in which the boundary between public and private has been blurred beyond recognition—mostly in favor of the private. In the case of the provision of public amenities for all to enjoy, the struggle goes on: these spaces are easy to identity and their disappearance can quickly be seen. The spaces of work and leisure have proven far more difficult to make sense of and to keep apart from one another. We bemoan with great energy the constant demands of work on our "free" time. We just as energetically scroll through the e-mail messages streaming down the screens of our smartphones even after the official end of the work day. We crave an escape.

Inside Out

On March 29, 2008, between the hours of 8 and 9 p.m., more than 24 cities across the world participated in "Earth Hour," encouraging businesses and individuals to turn off all nonessential electrical power as a step toward reducing the carbon emissions that con- tribute to global warming; by 2012, this event had expanded to include an enormous number of cities and town around the world, including 30 provinces and cities in Vietnam alone; and in 2016, a record 178 countries participated in the event. Whether you see this as a useful event or an empty symbolic gesture, it is significant as a mark of perhaps unprecedented global consciousness of the state of the globe itself—a space that we all inhabit, but can only know (in its totality as opposed to in its various smaller bits) in an abstract, mediated way. Our discussions of spaces and places so far have focused on con- crete, particular zones of experience—parks, roads, offices, and so forth—where we engage with different elements of popular culture. Our focus in this section shifts to aspects of the world that may seem to be the antithesis of the space of culture: nature and the environment (see Figure 9.4). We identify these areas separately not because they are practically distinguishable, but because they signify related but different ways of understanding the world around us, its nonhuman as well as its human elements.

It doesn't take a culture critic to tell you that nature is one of those concepts that is really difficult to define: many of us likely regard it as just one of those things that you know when you see it. Advertisers count on this fact when they market products from SUVs to shares in oil companies (many of which have pretty dodgy reputations as friends of nature) with images of sparkling lakes, mountain streams, and old-growth forests. We also see "nature" in the faces of threatened or endangered animals: pandas, tigers, or those remarkably colored tiny frogs whose disappearance scientists tell us is a barometer of catastrophic natural decline. Other animals interest us much less: rats, coyotes, cockroaches, and sparrows appear much less frequently, if at all, as ambassadors of nature. Then there are animals such as sharks that, until recently, served as emblems for the *other* nature—the uncontrollable, even diabolical force embodied in extreme weather events such as floods, earthquakes, and tropical storms. Now that they have been identified as endangered, sharks have become the beneficiaries of campaigns to rehabilitate their reputations, to show that, contrary to the serial-killer image portrayed in *Jaws* and countless other films and media stories, sharks are really big softies, more scared of us than we are of them. They thus join (with some difficulty thanks to their awkwardly large teeth) the ranks of ambassadors for *good* nature, which is almost always characterized as *fragile* nature, vulnerable to man's (and it is almost always characterized as *man's*) heedless and

Figure 9.4a A classic image of nature: Moraine Lake in Banff National Park, Canada. Source: By Gorgo, https://commons.wikimedia.org/wiki/File:Moraine_Lake_17092005.jpg. CC0-1.0 public domain https://creativecommons.org/publicdomain/zero/1.0/

Figure 9.4b An equally classic image of "culture": cityscapes such as this image of the Palace of Westminster (UK Houses of Parliament) taken from the dome of Methodist Central Hall, London. Source: Colin, https://commons.wikimedia.org/wiki/File:Palace_of_Westminster_from_the_dome_on_Methodist_Central_Hall.jpg. Used under CC BY-SA-4.0 https://creativecommons.org/licenses/by-sa/4.0/

greedy ways. Both categories of nature—threatening and threatened—invoke a whole host of other emotions including awe, aesthetic pleasure, and spiritual transcendence. Thus "nature"—even in its apparently most pared-down, nonhuman incarnation—almost always carries a lot of baggage, which is to say that it wears its unshakable connection with *culture* quite heavily. It is also highly unstable, as the case of the shark clearly illustrates, signifying different things in different times and different places. Rather than saying what nature is definitively, or going completely (infuriatingly) in the other direction and saying that it's purely an invention of culture, we can usefully examine how ideas of nature have traditionally worked to influence our relations with others (both human and nonhuman).

Moral Center, Uncivilized Chaos

As the random list of natural icons above suggests, nature, perhaps more than any other concept, lends itself to binary opposition, inviting mythological associations that swing back and forth between positive and negative values. This ambivalence is clear from a brief examination of two very different films, the animated children's comedy *Over the Hedge* (2006) and Werner Herzog's grisly documentary (excuse the pun) *Grizzly Man* (2005). Both films construct nature in a way that emphasizes its utter separateness and difference—whether positive or negative—from the human world.

As its title suggests, *Over the Hedge* is about the boundary that separates the places of human and animal habitation, and the danger—for animals—of crossing that boundary. Specifically, the hedge in the movie marks the border of a new subdivision that has sprung up while the animals (the principal characters, which include Vern, a turtle, Hammy, a squirrel, and Stella, a skunk) were hibernating. Imposingly tall and creepily green, the hedge is an object of suspicion to the animals, at least until a sleazy raccoon, RJ, persuades them to bust through it in order to find food (his plan is to use the animals as free labor, then give the food to a cranky bear who has threatened to kill RJ for an earlier theft of the bear's own food stash).

If there's a serious message to this film, it's that suburban developments have encroached on the habitats of animals, resulting in major disruptions to the food chain. Mostly though, it's a comedy, with much of the humor coming from the outrageous behavior of the human inhabitants of the subdivision (an aesthetic and environmental disaster, as movie suburbs generally are). Seen from the innocent perspective of the animals, we learn that humans are greedy ("We eat to live; they live to eat"); cruel (when told by an exterminator that a particular trap is illegal, the homeowner says "I don't care if it's against the Geneva Convention"), and lazy (humans ride around in SUVs, RJ tells the other animals, "because they're slowly losing their ability to walk"). The human world, for which the subdivision functions as an extreme emblem, is ugly, artificial, and aggressive in its domination of nature by technologies ranging from extensive sprinkler systems to a collection of brutal animal-control devices.

Most of the human vice in the movie is crammed into one comically horrible woman (Gladys, identified by the vanity plates on her SUV that read "GLADY$$"), so that a caricatured idea of femininity (shrill, bossy, obsessed with domestic details) becomes part of what is evil about the human side of the hedge. The animals, by contrast, aren't good in a simplistic way: under RJ's direction, they steal and—worse—become temporarily addicted to junk food, which is represented in the film not just as a nasty consequence of an industrial food system, but as a kind of metaphor for degraded humanity. The animals triumph (well, except the bear, but that's another story) by overcoming their junk-food addiction in favor of wholesome nuts and berries, reaffirming their work ethic and loyalty to one another, and effectively sealing off the border to the dangerous world of suburbia after dispatching Gladys and the exterminator in a particularly gruesome way. As the only humans in the movie, their fate doesn't give much hope for the possibility of reform.

While we would stop short of reading *Over the Hedge* as a serious defense of small semi-urban mammals, it would also be a mistake to write it off as a comedy that simply uses animals in place of humans to make a comment about the foibles of modern society. Neither is it a talking-animal movie like *Babe* or *Chicken Run*, whose comedy conveys uncomfortable truths about the human exploitation of animals. In fact, *Over the Hedge* is arguably not so much about the mechanics of human–animal relations as it is about the line that separates healthy and virtuous nature from the ugly, bloated, Chees-o-rama-coated goings-on of human society. While animals breach this line at their peril, the implication is that only by going over the hedge—that is, back to a more natural, pre-potato-chip existence—can humans redeem ourselves from the hell of our subdivided lives.

A version of this nature versus human philosophy guides the subject of *Grizzly Man*. Timothy Treadwell is a former athlete and sometime actor-turned-conservationist who spent 13 summers in a national park in Alaska living among grizzly bears. Supplemented by interviews with his friends and family, most of the footage in the film is drawn from the 100-plus hours of DVD footage Treadwell shot of himself—right up to the moment of his death at the hands of the bears (we don't see or hear the tape, which was recorded with the lens cap on, though we do watch Herzog as he listens in obvious horror to Treadwell and his girlfriend Amie's final moments). Part of what is so compelling about the movie is its invitation simultaneously to sympathize with Treadwell's sentimental identification with nature and to identify with Herzog's critical editorial perspective. While Treadwell speaks in crooning tones to the bears, to whom he's given names such as Mr. Chocolate and Aunt Melissa, and even rhapsodizes over their droppings ("I can feel the poop! It's warm"), Herzog offers a sober voiceover: "In nature there are predators. The common denominator of the universe is not harmony. It's chaos, hostility, murder." Herzog treats his subject respectfully. However, his skepticism—clearly shared by the wildlife experts and park officials interviewed for the film—finds ultimate vindication in Treadwell's death (which mocks his declaration early in the film: "I will not die at their claws and paws!"), which seems to support Herzog's contrary view of nature as violent and bloody. But this view is equally infused with emotion, equally mythological. For reviewer David Denby, the movie offers insight not intended by Herzog into the ideological opposition between the naive and optimistic American, Treadwell, and the

> hyper-cultivated European, who brings his own burden of despair to nature. Looking into the eyes of a bear that comes close to Treadwell's camera[, Herzog] discerns cruelty and mercilessness rather than hunger. Neither man, it seems, is willing to admit that a bear is a bear is a bear. (Denby)

Denby's analysis seems to make sense, but perhaps he overestimates not just the willingness but the ability of *any* of us to see nature in anything other than value-laden terms. In fact, Treadwell's view of nature resonates with many people, judging by the popularity of the workshops he ran for many years before his death. Despite Treadwell's somewhat loopy camera persona, many of his sentiments about the innocence of wild animals and the corruption of society (even the parks officials charged with protecting the grizzlies' habitat become objects of his suspicion) are widely shared by individuals and organizations a lot more mainstream than the radical Grizzly People that Treadwell founded.

Out in the Wilderness

This view of nature, which is particularly strong in North America, crystallizes around the concept of "wilderness." Idealized as "an island in the polluted sea of urban-industrial modernity" (Cronon 69), wilderness is, according to critic William Cronon, actually a *product* of the social forces it is seen to offer sanctuary from. To understand that irony it is necessary to go back a few centuries to a time when wilderness still retained its biblical significance as a place of desolation, darkness, and despair—the world outside the garden of Eden. Around the eighteenth century, that meaning changed. The processes of industrialization and colonization blurred the line between the known and the unknown as the entire globe was subject to systematic exploitation—for natural resource extraction, settlement, and the extension of European civilization. Within the United States, the concept of the frontier—the unsettled space at the edge of westward colonial expansion—came to embody the great hope for the American dream of democracy and freedom. In the course of contending with, and ultimately conquering, wild nature, the pioneer was seen to be reinvigorated by it, developing through the encounter the qualities of primitive energy, creativity, and independence thought to be the hallmark of the American character.

The wrinkle in this hypothesis was that by the time it was articulated (by Frederick Jackson Turner in *The Significance of the Frontier in American History* in 1893), settlement had extended to the point that the wilderness beyond it was being rapidly consumed—much like the animal's habitat in *Over the Hedge* that is shown on a map to be a tiny dot in a sea of subdivisions. Inherent in the idea of the frontier, then, was its imminent disappearance. And so the seeds were sown of the wilderness-preservation movement, nurtured by the idea that in wilderness lay the antidote to the corruption and decadence of Old World civilization; in wilderness, in short, lay the possibility of the salvation of human society. Cronon points out several problems with the idealization of wilderness, which persists today in a form not that different from that celebrated by nineteenth-century frontier enthusiasts (the evolution of Canadian ideas of nature took a somewhat different form, stemming from a very different history of European settlement; however, the wilderness ideal also has resonance in Canada, and to an extent in Europe and Australia).

First, the structure of the ideal is inherently nostalgic: celebration of the wilderness tends to go hand in hand with a condemnation of urbanization and modern life in general. Among the virtuous pleasures associated with wilderness are solitude (in contrast to the turbulent crowds of the city) and masculine ruggedness (vs. "the comforts and seductions" and "feminizing tendencies" of civilized life; Cronon 78). Ironically, these pleasures tended to be available only to the privileged: frontier nostalgia became a vehicle for expressing what Cronon calls "a peculiarly bourgeois form of antimodernism. The very men who most benefitted from urban-industrial capitalism were among those who believed they must escape its debilitating effects" (78). A version of this paradox persists today, whereby those who have profited most from the capitalist exploitation of natural resources are now in a position to escape from its consequences, which include the genuine problems of pollution and disappearing urban green space, but also more questionable objections to the sights, sounds, and smells of life in a modern city.

Authentic wilderness came to be seen as a place free from human society and economic activity in particular; this explained its particular affinity for urbanites: "The dream of an unworked natural landscape is very much the fantasy of people who have never themselves had to work the land to make a living" (Cronon 79). The view of the wilderness as home only to animals reflects disregard for the humans who lived, and continue to live and work, there. This contradiction is particularly evident in the way wilderness fantasies tend to gloss over the violent dispossession of First Nations peoples by European settlers. To the extent that the ideal wilderness contains Indians, they are generally presented as one with the land itself, romantic inhabitants because they, along with the buffalo and the forests, are seen to be on the verge of disappearance. The role of the settler/tourist in the displacement of traditional ways of life is awkwardly repressed in the construction of a sentimental image of the "noble savage" that condemns or strategically ignores the unromantic economic conditions of contemporary First Nations. In more concrete terms, preserving wilderness comes to seem like a cleaner, simpler goal than addressing Native land claims, with the result that Natives who attempt to hunt and fish on their ancestral lands today are often charged with poaching.

The history of Native cultures in North America and the violence of colonial contact are rarely acknowledged in our idealized constructions of wilderness. In fact, it is arguable that this erasure of history is key to the sacred appeal of wilderness, and its chief problem. The flight from history also represents a flight from present-day responsibility. Not only do we deny the reality of violence that gave birth to the myth of wilderness, but also, "by imagining that our true home is in the wilderness, we forgive ourselves the homes we actually inhabit" (Cronon 81). In other words, the creation of sacred natural spaces lets us off the hook for continuing to live unsustainably everywhere else. The paradox is especially evident in ads that display SUVs in remote wilderness settings—the trick being that a weekend spent in quiet contemplation of nature (alone, of course, since the sanctity of nature would be ruined if it was also accessible to other people!) can absolve us from the excesses of civilization, including the consumption of resources involved in escaping from it. The ludicrous contradictions in this scenario illustrate Cronon's argument that "wilderness poses a serious threat to responsible environmentalism" (81).

Suggested Activity 9.2

Slovenian philosopher Slavoj Žižek has expressed worries that our "ecology of fear"—our worries about everything from the potentially disastrous outcome of biogenetic experiments to exploitation of the Earth's resources—"has every chance of developing into the predominant form of ideology of global capitalism, a new opium for the masses replacing declining religion" (439). As long as we take comfort in our fears, he believes that we are unlikely to take the serious steps needed to deal with man's impact on the planet. For Žižek, one of the big problems we face is the view of nature we have constructed for ourselves, one that has made it an ultimate, final form of order that offers security to human social life even as it disappears. Our "cultural" lives might be contingent and made up as we go along through history, but nature has an order that is always beyond us and has no relation to us. Žižek would prefer that we engage in an "ecology without nature" (439), a movement to save the Earth that does not rely on ideas about restoring nature's balance or bringing it back into order.

This is one of the ways in which our categories of "nature" and "environment" might create more problems for us than they solve. In what ways are these categories put to use in the public debates about our environmental future today? What role do they play in other public anxieties as well (e.g., the concern that kids play too many video games and should be out getting some fresh air)?

Environmental Awareness

Cronon's comment highlights the need to be wary of the mythological foundations of one of our most common ways of representing nature. It does so by appealing to a different, less value-laden way of understanding the physical world, through the concept of "environment." A term with more scientific credibility, certainly, than words such as "nature" and "wilderness," environment seems to offer an objective way of characterizing nonhuman spaces and their contents—rocks, trees, animals, air, water, and so on. As ordinary people, even schoolchildren, have come to understand some of the causes and effects of global warming, it can be said that environmental awareness is growing: we're becoming more knowledgeable—amazingly so—about spaces and processes on a scale that we can't actually experience directly. Without diminishing the value of this knowledge, it is worth pausing to consider the cultural dimensions of this realm of existence that seems to be absolutely outside and beyond culture.

How did "the environment" emerge as a subject of popular consciousness? We can identify a few watershed moments. In 1962, marine biologist Rachel Carson's book *Silent Spring* used a mix of scientific data and an accessible narrative style to issue a warning about the effects of the pesticide DDT on animals and people. Part of what was so significant about her text, aside from the specific dangers of DDT (which manufacturers continue to dispute), was how it invited readers to envision the physical world as a vast, interconnected web, such that the effect of a single process, like the application of a pesticide to a farmer's field, could reverberate far beyond it in space and in time.

Silent Spring, which had been serialized in the *New Yorker* before being published as a book and went on to be featured in a 1963 CBS television special, found a large popular audience. An even more momentous contribution to the popularization of the idea of the environment was the transmission of photos of Earth from space. The taking of the 1968 photo "Earthrise" by Apollo 8 astronauts was shown live on television, and it became one of a series of images used on posters for the first Earth Day on April 22, 1970. Two years later, Apollo 17 captured the much more famous "Whole Earth" image that has come to be associated with the birth of a new awareness of the world as a single, fragile organism (Maher). Both photos feature in the lecture that structures Al Gore's 2006 documentary on climate change, *An Inconvenient Truth*, following an opening sequence depicting a traditional nature scene with trees, a gently flowing river, and the sound of birds and tree frogs. The images are woven together in a way that invites us to extend our sympathetic imagination from familiar wilderness scenes to the whole biosphere.

One of the striking elements of Gore's film is the way in which it acknowledges and even celebrates the role of technology in mediating our understanding of nature—the scene that bridges the river and the lecture is of Gore opening his Apple laptop, and images of computers feature throughout the film. This representation reflects—and maybe even produced—a new form of environmental consciousness, in comparison to which 1970s celebrations of the image of the "big blue marble" in space seem simple and childlike. The rapidly growing sophistication of visual technologies combined with unprecedented public access to the images they produce—if not to the technologies themselves—have enhanced popular understanding of and concern for spaces and places that we will never physically experience. This awareness has obvious benefits in encouraging individuals to change their own behavior and to lobby government to create policies necessary to reduce carbon emissions. But the increasing sophistication of popular global awareness may also have another, less positive ramification. The technology that gathers the data that informs our awareness, along with the perspective that interprets it, is not planetary in scope; rather, it is produced by organizations whose scientific focus is shaped and sometimes diverted by powerful political interests. The global environmental agenda as a consequence tends to be driven by wealthy nations in the global North, but directed toward poorer countries in the global South, whose development obviously consumes lots of resources. From logging in the Amazonian rainforest to heavy industry in China, environmental problems in the developing world have been the target of a lot of "First World" finger-wagging—at the expense of attention to the reliance of our own consumer-intensive lifestyles on unsavory environmental practices in other places. "Thinking globally" isn't the problem, then; it is that we don't think globally *enough*, or make the connections between where we live and what is happening in other places in the world.

The Big Picture: Globalization?

One of the major changes in how we talk about and conceptualize space is to think of the planet as a single, unitary system. Globalization is the term that has been used to make sense of those forces that have reshaped both individual and group experience in ways that have left everyone scrambling to understand. It is a complicated idea on whose behalf and in whose name many claims have been made.

Globalization has been discussed with equal fervor in the halls of academia, in the pages of business magazines, on the front pages of newspapers around the world, and on the web sites and Internet discussion groups of organizations and individuals dedicated to fighting global corporate dominance. At the beginning of the 1990s, globalization was a term most commonly associated with the decline of industrial manufacturing in the US "Rust Belt." Unlike typical recessions connected to the cyclical downturns characteristic of capitalist economies, the loss of blue-collar jobs was seen in these cases as the result of an unprecedented migration of North American industries to lower-wage countries, especially to China and the **maquiladoras** along the United States–Mexico border. By the end of the decade, globalization was linked to an ever-expanding range of political, economic, social, and cultural phenomena, from public demonstrations against multilateral trade and economic agreements to the potential dangers of genetically modified foods to worries over what Britney Spears's music and image are doing to the Philippines.

Though globalization is primarily the name of a *process* (just like modern*ization* and industrialization), the increasing use and visibility of the term in both the media and in public debates have sometimes made it seem as if it is the name for the particular moment in history we are now living through. Just as the Cold War was the name for the entire set of events and processes that made up the international order between the end of the Second World War and the fall of the Berlin Wall in 1989, globalization is sometimes taken to be synonymous with the "**New World Order**" announced by (the first) President George Bush and described by the author Francis Fukuyama as "the end of history." While it does seem to be the case that the term "globalization" began to be used with frequency only *after* the end of the Cold War and the dissolution of the Soviet Union, the claims made for and against globalization can be understood only if we treat it as an ongoing historical process. Indeed, much of the debate surrounding globalization concerns questions of just what kind of processes it names, how far back these processes can be traced, and, indeed, whether these processes can be described meaningfully as part of a single, worldwide process.

What kinds of processes are associated with globalization? At its most basic level, globalization is the name for the social, political, cultural, economic, and technological processes that, taken together, have created the changed conditions of contemporary existence. At the center of these altered conditions is an enormous change in both the physical and psychological experience of time and space. Globalization has brought previously distant parts of the world together. Instead of being composed of distant and distinct places, we have begun to imagine the world as a single space in which peoples and communities are connected to one another as never before. New communications technologies, such as the Internet, cell phones, and satellite transmissions, have made it possible for people (or at least some people) to communicate with one another instantaneously across huge distances, and to receive immediate information about political and social developments in other parts of the world. The communications revolution has also helped to produce greater integration of national economies, particularly with respect to financial markets. Multinational agreements that have been ratified by most countries in the globe, such as the General Agreement on Tariffs and Trade (GATT), have changed the nature of the world economy. Today, there is more than $5.1 trillion in foreign-exchange transactions per day, up from $750 billion in 1988 (Bank for International Settlements). As financial crises in Mexico (1994), Southeast Asia (1997), Russia and Brazil (1998), Argentina (2002), and the global crisis in 2007–08 have shown, economic developments in one country have an increasingly large impact on every other country in the world.

Culturally, globalization is experienced as the increased knowledge of and access to the culture and cultural products of peoples around the world, as well as the often-unwanted imposition of one especially powerful culture's values and products on nearly all the others. In the first instance, globalization can be witnessed in the popularity of world music (such as the Buena Vista Social Club or Cesária Évora), the global interest in Japanese *manga* and *anime*, and the fascination in Eastern Europe (and elsewhere) with *telenovelas* produced in Mexico and other parts of South America. On the other hand, the overwhelming, ubiquitous global presence of films, television programs, and fast-food franchises from the United States (with the same Starbucks coffee available in Beijing's Forbidden City as in the streets of Istanbul) has been seen by many people as one of the negative results of a smaller and faster world.

Popular culture today in every part of the planet exists in some relationship to globalization. Indeed, as John Tomlinson suggests at the beginning of his book *Globalization and Culture*, "globalization lies at the heart of modern culture; cultural practices lie at the heart of globalization" (1). In exploring contemporary popular culture, it is thus essential to understand the reciprocal relationship between globalization and culture. As a way of examining this relationship, we need to consider a perhaps surprising question that has a great impact on how we perceive the effects of globalization. We need to ask: Is globalization *real*? While no one disputes the fact that there have been significant changes in every sphere of human life over the past several decades, there are disagreements over just how *new* globalization is. Whether globalization is a genuinely new development in human life or whether it is the acceleration of much longer-term developments has a significant impact on how we understand its relationship to cultural practices around the world.

Is Globalization Real?

Claims about the "newness" of globalization have been raised in a number of related areas, including economics, politics, and technology. Though we take up each of these areas separately below, it is important to recognize that they are in fact connected in important ways. As we shall see in the discussion that ends this chapter, one of the things that globalization has meant is that it is no longer possible even to make such divisions *heuristically*—that is, as a simplified model that limits the range of events and concepts that we need to investigate in order to make sense of specific phenomena.

Economic Globalization

Globalization is a term that has perhaps been most frequently discussed in corporate boardrooms and in the pages of the business press. It is understood as presenting both new challenges and fresh opportunities in the never-ending quest to generate ever-greater corporate profits and to maximize shareholder value. In the eyes of the general public, too, globalization is connected to new forms of business practice. Businesses and economies were once linked to definite, national spaces, which meant that they could be controlled and regulated by the governments and citizens of nation-states. However, in the era of globalization many businesses have become transnational: able to relocate to whatever jurisdiction has the most favorable climate for business, and sometimes able to exist outside of any jurisdiction whatsoever. The former CEO of General Electric, one of the largest companies in the world, described the ideal location of his company as a gigantic barge that could be moved around the world as needed to take advantage of changes in economic climate (Welch). Similarly, shipping companies have increasingly registered their fleets in small protectorates such as the Marshall Islands in order to avoid taxation in the countries from which they really originate.

The ability of corporations to shift production around the world, often to take advantage of cheap wages and loose environmental and labor regulations in less developed countries (LDCs), has been accompanied by two other factors associated with globalization. First, many companies have become global enterprises in order to expand the range of consumer markets that they can reach. Several fast-food chains based in the United States operate in more than 100 countries worldwide, while cell phone and consumer electronics giants have established consumer outlets and the production facilities to support them on virtually every continent (Antarctica remains spared... for now). In recent years, even older industrial and resource enterprises, from steel producers to oil companies, have been consolidated into even more massive global businesses. Second, globalization has enabled unprecedented flows of financial goods and services. The world's stock markets are integrated as never before, with a small fluctuation in capital markets in one country able to produce major financial shifts and swings in others. For example, anxieties about the size of Greek's national debt—a country that occupies a very small part of the overall world economy—caused stock markets to decline not only in Europe, but in Shanghai, São Paulo, and Toronto, as well as New York City, and to do so repeatedly. Today, the equivalent of the combined global GDP flows across borders in the form of foreign-exchange transactions in roughly eight days.

The Roots of Globalization

The contemporary world economy is truly global in scope. But in many respects, it has been "global" for hundreds of years, even if we haven't used the term "globalization" to describe this fact. While prior to the time of Christopher Columbus's journey to the Americas most food and goods originated close to where people lived and worked, even in the ancient world there was a great deal of cross-cultural contact. This contact came about through military conquest (from Alexander the Great to the Roman Empire to the Crusades), travel along established trading routes between regions and even continents, and journeys of exploration—such as Marco Polo's travels to Asia and the voyages of the Vikings, who, 500 years prior to Columbus, had already established a settlement in the Americas at L'Anse aux Meadows, in what is today known as Newfoundland in Canada.

The "discovery" of the Americas by Europeans initiated a process of ever-accelerating, truly global trade in and production of goods. The establishment of far-sprung colonial empires by Spain, Portugal, England, Germany, Belgium, France, the Netherlands, and Italy (followed later by Japan and the United States) led to a market in Europe for goods produced abroad (bananas, oranges, coffee, tobacco, sugar, etc.). These empires also established a global division of labor that remains with us to this day. The colonies in South America, Africa, and Asia became sites of resource extraction and agricultural production for the European market. In turn, value-added manufacturing took place in Europe, with these goods often being exported back to the colonies in an effort to maximize the size of the markets (and thus of the profits) for European goods. The once powerful textile industries of India and the Philippines (e.g., cotton) were devastated by the cheaper textiles exported from England.

This global division of labor exists in very much the same form today, with an ever-increasing range of local economies (and thus local ways of life) feeling the impact of new global economic arrangements. In particular, the agricultural sector of many countries has been threatened by the availability of Western agricultural products that, due to protectionist tariffs and subsidies, can be sold much more cheaply than locally produced goods. Stephanie Black's documentary *Life and Debt* (2001), for instance, examines the flood of US agricultural products into Jamaica, a fertile country whose financial problems and debt crisis have meant that local farmers find it difficult to produce fruit and vegetables grown thousands of miles away.

Globalization is imagined as the era in which corporations have developed global reach and achieved newfound power. But here, too, the story is a much longer and more complicated one than many debates and discussions about globalization might lead us to believe. During the Cold War, a number of companies were already described as having operations that were multinational in scope. For example, Japanese automobile manufacturers such as Toyota and Nissan sold *and* produced cars in many countries outside of Japan during the 1960s, 1970s, and 1980s; the same holds true for all of the major corporations in the world.

A little further back, by the end of the nineteenth century a number of US corporations had developed not just national but global monopolies (or "trusts"), which led to the passage of "antitrust" legislation to limit the control of trade by a few large companies. The global might of Standard Oil, Carnegie Steel, American Tobacco, and other large corporations was reined in under this legislation, which has been used subsequently to challenge the power of corporations such as AT&T and Microsoft (though it has surprisingly *not* been invoked in the recent mergers of major oil companies). Even further back, enormous corporations developed alongside the creation of the European colonies. The insurance giant Lloyd's of London has been underwriting corporations and colonial expeditions since 1688; in Canada, the Hudson's Bay Company, which has been in existence since 1670, organized trade from the New World to Great Britain and Europe.

Corporations as "Persons"

In many ways, then, the world economy functions very similarly to how it has over the past century (if not even longer). Nevertheless, there are significant differences, as a result of developments in technology and geopolitical shifts, which have a direct impact on the shape and character of contemporary popular culture. Due in part to fears about the possibility that large corporations might relocate to other countries, there has been an unprecedented relaxation of governmental, legal, and economic controls on corporations worldwide.

This, too, is part of a longer history that extends back to 1886, when corporations in the United States were granted full legal rights as "natural persons," far in advance of rights for women and minorities. Prior to this date, corporations were extended short-term charters, which gave the public the ability to limit a company's profits and debt (among other things) and provided procedures for a full public accounting of the company's books.

Today, nation-states around the world have less legal recourse than ever in controlling the actions of corporations, which now exist to some degree outside of the laws of nation-states altogether. This has been one of the major consequences of the international trade agreements pursued by states since the end of the twentieth century. These agreements have the effect of spreading the US legal definition of corporations, as well as other aspects of corporate law (such as definitions regarding **intellectual property**), into other countries around the world.

As a result, the balance of power between corporations and states has shifted considerably. For example, under the provisions of Chapter 11 of the North American Free Trade Agreement (NAFTA), corporations are able to file suit against governments for infringing on "investor rights." United Parcel Services (UPS), the world's largest package-delivery company, in 2002 filed a $230 million suit against Canada Post (a public corporation), alleging that the Canadian federal government was involved in a service already provided by a private corporation in violation of NAFTA; however, it was unsuccessful ("Canada").

Similarly, citing NAFTA's fair and equitable treatment rules, Vancouver-based Methanex Corp. sued the US government as a result of a California decision to phase out the use of a gasoline additive produced by the company due to environmental concerns; the claims were dismissed and the company ordered to pay $3 million of legal fees to the US government and an undisclosed cost of arbitration (Huizen). While NAFTA and other trade agreements have included provisions to limit their applicability to cultural issues, this has in reality done very little to limit the erosion of state control over corporate activities.

The shift in the relationship between states and corporations has taken two other forms as well. First, as a way of attracting and retaining business, governments have committed significant public monies (through tax breaks, loan guarantees, or direct transfers) to entice companies to their countries, cities, and regions. This transfer of tax revenue, which is now generated predominantly by taxes on individual income rather than on corporate profit, has occurred in almost every sector of the business world. Its most public face in North America, however, has been seen in the debates over public financing of sports franchises and stadiums (see Chapter 2).

Second, while there have been challenges to the monopoly status of some companies (such as the European Union's legal challenge against Microsoft in 2008), for the most part there has been a loosening of restrictions on the size and power of corporations. In order to gain and maintain their competitive advantage globally, corporations from across the world have been merging into larger and larger entities. In 2000 alone, according to the consulting firm KPMG, the value of cross-border mergers was CAN$643 billion (though down in value in subsequent years, such mergers have continued). To put this in perspective, the value of cross-border mergers in 2000 was about the same as Canada's GDP for that year.

Integration and Convergence

The effects of these mergers have been especially pronounced in the culture industries. Changes in legislation regulating telecommunications in Canada and the United States have permitted the development of enormous multimedia conglomerates. Giant media corporations such as Time Warner, News Corporation, Viacom, and the Walt Disney Company have enormous global reach. Contemporary media conglomerates not only are vertically integrated, like the early twentieth-century film industry (see Chapters 2 and 4), but also are horizontally integrated, owning several record labels, television channels, or film studios. Technological changes (especially **digitalization**) have also made it possible for these conglomerations to make use of programming or content produced for one medium in several others. For example, a movie produced by Warner Brothers' film studio can receive positive press in *People* magazine, be publicized on the Internet via AOL, and be screened later on TNT, a television "superstation" that broadcasts across North America.

The culture industries belong to the sector of the economy known as *service industries*, which now constitute almost 30% of the total exports of the United States (World Bank 190–198). As culture becomes more closely identified with global economics, popular culture undergoes a shift. For example, the popularity of the action-film genre has much to do with the ease with which these films can be exported to countries outside the United States: dialogue is minimal and easily translated, and costly Hollywood special effects offer a spectacle that few indigenous cinemas can match. In other words, because they are able to generate enormous revenues in the global film market, action movies starring the likes of Sylvester Stallone, Steven Seagal, Jackie Chan, and Liam Neeson, or low-dialogue, high-scream horror films such as *Saw*, represent an increasingly large proportion of Hollywood productions.

Contemporary cultural industries require costly infrastructural investments in production facilities and distribution networks. They also require a high degree of technological innovation and expertise. Unsurprisingly, in a world in which the division of wealth has increased both among and within countries, only a very small number of countries have been able to participate actively in the production and export of some forms of popular culture. While the United States is the most visible of these, Canada has also aggressively marketed its cultural products abroad. This has sometimes placed the Canadian government in the awkward position of defending Canadian culture from outside influence through various cultural policies (such as Canadian content rules on television and radio), while simultaneously pushing for greater exports of Canadian-produced culture.

The global economy has developed over several hundred years, and is in many respects structurally similar today to what it was like at the end of the nineteenth century. There are, however, differences—especially with respect to the production and export of culture—that are an essential aspect of popular culture in globalization.

Suggested Activity 9.3

In what contexts have you heard the concept of globalization discussed (e.g., newspaper and television stories, books, etc.)? In these contexts, is globalization presented as an opportunity or a cost? How do different groups and organizations view globalization? Is globalization seen as just how things are, or as a political–economic project that needs to be contested and challenged? What do these differences (between, for example, Fortune 500 companies and environmental groups) suggest about the general public's understanding of the meaning of globalization, and how does this differ from what we've outlined so far (and what we go on to say in the rest of the chapter)?

Globalization and Politics

Many of the points made about the economic realities of globalization apply equally to its political aspects. Politically, discussions about globalization have tended to focus on two things: (i) the decline of the power of nation-states and the rise in power of corporations and international agencies such as the International Monetary Fund (IMF) and the World Trade Organization (WTO); and (ii) the increasing privatization of public services and public spaces.

There is some truth to both of these claims. Especially with respect to economic decision making, nation-states face considerable pressure from foreign economic developments and are often forced to act reactively rather than proactively to current events. At the same time, the massive privatization of the economy and culture offers evidence to the contrary. Though the decisions of governments to outsource services they once provided as a public good—everything from state-run utilities, to prisons, to the education system—are often presented to the public as matters of rational logic (i.e., the private sector can do things more efficiently than the government) or external compulsion (i.e., global competitiveness demands it), it is in fact only a strong state that could bring about such a massive change in the structure of Western politics and economics.

In other words, the claim that the power of the state has declined is in many respects little more than a ruse that has disguised a massive transfer of publicly accumulated wealth into private hands. In many cases, state spending has in fact increased more quickly than corporate growth over the past few decades, though this new spending has been directed toward different ends than in the past—policing, prisons, anti-immigrant spending, enforcement of drug politics, militarization, and transfers to business and infrastructural development that tend to benefit private corporations rather than the public at large. Nation-states continue to control the major institutions through which laws are enforced and legitimate force is exerted (armies, police, intelligence agencies, etc.).

National Identity

Not only has the decline of the power of the nation-state been exaggerated, but so too has the claim that globalization signals a decline in feelings of national identity or pride in national culture (see Chapter 7). Feelings of national belonging now compete with other forms of identification, which can range from various kinds of consumer identity (e.g., patterns of belonging derived *from* your belongings, such as occurs with Harley-Davidson or BMW owners) to identities based on ethnicity, sexual orientation, and political affiliations, all of which exceed the boundaries of individual nation-states. While it is true that national identity constantly interacts and competes with other forms of identification, this is true of the *entire* history of the nation, not just during the period of globalization.

Even where new nationalities (and, indeed, new nation-states, the multiple countries that now make what used to be Yugoslavia and the Soviet Union being just the beginning of the new nations that have come into existence since 1989) are not in the process of being formed, national identity remains an extremely powerful force. Pride in national identity is still reinforced by schooling (through the playing of the national anthem and the teaching of national histories and cultures), revived during the Olympics, and crystallized during times of tension and conflict—as the reaction of the citizens of the United States to the terrorist attacks on the World Trade Center and the Pentagon showed all too clearly.

The politics of globalization are complex and multifaceted. There are new political agents and institutions involved in shaping global politics, including a wide variety of nongovernmental organizations (NGOs) and institutions such as the International Intellectual Property Organization, which have been developed to manage international agreements of various kinds. Once again, however, it is best to stress continuities as opposed to a sudden, massive discontinuity in the nature of politics in the era of globalization.

The Technological Dimensions of Globalization

The possibility of imagining the world as one interconnected space can certainly be attributed to the global revolution in telecommunications. As with other developments we have traced so far, this "revolution" is not all that new. The ability to reach virtually any part of the globe with phone calls, television images, and computer-based information can be traced back to the launch of the first communications satellites in the early 1960s. The ability of these satellites to change the way in which we obtain information about the world became clear by the summer of 1964, when parts of the Tokyo Olympics were broadcast live on television.

Development of a global satellite communications network proceeded very rapidly. By the summer of 1969, an estimated 500 million people were able to witness the landing of *Apollo 11* on the moon. The rest, as they say, is history. In North America today, millions of individuals own tiny dishes that provide them with television images beamed from orbiting satellites; the use of cellular phones is ubiquitous; and live, continuous news coverage has become the norm since CNN covered the first cruise missile strikes live from Baghdad during the Gulf War in 1991. The widespread global mourning that accompanied the death of Princess Diana in 1997, the terrorist attacks on the United States in 2001, and the massive tsunami in Southeast Asia in 2006, as well as all the disasters that have occurred since, such as the recent earthquakes in Haiti and Japan, was in some sense the product of contemporary telecommunications technologies: without these technologies, the reaction to these events would likely have been very different in character and scope.

New Communication Technologies

The growth and spread of new modes of communication have had an impact on popular culture in a large number of ways. Cell phones have changed the nature of work and family life, and have introduced new cultural practices—such as the use of text messaging by teens to communicate with one another in secret or the writing of the cell phone novels now racing up the sales charts in South Korea and Japan. In many areas of the world, including parts of Eastern Europe, the advent of cell phones introduced phone communication for the very first time: the high infrastructural cost of traditional phones means that in these places cell phones are the primary means of interpersonal electronic communication. As a wide range of struggles since 1989—from the Zapatistas to the Arab Spring—have made evident, new communication technologies have also changed the nature of political struggles in the contemporary world (see Chapter 10).

The Internet has introduced new modes of consumerism and interpersonal interaction, greater flows of official and nonofficial information, and an astonishing number of new cultural practices, from online interactive gaming to Internet dating to the transnational bride market. The impact of these technologies has been so dramatic that globalization is often associated with these developments alone. Once again, however, current developments are the product of a process dating back at least a century: the invention of the telegraph in the mid-nineteenth century (see Chapter 2) and the laying of an underwater phone cable across the Pacific in 1902 were just two early instances of the long process of what Armand Mattelart has described as "networking the world."

It is certainly the case that contemporary technologies are both more intensive and more extensive in ways that do suggest the world has become networked in a very different way than before. For our purposes, what is perhaps most significant are the possibilities that digitalization has introduced for the dissemination of information and cultural products across the globe. Music, images, and printed text can now all be transmitted, distributed, and consumed electronically. The digitalization of popular culture has also made it increasingly inexpensive for individuals to produce and distribute to a global audience the movies and songs that they make. Indeed, ongoing developments in digitalization promise to continue to reshape popular culture in fundamental ways.

Connected to this process of digitalization has been a remarkable convergence of cultural forms and products: digital music can be played on cell phones, movie clips can be downloaded to iPads and iPods, and so on. Nevertheless, a sense of the longer history of developments in communications technologies is essential in order to temper some of the more exaggerated claims about the communications revolution espoused by magazines such as *Wired* and companies such as Apple and Google.

Globalization *is* real. The intent of this section has been to put globalization in a larger context so that we can see past the hype that often surrounds it. In order to understand contemporary popular culture, we will need to keep the influence and importance of all of these levels in mind—a complex but necessary procedure to make sense of the already complicated set of positions and issues that has surrounded popular culture in the second half of the twentieth century and the beginning of the twenty-first.

Globalization and Popular Culture

Given the long history of economic, political, and technological developments that led up to globalization, it should come as no surprise that there have been all kinds of cultural exchanges between peoples and cultures for thousands of years. When we speak about globalization with respect to culture, what we often imagine is not just an acceleration of these exchanges, but a whole new set of cultural practices produced as a result of them. Inevitably, the conjunction of globalization and culture also evokes the promise and/or threat of a single global culture, a culture that would be shared by everyone on Earth for better and/or worse. Both of these developments continue to garner the attention of scholars, politicians, and members of the public alike.

One of the most important things about all the various processes associated with globalization is that they have forced us to rethink long-held assumptions that continue to inform our understanding of culture. Our changing experience of time and space opens up new ways of looking at the past as much as it offers up rich opportunities to speculate about the future. The impact of globalization on culture is thus both empirical (effecting real changes in the real world) and theoretical (producing a change in our understanding and conceptualization of just what culture is). In this section, we will look at these changes and discuss the various ways in which culture has been perceived with respect to globalization.

Culture and Space

As we have seen throughout this book, there are so many definitions of culture that it is difficult to keep them apart: folk culture, mass culture, popular culture—culture as the name for a whole set of practices that people engage in, or as the word that describes particular kinds of artifacts and events that people produce to express themselves. It is hard to imagine that all of these very different ways of thinking about culture might have anything in common. But there is (at least) one thing that all of these senses of culture share: the idea that culture comes from some *place*. We usually think of culture—whether as practices or products—as having a definite and unambiguous point of origin. Today, we usually think of this place as being a nation or region—either a region within a nation, or regions that are collections of nations (e.g., the Middle East, Southeast Asia, Latin America, etc.).

Without thinking about it, and almost without being able to help it, we attribute attitudes and behavior to people based on their point of origin: Italians are loud and argumentative, Americans are brash, Japanese are idiosyncratic and technologically advanced, and so on (see the discussion of stereotypes in Chapter 7). This is done not only with people, but also with the ideas and culture that they produce. While we sometimes realize that these attributions are oversimplifications, when they come from experts in the study of these nations or regions we are often ready to believe that the unique characteristics that make one people different from another have in fact been discovered.

There are several problems with this way of locating culture in specific places—in this case, the space of the nation. First, as we discussed above and in Chapter 7, while it continues to produce pride, along with ethnic and racial tensions, the seemingly "natural" space of the nation is a recent political invention. Second, it is very difficult to isolate distinct cultural practices or products in the contemporary world—indeed, not just difficult, but impossible. Every culture has felt the impact and influence of other cultures. In Japan and other parts of the world, rock 'n' roll is often taken to be typically American. The origins of rock music are, however, quite complicated—a mix of indigenized African music (as in blues) combined with musical influences from various parts of Europe. Musical forms such as Jamaican dance hall music show even greater degrees of cultural migration: rock 'n' roll begets Jamaican reggae, which has an influence on American hip-hop, which in turn comes back to Jamaica as dance hall music (see Chapter 7 for a more detailed discussion of the role of diaspora in shaping hip-hop). As the sociologist Mel Van Elteren has put it, "national and other cultural identities are best grasped when seen as being constituted in and through their relation to each other, rather than analyzing cultural (or national) identities one by one and then subsequently thinking about how they are related to one another" (51–52).

Specific cultures are now connected with specific spaces so closely that it is very difficult to speak about cultural migration without using the reductive vocabulary of national cultures. By allowing us to see these migrations and movements much more rapidly—occurring not just slowly over centuries or in the space of one lifetime but within a matter of years or months—globalization has made it possible for us to question these links as never before. This is not to say that there aren't still vast "cultural" differences between, for example, Canada and Hong Kong. At the same time, as peoples and cultural practices move around the globe, we might also want to think about the connections as opposed to the disconnections among these spaces.

For example, with more than 300 stores, Market Village and Pacific Mall in the affluent suburb of Markham, Ontario, constitutes the largest indoor Chinese mall in North America. Given its location and the patterns of consumption that it structures and produces, it is worth considering the ways in which this mall is as Canadian as it is Chinese—just as many of the new affluent suburban houses being built in China borrow heavily from the new North American housing styles exhibited in Markham.

Global Culture and Cultural Imperialism

These points are well worth keeping in mind as we shift to the other extreme. For many people, globalization represents that birth of a truly global culture, a single culture shared to varying (if ever-increasing) degrees by everyone in the world. This global culture may not yet be in existence, but its arrival seems to be only a matter of time.

The effect of globalization's acceleration of time and collapse of space is to eliminate cultural distinctions—already more plural and complex than previously imagined—that might have once existed. Coincident with this process is the simultaneous decline of the world's languages and the establishment of a few major lingua francas: English, Mandarin, Spanish, Hindi-Urdu, and so on. Soon we will all be sharing a wide, but common, set of beliefs and practices that are reflected in a variety of international agreements, such as the United Nations' Universal Declaration of Human Rights (available in more than 300 different languages) or, indeed, that of the World Trade Organization (141 participating countries as of the Doha round). We'll also soon all be reading the same comic books, watching the same movies, drinking coffee from the same outlets…or so the story goes.

In its most general outlines, this *does* sound like a description of our world today—or, at least, our world as it sometimes appears from Europe and North America. There are in fact practices that seem already to have made their way to all corners of the world, the most significant being the practice of industrial management famously codified by

Frederick Winslow Taylor in 1911. But if the links between space and culture were in the past overly determinate, the belief in the possibility of a global culture overestimates the degree to which culture has or can be severed not just from space, but also from the specificities of history, economics, and politics that intersect in unique ways in different parts of the globe.

Class Issues

One of these, for instance, is class. Visions of global culture are more often than not an expression of the viewpoint of a group that the sociologist Zygmunt Bauman has described as "tourists": a relatively wealthy, socially mobile middle class, which exists to varying extents in different parts of the world, that is able to travel to remote locations where they interact with others like themselves in conference hotels or tourist resorts that are more or less indistinguishable from one another. For these people, the degree of global cultural convergence might seem to be startling enough to warrant belief in a truly global culture.

For the vast majority of people in the world, however, mobility is greatly limited—and, when movement does become a necessity, it is usually due to terrible economic, natural, or political circumstances that have generated refugee crises around the world. The UNHCR has estimated that there are currently more than 30 million "internally displaced people" worldwide.

The *possibility* of a global culture has to be clearly distinguished from questions of its *desirability*. Interestingly, with the exception of a few American commentators who positively equate global culture with the worldwide dominance of US values and beliefs (e.g., *New York Times* columnist Thomas Friedman or political scientist Samuel Huntington), very few critics, scholars, or citizens see global culture as an end worth achieving. Abstractly, the possibility of the universalization of certain "cultural" beliefs— such as human rights, freedom of the press, and democratic elections—seems desirable to most people. At the same time, everyone seems to be aware that a global culture can be achieved only through the globalization of mass culture—a form of culture in which the central motive of cultural production is profit and in which culture is produced primarily by "experts" (film directors, professional musicians, etc.).

One of the things that no doubt dismays Bauman's tourists even as it comforts them is the widespread diffusion of North American, European, and Japanese brand-name appliances, food franchises, clothing stores, and automobiles. One of the reasons to travel is, after all, to experience "difference" (in however problematic a form), and if every place looks like "home" (as airports and their duty-free shops certainly do), the thrill of encountering "exotic" peoples and places begins to lose its appeal. Westerners have an enormous amount invested in the idea of cultural diversity. The intrinsic desirability of cultural diversity seems to be one of the "facts" of contemporary human life that can't be challenged. Nevertheless, it is something that we should consider before rushing to judgment in open condemnation of the rapid "massification" of culture worldwide.

Suggested Activity 9.4

Globalization names the increased flow of ideas, goods, and cultural products around the world. But while borders may have become more porous to images, ideas, and products, the mobility of people has in many cases become more controlled than ever. Zygmunt Bauman suggests that globalization has divided the world into two new classes of people: "tourists," for whom globalization has meant increased mobility and for whom the world is almost entirely open to exploration; and "vagabonds," those who either can't move outside of fixed boundaries (for a variety of reasons) or who are forced to move by circumstances beyond their control (civil war, famines, etc.). Make a list of groups and individuals that would fit into these two categories and consider the implications of a world divided by degree of mobility. Do tourists exist only in the "First World" and vagabonds only in the "Third World"? What roles do race and gender play in the politics of mobility? In what way are these categories shifting and changing (if at all)?

Cultural Imperialism

The *undesirability* of global culture (and desirability of cultural diversity) is usually expressed as part of broader worries about cultural imperialism. This concept has come to mean many things since it was first articulated in the 1960s. However, there are two elements that seem to belong to any usable definition. First, most generally, cultural imperialism refers to the process by which political and economic power is used by a foreign culture to spread its culture and values to the detriment of cultures that it comes into contact with. Second, cultural imperialism also points to the important role that culture played in the process of colonialism and **imperialism** in the nineteenth and early twentieth centuries.

The second use of culture has been investigated extensively in postcolonial criticism and literature. The first definition has been used more frequently to characterize the unequal power relations—economic, political, *and* cultural—that continue to exist between developed and developing countries even after the official end of European colonial rule in most parts of the world. In the absence of direct political control, culture, especially mass culture, is seen as one of the forms through which these unequal power relations are maintained. While the British might once have had to stick troops and administrators in their colonies, the United States has often been seen as exerting its power through the values and life assumptions embedded in its globally popular films, television programs, and even novels.

In what ways can culture be seen to maintain (and indeed, to produce) this situation? John Tomlinson has identified four main ways in which culture has been seen as abetting imperialist relations: (i) through foreign ("American") mass media, whose global diffusion manages to produce the other three conditions; (ii) through the imposition of the values and beliefs of one nation on another; (iii) through the imposition of consumerism and capitalism as *the* "way of life"; and (iv) through the imposition of modernity on parts of the world that might be interested in developing along a very different path than that taken by the West. These four senses are very often confused and folded into one another (*Cultural*). From our discussions of the discourse of the nation and of the relationship between culture and space, one should be able to see quickly that—despite its intuitive power—the concept of cultural imperialism is problematic. First, as we have emphasized throughout this book, it is difficult to speculate about *any* particular outcome of an audience's encounter with mass media. Foreign audiences make sense of foreign mass media in their own contexts and for their own purposes; foreign audiences are also hardly uniform in their composition, with different segments of the audience reacting in different ways. Tomlinson suggests that "the simple notion of an immediate ideological effect arising from exposure to the imperialist text" is both "naïve and improbable" (*Cultural* 47).

Second, the idea that cultures are neatly divided into national units and possess characteristics that can be communicated in any easy way is one that can no longer be sustained, for all of the reasons that we outlined earlier in this chapter. The third and fourth claims about cultural imperialism are more interesting to consider, and we take these up in the final section of this chapter.

The Noble Savage versus Ronald McDonald

For many people, the most alarming aspect of globalization is the potential it represents of imposing the Western values of consumerism, capitalism, and modernity on cultures to which these values are not only foreign, but also hostile. In one sense, fears of the dilution of cultural diversity are real—borne out, for example, in the accelerated extinction of hundreds of indigenous languages in the face of the dominance of English. But it is also important to note that many of these fears do not actually arise out of the problem of cultural imperialism as it is normally framed: the imposition of one culture's forms and values on another. Rather, what is being expressed here is a more general worry about the value and viability of mass culture, not so much in foreign contexts but in North America itself. Until the twenty-first century, such worries didn't seem to have too much applicability to the rest of the world.

In addition to making North American mass culture more globally available, what contemporary communications technologies have done is to allow North Americans to take note of the shape of the rest of the world—a world with skyscrapers, freeways, and shopping malls on every continent (except Antarctica, of course). For a significant part of the group who fit the description of Bauman's "tourists," this vision is both comforting and depressing: comforting in that it attests to the universality of "our" culture, and depressing in that it fails to offer the temporary escape that the tourist craves. However, it is important to remember that what seems like a threat to Westerners may look very different in other parts of the world. As Tomlinson points out, "the Kazakhstani tribesman who has no knowledge of (and, perhaps, no interest in) America or Europe is unlikely to see his cassette player as emblematic of creeping capitalist domination" (*Cultural* 109).

The Western concern with preserving the cultural uniqueness of non-Western cultures has effects on those cultures that are in some cases more damaging than the imagined effects of global mass culture. For example, New Age celebrations of a romanticized Native American tradition have the effect of freezing real, living Native cultures outside of time, thus denying them the agency and opportunity to negotiate their way in the global economy. Ironically, the fantasy that there is something outside that economy is a luxury that is really available only to those who are firmly inside it.

Yet just because there are no insides or outsides to the global economy, just as there are no purely local, authentic cultures outside the network of global culture, does not validate the darkest visions of cultural imperialism. That global culture is both more fluid and more uneven in its effects than is represented either by its champions or its critics is clear if we look at an example that is often cited by both: McDonald's. For many people, the fast-food giant McDonald's has become a powerful cultural symbol of globalization. With more than 20 000 restaurants in more than 100 countries worldwide, McDonald's is a truly global company whose products represent more than quick meals at low prices.

The first appearance of a McDonald's in small towns across North America is seen by some people as a sign not only of a community's economic development and growth potential (since McDonald's is careful to build its restaurants only in places where it is certain to make a profit), but also its emergence into the mainstream of contemporary culture. News of openings of new McDonald's restaurants in Moscow and Beijing made headlines in the United States, as it was taken as a sign of the global victory of free-market values. Some commentators have gone even further, to see McDonald's as an ambassador of world peace: as *New York Times* columnist Thomas Friedman notes, no two countries possessing a McDonald's outlet have ever gone to war against each other (qtd. in Burkeman). Recent global strife has challenged this parable of globalization, however: the presence of McDonald's in Russia and Ukraine has not prevented these countries from engaging in an extended conflict that began in 2014.

McDonald's as a Target

In contrast to these positive views of McDonald's, the ubiquitous golden arches that make up the restaurant's logo have also been seen as a symbol of the dangers of the globalization of culture. The attacks on McDonald's storefronts during anti-globalization protests around the world, the dismantling of a McDonald's in Millau, France, by the Peasant Confederation (headed by activist José Bové) as a protest against genetically modified foods and corporate globalization, and the protests that greeted the announcement of a plan to build a McDonald's in Niagara-on-the-Lake, a small, well-preserved nineteenth-century tourist town in Ontario, all share the same commonly held view of the restaurant as a symbol of a global **monoculture**. The way in which the prefix "Mc" has come to be used suggests the same thing: "McWorld," "McAmerica," "McDonaldization"—these labels have become synonymous with the dark side of globalization that it seems everyone wishes to avoid.

When we speak about globalization as cultural imperialism, McDonald's immediately comes to mind (see Figure 9.5). As anyone who has taken a long-distance trip can attest, the ubiquity with which McDonald's restaurants (and other franchise stores and services) dot the landscape at highway interchanges can seem depressing, especially because travel is often undertaken precisely to discover different places and ways of living. In part because McDonald's spread to other countries so early (to Japan, Germany, and Australia in 1971), it has come to be seen as the leading-edge and primary example of a much larger

Figure 9.5 McDonald's restaurants are now at "home" around the world, including in such countries as Egypt. Source: © MARWAN NAAMANI/Getty Images

trend in which US popular culture is exported to other parts of the world, to the detriment of local cultures and practices. McDonald's has been followed by Starbucks in the "real" world and by Google, which seems to have extensions in every country (google.ae for the United Arab Emirates, google.ht for Haiti, google.tm for Turkmenistan, and so on), in the virtual one.

McDonald's is symbolic of the larger worry expressed by the cultural imperialism thesis that it is not just the choice of purchasing hamburgers that is being made available to peoples outside of the United States, but also the export of a whole way of life: American consumer society and the fantasies of the good life that accompany it. Gaining a McDonald's franchise means losing local dietary habits, patterns of daily behavior, and even norms of work and consumption—in other words, a whole range of the life activities that make cultures distinct from one another.

However, this view of McDonald's as a force that is inevitably corrosive to cultural difference is one that fails to account for the genuine complexities of culture and globalization. There is no country or culture that has not experienced influences from other cultures and nations. Even in the case of contemporary popular or mass culture, McDonald's is hardly the only form to have had an impact worldwide, though it is perhaps often the most visible symbol of foreignness to many people around the world. Worries about the influence of the kinds of popular cultural practices that are at least symbolically associated with McDonald's—consumerism, the consumption of mass-produced food, branding, and so on—also always underestimate or fail to account for the interests of local peoples and cultures, casting them in the role of helpless "victims" who are unable to resist the allure of the golden arches. In fact, there are some suggestions that customers are beginning to do just that: after years of unchecked expansion, the chain has closed hundreds of outlets since the early 2000s and has also had to modify its menu considerably, given the spread of other "cultures" (e.g., vegetarianism, healthy eating, organic growing, coffee culture).

Among the culprits cited for a loss of appetite among Big Mac eaters are the BSE (mad cow disease) scare in the United Kingdom and Canada, concerns about the effects of a fatty diet, and political resistance to McDonald's as a symbol—like Starbucks—of all the negative effects of globalization, both real and imagined, that we have discussed above. (See Chapter 1 for more on the symbolism of Starbucks.)

The shakiness of McDonald's stock-market share prices in recent years and its surprising ability to rally in the face of changing fashion and politics suggest that we need to develop a more complex account of the global role of popular culture than that expressed by worries over a coming "McWorld."

The Impact of McDonald's

To answer the question of whether the spread of fast-food chains around the world is helping to create a homogeneous, global culture, a group of anthropologists set out to study the impact of McDonald's in five different locales in East Asia: Beijing, Hong Kong, Taipei, Seoul, and Tokyo (Watson). What they discovered was that, while the introduction of McDonald's in these countries *was* having an impact on local customs and practices, the precise nature of this impact was very different in each context. For example, before McDonald's came to their country, Japanese consumers very rarely ate with their hands; in Hong Kong, the restaurant has replaced tea houses as the most popular place to have breakfast.

At the same time, McDonald's has been adapted to local circumstances in ways that differ not only among the different countries examined, but also in relation to the role that it plays in North America. In North America, McDonald's is generally a site to pass through for a quick meal on the way to doing something else. But it is also used for other purposes: a place for seniors to meet and talk in the mornings (most restaurants offer seniors discounts on coffee); a place for small children to play, especially in winter months; and, in the evenings, a place for teens to hang out. In East Asia, too, McDonald's has been transformed, often more forcefully, into a space serving local purposes. In Beijing, Seoul, and Taipei, McDonald's functions as a retreat from urban stresses; in Hong Kong, it is a place where middle-school students spend large amounts of time studying and gossiping—the function that coffeehouses sometimes assume in North America. Throughout the region, it is a place where women go to avoid other social spaces (such as bars) that are havens for men.

What even these few examples should indicate is that it is through the constant interaction of the global and the local that contemporary culture is produced. Even this distinction is misleading, however, since both of these terms suggest that there is something identifiably "global" (usually imagined as transnational corporations) as well as "local" (small communities across the globe).

Corporations such as McDonald's have global reach, but at the same time the company has shareholders from many localities and, like other corporations working on a global scale, its managers and investors tend to come from the localities in which McDonald's has a presence. The anthropologists examining McDonald's in East Asia discovered that virtually all of the managers came from Korea, Japan, China, and so on. The raw materials used to produce fast food tend to originate within geographical proximity of the restaurants, and McDonald's has generally adapted its menus to suit customers and cultures across the globe (though it has faced enormous problems as a result of concealing the use of beef fat in products created for the global Hindu community). Though it has been often (and deservedly) criticized, in many respects McDonald's has been a far more responsible and responsive transnational corporation than many others.

The point here is not to absolve McDonald's or other transnational corporations from criticism, or to suggest that their power and cultural influence are benign. As much as it sells a set of products, like so much else in contemporary popular culture McDonald's also sells an *experience* that has had noticeable effects around the world. With its hamburgers and fries, McDonald's sells friendly service, predictability, speed, cleanliness and hygiene, and toys and cultural symbols (e.g., Ronald McDonald) to its young customers. The experience of eating at McDonald's has had an impact on the experience of eating out almost everywhere the restaurant has been introduced. These are often subtle changes, but because dietary patterns and attitudes toward food are so important to everyday life, their impact is widely felt. Almost without exception, fast food is extremely unhealthy. There is no reason to celebrate the increase in consumption of mass-produced fast food around the world.

At the same time, the typical narratives that we use to imagine the impact of companies such as McDonald's on the shape of global popular culture have to be seen as far too simplistic. The idea that globalization leads to the production of a single "bad" global culture—that is, the collapse of the varied spaces of culture into a single culture—is not supported by more careful attention to the networks and processes through which cultural products and cultural experiences are produced in the world. Large, global corporations play an important role in this, but to see them as being almost omnipotent in the shaping of contemporary culture tends to negate the need to produce more complex accounts of culture in globalization that might in fact yield a better understanding of where we all stand today.

Globalization: What's Next?

Globalization has produced many new forms of culture and has changed older forms in significant ways as well. The fact of globalization has also changed how we talk about culture. The recent collapse of time and space that we associate with globalization has led to a reconsideration of the ways in which we once imagined that time and space kept cultures and people apart. Globalization has also led to a reexamination of the divisions we have used to study contemporary societies—divisions established initially for heuristic purposes, but which have since come to seem as if they were formed in response to actually existing divisions. The discussion in this chapter is an example of how globalization has made it impossible to discuss economics without politics, politics without culture, culture without economics, and so on. Increasingly, thinking about globalization also requires that we contemplate all of these realms of activity in relation to the environment and the devastating impact of global consumer culture on the future of the planet.

In all of the discussions surrounding globalization and culture—which now include such diverse issues as the devastating impact of the culture of consumption on the natural environment and the future of the planet, and the economic importance of creating urban spaces attractive to the members of the "**creative class**" who (according to Richard Florida) generate new wealth—the one thing that we seem to be no longer asking is: What hopes and dreams do we have for culture today? What do we see as the future of culture—and, indeed, if the connections and interconnections that we have described here are correct, the future of the social world itself? These are important questions to pose as the world becomes both a smaller and a more uncertain place in which to live for all of us; some of the many issues involved in framing answers to these questions will be the focus of our final chapter.

Suggestions for Further Reading

Appadurai, Arjun, ed. *Modernity at Large: Cultural Dimensions of Globalization.* Minneapolis: University of Minnesota Press, 1996.

Barlow, Maude, and Tony Clarke. *Global Showdown.* Toronto: Stoddart, 2001.

Bauman, Zygmunt. *Globalization: The Human Consequences.* New York: Columbia University Press, 1998.

Cazdyn, Eric, and Imre Szeman. *After Globalization.* Oxford: Wiley-Blackwell, 2011.

Davis, Mike. *Planet of Slums.* New York: Verso, 2006.

Giddens, Anthony. *Runaway World: How Globalization Is Reshaping Our Lives.* New York: Routledge, 2000.

Gray, John. *False Dawn: The Delusions of Global Capitalism.* New York: New Press, 1999.

Hardt, Michael, and Antonio Negri. *Empire.* Cambridge, MA: Harvard University Press, 2000.

Harvey, David. *A Brief History of Neoliberalism.* New York: Oxford University Press, 2005.

Harvey, David. *Social Justice and the City.* Oxford: Blackwell, 1992.

Held, David, Anthony McGrew, David Goldblatt, and Jonathan Perraton. *Global Transformations: Politics, Economics and Culture.* Stanford, CA: Stanford University Press, 1999.

Higmore, Ben. *Everyday Life and Cultural Theory: An Introduction.* New York: Routledge, 2002.

Jacobs, Jane. *The Death and Life of Great American Cities*. New York: Modern Library, 1993.

Jameson, Fredric, and Masao Miyoshi, eds. *The Cultures of Globalization*. Durham, NC: Duke University Press, 1998.

Klein, Naomi. *The Shock Doctrine: The Rise of Disaster Capitalism*. Toronto: Knopf, 2007.

Kohn, Margaret. *Brave New Neighborhoods: The Privatization of Public Space*. New York: Routledge, 2004.

Kunstler, James Howard. *The Geography of Nowhere: The Rise and Decline of America's Man-Made Landscape*. New York: Free Press, 1994.

LeGates, Richard T., and Fredric Stout, eds. *The City Reader*. 4th ed. New York: Routledge, 2007.

Lippard, Lucy. *The Lure of the Local: Senses of Place in a Multicentered Society*. New York: New Press, 1997.

Massey, Doreen. *Space, Place and Gender*. Minneapolis: University of Minnesota Press, 1994.

Merrifield, Andy. *Metromarxism: A Marxist Tale of the City*. New York: Routledge, 2002.

Scholte, Jan Aart. *Globalization: A Critical Introduction*. Basingstoke, UK: Macmillan, 2000.

Soja, Edward W. *Postmodern Geographies: The Reassertion of Space in Critical Social Theory*. New York: Verso, 1989.

Williams, Raymond. *The Country and the City*. London: Hogarth Press, 1973.

Wilson, Alexander. *The Culture of Nature: North American Landscapes from Disney to the Exxon Valdez*. Toronto: Between the Lines, 1991.

10

Popular Culture in the Twenty-First Century

Historical fact: people stopped being human in 1913. That was the year Henry Ford put his cars on rollers and made his worker adopt the speed of the assembly line. At first, workers rebelled. They quit in droves, unable to accustom their bodies to the new pace of the age. Since then, however, the adaptation has been passed down; we've all inherited it to some degree, so that we plug right into joysticks and remotes, to repetitive motions of a hundred kinds.

(Jeffrey Eugenides, *Middlesex*, 95)

In with the New?

At the start of the twenty-first century, popular culture is undergoing shifts and changes that are reshaping how we experience it, where we experience it, and what our experience of it means for the ways in which we engage with our lives. New technologies have played a major role in this shift: we are connected to one another as never before through mobile communication devices, e-mail, and social networking technologies; more of life is lived in front of screens both bigger (TV screens the size of rec room walls) and smaller (the near ubiquitous iPhone) than ever before; and there are new forms of popular culture coming into being as a result of new technologies—or at least the promise of new forms. Many educators, psychologists, and neurologists see a wholesale shift in thinking associated with the use of digital culture. So-called digital natives—those who have used computers since toddlerhood (many of the readers of this book)—are thought to have different thought patterns, even different brain structures, than those "digital immigrants" (including the authors) who were born before the widespread use of personal computers (Prensky).

It is important not to overestimate the significance of this change. A lot of what seems to be brand spanking new is simply a variation on something that has been a part of our lives before: no matter how addictive it might be, *Angry Birds* is still just a video game, and *Bridesmaids* watched on a tablet is still just a movie. But the fact that you can play such games and watch such movies whenever and wherever you want, and might do so instead of working, talking with your friends, or even getting enough sleep, might well prove to constitute genuine changes in how we experience popular culture—both signs and symptoms of larger social developments whose significance we may fully understand only decades from now.

Popular Culture: A User's Guide, International Edition. Imre Szeman and Susie O'Brien.
© 2017 John Wiley & Sons, Inc. Published 2017 by John Wiley & Sons, Inc.

While we have addressed a number of recent developments in popular culture throughout this book, in this concluding chapter we want to focus on some key issues in contemporary popular culture that capture the rapid social shifts through which we seem to be living. One danger in focusing in this way on the "new" is that it is all too easy to get things wrong by giving too much force to a particular development that might well prove to be less important in hindsight, thus misrepresenting the complex array of forces that in fact give shape to historical change. In discussing the social significance of new technologies, for instance, there is a tendency for scholars and critics to imagine that we are in the midst of a paradigm shift that will fundamentally alter how human beings live, work, and relate to one another. At the most extreme end of this euphoria over new technologies are futurists such as Ray Kurzweil, who has predicted that the "technological singularity" will be soon upon us—that is, the coming into being of a human–computer superintelligence as a result of (among other things) exponential increases in the speed of computing power. At the other end of the spectrum are critics such as Wendell Berry, who suggest that our reliance on digital technology is largely driven by advertisers, and that the manufacture, use, and disposal of personal computers contribute to the destruction of the Earth. Countering the usual assumption that increasing digitalization is the way of the future, Berry proclaims: "If the use of the computer is a new idea, then a newer idea is not to use one" (10).

While it is of course important to pay attention to the ways in which our activities are being reshaped by the technological devices embedded in our lives, it is just as important to keep in mind historical continuities and the persistence of older social and cultural practices, habits, and forms. Every parent who worries about the amount of time their kids spend in the imaginary world of video games instead of in their rooms reading should remember the fears that greeted the explosion of reading in the late eighteenth century. Today, we celebrate the idea of self-cultivation through reading and worry about the consequences of video-game playing—a practice that seems little more than a waste of time and brain cells; two centuries ago, however, there were "suggestions that, with all the new 'reading societies' springing up across what still counted as the Holy Roman Empire, a new disease, that of 'reading addiction' (*Lesesucht*), was arising, an ailment which was believed likely to strike impressionable young students, loose women, servants not properly respectful of their masters, and other questionable sorts of people" (Pinkard 50). There is a great deal about popular culture in the twenty-first century that *is* new in ways to which we have to be alert. But we have to be alert, too, to the excitement of the perpetually new, a force whose hazy energies have been repeatedly tapped in the vocabulary of marketing to support sales of consumer objects and experiences.

Suggested Activity 10.1

How has technology changed your experiences and expectations? In what ways has it reshaped your interaction with popular culture? Do you think that new technology has changed your life in fundamental ways, or has it only changed the content and not the form of daily life (i.e., you might now do different things in your spare time, but the way in which your spare time is organized in relation to study/work time has stayed the same)? Finally, to what extent and in what ways do your uses of technology differ from those of your parents or grandparents?

Many Popular Cultures?

Watching television in the mid-1980s was an easy task: click on the TV set, quickly look at the offerings available on the three or four broadcast stations available (or even fewer in some countries), and voilà! You were ready to ease into a few hours of *Happy Days* or *Dallas*. The next day at recess or around the water cooler at work, you could check in with friends or colleagues to see what they thought of the latest cool exploits of the Fonz or the devious shenanigans of J.R. Ewing. To a degree that wouldn't have surprised Horkheimer and Adorno (see Chapter 4), a common popular culture existed that provided a shared landscape of cultural experiences, desires, and experiences.

Even in the midst of this common popular culture landscape, there were always alternative and underground forms of culture, too; popular culture was never as uniform and singular as some critics feared it to be. Even so, talk in the school hallways or by the office water cooler is invariably more complicated today than it once was: instead of comparing favorite points about the past evening's shows, such discussions are as often as not occasions at which one learns about television shows, phone apps, web sites, and YouTube videos with which one hasn't yet come into contact. Cable TV has expanded the range of programs one can watch: a session in front of the television now begins with the navigation of a menu of hundreds of viewing options. The prevalence of DVDs, on-demand video, programs and films streamed via the web, and personal video recorders (PVRs or TVRs) has messed about with the temporality of viewing: many of us now watch programs when we want to, not when they are first broadcast. And we've yet to talk about all of the other forms of popular culture—the availability online of an enormous range of music of every conceivable style and genre (instead of being only from big record labels), the plethora of web sites where one can access information, the estimated (as of July 2015) 1.6 million iPhone apps available to play with and use, the 10 years' worth of viewing content now uploaded to YouTube, and so on. Given all of these developments, in our current cultural landscape it may make more sense to speak about the existence of *many* popular cultures as opposed to popular culture per se.

There remain seemingly obvious exceptions to this picture we're painting about the fragmentation of popular culture into many popular culture*s*. Major sporting events, such as the Olympics, the World Cup, or the Super Bowl, draw a huge number of viewers; in doing so, they bring people together through the mechanism and medium of these singular events on a national or even global scale. But even here, the raw numbers suggest a different story. Super Bowl 50 (2016) was the highest-rated TV show in US history, with an average audience of 120 million viewers—just over one-third of the US population. This is an impressive number, but it raises the question: What were the other two-thirds of the population doing during this (supposedly) can't miss event? According to the Nielsen Ratings, the top-ranked TV program (other than sports) for the week of January 25, 2016 was *NCIS*, which had 12 million viewers, while the highest-rated cable show was the *Republican Presidential Debate* at 12.4 million viewers (the highest regularly scheduled cable show was *The O'Reilly Factor*, at only 5.5 million viewers). While both these shows produce considerable buzz on industry programs like *Entertainment Tonight* or in magazines such as *People* and *HELLO!*, each forms a small piece of the large puzzle of popular culture in the twenty-first century—an era in which it is becoming safe to assume that most people *don't* watch the most popular television shows or listen to the bestselling albums of the day. If one needs any further evidence of the fragmentation of popular culture into smaller and smaller segments, consider YouTube's plans to create hundreds of new channels on its site, designed by professional writers and producers, and geared to niche interests (examples include "123UnoDosTres," a channel for Latin American young adults; a channel programmed by *The Onion*; and "Smart Girls at the Party," created by comedian Amy Poehler). According to Robert Kyncl, the senior executive at YouTube overseeing this development, "People went from broad to narrow and we think they will continue to go that way—spend more and more time in the niches—because now the distribution landscape allows for more narrowness" (Seabrook "Streaming").

Does it matter that today popular culture seems to consist of a bunch of niches? And is this really a new development? There is no question that the landscape of popular culture *has* altered. However, it is questionable whether this changes or challenges in a fundamental way the points we have made in the preceding chapters about the operations of popular culture in shaping and reinforcing—or challenging—cultural, ethnic, and gender stereotypes, or the primary role played by money and profit in the production of popular culture, or the way in which we understand our bodies and our place in the communities in which we live—and so on. On the one hand, the explosion of choice represented by the sheer size of the content available on TV, web sites, streaming radio, and so on suggests that popular culture has in some ways become newly and genuinely democratized. On the other hand, the choice on offer seems to be variations on what is already available. To return to the example of YouTube's niche channels, for instance, there are comedy networks (Official Comedy, Comedy Shaq Network), sports channels (Kick TV for soccer, the skateboard channel RIDE, and the action-sports channel Network A), news outlets (*Slate* and *Wall Street Journal*), and Look TV, one of many fashion-and-beauty channels. The genres represented by these channels are hardly under- or unrepresented on television or online at present; at best, they seem to be slices of the existing entertainment pie rather than an expansion of popular culture into new realms that, for instance, take up the many social, political, and environmental challenges the world faces today. Indeed, it needs to be remembered that YouTube's decision to launch these new channels was connected to the company's desire to maximize its profit. The challenge for YouTube—a company purchased in 2006 by Google for $1.65 billion—is to get visitors to linger longer than the few minutes on average they spend during each visit to the site. The average North American spends four to five hours watching television each day. Getting them to spend more of this time on YouTube, engaged in the specific niche programming that fits their needs best, means more advertising money for the web site—a lot more.

Learning to Love Céline: Twenty-First-Century Taste

There is one change produced by the existence of many popular cultures to which it is worth drawing specific attention. As we explained in Chapter 5, one of the outcomes of the choices made in the forms of popular culture one consumes—what styles of music one listens to or what clothes one wears—is to distinguish oneself from others. As Pierre Bourdieu argues, popular culture participates in a social game of distinction—a game with significant consequences, chief among them being the establishment of class boundaries or our position in social space. Our position within social hierarchies depends as much on our display of appropriate cultural tastes, manners, and behaviors as how much money we have or our class background. In addition to highlighting the ways in which our choices about the popular culture we consume participate in shaping our social and class status, Bourdieu's theories also challenged the degree of agency we feel in the cultural objects we consume and practices we engage in. Though it might feel as if we are articulating our greatest degree of autonomy and self-expression when we state our interest in music, films, or magazines, it is important to recognize that such choices are unconsciously motivated by social forces of distinction through which we express group belonging and distinction.

Distinction depends on a shared cultural landscape, one in which the choices one makes about one's cultural likes or dislikes can be read meaningfully by others as an expression of a move within a shared social game. What happens to the social power exerted by taste—"the basis of all that one has—people and things—and all that one is for others, whereby one classifies oneself and is classified by others" (Bourdieu 45)—when we no longer have one popular culture but many, each with its own coordinates and rules of distinction? Has the fracturing of popular culture into niche interests—to whatever degree this has happened—put an end to this key social function of cultural consumption?

A preliminary answer to this question can be found in Carl Wilson's book *Let's Talk about Love: A Journey to the End of Taste* (2007). A music critic for *The Globe and Mail*, Wilson is drawn to music of indie rock bands and experimental musicians. The task he sets for himself is not just to try to understand how pop musician (and fellow Canadian) Céline Dion can be loved by so many people, but to get to a place where he, too, can like (maybe even love) her music. At the outset of the book, Wilson is clear that he doesn't like Dion. Indeed, he *loathes* her, describing her music as "bland monotony raised to a pitch of obnoxious bombast—R&B with the sex and slyness removed" (11).

And he's not the only one: "As far as I knew, I had never even *met* anybody who liked Céline Dion" (11). The mystery that Wilson wants to understand is how Dion could possibly sell more than 200 million records, becoming in 2004 the best-selling female recording artist of all time.

Wilson describes *Let's Talk About Love* as "an experiment in taste" (18). In the course of providing some context to the unique pop culture environment out of which Dion emerges—French Canadian *vedette* (star) culture, in which homegrown celebrities get enormous attention for being one of the six million francophones in Canada—as well as tracking down her fans around the globe to learn just what they like about Dion, Wilson also engages in a quick survey of the philosophy of taste; that is, aesthetic theory. He is struck especially by the theories of Bourdieu, seeing them as offering particular insight into some of the reasons why some people love Dion, while others can't stand the sound of her voice. "Taste is a means of distinguishing ourselves from others, the pursuit of *distinction*," Wilson writes, "and its end product is to perpetuate and reproduce the class structure" (89). But he's also well aware of the fact that "your love of hip-hop or hatred for Céline Dion is part of your cultural capital, but it only gains value in the competition for distinction if it is *legitimated* in the contexts that matter to you" (93). Wilson notes that in the case of Dion, "a disproportionate part of her audience was in the lowest income bracket, under $25,000 a year, and again in the next-lowest category" (102)—a near perfect example of the social mechanics of taste to which Bourdieu drew attention in his work. In terms of income, however, this audience "is not as far from the average white pop critic as we might have expected" (103). This is where the context of legitimation comes into play: if one's attitude to Dion were only a matter of one's paycheck, Wilson would already have been trying to sing along with Quebec's famous *chanteuse*.

While Wilson might be part of the same economic class as many of Dion's fans (just like music critics, they don't tend to make very much money), his capacity to make judgments about the dominant aesthetics of this group—shaped partly by his education—is a way of defining his own life as other than "the life of subservient career, suburban lifestyle and quiet desperation we imagine befalls people like Céline Dion's white American fans, as well as fans of Billy Joel, Michael Bolton and other midlevel musicians whose names so often serves us as epithets" (103–104). A key theme in Wilson's "journey to the end of taste" is an exploration of the role he himself plays as a rock critic in the operations of popular culture and the distribution and legitimation of taste. He is clear that the work of the critic is based "on the power to exclude, not just to canonize" (15). His encounter with the music of Dion and the worlds inhabited by her fans causes him to come to doubt this role, not only because of how it helps to support class distinctions, but also because of the changing landscape of popular culture itself:

> What would criticism be like if it were not foremost trying to persuade people to find the same things great? If it weren't about making cases for or against things?... It might be more frank about the two-sidedness of the aesthetic encounter, and offer something more like a tour of an aesthetic experience, a travelogue, a memoir. More and more critics, in fact, are incorporating personal narratives into their work. Perhaps this is the benefit of the explosion of cultural judgment on the Internet, where millions of thumbs turn up and down daily: by rendering their traditional job of arbitration obsolete, it frees critics to find other ways of contemplating music. (156)

Today, *everybody* has the capacity to be a critic, whether through comments written on their own blogs, critiques about books on Amazon, restaurant reviews added to Urbanspoon, diatribes against dirty hotel rooms on TripAdvisor, and so on. The position of professional critic hasn't been eliminated altogether. But the ability for everyone to offer their own two cents about a television program on web sites that anyone can access (e.g., Google Maps search results for businesses almost always come with user reviews attached), combined with a decline in the readership of magazines and newspapers—the home of professional critics—has unsettled the game of social distinction and hierarchy. At the same time, the existence of multiple subgenres and cultural niches actively cultivated by the cultural industry—like the explosion of specific YouTube channels described above, or the appearance of streaming music services on national broadcast radio (NPR, CBC, BBC, etc.) that allow one to select the specific stream to which one wants to listen—is producing a situation in which popular culture is shaped less and less by the game of distinction to which Bourdieu alerted us.

It would be a mistake to imagine that such forms of distinction have disappeared entirely. Luxury brands of all kinds (such as Swarovski, Versace, and others—the kinds of brands that one typically finds in duty-free shops in airports) still signify wealth in taste as well as wealth in dollars, and what one listens to or watches (or doesn't) shapes not just one's sense of identity, but the groups to which one belongs (or doesn't). Still, when there is a growing capacity for people to engage in conspicuous consumption as a result of the growth of middle classes in the developing world and the massive extension of credit (with consequences we will discuss later in the chapter) in the developed one, and when capitalism depends increasingly on profit from its consumers, the "democratization" of taste is a development that should not come as a surprise.

If the existence of many popular cultures—even a "many" surrounded by all the caveats that we have presented here—cuts the feet out from under the role of the critic, Wilson seems to be more than happy to undertake a more "pluralistic criticism" that puts "less stock in defending its choices and more in depicting its enjoyment, with all its messiness and private soul tremors" (157). It is a form of criticism that, of necessity, has to be seen as "becoming democratic," which involves

> not a limp openmindedness, but actively grappling with people and things not like me, which brings with it the perilous question of what I am like. Democracy, that dangerous, paradoxical and mostly unattempted ideal, sees that the self *is* insufficient, dependent for definition on otherness, and chooses not only to accept that but to celebrate it, to stake everything on it. Through democracy, which demands we meet strangers as equals, we perhaps become less strangers to ourselves. (151)

New Technology and Its Discontents

Democracy—its presence or lack, its decline or enhancement—turns out to have become one of the key issues involved in discussions of popular culture in the twenty-first century. This is nowhere so true as in ongoing debates about the impact of new communications technologies and social media. On the one hand, the growing number of cell phones (for instance) has created new connections between individuals, with information about social and political developments finding their way directly and rapidly around the world, such that citizens can immediately challenge, debate, and question choices made by governments and nongovernmental agencies. Connections between individuals via new communications technologies have created communities that exist beyond borders, enabling an active exchange of information that surpasses the gate-keeping role played by daily newspapers or television news broadcasts. On the other hand, the organizations that operate social media are fewer and fewer in number, with a growing "concentration of power, especially in the hands of capital—as represented by the massive corporations that dominate stock exchanges and bourses worldwide, as well as the mobiles and telecommunications industry" (Goggin 176). In addition, the sheer number of events and developments that individuals can now follow, combined with the steady erosion of legitimacy of any given news agency, site, or critic, has made it difficult for political and social challenges to result in determinate action on the part of publics. We are living through a period in which technological changes are reshaping our experience of and relation to one another politically, socially, and culturally.

The challenges posed by new communication technologies can be witnessed in the different reaction of publics to decisions by governments that are trying to amend their practices in light of shifts in media. In 2012, Tim Uppal, the Canadian Minister of State for Democratic Reform, announced that in future federal elections the government would no longer penalize individuals who reported the results from eastern provinces before polls closed in the west. In the twenty-first century, such election blackouts are no longer feasible: publics in one part of the country can easily communicate the results to others using e-mail and social media sites. While this change was greeted positively as an appropriate reaction to new social and technological circumstances, Bill C-30, introduced a month later by Public Safety Minister Vic Toews, was criticized by members of the public from across the political spectrum. The intent of the bill was to give police and government easy access to the e-mails of individuals in order to catch criminals—specifically (according to the government) child predators. The public backlash against this intrusion into their privacy was so fierce and direct that it led the government to set the bill aside in order to rework it in light of privacy fears. In yet another example of the complex power of social media, Toews himself became the object of the kind of e-intrusion that might have been generated by Bill C-30. A Twitter account—@vikileaks30—later traced to a Liberal Party staffer, sent out dozens of embarrassing tweets from Toews's ex-wife concerning their divorce.

Over the coming decades, the possibilities and limits produced by new technologies are likely to become an ever-present part of public debate and discussion. In what follows, we look briefly at three key cases that raise questions about the powers and problems of new communications technologies in the twenty-first century, and that together provide a place from which to begin to map the increasingly complex landscape of contemporary popular culture.

Social Media and Political Change

New communications technologies and quick access to a huge range of online informa-tion open up possibilities for citizens to engage with one another and with their govern-ments in a potentially more democratic way. The mobile phone is one technology that has been especially celebrated as a device that has the potential to contribute to social and political change by enabling ideas—especially those ideas that stand in contrast or opposition to official new reports or government pronouncements—to spread like wild-fire through a community. In January 2001, thousands of Filipinos converged at a major crossroads in Manila to protest the actions of the Philippine Congress in relation to cor-ruption proceedings against President Joseph Estrada. What brought the crowds to Epifanio de los Santos Avenue was a text message sent rapidly around, which read: "Go 2 EDSA. Wear blk." Such incidences, which have become ever more frequent in the age of Twitter, have led some critics to equate the revolution in information and communica-tions technologies with the possibility of political revolution as such.

For new-media commentator and professor Clay Shirky,

> as the communications landscape gets denser, more complex, and more participa-tory, the networked population is gaining greater access to information, more opportunities to engage in public speech, and an enhanced ability to undertake collective action. In the political arena, as the protests in Manila demonstrated, these increased freedoms can help loosely coordinated publics demand change. (28)

While such examples of "microcoordination" have brought about significant develop-ments in culture (everything from the mobilization of consumers through coupons sent to their phones to the creation of "flash mobs" who perform spontaneously in public space) as well as politics, the enthusiasm of many pundits and scholars regarding the impact of hardware like cell phones or apps like Facebook to bring about social transfor-mation can (and all too often does) go too far, with claims that these new communica-tions media produce change by their very presence. Even President Estrada blamed text-messaging technology for his ultimate downfall, rather than public responses to the allegations of fraud directed at him or, indeed, his own illegal activities while leader of the Philippines. *How* citizens uses their devices and apps, and just as importantly *what* they communicate by means of them, is as important as the devices themselves, as is the larger historical context in which messages circulate. In contrast to Shirky's enthusiasm for technology's political possibilities, cultural critics such as Evgeny Morozov have chal-lenged a growing belief in the kind of technological determinism that once believed "that the Western radio informed Soviet citizens about the superior value of Western goods—and the Soviets eventually rebelled." The story of the collapse of the Soviet Union is much more complex than narratives that name the presence and content of radio ads would suggest, just as political change today comes about through processes, forces, and movements, not just the devices that mediate them.

Facebook Revolution

The presumed link between the communications revolution and political change became a key element of the story of the Arab Spring, the name given to a series of political confrontations between citizens and authoritarian governments in North Africa and the Arabian Peninsula, beginning in late 2010 (with the self-immolation of Mohamed Bouazizi in Tunisia in December) and continuing throughout 2011. The most widely and dramatically reported of the Arab Spring uprisings took place in Egypt, culminating on February 10, 2011 with the resignation of President Hosni Mubarak after 30 years in power (see Figure 10.1). The Western media's interest in the events in Egypt had much to do with the mechanics through which protest against the state was organized. "By the second day of the Egyptian uprising," writes Mona El-Gobashy, "CNN correspondent Ben Wedeman was calling it a 'very techie revolution.' In the following days, every major news outlet framed the uprising as the work of wired, savvy twenty-somethings awakening the liberating potential of Facebook."

There is no question that Facebook placed a huge role in helping to challenge the Egyptian government through the mobilization of youth in the country. One of the most important figures in the events of the Arab Spring was Wael Ghonim, an employee of Google in the Middle East with a background in marketing and finance. In his account of the Arab Spring in Egypt, Ghonim traces his own shift from tech geek to political activist. As with many others of his generation, "I enjoyed spending long hours in front of a screen

Figure 10.1 An Egyptian anti-government demonstrator takes part in a candlelight vigil at Cairo's Tahrir Square on February 9, 2011 on the 16th day of consecutive protests calling for the ouster of President Hosni Mubarak. Source: © MOHAMMED ABED/AFP/Getty Images

on chat programs. I built a network of virtual relations with people, most of whom I never met in person, not even once" (24). And while he believed himself to be immune to politics, the dire situation faced by most members of the Egyptian population—especially young people like himself—and the increasing corruption and violence of the state began to pull Ghonim into political intervention via the Web. Prior to the 2011 revolution, Egypt was ruled by an authoritarian government that fixed elections and blunted opposition groups (the existing regime had to formally approve new parties in order for the latter to be able to participate in voting). More than half of Egyptians lived in poverty, with 12 million of the 80 million citizens having no access to shelter and 1.5 million living in cemeteries. As of 2010, Egypt ranked 115th out of 139 countries on the Corruption Perception Index, was dead last in hiring transparency, and had the highest rate of newborn deaths in the world (Ghonim 165). Nobel Peace Prize recipient Dr. Mohamed ElBaradei's proposal in 2010 to run against Mubarak for the presidency of the country led Ghonim to support him by using his technical and marketing skills to create a Facebook site for ElBaradei; within three months, 100 000 people had signed up.

Ghonim's involvement with ElBaradei's camp led him to appreciate just how powerful Facebook could be in mobilizing political interest in a country in which political expression was otherwise controlled and suppressed. The Egyptian government had little sense of the significant of Internet use in its country; the number of users had increased from 1.5 million in 2004 to 13.6 million in 2008, the vast majority of whom were youths and young adults (38). Ghonim found a similar lack of vision regarding the political potential of new communications technologies in the ElBaradei camp:

> We constantly argued about the role of the Internet in the process of change. [Mostafa al-Nagar, ElBaradei's campaign manager] believed that the Internet was a virtual world with limited impact on reality, while I found it to be the key vehicle to bringing forth the first spark of change. The Internet is not a virtual world inhabited by avatars. It is a means of communication that offers people in the physical world a method to organize, act, and promote ideas and awareness. The Internet was going to change politics in Egypt, I wrote on Facebook and Twitter, and the 2011 elections would not be similar to those in 2005. (51)

The brutal beating and death of Khaled Mohamed Said, a young Egyptian man, by secret police on June 8, 2010 prompted Ghonim into further action. Given the number of people who were already members of ElBaradei's Facebook page, Ghonim initially considered posting images of Said's bloodied and broken body to the site. Instead, he decided to create a new page: *Kullena Khaled Said*, "We Are All Khaled Said." This Facebook page would play a crucial role in the Arab Spring, quickly becoming one of the main sites for the exchange of information concerning the actions of the Egyptian government and a safe place where protestors could organize events rapidly and with relative anonymity. Within two minutes of creating the page, 300 people had joined; by the end of the first day, 36 000 people had signed up. At the outset, the site circulated information (videos, photos, a certificate of Said's military service) that countered propaganda circulated by the police and the official state media about the events leading to Said's death.

From the beginning, Ghonim imagined the page as a space that would help Egyptians who wanted political change to move from communicating online to taking action in the streets. The first event generated by *Kullena Khaled Said* was a silent protest that consisted of people arriving individually along the coastal road in Alexandria, where they would meet up and form a chain of people holding hands and facing out to sea with their backs turned on Egypt. Images of hundreds of linked protesters lining the road, hand in hand, were posted to the Web. "Such images tend to annoy security forces," writes Ghonim. "Anything that is visually documented is evidence for the whole world to see" (79). The success of this initial peaceful gathering—made possible by the strategic use of social media—was critical to the events that would follow. On the *Kullena Khaled Said* Facebook page, Ghonim posted a celebratory message:

> Last Friday this page was launched....On Tuesday Mohamed sent his suggestion [for the Silent Stand] and it was announced to everyone....On Friday more than 100,000 members had joined this page and thousands went out in Cairo and Alexandria implementing an idea that was never done before in Egypt....So can we do just about anything or what? (81)

The capitulation of the Tunisian regime on January 13, 2011 gave the last bit of inspiration needed for members of the page and others opposed to the Egyptian government to realize that things could also change in Egypt. For much of the life of *Kullena Khaled Said*, from its origins through to Mubarak's resignation, state officials paid little heed to the role of the Internet and of Facebook in particular in shaping the protests. Soon after the Silent Stand, Ghonim conducted a survey of his users and discovered that more than 70% of them were under 24 (84). The largest portion of the Egyptian population as well as of its Web users are youths; the older generation of state officials and security had very little sense of the power of Facebook as a communication tool, and reacted too late to stop the developing opposition movement. Though access to the Internet was blocked for many users in advance of the important mass demonstrations on January 25, 2011, and Ghonim himself was arrested and interrogated in the days leading up to Mubarak's resignation, the Facebook site continued to play an important role in shaping participation in the protests even in his absence. The details that Ghonim provides in *Revolution 2.0* of the debates and discussions that took place among the ever-expanding number of members of his Facebook page (invitations to the January 25 protest reached more than 700 000 people) make it all too clear: the Egyptian revolution would not have happened as quickly and effectively as it did without social media, and may well not have happened at all. In the absence of a functioning civil society—a free and open space for debate and the exchange of ideas—Facebook and other social media became crucial spaces for Egyptians to voice their frustrations and to organize themselves to do something.

Given both his professional work and his experience using Facebook in order to generate a revolution, one might expect Ghonim to make a direct equation between technology and democracy. In his concluding remarks in *Revolution 2.0*, he appears to do just this:

> Now that so many people can easily connect with one another, the world is less hospitable to authoritarian regimes. Humanity will always be cursed with power-hungry people and the rule of law and justice will not automatically flourish in all places at all times. But thanks to modern technology, participatory democracy is become a reality. Governments are finding it harder and harder to keep their people isolated from one another, to censor information, and to hide corruption and issue propaganda that goes unchallenged. Slowly but surely, the weapons of mass oppression are becoming extinct. (292–293)

Yet while he does celebrate the power of technology, he is also careful to assign it its proper role in the developments that led to the Arab Spring in Egypt. For instance,

Ghonim is well aware of the digital divide within his own country. Since "reaching working-class Egyptians was not going to happen through the Internet and Facebook" (145), protestors also distributed information via text messaging and printed fliers as well. For the revolution to happen, it required people to be willing to risk their lives in the streets. "It was easy to write, rant, and mobilize people using the Internet," Ghonim writes. "The real heroes of the revolution were the people who had died and been injured" (257). And for people to be willing to risk their lives, conditions in Egypt had to have reached a level so abject that, for many, continuing with the way things had been heading was simply no longer an option.

For Ghonim, what distinguishes the revolution 2.0 model—revolutions enabled by social media and other new communication technologies—from its 1.0 predecessor is the wisdom of the crowd. Earlier revolutions were led by "charismatic leaders who were politically savvy and sometimes even military geniuses" (293). By comparison, the new model of radical political change, empowered by access to information that government once sought to manage or control, involves the participation of *everyone*. The democratization of access to information will not on its own address corruption—the United States ranks third in Internet use but ranked 18th on Transparency International's Corruption Perceptions Index in 2016 (i.e., 17 countries are considered to be less corrupt than the United States; "Internet", "Corruption")—nor will it directly address problems of poverty or inequality. However, it can't help but make possible more widespread challenges to political systems run for the benefit of the few at the expense of the many.

The Fate of Information

Friends who might have wanted to settle a bar bet about the name of the capital city of India, or kids looking for some quick help on their homework assignments, would have been surprised on January 18, 2012 to find that Wikipedia was… gone. In order to draw attention to the threat posed by two legislative acts then under discussion in the US House of Representatives (SOPA: Stop Online Piracy Act) and the US Senate (PIPA: Protect IP Act), Wikipedia and a number of other sites voluntarily engaged in a blackout. Had they been passed, these Acts would have increased copyright provisions to such a degree that many existing information services on the Web would have been legally threatened; at the same time, they would have given the US government considerable powers over the Internet, allowing the Attorney General to remove web sites deemed objectionable for whatever reason, and without any legal oversight. In her statement explaining the reason for the decision to blackout Wikipedia, Sue Gardner, Executive Director of the Wikimedia Foundation, spoke of the site as

> a resource that wants to be used for the benefit of the public. Readers trust Wikipedia because they know that despite its faults, Wikipedia's heart is in the right place. It's not aiming to monetize their eyeballs or make them believe some particular thing, or sell them a product. Wikipedia has no hidden agenda: it just wants to be helpful.

The blackout of Wikipedia had the desired effect—at least for the time being. Even before the blackout took place, the Obama Administration issued a statement saying that it would oppose any act "that reduces freedom of expression, increases cybersecurity risk, or undermines the dynamic, innovative global Internet" (Espinel).

The availability of almost instantaneous information online is one of the genuinely amazing features of the Internet. The information provided is, however, far from innocent or trustworthy. Indeed, the almost infinite number of sites from which one can get information, in conjunction with the threat posed by the Internet to the practices of "legitimate" critics, has had two contradictory effects. In some cases, sources trusted *off* the Web have become sites to which one turns *on* the Web as well. For example, the websites of the *New York Times* and *The Guardian* have become places to which one turns for news and opinions, in large part because of the high reputations that they both established prior to the creation of the Internet. The existence of so many sources of information, however, has led to challenges to the legitimacy of these self-same sources. During the race for the 2012 US Presidential campaign, for instance, Republican hopeful Rick Santorum frequently invoked lies and fictions to motivate his followers. To give but one example, Santorum said that 10% of deaths in the Netherlands were from euthanasia, a fate that he further claimed was forced on many helpless patients. A *Washington Post* article showing that this was *not* the case was greeted by a blogger supportive of Santorum as merely evidence of the questionable tactics of the "elitist" mainstream media. Similar patterns were evident in the 2016 US election campaign, when the regular exposure of Republican candidate Donald Trump's manipulation of the truth had no perceptible effect on his popularity among core supporters. In the view of journalist Ian Buruma, "the public is increasingly segmented into groups of like-minded people who see their views echoed back to them in blogs, comments and tweets. There's no need to be exposed to different opinions, which are, in any case, considered to be propaganda." Even as it has given us more information, the Internet has also made the always difficult task of separating truth from fiction all the more difficult. In the 2016 US election campaign, many more candidates played games with information in the same way as Santorum, with little worry about being corrected by mainstream media for their mistakes and false assertions.

There are other developments that are equally important in assessing the fate of information and knowledge in the twenty-first century. The fight over SOPA and PIPA raises important questions about who has access to information on the Internet, to what uses it is put, and under what conditions access is or should be provided. Wikimedia's intervention in the implementation of a potentially restrictive and invasive action by the government can't help but raise the question: If the government isn't regulating the Internet already, then who is? And to what end and for what purposes might they be involved in circulating information on the Web, including information about those who use it? In her explanation of the actions of Wikipedia, Gardner draws on ethical language to make her case: Wikipedia's heart is in the right place; it has no secret agenda; it's not involved in the market; "it just wants to be helpful." In the case of Wikipedia, these good intentions and lack of ambition to make a profit might well protect Internet users from having their search histories and record of Web visits used and abused by businesses or governments. At the same time, good intentions are far from being equivalent to laws or regulations generated by and for the good of publics; while Wikipedia's heart might be in the right place, anyone who has surfed the Web knows that other providers of services and information are neither so forthcoming about their intentions, nor shy about making money from Internet users.

In Wikipedia's appeal to its own ethical standards, one cannot help but hear echoes of an even more famous code of Internet conduct. Google is a company that has had an enormous impact on both the organization of and access to information on the Internet. As Daniel Soar, an editor at the *London Review of Books*, aptly puts it, Google's "ubiquitous search box has changed the way information can be got at to such an extent that ten years after most people first learned of its existence you wouldn't think of trying to find out anything without typing it into Google first" (3). The success of Google in becoming *the* site to which one turns for everyday information is such that it has played a major role in bringing about the end of such resources as the Yellow Pages (the physical version at least) and even the venerable *Encyclopaedia Britannica*, which announced in 2012 that it was ceasing publication of its printed version. Google has become so big so fast that, as early as 2006, even before it had acquired YouTube and became (in 2007) the most visited web site in the world, many were asking "whether Google is becoming too dominant in too many areas" (McArthur). In a review of books about Google, Soar lists the enormous amount and range of information to which the company now has access. The material it makes publicly searchable—everything from its index on the Web, to the texts on Google Books and videos on YouTube, to images of neighborhoods and strip malls on Google Street View is

> only a small fraction of the information it actually possesses. I know that Google knows, because I've looked it up, that on 30 April 2011 at 4:33 p.m., I was at Willesden Junction station, travelling west. It knows where I was, as it knows where I am now, because like many millions of others I have an Android-powered smart-phone with Google's location service turned on....If you use its products, Google knows the content of your emails and voicemail messages...[and] of every docu-ment you write or spreadsheet you fiddle or presentation you construct. If as many Google-enabled robotic devices get installed as Google hopes, Google may soon know the contents of your fridge, your heart rate when you're exercising, the weather outside your front door, the pattern of electricity use in your home.
>
> Google knows or has sought to know...your credit card numbers, your purchas-ing history, your date of birth, your medical history, your reading habits, your taste in music, your interest or otherwise (thanks to your searching habits) in the First Intifada or the career of Audrey Hepburn or flights to Mexico or interest-free loans, or whatever you idly speculate about at 3.45 on a Wednesday afternoon. Here's something: if you have an Android phone, Google can guess your home address, since that's where your phone tends to be at night. I don't mean that in theory some rogue Google employee could hack into your phone to find out where you sleep; I mean that Google, as a system, explicitly deduces where you live and openly logs it as "home address" in its location service, to put beside the "work address" where you spend the majority of your daytime hours. (Soar 3)

On the basis of this list alone—and there are spaces and places in which Google has asserted itself into our lives that amazingly *aren't* included even in this long list—worries about the size and power of Google are certainly justified. One of the ways in which Google has attempted to counter fears about the scope and scale of its operations is by adapting an ethical phrase as its corporate motto: "Do no evil." Whether the company has always managed to live up to this guiding mantra has come increasingly into question the larger it has grown. For instance, the company has at times complied with pressures—from sources as various as the governments of China, Germany, France, and Switzerland to the Church of Scientology—to block or limit some of the results that user searches might pull up. As Google has grown in size as a corporation, with so much liquidity that it can purchase any corporate target of interest to it (e.g., YouTube, or online ad rival DoubleClick) while simultaneously fending off sizable lawsuits (e.g., for copyright viola-tions in the creation of Google Books), objections to its practices and decisions have grown and multiplied (see McHugh; Palmer). The bulk of these objections fall under the category of what Google would characterize as a kind of "pragmatic censorship," a decision to comply with limits on searches now as a way of promoting what all tech corporations see as the long-term democratizing effect of Internet access around the world—short-term anti-democratic pain for long-term democratic gain. Others see things differently: following guidelines set by the European Court of Justice in 2014, more than a million people have exercised the "right to be forgotten" and have been asked to be removed from Google's search engine (Woollaston).

There are a number of things one might question about the statements in Close-Up 10.1, #6 of Google's 10-point philosophy. (To begin with, is it in fact possible to make money without hurting someone? Is capitalism a system that can ethically generate profit at no one's expense?) Perhaps the key thing singled out in Google's claim not to do evil has to do with the objectivity of its rankings and the integrity of its search results. This is the service for which Google is best known and the function that has made it such an integral service on the Internet: a portal through which users can find what they are looking for with a high degree of confidence and reliability. But good intentions notwithstanding, is Google's path to knowledge really that straightforward? As much as the Internet presents itself to us as a virtual candy land of information—a space in which we are able to prowl around in search of news, reviews, recipes, funny videos, or profiles of our friends and neighbors, free from censorship and guided only by our own choice—it is crucial to remember that the information we access is refracted through a social and cultural mechanism that inevitably pushes some sites and ideas to the forefront, while burying others on page 2 of the search results and beyond.

A different set of challenges and problems of dealing with information in an age when it is widely available can be seen by looking at an ongoing project of Google's that has

---

Close-Up 10.1 6. You Can Make Money without Doing Evil

"Google is a business. The revenue we generate is derived from offering search technology to companies and from the sale of advertising displayed on our site and on other sites across the web. Hundreds of thousands of advertisers worldwide use AdWords to promote their products; hundreds of thousands of publishers take advantage of our AdSense program to deliver ads relevant to their site content. To ensure that we're ultimately serving all our users (whether they are advertisers or not), we have a set of guiding principles for our advertising programs and practices:

- We don't allow ads to be displayed on our results pages unless they are relevant where they are shown. And we firmly believe that ads can provide useful information if, and only if, they are relevant to what you wish to find—so it's possible that certain searches won't lead to any ads at all.
- We believe that advertising can be effective without being flashy. We don't accept pop-up advertising, which interferes with your ability to see the content you've requested. We've found that text ads that are relevant to the person reading them draw much higher clickthrough rates than ads appearing randomly. Any advertiser, whether small or large, can take advantage of this highly targeted medium.
- Advertising on Google is always clearly identified as a 'Sponsored Link,' so it does not compromise the integrity of our search results. We never manipulate rankings to put our partners higher in our search results and no one can buy better PageRank. Our users trust our objectivity and no short-term gain could ever justify breaching that trust."

Source: Google, "Our Philosophy: Ten Things We Know to Be True."

drawn numerous objections (one of only many such objections: there is a Wikipedia page for "Criticism of Google"). In December 2004, Google announced a project to digitize and make publicly available 15 million printed volumes (approximately 4.5 billion pages), drawn primarily from the libraries of Stanford University and the University of Michigan, with the Widener Library at Harvard, the Bodleian at Oxford, and the New York Public Library involved to lesser degrees; the Bavarian State Library in Munich has also joined the project (Herwig). Such a project has incredible promise. In the words of Jean-Noël Jeanneney, the president of the Bibliothèque nationale de France, the Google project (initially called Google Library but since given the more modest name of Google Books) appeared initially as "the realization of an old dream…that a treasure trove of knowledge, accumulated for centuries, would be opened up to the benefit of all, and primarily to those whose family, sociological or geographical situation deprived them of easy access to the cultural and intellectual legacy of humanity" (5). The promise of easy access to the world's libraries is described by the director of the Bodleian, Sarah Thomas, as accelerating "the emergence of new knowledge tremendously" (Herwig). This narrative of universal knowledge aided by technology seems hard to resist, especially as it feeds into popular discourse linking new gadgets with the perpetual unfolding of the Enlightenment "maturity" of humanity.

Even so, significant concerns were raised about Google's project almost immediately. Chief among these for Europeans was the potential for a tool such as Google Books to further accelerate the prevalence of English as a language of research at the expense of other languages. Given the paucity of translations from other languages into English (e.g., in 2005, only 3.54% of new adult fiction titles published in the United States were translations; see Hoffman), this would in turn have implications for the circulation of and access to the non-English cultural resources of the world. As just one of many such cases, Jeanneney offers the example of a search for famous Spanish writer and cultural icon Miguel de Cervantes on the Spanish version of the Google Books. The first five items returned in the search were in French, followed by three books in English; in the ninth and final position was a collection of excerpts from *Don Quixote* in Spanish, with the whole work nowhere to be found in its original language on the first page—the only one visited by most users of Google (12).

Jeanneney's short book on Google is full of such anecdotes about the limits and problems of the online library that Google is in the process of assembling. His criticisms of the project are driven by a desire to maintain global cultural and linguistic diversity, in line with UNESCO's 2005 declaration (UNESCO), which states almost immediately (in Article 6) that "While ensuring that the free flow of ideas by word and image, care should be exercised that all cultures can express themselves and make themselves known." (Tellingly, perhaps, the United States is not a signatory to this declaration.) Among the many interesting solutions that Jeanneney offers to the current dominance of Google Books is the creation of a European online library, as well as the promotion of search engines that both make their search algorithms public and give users information about the limits of their search and some idea of the "representativeness of the corpus in which it is carried out" (68). These suggestions highlight the important of context in both shaping information online and how such information is used and interpreted.

Still, it is important to recognize the unexpected and perhaps problematic outcome of what amounts to a major reorganization of human knowledge at an unprecedented speed, at the very same time as access to this knowledge through information technologies is being massively expanded worldwide. Despite numerous competing online projects—the European Library, the European cultural platform MICHAEL, and so on—as with so many of the other services that it has collected under its banner, Google Books has quickly become *the* site to which members of the public, politicians, students, bureaucrats, and researchers turn to access information that one imagines to be comprehensive, if perhaps not universal; the lack of access by students and scholars in most parts of the world to password-protected private databases of research almost guarantees it. The very size of the Google library makes a claim to completeness that is seductive: there are only so many of those 4.5 billion pages that one can get through in a lifetime.

What looms large as a key issue for culture in the twenty-first century are the principles by which access to this information is organized for its users. In the case of Google, the information it provides is hierarchized according to two principles (although, of course, the precise algorithms remain secret). The first has to do with the frequency and density of links, which means in effect—and especially in the case of what would be a relatively fixed archive compared to the rest of the Internet—that "success breeds success, at the expense of newcomers, minorities, marginals" (Jeanneney 45). The second has to do with the demands of the advertising that pays for the digitalization project to begin with. Ads linked to specific books, themes, or topics—Jeanneney jokingly imagines a match manufacturer linking up to Hans Christian Anderson's *The Little Match Girl*—have an impact on the organization and hierarchization of search results as well.

There has (of course) to be a way of organizing the search results of such a potentially huge archive as Google Books (not to mention the even larger archive of the Internet itself, which was estimated on February 6, 2016 to have at least 48.9 billion Google-indexed pages; see www.worldwidewebsize.com). But once these particular principles of hierarchization, organized as they are by market imperatives as opposed to those that have guided the practices of archivists and librarians for centuries, are combined with the emphasis on English texts previously mentioned, we have in effect the sanctioning of a specific view of the world. To give one example, Jeanneney points to Simon Schama's book on the French Revolution, *Citizens*—a market success in the United States, but so skewed in its account that no publisher in France would consider a translation (41–42). If one were to get an account of the Revolution only through Schama as opposed to other sources—even fictional ones like Victor Hugo's *Quatre-vingt-treize*—they would have a very limited view of the past, just as getting an account of the Cuban missile crisis or 9/11 through the most popular American sources would quickly obscure our understanding of the politics of the global present. Yet this is the direction in which the "promise" of Google Book Search is leading us.

There's an "evil" at work here that is hard for Google or most of its users to identity. That the process of producing access to information on the Web works through a process of hierarchization that generates some problems is a point that Google—and no doubt the vast majority of its users—takes to be simply part of the pragmatic demands of life on the Internet. How could one possibly dismiss the value of having access to the great libraries of the world in one's bedroom? In the terms according to which Google has positioned its library project, the possibility of unfettered access to books is organized as a market promise—and not just because of the fact that money directly influences the importance of texts through advertising, but because of the illusion of choice combined with the attitude of "buyer beware." Google understands itself to be doing no evil because it is playing by standard social and political rules; indeed, it imagines that it is extending these rules substantially, contributing to global democratization and the reinforcement of rule of law by means of informational trickle-down (a belief that the events of the Arab Spring described above cannot help but reinforce).

As with every other aspect of social life, it is important to recognize that *especially* in the age of information, information is hardly innocent and is in fact at the heart of the political. "There can be no universal library, only specific ways of looking at the universal," Jeanneney reminds us (5). These specific ways demand explicit, ongoing, public contestation and debate of a kind that necessarily involves a discussion not only of the specifics of search engine algorithms, but, more broadly, of the kind of world that we want to inhabit and the futures we want to work toward.

From Information to Marketing

In *The Googlization of Everything*, Siva Vaidhyanathan writes, "we are not Google's customers. We—our fancies, fetishes, predilections and preferences—are what Google sells to advertisers" (3). In response to claims such as this one, Soar thinks that the implication that

> Google makes the information it has about us available to advertisers…[is] wrong. It isn't possible, using Google's tools, to target an ad to 32-year-old single heterosexual men living in London who work at Goldman Sachs and like skiing, especially at Courchevel. You can do exactly that using Facebook, but the options Google gives advertisers are, by comparison, limited: the closest it gets is to allow them to target display ads to people who may be interested in the category of "skiing and snowboarding"—and advertisers were always able to do that anyway by buying space in *Ski & Snowboard* magazine. (5)

Recent developments, however, suggest that it is in fact Soar who is wrong about the ends to which information about users is being put. There is no doubt that the services and applications many companies provide for free on the Internet are in fact lures intended to generate information about users that they intend to use for their own purposes, or to sell to other companies eager for any possible marketing and advertising advantage. Facebook provides perhaps the best example of a site that captures user information that it passes along to advertisers—for a fee that it pockets. In 2012, it revealed to advertising professionals "revamped Facebook pages and timelines that companies can use to interact innocuously with Facebook's vast user base" (Marlow "Google" B1). And Facebook is hardly the only such service. Not to be outdone, a month later Google instituted a new privacy policy that permits the company "to sweep together a person's data across its various services, from YouTube to Gmail and Google+, in an effort to better target the person with ads based on their personal preferences" (Marlow B3). In the intervening years, the use of personal data for advertising purposes has further intensified. As most websites and social media apps depend on advertising to help fund their endeavors, users of almost every web service are now routinely polled with personal information, whether legitimately (offers of air miles in exchange for participating in surveys) or illegitimately (hacks and hijacks of the information contained in services such as Reddit and Twitter).

In addition to the disturbing implications of corporate privacy violation, Evgeny Morozov laments another aspect of the way in which Google, along with social media sites like Facebook, filters our Internet experience. Perhaps a little romantically, Morozov compares the early Internet user to the *flâneur*, scrolling pleasurably and aimlessly (and anonymously) through virtual arcades, without any pressure to consume. Just as economic and architectural changes in nineteenth-century France diminished the quality of the *flâneur*'s experience (with the arcades replaced by "large, utilitarian department stores"), so Google and Facebook have transformed the Internet experience, each of them vying to become the one-stop shopping (and reading, listening, viewing, learning, and socializing) place for users, each diminishing the element of freedom, chance, and surprise that defined the joys of the "cyberflâneur" experience (Morozov "Death"). At least some of the promise and possibility heralded by the Internet are draining away into the control and corporatism that define all too much of contemporary experience.

Suggested Activity 10.2

Consider the ways in which you make use of the search tools on the Internet and the information that they bring up. Do you question the search results? Why or why not? Compare the results (or "hits") that appear when you use different search engines to find out about a specific topic or phrase (you can find a list of search tools at http://en.wikipedia.org/wiki/Search_engines_list). What do the differences and similarities tell you about the manner in which information is organized by different search engines?

The Real-World Costs of E-Life

There is no doubt that there have been a huge range of social, cultural, and political developments as a result of new technologies, especially as a result of the widespread global use of computing and communications technologies; we have only been able to touch on a few of these here. Though we've already addressed some of the downsides to the undeniable opportunities and new possibilities that have emerged as a result of these technologies, we would be remiss in not pointing (by way of concluding this section) to a few more ways in which the real world and e-life can be out of sync in ways that shape what is and isn't possible for people around the world.

While ever-increasing numbers of people have access to new communications and computing technologies, it is important to remember that in much of the world a digital divide still exists—that is, a divide between those who work in and live comfortably with e-life, and those who don't (see Figure 10.2). The long-standing attempt to create

Figure 10.2 A world map in which the size of countries is modified to reflect comparative internet usage shows a stark divide between the Global North and South. Source: © Benjamin D. Hennig (Worldmapper Project). http://www.worldmapper.org/display.php?selected=336

a cheap laptop (as supported, for instance, by the One Laptop per Child Foundation founded by Professor Nicholas Negroponte) is intended to make the services of and information on the Internet available to as many people in the world as possible. The aim is to make a fully functioning laptop that costs less than $100. While the Foundation has not managed to achieve its goal of creating a laptop that costs less than $100, it has managed to distribute 3 million laptops to date. Even so, the Internet remains inaccessible to large swaths of the globe's population, most notably the up to 2.7 billion people around the world that the World Bank estimates live on less than $2 per day. Despite a rapid expansion of owners of cell phones and computers, access to the physical devices required to visit the virtual landscape of the Web is still more limited than we might believe. While the creation of more and more devices such as the DataWind Aakash, an inexpensive ($50) Canadian-designed tablet intended for use in India, will continue to pull some people into the Internet era, the digital divide is likely to continue for some time to come.

Indeed, the continual expansion of technological offerings has had real-world costs that are becoming increasingly evident to the publics that use them. At roughly the same time as Apple's stock price was pushing the total value of the company into uncharted territories (in February 2017, the company was worth more than $700 billion), increasing attention was being drawn to the working conditions endured by many of the workers engaged in the manufacturing of Apple products. In a series of reports, journalists Charles Duhigg and David Barboza documented a range of labor abuses in high-tech factories based in China:

> Employees work excessive overtime, in some cases seven days a week, and live in crowded dorms. Some say they stand so long that their legs swell until they can hardly walk. Under-age workers have helped build Apple's products, and the company's suppliers have improperly disposed of hazardous waste and falsified records, according to company reports and advocacy groups that, within China, are often considered reliable, independent monitors.

In addition to harsh working conditions, the push to create cheap, shiny products to satisfy the high-tech desires of Western consumers—all while making a tidy profit— has repeatedly been said to endanger workers' lives. In 2010, 137 workers were injured while using a poisonous chemical to clean iPad screens; in 2011, two separate explosions at iPad factories injured 77 people and killed 4; and hazardous working conditions have been reported at factories of Apple suppliers for years (see Figure 10.3). Apple is hardly alone in this regard: reports of dangerous working conditions and labor abuses have been reported in factories involved in the production of devices for Hewlett-Packard, IBM, Lenovo, Dell, Sony, Motorola, Nokia, Toshiba, and other companies. Many of the devices on which we play games, watch films, send text messages to our friends, and check our e-mail have their origins in the kind of sweatshop factories that one would expect to find in the nineteenth century rather than the twenty-first.

In 2012, one of Apple's main suppliers, Foxconn Technology, announced that it would reduce overtime and raise salaries for its employees by 25% (Barboza). It is clear that the criticisms leveled at Apple and other companies—which have been quick to spread via the very same devices made by Foxconn employees—are having an impact.

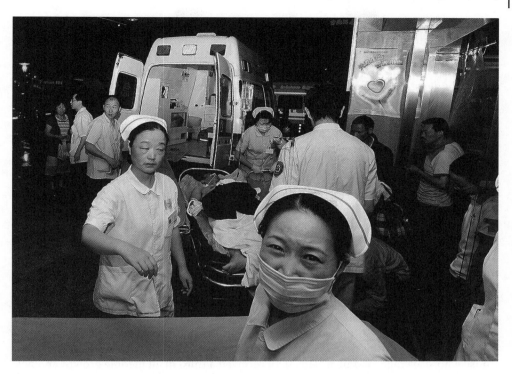

Figure 10.3 "An explosion [in 2011] at a Foxconn factory in Chengdu, China, killed four people and injured 18. It built iPads." *New York Times*. Source: AP/PA Images

Lost Generation?

On February 28, 2012, the magazine *Adbusters* posted "Tactical Briefing #26" on its blog. The brief outlines the next step in the Occupy movement, whose origins lie in an earlier call to action posted on *Adbusters*' blog on July 13, 2011. The impulse to Occupy Wall Street—the beginning of what became a worldwide movement, with sites in over 80 countries and more than 600 towns and cities in the United States—came from the successful people's revolution in Egypt a few months earlier. Citing the peaceful occupation of Tahrir Square as evidence of "a worldwide shift in revolutionary tactics," the blog suggests that "redeemers, rebels and radicals" get together in a symbolically important square where they would collectively reiterate a single demand until it was met. In the case of Tahrir, this demand was that President Mubarak step down from power; in the case of Wall Street, *the* space on the globe identified with the power of finance, *Adbusters* suggested that protesters "demand that Barack Obama ordain a Presidential Commission tasked with ending the influence money has over our representatives in Washington. It's time for DEMOCRACY NOT CORPORATOCRACY, we're doomed without it."

The different stakes of political struggle in Egypt and the United States could not be made any clearer than by the terms of this demand. In the first instance, as we saw in our discussion above, protestors risked their lives to upend a three-decade long dictatorship operating under a 45-year-old Emergency Law that suspended constitutional rights, legalized censorship, and allowed the police to do virtually whatever they wanted without repercussions; in the second, those assembled on Wall Street were supposed to ask the

President to form a commission to study a problem—an important problem, without question, but one with a solution imagined as being found *within* the existing system, as opposed to through this system's negation or elimination. As it moved around the world, the Occupy movement quickly took on a different form than the one initially imagined for it by *Adbusters*. Instead of asking for governmental bodies to study the influence of money on politics in their own countries—a worldwide phenomenon, to be sure—the common global message of the Occupy movement became something quite different. The now famous and powerful slogan "We are the 99%!" drew attention to the alarming divisions of wealth experienced in every country in the world. Spurred on by a definitive report issued in October 2011 by the US Congressional Budget Office that showed huge and growing disparities in wealth between the top 1% of US income earners and everyone else, the Occupy movement challenged a system that works only for the very few at the expense of everyone else.

The statistics are genuinely alarming. In the United States, from 1979 to 2007, after-tax income for the top 1% of the population grew by 275%; for the poorest quintile, it grew by only 18% (Pear). The disparity in income growth was not the only cause for concern. As might be expected from these growth figures, there was also an increasing disequilibrium in income distribution: in 2007 the household income of the top 1% was 17% of the total (up from 8% in 1979), while the top 20% of households received 53% of income—more than the combined incomes of the other 80% of their fellow citizens. While the situation is perhaps most extreme in the United States, similar patterns of income disparity exist across the globe. In the decade between 1997 and 2007, the richest 1% of Canadians (those whose average income is $405 000) received a third of all income growth and held 13.8% of incomes; the top 10% of income earners in the country received 42.5% of national income (Yalnizyan). "Like the Gilded Age a century ago, Canada is awash in money generated by an emerging new global economy," writes economist Armine Yalnizyan. "But during both slow and rapid periods of growth, incomes have increasingly become concentrated in the hands of the elite few rather than creating greater prosperity for all" (4).

What is as alarming as these facts of income disparity are the degree to which they seem not to have generated any significant response on the part of citizens—that 99% of us who are on the outside looking in. Indeed, perhaps up to the moment of the Occupy movement, Westerners seemed to have little understanding of their true economic and social circumstances, despite the fact that the growing economic inequalities had been articulated in numerous places and for more than a decade, including in mass-market books by figures such as former US Secretary of Labor Robert B. Reich (*Aftershock: The Next Economy and America's Future*) and Nobel Prize-winning economist Paul Krugman (*Conscience of a Liberal* and other books). The reasons for this lack of understanding or interest in income disparity are complex, but the fact that there is a general incomprehension on the part of populations of levels of social and economic equality is clear. In a 2011 study by Michael I. Norton and Dan Ariely, Americans were asked to estimate the current level of income distribution in the United States and to offer their opinion of the ideal income distribution. The study revealed that citizens massively underestimated the degree of income inequality: the estimate offered of the percentage of wealth owned by the top 20% (a different measure than income distribution) was *under* 60%, when it is in fact well *over* 80%. For those who participated in the survey, the ideal distribution, on the other hand, "resembled Sweden" (10), with the top 20% owning 30% of the wealth and the next two quintiles having roughly 20% each (see Figure 10.4).

The energy of the Occupy movement, as well as the considerable support that it received from the public (polls across the world indicated that the majority of the planet's

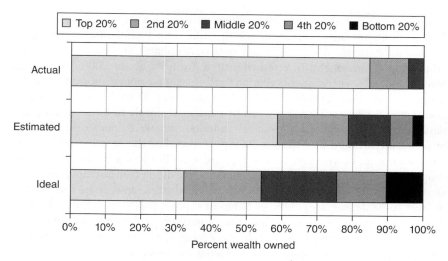

Figure 10.4 The actual distribution of wealth in the United States plotted against the estimated and ideal distribution across all respondents. Because of their small percentage of total wealth, neither the "4th 20%" value (0.2%) nor the "bottom 20%" value (0.1%) are visible in the "Actual" distribution. Source: Michael I. Norton and Dan Ariely, "Building a Better America, One Wealth Quintile at a Time," *Perspectives on Psychological Science* 6.1 (2011). Reproduceed with permission of SAGE

inhabitants agreed with the protestors), came from the force with which its slogan captured a problem that has been denied for too long. Publics long accustomed to thinking about social and political developments through narratives of progress that suggested that life could only ever become more just, equitable, and democratic were confronted with the realization that this was no longer the case: history had taken a turn for the worse. "Tactical Briefing #26," *Adbusters'* call to occupy the streets of Chicago on May 1, 2012 during the overlapping meetings of the G8 and NATO, places the problems of the current economic system front and center:

> The crisis of capitalism is deepening. Youth unemployment has reached 50% in Spain and Greece…30% in Portugal and Italy…22% in the UK…almost 20% in the US. Hundreds of millions of people around the world are waking up to the fact that their future does not compute…that their lives will be a never ending series of ecological, financial, political and personal crises…and that if we don't rise up and start fighting for a different kind of future, we won't have a future.

Though the current inequities we are experiencing have affected most people on the globe, it is young people who have been disproportionately affected by the 2008 economic crash and by the reshaping of societies via the forces that have created—and legitimated— the unprecedented concentration of wealth in the hands of fewer and fewer people. And so it is hardly surprising that young people around the globe are challenging the system that has produced a world that seems to hold little promise for them. What differentiates the Occupy movement from earlier cultures of protest in North America—particularly the 1960s and 1970s counterculture—is the way in which it unites youth with other disenfranchised groups. In the Woodstock era, Roger Lowenstein notes, "radical students preached an affinity with the 'working class,' but it was rare that the students and any members of the working class actually joined arms." The target of American students' protests back then was not the world of business and finance (which many of them would end up joining), but the government and the military, which were conducting an imperialistic war in Vietnam. Workers did not necessarily share—in fact they generally opposed—the student movement; in one instance, a group of about 200 construction workers clashed violently with students demonstrating against police shooting of anti-war protestors at Kent State University, with the result that 70 students ended up in hospital (Lowenstein). The tensions could not be explained simply in terms of different politics (conservative workers vs. progressive students), but were located in different horizons of possibility, rooted in different class positions. For the mostly middle-class and affluent students, as Lowenstein notes, "upward mobility was a birthright. People feared the cops, the draft, authority figures in general—we didn't fear unemployment."

Times have changed. The myth that hard work will lead to success, shared in various forms, to at least some degree, by people in different classes, has been definitively shattered: students, workers, unemployed people, even members of the once secure middle class, are united now in the feeling that the future is precarious (we expand on this below) and in the struggling effort to figure out why, and what can be done.

Close-Up 10.2 A Brief History of the 2008 Economic Crash

The crash of stock markets in Fall 2008 and the resulting global economic recession were the result of a burst financial bubble. In the decade leading up to the crash, real estate prices around the world had become massively inflated; in many cases, increasingly expensive properties were being purchased by individuals and corporations with the aid of large loans and mortgages that were not properly secured by significant downpayments, equities, or other assets. In an effort to expand the market for mortgages—and thus to generate more profits—some banks and finance companies created *subprime* mortgages (i.e., with interest rates set below the established prime lending rate) that allowed low income earners to enter the housing market and others to purchase larger properties than they otherwise might. Over time, the size of monthly payments would increase, as would the interest on the mortgages, making it difficult for many to manage the size of the debt they had taken on, especially given the fact that the annual income of most people has remained relatively flat for three decades. The expanded ability of individuals to borrow additional funds against their houses (home equity loans) also generated a huge expansion in consumer indebtedness.

Real estate value is to a large degree a form of collective fiction: the price of a piece of land and the object on it depends on what individuals are willing—or able—to pay for it. Housing prices can shift enormously alongside changes in the economy; in Detroit, an area hit especially hard over the past several decades as a result of the shift of industrial production to countries outside of the United States, houses that once sold for hundreds of thousands of dollars now sell for tens of thousands, or sit empty and abandoned, unwanted by anyone. When individuals were no longer able to continue to pay mortgages on properties they had purchased, they defaulted, leaving banks and credit companies with an ever-increasing stock of homes for which there was no market, thereby deflating the value of the existing stock of homes. The result was that many families had mortgages whose value far exceeded the market price of their homes; in extreme cases, some people simply left their keys in their home and walked away, unwilling to pay an inflated mortgage for an asset worth much, much less. Overleveraged and no longer able to access easy credit, consumers en masse started spending less, with immediate economic consequences, given the fact that companies, too, were in debt and had failing real estate investments.

The speed and severity of the crash were connected to one further factor. As one of few areas of real growth in the economy at the time, the real estate market became attractive to institutional and individual investors, who purchased securities related to the value of mortgages, with more risky mortgages generating greater returns on investments. In addition, a complex investment vehicle called a *credit default swap* was created that gave its purchasers a payout if a loan defaulted. When the price of real estate began to crash and mortgage holders defaulted in larger numbers on their loans, major banks and investment companies around the world did not have adequate funds to cover their losses, resulting in the collapse of several major companies (e.g., Northern Rock in the United Kingdom, CountryWide Financial and Lehmann Brothers in the United States), a precipitous decline in stock markets, a liquidity crisis (i.e., it was difficult for companies to get the loans they needed), and massive increases in government debt, as states had to intervene in markets to prevent the situation from becoming even worse.

The United States was far from the only place in which a real estate bubble burst. Excessive borrowing by individuals, corporations, and governments, made possible by cheap loans, generated even worse problems in Iceland, Ireland, Greece, Portugal, and Spain, and by consequence of a currency (the euro) shared by these countries with other nations, major economic problems for Europe as a whole.

The immediate context for the current economic and social problems faced by the world's youth is the financial crisis that followed the crash of stock market (and so of national economies around the world) in Fall 2008. Besides the creation of the high levels of youth unemployment noted above, there are two other things to note about the crash in relation to today's youth. First, it resulted in the disappearance of a huge amount of wealth from economies, and so, too, from the operating budgets of governments, with implications for unemployment programs and for funding of all manner of social programs. Second, rather than being challenged and widely questioned, the ideological imperatives that produced the crash continue to be those that, for the most part, guided how governments responded to the situation and tried to get their economies back on track. The ideology of neoliberalism, which emphasizes the reduction of the size of government (and thus of the level of taxation needed to keep government programs operating) and the elimination of rules on the operation of the private sector, continues to be the dominant one guiding state decision making. Despite the fact that this ideology was in many ways the cause of the crash, governments around the world continue to imagine it as the solution. The austerity measures proposed by many governments—cuts in programming in order to be able to pay down government debt—are deemed necessary in order to keep economies running. As often as not, however, these cuts are paired with tax cuts to the richest members of society, which means that programs that protect the poor and working classes are slashed for the sake of the 1% whose financial speculations generated the market crash (see Krugman "Four"). The persistence of neoliberalism means that the primary aim of societies around the world is to secure the ability of companies to make profit, rather than to work for the benefit of all of their citizens to live safe, healthy, and meaningful lives (see Figure 10.5).

The Future of Higher Education

One of the programs that governments claim they can no longer afford to support at the same levels as they once did is higher education. Cuts have been made to the budgets of universities and colleges across the world, and tuition fees have risen—sometimes

Figure 10.5 This Audi ad promotes private solutions to public programs, in line with the neoliberal ideology guiding government decision making across the world. Source: Audi 2011. Reproduced with permission of Audi AG

dramatically—at both public and private institutions. The most dramatic increases have taken place in California and the United Kingdom, in both cases due to lack of government funding. To address a $500 million funding gap, the California State University system—where tuitions have doubled since the 2007–08 academic year—announced in March 2012 that it would accept no new admissions in spring 2013 and would cut admissions by 20,000–25,000 students in 2013–14 (Asimov). Tuition rates in the University of California system (the research wing of the Cal State system) have climbed to historically high levels, with in-state students paying (in 2016) $12.264 a year and and out-of-state students paying $38,976. In the United Kingdom, the government of David Cameron lifted the pre-2012 cap on tuition fees (at £3290 per annum), leading to a tripling in the tuition rates at most universities. Once again, as part of government's austerity measures, cuts of more than £4 billion to university funding meant that students would have to pay more for their educations while receiving less. Throughout the world, students are enduring larger and larger class sizes and poorer service in every aspect of university life, as administrators make cuts to the number of faculty members and support staff. And because many students are forced to take on substantial debt loads in order to finance their education, an ever-increasing number of young people today enter the workforce in an economically compromised position—when, that is, they can find work at all—which means that their capacity to make choices about the kind of work they do is also compromised. They have to give themselves over to a system that is doing less and less to help them live truly meaningful lives (see Figure 10.6).

Figure 10.6 An estimated 200 000 people attended a march in Montreal on March 22, 2012 to highlight student indebtedness and to protest the Quebec government's decision to increase tuition fees by $1625 over five years—one of the largest demonstrations in the province's history. Source: © THE CANADIAN PRESS/Ryan Remiorz

One might ask: What does all this have to do with popular culture? Though to a lesser degree than one might have expected given its impact on people around the world, the market crash has become a theme explored within popular culture. Beneath the humor of the popular 2011 film *Bridesmaids* was a more serious message about the impact that financial crisis can have on an individual life. Because Annie Walker (Kristen Wiig) has had to close her bakery due to the economic downturn, she has to work in a low-paying retail job at a jewelry store; when she loses this job, too, she has to move out of the apartment she shares and back into her childhood home with her mother. The competition she engages in with Helen (Rose Byrne) over the planning of their friend Lillian's (Maya Rudolph) wedding is as much about class as it is about personal jealousy. Helen is wealthy and uses her riches to create lavish wedding events for Lillian, who will be entering the 1% through her marriage to a Chicago-based financier. As with many films, the life crisis that Annie endures has what one presumes is a happy ending (she finds a new boyfriend, one with a probably secure, working-class job as a police officer); and the glamorous parties and wedding that audiences get to witness are the typical stuff of pop culture fantasy. Annie's relegation to the sidelines of that world is represented as an instance of personal bad luck, rather than an indictment of the systematic inequality that sustains its excess. And yet, economic struggle is a part of her story as it would not have been in romantic comedies of the 1990s and early 2000s. Other popular films that feature the financial crisis as a theme also tend to use it in order to create a narrative arc in which, in the end, the ability to endure uncertainty results in individual growth and maturity, with things on the upswing in the closing frames. In *The Company Men*, downsized corporate executive Bobby Walker (Ben Affleck) is forced to join his brother-in-law's home renovation company, itself struggling with the effects of the downturn. After learning the value of "real" work, the film ends with Bobby's move to a new company, one in which he has a more prominent executive role to play, and one that promises (under the leadership of Tommy Lee Jones's character, Gene McClary) to engage in the capitalist game in a more fair and ethical fashion.

There are, of course, more critical narratives of life in the early twenty-first century, including ones that take a hard look at the consequences of neoliberalism. The bleakness of the contemporary economic environment is the subject of black comedy in the television series *Breaking Bad*, in which high school chemistry teacher Walter White (Bryan Cranston), recently diagnosed with lung cancer, sets up a methamphetamine lab in order to support his family. The 2011 film *Warrior* offers an only slightly less extreme take on contemporary working life, through the stories of two brothers competing (unbeknownst to each other) in a high-stakes mixed martial arts tournament. One, an ex-marine, is trying to earn money to support the widow of a fellow soldier who died in combat; the other is a high school physics teacher facing the threat of mortgage foreclosure. For both, ultimate fighting presents itself as the only viable means to make a living. Even though there have been an increasing number of pop culture narratives like these that address the realities of life in the wake of the financial crisis, it is telling that very few of them deal with the impact of neoliberalism on minorities—even though the latter were disproportionately affected by the crash.

Both *Breaking Bad* and *Warrior* caricature the myth of the resourceful entrepreneur, taking chances, getting his hands dirty—and in the myth it is generally a "he", though Nancy Botwin (Mary Louise Parker) in *Weeds* offers a suburban feminine counterpart to Walter White—to keep his family housed and fed. The reality, however, is not that different from the satire, as we see in Werner Herzog's documentary *Into the Abyss* (2011), which investigates the lives of two convicted murderers on death row in Texas. As one might expect, the film questions the ethics of the death penalty and probes the US penal system. In his complex and multifaceted exploration of the social context that produced the murderers and their victims, Herzog portrays a community that has largely been abandoned by mainstream America. The majority of the characters have been involved with the criminal justice system at some point and there is widespread un- or underemployment. The violent displays of masculinity and fetishism for status objects like cars (the theft of a car is what led to the murders the film investigates) are just some of the outcomes of a society in which accumulation is valued above all else, but available to the degree suggested by images in popular culture only to a very few.

We all know that real life does not match up to film and television. Our expectations and understanding of the good life are nevertheless shaped by the panoply of images and sounds we consume on a daily basis, which are filled with the fantasy of possibility, much more than a blunt assessment of the character of the reality we collectively inhabit. A few exceptions, some of which we've noted above, prove the rule of a commercial media landscape dominated by images of exceptional wealth and success (*Keeping up with the Kardashians, Extreme Makeover, Home Edition, The Real Housewives*, most sitcoms), which we might sometimes mock, but which also offer fodder for fantasy.

More than a half-century after Horkheimer and Adorno's comments on the culture industry (see Chapter 4), we need to ask ourselves once again: Do the images and symbols circulated in popular culture act as a salve for the wounds of the social and economic decisions we are living with today? Do they prevent even more of us from taking to the streets and questioning why we continue to accept as normal a society in which many are fated to live in debt, with poor work opportunities, and without the objects and experiences that popular culture so freely promises?

Suggested Activity 10.3

How have the effects of economic crisis been represented in popular culture? Is there a difference across genres or forms of popular culture (e.g., music, film, television, YouTube videos, etc.)? What kinds of issues or themes are prominent in these representations? And what kinds of things tend to be overlooked or occluded?

What Is Next?

One of the major political mysteries that we collectively face today is how a neoliberal rationality—"a new and virulent form of capitalism…with an even more disastrous impact on the fabric of a common life than its predecessors" (Budgen 150)—has in the space of a few decades become accepted as the new normal around the world. Jean and John Comaroff point to the extremity and depth of its effects:

> Neoliberalism aspires, in its ideology and practice, to intensify the abstractions inherent in capitalism itself: to separate labor power from its human context, to replace society with the market, to build a universe out of aggregated transactions … Formative experiences—like the nature of work and the reproduction of self, culture, and community—have shifted. Once-legible processes—the workings of power, the distribution of wealth, the meaning of politics and national belonging—have become opaque, even spectral. The contours of "society" blur, its organic solidarity disperses. (305)

We face a huge array of challenges in the twenty-first century. What we need perhaps most of all to navigate these—and the ones still to come—are new narratives of social being and belonging. The emerging technologies that we discuss in this chapter may help to organize, synthesize, and share these narratives, but it is popular culture's makers and "users"—including the readers of this book—who will create and, ultimately, enact them.

Suggestions for Further Reading and Viewing

Crary, Jonathan. *24/7: Late Capitalism and the Ends of Sleep*. New York: Verso, 2013.

Graeber, David. *Debt: The First 5,000 Years*. Brooklyn, NY: Melville House, 2011.

Inside Job. Dir. Charles Ferguson. 2010. Culver City, CA: Sony Pictures Classics.

Levy, Steven. *In the Plex: How Google Thinks, Works and Shapes Our Lives*. New York: Simon and Schuster, 2011.

Mandiberg, Michael, ed. *The Social Media Reader*. New York: New York University Press, 2012.

Morozov, Evgeny. *The Net Delusion: The Dark Side of Internet Freedom*. New York: Public Affairs, 2011.

Mukherjee, Roopali, and Sarah Banet-Weiser, eds. *Commodity Activism: Cultural Resistance in Neoliberal Times*. New York: New York University Press, 2010.

Nunns, Alex, and Nadia Idle, eds. *Tweets from Tahrir: Egypt's Revolution as It Unfolded, in the Words of the People Who Made It*. New York: OR Books, 2011.

Page One: Inside the New York Times. Dir. Andrew Rossi. Beverly Hills, CA: Participant Media.

Piketty, Thomas. *Capital in the Twenty-First Century*. Trans. Arthur Goldhammer. Cambridge, MA: Harvard University Press, 2014.

Rheingold, Howard. *Smart Mobs: The Next Social Revolution*. New York: Basic Books, 2002.

Turow, Joseph. *The Daily You: How the New Advertising Industry Is Defining Your Identity and Your Worth*. New Haven, CT: Yale University Press, 2012.

Glossary

Compiled by Nicholas Holm, Carolyn Veldstra, Tim Walters, Susie O'Brien, and Imre Szeman

aesthetics: The branch of philosophy concerned with sensory perception and appearances, especially as pertains to art, beauty, and notions of taste or judgment. Classically, aesthetics was thought to refer to an idea of universal beauty that exceeds personal tastes, but modern conceptions of aesthetics connect our tastes in art and culture to our class, gender, and racial backgrounds. To engage with an object or text in terms of aesthetics can also mean to consider how it appeals to your senses—how food tastes, music sounds, or a painting looks.

affect: A growing subject of scholarly research and investigation. The study of affect is intended to expand our understanding of identity formation and our relation to others through a focus on the operations of memory, perception, belief, and belonging. It challenges the historical emphasis in Western thought on reason and rationality by addressing a whole host of other ways in which we engage with the world, including the full range of our bodily sensations and emotions. Attention to such forms of affect have produced new insights into the shape and character of human experience by going beyond existing philosophical, physiological, and psychological concepts and categories. The focus in affect theory is not just on how feelings, such as happiness, hope, or depression, shape individuals, but also on the way that these and other affects assume social form, working to mobilize or restrict political projects.

agency: The ability of individuals to act as self-conscious, willful social actors and to exert their will through involvement in social practices, relationships, and decision making.

animal studies, critical: One of the foundational ways in which the category of "the human" has been established is in contrast to what in Western philosophy has been framed at its opposite: the animal. Through renewed attention to the social, cultural, and political significance of animals, critical animal studies highlights the ways in which the concept of the human (and the wide range of categories that depend on it) has been historically constructed, while also expanding theoretical and conceptual understandings of animals and the environment.

appropriation: The process by which innovative or resistant cultural forms are taken up, incorporated, and commodified by the culture industry. One of the most frequently cited examples is that of punk, which, though it developed as a dissident movement in working-class England, was quickly taken up as a style or genre by major fashion designers, music labels, and other producers of mass youth culture. In analysis of popular cultural forms, appropriation is often viewed pessimistically as evidence of the power of capitalism to absorb dissent into itself and turn it around for a profit. However, it is important to remember that resistance continues to circulate and change in form, even as its products are co-opted by dominant or mainstream culture.

assimilation: Also known as acculturation, this term refers to the sometimes forced integration of an immigrant or subordinate group into the dominant culture of the host community through the absorption of the host's cultural practices and history. This stands in opposition to the idea of **multiculturalism**, which suggests that different groups can coexist on an equal basis.

authenticity: A positive quality of genuineness and originality attributed to objects, practices, or ideas, often to demonstrate the extent to which an initially authentic phenomenon has been compromised or drained of its value. The notion of authenticity has been critiqued for its **ideological** grounding in a nostalgic vision of a more "real" cultural past now sullied by rank commercialism.

binary opposition: An analytical system that uses specific examples of symmetrically opposed pairs, or mirror opposites, which, although mutually exclusive, generate meaning through their difference and describe a complete, if extreme, system of understanding; for example, "us–them": in forming group identities, people are categorized either as part of the group ("us"), or outside of it ("them"). Binary oppositions can be dangerous in that they work to repress the ambiguities that exist between the two terms by positioning the binary as natural and any other forms of identification as deviant. In addition, binary terms often carry a positive–negative value assumption; for example, "we" are "safe, good, blameless," while "they" are "dangerous, bad, evil."

biopolitics: A term for the dominant mechanism through which contemporary states exert social and political control. Governments are still too often thought to exercise control over their populations primarily via force of law and threat of punishment. By contrast, biopolitics describes the multiple operations through which governments since the eighteenth century have exerted control through the scientific management of life, governing their populations through careful attention to their demographic and biological attributes (e.g., birth and death rates, hygiene, illness and health, attitudes toward sexuality, etc.). This less overt if more intensive and extensive form of control is most closely associated with the work of French theorist Michel Foucault.

branding: An economic trend that developed in the late 1980s and early 1990s wherein companies shifted their resources from producing goods or services to producing a corporate image defined by abstract emotional or spiritual qualities. Critics of this process have suggested that the reallocation of resources and the marketing strategies it entails contribute to trends such as the rise of child and sweatshop labor in developing nations, a decline in the number and quality of available jobs in North America, and a disturbing new invasiveness on the part of corporations into our lives and minds.

capitalism: See Close-Up 1.1.

class mobility: A characteristic of societies in which it is possible for an individual or a family to move from one social class to another and thus alter their social status and economic standing. For example, modern Western societies have greater class mobility than the rigid aristocratic societies that preceded them, which had firmly defined and immobile class boundaries. The idea of class mobility can also act as an **ideology** that paradoxically maintains the status quo. Even in Western societies, it remains difficult (and increasingly so) for the majority of people to change their class standing.

Cold War: A term that popularly refers to the tense, hostile relationship between the communist (USSR) and capitalist (US) superpowers and their respective allies from the end of the Second World War until the collapse of the Berlin Wall in 1989. Although marked by bitter animosities fueled by ideological differences, a voracious desire for world domination, and numerous moments of near disastrous military escalation (for instance, the Cuban Missile Crisis), the Cold War was known as such because it was fought largely by diplomatic and economic means rather than by sustained and overt acts of aggression. Though the Cold War spawned numerous proxy wars in developing countries, the USSR and the United States never came directly to blows.

colonialism: The historical process through which dominant groups have assimilated, dominated, and subjugated less powerful ones. Distinct from **imperialism**, which can also be used to describe nonterritorial kinds of control, colonialism involves physical settlement along with the military, political, and economic conquest of a people.

commodification: Rendering any artifact, action, object, or idea into something that can be bought or sold. Popular culture is often maligned for its commodification of formerly more **authentic** cultural forms, with the assumption that through commodification, things lose their implicit value.

commodities: Objects and services produced for consumption or exchange by someone other than their producers. Although humans have always exchanged the goods they produced for other goods, in the nineteenth century a new focus on the consumption of an increasingly diverse array of commodities by greater numbers of consumers was partly responsible for the gradual shift to a consumer culture. Marx employed the term **commodity fetishism** to describe the almost magical value attributed to objects in a capitalist economy—value derived not from how they are used or the labor that produced them, but from the price they command on the market. One of the most significant and damaging aspects of commodity culture is its tendency to attribute value to things and the relations between them rather than to people and human relationships.

commodity fetishism: See **commodities**.

conspicuous consumption: A pattern of behavior, initially observed by Thorstein Veblen, that began in the nineteenth century as a result of increased incomes and leisure time along with the growth of marketing. "Wasted" consumption (that which exceeds what is strictly necessary for life) began to be used by members of different classes in a way that was "conspicuous"—obvious, noticeable, visible—to signal or symbolize social distinction.

consumerism: The name for the complex set of dominant values and practices produced by and arising from life in a consumer society, a historically unique form of society in which consumption plays an important, if not central, role. Central to consumerism is the (generally implicit) belief that the organization of life around the purchase of commodities is the optimal way to address the needs and wants of individuals, and even to allocate social goods.

consumption: See **conspicuous consumption**.

copyright: See **intellectual property**.

counterculture: Groups that express antagonism toward the existing social and political order, and propose alternative ways of organizing society. The term "counterculture" is most commonly used to refer collectively to the alternative politics expressed by a variety of groups in the 1960s (feminist, civil rights, and anti-war activists, etc.). More generally, "the counterculture" describes all those groups that challenge and contradict the "common sense" of everyday life, with the aim of creating a better society.

creative class: A controversial term coined by urban studies theorist Richard Florida to describe a new social and economic class of artists, intellectuals, and "knowledge workers," a group that encompasses engineers, scientists, architects, and lawyers. In Florida's conception, members of the creative class are liberal, artistic types who act as the major force of economic growth in postindustrial cities through their production of new ideas, technology, and **intellectual property**.

critical animal studies: See **animal studies, critical**.

cultural imperialism: A term describing the ideological infiltration of the cultural products of dominant nations (typically, the United States) into less globally powerful ones at the expense of some aspects of indigenous cultures. Globalization theorists have cast some doubt on the concept of cultural imperialism, pointing to its problematic assumption of a passive, colonized global audience, as well as its simplistic reading of actual processes of global production and consumption.

cultural relativism: The acceptance of difference across a range of cultural activities, with the understanding that different cultures, individuals, and groups hold different values, all of which are of equal merit. This idea often works together with a postmodern refusal to accept fixed meanings or explanations, and opposes **essentialist** assumptions about culture, race, gender, and so on.

cultural studies: See Close-Up 1.2.

culture: Culture has been described by critic Raymond Williams as "one of the two or three most complicated words in the English language." The term has a wide and diverse range of meanings and associations that cannot easily be reduced to a single definition. In contemporary usage, the term carries three main significations: (i) a description of a whole way of social life (as in the idea that humanity is comprised of numerous, distinct cultures); (ii) the name for "serious" works of literature, music, fine arts, film, and so on, and the activities involved in producing these kinds of works; and, finally, (iii) as an extension of the latter definition, culture can be used to refer to a wide range of signifying and symbolic works and activities, whether these involve everyday social practices (e.g., **folk culture**) or the objects and practices of popular culture (e.g., detective novels as well as serious literature, television as well as film, etc.).

culture industry: A term first introduced by Max Horkheimer and Theodor Adorno in *Dialectic of Enlightenment* (1947) to describe the new conditions of cultural production in the twentieth century. In contrast to earlier periods, culture is now mostly produced and distributed in an industrial fashion and on a mass scale like any other **commodity**. Cultural industries (in the plural) include the music and film industry, advertising, television, and professional sports, among others. The concept of cultural industry (in the singular) draws attention to the overall social consequences of such a cultural commodity system, including the dominance of **instrumental rationality**.

culture wars: A series of disputes, primarily taking place in the United States, that attempt to reframe politics in terms of "values," especially as it pertains to contentious issues such as abortion, homosexuality, and public morality. Closely allied to the legacy of the 1960s counterculture, in universities the culture wars showed up in part as a conflict between traditional notions of literary value, often pejoratively linked to the writing of "Dead White Males," and a growing recognition of the overlooked contributions of **minority** and women writers and popular texts to the development of contemporary culture.

deconstruction: A method of analysis initially articulated in the work of philosopher Jacques Derrida that involves exposing the submerged philosophical assumptions that underpin texts and concepts. Derrida asserted that all Western thought is founded on countless sets of **binary oppositions** (black and white, speech and writing, man and woman, etc.) wherein one term is invariably considered superior to its "opposite," a valuation with vast cultural consequences. Deconstructionist readings attempt to discover how such unarticulated ideologies underpin seemingly straightforward surface meanings.

deterritorialization: The weakening of ties between a culture and a place so that a location becomes detached from the historical and social circumstances that make it a unique site. Deterritorialization leads to an emphasis on the generic rather than specifically local qualities of place, with the result that deterritorialized spaces, such as hotels and shopping malls, are often perceived to be interchangeable.

diaspora: From the Greek word for "to disperse," "diaspora" refers to the voluntary or forced migration of peoples from their homelands to new regions. In areas that are greatly affected by large diasporic movements (e.g., the West Indies via colonization and the slave trade), distinct, or creolized, cultures that blend indigenous with homeland cultures have developed. These unique diasporic cultures challenge **essentialist** models of culture or the nation.

digitalization: The translation of any kind of data (text, images, sounds, etc.) into an electronic language that can be used by a computer or other digital system for purposes of storage, distribution, or manipulation. Depending on one's perspective, digitalization is either an empowering tool with which to create and share diverse forms of information more democratically or a practice that threatens more authentic (or "real") forms of cultural production and challenges **copyright** protection laws. Because it offers unprecedented possibilities for the manipulation of sounds and images, digitalization also raises important issues for practices of **representation**.

disability: See Close-Up 6.1.

discourse: A concept articulated by Michel Foucault to describe the way speech and writing work in conjunction with specific structures and institutions to shape social reality. "Discourse" refers to distinct areas of social knowledge (typically, broad subjects such as law, science, or medicine) and the linguistic practices that are associated with them, but also to the rules governing the context of speech or writing, such as who is permitted and authorized to address these subjects. Knowledge, according to the concept of discourse, is power, since it comes into being through the operations of power and also exercises power by determining which truths will be endorsed. Discourses thus have immediate, material effects on the way a culture operates.

distinction: The condition of being set apart and considered different or special, usually through the achievement of a specific honor, and connected to value. In the study of popular culture, distinction is often linked to consumption, with the implicit idea that within a capitalist system, one can achieve distinction through one's purchases.

essentialism: The belief that categories, or individuals and groups of human beings, have innate, defining features exclusive to their category (e.g., the belief that different races have inherent characteristics that differentiate them from other races). Essentialism has been challenged by **social constructivist** theories that point to the ways in which identity and meaning are culturally produced.

ethnicity: A broad social category that addresses one's perceived membership in a larger group based on characteristics such as religious, cultural, or national background. Whereas one's **race** is generally "determined" by specific physical traits, ethnicity typically implies a somewhat more conscious and flexible affiliation with a particular group. Like race, however, the concept of ethnicity has often been used to discriminate against groups based on **stereotypical** perceptions of their common attitudes or attributes.

Eurocentrism: A critical term for any worldview that focuses on European philosophies and practices to the detriment of non-European perspectives. Eurocentrism is often thought to imply a tacit assumption that European ways of understanding the world are either superior to other beliefs or the norm from which other non-European cultures can be considered divergent. Eurocentrism is deeply implicated in the processes of **colonialism** and **racism**.

ex-nomination: A term used by Roland Barthes to identify one of the ways in which the dominance of the ruling class goes unexamined precisely because it is not named as such: the process of ex-nomination ensures that we see the values or attributes of dominant groups not as the product of particular class interests, but simply as apolitical, intrinsic human values that are therefore as unsuitable for critique as a grapefruit or any other "real thing." Ex-nomination also works to legitimate the dominance of specific racial and cultural groups by failing to acknowledge, or "mark," their distinctive qualities (e.g., white, heterosexual), thereby assuming their universality.

feminism: The name for a diverse range of political movements and approaches to the study of culture and society that concern themselves with the role played by sex and gender in the unequal distribution of power, particularly as concerns women. There are multiple feminisms: some promote gender equality, others seek to dispense with the concept of gender entirely, while still others seek to emphasize and value gender and sexual difference.

folk culture: Those cultural products and practices that have developed over time within a particular community or socially identifiable group and that are communicated from generation to generation and among people who tend to be known to one another.

Fordism: A highly mechanized and standardized manner of production, pioneered on the assembly lines of automaker Henry Ford to improve worker efficiency by duplicating the specialized precision of a machine. "Fordism" now refers not only to a seminal development in the history of industrialization that enabled hitherto unimaginable levels of mass production and consumption, but also to a type of culture (or a particular aspect of a culture) that displays similar—generally negative—qualities of uniformity and conformity. Fordism has been supplanted in much of the North American economy by post-Fordism.

Frankfurt School: See Close-Up 4.1.

gentrification: The movement of relatively affluent, middle-income individuals and families into poor urban neighbourhoods. Though often considered, especially in official civic discourse, as an improvement of underused or "rundown" space, the process almost inevitably displaces previous lower-income residents and is often thought to disrupt or destroy the character of local communities.

globalization: A recent (arguably), complex shift in the relationship between the world's many cultures fueled by complex economic, political, and technological factors. Its central effect is that temporal and geographical distances are no longer as divisive as they once were. Although seeming to possess enormous potential for improving the conditions of some of the world's poorest regions, globalization is increasingly seen as being primarily profit driven and is closely allied with the remarkable ascension to power of massive transnational corporations and with the connected phenomenon of **cultural imperialism**. Some critics of globalization argue that it is little more than a process of further concentrating wealth and power in the hands of those who already have it and that its effect on the indigenous cultures of developing nations is devastatingly corrosive. Others distinguish between different aspects of globalization (economic, political, technological, cultural, etc.) and point to the potential for new forms of cultural expression and new democratic alliances that are facilitated by a more globally connected world.

gross domestic product (GDP): The total monetary value of all the goods and services produced within a nation's economy during a one-year period, and a figure often used as an indicator of a nation's financial well-being. The GDP's value as a diagnostic tool to measure the health of a country is often criticized because it fails to account for the value of such activities as domestic work and volunteering, and attributes positive value to those transactions that produce profits but reflect a decline in social well-being (e.g., a boom in the divorce industry, the growth of prisons, etc.). Increasing concern about the inadequacy of GDP as a measure has led many economists and some countries to supplement or replace it with an alternative measure of national value, the GPI (genuine progress indicator). The GPI can be said to present a more accurate picture of national welfare by measuring previously unaccounted costs and benefits (e.g., to human health or the environment).

habitus: A concept outlined by Marcel Mauss, connoting both living space and habitat, that describes the way in which particular social environments are internalized by individuals in the form of dispositions toward particular bodily orientations and behaviors. The habitus we occupy radically affects such basic activities as sleeping, eating, sitting, walking, having sex, and giving birth, all of which should be understood not as natural but as a series of "body techniques" that are learned in particular social contexts and are therefore culturally and historically specific. Pierre Bourdieu extended this concept by investigating the relationship between habitus and social class.

hegemony: See Close-Up 2.2.

"highbrow"/"lowbrow": A colloquial reference to "high" and "low" culture—a distinction that is made on the assumption that high culture holds some sort of greater innate intellectual or moral worth, while low culture is base and degrading to those who partake in it. The distinctions between these two groups become unclear with, for example, pop art (e.g., Andy Warhol's painting of Campbell's soup cans), which borrows images from "low culture" and displays them in a venue for "high culture"—the museum. The term "nobrow" has been used recently to describe images, objects, or experiences that can't easily be classified into high or low. In fact, the quotation marks that often surround mentions of "high" or "low" culture suggest that these categories are not only constantly shifting but also arbitrary, often deployed as a means of legitimating class hierarchy.

horizontal integration: A **synergistic** venture wherein one company acquires (and integrates with) another company that is making the same kind of product or providing the same kind of service, in order to increase the purchasing company's presence in (and power over) a given market.

humanism: A collection of philosophies that espouse the idea that human life has an inherent worth and dignity that must be valued above all else. Humanism teaches that there exists a universal human condition that binds all of humanity together and that all people experience regardless of their **ethnicity** or culture. Consequently, humanists advocate that a concern for humanity needs to be the foremost concern of all cultural, political, and philosophical projects. Some critics have attacked humanism as a "speciesist" **ideology** that encourages the exploitation of nonhuman life.

hybridity: In horticulture, a term that means to graft two different plant types together to create a third, unique plant; in cultural studies, a term, generally associated with **diaspora** and **postcolonialism**, that refers to the blending of two or more cultures. The "third culture" that results from this interaction is not simply a combination of the two, but a space of possibility in which differences both between and within individual cultures express themselves.

idealization: To idealize an object, person, or social movement is to fail to critically account for its actual existence, holding it instead to impossibly high standards while ignoring the possible or potential flaws the idealized object might have. Idealization involves forgetting the actually existing material conditions in which relations occur and objects exist.

identity: An individual's unique personality or self (i.e., "who we are inside"). The concept of individual identity is complicated by the fact that, rather than inhabiting a single identity, we all assume multiple identities that are defined by particular circumstances and relationships. Marxist and psychoanalytic theories further challenge the concept of identity, showing how it is constructed by largely unconscious processes of **interpellation**. More recent theories of **performativity** offer possibilities for challenging the rigidity of the traditional identities on offer— identities that are founded in **essentialist** notions of gender, race, and sexuality.

identity politics: The strategic assertion of unity, defined by characteristics such as race, culture, ethnicity, or sexuality. Identity politics challenges prevailing power structures by demanding recognition and the extension of majority rights to minority groups.

ideological state apparatuses (ISAs): A term coined by French philosopher Louis Althusser to describe those social structures and organizations that indirectly (i.e., not by direct coercion) ensure that individuals subscribe to the ideology of the state or ruling class. Unlike repressive state apparatuses (for instance, the police or the military), which explicitly enforce the laws of a culture, ISAs work via the process of **interpellation** to compel individuals to conform to particular, class-specific social roles.

ideology: See Close-Up 2.1.

imperialism: The extension of rule over different countries, territories, or peoples, usually by force, for economic gain. Imperialism continues today through trade regulations that inhibit development in poor countries or that tie the course of their development to the economic agendas of wealthier nations. See also **colonialism** and **cultural imperialism**.

individualism: The belief, closely allied to **liberalism**, that the individual is the basic moral and political unit of society, and that the interests of the individual should take precedence over those of the community. The individual in these conceptions is thought to possess complete **agency**. Individualism promotes a society in which individual choice is not restricted by external constraints and in which individual members should practice self-reliance and responsibility.

industrialization: The movement within a culture or economic system toward an increased emphasis on large-scale/mechanized industry rather than agricultural/smallscale commercial activity. Although initially conceived as a primarily economic process in its broadest sense of organization, capitalization, and mechanization, industrialization has sweeping social and cultural implications. As well as determining the manner in which things are produced (and therefore what kinds of products are available), the process of industrialization also affects the way labor and other resources are divided up within a culture.

instrumental rationality: See Close-Up 4.2.

intellectual property/copyright: "Intellectual property" refers to one's legal ownership of an idea or any other kind of original creative work. This ownership may be protected by trademarks, patents, and copyright. Largely as a result of recent sweeping advances in technologies that can be used to reproduce or disseminate digital information, converting even the genetic material of living things into readable "code," intellectual property has become a hotly disputed issue.

interpellation: A term coined by Louis Althusser to describe the process by which an individual is addressed, or "called on," by **ideology** to assume a certain identity. Critical to the success of interpellation is the degree to which an individual recognizes and identifies with the roles she or he is assigned by the dominant culture.

intersectionality: A term coined by critical race theorist Kimberlé Crenshaw, informed by black feminists' conception of the interconnectedness of oppressive structures (e.g., **racism, patriarchy**, homophobia, transphobia, ableism) and their complex collective effects on social identity. For example, an intersectional understanding of identity recognizes how racism and misogyny inform one another in the experiences and perspectives of racialized women, instead of viewing each oppressive institution as distinct and singular.

language: A term that in cultural studies refers to more than literal words, "language" can be broadly applied to describe all forms of communication (or **sign** systems)—visual, oral, aural, physical. In the study of culture, the units of any type of language are a focus for study, as societal values, relations, and power distribution are reproduced through a culture's language(s).

liberalism: A school of political and philosophical thought that holds the individual to be the basis of society and takes individual freedom to be the ultimate ethical and political goal. Liberalism, often considered the dominant **ideology** of Western societies, emphasizes the importance of universal equality before the law, the existence of inalienable human rights, and electoral democracy. Two major forms of liberalism can be distinguished: social liberalism, which emphasizes the freedom to choose one's own lifestyle and the duty of the state to provide a certain quality of life to individuals; and economic liberalism, which emphasizes private property rights, the role of market forces, and noninterference by the state. As of late, economic liberalism has prevailed as an ideology, forcing social liberalism to the background.

maquiladoras: Spanish term describing the thousands of factories that have sprung up along the United States–Mexico border in the wake of NAFTA (the North American Free Trade Agreement). An inexpensive source of labor for **multinational** corporations, maquiladoras are known for meager wages, brutal management practices, dangerous working conditions, and widespread environmental violations.

market segmentation: Beginning in the latter half of the twentieth century, a paradigm shift in the marketing world that involves gearing cultural production toward increasingly narrow segments of the public, with the express goal of better catering to a consumer's specific tastes.

Marxism: A wide range of political and cultural philosophies that draw their inspiration from the work of Karl Marx. Marxist approaches to society and culture emphasize the primacy of economic relations and structures in determining all other social activity. In particular, Marxism emphasizes the exploitative foundations of **capitalist** systems of economics. The notion of **ideology** arises out of the Marxist tradition as a way to account for how the dominant economic class controls the production and distribution of ideas in society.

mass culture: A form of culture produced for profit and for a large and diverse audience by a vertically integrated factory system. Though in some ways more pervasive than ever, mass culture is also breaking down as a result of economic processes of market segmentation, cultural developments such as identity politics, and the growing accessibility of technologies that allow "the masses" to produce culture for themselves.

materialism: There are two understandings of materialism. The first is as an unhealthy, undesirable, or vulgar attachment to the consumption and ownership of material goods, or commodities, which equates happiness with owning a lot of things and distracts from the "finer," spiritual or intellectual aspects of life. The second is a philosophy that stresses the importance of physical objects and the actually existing conditions of life in shaping the concepts, discourses, and habitus of societies and historical periods.

media convergence: The combination of "new media" (primarily, cable and the Internet) with older media forms (radio, television, film, and newspapers and books), primarily by large corporations, with an intent to realize greater profits through the **synergistic** sharing of resources.

minority: In cultural terms, any relatively small and/or powerless group of people who differ from the majority, or dominant, culture in ethnicity, religion, language, political persuasion, and so on. Minority politics are linked to movements by groups to gain certain political, economic, or social rights that they have been denied because of their minority status. In cultural studies, "minority culture" may also refer to highbrow (serious, intellectual) culture, as opposed to lowbrow (mass) culture.

monoculture: From the agricultural term for the cultivation of a single crop. In cultural studies, the idea of monoculture is linked to **globalization** and refers to the concept of a single world culture shared by all. This term has negative implications in that it suggests the destruction of local and cultural diversity. It is often implied that monoculture is synonymous with American or consumer culture and is one of the potential results of **cultural imperialism**.

monopoly: An economic situation in which a single supplier controls the market for a particular product or service. This situation puts the producer in a position of unchallenged dominance from which it can inflate prices to cover more than just necessary costs (including a return on capital). Governments often legislate to restrict the emergence of monopolies, since they are usually detrimental to the consumer and the economy.

moral panic: See Close-Up 3.2.

multiculturalism: A sociopolitical concept (and, in some countries, a government policy) that describes the coexistence of many different cultures in one place.

Because it is linked to national politics, multiculturalism recognizes that there is no essential or unified definition of a national culture, but rather emphasizes that the nation is an idea of cultural freedom (e.g., Canada). Nominally a celebration of all cultures as equal, multiculturalist policies can often gloss over substantial power inequalities within a nation.

multinational (corporation): Any firm that extends itself outside of national boundaries by operating branches in many different countries simultaneously.

myth(ology): A term used by Roland Barthes to describe the ways in which **sign** systems work **ideologically** to reproduce and legitimate particular social relations. Myth is a mode of signification that works to express and surreptitiously to justify the dominant values of a given historical period. Unlike the relatively simple level of denotative, or literal, meaning, in which a word or image corresponds to a single, straightforward definition, myth brings into play a whole chain of associated concepts (e.g., tree–nature–goodness) by which members of a culture understand certain topics and that help to shape their collective identities.

nation/nationalism: See Close-Up 7.3.

neoliberalism: A political movement, originating with the policies of Margaret Thatcher in the United Kingdom, Ronald Reagan in the United States, and Brian Mulroney in Canada, that attempts to remove all government influence in economic matters through the **privatization** of state functions, deregulation of trade, and reduction of welfare spending. Neoliberalism is associated with economic rather than social **liberalism**. Critics of neoliberalism argue that it radically increases inequality and poverty, and places greater importance on free markets than on public well-being. In recent years, neoliberalism has come to be seen as the dominant **ideology** of **globalization**.

New World Order: A phrase associated with the postcolonial, post–Cold War configuration of world power, which remains dominated by the West, and particularly by the United States. Coined by former US President George H. Bush, the phrase describes genuine shifts in the geopolitical order, but also covers up long-term continuities in global power and capitalism (i.e., not everything is "new" in the New World Order).

orientalism: Refers to the way in which "the Orient" was and is constructed by the West as a means to claim authority and exercise control over Eastern cultures. The Orient is not a fact or a specific geographical place; rather, it is the complex layers of knowledge and **mythology** that have been constructed around Western ideas about the non-West. For example, the way North American media characterize the "Middle East" as a place of repressive government regimes and fundamentalist religion glosses over the vast cultural differences between the region's different groups and contributes to the Western assumption that domination of these "backward" nations is legitimate and necessary.

patriarchy: A social system in which men hold power in the family and in the social structure. Patriarchy has more recently been used in feminist criticism as a term to describe the total system of gender relations in which male dominance has historically worked to dominate and disempower women. The challenge in trying to dismantle this system is that it has been historically naturalized to seem as though the social position of both genders has been biologically determined.

performativity: Developed most extensively in the theory of Judith Butler, "performativity" refers to the process by which identities are enacted through repeated performance rather than inherently possessed or inhabited. The idea of performativity works on the premise that roles such as sex and gender are produced within an **ideologically** determined social script. While it is not possible to throw away the script—to be "oneself" instead of playing one's assigned role—by highlighting the tension between the scripted ideal and its embodied performance, the theory of performativity offers possibilities for resisting the straitjacket of traditionally defined identities.

populist: A political philosophy or rhetoric that claims to represent the interests of "the people" over those of "the elites." The term tends to be (but is not always) used pejoratively, and is thus rarely used for self-description. Populist politics can be either left-wing or right-wing.

Postcolonial(ism): Postcolonial refers to the period after the formal retraction of colonial rule in the developing world. This period varies considerably, but in the case of the former British colonies, it refers to the period after the Second World War. Postcolonialism is a term that refers to the working-through of the effects of colonization on a society or culture. The study of postcolonial culture examines the various mechanisms of colonialism (e.g., political rule, economic exploitation, colonial education systems) and their long-term, embedded cultural and social implications. While many former colonies are now independent states, postcolonial studies insists on the need to recognize and understand the ways in which colonialism's effects persist in the social, cultural, and political life of former colonial states today.

postfeminism: In popular and common use, "postfeminism" is an expression of the belief that feminist thought is now (at best) divisive and mean-spirited, and, in any case, no longer necessary because the main aims of feminism have been achieved: men and women are now social equals. By suggesting that feminism is no longer an important and essential form of social thought, postfeminism acts as an **ideology** whose intent is to defer, or delay, genuine gender equality through the articulation of fictitious claims about the reality of gender in contemporary society.

posthumanism: A philosophy that questions concepts that underpin the tradition of humanism, such as identity, subjectivity, consciousness, and the soul. While humanism is based on ideas of human beings as unique individuals and humanity as a clearly defined, superior life form, posthumanism rejects the autonomy of "the human" in favor of the cyborg—a being defined by a combination of human and machine and/or animal characteristics. Posthumanism has been taken up in different ways by feminists, for whom it represents a way of challenging biologically **essentialist** views of sex and gender, and by proponents of genetic engineering, who support the idea of designing "better," more powerful humans through technological enhancement.

postmodernism: Refers to a phase in Western history that coincides with the information revolution and new forms of economic, social, and cultural life produced by and in conjunction with it. Identified by Fredric Jameson as "the cultural logic of late capitalism," postmodernism names a period—the current era—and points to the fundamental differences of this era from even the recent past (i.e., modernism, ranging from roughly the mid-nineteenth to the mid-twentieth century); these differences, which characterize broad aspects of life, including architecture, artistic and literary style, cultural sensibility, and social experience, include the shift from a temporal or historical to a spatial consciousness, an intensified awareness of cultural form, and modes of ironic self-referentiality. Postmodernism also names a generalized lack of epistemic certainty—a questioning of long-standing assumptions about the search for and importance of "truth" in the operations of society, politics, culture, and science.

preferred reading: Any given text (be it a novel, film, image, or song) can be interpreted in a theoretically infinite number of ways, depending on the perspective and experiences of the reader. However, the preferred reading is the particular interpretation that emerges as the most obvious to the greatest number of people, based on prevalent and culturally specific modes of understanding (e.g., it is the reading that in many cases strikes interpreters as "common sense").

privatization: The process through which ownership of a public enterprise or the responsibility to enact a state function is transferred from government or community control into the private corporate sector and operated to generate profit. Privatization is a key aspect of **neoliberalism** and arises from a belief that the market can fulfill state functions more efficiently or cheaply than the government. State functions that have been privatized in some countries include education, television broadcasting, telecommunications, and even water supply and law enforcement. The reverse process, whereby a government takes ownership from the private sector, is called nationalization.

progress: An understanding of history, often considered to have arisen out of the Enlightenment, that holds that human conditions and society have steadily improved and will continue to do so, and that the future will inevitably be better than the past due to advances in technology, politics, economics, or culture. Following the devastation and barbarity of the Second World War and the Holocaust, some social critics began to question the notion of progress. However, the idea still defines most Western accounts of history and everyday understandings of the direction the future will take.

pseudo-individualization: Along with **standardization** (which it facilitates), one of the primary characteristics of the products of the **culture industry** as described by Max Horkheimer and Theodor Adorno. "Pseudo-individualization" refers to a mode of capitalist production wherein virtually identical cultural products are superficially varied to enable them to seemingly speak directly to a consumer's sense of individuality, unique taste, and apparent freedom to choose.

psychoanalysis: A body of ideas that derive their inspiration from the work of Sigmund Freud, specifically his work on the unconscious mind and its role in **identity** formation. Psychoanalysis seeks to account for individual behavior and social structures, such as gender and sexuality, through reference to a fundamental conflict between primal drives and desires and the need to repress and organize those drives for the purposes of social life.

queer theory: A body of theory that studies how sexuality inflects culture, politics, and society and investigates the ways in which sexual identity and orientation have been constructed and contested historically. Concerned most closely with gay, lesbian, and bisexual experience and the ramifications of homophobia, queer theory has, since its development in the 1980s, extended its focus to consider the situation and signification of transgender and other sexual minorities, as well as the construction of heterosexuality.

race: A constructed category that is widely used to distinguish among various groups of human beings based on inherited biological or physical characteristics (such as skin color or facial features). Although seemingly a neutral descriptive tool, race has functioned historically as a way to draw spurious connections between specific physical characteristics and the possession of certain behavioral traits assumed to be shared by all members of the race. The idea of race is therefore inseparable from the discriminatory attitude and practices of **racism**.

racism: The systematic practice of stereotyping and persecuting people on the basis of their **race**. Racism remains a central form of **ideology** today. Cultural studies has focused on the ways in which racist attitudes and **stereotypes** are both reinforced by and challenged in popular representations and institutionalized in a variety of popular cultural practices.

representation: The social production of meaning through **sign** systems (i.e., words, images, gestures, etc.). Representation involves making meaning by creating links between conceptual and linguistic or signifying levels of meaning—links that are established through codes shared by members of a culture. Inseparable from the socially specific processes of **ideology** and **mythology**, representation constructs the world in particular ways that have significant bearing on the organization of society.

sign: The smallest unit (such as a word, image, or sound) of communication to which meaning is attached. To be a sign, the unit must meet three criteria: it must possess a physical form, it must refer to something else, and it must do so in a way that is recognizable to others. The sustained and large-scale interconnection of signs facilitates the construction of shared sign systems that enable individuals to communicate with other members of their culture in a comprehensible manner. See also **representation**.

social constructivism: A way of explaining the production of meaning, identity, and value (often in explicit opposition to **essentialist** explanations). Social constructivists believe that identity is not inherent within an individual, group, or thing, but is instead largely a creation of cultural, political, and historical forces.

sovereignty: The possession of legal control and governance over a specific geographical territory. Sovereignty once rested in the body of the monarch, who possessed supreme power over his or her kingdom. In the modern context, sovereignty has been located in nation-states. **Globalization** has been understood by many scholars as having complicated and undermined the sovereignty of nation-states. The growth in the political power of international organizations (e.g., United Nations, World Trade Organization) and the rise of nongovernmental organizations has redistributed sovereignty to a multiplicity of local and global sites and political levels.

standardization: Along with **pseudo-individualization**, one of the primary characteristics of the products of the **culture industry** as formulated by Max Horkheimer and Theodor Adorno. "Standardization" refers to a widespread similarity between cultural products. Both a method of production and a manner of consumption, standardization not only dictates the kinds of cultural products that will be manufactured, but also inscribes in the consumer a shared mode of passive, apolitical, and disengaged reception.

stereotypes: A form of representation that reduces people to a few simple, essential characteristics that are **represented** as fixed by nature. Stereotyping is predicated on the simplistic notion that an individual's membership in any given social group (based on, for instance, class, gender, race, age, or sexuality) invariably predisposes him or her to possess certain personality characteristics, attitudes, or behaviors.

structuralism: An analytical approach characterized largely by a shift in focus from interpreting a text to unveil its hidden meaning to identifying and interrogating the ways in which meaning is brought into being structurally. Structuralism is a diverse approach encompassing numerous methodologies, connected by this concern with the ways in which the structure of any given text is implicated in the production of its meaning. Although it has been subject to intensive critique (focusing, for example, on its inability to take account of historical change), structuralism's once radical emphasis on the role of relationship and context in determining meaning has been enormously influential in many disciplines.

subculture: A term that describes groups or communities that deviate or differ from existing social norms. Subcultures are typically conceived of as groups of individuals who come together around shared practices and ideas that are rejected or treated with suspicion by official, mainstream culture. By creatively expressing their dissatisfaction with existing social norms and practices, subcultures challenge and modify what counts as normal everyday life. Subcultures are often identified with youth and youth culture.

subliminal advertising: A form of advertising that tries to persuade by having an impact on the subconscious or unconscious. Subliminal advertising passes underneath the threshold of the senses (sub-limen). Such forms of advertising hope to generate a desire in consumers to purchase a product or service without their conscious awareness of having been influenced to do so.

surveillance: The practice of monitoring persons, locations, or situations in order to gather information about the environment that is being observed. In cultural studies, surveillance is often understood, with reference to the work of Michel Foucault, as a means of ensuring that behavior remains within the bounds of established norms. Surveillance technologies have become much more advanced and their use much more widespread in recent decades with the implementation of government security programs following the events of September 11, 2001.

transnational (corporation): A firm that operates on a global scale and works, to a greater or lesser extent, outside of national jurisdictions. For example, former General Electric CEO Jack Welch's fantasy of operating the company from a permanently floating barge in order to avoid all national trade regulations and laws would be an example of a completely transnational company—it would operate worldwide without operating from within any specific country.

urbanization: The long-term but increasingly intensifying shift of human populations from the country to the city. In nineteenth-century Britain, urbanization contributed significantly to the reduction of open spaces available for recreation as land was expropriated for the building of industrial infrastructure. By 2007, more than 50% of the world's population lived in cities. Urbanization is associated with the production of new cultural forms, and also with problems such as crowding and the loss of agricultural land, green space, and species habitats.

vertical integration: A venture wherein one company acquires the means by which a particular product or service is manufactured, distributed, and sold. Its aim is to increase a corporation's control over its own products by diminishing its reliance on other companies, as well as to cut costs. Vertical integration is considered by some to be responsible for a reduction in the diversity of available cultural products.

Works Cited

Achebe, Chinua. "The Novelist as Teacher." 1965. *Hopes and Impediments: Selected Essays.* New York: Anchor, 1989. 40–46.

Adbusters. "#OccupyWallStreet: A Shift in Revolutionary Tactics." *Adbusters.* July 13, 2011. Accessed February 22, 2017. http://www.commondreams.org/views/2011/07/16/occupywallstreet-shift-revolutionary-tactics

Adbusters. "Tactical Briefing #26: Anarchic Swarms—The Emerging Model." *Adbusters.* February 28, 2012. Accessed February 22, 2017. http://www.adbusters.org/action/occupywallstreet/anarchic-swarms-the-emerging-model/

Adorno, Theodor. "Excerpt from 'On Popular Music.'" *A Critical and Cultural Theory Reader.* Ed. Anthony Easthope and Kate McGowan. Toronto: University of Toronto Press, 1992. 11–23.

Adorno, Theodor. "The Culture Industry Reconsidered." *The Adorno Reader.* Ed. Brian O'Connor. Oxford: Blackwell, 2000. 230–238.

Ahmed, Sara. *The Promise of Happiness.* Durham, NC: Duke University Press, 2010.

Akin, David. "From Igloo to Internet: First Nations Gain Entrée to the Electronic Age." *Hamilton Spectator September* 22, 1997: B1.

Althusser, Louis. *Lenin and Philosophy and Other Essays.* Trans. Ben Brewster. London: New Left, 1971.

An Inconvenient Truth. Dir. Davis Guggenheim. Perf. Al Gore. Paramount Classics, 2006.

Anderson, Benedict. *Imagined Communities.* London: Verso, 1983.

Arnold, Matthew. *Culture and Anarchy.* 1869. Ed. J. Dover Wilson. Cambridge: Cambridge University Press, 1990.

Ashcroft, Bill, Gareth Griffiths, and Helen Tiffin. *Key Concepts in Post-Colonial Studies.* London: Routledge, 1998.

Asimov, Nanette. "Cal State to Close Door on Spring 2013 Enrollment." *San Francisco Chronicle* March 20, 2012.

Atwood, Margaret. "Rich Kids Swim, Poor Kids Sink." *The Globe and Mail* April 19, 2008: M1.

"Australian Crime: Facts & Figures Report Show Teen Are the Most Violent Australians." news.com.au. May 18, 2013. Accessed February 22, 2017. http://www.news.com.au/national/australian-crime-facts-figures-report-shows-teen-are-the-most-violent-australians/story-fncynjr2-1226645615303

"Bad and Badder." *Harper's* September 2002: 21–22.

Bailey, Peter. *Leisure and Class in Victorian England: Rational Recreation and the Contest for Control, 1830–1885.* London: Methuen, 1978.

Popular Culture: A User's Guide, International Edition. Imre Szeman and Susie O'Brien.
© 2017 John Wiley & Sons, Inc. Published 2017 by John Wiley & Sons, Inc.

Balsamo, Anne. "On the Cutting Edge: Cosmetic Surgery and the Technological Production of the Gendered Body." *The Visual Culture Reader*. Ed. Nicholas Mirzoeff. London: Routledge, 1998. 228–233.

Bank for International Settlements. *Triennial Central Bank Survey of Foreign Exchange and OTC Derivatives Markets in 2016*. Basel: BIS, 2016. Accessed March 1, 2017. http://www.bis.org/publ/rpfx16.htm

Barboza, David. "Foxconn Plans to Lift Pay Sharply at Factories in China." *The New York Times* February 18, 2012. Accessed March 27, 2012. http://www.nytimes.com/2012/02/19/technology/foxconn-to-raise-salaries-for-workers-by-up-to-25.html

Barthes, Roland. *Mythologies*. Trans. Annette Lavers. London: Granada, 1973.

Baudrillard, Jean. *Simulations*. Trans. Paul Foss, Paul Patton, and Philip Beitchman. New York: Semiotext(e), 1983.

Bauman, Zygmunt. "Soil, Blood and Identity." *Sociological Review* 40.4 (1992): 675–701.

Beck, Ulrich. *Risk Society: Towards a New Modernity*. Trans. Mark Ritter. London: Sage, 1992.

Benjamin, Walter. *Illuminations*. Trans. Harry Zohn. New York: Schocken, 1968.

Bennett, Tony. "Putting Policy into Cultural Studies." *Cultural Studies*. Ed. Lawrence Grossberg, Cary Nelson, and Paula Treichler. London: Routledge, 1992. 23–37.

Berlant, Lauren. *Cruel Optimism*. Durham, NC: Duke University Press, 2011.

Berry, Wendell. Letter. *Harper's* Dec. 1988: 7–10.

Best, Geoffrey Francis Andrew. *Mid-Victorian Britain, 1851–1875*. London: Weidenfeld and Nicolson, 1971.

Blaut, James M. *The Colonizer's Model of the World: Geographical Diffusionism and Eurocentric History*. New York: Guilford, 1993.

Borduas, Paul-Émile. "Refus Global." 1948. Accessed March 1, 2017. http://www.dantaylor.com/pages/refusglobal.html

"Bouchard Taylor Commission." *Herouxville Town Charter*. November 1, 2007. Accessed February 22, 2017. http://herouxville-quebec.blogspot.fr/2007/11/bouchard-taylor-commission.html

Bourdieu, Pierre. *Distinction*. Trans. Richard Nice. Cambridge: Harvard University Press, 1987.

Boyd, Danah. "Why Youth ♥ Social Networking Sites: The Role of Networked Publics in Teenage Social Life." *MacArthur Foundation Series on Digital Learning—Youth, Identity, and Digital Media Volume*. Ed. David Buckingham. Cambridge, MA: MIT Press, 2007. 119–142.

Branston, Gill. *Cinema and Cultural Modernity*. Philadelphia: Open University Press, 2000.

Braun, Bruce. "Biopolitics and the Molecularization of Life." *Cultural Geographies* 14.6 (2007): 6–28.

Breaking Bad. Dir. and writ. Vince Gilligan. AMC. 2008–2013.

Bridesmaids. Dir. Paul Feig. Perf. Kristen Wiig and Maya Rudolph. Universal Pictures, 2011.

Briggs, Asa. *Mass Entertainment: The Origins of a Modern Industry*. Adelaide: Griffin, 1960.

Brown, Nicholas. "The Music of the Sphere." *Content Providers of the World Unite!* Ed. Susie O'Brien and Imre Szeman. [Globalization and the Human Condition Working Paper Series.] Hamilton, ON: McMaster University Institute on Globalization and the Human Condition, 2003. 23–28.

Budgen, Sebastian. "A New 'Spirit of Capitalism.'" *New Left Review* 1 (2000): 149–156.

Burke, Peter. "The 'Discovery' of Popular Culture." *People's History and Socialist Theory*. Ed. Raphael Samuel. London: Routledge, 1981. 216–226.

Burkeman, Oliver. "Not So Big, Mac." *Guardian Unlimited*. November 22, 2002. Accessed June 5, 2012. http://www.guardian.co.uk/media/2002/nov/22/marketingandpr.usnews

Buruma, Ian. "Populists Who Speak the (Relative) Truth." *The Globe and Mail* March 12, 2012. Accessed June 2, 2012. http://www.theglobeandmail.com/news/world/americas/us-election/populists-who-speak-the-relative-truth/article2364593

Butler, Judith. *Gender Trouble: Feminism and the Subversion of Identity*. New York: Routledge, 1990.

Butler, Judith. "Extracts from Gender as Performance: An Interview with Judith Butler." Interview by Peter Osborne and Lynne Segal. theory.org.uk. 2003. Accessed November 5, 2011. http://www.theory.org.uk/but-int1.htm

"Canada Post Claims Victory at Nafta over UPS." *CBC News*. June 13, 2007. Accessed March 1, 2017. http://www.bis.org/publ/rpfx16.htm

Carey, James W. *Communication as Culture: Essays on Media and Society*. Boston, MA: Unwin Hyman, 1989.

Carson, Rachel. *Silent Spring*. Greenwich, CT: Fawcett, 1962.

"The Case for War." Editorial. *The Economist* August 1, 2002: 9–10.

Cavett, Dick. "The Swimmers." Rev. of *Contested Waters: A Social History of Swimming Pools in America*, by Jeff Wiltse. Sunday Book Review. *The New York Times* June 3, 2007. Accessed September 16, 2011. http://www.nytimes.com/2007/06/03/books/review/Cavett-t.html?ref=%20review

"Celebrate: TV Commercial (We All Play for Canada)." Canadian Tire. Accessed February 22, 2017. https://www.youtube.com/watch?v=JIOfcvt7m0A

"Central Park." *Citimaps.com*. Guest Service Publications. Accessed February 22, 2017. http://www.citimaps.com/wp-content/uploads/maps/manhattan/centralpark.pdf

Cheng, Pheah, and Bruce Robbins. *Cosmopolitics: Thinking and Feeling beyond the Nation*. Minneapolis: University of Minnesota Press, 1998.

Cho, Nicholas. "The BGA and the Third Wave." CoffeeGeek.com. April 2, 2005. Accessed February 22, 2017. http://coffeegeek.com/opinions/bgafiles/04-02-2005/

CIA Factbook. "Rank Order—Roadways." CIA. Accessed February 22, 2017. https://www.cia.gov/library/Publications/the-world-factbook/rankorder/2085rank.html

Clairmont, Susan. "Road Hockey Sparks Conflict." *Hamilton Spectator* January 4, 2002. Accessed October 29, 2011. http://www.hamiltonspectator.com/clairmont/516812.html

Clark, Laura. "Soaring Youth Crime is Linked to Rising Inner-City Gang Culture." *Mail Online* November 11, 2008. Accessed February 22, 2017. http://www.dailymail.co.uk/news/article-1084639/Soaring-youth-crime-linked-rising-inner-city-gang-culture.html

"The Code." Molson Canadian TV Spots. Accessed February 22, 2017. https://www.youtube.com/watch?v=XAwg71Gg9ek

Cohen, Leah Hager. *Glass, Paper, Beans: Revelations on the Nature and Value of Ordinary Things*. New York: Doubleday, 1997.

Cohen, Stan. *Folk Devils and Moral Panics: The Creation of the Mods and Rockers*. London: MacGibbon and Kee, 1972.

Comaroff, Jean, and John L. Comaroff. "Millennial Capitalism: First Thoughts on a Second Coming." *Public Culture* 12.2 (2000): 291–343.

"Communities Ban Portable Hoops in Street." *USA Today*. June 2, 2003. Accessed February 22, 2017. http://usatoday30.usatoday.com/news/nation/2003-06-02-hoops-ban_x.htm

The Company Men. Dir. John Wells. The Weinstein Company. Battle Mountain Films. 2010.

Connell, Richard W. *Masculinities*. Berkeley: University of California Press, 1995.

Conniff, Richard. "Yes You Were Born to Run." *Men's Health*. May 2008. Accessed February 22, 2017. http://www.menshealth.com/fitness/the-biology-of-running

Connolly, Paul, Alan Smith, and Berni Kelly. *Too Young to Notice? The Cultural and Political Awareness of 3–6 Year Olds in Northern Ireland*. Belfast: Northern Ireland Community Relations Council, 2002.

"Corruption Perceptions Index 2016." Transparency International. Accessed March 1, 2017. http://www.transparency.org/news/feature/corruption_perceptions_index_2016#table

Coupland, Douglas. *Generation X*. New York: St. Martin's Press, 1991.

Crawford, Robert. "Healthism and the Medicalization of Everyday Life." *International Journal of Health Services* 10.3 (1980): 365–388.

Crenshaw, Kimberle. "Mapping the Margins: Intersectionality, Identity Politics, and Violence against Women of Color." *Stanford Law Review* 43.6 (1991): 1241–1299.

Cronon, William. "The Trouble with Wilderness; or, Getting Back to the Wrong Nature." *Uncommon Ground: Rethinking the Human Place in Nature*. Ed. William Cronon. New York: Norton, 1996. 69–90.

Cunningham, Hugh. *Leisure in the Industrial Revolution*. London: Croom Helm, 1980.

Darnton, Robert. *The Forbidden Best-Sellers of Pre-Revolutionary France*. New York: Norton, 1995.

Debord, Guy. *Society of the Spectacle*. Trans. Donald Nicholson Smith. New York: Zone Books, 1995.

The Decline of Western Civilization. Dir. Penelope Spheeris. Spheeris Films, 1981.

DeMott, Benjamin. "Put on a Happy Face: Masking the Differences between Blacks and Whites." *Harper's Magazine Sept.* 1995: 31–38.

Denby, David. "Loners." *The New Yorker* 8 Aug. 2005. Accessed December 5, 2011. http://www.newyorker.com/archive/2005/08/08/050808crci_cinema?currentPage=1

Denning, Michael. "The End of Mass Culture." *Modernity and Mass Culture*. Ed. James Naremore and Patrick Brantlinger. Bloomington: Indiana University Press, 1991. 253–268.

Derrida, Jacques. *On Cosmopolitanism and Forgiveness*. Trans. Mark Dooley and Michael Hughes. New York: Routledge, 2001.

de Zengotita, Thomas. "The Gunfire Dialogues: Notes on the Reality of Virtuality." *Harper's* July 1999: 55–58.

Dhamoon, Rita, and Yasmeen Abu Laban. "Dangerous (Internal) Foreigners and Nation Building: The Case of Canada." *International Political Science Review* 30.2 (2009): 163–183.

Dieter, Richard. "Struck by Lightning: The Continuing Arbitrariness of the Death Penalty Thirty-Five Years after Its Reinstatement in 1976." *Death Penalty Information Center*. July 2011. Accessed November 17, 2012. http://www.deathpenaltyinfo.org/documents/StruckByLightning.pdf

Dobbs, William. "400 Days Later, UNPJ Still Seeking RNC Permit." Interview with Amy Goodman. *Democracy Now* July 14, 2004. Accessed December 14, 2011. http://www.democracynow.org/2004/7/14/400_days_later_ufpj_still_seeking

Dogtown and Z Boys. Dir. Stacy Peralta. Prod. Agi Orsi and Jay Wilson. Sony Pictures Classics, 2002.

Dorfman, Lori and Vincent Schiraldi. "Off-Balance: Youth, Race and Crime in the News." *Building Blocks for Youth* April 2001. Accessed February 22, 2017. http://www.bmsg.org/sites/default/files/bmsg_other_publication_off_balance.pdf

Dretzin, Rachel, and Barak Goodman. "A Talk with the Producers of *The Merchants of Cool*." Interview by Frontline staff. *PBS*. Accessed August 9, 2012. http://www.pbs.org/wgbh/pages/frontline/shows/cool/etc/producers.html

Duany, Andres, Elizabeth Plater-Zyberk, and Jeff Speck. *Suburban Nation: The Rise of Sprawl and the Decline of the American Dream*. New York: Farrar, Straus and Giroux, 2000.

Dube, Rebecca Cook. "Muslims Laud 'Little Mosque on the Prairie.'" *Christian Science Monitor* January 17, 2007. Accessed December 18, 2011. http://www.csmonitor.com/2007/0117/p07s02-woam.html

Dubuc, Alain. "Fear and Ignorance: A Rural Revolt." *Vancouver Sun* March 1, 2007. Accessed August 29, 2012. http://www.canada.com/vancouversun/news/editorial/story.html?id=2d10e22f-1e87-4faf-a6dc-15ffebaa8ab7

du Gay, Paul, ed. *Production of Culture/Cultures of Production*. London: Sage, 1997.

du Gay, Paul, Stuart Hall, Linda Janes, Huch Mackay, and Keith Negus. *Doing Cultural Studies: The Story of the Sony Walkman*. London: Sage, 1997.

Duggan, Lisa. "The New Homonormativity: The Sexual Politics of Neoliberalism." *Materializing Democracy: Toward a Revitalized Cultural Politics*. Ed. Russ Castronovo and Dana D. Nelson. Durham, NC: Duke University Press, 2002: 175–194.

Duhigg, Charles, and David Barboza. "In China, Human Costs Are Built into an iPad." *The New York Times* January 25, 2012. Accessed March 26, 2012. http://www.nytimes.com/2012/01/26/business/ieconomy-apples-ipad-and-the-human-costs-for-workers-in-china.html?_r=2&pagewanted=all%3Fsrc%3Dtp&smid=fb-share

Duncombe, Stephen. *Cultural Resistance Reader*. New York: Verso, 2002.

During, Simon, ed. *The Cultural Studies Reader*. New York: Routledge, 1993.

Edwards, Verity and Michael Sainsbury. "Weak Coffee and Large Debt Stir Starbucks' Trouble in Australia." *The Australian* July 31, 2008. Accessed February 22, 2017. http://www.theaustralian.com.au/archive/news/coffee-debt-stir-starbucks-troubles/story-e6frg6no-1111117065025

El-Gobashy, Mona. "The Praxis of the Egyptian Revolution." *Middle East Research and Information Project* 258 (2011). Accessed January 8, 2012. http://www.merip.org/mer/mer258/praxis-egyptian-revolution

Elias, Norbert. *The Civilizing Process*. Vol. 1. New York: Pantheon, 1982.

Elmore, Lauren. "Raise Your Glass If U R A Firework Who Was Born This Way." *Bitch Magazine*. November 9, 2011. Accessed March 19, 2012. http://bitchmagazine.org/article/raise-your-glass-if-u-r-a-firework-who-was-born-this-way

Engels, Friedrich. *The Condition of the Working Class in England*. Trans. and ed. W.O. Henderson and W.H. Chaloner. Oxford: Basil Blackwell, 1958.

"Environmental Charities 'Laundering' Foreign Funds, Kent Says." *CBC News*. May 1, 2012. Accessed July 19, 2012. http://www.cbc.ca/news/politics/story/2012/05/01/pol-peter-kent-environmental-charities-laundering.html

Espinel, Victoria, Aneesh Chopra, and Howard Schmidt. "Combating Online Piracy while Protecting an Open and Innovative Internet." *The White House Blog*. January 14, 2012. Accessed May 14, 2012. http://www.whitehouse.gov/blog/2012/01/14/obama-administration-responds-we-people-petitions-sopa-and-online-piracy

Eugenides, Jeffrey. *Middlesex*. Toronto: Vintage Canada, 2003.

Faludi, Susan. *Stiffed: The Betrayal of the American Man*. New York: Harper, 2000.

Fanon, Frantz. *Black Skin, White Masks*. Trans. Charles Lam Markmann. New York: Grove, 1967.

Featherstone, Mike. "Body Modification: An Introduction." *Body Modification*. Ed. Mike Featherstone. London: Sage, 2000. 1–14.

Femmephane. "Why I Don't Like Dan Savage's 'It Gets Better' Project as a Response to Bullying." *tempscontretemps*. September 30, 2010. Accessed April 7, 2012. http://tempcontretemps.wordpress.com/2010/09/30/why-i-dont-like-dan-savages-it-gets-better-project-as-a-response-to-bullying

Fight Club. Dir. David Fincher. Prod. Art Linson, Cean Chaffin, and Ross Bell. 20th Century Fox, 1999.

"Fighting for the Right to Play Road Hockey in Hamilton." CBC Sunday Report. *The National* transcripts. Host Alison Smith. January 6, 2002. Accessed April 8, 2012. http://tv.cbc.ca/national/trans/T020106.html

Fiske, John. *Understanding Popular Culture*. London: Routledge, 1989.

Florida, Richard. *The Rise of the Creative Class: And How It's Transforming Work, Leisure and Everyday Life*. New York: Basic Books, 2002.

Forrest Gump. Dir. Robert Zemekis. Prod. Wendy Finerman. MGM Studios, 1997.

Foucault, Michel. *History of Sexuality*. Trans. Robert Hurley. Vol. 1. Harmondsworth, UK: Penguin, 1984.

Frank, Thomas. *The Conquest of Cool*. Chicago: University of Chicago Press, 1997.

Freccero, Carla. *Popular Culture: An Introduction*. New York: New York University Press, 1999.

Fukuyama, Francis. *The End of History and the Last Man*. New York: Free Press, 1992.

"Game On! Road Hockey Charges Dismissed." *CBC News*, Toronto. January 8, 2002. Accessed January 8, 2012. http://toronto.cbc.ca/template/servlet/View?filename=hockey_010802

Gardner, Sue. "English Wikipedia Anti-SOPA Blackout." *Wikimedia Foundation*. January 16, 2012. Accessed February 22, 2017. https://wikimediafoundation.org/wiki/English_Wikipedia_anti-SOPA_blackout

Garnham, Nicholas. "Concepts of Culture: Public Policy and the Cultural Industries." *Cultural Studies* 1.1 (1987): 23–38.

Gellner, Ernest. *Nations and Nationalism*. Oxford: Blackwell, 1983.

Gendron, Bernie. "Theodor Adorno Meets the Cadillacs." *Studies in Entertainment*. Ed. Tania Modleski. Bloomington: Indiana University Press, 1986. 18–36.

Ghonim, Wael. *Revolution 2.0: The Power of the People Is Greater Than the People in Power: A Memoir*. Boston, MA: Houghton Mifflin Harcourt, 2012.

Ghost World. Dir. Terry Zwigoff. Prod. Mr. Mudd. MGM/UA, 2001.

Gill, Rosalind. "From Sexual Objectification to Sexual Subjectification: The Resexualisation of Women's Bodies in the Media." *MRzine*. Monthly Review. May 23, 2009. Accessed September 28, 2011. http://mrzine.monthlyreview.org/2009/gill230509.html

Gill, Rosalind. "Postfeminist Media Culture: Elements of a Sensibility." *European Journal of Cultural Studies* 10.2 (2007): 147–166.

Gilroy, Paul. *The Black Atlantic: Modernity and Double Consciousness*. London: Verso, 1993.

Gilroy, Paul. *Small Acts: Thoughts on the Politics of Black Cultures*. London: Serpent's Tale, 1993.

Giroux, Henry. *Disturbing Pleasures: Learning Popular Culture*. New York: Routledge, 1994.

Giroux, Henry. *America's Education Deficit and the War on Youth*. New York: Monthly Review Press, 2013.

Giroux, Susan Searls. "The Lessons of Law and Order: What Canadians Can Learn from Failed US Crime Policy." *truthout*. October 5, 2011. Accessed February 23, 2012. http://truth-out.org/news/item/3750:the-lessons-of-law-and-order-what-canadians-can-learn-from-failed-us-crime-policy

Goggin, Gerard. *Global Mobile Media*. New York: Routledge, 2011.

Goodall, Jane. "An Order of Pure Decision: Un-Natural Selection in the Work of Stelarc and Orlan." *Body Modification*. Ed. Mike Featherstone. London: Sage, 2000. 149–170.

Google. "Ten Things We Know to Be True." *Google*. Accessed May 19, 2012. http://www.google.ca/about/company/philosophy

Government of Canada home page. Accessed June 12, 2012. http://www.canada.gc.ca/home.html

Government of Canada. "Discover Canada: The Rights and Responsibilities of Citizenship." Government of Canada. 2012. Accessed May 28, 2012. http://www.cic.gc.ca/english/resources/-publications/discover/index.asp

Grierson, Bruce. "Headrush." *Adbusters* 25 (Spring 1999): 23–29.

Grizzly Man. Dir. Werner Herzog. Prod. Erik Nelson. Lionsgate, 2005.

Grossberg, Lawrence, Ellen Wartella, and D. Charles Whitney. *Media Making: Mass Media in a Popular Culture.* Thousand Oaks, CA: Sage, 1998.

Grossman, David. *On Killing: The Psychological Cost of Learning to Kill in War and Society.* New York: Little, Brown, 1998.

Grosz, Elizabeth. *Volatile Bodies.* Bloomington: Indiana University Press, 1994.

Hall, Ann, Trevor Slack, Garry Smith, and David Whitson. *Sport in Canadian Society.* Toronto: McClelland & Stewart, 1991.

Hall, Stuart. "Cultural Identity and Diaspora." *Identity, Community, Culture, Difference.* Ed. Jonathan Rutherford. London: Lawrence and Wishart, 1990. 222–237.

Hall, Stuart. "Cultural Studies and Its Theoretical Legacies." *Cultural Studies.* Ed. Lawrence Grossberg, Cary Nelson, and Paula Treichler. London: Routledge, 1992. 277–294.

Hall, Stuart. "Cultural Studies and the Centre: Some Problematics and Problems." *Culture, Media, Language.* Ed. Stuart Hall, Dorothy Hobson, Andrew Lowe, and Paul Willis. London: Hutchinson, 1980. 15–47.

Hall, Stuart. "Encoding, Decoding." *The Cultural Studies Reader.* Ed. Simon During. London: Routledge, 1993. 90–103.

Hall, Stuart. "Gramsci's Relevance for the Study of Race and Ethnicity." *Journal of Communication Inquiry* 10.2 (1986): 5–27.

Hall, Stuart. "Notes on Deconstructing the Popular." *People's History and Socialist Theory.* Ed. Raphael Samuel. London: Routledge & Kegan Paul, 1981. 227–240.

Hall, Stuart, Chas Critcher, Tony Jefferson, John Clarke, and Brian Roberts. *Policing the Crisis: Mugging, the State, and Law and Order.* New York: Holmes & Meier, 1978.

Harris, Tamara Winfrey. "Precious Mettle: The Truth Behind the 'Strong Black Woman' Stereotype." *Bitch Magazine* May 13, 2014. Accessed February 22, 2017. https://bitchmedia.org/article/precious-mettle-myth-strong-black-woman

Heath, Joseph, and Andrew Potter. *The Rebel Sell: Why the Culture Can't Be Jammed.* Toronto: HarperCollins, 2004.

Hebdige, Dick. *Hiding in the Light: On Images and Things.* New York: Routledge, 1994.

Hebdige, Dick. *Subculture: The Meaning of Style.* New York: Routledge, 1981.

"Hérouxville Town Charter." March 24, 2007. Accessed June 22, 2012. http://herouxville-quebec.blogspot.com/2007/03/about-beautiful-herouxville-quebec.html

Herwig, Malte. "Google's Total Library: Putting the World's Books on the Web." *Spiegel Online.* March 28, 2007. Accessed October 11, 2011. http://www.spiegel.de/international/-business/0,1518,473529,00.html

Hirschberg, Lynn. "The Thinking inside the Box." *The New York Times Magazine* November 3, 2002: 67–71.

Hobsbawm, Eric. *The Age of Extremes: A History of the World, 1914–1991.* New York: Vintage, 1996.

Hobsbawm, Eric. *Industry and Empire: An Economic History of Britain Since 1750.* London: Weidenfeld and Nicolson, 1968.

Hochschild, Arlie Russell. *The Time Bind: When Work Becomes Home and Home Becomes Work.* New York: Holt, 2001.

"Hockey Canada Reaches Out to Immigrant Youth." CBC News. February 16, 2011. Accessed February 22, 2017. http://www.cbc.ca/news/canada/ottawa/hockey-canada-reaches-out-to-immigrant-youth-1.1112328

Hoffman, Jascha. "Data: Comparative Literature." *The New York Times.* April 15, 2007. Accessed June 11, 2012. http://select.nytimes.com/search/restricted/article?res=F50C12F93D5B0C768DDDAD0894DF404482

hooks, bell. "No Love in the Wild." *NewBlackMan (in Exile).* September 5, 2012. Accessed February 22, 2017. http://www.newblackmaninexile.net/2012/09/bell-hooks-no-love-in-wild.html

Horkheimer, Max, and Theodor Adorno. *Dialectic of Enlightenment.* New York: Continuum, 1971.

Hough, Mike and Julian V. Roberts. *Youth Crime and Youth Justice: Public Opinion in England and Wales.* Bristol, UK: Policy Press, 2004.

Huizen, Jennifer. "Global Trade 101: How NAFTA's Chapter 11 Overrides Environmental Laws." *Mongabay.* November 8, 2016. Accessed March 1, 2017. https://news.mongabay.com/2016/11/global-trade-101-how-naftas-chapter-11-overrides-environmental-laws/

Hunter, Latham. "The Celluloid Cubicle: Regressive Constructions of Masculinity in 1990s Office Movies." *American Culture* 26.2 (2003): 71–86.

Huntington, Samuel. *The Clash of Civilizations and the Remaking of World Order.* New York: Simon and Schuster, 1998.

Hutson, Matthew. "The Power of the Hoodie-Wearing CEO." *The New Yorker.* December 17, 2013.

"I Am...an Asshole?" www.egulphy.com. April 16, 2000. Accessed March 29, 2012. http://www.angelfire.com/rock/cpar/p2k/2kapr16paperless.html

"I Am Canadian: The Rant." SHNKArchives. Accessed March 1, 2017. https://www.youtube.com/watch?v=WMxGVfk09lU

Ibbitson, John. "Harris Vows to Rid Streets of Pushy Beggars, Squeegees." *National Post* 20 May 1999: A1, A8.

"Internet Users by Country (2015)." Internet Live Stats. Accessed March 1, 2017. http://www.internetlivestats.com/internet-users-by-country/2015/Into *the Abyss.* Dir. Werner Herzog. Sundance Selects, 2011.

Irigaray, Luce. *This Sex Which Is Not One.* Trans. Catherine Porter with Carolyn Burke. Ithaca, NY: Cornell University Press, 1985.

Jafri, Beenash. "National Identity, Transnational Whiteness and the Canadian Citizenship Guide." *Critical Race and Whiteness Studies* 8 (2012): 1–15. Accessed August 19, 2012. http://acrawsa.org.au/files/ejournalfiles/179CRWS201281Jafri.pdf

Jameson, Fredric. *Postmodernism, or the Cultural Logic of Late Capitalism.* Durham, NC: Duke University Press, 1991.

Jeanneney, Jean-Noël. *Google and the Myth of Universal Knowledge: A View from Europe.* Trans. Teresa Lavender Fagan. Chicago: University of Chicago Press, 2007.

Jenkins, Henry. "Professor Jenkins Goes to Washington." *Harper's* July 1999: 19–23.

Jenkins, Simon. *Mission Accomplished: The Crisis of International Intervention.* London: I.B. Taurus, 2015.

Jhally, Sut. *The Codes of Advertising: Fetishism and the Political Economy of Meaning in the Consumer Economy.* New York: St. Martin's Press, 1987.

Johnson, Reed. "Oscars 2012: Despite Halle and Denzel, Gold Mostly Eludes Non-Whites." *LA Times* February 24, 2012. Accessed May 13, 2012. http://latimesblogs.latimes.com/movies/2012/02/oscars-2012-despite-hattie-halle-and-denzel-few-non-white-actors-win-gold.html

Jones, Gareth Stedman. "Working-Class Culture and Working-Class Politics in London, 1870–1900: Notes on the Remaking of a Working Class." *Journal of Social History* 7.4 (1974): 460–508.

Kanji, Nazneen, and Kalyani Menon-Sen. "What Does the Feminisation of Labour Mean for Sustainable Livelihoods?" *World Summit on Sustainable Development.* August 2001. Accessed February 22, 2017. http://www.iatp.org/files/What_does_the_Feminisation_of_Labour_Mean_for_.htm

Kant, Immanuel. *Toward Perpetual Peace and Other Writings on Politics, Peace, and History.* Trans. David L. Colclasure. Ed. Pauline Kleingeld. New Haven, CT: Yale University Press, 2006.

Katz, Jon. "The Digital Citizen." *Wired.* December 1, 1997. Accessed February 22, 2017. https://www.wired.com/1997/12/netizen-29/

Keay, Douglas. "Margaret Thatcher Interview, 'Aids, education and the year 2000!'" *Woman's Own.* October 31, 1987. Accessed March 1, 2017. http://www.margaretthatcher.org/document/106689

Kelly, David. "O.C.'s Mix of Cultures Yields Co-operation, Tensions." *LA Times.* June 24, 2007. Posted on *American Renaissance.* Accessed November 6, 2011. http://www.amren.com/mtnews/archives/2007/06/ocs_mix_of_cult.php

Klesse, Christian. "'Modern Primitivism': Non-Mainstream Body Modification and Racialized Representation." *Body & Society* 5.2/3 (1999): 16–38.

Klosterman, Chuck. "The Ratt Trap." *The New York Times Magazine.* 29 Dec. 2002: 24–25.

Kohn, Margaret. *Brave New Neighborhoods: The Privatization of Public Space.* New York: Routledge, 2004.

Kozol, Jonathan. *The Shame of the Nation: The Restoration of Apartheid Schooling in America.* New York: Broadway, 2006.

Krugman, Paul. "The Centrist Cop-Out." *The New York Times.* July 28, 2011. Accessed November 1, 2011. http://www.nytimes.com/2011/07/29/opinion/krugman-the-centrist-cop-out.html?_r=2&src=me&ref=general

Krugman, Paul. *Conscience of a Liberal.* New York: Norton, 2007.

Krugman, Paul. "Four Fiscal Phonies." *The New York Times.* March 1, 2012. Accessed July 29, 2012. http://www.nytimes.com/2012/03/02/opinion/krugman-four-fiscal-phonies.html?src=me&ref=general

Kurzweil, Ray. *The Singularity Is Near.* New York: Penguin, 2006.

Lacayo, Richard. "Violent Reaction: Bob Dole's Broadside against Sex and Violence in Popular Culture Sets off a Furious Debate about Responsibility." *Time.* June 12, 1995. Accessed February 22, 2017. http://content.time.com/time/magazine/article/0,9171,983035,00.html

Larner, Wendy. "Spatial Imaginaries: Economic Globalization and the War on Terror." *Risk and the War on Terror.* Ed. Louise Amoore and Marieke de Goede. New York: Routledge, 2008. 41–56.

Leapman, Ben. "Violent Youth Crime Up a Third." *The Telegraph.* January 20, 2008. Accessed February 22, 2017. http://www.telegraph.co.uk/news/uknews/1576076/Violent-youth-crime-up-a-third.html

Leavis, F.R., and Denys Thompson. *Culture and Environment.* Westport, CT: Greenwood, 1977.

Lefebvre, Henri. *Introduction to Modernity.* Trans. John Moore. New York: Verso, 1995.

Lefebvre, Henri. "Towards a Leftist Cultural Politics." *Marxism and the Interpretation of Culture.* Ed. Cary Nelson and Lawrence Grossberg. Chicago: University of Illinois Press, 1998: 75–88.

Lessing, Lawrence. *The Future of Ideas: The Fate of the Commons in a Connected World.* New York: Vintage, 2001.

Levine, Judith. *Not Buying It: My Year without Shopping.* New York: Atria, 2007.

Levine, Lawrence W. *Highbrow/Lowbrow: The Emergence of Cultural Hierarchy in America.* Cambridge, MA: Harvard University Press, 1988.

Lewis, Bernard. *What Went Wrong? Western Impact and Middle Eastern Response.* Oxford: Oxford University Press, 2002.

Life and Debt. Dir. Stephanie Black. Tuff Gong Pictures, 2003.

"Little Mosque." *Little Mosque on the Prairie.* CBC. Toronto. January 9, 2007.

"Local Ad." *The Office.* NBC. Global, Toronto. October 25, 2007.

Longman, Jere. "Athletics: Disabled Runner Makes Case for Competing in Olympics." *International Herald-Tribune.* May 14, 2007. Accessed February 22, 2017. http://www.nytimes.com/2007/05/14/sports/14iht-track.4.5704964.html

Lowenstein, Roger. "Occupy Wall Street: It's Not a Hippie Thing." *Business Week.* October 27, 2011. Accessed December 6, 2011. http://www.businessweek.com/magazine/occupy-wall-street-its-not-a-hippie-thing-10272011.html

Lury, Celia. *Consumer Culture.* New Brunswick, NJ: Rutgers University Press, 1996.

Lütticken, Sven. "The Art of Theft." *New Left Review* 13 (2002): 89–104.

Lyotard, Jean-François. *The Postmodern Condition: A Report on Knowledge.* Minneapolis: University of Minnesota Press, 1984.

MacEachern, Alan. "Ye Old Season's Greetings." *The Globe and Mail.* December 31, 2007. Accessed February 22, 2017. http://www.theglobeandmail.com/opinion/letters/ye-olde-seasons-greetings/article964688/

MacFarquhar, Neil. "Sitcom's Dubious Premise: Being Muslim over Here." *The New York Times.* December 7, 2006. Accessed February 7, 2012. http://www.nytimes.com/2006/12/07/arts/television/07mosq.html

MacGregor, Robert M. "I Am Canadian: National Identity in Beer Commercials." *Journal of Popular Culture* 37.2 (2003): 276–286.

MacGregor, Roy. "Here's the Skinny on Shinny: It's Starting to Pick Up Again, But Shame about Those Rinks." *The Globe and Mail.* January 2, 2003: A2.

Maher, Neil. "Neil Maher on Shooting the Moon." *Environmental History* 9.3 (2004).

Malcomson, Robert W. *Popular Recreations in English Society 1700–1850.* Cambridge: Cambridge University Press, 1973.

Marcus, Greil. *Lipstick Traces: A Secret History of the 20th Century.* Cambridge, MA: Harvard University Press, 1989.

Marlow, Iain. "Google, Facebook Get Personal by Revamping Their Advertising Tactics." *The Globe and Mail.* March 1, 2012: B1, B6.

Martin, Emily. "Body Narratives, Body Boundaries." *Cultural Studies.* Eds. Lawrence Grossberg, Cary Nelson, and Paula Treichler. New York: Routledge, 1992. 409–423.

Marx, Karl. "Excerpt from the Preface to *A Contribution to a Critique of Political Economy.*" *A Critical and Cultural Theory Reader.* Ed. Anthony Easthope and Kate McGowan. Toronto: University of Toronto Press, 1992. 45–46.

Marx, Karl, and Friedrich Engels. *The Communist Manifesto: A Modern Edition.* 1888. New York: Verso, 1998.

Mathieu, Emily. "Pair Jailed 10 Years in Homeless Beating Death." *Toronto Star.* May 2, 2008. Accessed July 22, 2012. http://www.thestar.com/News/GTA/article/420621

Mattelart, Armand. *Networking the World, 1794–2000.* Trans. Liz Carey-Libbrecht and James A. Cohen. Minneapolis: University of Minnesota Press, 2000.

Mauss, Marcel. "Techniques of the Body." *Incorporations*. Ed. Jonathan Crary and Sanford Kwinter. New York: Zone, 1992. 455–477.

McArthur, Keith. "Is Google 'Evil'? Not If You're Its 'Partner.'" *The Globe and Mail*. November 22, 2006. Accessed December 28, 2011. http://www.theglobeandmail.com/report-on-business/is-google-evil-not-if-youre-its-partner/article4113018/

McHugh, Josh. "Google vs. Evil." *Wired* 11.1 (2003). Accessed January 13, 2012. http://www.wired.com/wired/archive/11.01/google_pr.html

McKay, George. *Senseless Acts of Beauty: Cultures of Resistance since the Sixties*. New York: Verso, 1996.

McLuhan, Marshall. *Understanding Media: The Extensions of Man*. New York: McGraw-Hill, 1964.

McRobbie, Angela. *Postmodernism and Popular Culture*. London: Routledge, 1994.

McRobbie, Angela. "Clubs to Companies: Notes on the Decline of Political Culture in Speeded Up Creative Worlds." *Cultural Studies* 16.4 (2002): 516–531.

Media Matters. "Study: The Press and the Pipeline." Accessed September 9, 2012. http://mediamatters.org/research/201201260005

Mercer, Kobena. "Welcome to the Jungle: Identity and Diversity in Postmodern Politics." *Identity: Community, Culture, Difference*. Ed. Jonathan Rutherford. London: Lawrence and Wishart, 1990. 43–71.

Merchants of Cool, The. Dir. Barak Goodman. Prod. Barak Goodman and Rachel Dretzin. Frontline/PBS, 2001.

Merrifield, Andy. *Metromarxism: A Marxist Tale of the City*. New York: Routledge, 2002.

Metcalfe, Alan. *Canada Learns to Play: The Emergence of Organized Sport, 1807–1914*. Toronto: McClelland & Stewart, 1987.

Mickey Mouse Monopoly: Disney, Childhood and Corporate Power. Dir. Miguel Picker. Prod. Chyng Sun. Artmedia, 2001.

Mills, George. "Word-Beater Spain Set to Fight Street Football with Fines." *The Local*. December 2, 2013. http://www.thelocal.es/20131202/spain-set-to-fight-street-football-with-fines

mitch@habs. "Road Hockey Goes to Court!" *Hockey Talk!* Gameworn.net. January 7, 2002.

Modern Times. Dir. Charles Chaplin. Charles Chaplin Productions, 1936.

Morozov, Evgeny. "The Death of the Cyberflâneur." *New York Times*, February 5, 2012. Accessed March 1, 2017. www.nytimes.com/2012/02/05/opinion/sunday/the-death-of-the-cyberflaneur.html

Morozov, Evgeny. "Picking a Fight with Clay Shirky." *Foreign Policy*. January 15, 2011. Accessed February 22, 2017. http://foreignpolicy.com/2011/01/15/picking-a-fight-with-clay-shirky/

Mulvey, Laura. "Visual Pleasure and Narrative Cinema." *A Cultural Studies Reader*. Ed. Jessica Munns and Gita Rajan. New York: Longman, 1995. 322–332.

Murphy, Meghan. "We're Sluts, Not Feminists. Wherein My Relationship with Slutwalk Gets Rocky." www.rabble.ca. May 16, 2011. Accessed October 29, 2011. http://rabble.ca/news/2011/05/we%E2%80%99re-sluts-not-feminists-wherein-my-relationship-slutwalk-gets-rocky

Murphy, Shaunna. "Could the 'Every Single Word Spoken' Project Make the Next 'Harry Potter' More Diverse?" MTV News. August 28, 2015. Accessed February 22, 2017. http://www.mtv.com/news/2252921/every-word-spoken-person-of-color/

Nachbar, Jack, and Kevin Lause. "Getting to Know Us: An Introduction to the Study of Popular Culture: What Is This Stuff That Dreams Are Made Of?" *Popular Culture: An Introductory Text*. Ed. Jack Nachbar and Kevin Lause. Bowling Green, OH: Bowling Green State University Popular Press, 1992. 1–36.

Naremore, James, and Patrick Brantlinger, eds. *Modernity and Mass Culture*. Bloomington: Indiana University Press, 1991.

Negus, Keith. "The Production of Culture." *Production of Culture/Cultures of Production*. Ed. Paul du Gay. London: Sage/Open University, 1997. 67–118.

Nguyen, Mimi. "The Hoodie as Sign, Screen, Expectation and Force." *Signs* 40.4 (2015): 791–816.

NM Incite. "Buzz in the Blogosphere: Millions More Bloggers and Blog Readers." March 8, 2012. Accessed April 28, 2012. http://www.nielsen.com/us/en/insights/news/2012/buzz-in-the-blogosphere-millions-more-bloggers-and-blog-readers.html

Norton, Michael I., and Dan Ariely. "Building a Better America—One Wealth Quintile at a Time." *Perspectives on Psychological Science* 6.1 (2011): 9–12.

The O.C. Fox. E!, Toronto. Pilot. August 5, 2003.

Office Space. Dir Mike Judge. Prod. Daniel Rappaport and Michael Rotenberg. 20th Century Fox, 1999. Film.

Ohmann, Richard. *Selling Culture: Magazines, Markets and Class*. New York: Verso, 1996.

O'Sullivan, Tim, John Hartley, Danny Saunders, Martin Montgomery, and John Fiske. *Key Concepts in Communication and Cultural Studies*. London: Routledge, 1994.

Over the Hedge. Dir. Tim Johnson and Karey Kirkpatrick. Prod. Bonnie Arnold. DreamWorks, 2006.

Packard, Vance. *The Hidden Persuaders*. London: Longmans, Green, 1957.

Page, Don. "A View from the South." *Coast to Coast* 5.3 (1999).

Palahniuk, Chuck. *Fight Club*. New York: W. W. Norton, 1996.

Palmer, Maija. "Google Retreats in EU Fight over Storage of Personal Search Data." *Financial Times* (Europe) June 13, 2007: 1.

Papper, Bob. "Number of Minority Journalists Down in 2009; Story Mixed for Female Journalists." Radio-Television News Directors Association and Foundation Newsroom Diversity Project, 2009.

Pear, Robert. "Top Earners Doubled Share of Nation's Income, Study Finds." *The New York Times*. October 25, 2011. Accessed December 2, 2011. http://www.nytimes.com/2011/10/26/us/politics/top-earners-doubled-share-of-nations-income-cbo-says.html?_r=2

Peters, Jeremy W. "Coming Out: When Love Dares Speak, and Nobody Listens." *The New York Times*. May 21, 2010: n.p.

Pinkard, Terry. *Hegel: A Biography*. Cambridge: Cambridge University Press, 2000.

Pocahontas. Dir. Mike Gabriel and Eric Goldberg. Prod. James Pentecost. Burbank, CA: Walt Disney Films, 1995.

"Police Reported Crime Statistics in Canada, 2012." Juristat. Statistics Canada. Accessed July 25, 2013. http://www.statcan.gc.ca/pub/85-002-x/2013001/article/11854-eng.htm?fpv=269303#a7

Prensky, Marc. "Digital Natives, Digital Immigrants." *On the Horizon* 9.5 (2001). Accessed February 22, 2012. http://www.marcprensky.com/writing/Prensky%20-%20Digital%20Natives,%20Digital%20Immigrants%20-%20Part1.pdf

Puar, Jasbir. "In the Wake of It Gets Better." *The Guardian*. November 16, 2010. Accessed October 17, 2011. http://www.guardian.co.uk/commentisfree/cifamerica/2010/nov/16/wake-it-gets-better-campaign?INTCMP=SRCH

"Public Perception of Crime and Justice in Canada: A Review of Opinion Polls." Department of Justice. November 11, 2001. Accessed February 22, 2017. http://www.justice.gc.ca/eng/rp-pr/csj-sjc/crime/rr01_1/index.html

Putnam, Robert D. *Bowling Alone: The Collapse and Revival of American Community.* New York: Simon and Schuster, 2001.

"Quebec Town Forbids Stoning and Throwing Acid in People's Faces." *Progressive Muslima News.* January 30, 2007. Accessed February 18, 2012. http://proggiemuslima.wordpress. com/2007/01/30/quebec-town-forbids-stoning-and-throwing-acid-in-peoples-faces

QuietRiotGirl. "It Gets Better: What Does? For Whom?" *QuietRiotGirl.* October 6, 2010. Accessed January 19, 2012. http://quietgirlriot.wordpress.com/2010/10/06/it-gets-better-what-does-for-whom

Rak, Julie. "The Digital Queer: Weblogs and Internet Identity." *Biography* 28.1 (2005): 166–182.

Rankine, Claudia. "Blackness as the Second Person." Interviewed by Meara Sharma. *Guernica.* November 17, 2014. Accessed February 20, 2017. https://www.guernicamag. com/blackness-as-the-second-person/

Reich, Robert. *Aftershock: The Next Economy and America's Future.* New York: Knopf, 2010.

Reynolds, Joshua. *Discourses on Art.* 1797. Ed. Robert Wark. New Haven, CT: Yale University Press, 1975.

"Rising Crime Blamed on Youth Violence, Gangs." NBC News. May 15, 2007. Accessed February 22, 2017. http://www.nbcnews.com/id/18671013/ns/us_news-crime_and_courts/t/rising-crime-blamed-youth-violence-gangs/#.U86Ql1ZOjq0

Roberts, Greg. "Violent Youth Crime on the Rise." *The Australian.* July 19, 2008.

Roberts, Julian V. "Public Opinion and Youth Justice." *Crime and Justice* 31 (2004): 495–542.

Robbins, Richard. *Global Problems and the Culture of Capitalism.* 2nd ed. Boston: Allyn and Bacon, 2002.

Robertson, Roland. *Globalization: Social Theory and Global Culture.* London: Sage, 1992.

Robinson, Laura. "Girls Should Take to the Streets." *The Globe and Mail.* January 11, 2002: A15.

Rosenberg, Matt. "Berlin Conference of 1884–1885 to Divide Africa." October 20, 2016. Accessed February 22, 2017. http://geography.about.com/library/weekly/aa021601a.htm

Ross, Andrew. *No Collar: The Humane Workplace and Its Hidden Costs.* Philadelphia, PA: Temple UP, 2004.

Rutherford, Jonathan. "Identity and the Cultural Politics of Difference." *Identity: Community, Culture, Difference.* Ed. Jonathan Rutherford. London: Lawrence and Wishart, 1990. 9–27.

Rutherford, Fiona. "This Tumblr is Exposing Hollywood's Problem with People of Color." *Buzzfeed.* July 8, 2015. Accessed February 22, 2017. http://www.buzzfeed.com/fionarutherford/a-man-is-editing-hollywood-movies-so-only-people-of-colour-s#. dsaz2pPAp

Said, Edward. *Culture and Imperialism.* London: Chatto and Windus, 1993.

Said, Edward. *Orientalism.* New York: Vintage, 1979.

Saletan, William. "The Beam in Your Eye: If Steroids Is Cheating, Why Isn't LASIK?" *Slate.* April 18, 2005. Accessed January 26, 2012. http://www.slate.com/id/2116858/

Schivelbusch, Wolfgang. *Tastes of Paradise: A Social History of Spices, Stimulants, and Intoxicants.* New York: Pantheon, 1992.

Schneller, Johanna. "Only Money Breaks the Colour Barrier." *The Globe and Mail.* December 21, 2001: R3.

Schor, Juliet. "Towards a New Politics of Consumption." *The Consumer Society Reader.* Ed. Juliet B. Schor and Douglas Holt. New York: New Press, 2000. 446–462.

Scott, Paul. "You're Sitting on a Time Bomb." *Men's Health.* April 24, 2015. Accessed February 22, 2017. http://www.menshealth.com/health/back-pain-and-spinal-health

Screen Actors Guild. "2007 & 2008 Casting Data Reports." Accessed March 19, 2012. http://www.sagaftra.org/files/sag/documents/2007-2008_CastingDataReports.pdf

Seabrook, John. *Nobrow: The Culture of Marketing, the Marketing of Culture*. New York: Vintage, 2001.

Seabrook, John. "Streaming Dreams: YouTube Turns Pro." *The New Yorker*. January 16, 2012. Accessed April 29, 2012. http://www.newyorker.com/reporting/2012/01/16/120116fa_fact_seabrook

Sedgwick, Eve Kosofsky. *Tendencies*. Durham, NC: Duke University Press, 1993.

Shapiro, Joseph P. *No Pity: People with Disabilities Forging a New Civil Rights Movement*. New York: Three Rivers Press, 1994.

Sheard, Sally. "Profit Is a Dirty Word: The Development of Public Baths and Wash-Houses in Britain 1847–1915." *Social History of Medicine* 13.1 (2001): 63–86.

Shears, Mary Deanne. "Our Duty: Examine All Issues." *Toronto Star*. October 19, 2002. Accessed November 24, 2011. http://www.thestar.com/NASApp/cs/ContentServer?pagename=thestar/Layout/Article_Type1&c=Article&cid=1026146584089&call_page=TS_RaceAndCrime&call_pageid=1034935301156&call_pagepath=GTA/Race_and_Crime&col=1034935301113

Shilling, Chris. "The Body and Difference." *Identity and Difference*. Ed. Kathryn Woodward. London: Sage, 1997. 63–120.

Shirky, Clay. "The Political Power of Social Media." *Foreign Affairs* 90.1 (2011): 28–41.

Shohat, Ella, and Robert Stam. *Unthinking Eurocentrism: Multiculturalism and the Media*. London: Routledge, 1994.

Simons, Penelope. "Human Security, Corporate Accountability and the Regulation of Trade and Investment." Canadian Consortium on Human Security, 2004. 85–86.

Skeie, Trish R. "Norway and Coffee." *Flamekeeper*. Newsletter of the Roasters Guild. Spring 2003. Accessed February 22, 2017. https://www.timwendelboe.no/for-press

Skiba, Russell. "Zero Tolerance, Zero Evidence: An Analysis of School Disciplinary Practice." Policy Research Report #SRS2. Indiana Education Policy Center. August 2000. Accessed February 22, 2017. http://youthjusticenc.org/download/education-justice/suspension-and-expulsion/Zero%20Tolerance,%20Zero%20Evidence%20-%20An%20Analysis%20of%20School%20Disciplinary%20Practice(2).pdf

Smith, Jocelyn. "When Neoliberalism and Radical Feminism Collide: Reclaiming Feminist Discourse and Sexual Choice Online." 2011. Unpublished paper.

Soar, Daniel. "It Knows." *London Review of Books* 6 Oct. 2011: 3, 5–6.

Solnit, Rebecca. *River of Shadows: Eadweard Muybridge and the Technological Wild West*. New York: Penguin, 2004.

Spirn, Anne Whiston. "Constructing Nature: The Legacy of Frederick Law Olmstead." *Uncommon Ground: Rethinking the Human Place in Nature*. Ed. William Cronon. New York: Norton, 1996. 91–113.

Stallabrass, Julian. "Digital Commons." *New Left Review* 15 (2002): 141–146.

Statistics Canada. "National Balance Sheet Accounts." Third quarter 2011. Accessed June 27, 2012. http://www.statcan.gc.ca/daily-quotidien/111213/dq111213a-eng.htm

Stevenson, Seth. "I'd Like to Buy the World a Shelf-Stable Children's Lactic Drink." *The New York Times Magazine* March 10, 2002: 38–43.

"Study Reveals Continued Lack of Characters with Disabilities on Television." SAG.AFTRA. September 27, 2011. Accessed February 22, 2017. http://www.sagaftra.org/study-reveals-continued-lack-characters-disabilities-television?page=0

Suskind, Ron. "Faith, Certainty and the Presidency of George W. Bush." *New York Times Magazine.* October 17, 2004. Accessed February 22, 2017. http://www.nytimes.com/2004/10/17/magazine/17BUSH.html?scp=3&sq=suskind&st=cse

Symons, Emma-Kate. "Aussie Flat White Is the Toast of the Trendy Coffee Set in London and Berlin." *The Australian* February 7, 2011. Accessed September 14, 2016. http://www.theaustralian.com.au/life/food-wine/aussie-flat-white-is-the-toast-of-the-trendy-coffee-set-in-london-and-berlin/story-e6frg8jo-1226001046539

Szatmary, David P. *Rockin' in Time: A Social History of Rock and Roll.* Upper Saddle River, NJ: Prentice Hall, 2000.

Talaga, Tanya. "UN to Investigate Missing Aboriginal Women." *Toronto Star.* January 6, 2012. AccessedApril18,2012.http://www.thestar.com/news/insight/article/1111907--un-to-investigate-missing-aboriginal-women

Terkel, Amanda. "Video Games Targeted by Senate in Wake of Sandy Hook Shooting." *Huffington Post.* December 19, 2012. Accessed February 22, 2017. http://www.huffingtonpost.com/2012/12/19/video-games-sandy-hook_n_2330741.html

Thompson, E.P. *The Making of the English Working Class.* Harmondsworth, UK: Penguin, 1963.

Thomson, Rosemary Garland. *Extraordinary Bodies: Figuring Physical Disability in American Culture and Literature.* New York: Columbia University Press, 1997.

Thornton, Sarah. *Club Cultures: Music, Media and Subcultural Capital.* Cambridge, UK: Polity, 1995.

Tomlinson, John. *Cultural Imperialism: A Critical Introduction.* Baltimore: Johns Hopkins University Press, 1991.

Tomlinson, John. *Globalization and Culture.* Chicago: University of Chicago Press, 1999.

Transamerica. Dir. Duncan Tucker. Prod. William H. Macy. Perf. Felicity Huffman. The Weinstein Company, IFC Films, 2005.

Tsoukalas, Spyridoula, and Paul Roberts. "*Legal Aid Eligibility and Coverage in Canada.*" Legal Aid Research Series. Ottawa: Department of Justice Canada, 2003. Accessed February 22, 2017. http://www.justice.gc.ca/eng/rp-pr/csj-sjc/jsp-sjp/rr03_la5-rr03_aj5/rr03_la5.pdf

Turkle, Sherry. *Alone Together: Why We Expect More from Technology and Less from Each Other.* New York: Basic Books, 2011.

"TV Guide Most Popular Shows." *TV Guide.* Accessed September 30, 2011. http://www.tvguide.com/top-tv-shows

Twitchell, James. *AdCult USA: The Triumph of Advertising in American Culture.* New York: Columbia University Press, 1996.

Tzara, Tristan. "Dada Manifesto 1918." *The Dada Painters and Poets.* Ed. Robert Motherwell. New York: G. Wittenborn, 1951.

UNESCO. "UNESCO Universal Declaration on Cultural Diversity." Accessed January 19, 2012. http://unesdoc.unesco.org/images/0012/001271/127160m.pdf

UNHCR United Nations High Commission for Refugees. "Internally Displaced People Figures." Accessed February 22, 2017. http://www.unhcr.org/internally-displaced-people.html

United for Peace and Justice. "UFPJ Announces Full March Route for August 29th." August 26, 2004. Accessed February 22, 2017. http://lists.peacelink.it/pace/msg08142.html

Vaidhyanathan, Siva. *The Googlization of Everything (and Why We Should Worry).* Berkeley: University of California Press, 2011.

Valenzuela, Sebastiàn, Namsu Park, and Kerk F. Kee. "Is There Social Capital in a Social Network Site? Facebook Use and College Students' Life Satisfaction, Trust and Participation." *Journal of Computer-Mediated Communication* 14.4 (July 2009): 875–901.

Vaneigem, Raoul. *The Revolution of Everyday Life*. Trans. Donald Nicholson-Smith. Oakland, CA: PM Press, 2012.

Van Elteren, Mel. "Conceptualizing the Impact of US Popular Culture Globally." *Journal of Popular Culture* 30.1 (1996): 47–89.

Veblen, Thorstein. *The Theory of the Leisure Class*. New York: New American Library, 1953.

"Victoria's Secret." *W5*. CTV, Vancouver. March 10, 2002.

Virilio, Paul. *Open Sky*. London: Verso, 1997.

Wald, Johanna and Dan Losen. "Defining and Re-Directing a School-to-Prison Pipeline." *New Directions for Youth Development* 99 (2003): n.p.

Wallace, Amy. "True Thighs." *More*. September 2002. Accessed May 19, 2012. http://www.more.com/more-women/celebrities/jamie-lee-curtis-true-thighs/

Walzer, Andrew. "Narratives of Contemporary Male Crisis: The (Re)Production of a National Discourse." *Journal of Men's Studies* 10.2 (2002): 209–224.

Warrior. Dir. Gavin O'Connor. Perf. Tom Hardy, Nick Nolte, and Joel Edgerton. Lionsgate, 2011.

"Water Related Injuries: Fact Sheet." Centers for Disease Control and Prevention. Department of Health and Human Services. Accessed July 20, 2012. http://www.cdc.gov/ncipc/factsheets/drown.htm

Watson, James, ed. *Golden Arches East: McDonald's in East Asia*. Stanford, CA: Stanford University Press, 1997.

Waydowntown. Dir. Gary Burn. Alliance Atlantis Home Video, 2000.

Weber, Max. *The Protestant Ethic and the Spirit of Capitalism*. 1930. Trans. Talcott Parsons. New York: Scribner, 1958.

Weeds. Created by Jenji Kohan. Showtime, 2005–12.

Weiss, Brad. "Coffee Breaks and Coffee Connections: The Lived Experience of a Commodity in Tanzanian and European Worlds." *Cross-Cultural Consumption: Global Market, Local Realities*. Ed. David Howes. London: Routledge, 1996. 93–105.

Welch, Jack. Interview on CNN *Moneyline*. December 8, 1998.

Wente, Margaret. "It's Okay to Hate Hockey." *The Globe and Mail.* January 10, 2002: A21.

"Western Eyes." *Rough Cuts*. CBC, Toronto. April 16, 2002.

"Why Is Google So Great?" *Great Place to Work Institute*. 2007. Accessed December 11, 2011. http://www.greatplacetowork.com/best/100best2007-google.php

Williams, Raymond. "Advertising: The Magic System." *The Cultural Studies Reader*. Ed. Simon During. London: Routledge, 1993. 320–336.

Williams, Raymond. "British Film History: New Perspectives." *British Cinema History*. Ed. J. Curran and V. Porter. London: Weidenfeld and Nicolson, 1983. 9–23.

Williams, Raymond. *Culture and Society 1780–1950*. New York: Columbia University Press, 1983.

Wilson, Carl. *Let's Talk About Love: A Journey to the End of Taste*. New York: Continuum, 2007.

Wiltse, Jeff. *Contested Waters: A Social History of Swimming Pools in America*. Chapel Hill: University of North Carolina Press, 2007.

Wolfe, Cary. *Before the Law: Humans and Other Animals in a Biopolitical Frame*. Chicago: University of Chicago Press, 2012.

Wolgamott, L. Kent. "Museums Re-Evaluate Display Methods." *Journal Star*. June 25, 2006. Accessed October 8, 2012. http://www.journalstar.com/articles/2006/06/25/

Wong, Danielle. "10 Myths About Immigration." *Hamilton Spectator.* October 16, 2011. Accessed January 17, 2012. http://www.thespec.com/news/local/article/609860--10-myths-about-immigration

Woollaston, Victoria. "Could the 'Right to Be Forgotten' Become Automated? Oblivion Software Could Help Google Remove Hundreds of People from the Web in Seconds." *Daily Mail*, June 26, 2015. Accessed March 1, 2017. http://www.dailymail.co.uk/sciencetech/article-3140534/Could-right-forgotten-automated-Oblivion-software-help-Google-remove-hundreds-people-web-seconds.html

World Bank. *World Development Indicators 1998*. Washington, DC: World Bank, 1998.

World Trade Organization. "Canada—Certain Measures Concerning Periodicals." Dispute Resolution Panel Report WT/DS31/R. March 14, 1997. Accessed August 19, 2012. http://www.worldtradelaw.net/reports/wtoab/canada-periodicals(ab).pdf

Wrenn, Eddie. "Stiff Penalty: Two PCSOs Ban Eight-Year-Old Boy from Playing Football outside House after He 'Kicked Too Loudly.'" *Daily Mail.* April 3, 2012. Accessed September 14, 2016. http://www.dailymail.co.uk/news/article-2124488/Two-PCSOs-ban-boy-playing-football-outside-Bolton-house-kicking-ball-loudly.html

Yalnizyan, Armine. *The Rise of Canadan's Richest 1%.* Ottawa: Canadian Centre for Policy Alternatives, 2010.

Young, Iris Marion. "Throwing Like a Girl: A Phenomenology of Feminine Body Comportment, Motility and Spatiality." *Human Studies* 3 (1980): 137–156.

"Youth Justice Statistics 2012/2013." Youth Justice Board/Ministry of Justice Statistics Bulletin. Accessed January 30, 2014. https://www.gov.uk/government/uploads/system/uploads/attachment_data/file/278549/youth-justice-stats-2013.pdf

"Youth Violence National and State Statistics at a Glance." CDC Centers for Disease Control and Prevention. Accessed July 24, 2014. http://www.cdc.gov/VIOLENCEPREVENTION/youthviolence/stats_at_a_glance/

Žižek, Slavoj. *In Defense of Lost Causes*. New York: Verso, 2008.

Index

Popular Culture: A User's Guide, International Edition. Imre Szeman and Susie O'Brien.
© 2017 John Wiley & Sons, Inc. Published 2017 by John Wiley & Sons, Inc.